THE GREAT DEBATES

The
Great Debates

CARTER vs. FORD, 1976

Edited by Sidney Kraus

INDIANA UNIVERSITY PRESS

Bloomington *London*

Library of Congress Cataloging in Publication Data
Main entry under title:

The Great Debates.

Includes the text of the 3 televised debates between
J. Carter and G. R. Ford, and of the Vice-Presidential
debate between R. J. Dole and W. F. Mondale, in the 1976
Presidential campaign.
Includes bibliographical references and index.
1. Presidents—United States—Election—1976.
2. United States—Politics and government—1974–1977.
3. Carter, Jimmy, 1924– 4. Ford, Gerald R.,
1913– 5. Television in politics—United States.
I. Kraus, Sidney. II. Carter, Jimmy, 1924–
III. Ford, Gerald R., 1913–
E868.G73   329'.023'730925   78-62422
ISBN 0-253-30363-X   ISBN 0-253-20229-9 pbk.

For the Debaters

JIMMY CARTER   GERALD FORD

The debates between President Ford and myself were a central element in the 1976 election. As perhaps nothing else could have, they provided an opportunity for the American people to weigh the merits of the candidates.

Because of the special circumstances of that election year, such an opportunity was particularly valuable to the electorate in reaching an informed judgment.

President Ford had come to office only two years before, without a chance to define his views in a national campaign. I had never held national office, and was relatively unknown.

These factors had limited our chances to explain ourselves and our policies to the American people. But the debates gave us both the opportunity to overcome these difficulties, and present ourselves at length to tens of millions of Americans.

There will never be any way of knowing for sure which of us gained most from the debates. The polls do not present a clear picture. This volume of studies, like the previous one on the Kennedy–Nixon debates, ought to add to our assessment of the debates. The only certain winner was the American voter, to whom the debates afforded an invaluable chance to examine the candidates in intimate detail.

    —JIMMY CARTER, letter to Sidney Kraus, April 8, 1976

I think presidential campaigns are as good as we can do under the circumstances. They are not as informative in a substantive way, perhaps, as they should be, but there are for obvious political purposes some statements made or commitments set forth that sound good in a campaign that have some difficulty of achievement when you become president; nevertheless, I really don't see how you can significantly improve the process in a three-month period.

I was a strong advocate and took the initiative for the debates that Mr. Carter and I had. I thought that was a way in which the public could become more accurately informed as to the views of both President Carter and myself. I think the fact that we did debate, that I was an incumbent president willing to institutionalize those debates in subsequent presidential elections, makes a strong case for their being held in the future and that incumbents ought to be willing to do it as I did it.

Maybe the format could be improved. I would like the judgment of those who could study the debates over the next two or three years to make recommendations. But debates, in whatever form—I hope an improved form—will be a part of the educational process for a presidential election, and I believe they will and I hope they will.

    —GERALD FORD, University of Michigan, April 6, 1977

CONTENTS

PREFACE

The purpose of this book is fourfold. First, it attempts comprehensively to document and record the events and the actions that brought about the 1976 Carter-Ford debates. Second, it investigates the way in which the electorate used the debates and assesses the effect they had on voting decisions and on the campaign generally. Third, it provides a verbatim transcript of the four debates. Last and perhaps most important, wherever possible, the research on the 1960 Kennedy-Nixon debates is related to the 1976 experience to provide comparative data for future presidential debates policy making.

Unlike the situation in 1960, advance announcements of the 1976 debates provided some opportunity for both planners and researchers to rehash the former effort with a view toward guiding the latter one. Lest anyone think that mounting televised presidential debates is merely a matter of matching expertise to needs, or that researching and documenting what happened simply requires locating and committing participants and scholars to writing tasks, let me dispel such notions at the start.

Critical events such as televised debates have a way of developing over time that hampers one's ability to predict changes or events. Several of the articles in this book were difficult to obtain because of the nature of the event and the complexity of the interactions among participants. Some 400 items in the manuscript had to be checked for accuracy. Memories are short and a given contribution as perceived by one or another participant may reflect more of a vested interest or an intense desire to shape history than an "objective" view of what happened. While I am satisfied that we have reduced the 400 items to less than a handful, I am certain that some may disagree with a point here or there.

I am most grateful to several institutions and to dozens of people. Among them a number deserve to be identified.

The John and Mary R. Markle Foundation graciously and generously supported my effort to bring out this volume. The foundation provided funds for travel, assistance, and research, and for a two-day debriefing conference with participants and some researchers; it also helped offset publishing costs when it became apparent that the volume would be larger than anticipated. Both Jeanie Firstenberg and Lloyd Morrisett were very responsive and most helpful.

The Columbia Broadcasting System, Inc. and in particular, my friend Joseph T. Klapper, director, Office of Social Research, encouraged this project with a substantial unrestricted grant. Joe wrote, "When we use the words 'unrestricted grant' we mean them in their fullest sense, and explicitly state that we have no rights of interposition in the pursuit, report, or publication of your work, in regard to all of which you remain, as far as we are concerned, totally and completely autonomous." I consider that statement in the best tradition of public service, and I hope that this research will contribute to the general effort of providing the electorate with a better understanding of political telecasts.

I am also grateful to the William Benton Foundation, particularly to Charles Benton, for a grant that enabled us to make this book more comprehensive than otherwise would have been allowed.

This research would have been virtually impossible without the cooperation of the League of Women Voters Education Fund. Their kind invitation for me to attend each of the debates and their subsequent generosity in making available files and documents as well as a significant amount of interviewing time with very busy people can never be fully repaid. Peggy Lampl, then executive director, and now deputy assistant secretary for congressional relations, U.S. Department of State, spent hours upon hours helping me to gain access here or to obtain a document there and generally providing information. Ruth Clusen, president, found time for interviews during the debates and afterwards. Betsy Dribben, charged with the enormous task of coordinating newsrooms and working with the press, deserves my thanks for tolerating my persistence—she had to keep kicking me out of the newsrooms. (In that regard I want to thank the Democratic and Republican parties for allowing me newsroom access at the last debate.)

Most of my indebtedness to a single individual must go to Jim Karayn, project director of the debates and now president of WHYY, the PBS station in Philadelphia. He gave generously of his time both during the debates and later. He was instrumental in my gaining access to almost every part of the entire effort. His recall is uncanny and his energy in promoting televised debates is unmatched. His broadcasting skills, administrative know-how, and journalistic competencies made him a joy to be with as well as a vital resource person.

There are so many other people to thank:

—Charles and Marjorie Benton and Gene Pokorny for their kind hospitality in Chicago, New York, and Washington and their hours of attention to this effort.

—Barry Jagoda and Bill Carruthers, Carter and Ford television advisors, respectively, for their kindness and help.

—Michael Raoul-Duval, then special assistant to President Ford, and Stuart Eizenstat, now special assistant to President Carter, for their time and input on issues.

—John Boesel and Gene Telser of A. C. Nielsen for access to data on debate viewing.

—Steve Chaffee and Dave Sears for endless hours working with the quantitative data on uses and effects.

At Cleveland State I owe special thanks to John Courtright, Jae-won Lee, and John Robinson for their expert advice at various stages of the volume.

PREFACE

Three other colleagues deserve special mention—Dennis Davis, who took on considerable editing chores; Jess Yoder, who kept our department intact during my frequent absences; and Leo Jeffres, who took my classes when necessary. Sandy Coy, my administrative assistant, was most skillful with the manuscript, files, and itineraries.

The staff of the Indiana University Press has been most helpful.

Finally, a very personal note. In December 1961 I concluded my preface to the Kennedy-Nixon debate book (*The Great Debates: Background, Perspective, Effects* [Bloomington: Indiana University Press, 1962]) with "Finally, to Cecile, Kenny, Pammy, and Jody, whose activities for the past year were neglected by a busy husband and a 'bye-bye' father, I offer my undivided attention." We have all grown up in the past seventeen years. So have the debates.

SIDNEY KRAUS

Cleveland, Ohio
November 21, 1978

THE GREAT DEBATES

Part I

Background and Perspective

1.

Introduction
Presidential Debates:
Political Option or Public Decree?

SIDNEY KRAUS

The decision of presidential candidates to debate on television has been a political option left to them alone. Politicians make that decision with more concern for political expediency than regard for the public good.

Confrontations between John F. Kennedy and Richard Nixon in 1960[1] and between President Gerald Ford and challenger Jimmy Carter in 1976 came about because each candidate determined it was in his political interest to debate.

In 1964 Goldwater and his supporters vigorously tried to involve President Johnson in debates, but the major-party incumbent was at the peak of his popularity and so ignored the appeals to debate. Likewise, for reasons of political advantage by one side or the other, the elections of 1968 and 1972 were conducted without presidential debates.

Three presidential elections separated the two in which debates were held. After winning the election in 1960, President Kennedy said that should he be the 1964 nominee, he would debate his opponent. Were it not for an assassin's bullet, presidential debates may have been institutionalized in elections.

At a conference examining the 1976 debate experience, a Carter representative indicated that the then president-elect was inclined toward 1980 debates but that he reserved the option.[2] Presently, Congress is considering eliminating Section 315 of the Communications Act, which now requires equal broadcast time for all candidates for the same public office.[3] Carter's attitude toward debates may well influence Congress's deliberations and will ultimately affect the political process and how voters will be able to get political information.

As Carter and Congress deliberate, several questions will emerge: What is best for the public good? Should presidential candidates have the option to debate or not? Should the public decree that debates must be held in presidential campaigns? Should third- and minor-party candidates debate? While arguments pro and con are not without merit, it might be novel for a change to lean more heavily toward those in favor of the public good.

There is some evidence, if only by inference, that presidential debates may help to avoid power-inflated presidencies by bringing about closer electoral outcomes. Teddy White suggested that electoral mandates—winning by large

3

margins—may have bad effects on presidential administrations.[4] Roosevelt's mandate led him to believe he could stack our courts with jurists of a certain philosophy and political ideology. Subsequent to Johnson's mandate we found ourselves significantly involved in Indochina. Nixon's 1972 mandate gave his administration such confidence that even the Watergate cover-up was considered strategically acceptable.

This analysis posits that presidents elected by large margins may feel free to behave in ways which otherwise might be perceived as too risky politically.

Extending White's analysis, it is interesting to note that with the two televised presidential debates, we had close elections. Kennedy's wafer-thin margin in 1960 and Carter's "but for one state" victory may well have been a consequence of the televised debates. Such televised appearances may serve as "equalizers" which in the long run protect the presidency from arrogant actions.

Another lesson from 1960 and 1976 may be that debates serve to offset certain prejudices and stereotypes in the process of selecting a person to lead our nation. Without the debates, Kennedy's youth, inexperience and religion may have been insurmountable handicaps compared to Nixon's perceived maturity, his experience as a vice-president, and his religious affiliation. Televised debates evidently helped convince most voters that those characteristics did not account for the differences between the two men, especially as they related to qualifications for president. Similarly, Carter's southern heritage and his lack of a current office—considered disadvantages compared to Ford's midwestern background and his incumbency—were obviously not as important to enough of the electorate as were other considerations.

Perhaps such televised exposure brings out candidates' qualities and positions on issues that voters perceive as more important for their electoral choice than party affiliation, age, religion, geography, or incumbency. Voters, given the opportunity to see and compare candidates in joint appearances on television, look for those positions on issues which they feel will affect their lives.

A respected political scientist, V. O. Key, Jr., once said that "voters are not fools," that they use political information in a responsible way when making their decisions.[5]

In this writer's opinion, politicians are sometimes duped by their low assessment of voters. It is their failings in judgment and inability to predict what moves voters which account for many poor decisions affecting the political process. Politicians and media, not voters, are responsible for the quality of political information in elections.

Key makes an observation that should interest all candidates and especially those considering debates. "The predictability of electoral response to a particular action remains so uncertain that the avoidance of a sensible decision because it will lose votes is usually the work of a man whose anxieties outweigh his capacities of prediction."[6]

While voters are not fools, they are bombarded with a variety of communications urging them to behave or act in given ways. Obviously, it is a rare voter who persistently follows a presidential campaign, closely checking out the candidates, their positions on issues, and the like. It is the exceptional voter who remembers what Candidate A said five weeks ago and compares that with what Candidate B said today. Most voters do not retain political information over long periods. Televised debates, spaced properly in the campaign, help voters retain information.

We've learned a lot about how voters use the mass media and how television serves both the voter and the candidate. Studies confirm several important relationships between voters and television. For one, most voters (and nonvoters too) get most of their political information from television. For another, voters learn about candidates and issues from televised debates. Though television viewing is differentiated by level of education, even the highly educated use television along with newspapers and magazines for their information about politics.[7]

The empirical evidence to date strongly supports the continuation of debates in future presidential elections. Reviewing some 43 studies, Sears and Chaffee (Chapter 13) conclude that "the election of 1976 was the better for the addition of the debates." In determining the usefulness of the debates for voters, Chaffee argues that "the burden of evidence to date, when intersected with traditional democratic values, should encourage us to attach a rather high net value to the debates as an emerging institution in the political process."[8] Despite these apparent pluses for televised debates, some would have it otherwise.

It has been fashionable to criticize both politicians and the media in their handling of the 1976 presidential campaign. A colleague of mine, so upset with the discourse in the first Ford-Carter debate, vehemently suggested that "Hitler's propaganda contained better rhetoric, at least, and was certainly less boring than Mr. Dull and Mr. Duller." Two respected journalists were not much kinder with their views. Tom Wicker, *New York Times* columnist, argued that debates are "thin on issues" and since presidents never have to debate in office, they shouldn't in campaigns.[9] Sander Vanocur wants the debates banned in future elections. "Failing that," he urges, "lovers of the American political system should take the issue to the courts in an effort to forever proscribe two consenting adults from committing unnatural acts in public."[10] Vanocur feels that the debates are replacing "the political process of electing a president." Though these indictments fall short of the point, they keep popping up in campaigns containing debates.

It was said in 1960 and again in 1976 that televised debates focus on candidate images and not on issues. Another criticism voiced in both debate years claimed that two men talking for an hour or more is too boring. Perhaps the loudest invectives came from those who felt the televised debates were not debates at all, but a "Meet the Press" panel of questions and answers. This latter group sees the newsperson format as an intrusion, forcing viewers to judge personalities and abilities of the questioners, taking attention away from the candidates.

There's some truth in most of the criticism, but not enough in this writer's opinion to detract from the more positive aspects of the confrontations. What would the Ford-Carter campaign have been like without the debates? Both candidates were perceived by political pundits and others as dull and unexciting. Ford was the nice but incompetent guy. To many politicial observers, Carter was vacillatory on issues, even contradictory.

Evidence about the effects of the recent debates showed that these predebate criticisms disappeared in media reports as the debates continued.

But the major points in favor of debates, confrontations, or whatever, is that voters, for the most part, want them, pay attention to them, and act (vote) as a result of them. Even if the debates resulted in revealing personalities only, it should be considered as an important revelation of the very quality to affect the highest public office of the country.

Over 80 million people saw at least one or more of the Kennedy-Nixon debates. More than 100 million viewed the first Ford-Carter debate.[11] A Gallup poll taken a few weeks after the recent election suggested that "if it were up to U.S. voters, presidential debates could become a permanent feature of the electoral process." The postelection nationwide survey found that 66 percent favored presidential televised debates in 1980.

Democracy is essentially well served by televised debates. They provide the American electorate, at their convenience and in their homes, with facts about candidates and issues. *Debates on television should be institutionalized, if not by law, by public decree.*

In 1858, just before secession, Lincoln and Douglas debated. A major issue confronting the nation was slavery. The country was in severe inner turmoil. Information was slow to reach the public and when it did, it was usually altered and second hand. The 1857 Supreme Court decision in *Dred Scott* v. *Sanford* led Lincoln in the debates to believe that preventing slavery in the territories by any governmental action would be unconstitutional. Douglas responded that "the people have the lawful means to introduce it or exclude it as they please."

The Freeport exchange between Lincoln and Douglas and the other six debates were witnessed by relatively few voters (about 15,000 at each site except in the town of Jonesboro which attracted only 1,500). Though they were not presidential debates (Lincoln and Douglas were candidates for the U.S. Senate), it was the first time in our history that opposing candidates went before the public to debate.

Considering the impact of television in the last twenty-five years, how might history have been altered had the Lincoln-Douglas debates been televised? History records that advances in technology have been followed by massive changes in society. The introduction of movable metal type in the fifteenth century, Foudrinier's machine enabling continuous production of paper in the late nineteenth century, and the telegraph, telephone, teletype, radio, and computer have all had significant impact on our social and political lives. Certainly, new methods of communication were responsible, in large part, for the various changes in our society in the mid-sixties.

Communication technology and the Industrial Revolution have been responsible for advances in literacy in America. Ben H. Bagdikian noted that "in the late eighteenth century South Carolina and most other Southern states passed laws making it a crime to teach a Negro to read. By the mid-twentieth century instruction for competent literacy was considered therapy against ghetto violence." The pattern throughout history has been, as Bagdikian documents, that new modes of communication providing new information reach new audiences; this process "ultimately alters the status quo and broadens the participation of individuals in the social process."[12]

It remains for us to capture communication innovations, such as televised presidential debates, and harness them within the political process for the benefit of democracy. It is not an easy task. For example, Benton and Pokorny (Chapter 5) outline an interesting "innovation" in voter education that was attempted in the 1976 primaries. Attempts by various groups to educate and inform voters during political campaigns are often thwarted by candidates' behaviors. Political candidates are concerned with *getting elected*; they are less concerned with political education, political discourse, or the public good. As harsh as that may seem, given their view that debates may hurt their chances for election, for example, candidates will choose not to debate.

The point is should they have that option? Or should they—at least presidential candidates—be required to debate because the public wants debates?

Assuming that it is desirable for presidential contenders to debate on television, what ought we to do to insure that debates occur in 1980 and every four years thereafter? The issue of institutionalized debates is rapidly gaining attention among political leaders, researchers, and the public generally. The Twentieth Century Fund, for example, has established a task force on presidential debates to make recommendations for the future. Jim Karayn (Chapter 12) has offered some suggestions for the future, but future presidential debates will depend upon a variety of considerations. Some of these are listed below.

Legislation.—A review of legal actions over the years would be most useful for any discussion of the legislative role in the political process and the use of mass media. Becker and Lower's earlier review[13] of broadcasting's role in presidential campaigns combined with their current update (Chapter 2) provide a starting point. A major deterrent to presidential debates is the equal-time provision (Section 315) of the Communications Act. It mandates that when one candidate is given air time, an equal amount must be given other candidates for that office. This limits the flexibility of the networks and economically "prohibits" major candidate debates. Section 315 should be repealed.[14] Some provision is necessary for minor party candidates; perhaps, a formula based on a certain percentage of votes in primaries could include or exclude non-major-party candidates. Terry and Kraus (Chapter 3) discuss the 1976 problems associated with Section 315.

Format.—While it may be desirable to have the presidential debates conducted in the "Oregon style" (Thomas E. Dewey and Harold Stassen debated in the 1948 Oregon presidential primary), a format requiring arguments on a single proposition or critical question, cross-examination and rebuttal between the two candidates, any format which provides enough time to expose candidates' issues and personalities, will do. Format decisions can be negotiated between participants; the crucial consideration should be the issues to be discussed. The problems associated with debate format and issues are revealed by studying the interactions of several 1976 participants (see, for example, Lampl, representing the League of Women Voters Education Fund [Chapter 6]; Eizenstat's and Raoul-Duval's candidate briefings [Chapter 7]; and Karayn's plan for the future [Chapter 12]).

Issues.—In the past, candidates have determined the issues discussed in debates. While one may successfully argue for candidate control in the selection of issues, there are good reasons for the public's participation in the process. Public opinion is the bulwark of democracy. Why not let the public define the issues, set the agenda for the debates? In 1976, Cyrus Vance, Daniel Yankelovich, Thomas Watson, Clark Kerr, Coleman Young, and twenty-three other prominent Americans formed a Policy Review Board within a nonprofit, nonpartisan organization called the Public Agenda Foundation. Their stated purpose was to clarify "key national issues" in order to "enhance citizens' participation in the political process." They interviewed a wide spectrum of leaders and citizens and came out in early September with three reports—*U.S. Foreign Policy: Principles for Defining the National Interest*; *Inflation and Unemployment*; and *Moral Leadership in Government*. It was not without intent to influence the discussion in the Ford-Carter debates that Dan Yankelovich went to the White House and discussed the reports with Michael Raoul-Duval, special counsel to the president. A procedure similar to the Foundation's would be most beneficial in determining the issues. That is, the use of public opinion research may prove valuable in setting an agenda of issues for the debates. In Chapter 4 Cohen recounts the Foundation's effort.

News panel.—In 1960, an elaborate lottery system developed by press secretaries Pierre Salinger and Herbert Klein, pressure from the networks and the candidates, all interacted in the selection process of the news panel—those who would ask questions of the candidates. No less an harangue occurred in selecting the journalist-questioners for the 1976 debates (see especially Salant's comments in Chapter 10 and Lampl's discussion in Chapter 6). An elimination of the panel in at least some of the debates, with a strong moderator and/or questioners from fields such as political science, economics, history, and the like may add a worthwhile dimension. Milic's analyses of the debates' Q and A process (Chapter 11) and Yoder and Mims's rendition of the debates texts (Chapter 27) are instructive here.

Television production.—Candidates' representatives were extremely concerned with how the cameras presented the candidates. Seltz and Yoakam (Chapter 8) once again document the myriad concerns in getting the debates televised.[15] In both debate years an inordinate amount of attention was given to almost every minute detail of the productions. Lighting, makeup, shot-selection,[16] set, lectern, and sound were all elements of immense concern. To the chagrin of many, the loss of sound in Philadelphia most likely would have been avoided had the debate been housed in a television studio. Further, criticisms of news coverage during the sound gap (see Lang and Lang, Chapter 9) did not help network or debate credibility. To insure maximum efficiency in production, future debates should be held in studios.

Audience.—The important audience for presidential debates is located in homes throughout the nation. Elimination of audience at the debate sites would avoid all network demands for audience coverage during the debates. It would also help the candidates to look into the cameras without distractions.

Requiring debates.—There is much disagreement as to whether or not televised debates should be required by law. Raoul-Duval wants politicians to retain the option, suggesting that public opinion should be the persuader or dissuader. He said it would require an amendment to the Constitution. Bob Chandler, vicepresident of CBS News, countered that the provision could be attached to the Campaign Financing Act. Presidential candidates who qualify for public funds (Carter and Ford each received some $21 million in 1976) could be required to debate in order to receive the money. They could choose not to debate, but they would not get any of the funds.[17]

Much of the 1976 presidential campaign fund financed by the public was spent in saturating the television networks on election eve. The same money spent for the thirty minutes of partisan programs could have been used for debates.

In addition, the 1976 presidential debates saw a parallel development of the same kind in New York—debates between senatorial candidates Buckley and Moynihan. An institutionalized presidential debate may promote local-level debates that are likely to help voters decipher their less-known candidates for local offices.

These are but a few of the many suggestions and problems which need attention in the next few years. The way we use our wits to move meaningful information *between* potential leaders and the populace at large may significantly contribute to the quality of our political process. Presidential televised debates have twice been part of our presidential selection process and by most reports the voters have benefited.

Harold Lasswell, commenting on the 1960 debates, wrote:

> Given the presently prevailing institutions of the American polity, we must not overlook the possibility that a true debate between presidential candidates would threaten the genius for ambiguity that is essential to the operation of our complex, semiresponsible, relatively democratic system of multigroup coalition. The implication is that the introduction of "genuine debate at the top" on TV calls for simultaneous changes elsewhere in the effective practices of American government.[18]

We ought to begin those changes now. It is hoped that the views and studies contained in this book will provide a basis for those changes.

NOTES

1. Sidney Kraus (ed.), *The Great Debates: Background, Perspective, Effects* (Bloomington: Indiana University Press, 1962); reprinted as *The Great Debates, Kennedy vs. Nixon, 1960* (Bloomington: Indiana University Press, 1977).

2. See Sidney Kraus, Transcript, *Presidential Debates De-Briefing*, Crystal City Marriott, Arlington, Virginia, November 29–30, 1976, pp. 147–49.

3. "Communications Act of 1978," for Subcommittee on Communications, H.R., 95th Congress, 2nd Session, June 6, 1978.

4. Theodore H. White's analyses of election results on network television, election night, 1976.

5. V. O. Key, Jr., *The Responsible Electorate* (Cambridge: Harvard University Press, 1966), p. 7.

6. V. O. Key, Jr., *Public Opinion and American Democracy* (New York: Alfred A. Knopf, 1961), pp. 557–58.

7. For a review of studies on information and politics see Sidney Kraus and Dennis Davis, *The Effects of Mass Communication on Political Behavior* (University Park: Penn State University Press, 1976).

8. Steven H. Chaffee, "Presidential Debates—Are They Helpful to Voters?" *Communication Monographs*, 45, November 1978, p. 346.

9. Tom Wicker, "Do We Really Need the Debates?" *New York Times*, October 24, 1976, Section E, p. 15.

10. Sander Vanocur, "Televised 'Debates': Their Time Is Up," *Washington Post*, October 17, 1976, Section F, p. 1.

11. According to A. C. Nielsen, in both debate years approximately 90 percent of the nation's TV households viewed the debates. In 1976, 90 percent represented 64.1 million households; in 1960, the percentage was 40.6 households.

12. Ben H. Bagdikian, *The Information Machines* (New York: Harper and Row, 1971), p. 7.

13. Samuel L. Becker and Elmer W. Lower, "Broadcasting in Presidential Elections," in Kraus, *The Great Debates, Kennedy vs. Nixon, 1960*, pp. 25–55.

14. After the election, Barry Jagoda, President Carter's television aide during the debates and now in the White House, said: "Section 315 should be repealed, to make the process [the negotiations for debates] as open as possible, as flexible as possible." See Kraus, *Presidential Debates De-Briefing*, p. 147.

15. See their earlier piece in Kraus, *The Great Debates, Kennedy vs. Nixon, 1960*, pp. 73–126.

16. For an interesting analysis of the pictorial treatment of candidates in the 1976 debates see Robert K. Tiemens, "Television's Portrayal of the 1976 Presidential Debates: An Analysis of Visual Content," *Communication Monographs*, 45, November 1978, pp. 362–70.

17. Kraus, Transcript, *Presidential Debates De-Briefing*, p. 69.

18. Harold Lasswell, "Introduction," in Kraus, *The Great Debates, Kennedy vs. Nixon, 1960*, p. 21.

2.

Broadcasting in Presidential Campaigns, 1960–1976

SAMUEL L. BECKER and ELMER W. LOWER

The growth of television . . . has transformed politics in America. Like a colossus of the ancient world, television stands astride our political system, demanding tribute from every candidate for major public office, incumbent and challenger. Its appetite is insatiable and its impact is unique. No amount of spending on other media can possibly offset the role of television and the impression it makes on voters.

SENATOR EDWARD M. KENNEDY

This belief, expressed by Senator Kennedy during the Senate committee hearings on the campaign reform bill of 1971, is an apt keynote for this history of broadcasting and presidential campaigns, 1960–1976. It is this belief that motivated most of the political, legislative, and journalistic activity reported here.

The sixteen years and five presidential elections covered by this chapter were marked by political and social upheaval that at times shook the American system of government. More than fifty thousand young Americans died in an unpopular war in Vietnam. The inner cores of the great American cities were wracked by riots, fires, wanton destruction, plundering, and sniping. Life styles and sexual mores changed as the under-thirties rejected the old ways of their parents. Confidence in government, the church, educational institutions, and business declined as Watergate and associated scandals shocked the country. One American president was assassinated, another declined to run for re-election because of his war-related unpopularity, scandal forced a third to resign, and added scandal forced a vice-president to quit under fire.

Radio and television played an increasingly vital role in all of those disturbing events, and broadcasting, in turn, came under question, criticism, and attack for the manner in which it mirrored an America in political and social transition.

In contrast, the first four decades (1920–1960) during which broadcasting had played a role in presidential elections seemed mild indeed, marked by a great depression and two wars. During that period costs of political campaigning skyrocketed, and attempts at regulating them led to decentralization, evasion, and concealment rather than control. Merchandising of candidates became more sophisticated. Broadcasters, themselves, became increasingly adept at presenting the relevant facts of the campaigns to the voters. Arguments continued about the relative freedom and responsibility of the broadcast industry to cover these campaigns.

These developments were documented in our study published in *The Great Debates*, following the 1960 election.[1] We also documented the face-lifting of political conventions necessitated when the conventions became a show, designed to create an attractive and persuasive image of the party, rather than an occasion for vital political machinations. We showed the developing role of the advertising agency, the public relations firm, and the communications consultant in political campaigns and the way in which these agencies, the candidates, and the other advisers of candidates worked together to develop most of the methods of presidential communication with the public that we know today: the broadcast press conference, the staged cabinet meeting, the fireside chat, among others. And we covered the continuing controversy over the equal-time provision in Section 315 of the Communications Act of 1934 and the way in which it was amended in 1959 to exclude bona fide newscasts, news interviews, and news documentaries in which the appearance of a candidate is incidental to the subject, as well as on-the-spot coverage of bona fide news events. This last exemption was especially important because, as documented elsewhere in this book, it was the loophole in Section 315 that made the Carter-Ford debates of 1976 possible.[2]

Though radio and television had largely overcome their growing pains by 1960 and had become well-established factors in the political processes, the relationship between the media and politics was far from stable. Change, as mentioned earlier, was the order of the day throughout the sixteen-year period. This essay is an attempt to document those developments which have been most important for presidential election campaigns.

To put the details that are to follow in some perspective, it is useful to consider first some of the major trends in population, voting, and broadcasting during the 1960–1976 period.

Among the most important of these trends is the increase in the number of eligible voters, from 109,674,000 in 1960 to 146,548,000 in 1976. Part of that increase is due, of course, to the added numbers of eighteen- through twenty-year-olds who became eligible to vote in 1971.

The increase in the availability of radio and television receivers to reach these voters more than kept pace with the mounting population. Radio was already at virtually 100 percent saturation of American homes at the beginning of this period, and it remained so. Television was available in approximately 87 percent of American homes in 1960, and increased to almost 98 percent saturation by November 1976. Perhaps even more important than the general increase in saturation is the reduction that occurred in the uneven geographical distribution of receivers. In 1960, 92 percent of homes in the North had television receivers, but only 79 percent of those in the South. By 1976, as distribution of television receivers approached the saturation point, such regional differences had virtually disappeared.

The computer established itself as a major tool of political parties, for planning campaign appeals and maintenance of up-to-date voter lists, and of broadcasters, for increasing the speed and reliability of election night projections. The tabulation of elections witnessed the greatest advance in the twentieth century

when the three major networks and the two major wire services pooled th
efforts to establish the cooperative News Election Service. NES was born ⎯
June 1964 and has tabulated four presidential elections, three off-year congressional elections, and hundreds of primaries and local contests.

Most important, major reforms in the laws governing the conduct of elections were enacted during the period, which contributed substantially to a leveling off toward the end of the period in the steep rise in election costs. But the
steady attacks on the equal-time provision of the Communications Act of 1934
continued to meet with failure. The attempts to find some means of equalizing
the advantage that easy access to the media gives the incumbent president over
potential challengers, the opposition party, and the Congress also met with
failure.

The 1960 Election

Though the 1960 Kennedy-Nixon election campaign has been well documented, in *The Great Debates* and elsewhere, there are a few historical facts
about it which it is important to stress here because they help to explain much
of the history of broadcasting and politics in the succeeding sixteen years.

Among the many things that the 1960 experience demonstrated was that,
although great amounts of free coverage of the campaign by radio and television
can sharply reduce expenditures for broadcast time, at least for the major parties, total campaign expenditures are not necessarily reduced commensurately.
The three commercial television networks devoted 17 hours 32 minutes of
sustaining time to coverage of the presidential campaign in 1960 (8 percent of
this for minor party candidates); the radio networks devoted 21 hours 57 minutes (4 percent to minor candidates). This was a sharp increase from the previous presidential campaign (and there was a sharp drop four years later).[3]
Apparently as a result, the Republicans spent only $1,865,000 and the Demo-
crats $1,142,000 for broadcast time in the presidential general election cam-
paign. This total was 35 percent below the parties' time costs in 1956. On the
other hand, total campaign costs rose from almost $13 million in 1956 to almost
$20 million in 1960.[4]

In our earlier study, we documented the growing importance of media consultants to presidential political campaigns: the trend continued in 1960. Dan
Nimmo reported that one of Nixon's consultants, Carroll Newton, a former
BBD&O advertising agency executive, proposed that the candidate be "mar-
keted" by the creative use of television, "relying on thorough research, testing
of attitudes, and appropriate media techniques. But Nixon turned to more traditional communication techniques and failed to execute the elaborate media
plan."[5] Yet, perhaps because of Kennedy's increasing strength in the latter part
of the campaign, Nixon did agree to a last-minute media blitz, including a four-
hour telethon on ABC which cost $200,000. It featured everything from a chat
with Ginger Rogers to discussions of major issues facing the country.[6]

The 1960 Kennedy campaign gave great impetus to the trend toward using
public opinion polling and computer analyses to guide the conduct of campaigns. Kennedy appears to have been the first candidate to use computer simulation of the electorate to test the effects of various issues on voter sentiment,
though it is not clear to what extent the results of those analyses were used to

shape the media campaign or other messages of the campaign.[7] Both Democrats and Republicans also began using computers to facilitate the maintenance of up-to-date voter lists.

Computers were used increasingly by the networks during their election night coverage to project the results on the basis of early scattered returns. The idea appears to have been conceived originally in 1952 by Paul Levitan, election night producer for CBS television, working with Arch Hancock of the Remington Rand Corporation. The first test of the plan, using UNIVAC I, was election night, 1952. The basic data for the projections were, and continue to be, detailed voting data for key precincts in earlier elections and the trends indicated by differences between present voting returns and those from the past. The system proved even more successful than its originators imagined. On its first trial in 1952, by 8:30 P.M., Eastern Standard Time, UNIVAC I was predicting a landslide for Eisenhower at odds of 100 to 1. Because the election was expected to be reasonably close, the statistician and Remington Rand programmers were afraid that some human error had been made and did not release those results until almost four hours later.[8]

All three networks turned to computers for projection of Eisenhower's second victory over Stevenson, though this time it was less of a surprise, since the landslide was clearly evident before the election.

By 1960, the reliability of these early election-night projections was proven, and politicians became aware of a potential danger. Their concern is exemplified by a statement from Oregon Governor Mark O. Hatfield two days before the 1960 election: "The West should not be stampeded nor tranquilized by electronics."[9] There was fear that radio and television projections of the outcomes of presidential elections broadcast before polls closed in the Western states would influence voters in those states. Concern about such influence continues to the present day, though no study has yet demonstrated that such influence has occurred.[10]

As a result of the race to be first on the air with the "final" results, network computer projection had its first setback. ABC "won" the race in 1960, projecting at 6:54 P.M., Eastern Standard Time, ten-to-one odds on a Nixon victory. It was 3:54 P.M. on the West coast, so voters had three to four more hours during which to cast ballots. Twenty-two minutes later, at 7:16 P.M., Eastern Time, with fewer than one percent of the country's precincts reporting, CBS also projected Nixon as the winner. It was not until 7:50 P.M., almost an hour after ABC's initial projection, that CBS, this time with three percent of the precinct results in, switched its forecast and projected odds of 11 to 10 for Kennedy.

As the tabulation was the closest presidential count since Woodrow Wilson overtook Charles Evans Hughes in 1916, all three networks and the two wire services continued their individual tallies throughout the long night. Finally, NBC News projected California for Kennedy at 7:30 A.M., thus giving the Democrats the national victory. When the absentee ballots were counted later, Nixon actually carried California, but Kennedy had enough other electoral votes to clinch his victory, 303 to 219.

Ballots were cast by 62.8 percent of the eligible population in 1960. This was the highest percentage of participation in the United States since 1916, the last year in which suffrage was limited to males. It is impossible to demonstrate

14 **THE GREAT DEBATES**

a causal relationship to the broadcasts of the Kennedy-Nixon debates, but no other explanation seems as likely, especially since the percentages declined again for the elections following 1960.[11]

The 1964 Election

The tragic shadow of John F. Kennedy lay over the 1964 presidential campaign. Less than a year before—on November 22, 1963—he had been assassinated in his vice-president's home state of Texas. Television coverage of the assassination and the events of the following four days brought increased respect and credibility to the television medium. Almost physically, it was the glue that held a shocked and mourning nation together. The three major networks preempted all regular programming and commercials from the moment of the assassination on Friday afternoon, November 22, through the final poignant hours of the state funeral on Monday, November 26.[12]

Now the tall Texan who had succeeded his slain chief, Lyndon Baines Johnson, was running virtually unopposed for the Democratic nomination. With the defeated Richard M. Nixon wounded on the sidelines, the Republican nomination was a heated fight between an eastern liberal, Governor Nelson A. Rockefeller of New York, and a western conservative, Senator Barry M. Goldwater of Arizona.

President Theodore Roosevelt, long before the advent of radio and television, called the White House "a bully pulpit." It became far more so in the half century that followed. March 15, 1963, marked the fiftieth anniversary of an institution that has played an ever-increasing role in presidential politics, the presidential press conference. The first such White House press conference was introduced by President Woodrow Wilson on March 15, 1913, only eleven days after his inauguration. Later Franklin D. Roosevelt, Dwight D. Eisenhower, and John F. Kennedy added their unique touches. FDR exploited radio as had no other chief executive. Eisenhower was the first to permit recordings of press conferences. Recognizing the legitimacy of electronic journalism and, undoubtedly, the influence of his television image on the public, Kennedy, five days after his 1961 inauguration, opened the doors to live television and radio during his meetings with the press.

The opposition party was no less cognizant of the power which these broadcast press conferences bestowed on the president. To counterbalance it, the "Ev and Charlie Show" was born, weekly press conferences held by the Senate and House majority leaders, Everett McKinley Dirksen of Illinois and Charles A. Halleck of Indiana (later replaced by Rep. Gerald R. Ford of Michigan).[13]

It was the Kennedy performance in the 1960 presidential debates, however, that probably had the most lasting effect on media use in presidential campaigns.

Though there were no debates between presidential candidates in the general election campaigns from 1960 until 1976, the 1960 confrontation between Kennedy and Nixon spawned a large array of debates and pseudo-debates between candidates for other offices and for primary opponents. In 1961 New York mayoralty candidates Robert Wagner and Louis Lefkowitz debated on television and radio. They even used the podiums and some of the furniture from one of the Kennedy-Nixon debates. Among the many other participants in such debates were Ted Kennedy and Edward McCormack, who were vying for the Democratic senatorial nomination in Massachusetts in 1962; Michigan Governor John Swainson and his challenger, George Romney, in 1962; California senatorial candidates George Murphy and Pierre Salinger in 1964; and Robert Kennedy and Eugene McCarthy during their primary campaign for the Democratic presidential nomination in 1968.[14]

In the jockeying that normally preceded them and, even more, when one of the candidates declined to participate, the debates often appeared to become the major issue of the campaign. This was especially true in the sixties, when the "empty chair debate" flowered as a form of political communication. This was the "debate" form in which, to dramatize the refusal of an opponent to participate in a more traditional debate, the script called for the candidate to appear on television with an empty chair as a symbol and reminder of the opponent's cowardice.

A more extreme and questionable practice was exemplified in Ohio by the challenger of Senator Frank Lausche. For this pseudo-debate, he utilized film clips of Lausche speaking, instead of an empty chair, and spliced his own arguments between those film clips. George Bush, a Texas Republican, was party to a similar "debate" during his campaign against Texas Senator Ralph Yarborough.[15]

The success of the Kennedy-Nixon debates also stimulated further attacks on the equal-time provision of the Communications Act and, perhaps, was partly responsible for the increasing efforts to reduce costs and reform campaign financing practices through legislation. The 1960 election was hardly over before Senator Warren Magnuson, chairman of the Committee on Interstate and Foreign Commerce, introduced a bill, S. 204, to make permanent the exemption of presidential and vice-presidential campaigns from Section 315.[16] Shortly thereafter, CBS president Dr. Frank Stanton, NBC president Robert Kintner, National Association of Broadcasters president LeRoy Collins, and other broadcasting executives urged the Communications Subcommittee of the Senate Committee on Interstate and Foreign Commerce to recommend repeal of the equal-time rule.

Frank Stanton, the most articulate spokesman broadcasting has ever had, put it this way:

> The public is the only touchstone for the solution of the persistent problem of Section 315. It is not a question of what is in the interest of a particular candidate. It is not a question of what is in the interest of the broadcasters. The one, the only, valid standard is whether the public was served, whether radio and television, unfettered by Section 315, could do and did a better job of interesting and informing the American voter. By that single standard, the 1960 experiment was not just a success—it was a triumph. . . . I hope most earnestly that the Congress will promptly, completely and permanently free broadcasting from restraints that, however noble in purpose, were abortive in operation and have now proved unnecessary in fact.[17]

In its recommendations, filed on April 17, 1962, the Subcommittee on Freedom of Communication (a subcommittee of the Senate Subcommittee on Communications), which had studied the way in which broadcasters had covered the 1960 presidential campaign, took issue with Stanton and his colleagues concerning the adequacy of the 1960 experiment. The subcommittee argued:

> Despite claims to the contrary, the exemption from Section 315 of the presidential campaign in 1960 did not give us a comprehensive picture of what would happen if the exemption were made permanent. The 1960 exemption became effective on August 26, 1960, *after* both national conventions of the two major political parties. Performance of the networks and licensees in the period prior to the conventions under such an exemption has not been tested.[18]

The subcommittee concluded that consideration of a permanent statute to qualify Section 315 was premature. Even more, the subcommittee questioned some of the assumptions made by advocates of the section's abolition. The subcommittee stated:

> The drive for suspension of Section 315 permanently has some curious overtones. There seems to be a feeling on the part of some proponents of this type of legislation that those who are eminently qualified in the field of entertainment are better able to judge the format and content of political programs designed to enlighten the public than the candidates themselves. Those who test the public response and rate programs accordingly for entertainment value or the sale of commercial products may not be the best judge to analyze the citizen's quest for information or his taste for political controversy. . . . The interposition of the licensee between the candidate and the public does not mean that the licensee is to act as a filter, substituting his judgment for that of the candidate as to what the American people want to hear.
> The substitution of licensee judgment for that of the candidates themselves, as to how best to present the candidates and the issues, the format and content of political programming, is freedom abused.[19]

This concern that abolition of Section 315 would increase the power of broadcasters to control political dialogue at the expense of the power of politicians may account in part for the lack of success by Senator Jacob Javits when he introduced a bill to suspend Section 315 for the congressional campaign in 1962, or by Senator John Pastore when he introduced a bill to repeal it, or by Senator Pastore and Senator Warren Magnuson when they cosponsored a bill to continue the suspension of the equal-time provision for presidential and vice-presidential candidates. Evidence was presented at a 1963 hearing of the Senate Subcommittee on Communications that more than half the governors in the country favored suspension of Section 315 for gubernatorial campaigns.[20] According to a Gallup Poll, 71 percent of the American public favored broadcast debates between presidential candidates of the sort that suspension of 315 would make possible.[21]

As the 1964 election approached, it appeared that Congress would agree on a suspension of some sort. During the summer of 1963 the Senate approved a bill to suspend the equal-time rule for sixty days preceding the election. The House approved a somewhat different suspension.[22] In May 1964, a congressional conference committee representing the Senate and the House agreed on a compromise version of the two bills.[23] Two months later, a coalition of Democrats in the Senate was able to get the bill tabled by a vote of 44 to 41, thus effectively killing the chances for broadcast debates between the presidential candidates in 1964.[24] Many observers attributed this defeat of the bill to the reluctance of President Johnson to participate in such debates.[25] As the incumbent, endowed with all of the power and media exposure of the presidency, Johnson was determined not to give Goldwater any opportunities for equal exposure, which might have resulted had presidential debates been possible.

The loss in exposure of the candidate to the public can be seen in the fact that the largest audience for any appearance by either Johnson or Goldwater in 1964 was only 20 to 25 percent as large as the audience for the first Kennedy-Nixon debate four years earlier.[26]

A month and a half after the Senate killed efforts to suspend Section 315, the Federal Communications Commission, by a vote of 4 to 3, ruled that any station carrying President Johnson's news conferences in full must meet equal-time demands.[27]

In one of the many efforts during the sixties to alleviate the financial burdens of political campaigns, Senator Mike Mansfield, in 1961, proposed legislation, S.222, to make available a million-dollar subsidy to each of the two major parties for the purchase of broadcast time.[28] This legislation was not enacted.

The effort during this period to gain some measure of control over mounting campaign costs that ultimately proved most important was initiated by President Kennedy when he appointed a Commission on Campaign Costs. The charge of the commission was to recommend means for reducing presidential campaign costs and for financing those costs. The commission report, *Financing Presidential Campaigns*,[29] filed in April 1962, was endorsed by all six of the men then alive who had been presidential candidates of one of the two major parties: Truman, Eisenhower, Stevenson, Dewey, Nixon, and, of course, Kennedy. The major innovation in the report was the idea of matching funds.[30]

The legislative remedies for the problems of campaign finance were not enacted for many years, and the major party expenditures in the 1964 presidential general election rose to $24,783,000, an increase of 24 percent over 1960. The costs of broadcast time, on the other hand, rose 267 percent to a total of $11,044,000, 45 percent of the total campaign costs. If production and other related costs were added to the broadcast time costs, of course, that percentage would be far greater. Broadcasting expenditures by the Republicans exceeded those of the Democrats by 36 percent; total campaign expenditures of Republicans were almost double those of the Democrats.[31]

These greater costs are explained in part by the sharp reduction in sustaining network time devoted to the presidential and vice-presidential candidates. Such sustaining time on the commercial television networks dropped from 17 hours 32 minutes in 1960 to 1 hour 18 minutes in 1964; for radio networks it dropped from 21 hours 57 minutes in 1960 to 7 hours 38 minutes. Minor party candidates received 8 percent of that sustaining television time in 1960, none in 1964. On the other hand, they received more sustaining radio time in 1964 than in 1960, 7 percent compared to 4 percent.[32]

THE GREAT DEBATES

Political commercials became an issue in the 1964 campaign not only because of their mounting costs but also because of their content. Eisenhower's advertising agency had used an amusing one-minute animated commercial in 1952, accompanied by a catchy jingle, "I like Ike, You like Ike, Everybody likes Ike." Nevertheless, it was not until 1964 that short commercials were widely used.

Cries of "foul" were heard when the Johnson advertising agency created the "Daisy Girl" commercial and presented it on NBC-TV. The one-minute commercial began with a small girl picking daisies in a field. Then she began to count the petals as she picked them from the flower. As she reached nine, an ominous voice was faded in, counting backwards as in the countdown for a nuclear blast. As the child reached ten and the man's voice tolled zero, the screen dissolved into an atomic explosion.

"These are the stakes," warned the voice of President Johnson, "to make a world in which all God's children can live, or go into the dark. We must either love each other or we must die."[33] No mention was made of candidate Goldwater. None needed to be. The implication was clear.

A similar anti-Goldwater commercial showed a child eating an ice-cream cone, while the sound track carried a maternal voice, explaining that strontium 90, a fall-out element from nuclear testing, is found in milk, and that Goldwater had voted against the test-ban treaty. Yet another tagged Goldwater as an opponent of the Social Security system. All of these commercials were created by the advertising agency, Doyle Dane Bernbach, marking its entry into the field of political commercials.[34]

Not to be outdone, the Republicans produced a film titled *Choice*, which they claimed was sponsored by the "Mothers for a Moral America" and which played on middle-class fears. It showed, among other sights, a girl in a topless swimsuit, beatnik revels, a striptease, and black people rioting and looting. Goldwater, however, citing his belief that the film would increase racism, refused to permit its release.[35]

Interestingly, earlier, during the presidential primary campaign in California, Nelson Rockefeller insisted on canceling a half-hour television film made for his campaign against Goldwater by the Spencer-Roberts firm. Titled *The Extremists*, it showed the fate of a number of Californians persecuted by southern California witch-hunters. Rockefeller labeled the film "McCarthyism in reverse."[36]

When asked to rule on the acceptability of some of these television commercials, the Code Office of the National Association of Broadcasters refused to do so, "because of the difficulty in applying Code standards to politics."[37] However, the American Advertising Federation issued an "Advertising Code of American Politics," in which it suggested that "political spots should be truthful, inoffensive to good taste or public decency, and should not disparage opposition candidates." Political observer Edward Chester has questioned whether this code "covers a commercial of the sort which California Governor Edmund Brown used in his campaign against Ronald Reagan [in 1966] in which Brown reminded the audience, 'Remember it was an actor who shot Lincoln.' "[38]

Short political commercials were used in the 1964 campaign more than ever before. In the top 75 markets, nearly 10,000 of them were aired on television stations. The Democrats alone sponsored 410 commercials in New York, 1,345 in Texas, and 832 in California.[39]

Increasingly sophisticated use of computers by the parties was evidenced in 1964. The Goldwater strategists, aided by the largest marketing-communications conglomerate in the world, the Interpublic Group of New York, utilized computers to analyze the 1952, 1956, and 1960 presidential elections by party, state, and ethnic group to determine the major television markets which could help them to reach the audience most crucial for a Goldwater victory at the lowest price.[40]

The broadcasting networks also demonstrated more sophisticated use of computers for projecting election returns. Throughout the 1964 primaries, ABC News, CBS News, NBC News, the Associated Press, and United Press International all operated expensive independent vote tabulation systems. After initial discussions by the CBS and ABC presidents, network news heads Fred W. Friendly and Elmer W. Lower organized a meeting among the news organizations and worked out the pool sponsorship and structure of the new News Election Service in time for the 1964 general election night coverage. Network coverage began that night at 7:00 P.M., EST, by which time News Election Service had tabulated two percent of the ultimate vote total. At 7:09 David Brinkley reported that NBC's Electronic Vote Analysis projected a Johnson victory with between 60 and 70 percent of the votes. CBS News and ABC News soon reached the same conclusion.[41]

Three months before the election, Senator Pierre Salinger, California Democrat, a candidate in the 1964 election, introduced a Senate resolution, cosponsored by five western colleagues, that stated it was "the sense of Congress that national radio and television networks and other news-gathering agencies should refrain from broadcasting or distributing projections or predictions based on electronic computation of an election for president or members of Congress until after the latest official closing time of any polling place for such an election in any other state on the same day."[42] This would have delayed all projections until 2 A.M., EST, when the westernmost precinct closed in Alaska. The resolution did not pass.

Because of the landslide margin for Johnson, the speed of the NES tabulation, and the early airing of projections of a Democratic victory, numerous complaints were voiced after the election. There were demands that the computers be restrained. Senator Salinger complained for several months that the early projections had hurt him. It was hard to see, however, how the damage could have changed the result. He ran more than a million votes behind the head of his ticket in California, President Johnson.

The percentage of voting-age citizens who cast their ballots in 1964 was 61.9, down only 9 percent from the record high of 1960. The absolute number of people voting was the highest ever, almost 71 million, and Johnson's margin of victory over Goldwater, both in absolute number and in percentage of votes cast (61.1 vs. 38.4) was the largest ever.[43]

THE GREAT DEBATES

There was an interesting footnote to the 1964 election campaign. Journalists and media technicians covering the 1964 Democratic convention outnumbered the delegates and alternates 5,500 to 5,260.[44]

The 1968 Election

As the shadow of John Kennedy's assassination hung over the 1964 election campaign, the assassinations of Martin Luther King, Jr., and Senator Robert F. Kennedy, racial and antiwar violence, and, finally, the decision by President Lyndon B. Johnson not to seek re-election all weighed heavily on the nation in the period leading up and through the 1968 presidential election campaign.

Television and radio coverage of these events, especially of the scenes of rioting and its aftermath, provided a context for the election which stimulated the desire for change. "Law and order" became the password, and the media, especially television, were damned for exacerbating the violence by glorifying its leaders and encouraging its spread.[45]

The creation of the context of fear for the 1968 election had its first major impetus on August 11, 1965, when the black Watts district of Los Angeles exploded in racial fury. For six days, television showed the results. These scenes were repeated July 12 to 17, 1967, from Newark, N.J., and July 23 to 30, 1967, from Detroit. The most sustained and widespread scenes of such disorders were broadcast during the first ten days following Martin Luther King's assassination on April 4, 1968, as racial violence erupted in 125 cities in 29 states.

As racial protests and disorders escalated, so did the war in Vietnam and the protests of those who opposed it. These, too, filled America's television screens and the other media. By the summer of 1968, there seemed to be little left that could shock the American public. The assassination of Sen. Robert Kennedy on June 5, however, in the midst of the celebration of his victory in the Democratic presidential primary in California, did so.

Two months earlier, on March 31, television and radio carried Lyndon Johnson's surprise announcement that he would not seek or accept the nomination of the Democratic party for another term as president. Mounting protests against his Vietnam policy by the young, by many reporters and media commentators, and even by other leaders within his party, had made his role untenable.

It was in this unsettled context that the presidential campaign took place.

Equally unsettled through most of the 1964–68 period was the fate of the equal-time provision of Section 315 of the Communications Act. No sooner was the 1964 presidential vote tallied than efforts were renewed to eliminate or modify this provision.

The opening blow was struck by FCC Chairman E. William Henry on January 15, 1965. Henry proposed that the equal-time provision be reformed, rather than suspended or repealed. He suggested that Section 315 be amended to require political parties to have won a certain minimum percentage of votes in the most recent election to qualify for free time. New parties, he proposed, could qualify by petition if they had some minimum number of signatures of registered voters. Henry warned against outright repeal of Section 315 because it could give too much power to the nine organizations that controlled three-quarters of the television stations reaching 40 percent of America's homes.[46]

Such a bill was proposed by Senator Hugh Scott later that year. It specified that candidates of parties that received less than 10 percent of the vote in the previous election would be excluded from the provisions of Section 315.[47] Scott's bill and three others were the subject of hearings before the Senate Communications Subcommittee July 18–20, 1967. One bill introduced by Senator James Pearson, Kansas Republican, would have permanently suspended Section 315 for presidential and vice-presidential candidates, thus making possible Kennedy-Nixon type debates for all presidential elections. A bill by Senator John Pastore, chairman of the subcommittee, would have exempted gubernatorial and congressional candidates as well as presidential candidates from the equal-time provision. Just before the hearing, Senator Vance Hartke submitted a bill that would simply have repealed Section 315 in its entirety, doing away with both the equal-time provision and the fairness doctrine.[48]

None of these bills were passed, despite initial Republican and later Democratic efforts. Prior to President Johnson's announcement that he would not seek re-election, the House Republican Policy Committee urged passage of a bill that would permit presidential debates in 1968, but the Democratic majority failed to act. House Minority Leader Gerald Ford, pressing for passage of enabling legislation, claimed that any Republican nominee would be willing to debate Lyndon Johnson. On May 29, following the Johnson announcement, the Senate passed a bill suspending the equal-time provision for presidential and vice-presidential candidates for 1968 only. After some delay, the House Commerce Committee amended the Senate bill to allow for a three-way debate among the Democratic nominee, the Republican nominee, and minority party candidate George Wallace.

After the nominating conventions, Democratic nominee Hubert Humphrey, who had refused to debate either Robert Kennedy or Eugene McCarthy in the primaries, urged passage of a bill to permit debates among presidential nominees. However, by this time, Republican candidate Nixon was reported to be unwilling to participate in such debates, and House Republicans engaged in the equivalent of a filibuster on October 8 and 9 to prevent action on the Senate bill. The House session, which also included consideration of bills on campaign spending reform and congressional reorganization, which the Republicans favored and Democrats opposed, lasted 32 hours 17 minutes, the longest continuous session in 93 years and the third longest in history. Finally, after 45 roll call votes, the House passed an amended version of the bill and returned it to the Senate, where threats of more "extended debate" by Republicans prevented its consideration, and the Senate was adjourned without action.[49]

Though there were no presidential debates in 1968, one major debate between two of the aspirants for the Democratic nomination, Eugene McCarthy and Robert Kennedy, was televised. Although he had refused to debate McCarthy earlier, saying that he would participate in such a confrontation only if Hubert Humphrey also participated, Kennedy changed his mind following his defeat in the Oregon presidential preference primary, and the hour-long, nationally televised debate was held on June 1, just before the California primary. Following Robert Kennedy's assassination, both McCarthy and Humphrey claimed to be willing to debate, but no agreement on details could be reached and no debate took place.[50]

McCarthy was responsible for another controversy involving television and radio and Section 315 during the time it still appeared that Johnson would be standing for re-election. This was an important controversy, for it raised the question of when an incumbent president becomes a candidate. On December 19, 1967, the three commercial television networks carried an hour interview with Johnson titled "Conversation with the President." The following day, McCarthy asked for equal time and the networks refused, saying that Johnson had not announced his candidacy and thus was not a legally qualified candidate. The FCC agreed with the network decision, and the U.S. Court of Appeals in Washington upheld the FCC. However, in its decision, the appeals court appeared to question the wisdom of applying the test of formal announcement of candidacy too firmly. The court stated:

> No rule in this sensitive area can be applied mechanically without, in some instances at least, resulting in unfairness and possible constitutional complications . . . . But program content and perhaps other criteria may provide a guide to reality where a public figure allowed television or radio time has not announced for public office.[51]

A year earlier, it was Republican Gerald Ford who challenged President Johnson's access to the electronic media without equal opportunity for the opposition party. When the television networks refused live coverage of the Republican leaders' answer to the president's State of the Union address in January 1967, just as they had refused the previous year, Ford claimed that the Republican party not only favored nationally televised debates between presidential candidates, it also favored legislation that would require free and equal access to the major parties between elections.[52]

Equal time was not the only political issue prompting congressional attacks on broadcasters during the 1964–1968 period. Despite studies which indicated that computer projections of vote totals before all polls were closed had little, if any, effect on election outcomes, pressures to eliminate even the possibility were continued. The General Assembly of the States, a conference of governmental officials from throughout the nation, adopted a resolution that condemned voting projections and called for state and federal laws to prohibit any that might influence election results in areas where the polls have not closed.[53] Broadcasters proposed that uniform polling hours would resolve the problem and Senator Jacob Javits introduced two bills to facilitate such uniformity. One required all polls to close at a time equal to 11 P.M., EST, and 5 P.M., Bering time, and the other to make presidential election day a national holiday, so that the early poll closing time in the West would not inhibit voting. Neither the Javits bills nor any of the other proposals were enacted.[54]

Even stronger attacks on broadcasters accompanied and followed broadcast coverage of the 1968 Democratic convention in Chicago. There had been periodic conflict between the political parties and television personnel over coverage of the conventions since at least 1954. This conflict reached a head during the tension-filled days of August 1968, as the Democrats nominated Hubert

Humphrey and Edmund Muskie to head their ticket. *Broadcasting* magazine reported:

> Night after night, TV and radio commentators used their nationwide electronic platforms to expound on aspects of control by force and hidden control that they felt to be hindering their coverage efforts. Instead of leaving the public with an image of law and order inside and outside the amphitheater, and a democratic choosing of a national candidate, the impression given was of a police state with TV reporters slugged and pushed inside the hall and defiant young demonstrators and attendant reporters being indiscriminately clubbed by police in other parts of the city.[55]

An estimated dozen reporters and photographers were arrested during the course of the convention, including at least one on the floor of the convention, CBS News's Mike Wallace, during a disagreement with police. Charges of hostility, bias, and poor news judgment were hurled at journalists, with major television figures David Brinkley and Chet Huntley of NBC and Walter Cronkite, Roger Mudd, and Eric Sevareid of CBS being singled out for particular criticism.[56]

Drew Pearson and Jack Anderson, in their syndicated column dated September 6, 1968, charged:

> After the Miami Beach convention, we reported that the TV networks, angry over the $3 million it was costing them to pull up their cables and transfer everything to Chicago, intended to retaliate by focusing attention on Democratic "disturbances." The networks got their revenge. In Chicago they played up the violence which they had virtually ignored in Miami. They complained about tight security restrictions, which, incidentally, had also been imposed by the Republican Convention. They sought out the dissidents and featured them while the Democratic orators were expounding.[57]

Following the convention, at least three independent investigations were conducted. One was by a Federal Grand Jury for the Northern District of Illinois. It subsequently indicted some members of the Chicago police force, demonstration leaders, and one NBC employee for alleged violations of the Criminal Code. The NBC employee was accused of illegally placing microphones in the hearing room used by the Democratic platform committee.

The Federal Communications Commission attempted to determine whether any violations of the Communications Act had occurred. The Special Subcommittee on Investigations of the U.S. House of Representatives Committee on Interstate and Foreign Commerce aimed its study at determining whether there was any evidence that television convention coverage warranted consideration of changes in the communications law or policy.

The staff of the House subcommittee concluded that evidence supported charges of some bias by network employees against the city of Chicago and the Democratic party and in favor of demonstrators and protestors. They also concluded that there was unfairness in the intercutting by CBS-TV between scenes from police-demonstrator confrontations in downtown Chicago and shots of Mayor Richard Daley assuring interviewer Dan Rather that police were not using undue violence and that everything was well in hand, when the mayor was unaware that such intercutting was being done. On the other hand, charges that the networks had staged and filmed events that they later presented as bona fide news, or that executives of the networks encouraged or condoned illegal or biased coverage, were not supported.[58]

By the time of the 1968 election, television set saturation in the United States was almost complete, with approximately 95 percent of all homes equipped with at least one receiver. The South, however, continued to lag behind other parts of the country.[59] The Radio Advertising Bureau reported as early as 1966 that there were 242 million radios in the country, more than one each for the 195 million people.[60]

The only clear innovation in the 1968 political advertising campaign occurred in the primaries when Eugene McCarthy adopted a radio variation of the chain letter technique in a last-minute attempt to head off the nomination of Humphrey. The idea was radio spots that would be self-generating. Each supporter of McCarthy who paid for a commercial was also the voice on the air, stressing that he or she had paid for the time, indicating a reason for supporting McCarthy, and urging other supporters to take to the air with their support.[61]

Radio was used more fully in 1968 than in any presidential campaign in recent years, especially by the Republicans. Five-minute excerpts from Nixon's speech accepting the Republican nomination, detailed presentations of issue positions, and messages from Nixon's campaign plane tailored to the particular region over which he was flying were broadcast regularly, along with appearances by key supporters on interview programs, call-in shows, and other talk programs. In assessing the success of the radio campaign following the election, Nixon's campaign manager, John N. Mitchell, noted that the only change he would make if the campaign were just starting would be to spend even more money on radio.[62]

Other uses of broadcasting in the presidential campaign were continuations or developments of techniques from earlier campaigns. The Democrats sponsored a television commercial that was reminiscent of the "Daisy Girl" spot against Goldwater which suggested that Nixon favored nuclear war because of his failure to support ratification of the nuclear nonproliferation treaty. It even repeated the use of the mushroom cloud.[63] The Republicans aired a spot during NBC's "Laugh-In" showing shots of Humphrey laughing, intercut with shots of riots and war carnage. Protests caused the commercial's withdrawal after one showing. Similarly, the Democrats withdrew a spot that showed an "Agnew for Vice-President" sign coupled with a soundtrack of a man laughing.[64]

The American Association of Advertising Agencies' ad hoc group on political advertising early in the campaign warned advertising agencies and the media to "get cash in advance since political accounts are notoriously lax about their debts and the lost money can't be deducted at tax time." The AAAA also suggested that no ad agency represent a candidate who had not signed or who did not observe the code promulgated by the Fair Campaign Practices Committee.[65]

Campaign reform and campaign funding continued to occupy the Congress during the 1964–68 period, sparked by campaign finance scandals involving Senator Thomas Dodd of Connecticut and Bobby Baker, a former Lyndon Johnson aide. Attempts were made to establish a bipartisan Federal Election

Commission to receive, analyze, and publicize election spending reports from candidates and committees. In 1966, a bill to provide federal subsidies for presidential elections was passed on the final day of the second session of the 89th Congress. Attempts the following spring to repeal the act failed, but the same end was achieved. Its provisions were no longer in force after May 1967.[66]

Meanwhile, election campaign costs made their sharpest rise in history, from $200 million in 1964 to $300 million in 1968. This 50 percent increase contrasts with a 14 percent increase for 1964 over 1960, a 13 percent increase for 1960 over 1956, and an 11 percent increase for 1956 over 1952, the first presidential year for which such costs were calculated.[67] Of the total spent on broadcasting in 1968, 91 percent was spent for spot commercials, 9 percent for longer programs.[68]

According to FCC reports, time costs alone in 1968 approached $59 million, with production and promotion costs probably adding another $20 million. For the presidential general election campaign, over $12 million was spent for broadcast time for the Nixon ticket, almost $6 million for the Humphrey ticket, and over $1.5 million for the Wallace ticket.[69]

There were 60.9 percent of the voting age population who cast ballots in 1968, down 1 percent from 1964. Nixon's edge was less than 1 percent— 43.4 percent to Humphrey's 42.7 percent, with 13.5 percent going to George Wallace.[70]

The 1972 Election

With passage of the Federal Election Campaign Act of 1971 and the Revenue Act of 1971, the United States witnessed the culmination of years of effort to resolve the problems of financing political campaigns for federal office. The former act, passed by Congress on January 19, 1972, and signed by President Nixon on February 7, became effective on April 7. It was the first major legislation in almost half a century to deal with the problems of rising federal election costs. It replaced the Federal Corrupt Practices Act of 1925.

The new act limited the amount that could be spent by federal candidates for advertising time in communications media to 10 cents per eligible voter, or $50,000, whichever was greater. Media costs, defined to include agency commissions, covered broadcasting stations, newspapers, magazines, outdoor advertising facilities, and telephones (excluding telephone costs incurred by volunteers). Expenditures for broadcast media could not exceed 60 percent of the total media costs incurred. The act also prohibited radio and television stations from charging political candidates more than the lowest unit cost for the same advertising time available to commercial advertisers during the 45 days preceding a primary election and the 60 days preceding a general election, and required that they allow reasonable access or permit the purchase of reasonable amounts of time by candidates for federal elective office.

Limits were also placed on campaign contributions. Disclosure of contributions and expenditures was required.[71]

The Revenue Act of 1971 provided a tax incentive for contributors to political campaigns, a tax credit for 50 percent of one's contributions up to a maximum of $12.50 on a single return and $25.00 on a joint return or, alter-

THE GREAT DEBATES

natively, a deduction up to a maximum of $50 or $100. The act also provided a mechanism for taxpayers to contribute $1 of their income tax payment for a general fund for presidential and vice-presidential candidates, and prohibited major party candidates who accepted public financing from accepting private campaign contributions unless there were insufficient funds available from the income tax check-off to pay campaign expenses to which candidates were entitled.[72]

A third piece of legislation which affected the use of broadcasting by political candidates and the probable impact of that use was the constitutional amendment lowering the voting age for national elections in the United States to eighteen. Ratification of this proposal by states was completed on June 30, 1971, and it became the 26th Amendment to the Constitution.

A bill similar in most respects to the Federal Election Campaign Act of 1971 was passed in 1970 but was vetoed by President Nixon, and the Congress was unable to overturn the veto. The major difference between the two bills, which is especially pertinent to the topic of this book, is that the 1970 Act would have repealed the equal-time provision of Section 315 of the Communications Act, thus facilitating the broadcasting of debates between major party presidential and vice-presidential candidates without the need to give equal time to minor party candidates.[73] The bill was S.3637.

Another proposal which failed to become part of the Federal Election Campaign Act of 1971 was a ban on the use of television spots in political campaigns, proposed by Senator Vance Hartke and supported by Senator Robert Dole, Senator Edmund Muskie, and former FCC chairman Newton Minow.[74]

Despite the lack of enabling legislation during the Democratic primaries, the ABC and CBS television networks each carried a debate-type confrontation between Hubert Humphrey and George McGovern which was billed as a news interview, a category specified by the Communications Act as exempt from the equal-time provision. Representative Shirley Chisholm, also a candidate in the California presidential primary at the time, requested equal treatment from ABC and CBS, but her request was denied. The network decisions were supported by the FCC, but overturned by a unanimous decision of the Federal Appeals Court panel, which held that the Humphrey-McGovern appearances on CBS and ABC were "debates," not "interviews," and hence not exempt from the equal-time law.[75]

The FCC took a somewhat harder line against comedian Pat Paulsen, causing him to lose a chance to appear on "The Mouse Factory" television program. The commission ruled that Paulsen had qualified to be on the ballot in New Hampshire and was apparently actively campaigning, hence he was a bona fide candidate for the Republican presidential election and the equal-time rule would apply if he appeared on "The Mouse Factory."[76]

Plans for a debate among all seven of the candidates for the Democratic nomination in the Florida primary were foiled when candidates Muskie and Humphrey refused to participate.[77]

During the sixties and seventies, primary elections became increasingly important for the Democratic party, climaxed by James Earl Carter's striking victory in 1976. The major boost to the importance of these primaries came from the Democratic reforms of 1970, which substantially altered the way in which many delegates to the national convention were selected. This altered the makeup of that convention.

These reforms were initiated the night of August 27, 1968, at the Democratic convention, when delegates passed what appeared to be a mild resolution proposed by the credentials committee to set up a committee to reform and improve delegate selection processes for national conventions. The committee became known as the McGovern Committee.[78]

We have had the same difficulty generalizing about the use of broadcasting in the twenty-two Democratic presidential primaries as the candidates had in planning such use, because of the varied forms those primaries took. In some states delegates were elected directly in the primaries. Some were preferential primaries in which voters simply indicated which presidential candidates they wanted their delegates to support. In others that preference was binding on the delegate representing a particular group; in still other states it was not. In some states there was a combination of preferential and delegate-selection primaries. In some states one voted by slate—all or none, with each slate pledged to a different candidate. In other states, one voted for delegates individually, in some cases not even knowing which candidates they favored. Each of these types of primaries called for a different campaign strategy and, hence, a different strategy for using broadcasting.[79] The importance of this burgeoning primary system is seen in the fact that, among all Democratic candidates in 1972, the Gallup Poll in January showed Muskie supported by 32 percent of the public, Kennedy by 27 percent, Humphrey by 17 percent, and McGovern by only 3 percent.[80]

In 1972 campaigning costs, especially those for broadcasting, began to come under control. The country's total election campaign bill for 1972 was estimated at $425 million, with a third of that—roughly $138 million—spent in the presidential campaign. This total represents a slight leveling off of the trend in increased election year costs, the first such slackening of the trend in the twenty years that such costs were computed. It is an increase of 42 percent over 1968, 8 percent less than the increase of 1968 over 1964.[81]

One out of each seven dollars spent in election campaigns in 1972 was for radio or television time (these figures do not include production and other costs associated with broadcasting). This was almost $53 million, of which over $14 million was for the presidential campaign (almost $11 million for television and over $3 million for radio time). Over twice as much was spent for broadcast time for the Democratic presidential campaign as for the Republican one, partly because of the greater primary election costs for the Democrats, partly because of the Nixon campaign strategy in 1972.[82] Of the total spent for broadcasting, roughly 88 percent was for short commercials, 12 percent for longer programs. This compares to 91 and 9 percent for 1968.[83]

In the general election of 1972, excluding the primaries, the total amount spent for broadcast time in the campaigns for all offices was just over $38 million. This was a decrease of more than $2 million from 1968. This was the first presidential election year in which there was a reversal of the rapidly escalating cost of broadcast time (almost $10 million in 1956, over $14 million in 1960, over $24.5 million in 1964, and over $40 million in 1968). This drop in campaign spending from 1968 to 1972 was due completely to the sharp drop in

THE GREAT DEBATES

broadcast time purchased by the Republicans: $22.5 million in 1968, $17.5 million in 1972.[84]

The broadcasting expenditures for the presidential campaigns of both major parties in the 1972 general election were well below the $8.5 million limit set by the Federal Election Campaign Act of 1971. Though McGovern spent more for broadcasting than any previous Democratic candidate, his expenditures totaled only $6.2 million. Large amounts of money were also spent to get him to events where free television coverage was likely. Nixon spent $4.3 for broadcasting in 1972, which was only a third of the $12.6 million he had spent in 1968.[85]

Although broadcasting expenditures for the Democratic presidential ticket exceeded those for the Republican ticket, the Republicans maintained their traditional edge in overall spending on the general presidential election campaign: $61.9 million to $30 million.[86]

The new campaign law took effect on April 7, 1972, with the expectation of some evasion, at least during the initial year. Evidence that the spirit, if not the letter, of the law was being broken by political fund raisers was observed as early as March 1972.[87] It was not until the Watergate disclosures following the election, though, that the full extent of the evasion was even suspected.

The 1972 election saw a candidate use the presidency to control his media coverage probably more expertly than anyone ever had before. This control can be seen in the striking story of Richard Nixon meeting with Chou En-lai in China, fed directly back through communication satellites to television receivers in American homes, during the same day that those receivers were getting pictures of Edmund Muskie trudging through the snows of New Hampshire or choking in anger over the attacks upon his wife by New Hampshire publisher William Loeb. Here we saw, more clearly than anywhere, the striking difference in the power of officeholder and challenger to control their media coverage. Later, as one observer commented:

> While Senator McGovern is fraying his nerves and his finances out on the hustings, the President sits in the White House reaching just as many voters through the media and, what's more, reaching them in the role of a confident, powerful leader rather than as a scrambling self-assertive office-seeker.[88]

President Nixon's control of his broadcast coverage was but a continuation of the practices he had developed throughout his term in office. That control is probably best exemplified by comparative data on televised speeches that can be firmly controlled by the president and the relatively uncontrollable press conference. One study reached these conclusions:

> In his first eighteen months in office, President Nixon appeared on prime-time television as many times as the *combined* appearances of Presidents Eisenhower, Kennedy, and Johnson in their first eighteen months in office. During his first forty months in office prior to his Moscow trip, President Nixon had made thirty-two special appearances in prime time, compared to only twenty-four by President Johnson in over five years, ten by President Kennedy in under three years, and twenty-three by President Eisenhower in eight years. . . .

In his three terms and one month in office, Franklin Delano Roosevelt held 998 presidential news conferences; Truman, 324 in under eight years; Eisenhower, 193 in eight years; Kennedy, 64 in three years; Johnson, 126 in six years; and Richard Nixon, in his first four years, only 28.[89]

Such facts as these brought increasing cries for legislation insuring equal time for opposition voices between as well as during election campaign periods. These cries became most vociferous during the Vietnam war, when opponents of administration policies, during both the Johnson and Nixon terms, believed that they should be granted greater access to present their views on television. The frustration of these protestors can be seen in the lament of Senator Harold Hughes of Iowa, when a group of congressmen under his leadership attempted to buy television time, after their requests for free time were rejected, so that they could adequately present their anti-administration position to the public. Said Hughes, "I could buy time to sell soap or women's underwear, but not to speak as a United States Senator on issues of war and peace."[90]

The 1968–1972 period also saw the continued growth of the campaign management business. By the off-year elections of 1970, there were at least 200 organizations that were primarily in the business of designing and managing marketing campaigns for political candidates.[91] The acknowledged television experts in the business by this time were Harry Treleaven and Robert Ailes, who worked on the Nixon campaigns; Robert Goodman who created television materials for other Republican campaigns; Charles Guggenheim, McGovern's television adviser in 1972; and David Garth and Robert Squier, each of whom worked for a variety of Democratic candidates.[92]

The percentage of voting-age citizens casting ballots dropped to 55.5 percent in 1972, down from 60.9 percent in 1968. This drop is due in part to the below-average voting proportions among the newly enfranchised eighteen- to twenty-year-olds, although this group does not account for the entire drop.[93] The Nixon popular vote margin over McGovern, however, exceeded by 0.5 percent even the record 1964 Johnson margin over Goldwater. The Republican candidate won 60.7 percent of the vote, and the Democratic candidate 37.5 percent, with minor party candidates accounting for the rest.

The 1976 Election

The 1976 presidential election campaign was interesting for many reasons, not the least of which was that the incumbent president, running for a new term, had never been a candidate in a national election. Gerald Ford had been appointed vice-president when Spiro Agnew resigned in disgrace and had succeeded to the presidency when Richard Nixon resigned in disgrace. Probably more important, in terms of its impact both on American presidential politics and on the role of radio and television in this politics, is that this was the first presidential campaign in United States history to be subsidized almost totally by tax funds.

In place of funds raised from private and corporate sources, Gerald Ford and Jimmy Carter each received $21.8 million in federal funds to finance his campaign. (This amount will be adjusted in the future as a result of changes

30

in the Consumer Price Index.) In addition to that subsidy, each could raise up to $3.2 million from private sources through his respective national party committee. Up to $4.5 million could be raised from private sources to be spent on behalf of state, local, city, and congressional district committees. To put these figures into perspective, this total for each candidate is not only considerably less than the $61.4 million spent for Richard Nixon's campaign in 1972, it is even below the $30 million spent by McGovern in 1972.[94] This was the first time since 1948, when television first became an important factor in election campaigns, that the sharply escalating costs of the presidential general election campaign declined.

While the costs of the general election campaign went down due to the Federal Election Campaign Act of 1971 as amended, the costs of the primary campaign for the presidential nominations increased. Aided by federal subsidies for the first time, the aspirants spent approximately $70 million in their chase for the party nominations. Roughly $24 million of the total came from federal subsidies. In 1976, each primary candidate was eligible for funds of up to $5.45 million from the U.S. Treasury, to match private funds raised by the candidate in amounts of $250 or less.[95]

Because of delays growing out of political considerations and court challenges, the 1976 presidential contenders came close to missing out on federal subsidies. The system for public financing of elections became part of the Federal Election Campaign Act with the amendments of 1974 (together with the Revenue Act of 1971), which also set new contribution and spending limits. The amendments also provided for some financial support of presidential nominating conventions, and created a full-time bipartisan Federal Election Commission to administer the act's provisions. Of special relevance to the mass media was the amendment repealing the media spending limitations in the Federal Election Campaign Act of 1971. As we shall suggest later, this change has major implications for future presidential election campaigns. These amendments were passed and signed into law in October 1974.

The new law took effect on January 1, 1975, but was immediately challenged in the courts by an assortment of plaintiffs, ranging from Conservative-Republican Senator James Buckley of New York to former Democratic Senator and presidential aspirant Eugene McCarthy, and from the Conservative Victory Fund to the American Civil Liberties Union. The U.S. Court of Appeals for the District of Columbia sustained the bulk of the law, but the decision of the United States Supreme Court, to which the case was appealed, on January 30, 1976, struck down some of its major provisions. The Court upheld the constitutionality of public financing for presidential elections, limits on individual political contributions, and the strict requirements for reporting contributions and expenditures, but struck down as unconstitutional the limits on campaign spending by congressional candidates and nearly all spending limits for presidential candidates who do not accept public funds. The greatest crisis for the 1976 election was created by the Court ruling that the system of appointing Federal Election Commissioners must be changed or the commission must cease most of its operations within thirty days. The aspect of the decision with the most far-reaching impact was the equation of campaign spending with free speech. The Court ruled that the government could not limit amounts spent on the campaign by individuals and groups, as long as the spending was not controlled by the candidate or coordinated with him or his campaign.[96]

Congress had until March 1 to reconstitute the Federal Election Commission, as required in the Supreme Court decision, if the commission was not to lose its major powers, including the power to grant matching funds to the candidates then running in the primaries. At the last moment, on February 28, when it became clear that the deadline would not be met, the Court extended it until March 22.[97]

The second deadline passed also, as Congress debated additional amendments to the act, creating problems for some of the primary candidates to whom matching funds were no longer available.

Finally, on May 4, Congress approved a bill to revive the Federal Election Committee and its authority to subsidize presidential candidates, though with less independent decision-making power. President Ford did not rush the signing of the bill or the reappointment of the commissioners; one of the candidates in need of matching funds was his major Republican challenger, Ronald Reagan. Finally he signed the bill on May 11 and on May 17 reappointed five members of the commission, whom the Senate confirmed.[98]

Through August 26, 1976, the two major contenders for the Republican nomination received the most matching funds for the primary campaign. Ronald Reagan led with $5,088,911, followed closely by Gerald Ford with $4,657,008. Among the Democratic contenders, Jimmy Carter, receiving $3,465,585, edged out George Wallace, who qualified for $3,291,309. Both Senator Henry Jackson of Washington and Representative Morris Udall of Arizona, the two next highest, qualified for just under $2 million each.[99]

The persistent efforts to amend Section 315 of the Communications Act were less successful than the efforts to revise the Campaign Act. A major thrust of most of the proposed amendments was to make possible and probable broadcast debates between the presidential candidates of the major parties.

In the Senate alone, at least five bills were introduced during this period which would have eliminated or modified the equal-time provision. Senator Pastore introduced a bill on January 16, 1973, which would have permanently exempted broadcasters from the equal-time requirement with respect to presidential and vice-presidential candidates (S.373). Senators Hugh Scott and Mac Mathias presented a similar bill on March 6, 1973, which would have applied to candidates for any federal elective office (S.1095). On January 15, 1975, Senator Proxmire proposed a bill that would have repealed Section 315 of the Communications Act in its entirety (S.2). Senators Pastore and Huddleston, in a bill introduced on February 7, 1975, suggested again an amendment that would have exempted from the equal-time provision only candidates for the offices of president and vice-president (S.608). The bill that went furthest in proposed deregulation of broadcast news coverage, nonpolitical as well as political, was introduced on March 18, 1975, by Senators Hruska, Curtis, Fannin, and Young. They labeled their bill the "Fully Free Press Act of 1975." They not only proposed repealing Section 315 but they also specified that:

Nothing in this Act shall be understood or construed to grant to the Commission the power to require any licensee to develop program-

ming specifically designed to provide balance to points of view previously broadcast or to require any licensee to make broadcast time
available to spokesmen for contrasting views on controversial issues
of public importance presented on his station (S.1178).

In hearings before the Subcommittee on Communications of the Senate
Committee on Commerce in March 1973, CBS executive Frank Stanton reminded the Senators that he had testified before this one committee alone regarding Section 315 eight different times in fourteen years![100]

Despite the maintenance of the equal-time provision in the Communications
Act, the 1959 Amendment of Section 315, which exempted news coverage of
bona fide news events, became the loophole that made possible the 1976 debates between candidates Carter and Ford without the necessity of providing
equivalent treatment for any of the other 205 candidates registered with the
Federal Election Commission.[101] The events leading up to these debates are
documented elsewhere in this book, and will not be discussed here except to cite
one explanation for the Carter-Ford agreement to debate that might be useful
to those who hope that such debates will become a fixture of presidential campaigns. Said one correspondent, "All it takes is an incumbent president who is
thirty-three points behind in the polls, and an opponent who nevertheless figures
he may have a recognition problem."[102]

Early in the primaries, Ronald Reagan's campaign directors proposed a debate between Reagan and Ford. This idea was reported to have been considered
and then rejected by White House advisors. The debate challenge was repeated
in July, this time with the proposed debate to take place at the Republican
National Convention, but again the president declined.[103]

During the 1972–1976 period, the use of television to raise funds for political campaigning developed into a rather fine art. The first "telethon" for this
purpose was produced in 1972 by the Democratic National Committee just
before its convention to help pay off party debts, some of them going back
to the 1968 campaign. The nineteen-hour show on the ABC network raised
approximately $2 million for the party in pledges of over $4 million. The telethon was repeated in 1973, 1974, and 1975. In 1976, instead of a telethon,
the Democratic National Committee bought thirty- and sixty-second blocks of
time during its presidential nominating convention for commercials appealing
for contributions.

The most successful use of television for political fund raising was that by
Ronald Reagan. In late March 1976, with his challenge of President Ford faltering, Reagan purchased a half-hour of prime network time to discuss his campaign and appeal for contributions to aid it. Time and production costs totaled
approximately $100,000, but the program resulted in contributions of more
than $1 million.[104]

The biggest news in the 1976 primaries was the early and effective grass-
roots campaign of Jimmy Carter, capitalizing on a four-year head start and a
sophisticated understanding of the Democratic Party's new delegate selection
system and of the way to balance personal contacts with optimum media use.
Carter's advertising director, Gerald Rafshoon of Atlanta, had a total advertising budget for the primaries and the general election of $14.3 million, of

which $11.25 million was spent on broadcasting. In Iowa, the first of the states to select delegates for the Democratic convention, Rafshoon spent $8,000 for commercials. He claimed that this was the first time a candidate had ever made a concerted media drive to attract caucus delegates.[105]

As *Broadcasting* magazine reported, President Ford tried "grass-rooting," but "in reverse," when he invited reporters from radio and television stations to the White House for exclusive news conferences. Those from New Hampshire received invitations just before the New Hampshire primary. The interviews with Florida, North Carolina, and Texas stations were timed just before each of those critical primaries. When one Miami station ran six-minute segments of those interviews on five consecutive evening newscasts, Reagan supporters complained to the FCC, citing the equal-time provision of Section 315, but the complaint was rejected.[106]

In prior years, the media have often been accused of turning public attention during a presidential election from issues to images. In the general election of 1976 it was clearly the candidates, not the media, who chose to run image campaigns. The key question was "Whom do you trust?" The media, especially television and radio, were more important than ever, in good part because of the spending restrictions of the new campaign laws. The campaign planners spent much of their energy and the energy of their candidates creating "media opportunities."

Ford advisors, utilizing the built-in advantages of White House incumbency, developed what the press came to term the "Rose Garden campaign." The *Columbia Journalism Review* reported:

> Ford's political managers contrived to set up bill-signing ceremonies in the White House Rose Garden to suggest that Ford was being "presidential" and doing his job, while Carter was rampaging around the country on what Ford meant to suggest was less "significant" business—a campaign. . . . The White House orchestrated the Rose Garden signings in a simple way. Ford's managers knew the networks would want to "balance" coverage of the two candidates during the campaign. To control what was available on Ford, the president was produced in public only once a day for a few moments in the Rose Garden. The networks had no other options. . . . For the most part, the networks did not have the courage to omit the phony Rose Garden shows, although every reporter involved knew they were phony.[107]

The "trust" issue was dominant in the commercials for both the Democratic and Republican candidates, the Carter spots playing on the disillusionment which many people felt in government, the Ford spots playing upon the theme: "He is making us proud again."[108]

Though the new campaign financing law brought about greater stress on television advertising by candidates, since it appeared to be the most "cost efficient" method of selling candidates, some broadcasters claim that the increased political business resulted in a net loss of revenue. Data compiled in the Chicago market indicate that many viewers turned off their sets during the five-minute political announcements and left them off. Drop-offs from two to five rating points were reported, and the loss appears to have been especially great among younger adults.[109] An interesting and related sidelight to this report on

THE GREAT DEBATES

the effect of longer political broadcasts is that WGN-TV, Chicago, refused to sell political candidates time in less than five-minute segments, while KGW-TV in Portland, Oregon, refused to sell at least one candidate in the primary *more* than five minutes. In both cases, the station policies were overturned by the Federal Communications Commission.[110]

In the media coverage of the 1976 election, especially in the primaries, there was greater self-reflectiveness demonstrated by journalists than in previous elections. They warned viewers, listeners, and readers of the dangers of being swayed by reporters' interpretations of events, rather than by the events themselves. These warnings followed the charges made after the 1972 primaries that media interpretations of the meaning of each primary vote had greater effect on subsequent events than the vote itself. Many journalists in 1976 appeared to be trying to avoid such interpreting and to stick to "objective" reporting. Their resistance soon broke down.

In addition to issuing warnings that media interpretation of results can influence subsequent primary elections, journalists often spent almost as much time and space reporting on the activities of the media as on the activities of candidates. It was as if journalists were playing two roles, both the reporter and the reported, without even a change of costume. They told the audience about "pack journalism." They showed how the gaggle of photographers and reporters trailing every candidate was "used" by the candidates who regularly staged "photo opportunities." They reported not only a candidate's statement, but the way in which the media treated that statement. They condemned themselves for contributing to the mundane quality of the campaign, for ignoring issues in favor of trivia.

In television, electronic news gathering—"ENG," in the jargon of the trade—proved itself in the 1976 campaign. Videotape replaced film for covering the campaign, not only for the networks, but for many local stations as well. It enabled them to get stories on the air faster and, for network newscasts, to move back deadlines. Freed of developing and editing film, and aided by telephone company video circuits in remote locations, networks gained an hour or more each day.

There were two Federal Communications Commission rulings in 1975 and 1976 and a court ruling which had especially important implications for the 1976 election campaign and probably future campaigns. In September 1975, the FCC reversed an earlier ruling, concluding this time that news conferences held by the president can be treated as bona fide news events, exempt from the equal-time provision during a presidential election campaign. Even more important for the 1976 campaign, the commission ruled, and was sustained by a U.S. Court of Appeals in April 1976, that debates by political candidates, provided that they were arranged by an independent organization, were exempt from the equal-time rule, that radio and television could cover them as they cover any other bona fide news event.[111]

As the 1976 presidential election campaign drew to a close, "authoritative sources" were predicting that less than 50 percent of Americans eligible to vote would cast ballots, which would be the first time that turnout had been so low since 1920, when women first had the vote.[112] Considering the trends in recent years, these predictions were not unreasonable. Though the turnout was low, percent of the voting-age population, it exceeded both the predictions and the 1948 vote, which was 51.1 percent. It is not unreasonable to assume that at least part of that increase over predictions was due to the interest created by the broadcast debates between the presidential and vice-presidential contenders.

Conclusions

Public financing of presidential campaigns promises to have an increasing effect on the use of television and radio for political purposes. Because more limited resources will be available for such campaigns than have been available in the past, it will be necessary to use funds more efficiently. This means that candidates will probably turn more and more to the electronic media, which can insure large coverage at small cost, and there will be strong pressures for broadcast debates between major party candidates, which will help to stretch further the campaign dollars.

In addition, because the presidential election campaign will be financed almost entirely without direct private contributions, the traditionally large contributors—the corporate and union political action committees—will have more to contribute to congressional candidates, who, in turn, will then have more to invest in media advertising. This latter effect was seen already in the 1976 election, during which congressional candidates attracted record contributions.[113]

A somewhat cynical summary of the relationship of broadcasting to presidential election campaigns is this quotation of Malcolm MacDougall, creative director for the Gerald Ford media campaign in 1976.

> What's the difference between selling a president and selling soap? Frankly, the disciplines are basically the same. But you don't get quite so emotionally involved with a box of soap.[114]

NOTES

1. Samuel L. Becker and Elmer W. Lower, "Broadcasting in Presidential Campaigns," in *The Great Debates*, ed. Sidney Kraus (Bloomington: Indiana University Press, 1962), pp. 25–55.

2. The Kennedy-Nixon debates of 1960 were exempted from Section 315 considerations by an act of Congress, 74 Stat. 554, for that one presidential campaign. That it was not the intent of Congress in its 1959 amendment of Section 315 to exempt the broadcasting of debates between political candidates from coverage by that section is demonstrated by the evident belief in 1960 that a special act of Congress was required to make possible the broadcasting of the Kennedy-Nixon debates.

3. Thomas H. Guback, "Political Broadcasting and Public Policy," *Journal of Broadcasting*, 12 (1968), pp. 196, 198.

4. Herbert E. Alexander, *Financing Politics: Money, Elections and Political Reform* (Washington, D.C.: Congressional Quarterly Press, 1976), pp. 20, 28.

5. Dan Nimmo, *The Political Persuaders: The Techniques of Modern Election Campaigns* (Englewood Cliffs, N.J.: Prentice-Hall, 1970), p. 112.

6. Ibid., p. 148.

7. The computer simulation was developed by academics, Ithiel de Sola Pool and Robert Abelson.

8. Most of the information on the development of computer projection of election returns given here is from Elmer W. Lower, "Use of Computers in Projecting Presidential Election Results, 1952–1964," unpublished M.A. thesis, Columbia University, 1970.

9. *New York Times*, Nov. 8, 1960, p. 17.

10. See, for example, Kurt Lang and Gladys Engel Lang, *Voting and Nonvoting: Implications of Broadcasting Returns Before Polls are Closed* (Waltham, Mass.: Blaisdell, 1968); Harold Mendelsohn, "Election-Day Broadcasts and Terminal Voting Decisions," *Public Opinion Quarterly*, 30 (1966), 212–225; and Douglas A. Fuchs, "Election-Day Radio-Television and Western Voting," *Public Opinion Quarterly*, 30 (1966), 226–236.

11. Data from 1932 through 1972 are from *Statistical Abstract of the United States 1976* (Washington, D.C.: U.S. Department of Commerce, Bureau of Census, 1976). Estimates of voting percentages for earlier elections are based on extrapolations from *U.S. Bureau of Census Historical Statistics of the United States, 1789–1945*, Series B 237–278, p. 32; Thomas H. McKee, *The National Conventions and Platforms of All Political Parties 1789–1905: Convention, Popular and Electoral Vote* (Baltimore: Friedenwald Co., 1906), pp. 198, 229; and *Statistical Abstract of the United States 1949* (Washington, D.C.: U.S. Department of Commerce, Bureau of the Census, 1949), p. 317.

12. The performance of television and the other media during the period immediately following the assassination of President Kennedy is best described in *The Kennedy Assassination and The American Public*, ed. Bradley S. Greenberg and Edwin B. Parker (Stanford: Stanford University Press, 1965).

13. Edward W. Chester, *Radio, Television and American Politics* (New York: Sheed and Ward, 1969); the co-author of this chapter, Elmer W. Lower, was a member of the three-network pool that produced the first "live" Kennedy press conference. He was then NBC bureau chief in Washington.

14. These and many other examples are cited by Chester, pp. 132–135, 271.

15. Chester, pp. 134, 155. These latter incidents, of course, were not novel. In our paper on "Broadcasting in Presidential Campaigns" (Becker and Lower, 1962, p. 35) we described the 1936 CBS broadcast by Senator Arthur Vandenberg of Michigan, in which he carried on just such a pseudo-debate with President Roosevelt.

16. *Review of Section 315 of the Communications Act.* Hearings before the Communications Subcommittee of the Committee on Interstate and Foreign Commerce, United States Senate, 87th Cong., 1st Sess., January 31 and February 1, 1961 (Washington, D.C.: U.S. Government Printing Office, 1961), pp. 1–2.

17. *Review of Section 315 of the Communications Act*, pp. 40–41.

18. *Freedom of Communications*, Final Report of the Freedom of Communications Subcommittee of the Subcommittee on Communications of the Committee on Commerce, U.S. Senate, 86th Cong., April 17, 1962. Part VI, Recommendations (Washington, D.C.: Government Printing Office, 1962), p. 10.

19. Ibid., pp. 9–10.

20. Chester, pp. 254ff., discusses these and other efforts during this period to remove or ease the equal-time provision.

21. Ibid., p. 148.

22. *New York Times*, June 20, 1963, p. 67.

23. *New York Times*, May 8, 1964, p. 18.

24. *New York Times*, August 19, 1964, p. 1.

25. Typical of such observers is Chester, pp. 148–149.

26. Chester, p. 149.

27. *New York Times*, October 2, 1964, p. 1.

CARTER vs. FORD, 1976

28. Thomas H. Guback, "Political Broadcasting and Public Policy," *Journal of Broadcasting*, 12 (1968), 206.

29. *Financing Presidential Campaigns*, Report of the President's Commission on Campaign Costs (Washington, D.C.: Government Printing Office, April 1962).

30. Alexander, pp. 134–135.

31. Ibid., pp. 20–28.

32. Guback, p. 198.

33. *New York Times Magazine*, October 25, 1964, p. 30.

34. Theodore H. White, *The Making of the President 1964* (New York: Atheneum, 1965), pp. 322–323.

35. Ibid., pp. 332–333.

36. Ibid., pp. 123–124.

37. *Highlights* (Newsletter of the NAB), October 12, 1964, p. 2.

38. Chester, p. 162.

39. "Road to the Presidency," *Sponsor*, January 18, 1965, pp. 27–28; Chester, p. 146.

40. White, 1965, p. 322.

41. Lower, pp. 127–149.

42. United Press International Dispatch, August 2, 1964.

43. *Congressional Quarterly's Guide to U.S. Elections* (Washington, D.C.: Congressional Quarterly, Inc., 1976).

44. White, 1965, p. 276.

45. See, for example, Chapter 15, "The News Media and the Disorders," in the report of the Kerner Commission, *Report of the National Advisory Commission on Civil Disorders* (Washington, D.C.: Government Printing Office, 1968), pp. 201–213.

46. *Congressional Quarterly Almanac*, vol. 20, 88th Cong., 2nd Sess., 1964 (Washington, D.C.: Congressional Quarterly Service, 1964), p. 414.

47. Chester, p. 256.

48. *Broadcasting*, July 24, 1967, pp. 22–23.

49. A detailed chronology of these events can be found in the *Congressional Quarterly Almanac*, vol. 24, 90th Cong., 2nd Sess., 1968 (Washington, D.C.: Congressional Quarterly Service, 1968), pp. 647–656; *New York Times*, October 10, 1968, p. 1, and October 11, 1968, p. 1.

50. *CQ Almanac*, 1968, p. 656.

51. *Broadcasting*, February 26, 1968, p. 25.

52. *Broadcasting*, January 23, 1967, p. 72.

53. *Broadcasting*, December 12, 1966, p. 48.

54. *Broadcasting*, July 24, 1967, p. 25; *Variety*, July 26, 1967, p. 25; *New York Times*, September 1, 1967, p. 27.

55. *Broadcasting*, September 2, 1968, pp. 17–18.

56. Ibid., pp. 20–21.

57. Drew Pearson and Jack Anderson, "Networks Slanted Chicago Coverage," *Washington Post*, September 6, 1968, p. B–13.

58. *Television Coverage of the Democratic National Convention, Chicago, Illinois, 1968*. Staff Report of the Special Subcommittee on Investigations of the Committee on Interstate and Foreign Commerce, House of Representatives (Washington, D.C.: Government Printing Office, 1969), pp. 1, 26.

59. *New York Times*, April 25, 1967, p. 86.

60. *New York Times*, February 14, 1966, p. 42.

61. *Broadcasting*, August 12, 1968, p. 50.

62. Nimmo, p. 135.

63. *Advertising Age*, October 21, 1968, p. 2.

64. *Advertising Age*, November 4, 1963, p. 88.

65. *Broadcasting*, April 22, 1968, p. 24.

66. Alexander, pp. 136–137.

67. These figures are based on data compiled by the Citizens' Research Foundation and reported in Alexander, pp. 16–17.

68. *Federal Election Campaign Act of 1973*, Hearings Before the Subcommittee on Communications of the Committee on Commerce, U.S. Senate, 93rd Cong., 1st Sess. on S.372, March 7–13, 1973 (Washington, D.C.: Government Printing Office, 1973), Appendix A.

69. *Advertising Age*, September 8, 1969, p. 59; *Broadcasting*, November 11, 1968, p. 36.

70. *Congressional Quarterly's Guide to U.S. Elections.*

71. Public Law 92–225.

72. Public Law 92–178.

73. *New York Times*, October 13, 1970, p. 1.

74. *Broadcasting*, March 8, 1971, p. 27.

75. *Television Digest*, June 5, 1972, pp. 1–2.

76. *New York Times*, February 3, 1972, p. 27.

77. *Variety*, March 15, 1972.

78. An excellent description of the birth and working life of this committee can be found in Theodore H. White, *The Making of the President 1972* (New York: Atheneum, 1973), pp. 18–95.

79. Ibid., p. 72.

80. "Muskie is Top Choice of Democrats for the First Time," *New York Times*, January 23, 1972, p. 26.

81. Alexander, pp. 16–17.

82. Federal Communications Commission, *39th Annual Report/Fiscal Year 1973* (Washington, D.C.: Government Printing Office, 1973), p. 204.

83. "FCC Report on Political Broadcasting and Cablecasting, Primary and General Election Campaigns of 1972," Appendix A of *Federal Election Campaign Act of 1973*, Hearings Before the Subcommittee on Communications of the Committee on Commerce, U.S. Senate, 93rd Cong., 1st Sess. on S.372, March 7–13, 1973 (Washington, D.C.: Government Printing Office, 1973).

84. Federal Communications Commission, *39th Annual Report/Fiscal Year 1973*, p. 207.

85. Alexander, pp. 41, 217.

86. Ibid., p. 20.

87. *New York Times*, March 22, 1972, p. 32; March 26, 1972, p. 1.

88. Warren Weaver, Jr., "How to Tune in the Voters," *New York Times*, October 22, 1972, section E, p. 3.

89. Newton N. Minow, John Bartlow Martin, and Lee M. Mitchell, *Presidential Television* (New York: Basic Books, 1973), p. ix.

90. Taylor Branch, "Profiles in Caution," *Harpers*, July 1973, p. 70. Some of the background of this case may be found in the Federal Communications Commission Memorandum Opinion and Order adopted August 14, 1970, released August 18, 1970. FCC 70–881. A study of the growing gap between the Congress and the administration in their communication with the public and the ways in which access to broadcasting might close that gap is contained in *Congress and Mass Communications: An Institutional Perspective*, a study conducted for the Joint Committee on Congressional Operations by the Congressional Research Service, Library of Congress (Washington, D.C.: Government Printing Office, 1974).

91. Stanley Cohen, "Advertising Becomes More Important in Promotion of Political Candidates," *Advertising Age*, June 1, 1970, p. 10.

92. *Newsweek*, October 19, 1970, pp. 34–39.

93. U.S. Bureau of the Census, *Current Population Reports*. Series P–20, No. 253 and series P–25, Nos. 311 and 626.

94. Warren Weaver, Jr., "By Law, This Will Be a Cheaper Campaign," *New York Times*, September 5, 1976, Section 4, p. 1; Federal Election Campaign Act, Amendments of 1974, Public Law 93–443.

95. Warren Weaver, Jr., *New York Times*, August 29, 1976, p. 1.

96. *New York Times*, January 31, 1976, p. 1; February 1, 1976, p. 1; Alexander, pp. 140–152, 243–245, 278–281; *Buckley v. Valeo*, 424 U.S. 1 (1976).

97. *New York Times*, February 28, 1976, p. 1.

98. *New York Times*, May 5, 1976, p. 1; May 12, 1976, p. 1; May 18, 1976, p. 1; Alexander, pp. 152–154.

99. Alexander, p. 248.

100. Hearings March 7–13, 1973, before the Subcommittee on Communications of the Committee on Commerce, U.S. Senate, 93rd Cong., 1st Sess., S.372 (Washington, D.C.: Government Printing Office, 1973), p. 188.

101. *Des Moines Register*, October 31, 1976, section E, p. 1. Among the "candidates" reported by the *Register* were J. John Gordon, whose goal was to remove "shyster lawyers" from government posts; Clarence L. Courton, whose platform was the admission of Israel as the fifty-first state, "so we can eliminate the present imbalance where [Israel] has 70 senators instead of the usual two"; and Philip Vernon Baker, whose plans for eliminating crime included giving every law-abiding adult a "Saturday Night Special."

102. Walter R. Mears, "The Debates: A View from the Inside," *Columbia Journalism Review*, January–February 1977, p. 21.

103. *Broadcasting*, January 3, 1977, p. 38.

104. Alexander, pp. 32, 96.

105. "Television: Medium of Choice and Necessity," *Broadcasting*, January 3, 1977, pp. 73–76.

106. *Broadcasting*, February 16, 1976; March 8, 1976; March 15, 1976; March 22, 1976; April 12, 1976; May 17, 1976.

107. James McCartney, "The Triumph of Junk News," *Columbia Journalism Review*, January–February 1977, p. 20.

108. Joseph Lelyveld, "The Soft-Sell Presidential Commercials," *The New York Times*, October 3, 1976, section E, p. 4.

109. *Variety*, November 24, 1976, p. 89.

110. *Broadcasting*, January 3, 1977, p. 38.

111. *New York Times*, September 26, 1975, p. 1; April 13, 1976, p. 67.

112. See, for example, Robert Reinhold, "Just Half an Electorate May Vote Nov. 2," *New York Times*, September 26, 1976; Editorial Section, p. 4; Tom Wicker, "It Sells Toothpaste, Doesn't It?" *New York Times*, October 17, 1976, Editorial Section, p. 15.

113. *Des Moines Register*, February 15, 1977, p. 1.

114. Malcolm D. MacDougall, "How Madison Avenue Didn't Put a Ford in Your Future," *New York Times*, February 21, 1977, p. 54.

3.

Legal and Political Aspects: Was Section 315 Circumvented?

HERBERT A. TERRY and SIDNEY KRAUS

One of the most intriguing aspects of the 1976 presidential debates was that they occurred without an act of Congress. The 1960 Kennedy-Nixon debates happened only after passage of a joint resolution of Congress suspending application of Section 315 of the Communications Act to the presidential and vice-presidential races of that year.[1] Absent such legislation, broadcasters feared candidate debates because of the legal requirement to provide "equal opportunities" to a pack of minor candidates. The joint resolution allowed broadcasters to cover the Kennedy-Nixon debates without granting such equal opportunities, but probably furthered a mind-set among politicians and broadcasters that future presidential candidate debates would require similar legislation. The 1976 debates, however, transpired largely because the FCC, supported by the courts and at least passively tolerated by the Congress, found a proximate solution to what had been an insoluble problem to the legislative branch of government for about fifteen years.

The depth of the belief that Congress had to act to remove constraints on presidential-candidate debates emerges from analysis of often inconclusive congressional activities between 1959 and 1976. Congress has allegedly been concerned with providing "equal opportunities" for use of the airwaves by candidates for public office since 1927.[2] In 1959, the FCC ruled that a minor candidate for mayor of Chicago, Lar "America First" Daly, was entitled to "equal opportunities" because of appearances of the real Mayor Daley and other major candidates on news programs broadcast by Chicago TV stations.[3] A shocked broadcast industry quickly pressured Congress into creating four types of programming in which the appearance of a candidate—in FCC parlance a "use"—would not create equal opportunity rights for opponents: "(1) bona fide newscast[s], (2) bona fide news interview[s], (3) bona fide news documentar[ies] (if the appearance of the candidate is incidental to the presentation of the subject or subjects covered by the news documentary," and, most important to understanding the 1976 debates, "(4) on-the-spot coverage of bona fide news events (including but not limited to political conventions and activities incidental thereto)."[4]

Congress did not seem to think that these 1959 changes in Section 315 authorized broadcaster-conducted candidate debates, for, as already noted, it passed a special joint resolution in 1960 legitimating the Kennedy-Nixon debates. That action strengthened the assumption that all candidate debates normally, if broadcast, created "equal opportunity" rights for opposing candidates. The assumption that this could only be changed by Congress was deepened in subsequent years when Congress, repeatedly, considered amending or repealing Section 315 in order to facilitate candidate debates. For a variety of reasons—differences in perceived self-interest of the Senate and House, related but not inextricably intertwined disputes over campaign financing reforms, incumbent presidents unwilling to provide broadcast exposure for opponents, a presidential assassination, untimely spurts of support for significant minor candidates, and, of course, simple distrust of broadcasters—none of the congressional efforts at Section 315 reform between 1960 and 1976 produced changes in the law. The fact, however, that Congress considered these issues at least quadrennially suggested strongly that the eventual removal of impediments to presidential candidate debates had to be congressional.

Actually debates were almost established as a tradition with the 1964 presidential campaign. It seems clear that John Kennedy expected to debate in that year and that the Democratic Congress was willing to at least create a 1960-style partial suspension of Section 315. On June 19, 1963, the House passed a resolution that would have suspended Section 315 for presidential and vice-presidential candidates for a seventy-five-day period prior to the 1964 elections.[5] Three and one-half months later, the Senate passed a slightly different version of the same resolution.[6] Kennedy's assassination in Dallas on November 22, 1963, however, made Lyndon Johnson president, and at his early press conferences Johnson made it clear that he lacked Kennedy's ardor for debates that might give TV exposure to a Republican challenger.[7] Behind the scenes, Johnson engineered tabling the resolution which killed the prospects that Section 315 might be suspended for a perhaps precedent-setting two consecutive presidential campaigns.[8]

Interest in amending Section 315 for the 1968 campaigns began in mid-1967 with Senate consideration of alternatives ranging from a 1960-style suspension to total repeal.[9] Prior to Johnson's March 31, 1968, announcement of his decision not to seek reelection, however, prospects for changing Section 315 were dim, as Johnson's aversion to debates from 1964 seemed intact. The day following Johnson's speech, however, all three TV networks sensed that debates might be possible and called for Congress to amend, or at least suspend, Section 315. By May 29, 1968, the Senate did pass a resolution suspending Section 315 for presidential and vice-presidential candidates starting August 31, 1968.[10]

The possibility of debates in 1968 collapsed, however, when significant minor candidates emerged in the wake of LBJ's decision not to run. Most important here was the campaign of then Alabama Governor George C. Wallace as a serious third-party candidate. On October 9, 1968, after Wallace's strength was becoming apparent, the House passed a resolution to suspend Section 315 with respect to "all presidential and vice-presidential candidates who have qualified to appear on the ballots of at least two-thirds of the states,"[11] wording intended to encourage three-way Humphrey, Nixon, and Wallace debates. Senate Republicans, however, feared that Wallace would draw votes from their candidate, Nixon, and accordingly blocked Senate action on the House version

THE GREAT DEBATES

of the suspension resolution so that the 90th Congress adjourned without changing Section 315 for the 1968 campaign.

After the very expensive 1968 Nixon-Humphrey campaign, and associated campaign scandals, Congress turned to broad issues of campaign reform that tended to absorb, and eventually overwhelm, more limited efforts to amend or suspend Section 315. For Congress, the basic issue was what, if anything, could be done to control campaign costs and avoid the appearance of influence buying. Section 315 issues were secondary and easily compromised away in the difficult task of seeing broad election reform through a skeptical Congress. Still, in 1970, Congress actually approved a general campaign reform bill which, among many other things, repealed Section 315 for presidential and vice-presidential elections.[12] That bill, however, was vetoed by President Nixon[13] and when its replacement, the Federal Election Campaign Act of 1971, was finally approved by Nixon in 1972, Section 315 remained intact. That it did so was largely due to Nixon's shrewd manipulation of Senate-House differences and to the power of a single member of Congress, former Ohio Democratic Representative Wayne Hays.

Attempts to hammer out general campaign reform legislation following the 1970 Nixon veto began early in the 92nd Congress. Since campaign reform issues were broad, both the Senate and House found that the proposals required hearings by more than one subcommittee. Such multiple jurisdiction opened opportunities for the Nixon administration, not truly anxious for debates, to appear publicly to favor them while actually acting in a way sure, for political reasons, to scuttle debate-related legislation. By April 23, 1971, then Senator John Pastore's (D-NH) Communications Subcommittee had shepherded through the full Commerce Committee a version of campaign reform that not only attempted to control costs but also repealed Section 315 for presidential and vice-presidential candidates, a position Pastore reasonably believed might be acceptable to the House, which had consistently opposed broader suspensions or repeals reaching their own House races.[14] In May, 1971, however, the action shifted to the Senate Rules and Administration Committee, where then Deputy Attorney General Richard G. Kleindienst pushed an Administration proposal that Section 315 be repealed for all federal candidates.[15] This position eventually prevailed in that committee[16] and on the Senate floor.[17] The Nixon position was politically masterful, for it meant that the Administration was publicly on the record as encouraging debates in all federal races, and in favor of the position taken by the broadcasting industry, when in fact the Administration knew perfectly well that such a broad repeal would never pass the House of Representatives.

In the House, jurisdiction was split between the Interstate and Foreign Commerce Committee's Subcommittee on Communications and Power, then chaired by Massachusetts Democratic Representative Torbert Macdonald, and an elections subcommittee of the House Administration Committee chaired by Congressman Hays. Macdonald, unwilling to repeal Section 315 for all federal candidates, steered his subcommittee, and eventually the full Commerce Committee, into recommending repeal of Section 315 as applied to just presidential and vice-presidential candidates.[18] Hays, however, opposed any change in Section

315, as well as opposing, perhaps more violently, most other aspects of election campaign reform. In floor debate, Representative James Harvey (R-MI) sensed the profound Macdonald-Hays split and warned of its chances to harm the entire campaign reform package. He proposed to leave Section 315 unchanged,[19] a position the House finally adopted. Because of the resulting Senate-House differences, a conference committee was required, and it elected to follow the House position on Section 315 and make no changes in the law. During final Senate debate, Pastore—in a testament to Hays's power in the House— expressed substantial displeasure that Section 315 had not been repealed or at least amended, but noted that the House, meaning Hays mostly, was violently opposed to repeal for all federal candidates, as Nixon had forced upon the Senate, and that to insist on it would have jeopardized the whole reform package.[20] As a result, when Nixon finally signed the Federal Election Campaign Act of 1971 on January 19, 1972, it made no change in Section 315.

A similar scenario was played out between 1972 and 1974, as Congress considered public financing of federal campaigns. At Pastore's urging, the Senate Commerce Committee twice reported, and the Senate once approved, versions of campaign reform that repealed Section 315 for president and vice-president.[21] Nixon spokespersons, through the Subcommittee on Privileges and Elections of the Senate Rules and Administrations Committee, successfully advanced the broader, but still unacceptable to the House, repeal or suspension for all federal candidates.[22] Hays, in the House, objected to both public financing of campaigns and to tampering with Section 315 but eventually accepted limited financing of presidential and vice-presidential campaigns and succeeded in blocking Senate supported changes in Section 315.[23] Following Nixon's resignation on August 8, 1974, then President Gerald Ford signed the Federal Election Campaign Act Amendments of 1974, which made no changes in Section 315.[24]

On March 26, 1975, Macdonald introduced a bill, H. 5600, that simply looked like the beginning of yet another of these congressional exercises in futility. He proposed to repeal Section 315 for president and vice-president, guarantee equal opportunity for party spokespersons to reply to partisan presidential speeches, and exempt from Section 315 programs exploring controversial issues of public importance when stations or networks controlled content, participants, or format. Even considering the odd nature of the 1976 campaign and the Ford "incumbency," there was little reason to believe that these congressional efforts would be any more successful than those of the preceding Congresses. However, events were already in motion elsewhere that eventually took the matter out of the hands of Congress—unable anyway to solve it for fifteen years—and put it in the hands of the FCC and the courts.

The complete story of the 1976 debates actually began ninety years earlier when two brothers, Robert L. (Dem.) and Alfred A. (Rep.) Taylor, competed for the Tennessee governorship in an 1886 campaign featuring debates from a flatbed wagon and affectionately known as the "War of the Roses." In 1970, two other Tennessee gubernatorial candidates, Winfield Dunn (Rep.) and John J. Hooker, Jr. (Dem.), decided to conduct debates in the spirit of the 1886 campaign. Serving as campaign communications director to Dunn was a young University of Virginia law student, Stephen A. Sharp. Sharp encountered hesitancy of some broadcast stations to carry the debates, or even news actualities, out of fear about Section 315. A year later, Sharp prepared a law school paper on the history of FCC interpretations of Section 315, and concluded that the most important debate rulings, holding that such debates were not "bona fide news events" under the 1959 changes in the law, had been erroneous, because they were based on language not eventually included in the revisions of the equal-time law. In 1972, Sharp joined the FCC's General Counsel's office, and made known his law school findings. Office colleagues were willing to admit that Sharp might have been legally correct, but tended to think his views not particularly practical, since it seemed so well established by the FCC, and recognized by candidates and the Congress, that candidate debates were not bona fide news events. Sharp's views, however, stuck in the mind of another FCC attorney, Lawrence Secrest, who by 1975 was legal and administrative assistant to then FCC Chairman Richard Wiley.

On March 14, 1975, Douglass Cater of the Aspen Program on Media and Society convened a meeting at the Brookings Institution in Washington, D.C. The Brookings roundtable discussed ways to make the Bicentennial election a model of ideal political broadcasting. Among the participants were two individuals with many years of broadcasting law and policy experience: Henry Geller, former FCC general counsel and then an Aspen senior associate, and Nicholas Zapple, former chief counsel of the Senate Communications Subcommittee and a protege of Senator John Pastore. Also included were relative newcomers Secrest and Dr. Barry Cole, an occasional FCC consultant, university professor, and policy researcher.

A few days prior to the Brookings meeting, Cole, Secrest, and Geller discussed Sharp's views privately. While conceding the quality of his legal analysis, they were agreed that the 1975 political environment inhibited the FCC from revisiting the old Section 315(a)(4) rulings. Secrest, Cole, and Geller decided not to suggest such a revision at the Brookings meeting, feeling that any such FCC action would be unacceptable to, and viewed as partisan by, Congress, which had considered Section 315 changes so many times since the 1960 debates.

At the Brookings meeting, however, Zapple suggested that he and members of Congress, presumably Pastore, believed there were good grounds to revisit the old FCC Section 315 debate rulings and to change the commission's interpretation of the concept of a "bona fide news event." Coming from a man with such deep congressional roots, Zapple's comments suggested to Geller, Cole, and Secrest that their earlier political judgment was wrong. After the meeting, and just outside of the Brookings Institution, Geller told Secrest that he would file a petition for Aspen, asking the FCC to reconsider the old rulings, and Secrest, without making any promises as to its disposition, said the FCC would be pleased to receive such a request.[25]

Aspen's petition, filed April 22, 1975, urged the FCC to reverse its 1962 *Wyckoff*[26] and *Goodwill Station*[27] decisions with their restrictive interpretations of Section 315(a)(4) of the Communications Act. Under those cases, the FCC said, in effect, that candidate appearances not "incidental to" some other news event weren't news events in their own right and were therefore not exempt from the equal opportunities requirement.

Geller, writing for Aspen, urged abandonment of the "incidental to" test and proposed instead a "common sense" reliance on the "bona fide news judgment" of licensees as to what was news and what was not. Aspen advanced three justifications for this shift: first, that the commission had incorrectly read legislative history and the intent of Congress when it promulgated *Wyckoff* and *Goodwill*; second, that changes in FCC policies since those cases, particularly the issue-by-issue application of the Fairness Doctrine now employed, eliminated any justification for a restrictive approach to Section 315(a)(4); third, that the commission should prefer Aspen's proposed "bona fide news judgment" test to the FCC's older rulings, which, said Aspen, raised "the most serious First Amendment issues." This last argument, Aspen contended, was vital because the present construction of Section 315 had not promoted "robust, wide-open debate" and was therefore counterproductive to the intent of the First Amendment.

The Aspen petition split the FCC staff. Members of the commission's Broadcast Bureau viewed it as an unnecessary and unjustifiable change from established commission policies. The General Counsel's Office, however, was aware of Sharp's previous work in this area and inclined toward leading the commission to correct its past errors. A June 13, 1975, draft opinion from the General Counsel's Office on the Aspen petition put the FCC on the verge of setting the requested "newsworthiness" standard. Faced with that draft, the Broadcast Bureau asked for additional time to respond with its own more conservative views. A commission vote was, accordingly, set for a planned July 29, 1975, meeting.

On July 16, 1975, however, CBS through its New York rather than its Washington, D.C. counsel, confused matters by filing a petition asking the FCC to revisit its 1964 *CBS* decision and to declare that, contrary to that decision, press conferences of incumbent presidential candidates did not create Section 315 equal-opportunities obligations for broadcasters.[28] The CBS action strengthened the hand of the Broadcast Bureau in the internal fight within the FCC over Aspen. If granted, the Aspen petition could be readily characterized as nonpartisan or at least bipartisan, but the CBS petition created a greater risk for the FCC that its actions could be characterized as pro-Ford. Concerned, again, about political fallout from its actions, the FCC delayed its planned consideration of the Aspen petition.

The CBS petition brought an odd assortment of opponents. Robert N. Smith, counsel for the Democratic National Committee, asked the FCC on July 18, 1975, for a copy of the CBS petition and on September 2 formally opposed it. Media Access Project, on behalf of Representative Shirley Chisholm (D-NY) and the National Organization for Women (NOW) filed an opposition September 12; Representative Charles Rangel (D-NY), on behalf of the Congressional Black Caucus, on September 19; Loren A. Smith, general counsel of Citizens for Reagan for President, on the twenty-second and, with trade press accounts indicating impending FCC action on Aspen/CBS, the commission on September 23, 1975, received letters from Ruth C. Clusen, president of the League of Women Voters, and then candidate for the Democratic nomination Jimmy Carter asking the commission not to grant the Aspen/CBS requests without going

THE GREAT DEBATES

through rulemaking proceedings, an act that would have delayed the commission's decision for many months.

Despite all this opposition, the FCC partially granted Aspen's petition by a 5-2 vote on September 25, 1975. At the same time, the commission granted, indeed expanded upon, the CBS petition and exempted from creating "equal opportunities" all candidate press conferences, subject to certain coverage conditions.[29] Gone, however, was the broad newsworthiness test that Aspen had sought and that the commission had been on the verge of granting in July. Instead, the FCC limited its decision to just overturning the earlier *Wyckoff*, *Goodwill*, and *CBS* decisions and established a rather narrow principle that broadcasters could cover, without creating Section 315 rights for others, candidate debates, provided that the debates were not conducted by broadcasters but were covered live and in their entirety. The stage was set for presidential debates in 1976 if some party agreed to conduct them and broadcasters chose to cover them under the *Aspen* decision strictures. First, however, the ruling was subjected to a rather abstract legal challenge mounted by Chisholm and NOW and, in a somewhat half-hearted fashion after Carter gained its nomination, by the Democratic National Committee.

The eventual FCC court victory in the resulting case, *Chisholm* v. *FCC*, actually clinched most of the legal issues that surrounded the 1976 debates and loomed in a towering fashion over more specific court cases brought by minor candidates not included by the League of Women Voters in the debates.[30] On April 12, 1976, the U.S. Court of Appeals for the D.C. Circuit, in a 2-1 split panel decision, affirmed the FCC's *Aspen* ruling. Concluding that the 1959 legislative history was ambiguous, but that the FCC's new reading of that history was not unreasonable, Judges Tamm and Wilkey supported the commission. Judge Wright disagreed, both as to the substance of the commission's decision and its choice of a declaratory ruling rather than a rulemaking proceeding for making it. Appeals of *Chisholm* continued until the end of the 1976 campaign season. The U.S. Supreme Court, in fact, did not finally decide not to review the case until October 12, 1976, one day after the third (vice-presidential) debate and just ten days before the final Carter-Ford debate of October 22.

Most of the court challenges to the actual conduct of the debates involved minor presidential candidates who had not been, as indeed *Aspen* did not require, included in the League's debates. Given the *Chisholm* decision, those candidates generally accepted *Aspen* as the law and just argued, particularly after the twenty-six-minute audio gap in the first debate, that the 1976 debates were not being properly conducted by the League, broadcasters, and the candidates so as to fall within the *Aspen* guidelines. A flurry of FCC decisions and court appeals—at least four different important court cases—involved candidates such as Lester Maddox of the American Independent Party, Tom Anderson of the American Party, Socialist Workers' Party candidate Peter Camejo, and independent candidate Eugene McCarthy, all of whom filed complaints and appeals in rapid succession between the August 19, 1976, invitation by the League to Carter and Ford to debate and Carter's election on November 2, 1976. All FCC and court decisions produced results favorable to the commission, the League, and the broadcasters and opposed to the claims of the minor candidates that they should have been included or that Section 315 was somehow being circumvented.[31]

The most persistent legal argument that Section 315 was being circumvented was posed by Eugene McCarthy following the first, Philadelphia, debate of September 23, 1976. In that debate there was an audio failure of some twenty-six minutes.[32] McCarthy, in a complaint the next day to the U.S. Court of Appeals, D.C. Circuit, made much of the fact that during the gap "neither Ford nor Carter said one word to the 400 journalists in the audience . . . a clear indication of the obvious, that the debate was set up only because the networks agreed to cover it, subject to censorship and control exercised by Ford and Carter."[33]

Our research indicates that the courts and FCC were correct and that there was not, by the networks, the candidates, or the League, any violation of the letter of the *Aspen* ruling. Because of litigation threatened or initiated by minor candidates, the League and broadcasters were constantly fearful of even the appearance that they together were putting on the debates. Each group was concerned that it maintain its distinct, separate role and function, so that it would be legally clear that the League was sponsoring a news event and the networks were just covering it.[34]

Indeed the twenty-six-minute gap, as the FCC eventually concluded, did more to prove than to disprove that there was a separation between the event and its coverage.[35] In a prior audio check of the Walnut Street Theater, ABC technicians discovered feedback into the auditorium from the TV sound which made stage sounds unintelligible. The network technician, therefore, hooked up the sound for the theater audience through the TV audio distribution system, as was often done in covering other events. That act, perhaps, placed the networks and the League astride a precarious fence separating sponsorship from coverage, but it would clearly be unfair to conclude that it had truly given broadcasters control over the event. When the ABC equipment failed, some of the problems of restoring the sound systems were related to the fact that many, from both the League and the networks, did not really know how the sound system had been wired. The audio-system failure made it impossible for the League to continue its debate, as there was no auditorium sound-system operating. It might have been clearer had the networks chosen to cover the "gap" itself as a kind of news event within the debate news event, or had the League made some independent effort to explain what was happening to the theater audience,[36] but the basic fact is that the reactions to the audio failure were human, understandable, and probably not legally questionable. The principals waited because they expected the problem to be solved momentarily. The League tried to get its sound system restored, but was partly unable to do so because network technicians had no clear understanding of where the failure had occurred or exactly why it should have caused simultaneous loss of both the broadcast and theater audio.

Legally, then, Section 315 as reinterpreted by the FCC in *Aspen* was followed rather than circumvented. For the first time since the 1960 Kennedy-Nixon debates there were broadcast debates, in prime time, between the two major contenders for the U.S. presidency. Does that suggest that, if there is a positive social value in such debates, *Aspen* is enough and that further congressional concern with Section 315 is unneeded?

We would say no, and that Congress should complete the FCC's half-way reform of Section 315 by repealing it for federal candidates.[37] Given our knowledge of the inability of Congress in the past to take this step, we are not greatly optimistic of its political viability, but we suggest it nonetheless, because even in the wake of *Aspen*, the present version of Section 315 still seems to cause more harm than good. Like Henry Geller, we have become convinced that the law, with its glowing promise of "equal opportunities" to all, has created but a hollow promise for minor candidates who, in the end, get little or no broadcast exposure, as most of their "uses" are limited to paid ads that they can not afford.[38] Such a situation benefits neither the minor candidate nor the public, deserving of better knowledge of that candidate's views.[39]

Further, the *Aspen* ruling and its interpretations have led to an odd kind of political broadcast coverage, in which the skills of the broadcast journalist are difficult to employ, and in which technical problems, like the twenty-six-minute gap, are made more probable than would be the case if broadcasters were fully in charge. We would agree with former FCC Commissioner Benjamin L. Hooks that the present law creates an unseemly fantasy world, in which debates of only the oddest nature are conducted under artificial circumstances, and that it forces all debate participants

> to engage in all manner of subterfuge and charade to make it appear that . . . presidential polemics are autonomous news events rather than the premeditated media extravaganza they clearly are to everyone still enjoying the blessings of earthly life. We are all victims—the League, the candidates, the voters, the media—of the *Aspen* ruling which makes everyone *pretend* that these debates are a spontaneous occurrence (like a forest fire) or a routinely scheduled newsworthy event (like the Super Bowl) which would have occurred anyway, with or without the conspired presence of the media. The world-at-large is not fooled into believing that these debates would have taken place without the direct involvement and commitment of the networks. However, like Shakespeare, the FCC . . . affirms that "(t)he play's the thing."[40]

NOTES

1. P.L. 86–677, 74 Stat. 574 (1960).

2. "Equal opportunities" were first guaranteed by §18 of the Radio Act of 1927, 44 Stat. 1162 (1927). The protection was carried over without change as §315 of the Communications Act of 1934, 48 Stat. 1064 (1934).

3. *Columbia Broadcasting System, Inc.*, 18 RR 238 (1959).

4. P.L. 86–274, 73 Stat. 557 (1959). Now §315(a)(1–4) of the Communications Act.

5. H.J. Res. 247. See House Report 359, 88th Cong., 1st Sess.

6. Passed October 2, 1963, as H.J. Res. 247. See Senate Report 501, 88th Cong., 1st Sess.

7. Johnson's consistent tactic was to say that he was not yet a candidate for president but was just running for the Democratic nomination, and that he would decide

upon debates later. See Johnson's press conferences of December 18, 1963, and February 29, July 24, July 30, and August 15, 1964.

8. Senate-House conferees met May 7, 1964, and issued a report on May 19, 1964, which mostly followed the Senate language. See House Report 1415, 88th Cong., 2nd Sess. The Senate, however, tabled the conference report on August 18, 1964.

9. See S. 1548, S. 1859, S. 1926, S. 2090, S. 2128, all 90th Congress. Hearings were held by the Subcommittee on Communications, Senate Commerce Committee, July 18–20, 1967.

10. S.J. Res. 175, 90th Cong., 2nd Sess.

11. S.J. Res. 175, 90th Cong., 2nd Sess. See H. Rept. 1928, 90th Cong., 2nd Sess.

12. On April 14, 1970, the Senate approved S. 3637 which (1) limited radio and TV spending by presidential and congressional candidates, (2) required broadcasters to sell campaign spots at the "lowest unit charge" and (3) permanently repealed §315 as it applied to presidential and vice-presidential candidates. See Senate Report 751, 91st Congress, 2nd Sess. The House passed generally similar legislation—S. 3637 as a substitute for H.R. 18434, August 11, 1970, House Report 1347, 91st Cong., 2nd Sess. A conference committee was required due to differences in the versions unrelated to §315. House Report 1420, 91st Cong., 2nd Sess. The House adopted the report September 16, 1970, and the Senate followed with adoption on September 23.

13. The veto came October 12, 1970. Nixon in his veto message did not raise objections, as he would do later, to repeal of §315 as it applied to presidential and vice-presidential candidates.

14. The bill was S. 382, introduced and discussed with a Conference Committee Report issued May 6, 1971. Senate Report 96, 92nd Congress, 1st Sess.

15. Hearings were held May 24–25, 1971.

16. See Senate Report 229, 92nd Congress, 1st Sess. issued June 21, 1971.

17. S. 382 was approved by the Senate August 5, 1971. As a result of a floor amendment by Nixon supporter Sen. Winston L. Prouty (R-VT), the bill repealed §315 as it applied to major candidates for president, vice-president, senator, representative, delegate and resident commissioner.

18. The committee issued a report on H.R. 8628 by a 23-20 report. See House Report 595, 92nd Congress, 1st Sess., October 13, 1971.

19. Debate was on November 30, 1971, over H.R. 11060, the Federal Election Campaign Act of 1971.

20. The Conference Report is Senate Report 580 and House Report 575, 92nd Congress, 1st Sess. Senate debate and approval of the report came December 14, 1971. The House acted January 19, 1972.

21. The Commerce Committee made the recommendation in reports on S. 3178 (Senate Report 684, 92nd Congress, 2nd Sess.) issued March 6, 1972, and on S. 372—a general public financing proposal—(Senate Report 170, 93rd Congress, 1st Sess.) issued May 22, 1973. S. 3178 actually passed the Senate March 23, 1972, on a 67-13 roll-call vote, but no House hearings on parallel proposals were held before the end of the 92nd Congress.

22. See Senate Report 310 (93rd Congress, 1st Sess.) on S. 372 issued by the Senate Rules and Administration Committee on July 11, 1973. S. 372, proposing §315 repeal for all federal candidates but requiring broadcasters to offer fifteen minutes of free time to candidates who did not get equal time, passed the Senate on a roll-call vote July 30, 1973. The 1st Session of the 93rd Congress, however, ended without action on electoral reform. On February 21, 1974, Senator Howard Cannon introduced S. 3044, essentially S. 372 all over again, which was quickly approved and reported by the Senate Rules Committee (Senate Report 689, 93rd Congress, 2nd Session). Its main point was public campaign financing, but it also repealed §315 for all federal candidates. On April 11, 1974, the Senate, by a 53-32 vote, passed S. 3044, a

campaign reform and public financing bill. It included an amendment proposed by Senator Walter Huddleston on March 29 that repealed §315 for president and vice-president only, but would have allowed it to be waived for other races on a case-by-case basis when stations offered five free minutes to all candidates in a race.

23. In October and November, 1973, Hays's Subcommittee on Elections held hearings on S. 372, with Hays expressing opposition to any repeal of §315 out of concern for how local broadcasters would treat House campaigns. *Federal Election Reform*, Hearings before the Subcommittee on Elections, U.S. House of Representatives, 93rd Congress, 1st Sess. The next year, Senate-passed S. 3044 was referred to Hays's House Administration Committee. On July 24, 1974, Hays introduced H. 16090, an alternative campaign reform bill which rejected public financing for congressional elections. That bill, which proposed no change in §315, was reported out July 30, 1974 (House Report 1239, 93rd Congress, 2nd Sess.) and approved by the House 355-48 on the day of Nixon's resignation. As a result, the Senate version (S. 3044) called for a very odd kind of repeal of §315, but the House recommended no change. The Senate named conferees on August 15, 1974. Included was Senator Pastore. Hays was reported to be incensed at the Senate conferees, which he saw as biased toward broad public financing and toward tampering with §315. He is said to have demanded new conferees from the Senate or at least an order from then Senate Majority Leader Mike Mansfield (D-MT) that §315 not be discussed in conference, and meanwhile delayed naming House conferees. Eventually, on October 7, 1974, a Conference Report was issued (House Report 1438, Senate Report 1237, 93rd Congress, 2nd Sess.), in which Hays had his way—no change—on §315.

24. The Senate approved, 60-16, on October 8, 1974, and the House followed, 365-24, on October 10, 1974. The bill was forwarded to and signed by President Ford on October 15, 1974. Federal Election Campaign Act Amendments of 1974, P.L. 93–443, 88 Stat. 1263 (1974).

25. The previous account, and much of what follows about the internal FCC debate over the Aspen petition, is based on interviews conducted in November 1976, and January 1977 in Washington, D.C. with Cole, Secrest, Geller, and Sharp. Confidentiality as to specific information was requested in many instances. Some anonymous sources at the FCC were also interviewed.

26. *Goodwill Station, Inc.*, 40 FCC 352, 24 RR 413 (1962).

27. *National Broadcasting Company*, 40 FCC 370, 24 RR 401 (1962).

28. *Columbia Broadcasting System, Inc.*, 40 FCC 395, 3 RR 2d 623 (1964).

29. *Political Debates and Press Conferences*, 55 FCC 2d 697, 35 RR 2d 49 (1975). Press conferences had to be covered live and in their entirety and controlled by the candidates.

30. *Chisholm et. al. v. FCC*, 538 F. 2d 349, 36 RR 2d 1437 (CADC, 1976). Chisholm filed her case (No. 75–1951, CADC) the day following FCC release of *Aspen*. On October 8, 1975, the Democratic National Committee filed an appeal, starting the case of *Democratic National Committee v. FCC* (No. 75–1994, CADC). The Court of Appeals consolidated the cases, on motion of the FCC, October 17, 1975. Oral arguments were heard November 26, with FCC General Counsel Werner Hartenberger making the presentation for the FCC, assisted by Stephen Sharp.

31. Lester Maddox was the first to complain to the FCC, writing them September 7, 1976, that he was being excluded from the League's planning sessions. On September 10, the Socialist Workers' Party telegraphed a complaint to the commission that their candidate would be denied equal time in the upcoming debates. The FCC Broadcast Bureau rejected the Maddox complaint on September 17—*Lester Maddox*, 38 RR 2d 873 (1976)—and on the twentieth, rejected the complaint of the Socialist Workers' Party. To be sure that it had exhausted administrative remedies, the Socialist Workers' Party asked for immediate review of the bureau's decision by the full

commission, which, in a two paragraph order, supported the staff. *Socialist Workers 1976 National Campaign Committee,* 38 RR 2d 876 (1976). The full FCC supported the staff on the Maddox complaint on October 5, 1976. *American Independent Party* v. *ABC,* 38 RR 2d 923 (1976). As a result, Maddox and the Socialist Workers' Party were in a position to go to court claiming to have exhausted administrative remedies.

Tom Anderson, of the American Party, and Eugene McCarthy decided initially to bypass the FCC and go directly to court to attempt to block the debates. Anderson filed a complaint with the U.S. District Court, D.C. (*Tom Anderson et al.* v. *Gerald Ford et al.,* Civil Action No. 76–1672, DCDC) on September 8, 1976, followed shortly thereafter on September 10 by Eugene McCarthy (*McCarthy et al.* v. *Carter et al.,* Civil Action No. 76–1697, DCDC). The cases were combined and dismissed by District Court Judge Aubrey E. Robinson, Jr. on September 17, 1976, on two grounds: failure to complain first to the FCC and to exhaust administrative remedies and a conclusion that the relief sought would amount to an unconstitutional prior restraint. Anderson seems to have accepted this defeat, but McCarthy, on September 17, 1976, filed notice of appeal with the U.S. Court of Appeals, D.C. Circuit (*McCarthy* v. *Carter,* No. 76–1865, CADC). This appeal was rejected by the Court of Appeals on the eve of the first presidential debate, September 22, 1967, with an opinion that generally supported Judge Robinson.

Following the September 23, 1976, debate, with the audio gap, McCarthy on the twenty-fourth filed a complaint with the FCC. That complaint was rejected October 5, 1976—in the same opinion rejecting the earlier Maddox complaint—meaning that at last McCarthy could go to court without the burden of having failed to exhaust remedies at the FCC. Accordingly he filed, on October 6, a Petition for Review of this FCC decision with the U.S. Court of Appeals, D.C. Circuit. *McCarthy* v. *FCC,* No. 76–1915 (CADC).

Meanwhile, in what the FCC considered good strategy, the Socialist Workers' Party filed an appeal of the FCC's September 10 decision denying their complaint with the 2nd Circuit U.S. Court of Appeals in New York City. The Socialist Workers' Party had anticipated, correctly, that McCarthy would end up in the D.C. Circuit and that that circuit, having recently decided *Chisholm,* would support the FCC. Evidently the Socialist Workers' Party hoped to provoke conflict between the circuits, which would have increased the chance of review by the U.S. Supreme Court. However, on September 24, the FCC asked that the case be transferred to the D.C. Circuit and, on the twenty-seventh—just one day before its scheduled oral argument —the 2nd Circuit so ordered. On September 30, 1976, the D.C. Circuit supported the FCC in a brief order which cited only *Chisholm. Socialist Workers' Party* v. *FCC,* No. 76–4213 (CADC). The party filed a petition for *certiorari* with the U.S. Supreme Court on October 4, just one day before McCarthy also asked that court for review of his September 22 loss at the Court of Appeals of *McCarthy* v. *Carter.* McCarthy also asked the U.S. Supreme Court to intervene in another case, *McCarthy* v. *FCC,* which was about to begin at the D.C. Circuit of the U.S. Court of Appeals.

On October 12, the U.S. Supreme Court simultaneously denied review to the Socialist Workers' Party of their losses at the FCC and the U.S. Court of Appeals and, at long last, also to the requests of Chisholm and the Democratic National Committee for review of the Court of Appeals decision supporting the FCC in *Aspen.* Only Justice White would have granted review. For practical purposes, this ended any meaningful chance of Supreme Court intervention in the 1976 debates.

There was still some McCarthy debris, however. On October 21, McCarthy asked the U.S. Supreme Court for an injunction to block the final debate scheduled for the next evening. The Court denied that request on the twenty-second. Also on the twenty-second, the U.S. Court of Appeals at last decided *McCarthy* v. *FCC* (No. 76–1915, CADC), sustaining the FCC's rejection of the McCarthy and Maddox requests for equal time. At this point, since the U.S. Supreme Court denied review of *Chisholm*, the U.S. Court of Appeals cited it as authority. On January 19, 1977—after the election—McCarthy asked the U.S. Supreme Court to review this Court of Appeals decision, but the Supreme Court on April 4, 1977, decided not to grant that request, ending the last McCarthy case.

32. See chapters 8 and 9.

33. See complaint associated with *McCarthy v. FCC*, No. 76–1915, CADC.

34. See chapter 8.

35. In *American Independent Party* v. *ABC*, 38 RR 2d 923, 932 (1976) the FCC recognized three reasons why the audio gap indicated that the League's sponsorship was in fact separate from ABC's broadcast: (1) the auditorium and TV sound systems were interconnected and it was logical for the candidates to wait for restoration of auditorium sound; (2) so far as the FCC could tell, no broadcaster exercised any control over the candidates' decisions not to attempt to continue debating; and (3) the League stated that it tried unsuccessfully to restore the auditorium sound system "so that the debate could continue without regard to the broadcast coverage."

36. No such effort was made according to Sidney Kraus, who was in the theater audience.

37. In a proposed revision of the Communications Act of 1934 considered by the House of Representatives in the 95th Congress, 2nd Session, (H.R. 13015), it was proposed to eliminate §315 for radio and restrict it to candidates not elected on a statewide basis (which would include House members, obviously) for TV.

38. In a conference following the 1976 elections, Geller said: "Whatever the worry about the minority-party candidates, and that is a serious worry . . . the fact is they don't fare well under the commission's 1962 construction either. They get nothing. The majority-party candidate gets nothing, the minority-party candidates get nothing." Transcripts of Presidential Debates De-Briefing Conference, Crystal City Marriott, Arlington, Va., November 29–30, 1976, Sidney Kraus (ed.), p. 10.

39. We might also propose some sort of mandated minimum candidate access, but the political prospects of that approach zero.

40. *American Independent Party* v. *ABC*, 38 RR 2d 923, 935–936 (1976). Emphasis in the original. Hooks is dissenting, and would not endorse our suggestion to repeal §315.

4.

The Public Agenda Foundation:
An Experiment in Issues Analysis

RICHARD L. COHEN

In the fall of 1975—long before anyone knew for certain that 1976 would witness the rebirth of nationally televised presidential debates—an unusual experiment in campaign issues analysis was undertaken by a small group of concerned Americans known as the Public Agenda Foundation. This experiment was born of the assumption that changes were occurring within the American political system which would hinder a sober, realistic assessment of key issues facing the country during the 1976 presidential campaign and that a special effort had to be made to counterbalance the negative effects of such changes.

The Public Agenda's objective was to provide the candidates, the media, and the voters—particularly independent voters—with reliable, nonpartisan analyses of critical national issues. Its founders hoped that these efforts would sensitize the candidates to the thinking of various constituencies throughout the country and would supply the voters with a framework for evaluating and choosing among the candidates. The principal goals of the Public Agenda were to encourage debate sharply focused on the crucial issues and to assist voter decision making in what many people felt would be an unusually critical election year.

The crucial issues were outlined in three Public Agenda Foundation reports published in early September 1976: *Inflation and Unemployment*; *Moral Leadership in Government*; and *U.S. Foreign Policy: Principles for Defining the National Interest*.[1] Each report identified key issues and suggested proposals and alternative perspectives. The *Inflation and Unemployment* report, for example, defined the key economic issues and recommended eight proposals. Similarly, the two other reports listed the pertinent issues and discussed possible strategies for coping with them.

These reports were presented to the candidates' staffs. According to informed feedback, they made a limited but meaningful contribution to the thinking and debate preparations of the two major-party presidential candidates.

The purpose of this essay is to describe in some detail the process that led to the Public Agenda's reports and the manner in which they were used.

The First Phase

The Public Agenda Foundation was conceived of during a series of meetings between Daniel Yankelovich, president of the public attitude research firm of

Yankelovich, Skelly & White, and Cyrus Vance, then a senior partner in the New York law firm of Simpson Thacher & Bartlett and now secretary of state. In the course of these discussions, Yankelovich and Vance found that they shared a common concern about the coming 1976 presidential election campaign. They were troubled by the mistrustful mood of the electorate and by trends that might warp or distort the soundness of the presidential selection process and, in the long run, lead to further disillusionment among the voters. They sensed—indeed were largely convinced—that their concern was fairly widely shared by the public at large and by much of the leadership of American society. They were particularly concerned by the following four developments:

1. *The rapid increase in the number of presidential primaries.* Thirty presidential primaries would be held in 1976. In 1968 there had been fifteen, and in 1972, twenty-three. This increase, many analysts argued, represented a welcome democratization of the parties' candidate-selection process, for the primaries placed the selection process more firmly in the hands of the voters. But for any change there is always a price to be paid. The increasingly large number of primaries meant that in the absence of a candidate who was a clear-cut winner at an early stage (in which case the primaries would be largely irrelevant), the candidates would be forced to spend the first six to eight months of the year scurrying about the country trying to win local elections, with the results hinging mainly on local issues and personalities. The candidates' time, energy, and resources, it was feared, would be largely consumed by this effort. Little serious attention would be paid to overriding national issues until *after* the nominating convention. Such a late shift in attention threatened to detract from the quality of the issues debate during the general election campaign.

2. *The large number of serious primary candidates expected.* Barring some major unforeseen development, it was evident late in 1975 that former California Governor Ronald Reagan had launched a sustained, viable challenge to President Ford for the Republican party nomination. It was even more obvious that there was no clear front-runner for the Democratic party nomination, and that a Democratic standard-bearer would likely emerge only after a lengthy primary season. Highly competitive races in each of the major political parties meant that the candidates would have to focus even more intently on winning the primaries, diverting their attention from the major national issues.

3. *The dramatic increase in the number of independent voters.* Whatever the causes—Vietnam, Watergate, continuing economic uncertainty, the social upheavals of the late 1960s, and other long-term trends eroding party loyalty—a growing number of voters had become disillusioned with both major political parties. Surveys placed the number of self-classified "independents" in the range of 35–40 percent of the electorate as of late 1975. This was a pivotal chunk of voters that clearly held the key to the outcome of the 1976 election. But if such a large number of voters failed to turn for guidance to either of the major political parties, by what standards were they going to judge the candidates? To what or whom would these voters turn for information to help them evaluate the issues—a role played in the past by the political parties? These questions were potentially crucial to the outcome of the election and possibly to a reversal of the public's steadily declining trust and involvement in voter participation.

CARTER vs. FORD, 1976

55

4. *The absence of any systematic attempt to discuss and deal with important public policy issues from the point of view of reconciling expert opinion with public attitudes.* On the one hand, there were any number of mechanisms by which the voters and the candidates could be apprised of expert opinion on any given issue. On the other hand, each candidate employed his own in-house pollster to keep him up to date on public attitudes, and this information would be supplemented continually by the published results of independent researchers. But who, for the benefit of both the candidates and the voters, could reconcile expert approaches to the economy, foreign policy, crime, tax reform, and other issues with voter attitudes when these were in conflict? On any given issue, who was going to lay out in a systematic, politically disinterested fashion the principal dimensions of the issues and the policy options that seemed feasible from both a technical and a political point of view? The founders of the Public Agenda felt that such work was essential to an intelligent discussion of the issues during the presidential campaign—indeed, to the entire process of public policy formulation. Its importance was further underlined by the highly suspicious, post-Watergate mood of the public, by the public's heightened insistence on more openness and responsiveness in government, and by the increasing complexity of national issues. No one appeared to be doing this kind of work, and its absence served to diminish the relevance of issues discussion during the presidential campaign.

The founders of the Public Agenda were concerned that these four developments—the large number of primaries, the sizable field of candidates, the decisive block of independent voters, and the lack of attention devoted simultaneously to expert and public attitudes on any given issue—would combine with the more traditional distractions of presidential campaigns to obscure, rather than clarify, the candidates' approaches to critical national issues. They also thought that such a development would be unusually damaging to the country, given the widely perceived "watershed" nature of the 1976 election—the fact that it was the first presidential election to be held following the Vietnam war, the trauma of Watergate, and the deep economic recession.

In December 1975 and during the first few months of 1976 Yankelovich and Vance—joined by others—formed the Public Agenda Foundation and its Policy Review Board. Active participants included Kingman Brewster, Robert Burnett, Gilbert Carmichael, C. Douglas Dillon, John Gardner, Robert Hodes, Vernon Jordan, Jr., Clark Kerr, Maurice Lazarus, Sol M. Linowitz, John J. McCloy, Waldemar Nielsen, William Ruder, Frank Stanton, Thomas J. Watson, Jr., and Harold Williams.

The Public Agenda was organized as an independent, nonprofit, nonpartisan research foundation. It was to have minimal staff and a barebones budget. The funds required to carry out the work were to be raised by the founders from individual citizens and organizations. It was agreed that in order to avoid undue influence, no contribution in excess of $10,000 was to be accepted from any one source.[2]

The objectives of the Public Agenda were to be threefold: (1) to identify several critical national issues that were likely to be pivotal to the outcome of the 1976 presidential election; (2) to analyze each of these issues from the point of view of both expert opinion and public attitudes, focusing on the major *alternative* approaches for dealing with the issues and the pros and cons (trade-offs, benefits and sacrifices) of each approach; (3) to make available the completed analyses to both presidential candidates, as unique material bearing on the formulation of their respective policy positions, and also to the media and the voters, as tools with which to probe, judge, and evaluate the candidates. The Public Agenda was to be an *ad hoc* temporary organization. Its future would be decided after the election, when the degree of success of the experiment could be assessed.

Identification of Issues

The Public Agenda project was to have three distinct, although somewhat overlapping, phases: (1) identification of issues; (2) analysis of issues; and (3) dissemination of the completed analyses.

The three issues chosen for analysis were inflation and unemployment, moral leadership in government, and the principles for defining U.S. national interest in foreign policy. The Public Agenda limited its study to these issues not because they were perceived to be the only issues worthy of study, but simply because of time and resource limitations. The three issues were selected on the basis of a survey conducted among a select but diverse group of public opinion professionals and noted American leaders, supplemented by an extensive analysis of public opinion data. The survey utilized a specially designed inventory of issues and an issues ballot. The twenty-three-page inventory contained brief descriptions of twenty-four issues organized into three categories: the economy, social issues, and foreign policy.[3] The ballot accompanying the inventory enabled respondents to rate each of the twenty-four issues according to four criteria: (1) the issue's importance to the future well-being of the United States; (2) its potential importance to voters as it influenced their vote for a party or candidate; (3) the extent to which the issue offered an opportunity for fresh thinking and citizen input; and (4) the degree to which the respondent was responsive to the issue on purely personal grounds. The ballot instructions also encouraged the respondents to add, and score accordingly, any important issue they thought had been neglected on the prepared inventory and ballot.

In mid-January 1976, inventories and ballots were mailed to prominent Americans representing a wide range of professions, geographic regions, and interests, including the heads of more than one hundred broad-based, national special-interest organizations;[4] approximately thirty of the country's leading public opinion analysts in the academic and commercial fields; and some seventy-five individuals widely respected for their leadership abilities and positions. In February the completed ballots were tabulated and analyzed. The results were then cross-checked with the Public Agenda's separate analysis of existing public opinion data. All ballots received before the end of February were included in this process.

Inflation and unemployment and the issue of moral leadership in government ranked among the top-priority issues, according to both the Public Agenda's special survey and its analysis of existing public opinion data. The identification of a third issue was more difficult. Foreign policy seemed an obvious choice to many involved in the Public Agenda, but there was a significant difference of opinion between the leadership groups surveyed and the American public at large on the importance of the foreign policy issue. Those in positions of leadership clearly considered foreign policy a top-priority issue. But all other data indicated that foreign policy ranked much lower on the general public's scale of priorities, superseded by such issues as crime, taxes, welfare, and energy. Based on its analysis, the Public Agenda ultimately concluded that foreign policy was likely to become an increasingly important and visible issue as the presidential campaign progressed, and, therefore, that it should be included for study. The particular foreign policy issue chosen for analysis was the one ranked highest among foreign policy issues included in the Public Agenda's special survey—definition of United States national interest as a framework for the conduct of foreign policy.[5]

Analysis of Issues

The research/analysis process had to meet certain criteria to achieve the over-all objectives of the project. First, the Public Agenda had to draw on a wide range of expert opinion to define the particular issue under study, the most promising policy options for dealing with the issue, and the principal pros and cons of each option. Second, the Public Agenda had to find a reliable way to gauge voter reaction and receptivity to the policy options outlined by the experts. Third, the method of issues analysis had to incorporate mechanisms for minimizing the effects of bias, a particularly difficult task given the intense emotion and ideological commitment with which critical national issues are inevitably viewed.

Expert Interviews

To meet the first of the three criteria, the Public Agenda decided to conduct personal, in-depth interviews with a wide variety of experts, or professional observers, in each issue area. The principal reason for resorting to the laborious, expensive, and time-consuming method of personal interviews was that the Public Agenda wanted to amass the views of experts within a common framework—by having them all respond to the same questions and react to a common set of problems and possibilities. Also, the Public Agenda was seeking the most recent, up-to-date—and unofficial—views of the experts, which might not be forthcoming in written material.

Ultimately, seventy experts were interviewed for the Public Agenda's foreign policy study, fifty for its study of inflation and unemployment, and seventy-six for its study of moral leadership in government. These experts were selected primarily for the preeminence of their work on the relevant issue. The Public Agenda also did its best to insure that the experts reflected a fair ideological cross section, as well as some degree of geographic and age balance. With some variation of emphasis among the three issue groups, the experts represented a broad range of views, perspectives, backgrounds, and professional involvements. They included academic specialists, current and former government officials, members of Congress, foundation officials, business and labor leaders, religious leaders, and spokespersons for minorities and women.[6]

58

Gauging voter receptivity to the policy options outlined by the experts was a particularly difficult problem, since the Public Agenda felt its analyses, in order to meet objectives, had to push beyond the level of generality of standard polling questions. The Public Agenda wanted to determine not only how the public felt about a specific issue at a given time, but how people might feel if they had an opportunity to really "work through the issue." In other words, if the issue were debated and discussed prominently in the course of the campaign, and if the voters, as a result, were able to wrestle with it within the context of clearly stated policy options, would their attitudes, reactions, and choices be any different?

The Public Agenda decided upon a three-pronged approach to this problem: (1) it would tap the knowledge of some of the country's leading public opinion analysts; (2) it would conduct its own referendum among community leaders in key cities around the country; and (3) it would apply its own analysis of existing public opinion survey data.

The first part of this effort—drawing on the insights of the country's most respected public opinion analysts—was an innovative and instructive experiment. In the late spring of 1976, the Public Agenda established an Electorate Analysis Panel, composed of fourteen public opinion professionals from both academic and commercial fields.[7] This group, chaired by Professor Everett C. Ladd, of the Social Science Data Center at the University of Connecticut at Storrs, performed two key functions. First, it analyzed public attitudes through responses to a written survey specially designed for the Public Agenda's purposes and administered to members of the panel. Through this survey, the members of the panel drew upon their own individual work and experience in public opinion analysis to gauge public attitudes toward specific policy options that had emerged from the Public Agenda's interviews with the experts in each issue area. The survey provided for an assessment of public attitudes as they existed during the first half of 1976, and for a judgment with regard to how these attitudes might change—if at all—should the specific issues and policy options be discussed prominently during the course of the presidential general election campaign.

After the results of this written survey had been compiled and analyzed, panel members met in late June 1976 to review and discuss the results of the survey and to further evaluate the range of specific policy options which had been put forth during the Public Agenda's expert interviews. The results of these activities were a major source of the public attitude conclusions in the Public Agenda's final reports.

Two other sources also played an important role in these evaluations. One was the Public Agenda's analysis of existing public opinion survey data. The other was a special referendum conducted among 133 community leaders in thirteen cities around the country.[8] This referendum, carried out at the end of May and the beginning of June, served a dual purpose. The Public Agenda drew upon it as a gauge of attitudes among a special, more informed, and more activist group of the American public. But it also used the referendum as a source of policy options for dealing with the issues under study. The community leaders, then, were a kind of "bridge group" between the public at large and the experts interviewed in each issue area.

Minimizing Bias

The Public Agenda was aware from the beginning that its analyses had to be objective and credible, and, therefore, as free as possible from bias—personal, political, ideological, or regional. Considering the highly charged nature of the issues to be studied and the ideological preconceptions with which people —experts included—normally approached them, this was a formidable task. But, judging from the reaction to the completed analyses, the Public Agenda seems to have succeeded well in this effort. In doing so, it relied on two fundamental safeguards.

First, the Public Agenda decided to establish for each issue under study a task force consisting of experts on the issues, with the task-force members representing the principal ideological/political frameworks within which the issue was normally perceived and analyzed. These task forces were to have several important functions: they were to help identify the group of experts to be interviewed so that all significant points of view would be represented; to help formulate the depth guide to be used in the expert interviews; to participate in the distillation and analysis of the expert interviews; to help draft the final report on each issue; and to review the draft of the final report for balance, fairness, and completeness. The Public Agenda worked to involve as many task-force members as possible in each of these steps. Time pressures, however, and the fact that some of the task forces were not completely established until May meant that some members participated more fully than others.[9]

Second, the Public Agenda also decided to set up a Policy Review Board composed of a varied group of prominent American leaders, reflective of a wide range of backgrounds, interests, professions, perspectives, and ideological/ political allegiances. Members of the Policy Review Board made many contributions to the overall Public Agenda effort, but the single overriding task of the board was to judge and evaluate the Public Agenda's final reports in terms of balance, fairness, coherence, and overall professional competence. The members of this board were not asked to arrive at a consensus on the substance of any report, nor to agree among themselves on any issue or policy option, but rather to determine whether each of the reports was sufficiently fair, complete, and worthy of distribution to the presidential candidates, the media, and the voters. No report was to be released without the Policy Review Board's approval.[10]

A few key points about the substance of the three reports should be mentioned briefly. The report on inflation and unemployment highlighted a sharp conflict between the views of experts and the public on how to deal with the problems of the economy. The public did not accept the premise of some of the experts that, in order to bring inflation under control, millions of people would have to remain jobless, or the alternative premise that, if the level of unemployment were to be brought down, inflation would be inevitable. The report on foreign policy demonstrated the existence of a surprisingly widespread consensus, among both the experts and the public, on the principles that should underlly the U.S. role in the world—though here, too, there were some significant differences between the professionals and the public at large. The report on moral leadership in government outlined in some detail how and why this issue was of such critical importance in 1976 and suggested some specific steps that could be taken to restore public confidence in the presidency.

Dissemination

To get the reports into the hands of the candidates, the media, and the voters, the Public Agenda concentrated on three main target audiences for its dissemination effort: the major-party presidential candidates and the debates; the media; and "organized America."

The Candidates and the Debates

Top campaign aides to both the Republican and Democratic presidential candidates had been informed of the Public Agenda project in the spring and summer of 1976 while the issues analysis was proceeding. There was no close or formal coordination, however, between the Public Agenda and the two campaign staffs. Neither of the campaign staffs participated in any way in the Public Agenda's issues-identification and analysis work. These two phases of the project were carried out on a strictly independent basis.

As soon as the Public Agenda's three final reports were ready for public distribution, however, multiple copies of each were forwarded to President Ford and to Governor Carter's campaign headquarters in Atlanta. This occurred during the first week of September 1976. Concurrently, meetings took place between officials of the Public Agenda and top advisers to each of the candidates.

When the Public Agenda was organized, the prospect of presidential debates was highly uncertain. Talk and pressure for such debates had begun, but no one could be sure that they would in fact occur. As late as August 1976, after the League of Women Voters had experimented with televised regional forums during the presidential primaries, there was still no assurance that nationally televised general election debates would occur. The Public Agenda effort, therefore, was undertaken and carried out irrespective of whether there would or would not be debates. Once the debates became a reality, however, they were a natural focus, and a critical outlet, for the Public Agenda's work.

While there was no formal link between the Public Agenda and the League's year-long debate effort, the Public Agenda and the debate organizers had generally kept abreast of each other's work. The Public Agenda established contact with Jim Karayn, project director of the debates, as early as January 1976. Shortly thereafter, a Public Agenda representative attended the news conference formally announcing the League's televised primary forums. Occasional contact was maintained between debate and Public Agenda officials throughout the spring and summer of 1976.

The first detailed discussion of how the Public Agenda's work might be incorporated into the debate effort, however, came in August, at a meeting in New York involving Karayn; Yankelovich; Ruth Clusen, president of the League of Women Voters; and Richard L. Cohen, staff director of the Public Agenda Foundation. Karayn and Clusen were at the time negotiating seriously with both the candidates and the television networks; they were also attempting to mount a nationwide public pressure campaign in support of the debates. They were interested in the Public Agenda's work—the issues it was studying, how it was studying them, when the materials would be ready and in what form—as a possible substantive basis for organizing the debates, should they take place.

The Public Agenda and the debates did come together in a somewhat informal fashion. The Public Agenda supplied the debate organizers with multiple copies of all three Public Agenda reports. The debate organizers, in turn, gave the reports to the moderators and panelists for each of the debates, with encouragement that they be read and utilized as tools for probing the candidates' positions on the issues.

The Media

Together with the candidates and the debates, the news media were viewed as critically important to the success of the Public Agenda effort. The Public Agenda's formal introduction to the media came on May 20, 1976, when a news conference was held at Automation House in New York to announce the project. Throughout August, while the three reports were undergoing final reviews and revisions, Yankelovich and Vance held a number of meetings with key people at some of the country's leading news organizations. Included in this group were the *New York Times, Washington Post, Wall Street Journal, Time, Newsweek*, NBC, CBS, ABC, and PBS. Policy Review Board members were also contacting important media outlets in the Boston area, on the West coast, and in the South. The purpose of these meetings was to explain in some detail the work that had been carried out by the Public Agenda, why it had been done, and the nature and value of the materials that would be forthcoming. The Public Agenda hoped that such explanations would enable the media to anticipate their distribution and to be in a position to utilize them quickly and appropriately.

Early in September, the finished reports were distributed to the appropriate people in as many news organizations as possible across the country. By the end of September, copies of the reports were placed in the hands of over 500 key journalists throughout the country—including over 100 editorial writers and editors, 125 political editors, 200 business and economic writers, and a number of the more prominent nationally syndicated columnists, national news services, and magazine editors.[11]

Organizations

Since the Public Agenda had neither the time nor the resources to reach large numbers of voters directly, it supplemented its work with the media by turning to the distribution network of "organized America," i.e., broad-based national, special-interest organizations representing a wide array of the most powerful groups in America. During September the Public Agenda forwarded copies of its reports to the heads of over 100 such organizations with the intent that they would communicate summaries or relevant portions of the reports to their memberships.[12]

The Public Agenda's extensive distribution effort to the media and to the national organizations was coordinated by Public Interest Public Relations, a New York-based firm whose president, Margaret Booth, played an active role in the Public Agenda from its beginnings.[13]

THE GREAT DEBATES

Evaluation and Lessons for the Future

What did the Public Agenda accomplish? What role did it actually play in the general election campaign? Did it meet its original objectives of providing meaningful analyses for the benefit of both the candidates and the voters, particularly independent voters? What lessons does it provide for similar such efforts that might be undertaken in the future—or for the public policy process in general?

Any evaluation of the effort must be, on our part, both tentative and subjective. We believe, however, that enough reaction and evidence were accumulated to draw some general—though perhaps not definitive—conclusions with regard to the impact and potential of the Public Agenda's Work.

Identification of Issues

By virtually all measurements, two of the three issues identified by the Public Agenda for analysis—the economy and moral leadership in government—proved to be priority issues during the general election campaign. The third issue, foreign policy, was perhaps somewhat more peripheral, although it was the sole focus of one of the three nationally televised presidential debates, a pivotal election event itself. Clearly, refinements in the Public Agenda's issues-identification method can be made in the future. More advanced planning, greater financial resources, and the 1976 experience itself can contribute to such refinements. Nonetheless, the Public Agenda's issues-identification work was, we believe, a sound approach.

Analysis of Issues

Reaction to the substance of the Public Agenda's reports was extraordinarily favorable—from the media, from the candidates' staffs, from organizational heads, from people in a variety of leadership positions who are widely respected for their abilities and judgment. Those who commented applauded, in particular, the Public Agenda's success in combining expert opinion with public attitudes in its analysis of issues, as well as its attempt to clarify public understanding and discussion of these issues during a presidential campaign. As with issues-identification, there is opportunity for improvement in the Public Agenda's analysis and report-preparation. The level of generality with which an issue is defined; the number and mix of experts interviewed; the nature of the depth-guide used in the expert interviews; the size, mix, and focus of the Community Leader Referendum; the composition and input of the Electorate Analysis Panel; the length and complexity of the final reports—these and other areas are proper subjects for further thought, study, and refinement. But we believe that a sturdy foundation has been laid.

Dissemination

If there was any serious shortcoming to the Public Agenda's 1976 effort, clearly it was in the dissemination of its work. The reports might well have had a significantly larger effect on the campaign if the target audiences had known well ahead of time what to expect, if the materials had been completed and available earlier than they were, if the Public Agenda had been able to work more closely with the candidates' staffs, with the media, with a variety of broad-based national organizations and with the organizers of the debates.

Despite this important qualification, the Public Agenda's dissemination effort did achieve a measure of success. According to close aides of both major-party presidential candidates, the reports were studied carefully in preparation for the televised debates. We know from sources within the campaign staff that Carter thoroughly digested the Public Agenda's foreign-policy report prior to the second televised debate. We also know that much of what Carter said during the second debate reflected the Public Agenda's analysis. Whether the report significantly altered his thinking, whether it served as a catalyst for solidifying inclinations and advice already received, or whether it merely supplemented and further substantiated positions already firmly worked out are questions about which we can only speculate. Our best, most informed feedback indicated that the report at the very least played a significant role in Carter's preparation for the debates.

The same is true, perhaps to a lesser extent, of the moral-leadership report. Our understanding was that it was studied carefully by the Carter campaign staff. A number of telephone discussions to elaborate on and explain in more detail the report's findings did occur between the Public Agenda and top Carter campaign officials. Certainly, much of Carter's position on this issue during the latter days of his candidacy and the early days of his presidency reflected the Public Agenda's analysis of the issue. What we do not know is the degree to which the Public Agenda study may have affected Carter's thinking.

Reports from the Ford camp indicated that the Public Agenda's studies were "extremely useful, helpful, and interesting." Michael Raoul-Duval later told the Public Agenda that its studies played a "major role" in shaping his own thinking in preparing debate briefings for Ford. According to Raoul-Duval, all three reports went to the president, with cover notes outlining their principal findings. Raoul-Duval thought it likely that Mr. Ford had studied the reports themselves, as well as the cover notes.

Other feedback from the Ford campaign indicated that the moral-leadership report was the most productive and informative for Mr. Ford. According to this information, the economic issue had been such a pressing, day-to-day problem for the Ford administration, had been so continually and thoroughly worked over by the president and his top advisers, that the president's position on the issue was firmly rooted and therefore largely unaffected by the Public Agenda analysis. The moral-leadership analysis, however, provided him with an unusual perspective on a critical but highly elusive issue—one in which the president himself was clearly interested—and it was on this analysis that Mr. Ford apparently focused most of his attention.

Aside from their use by the candidates, the Public Agenda reports also received a fair amount of attention from the media. Significant articles, columns, or editorials appeared in or were distributed by such publications and news services as the *New York Times, Wall Street Journal, Washington Post, Christian Science Monitor, Boston Globe, Cincinnati Enquirer, Cleveland Plain Dealer, Los Angeles Times, New Orleans Times-Picayune,* Associated Press, Knight News Service, and Copley News Service. Stories using, relating to, or discussing the Public Agenda's work appeared in more than fifty newspapers around the country.

In addition, the Public Agenda reports were discussed on PBS's "MacNeil/ Lehrer Report" and "People and Politics" and on NBC's "Today Show." The October 1 installment of "Campaign '76," a weekly program aired by CBS throughout the campaign, was devoted entirely to a discussion of the moral-leadership issue, based on the Public Agenda's analysis. And the foreign-policy report was the subject of an entire "Focus" program, a public policy series distributed nationwide via cable-television outlets.

Despite this level of nationwide coverage, we concluded that the play given to the reports by the media was, for the most part, insufficient either to inform the voters adequately or to bring major public and media pressure to bear on the candidates. A longer period of preparation and more advance work clearly needs to be done in this area should a similar effort be undertaken in the future.

To summarize, we believe that the Public Agenda effort did make a contribution of some significance to the discussion of key issues in the 1976 presidential campaign. It was not highly visible. It did not transform the course of the campaign. It probably did not radically alter the thinking of either of the major-party candidates. But we do believe that its contribution, while not precisely definable, was more than marginal. Perhaps even more importantly, we are convinced that the effort broke new ground which can and should be cultivated in the future.[14]

It is always difficult for a sober, reasoned discussion of critical national issues to break through the hubbub of a presidential campaign. Some people think it is impossible. At the very least, it is extraordinarily difficult. The pressures on the candidates to fuzz and obscure—rather than to clarify—the issues, the distractions of often decisive but less substantive aspects of campaigning, the inclinations of people to judge and vote on image and personality, all are formidable factors that detract from thoughtful consideration of issues. Yet, at the same time, no one who has carefully and objectively analysed the results of presidential elections can fail to conclude that the candidates' stands on the issues play a critical role in the voters' choice. Voters may not evaluate a candidate as a technical expert or a journalist might—on the basis of a detailed analysis of each issue—but voters know what is important to them, and they can and do make shrewd discriminations between candidates on the basis of their stands on the issues. With the decline of party-line voting, a need has arisen in the country for new sources of information that will clarify the issues for the voters, sensitize the candidates to voter opinions on these issues, balance technical expert approaches to issues with voter-based preferences and values, and help to focus national campaigns on the most vital issues of our time. We believe the Public Agenda made a promising start in attempting to fill this need.

NOTES

1. For a list of some of the publications that discussed the reports, see below, p. 64.

2. The full-time staff of the Public Agenda consisted of a staff director and one staff assistant. Some interviewers and analysts were paid on a project basis. Much of

the work was done voluntarily. The budget for the Public Agenda—$120,000—was covered by contributions from a variety of individuals, foundations, and corporations. A list of contributors is included in the three reports.

3. Included in the economy category were inflation, unemployment, stimulating the economy, the environment, energy, economic planning and federal/state/city economic relations. Included under social issues were big government, moral leadership, tax policy, crime, welfare and other transfers, medical care, racial equality/desegregation/busing, women's rights, housing, legal solutions to moral issues, and education. Included under foreign policy were defining our self-interest, detente, nuclear proliferation, relations with allies, relations with less-developed countries, and responsibility for foreign policy.

4. The organization heads to whom the ballots were sent represented the communications industry; the elderly; labor; business; agriculture; builders; environmentalists; professional groups; medical and public health groups; religious groups; education; young people; minorities; women; civic, social-service; and voluntary groups.

5. It is of interest to note that this issue—the most general of the foreign policy issues listed on the inventory and ballot—ranked ahead of more specific issues such as detente, relations with allies, etc.

6. For a list of the experts interviewed on each issue, see Chapter IV of the relevant Public Agenda report.

7. The members of the Electorate Analysis Panel were: Everett Ladd (chairman), Irving Crespi, Phillips Davison, Mervin Field, Sidney Kraus, Seymour Martin Lipset, David Mayhew, Warren Miller, Ithiel Pool, John Robinson, Burns Roper, William Schneider, William Watts, and Daniel Yankelovich.

8. The questionnaire used in the Community Leaders Referendum, like the written survey of the Electorate Analysis Panel, was based on the Public Agenda's initial group of interviews with experts in each of the issue areas. The occupations and interests represented among the community leaders participating in the referendum included business, labor, minorities, women, religion, government, consumer, elderly, environmental, education, health and other professional (e.g., lawyers, engineers, scientists). The cities included in the referendum, selected for geographic balance, were Boston, Chicago, Cincinnati, Cleveland, Denver, Des Moines, Detroit, Memphis, Newark, Philadelphia, Pittsburgh, Phoenix, and San Francisco.

9. For a list of the members of each task force, see Chapter IV of the relevant Public Agenda report.

10. For a list of the Policy Review Board members, see Chapter IV of any of the Public Agenda reports.

11. During August, the Public Agenda had considered holding either a formal news conference or a series of specialized briefings for the news media concurrent with public release of the reports. The latter would have been desirable. But the reports were finally completed so close to Election Day (two months before) that the Public Agenda simply concentrated on getting the reports out as rapidly and as widely as possible.

12. Common Cause and the League of Women Voters each distributed over 100 copies of all three reports among their respective leaderships and state chapters around the country. The National Urban League also requested 120 copies each of the moral-leadership and inflation and unemployment reports.

13. In addition to making the reports available to the candidates, the media, organization heads, and the debate organizers, the Public Agenda, in cooperation with the Carnegie Endowment for International Peace, distributed reports to a number of other groups: all three reports were sent to all members of and candidates for Congress, and to all gubernatorial candidates in 1976; copies of the foreign-policy report

66

were also sent to all U.S. ambassadors abroad, all foreign ambassadors in the United States, all United Nations ambassadors in New York, top administration officials in the White House, the National Security Council and the Treasury Department. One hundred additional copies of the foreign-policy report were sent to the State Department, at its request, and 150 copies were made available to the United States Information Agency, for distribution to its offices overseas.

14. A feasibility study was conducted in 1977 to determine whether it is possible and desirable to establish the Public Agenda as a permanent organization. Many of those involved in the 1976 project felt that a permanent Public Agenda could play an important role in the between-elections public-policy process, as well as in future presidential and possibly congressional elections.

5.

The Presidential Forums

CHARLES BENTON and GENE POKORNY

EDITOR'S NOTE:
A series of four Presidential Forums preceded the 1976 presidential debates. The Forums, open to all presidential candidates, were held in four cities and were nationally televised by the Public Broadcasting Service. The Forums, organized by the League of Women Voters Education Fund, were, in many ways, precursors of the 1976 debates.

The idea for the Forums first took shape during a weekend in Phoenix in April 1975 when Marjorie and Charles Benton and Gene Pokorny discussed what could be done to enhance not only the quality of the coming campaign's political dialogue, but also the direct, active participation of concerned citizens. On the assumption that in many ways process determines content, what new process in 1976 would enable concerned citizens to force the candidates to address issues that citizens cared about? How could the awesome power of television be utilized as a communicator of facts, images, and reality, while providing greater public control over it? The weekend conversations generated some exciting ideas that eventually came to fruition as the 1976 Presidential Forum Project.

The Beginnings of the Presidential Forum Project

A planning memorandum written by Pokorny on May 1 set forth the ideas discussed in Phoenix and placed them in a conceptual and strategic framework. The main points were:

1. The Presidential Forum Project was to be a citizen-directed political education program consisting of 8–10 individual presidential candidate Forums held around the country. The Forums would be, in a sense, regional "town meetings," at which presidential candidates could address themselves to the major issues on the minds of voters.

2. The Forums would be nonpartisan and open to all major candidates seeking the presidency in 1976.

3. The sequence of the Forums would follow the course of the 1976 campaign as it progressed from East to West, with the first Forum in New England and the last in California. In addition, the plan called for two convention-eve Forums and a series to be held in the fall prior to the general election.

4. The Forums would be televised by the Public Broadcasting Service (PBS) so that they would reach and involve a national audience. Public television was not to control and manage the Forums as broadcast events, but rather merely to cover the citizen-organized Forums as live public affairs events.

5. The Forums would be financed by money raised privately from foundations and other sources, with the Benton Foundation underwriting most of the costs.

The idea seemed viable, since 1976 would be:

. . . our nation's Bicentennial, and a series of Presidential Forums would be an appropriate way of rekindling and building citizen participation in the public life of the nation.

. . . the first presidential election after the experiences of Watergate, thus candidates should be more responsive to cooperating with open, citizen-organized forums.

. . . the first presidential election held under the new campaign finance law, which we felt would increase candidate willingness to take advantage of "free" public exposure.

. . . the first election in our nation's history with a nonelected president in office, thus increasing the chances that the incumbent president would feel the need to participate.

Underlying the plan was a clear political philosophy of direct, active citizen sponsorship and control of the Forums. We wanted them to be run by local citizens at the "grass roots" level in the cities involved. The process of organizing and holding the Forums was to be an exercise in citizenship for the largest possible number of people. We thereby hoped to set in motion a series of events that would present an alternative to the usual conduct of presidential campaigns.

In implementing the Forum plan, we faced three immediate tasks: first, to determine whether PBS was interested in televising the Forums; second, to arrange for initial funding from the Benton Foundation; third, to begin organizing the grass-roots base for the Forums. During June and July, 1975, we started working on the first two tasks. Since organizing at the local level depended upon accomplishing the other two objectives, we let this last matter rest, though some initial contacts were made with political grass-roots organizers around the country.

Initial PBS Support

Charles Benton explained our plans in May to Bill McCarter, general manager of WTTW, the PBS station in Chicago. McCarter, one of the outstanding leaders in public broadcasting, gave us immediate and full encouragement. He suggested that Benton attend a public affairs workshop in Woodstock, Illinois, sponsored by the Corporation for Public Broadcasting (CPB) in late June.

During the two-day workshop, Benton met most of the key national CPB and PBS people involved in public-affairs programming. The Forum plan was presented to many of the participants, including Cal Watson of the CPB; Prentiss Childs, head of public affairs for PBS; and Jim Karayn, former head of NPACT, the National Public Affairs Center for Television. Karayn, in particular, was enthusiastic about the proposal and expressed an interest in helping to launch the Forums. While workshop participants liked the Forum plan, most thought it impractical. There were just too many difficult problems to be resolved. It was clear, however, that if solutions could be found, PBS was receptive to televising the Forums. PBS was interested in new public affairs programming ideas, and the Forums seemed complementary to the emerging PBS plan for covering the 1976 campaign. In addition to the PBS people contacted at Woodstock in June, other key officials of PBS were approached.

On July 16, Karayn was interviewed in Washington and invited to begin working on the Forum project. His initial responsibility was to continue making contact with top PBS officials around the country to coordinate the broadcast aspect of the project.

Arranging Financial Support

A major immediate hurdle was to arrange for some seed money from the Benton Foundation in order systematically to research and, it was hoped, resolve the legal, organizational, and financial problems inherent in the plan. The trustees were concerned that foundation support for such a project be acceptable to the IRS; they did not want to risk violating laws prohibiting participation of a nonprofit foundation in politics. Legal advice prompted the foundation to seek an acceptable nonprofit organization to which it could donate its money and which could run the Forum project. On July 29 the trustees voted a grant of $50,000 with the provision that the project be nonpartisan and that it not violate campaign laws or threaten the foundation's tax-exempt status. The next task was to identify an appropriate nonprofit organization.

In August, while we struggled to find a legitimate recipient for the grant, the Presidential Forum was rapidly developing into a public television project, a result of progress in negotiations with PBS. Bill McCarter offered to organize the Forum as a special autonomous program of WTTW in Chicago. As a nonprofit, tax-exempt organization, WTTW could become the acceptable legal recipient of the Benton Foundation grant. Also, Jim Karayn, who was the only person working full time on the Forum project, visualized the project as a broadcast event, in which PBS stations would play a major role. His experience in public television facilitated contacts in August with PBS stations in the cities chosen as sites of the five primary Forums: WGBH (Boston), WPBT (Miami), WNET (New York), WTTW (Chicago), and KCET (Los Angeles). These five cities were selected because each had a strong station with widespread public support in its area. Also, a series of Forums in these five cities in the spring of 1976 would generally follow the course of the presidential primary season. Each of these stations expressed an interest in participating.

By September we were considering five primary Forums, with two additional Forums on the eve of the two major-party nominating conventions. They were still to be nonpartisan, community-organized events that would involve ordinary citizens in their planning and implementation. It was intended that each Forum, and the broadcast resulting from it, should be truly regional or local in emphasis. The PBS station in each of the host cities would be responsible for producing and funding its Forum. Also, within each region, committees of prominent public officials, civic leaders, citizens, and politicians would be formed to organize the event, extend invitations to the candidates, and work with the national coordinating staff in structuring the Forums.

70

In order to keep the structure and ground rules consistent, a national body would be created to oversee the entire project. To be called the 1976 Presidential Forum Committee, the national body would consist of a board, an executive committee, and a staff of three—an executive director (Jim Karayn), a director of development and promotion, and a political and community organizer. The overall 1976 Presidential Forum Committee was to be a separate unit of the Chicago PBS station, WTTW, thus acquiring its nonprofit, tax-exempt status.

Most committee members considered strong grass-roots support essential to the Forums' success. Each local Forum committee was to be organized in such a way that the various candidates would see the value of participating. We wanted the Forums and their citizen supporters to be in the controlling position, rather than the candidates, as is usually the case. Forum committee members expressed varying degrees of support for the political/community organizational component. Some believed that the allure of the television medium or high-level national political contacts would be more effective in persuading candidates to participate than would grass-roots pressure.

On September 24, at a meeting in Chicago with leaders of the five PBS stations, all aspects of the project were reviewed, including structure, legal and financial problems, and questions of format and approach. This meeting turned out to be a crucial turning point for the Forum project, radically altering its organizational structure. Wayne Coy, the Forum's legal counsel, predicted that the Federal Communications Commission was about to rule favorably on a petition from the Aspen Institute requesting clarification and broadening of the definition of "bona fide news events" that would be exempt from the equal-time provisions of Section 315 of the Communications Act. The revised definition of "bona fide news events" was expected to include all political events not controlled by the television stations themselves. Coy's prediction was correct. As a result, the Forum project could not have PBS nationally or the five selected PBS stations involved in planning and organizing the political events—the Forums—themselves. The Forum project could not be a special program under the auspices of WTTW in Chicago.

The FCC decision solved Section 315 problems for the broadcasters. They could cover the Forums as legitimate "bona fide news events" without incurring any liabilities. But at the same time the FCC decision threw the Forum project backwards organizationally, for now, once again we were without a sponsoring organization to receive the Benton Foundation's grant.

Anticipating the FCC action, we decided to divide the Forum project into two parts. The first would concentrate on the organization of the Forums, including the appointment of a National Steering Committee and the recruitment of the local host committees, made up of political and civic leaders. These local committees, with help from the national Forum staff, would build and generate the grass-roots support for the Forums that would insure wide candidate participation. The second part of the project would involve encouraging the media, including PBS, to cover the individual forums as legitimate "bona fide news events."

Forum project organizers had two choices with regard to a sponsoring organization. Either they could establish the project as a new nonprofit, tax-exempt group, or they could locate an established group having those qualifications that would take over and adopt the project. After much discussion, it was decided to pursue the latter alternative. Time was limited, as the first Forum was scheduled for February in Boston. The Forum project still didn't have any seed money and it might have to wait an indefinite period to obtain tax-exempt status from the IRS. Numerous groups were discussed; because of its long-term involvement and preeminence in nonpartisan voter education, the League of Women Voters Education Fund was selected.

On September 26, Charles Benton called Peggy Lampl, national executive director of the League, to explain the Forum project. Lampl reacted enthusiastically, pointing out that just the previous day the League had adopted "Issues Not Images" as the theme of its 1976 election year activities. Lampl agreed that the project might indeed be an excellent activity in keeping with the new theme.

A meeting was arranged for October 3 in Washington. Lampl, Ruth Clusen, president of the League, and other League leaders met with the Bentons and Pokorny to learn more about the Forum project and to exchange ideas. The League indicated it was willing to consider adopting the project and also to direct it. In essence, the League said it would fulfill the role of what we had been calling the "political-community organizer" for the Forums: it would organize the events. The project itself would not have to create a separate organizing component. The League felt it had the experience, credibility, and talent needed to organize the local host committees in the five cities and that it could successfully entice the presidential candidates to appear on the various Forums.

On October 15, Clusen officially requested that the Benton Foundation provide a grant to cover the costs of producing and coordinating the five Presidential Forums. The request was for the $50,000 that had been waiting for a recipient since July 29, and for an additional $150,000 payable on January 1, 1976.

A few legal problems still had to be cleared up in November. The Federal Election Commission (FEC) ruled that the League Education Fund did not have to report its activities and spending on voter education as campaign expenditures. Further the Benton Foundation lawyers advised the foundation that a grant to the League would not violate tax laws or any federal laws regulating foundations. With these hurdles cleared, on December 2, the Benton Foundation met and approved the additional $150,000 grant to the League of Women Voters Education Fund, of which Clusen was the chairman. The final conception of the Forum under League sponsorship in December was quite different from what we had planned in May or even early September.

The League Takes Over

The first meeting of the reorganized National Steering Committee of the 1976 Presidential Forum project took place on December 15, in Washington, D.C. The meeting was conducted by Clusen and Lampl; the agenda and discussions reflected the direction the Forum project would follow under League leadership. Most of the meeting was devoted to discussing the best way to organize the Forums as viable news events. How would the Forums be run? What would be the format and the issues discussed? Which candidates would be eligible to participate in each of the five Forums? The minutes show that the following key subjects were discussed or reported on:

1. PBS was committed to televising each Forum live in its entirety, if it was a worthy "bona fide news event" and, of course, pending receipt of the funding needed to cover each station's actual production and set-up costs.

2. Candidates eligible to participate in each of the five Forums would consist of those persons on the ballot(s) in the primaries taking place in the state/region of the host city. (At the second Steering Committee meeting on January 8, it was decided that, in addition, only candidates would be invited to participate who met the Federal Election Commission's qualifications for federal campaign matching funds under the 1974 Federal Campaign Act.)

3. All the presidential candidates, when initially contacted in December, had expressed interest in participating in the Forums, except Governor Wallace on the Democratic side and President Gerald Ford and Governor Ronald Reagan on the Republican side.

4. Each Forum would concentrate its questioning and dialogue on one set of issues. (For example, the set eventually developed for Boston was "High Employment, Low Inflation, and Cheap Energy: Can We Have Them All?")

5. Each Forum would last for no less than ninety minutes and no more than two and one-half hours. On the stage would be the candidates, a moderator (Dean Elie Abel of the Columbia University School of Journalism was eventually selected), and a "resource panel" made up of regional authorities on the topic being discussed at the Forum.

6. The audience would be an invited cross-section of the community. In this way security would be more manageable, and the chances that any one candidate's campaign could "pack the hall" would be eliminated. Questioning of the candidates by the audience would be allowed through the submission of written questions screened by a panel of local League members.

Virtually no time was devoted at the December meeting to discussion of the local grass-roots organizing component, which had been such an important part of the original idea earlier in the year. The League's position was that, given the grass-roots nature of the League, state and local chapters were autonomous.

While the National Steering Committee of the Presidential Forum project could suggest ancillary public participation activities, it was up to each local chapter to decide whether it wanted to pursue them. The League felt it had essentially contracted with the Benton Foundation to put on a television series of "candidate town meetings," and it was to this narrower vision of the project that the League devoted its attention.

Three political consultants/organizers, however, were hired in early December to help elicit candidate participation in the Forums (Terry Straub, Paul Wagner, and Ralph Murphine—all Washington-based). Straub and Murphine prepared for the Steering Committee elaborate grass-roots organizational blueprints that outlined strategies for achieving greater public participation than would come from League sponsorship alone. Their concern was to use the

Forums locally as catalysts for greater citizen involvement in political life—an original goal of the Forums. However, because of limited time, budget, and volunteers, the League chose not to pursue the Straub-Murphine plan, though it said it would have no objections if local chapters in the five host cities wanted to pursue the plan on their own. We felt that was a costly decision, because it made it easier for candidates such as Ford, Reagan, and Wallace to ignore the Forums.

In retrospect, perhaps no amount of grass-roots community involvement and participation in the individual Forums could have forced Ford, Reagan, and Wallace to participate. Perhaps no level of community demand could have overcome their unwillingness to expose themselves to the public and the other candidates in the Forum context. Still, well-organized, broad-based community support and involvement in the individual cities could no doubt have kept the Forums from experiencing the candidate attrition that occurred throughout the primary season and that ultimately killed the final, fifth Forum scheduled for Los Angeles in May. This record of declining candidate participation in the Forums, as they progressed from Boston in February (where seven candidates participated) to Chicago in May (where two came), is one of the most important experiences of the entire Forum project.

February 23 / Boston

On Monday, February 23, at John Hancock Hall in Boston, the first 1976 Presidential Forum, billed as the New England Forum, took place. Invitations were extended to all presidential candidates who were entered in the upcoming New Hampshire or Massachusetts primaries and who were certified by the Federal Election Commission to receive federal campaign matching funds. Seven candidates attended: Senators Birch Bayh and Henry Jackson, Governors Jimmy Carter and Milton Shapp, Congressman Morris Udall, former Senator Fred Harris, and former Ambassador Sargent Shriver. The theme of the discussion was "High Employment, Low Inflation, and Cheap Energy: Can We Have Them All?"

Getting the seven candidates to attend had not been easy, even though both major party chairmen, Robert Strauss for the Democrats and Mary Louise Smith for the Republicans, had endorsed the 1976 Presidential Forum project at a February 3 press conference in Washington, officially announcing the project.

It had become quite clear by early January, at the time of the second meeting of the National Steering Committee, that persuading candidates to participate was going to be difficult. Candidate responses seemed to be closely related to each candidate's perception of his standing in the race and of his need for the exposure. Harris, Shapp, Carter, and Shriver, all acknowledged underdogs, were early recruits for the New England Forum, with Bayh and Udall not far behind. Jackson, "the man to beat" in the early primaries, however, was a holdout. Only at the last minute did he and his staff make the decision to join the Forum, and this only after many phone calls and much cajoling and pressure from every contact the National Steering Committee could muster. As would be the case throughout all four Forums, the local host committee in Boston was of some help in obtaining candidate participation, since it tried to do at the local and regional level what the National Steering Committee was doing across the country—to bring targeted, selective pressure to bear on a candidate here, a candidate there. However, because no broad community-based, grass-roots support existed for the Forum in Boston, there was little popular leverage to use on candidates. In short, there was no public outcry for the Forum that could be used to demand participation. Rather the Forum was a television event that candidates could decide to participate in, if they so desired.

The actual Forum was televised live by PBS to its 258 outlets, and was also broadcast over the National Public Radio network. As expected, the commercial networks refused to broadcast the Forums, citing, in most cases, Section 315 of the Communications Act.

The New England Forum lasted two hours, with questions asked of the candidates by moderator Elie Abel, the resource panel of three Boston-area economists, and the audience. The reviews of the Forum were mixed. Many political reporters, as well as some candidates and their staffs, were disappointed. From their point of view, the New England Forum was pedestrian, colorless, perhaps even "boring." The dialogue dealt with complex economic issues, which are often not well understood by ordinary voters, or by reporters and commentators for that matter.

Press coverage of the Forum emphasized the major mistake of the evening. Jimmy Carter stated for the first, and last, time that his proposed reform of the federal tax laws would include elimination of the tax deduction for interest on home mortgages. This statement by Carter would haunt him two weeks later in Florida, where Jackson made it *the* issue on the final days of that campaign. Carter's Florida campaign coordinator Phil Wise stated after the Florida election that the Boston statement cost him at least 10 percent of the vote.

Those trained and experienced in the issues discussed, however, found the dialogue a most interesting statement of the general Democratic attack on Republican national economic policy, and a statement of the variations among the Democratic candidates themselves. Many commentators found real value in the Forum, particularly if they were prepared to accept it for what it was— a "live" telecast of the typical candidate forums which are so much a part of the reality of American political life. The purpose of the Forums was, after all, not to make news, but rather to give the audience (A.C. Nielsen estimated that a total of 1,040,000 households viewed part of the New England Forum) a chance to see and hear the candidates running for the presidency discuss—not debate—the major issues facing the country.

One criticism of the New England Forum was that, with seven candidates on the stage at the same time, the format tended to blur distinctions among them and provided little time for any one candidate to discuss his views thoroughly. While there was validity to this charge, it failed to take note of the fact that blurring, if blurring it be, was an accurate reflection of the reality of the early days of the 1976 presidential campaign—a plethora of Democrats chasing each other to earn the right to go after Ford.

March 1 / Miami

The second, Southern Forum, took place as planned in Miami on March 1, one week after the Boston event and after Jimmy Carter had pulled a surprising upset in the New Hampshire primary on February 24. But, while the Grand

Ballroom of the Sheraton Four Ambassador Hotel—scene of the Southern Forum—was larger than John Hancock Hall in Boston, the crowd of candidates had dwindled to three—Jackson, Carter, and Shapp. All the eligible candidates had been invited to participate, but since most of them were not actually campaigning in Florida, many skipped the Southern Forum. The liberal candidates in particular stayed in Massachusetts on March 1, election eve of the Massachusetts primary—predicted to be the key testing-ground for the liberal field of Democratic hopefuls.

The absence of liberals in Miami was quite all right from the Forum project's point of view, because it had always been hoped that the individual Forums would have a regional feeling to them, that they would show the character of the unfolding 1976 presidential campaign. This would mean, as it did in Miami, that only those candidates who were actually fighting for votes and delegates in that particular state or region would participate. Since the Democratic contest in Florida was among Jackson, Carter, and Wallace, the Forum would have been a success if these three Democrats had participated. However, only the first two attended. Jackson had wanted to stay in Massachusetts, but at the last minute he canceled an election eve rally there and went to Miami. Carter, who from the beginning of his campaign had seen Florida as his "breakthrough" victory, eagerly agreed to participate. Wallace did not come, for he still believed he had more to lose than to gain from the Forums. He believed, wrongly as it turned out, that he was ahead in Florida, the sure winner, and that he didn't need to campaign much in the state.

PBS coverage of the Southern Forum was uncertain up to the last few days, because WPBT in Miami had trouble raising the money to pay for the broadcast. The Ford Foundation in January had granted $100,000 in matching funds to the five stations. This meant that, whatever amounts each station raised from other sources, Ford would contribute matching money up to $20,000. If each station raised $20,000, the resultant $40,000 would cover the expenses incurred in providing coverage of the forum. Miami had difficulty raising its $20,000, despite appeals to various individuals and foundations. Finally, in the week before the event, the Lilly Endowment contributed $5,000, and WPBT told PBS it would televise the Forum. While the Miami experience was the closest call of the four, during February, March, and April, fund-raising by local PBS stations for Forum broadcast coverage was a huge problem. The Forum project itself could not get involved in this situation. It was a continual source of concern, especially since the League had concentrated on the Forums as television events.

In addition, the Forum project also faced financial problems of its own in the spring, as it tried to raise additional funding for the local organization and promotion of the individual Forums. Organizations that helped with this funding were the National Council of Churches, the Carnegie Corporation, and the ARCO Foundation.

The topic for the Southern Forum was "From Social Security to Welfare: What is the National Responsibility?" This was a broad subject area and gave the three candidates great flexibility to delineate their views. Carter used the opportunity to articulate his views on the need for government reorganization, and he struck the "anti-Washington" themes that were to become a key component of his campaign for the White House. Jackson criticized Carter's promise to improve government by merely reorganizing it. He tried to force Carter to deal more substantively with the commitments and responsibilities of the federal government, even if reorganized. Jackson also continued attacking Carter in Miami on the home-mortgage interest deduction issue, which had surfaced the week before at the New England Forum. As he had done in Boston, Shapp made clear his businessman's vision that the government should be run like a business. In some ways, the dialogue among the candidates in Miami was superior to the one in Boston. This was largely because only three candidates occupied the stage, compared to seven in Boston. Thus, each got a chance to articulate his views more fully on the subjects under discussion.

On March 3, two days after the Southern Forum, the National Steering Committee met in Washington to evaluate the first two efforts and to make plans for the remaining Forums. Many members felt that the format needed tightening and that Elie Abel, as moderator, should exercise more control over the discussions. Plans for the remaining Forums, therefore, were based on the experience of the first two. In addition, it was at this Steering Committee meeting that the topic of fall 1976 presidential debates once again arose. Everyone on the committee felt that fall debates would be a logical extension of the spring Forums, especially because of the precedent they set as televised "bona fide news events." Thus, the committee, on March 3, discussed sponsorship by the League of a series of fall presidential debates—a concept that had been part of the original Presidential Forum idea in early 1975. Consideration was given at the meeting to announcing plans for the fall debates at the third Forum to be held in New York on March 29, but the Steering Committee ultimately decided more work on the concept was needed.

March 29 / New York

By the time the Mid-Atlantic Forum took place in New York at the Waldorf Astoria Grand Ballroom on March 29, Jimmy Carter was clearly the man to beat in the Democratic primaries. He had won the New Hampshire and Florida primaries, and his campaign was gaining momentum. By now, too, the field of eligible candidates was smaller. Some, like Bayh, Shriver, and Shapp, had dropped out of the race, while others, like Senator Frank Church and anti-abortion advocate Ellen McCormack, were now qualified by the FEC for federal matching funds.

Five candidates attended the Mid-Atlantic Forum: Carter, Jackson, Church, Udall, and Harris. As with the New England Forum, the underdogs, Udall and Harris, signed up early. Church, who had just entered the race, felt he needed the exposure and quickly agreed to attend. At the Forum, Church described himself as the "new boy on the block." Jackson (who had won the Massachusetts primary on March 2) and Carter, now the front-runners, were hardest to line up. Carter finally agreed to come when the last ounce of "influence" was applied by members of the National Steering Committee and their contacts. Jackson, who needed to score against Carter in industrial states like New York, considered his strongest territory, agreed to participate once he knew for sure

Carter would be there. Ford, Reagan, and Wallace, as had been their pattern, still refused, though the Republican race changed dramatically in North Carolina on March 23 with Reagan's victory over Ford.

Prior to the New York event, some of Ford's staff had inquired about whether the president could participate in the Forum by way of a television hook-up from the White House. Karayn turned down the request because he felt it would give the president, seated in the Oval Office, an unfair advantage over the other candidates, on the New York stage. Had the White House pursued the matter, the Forum project might have accepted a Ford-from-Washington appearance, with the caveat that it be from a more neutral setting than the Oval Office. But the White House did not follow up on the initial feeler.

The topic in New York was "Who is Responsible for the Cities?"—in essence, a discussion of the urban problems facing America. With little to lose, candidates Jackson, Udall, and Harris all attacked Carter for his positions on the New York fiscal crisis. While these attacks seemed to please the audience in the Waldorf (the *New York Post* called it the "battle of the city-savers"), Carter quietly sat through it all, refusing to be drawn into battle with his challengers. Smiling serenely, perhaps he knew that once the television signal got beyond the Hudson, his position on the issue was closer to that of the average national voter. As in Boston, one misspoken idea attracted attention. In this case, it was Jackson's statement that it wasn't "normal" for families to raise children "in tenth floor apartments." To a New York audience, something about this seemed in error, and titters of laughter—in some cases, anger—rose. Jackson's clarification that he really meant poor people living in crowded apartments didn't seem to help. He had failed to score; in fact, he bled from a self-inflicted wound.

As a television event, the Forum in New York made progress in terms of viewership. The Nielsen organization reported "a sizeable audience for a public television program." This translated into 3.5 percent of the New York viewing audience.

The National Steering Committee met again on April 9. By then, much work had been done on the idea of fall presidential debates. Informal sessions, for example, had been held in late March and early April between Forum project committee members and executives of all three commercial networks. A formal proposal outlining the proposed fall debates was adopted by the committee. It was decided that formal announcement of the proposed fall presidential debates as a special project of the League of Women Voters Education Fund would be made by Clusen on May 5 at the League's 32nd Annual National Convention in New York.

May 3 / Chicago

By the time the Forums reached Chicago on May 3 for the Midwest states event in the Guildhall of the Ambassador West Hotel, the project appeared doomed. Events were moving rapidly in the primaries. The week before, Carter had beaten Jackson decisively in Pennsylvania. Not only was he now the front-runner, but most commentators also gave him the nomination. The only remaining threat to his candidacy was the late-starting effort of California Governor Jerry Brown, who was bent on beating Carter in the Maryland primary on May 18.

Donna Schiller, president of the Illinois League of Women Voters, had organized what was without question the broadest community support for any of the Forums. She and her workers had a little more time than the people in the earlier cities, and they used it wisely. But even this effort failed to get the front-runner to appear in Chicago. By this point in the sequence of primaries, Carter was unquestionably far ahead. He and his staff, like Ford, Reagan, and Wallace before him, decided the risk was greater than the potential gain. While one can understand the candidate's point of view, the verdict he reached and the ease with which he carried off his decision demonstrated that the Forum project really needed much more national support than League sponsorship gave it. Once again, candidates were using the political/communications process, instead of being constrained by it.

The Midwest Forum took place on May 3, with Carter ignoring it and Brown concerned with the Maryland primary. Wallace, whose campaign was in deep trouble, agreed to appear in Chicago, an interesting about-face from his earlier position. Now he, like Carter two months earlier, needed the help and exposure the Forums might provide. But at the last minute he returned home to Alabama from Indiana, where he had been campaigning for that week's primary. Thus, only Udall and Church were present to discuss the topic "Defense, Detente, and Trade: What Are Our Goals?"

The Forum (cut down to only one hour) was a kind of seminar on American foreign policy between men who almost ashamedly found nothing to disagree about. At one point each said he would like the other to be his secretary of state.

Two days after the Midwest Forum, on May 5, Ruth Clusen, as planned, officially announced the League Education Fund's plans for a fall series of presidential debates. In her announcement, Clusen said,

> . . . The 1976 Presidential Forum program, a special project of the League's Education Fund, is proof of the viability of our debate proposal.
> The Forum series was acclaimed as a unique and important contribution to voter understanding of issues and candidates' positions.
> The fall debates will be a natural extension of the Forum project, which marked the first time a nonpartisan organization presented the candidates to the public on a national scale.

Clusen pointed out that the Forum project had demonstrated the viability of candidate forums and debates as "bona fide news events" which could be covered by the television networks without their incurring Section 315 liabilities. She challenged the networks to cover the fall debates as League-sponsored events.

The Forums End

The Forum project faced increasing difficulties in arranging its fifth, and final, event—the Los Angeles Forum, scheduled for May 24. Looking to the political history of the 1968 and 1972 presidential primaries, the Forum project had always assumed that the California primary in 1976 would be the final, climactic struggle. Brown's late entry in the 1976 primary race, however, changed all that. With his candidacy, Brown turned California into favorite-son territory. The effect of this on the other Democratic hopefuls was that in April and May they increasingly devoted their attention to the May 25 Oregon primary as the "Western test" of their voter appeal. With candidate interest in Oregon, the Forum project had problems getting commitments for a May 24 event in Los Angeles. In mid-May, however, it still looked as if Udall, Church, and Brown would attend. But during the week before the event, all plans changed. Church and Brown indicated they were spending the evening of May 24— Oregon's election eve—in Portland, not Los Angeles. The Forum project responded by trying to reschedule the final Forum in Portland. A live interconnection between a Portland location and the hotel in Los Angeles was also considered briefly, but to no avail. Events were moving too fast, and the candidates clearly preferred, in the final days of the primary season, to participate in their own paid for and "controlled" television shows. The Forums had become television events under League sponsorship, not the community-organized political education events we had originally planned for in 1975 and early 1976. By that standard they couldn't compete with the "real thing" from the candidates' point-of-view—paid television advertising. Thus, on Friday, May 21, the League abandoned the final 1976 Presidential Forum.

Ruth Clusen in her announcement of the cancellation, perhaps unwittingly, acknowledged the essential weakness of the League's philosophy of the Forums as "television events" when she said:

> It's both sad and a bit shocking that none of the men running for the presidency believed that the opportunity to outline their choices for national priorities at a Forum which would have had a national television audience was important.
>
> I realize that campaign plans are subject to constant change and reevaluation. However, our Forum dates were announced well in advance and it seems apparent that, given *the choice between controlling their own candidate appearances and facing a live audience with some hard questions, the candidates and the campaign managers chose the former course.*

With that the 1976 Presidential Forum project ended.

Success and Failure

While the Presidential Forum project didn't achieve all its goals, it did make at least three contributions to the 1976 presidential campaign and to the country's political process generally.

First, the Forums paved the way for the Carter-Ford debates in the fall, which were acknowledged by President Carter as having been the "key" to his victory. As a result of the Forums, the Federal Communications Commission ruling on the Aspen Institute petition ("bona fide news events") was challenged in the spring and left standing. Thus, by the time the fall debates were arranged, it was clear that they could be covered by the commercial television stations without their incurring Section 315 liabilities. Further, early seed money for the debate project came to the League Education Fund in June 1976 as a result of the Forums. The Forum project, upon completion in June, had funds left over especially because of the cancellation of the last Forum in Los Angeles. When asked, the Benton Foundation agreed to release these funds and allow the Education Fund to use them for preliminary planning for the fall debates.

Second, the Forum Project made a contribution to the 1976 campaign and beyond as a challenge to the prevalent mood of political apathy in the country. It was an example of how citizen volunteerism can make a difference.

Third, the Forum discussions themselves provided for the millions who viewed them a chance to see, hear, and evaluate some of the men running for the presidency. While not all the candidates, as we've seen, participated in the Forums, the man who won on November 2 did participate in three of the four that took place. Carter attended as many Forums as any other single candidate and, as a result, the public gained a better insight into the man and into what his policies as president would be.

When one looks for failures, the Forums had their share. Perhaps the most important was the progressive loss of the original emphasis on direct citizen involvement and control. In many ways, the story of the Forums is the story of an original idea of broad-based citizen participation in a political project, which loses out to the realities of organizational and institutional pressures and power. The project became the program of one national organization directed from Washington. As the project progressed, its potential for citizen involvement was largely unrealized. The Forums became the "television events" they were meant to replace. If the Forum project had achieved its original organizational goals, its entire life might have been different. Strong, broad-based community support in each of the five host cities would have helped to increase candidate willingness to participate and to generate increased viewership. Community support could have helped the local PBS stations raise production money. In short, deemphasizing the citizen-organizing component of the project was costly on almost all scores.

The Forums' inability to overcome the "front-runner" problem also inevitably relates to the question of organizational strength. Without a strong public demand for participation, the front-runners (Ford, Reagan, Wallace, and eventually Carter) avoided the Forums, and left them to the underdogs and the also-rans. If this condition is to be changed, it seems that only better-organized, broader-based community support for events like the Forums can be successful. Candidates should be constrained by public pressure to participate in such events. If events like the Forums inevitably become a process to be used by candidates for their own purposes, then perhaps they should be institutionalized by federal law.

A final question raised by the Forum project, of course, is that of the role of television in the political process. Can television be used to communicate ideas? Many commentators argue negatively, saying that it is a medium for communicating personality and whatever the camera happens to pick up and distill. If that is true, what are the implications in a country where overwhelming majorities get their information and understanding of political events through television? Perhaps there are ways in which the television viewing experience can be supplemented by a more systematic presentation of the candidates' views in print. Other approaches need to be tested and new ideas tried.

The Presidential Forums, like the subsequent fall debates, lead one to wonder how in American society today mass communications technology can best play a role that supports, rather than erodes, the basic foundations of political democracy—public education, public understanding, and enlightened public choice.

The 1976 Presidential Forums, in the final analysis, were yet another experiment in our country's continuing imperfect attempt at realizing popular democracy. As with most similar experiments, they were not wholly successful, but they were not complete failures either—much was learned by many. It is hoped that these lessons will be used to improve the quality of the American political and communications processes in the years ahead.

6.

The Sponsor: The League of Women Voters Education Fund

PEGGY LAMPL

Perhaps the most surprising thing about the 1976 presidential debates is that they happened at all. The key to success or failure was the decision of each nominee that face-to-face meetings were in his best interests—a decision not forthcoming in three prior presidential elections. Thus, whatever steps the League of Women Voters Education Fund undertook to promote the debate concept were always weighed in the light of political palatability and reality.

While President Ford's August 19 announcement that he wanted to debate his opponent was the beginning of a chain of events that led to three 90-minute meetings between the candidates, it was also the end of months of work and planning by the Education Fund's staff, the project's co-chairs, and the steering committee.

For the Education Fund, involvement in the project began on September 25, 1975, when the Federal Communications Commission, acting favorably on a petition by the Aspen Institute, ruled that debates could be exempt from the "equal opportunity" restrictions of Section 315 of the Communications Act of 1934, if sponsorship was independent of both broadcasters and candidates and if the debates could be classified as bona fide news events. The following day, Charles Benton, president of the William Benton Foundation, approached the League on behalf of the foundation. Anticipating the FCC ruling, Benton and Jim Karayn, former president of NPACT, had developed a proposal for a series of town meetings to be conducted during the primaries and to feature the Republican and Democratic candidates vying for their party's nomination. The idea appealed to the Education Fund, and it agreed to sponsor the meetings or, as they were called, the Presidential Forums. With acceptance came a $50,000 planning grant from the foundation and the employment of Karayn to direct the project.

The League's receptivity to the Benton proposal was a natural outgrowth of its long-standing involvement in and dedication to voter education. Since its founding in 1920, the League of Women Voters has played an active role in informing the electorate about candidates and about the issues that make up the electoral mix. These voter service activities are carried on by the more than 1400 state and local Leagues nationwide and include candidates meetings and forums, election guides, and nonpartisan analyses of ballot issues.

The League had also been a part of the electronic media's pioneer effort in election public-service broadcasting. Prior to the 1928 presidential contest, NBC radio asked the League to hostess a half-hour program to "present all sides" of the issues being discussed in the campaign. In 1954, the League was the convener of a preconvention television program, also on NBC, featuring Republican and Democratic primary hopefuls. In 1972, the League explored the possibility of doing another primary-oriented televised broadcast but was stymied by the equal-opportunity provision of Section 315.

Additional staff was hired and an advisory committee assembled for the Forum project; it included bipartisan representation from both political parties and union, business, and civic leaders. Preliminary contacts were established with announced and expected-to-announce candidates, and the plans were broached to public and commercial television stations in the locations under consideration. By January 1976, enough progress had been made in developing the Forum concept for the League to receive an additional $150,000 grant from the Benton Foundation. The first event was held in Boston on February 23 to coincide with the Massachusetts and New Hampshire primaries and included seven of the eight Democratic candidates qualified to receive public financing. The exception was George Wallace. Three more Forums were held: in Miami on March 1; in New York on March 29; and in Chicago on May 3. All four were carried in their entirety by the Public Broadcasting Service and National Public Radio. As primary candidates waxed and waned, the final appearance scorecard read: Carter 3, Udall 3, Jackson 3, Harris 2, Church 2, Shapp 2, Bayh 1, and Shriver 1. Although invited, both Governor Reagan and President Ford declined to appear in any of the Forums.

In March, while the Forums were underway, Ruth C. Clusen, chairman of the Education Fund; Peggy Lampl, executive director; and Karayn held a series of informal discussions exploring the idea of carrying the Forum experiment to its logical conclusion—a series of presidential debates following the two national conventions. They agreed that it was certainly worth a try and that one of the ingredients for success would be building a strong public awareness of and demand for candidate debates. The idea was discussed with the Forum's steering committee and the League's Board of Trustees, and it received strong support from both quarters.

Another point of early agreement was that it would be an exercise in futility for the League, with limited staff and resources, to mount a major debate effort if the three networks were going to wage a substantial campaign to have Congress waive Section 315. Accordingly, Clusen wrote the heads of the three networks requesting a meeting to outline, in broad terms, the League's debate plans.

On April 26, Clusen, Lampl, and Karayn held separate meetings with network officials, including Herbert Schlosser, president, National Broadcasting Company; Elmer W. Lower, vice-president, American Broadcasting Company; and John A. Schneider, president, CBS Broadcasting Group. At each of the meetings, the League representatives sketched out their plans for a series of debates to be announced at the League's national convention the following week and also their intention to mount a public-opinion campaign as part of the debate strategy. In the course of the discussions, it became clear that none of the networks thought that debates were in the cards for 1976 and, therefore, would not be aggressively seeking a waiver of 315. (In 1960, the congressional waiver followed the acceptance in July by Nixon and Kennedy of the network's debate offer.)

Among the reasons given by the network executives was one that echoed over and over again as the League pursued the project. Most observers believed that Ford would win the Republican nomination. If so, tradition dictated that an incumbent president would never agree to debate his opponent. The League reasoned, however, that Ford's situation was different—he was the incumbent but he was also an appointed, not an elected, president. Additionally, his showings in various polls did not give him an overwhelming advantage—not even within the Republican party.

At that juncture, the League believed that it had a potentially clear but rock-strewn field and that, in fact, there probably would not be any debates if it didn't try to act as the catalyst. On May 5, at the League's national convention, Clusen announced the debate plans, stating: "The country is ready for face-to-face discussions of issues, the public has said it wants this kind of dialogue, and the candidates themselves have claimed there is a desperate need for full airing of the issues."

While the announcement did not burst like a bombshell, it did generate editorial comment, such as the following from the May 11 *Cincinnati Post*: "The League has set itself a hard task. Generally, the favored candidate shuns debates out of fear of making his underdog opponent better known. That may be good politics but it isn't fair play nor does it aid voters in making an informed choice.

"If the candidates try to duck the debates, the women plan to bring enough pressure to change their minds. The League is on the correct track and we wish it luck."

One of those pressure points was a nationwide petition drive, with a goal of 4 million signatures, to be conducted by the 1400 Leagues across the country. In June, a twelve-page petition kit was mailed to Leagues with detailed instructions for signature-gathering and for generating media and public support for presidential debates. The petition timetable called for the campaign to peak the third and fourth week in August, when both candidates would be known. President Ford's August 19 announcement aborted the full drive, but the League network was able to generate a slow but steady growth of interest in the debate issue across the country.

The Forums had run their course by the end of May, and the full-time job of mobilizing for the debates began in June. An immediate, and as it turned out continuing, problem was securing the necessary funding for predebate activity. On June 9, following discussions with Karayn and Benton, Clusen wrote to Anna Rosenberg Hoffman, chairman of the William Benton Foundation, requesting permission to use monies still remaining in the Forum grant (approximately $17,000) as seed money for the debates. The request was granted, and the League was able to retain the office space rented for the Forums and a small staff, which through June and July consisted of Karayn and two other persons, with additional help from members of the League's own staff.

By mid-June, Karayn had developed a basic debates briefing book entitled "A Proposal For Action," which outlined the rationale behind debates, established the framework for building public and candidate support, and called for a series of three presidential debates and one vice-presidential debate to be held in the weeks of September 27, October 11, October 19, and October 25.

The plan included the formation of a new steering committee composed, as for the Forums, of political, civic, union, and business leaders. As in the Forum planning, it was recognized that it was essential to have individuals associated with the project who had access to the candidates and to their political advisors. The original scenario called for a single chair for the committee who would play an active role in the public and candidate support-building process.

In internal discussions and in soliciting suggestions from others, the name of Frank Stanton, former president of CBS and a key figure in the 1960 debates, was mentioned repeatedly. An informal approach to Stanton was made by Douglass Cater, director of the Aspen Institute's Center for Communications, and when he expressed interest, a follow-up meeting was arranged in New York with Karayn, Clusen, and Lampl. The two-hour meeting ended on a positive note pending Stanton's resolution of two points. As a broadcaster, he wanted to test the 315 waters once again. He did so and was informed by Senator John Pastore, chairman of the Subcommittee on Communications, that there was virtually no possibility of a waiver. Second, as a member of the CBS Board and former employee, he had an obligation to see if CBS had any objection to his accepting the task. CBS did object, with the network's attorneys indicating that Stanton's association with the project might, if it was successful, lead to charges of collusion between CBS and the League. So, Stanton was out.

Next on the list of possible chairs was Newton Minow, former FCC commissioner and currently a partner in the Chicago law firm of Sidley & Austin. Karayn and Clusen broached the idea to Minow in early July. In agreeing, Minow suggested that because of his identification as a Democrat and because of the bipartisan nature of the project, he thought it would be better politically to have Republican identification as well. Accordingly, the League asked Charls Walker, former undersecretary of the treasury and a member of the Forum Advisory Committee, and Rita Hauser, former U.S. delegate to the United Nations and a law partner in the New York firm of Stroock & Stroock & Lavan, to serve as co-chairs.

The establishment of a steering committee followed. The members, in addition to the chairs, were: Ruth C. Clusen; Peggy Lampl; Jim Karayn; Charles Benton; Mary Lou Burg, Democratic National Committee; Douglass Cater, Aspen Institute; Gary Engebretson, Republican National Committee; George Gallup, Jr., president, American Institute of Public Opinion, Inc.; John Gilligan, former governor of Ohio; Eppie Lederer [Ann Landers], columnist; Dr. Henry Simmons, president-director, Hunterdon Medical Center; Glen Watts, president, Communications Workers of America; and Theodore H. White, author.

During June and July, additional contacts were made and maintained with Governor Carter's staff, who were fully briefed on the proposal during a trip by Karayn to Plains in July. During a visit to Washington on June 24, Carter had publicly indicated that he favored debating his Republican opponent, although "he wouldn't give his word on it."

Simultaneously, overtures were made to the White House and to other Republicans active on the political scene. Charls Walker made sure that Bryce Harlow, Dick Chaney, and John Connally were briefed on the debates. In July, Karayn had a long discussion with Dean Burch about the debate proposal. His arguments were apparently persuasive and led to a memorandum from Burch to President Ford suggesting that he consider debating his opponent.

Communications were also kept open to the Reagan camp, with the ex-governor of California being the only one of the three potential contenders who had committed himself to debating his opponent.

In Karayn's "Proposal for Action," activity was segmented into two phases. Phase I, subtitled "The building of the voters' mandate," was originally scheduled to run through Labor Day. It included the petition drive, media contacts, the securing of a broad list of organizational and individual endorsements for debates, and a series of cross-country appearances by Clusen and Karayn.

Phase I was also predicated on the League's ability to raise funds for the project. Karayn and the League's Development Office took the proposal to a variety of corporate and foundation donors—eighty-three in all. By mid-August, there were commitments for about $175,000 of the original $280,000 budget—commitments contingent, however, on the candidates actually agreeing to debate. At least some of these commitments could not be honored once the Federal Election Committee ruled on August 30 that corporate dollars could not be used to fund the debates.

Without the money in hand, a number of the phase I outreach programs had to be cut back or canceled. However, by August 2, 112 national organizations had been contacted, and their support for debates and/or participation in the petition drive solicited—roughly half responded favorably and action was pending in another thirty when the debates became a reality.

Media interest had gradually picked up and was quickened by an August 5 Gallup Poll, suggested by the League, which showed that 68 percent of the electorate, evenly divided between Republicans and Democrats, wanted the candidates to debate.

On August 3, the League held a morning press conference in Washington to formally announce the co-chairs for the debates and to outline progress to date and future plans. The press conference was followed by the first meeting of the steering committee.

One question raised repeatedly at the conference, and thereafter, was how the League proposed to deal with minor party or independent candidates. It was a question which had been thoroughly discussed in the preceding months and answered in Clusen's May debate announcement, in which she stated that the debates were to be between the nominees of the major parties—a position repeated in the petition text.

It was a decision born of practicality and necessity, and one which the League knew would be contested on both legal and ethical grounds. More than 102 individuals had filed statements with the Federal Election Commission indicating their intention to run for the presidency—all were "legally qualified candidates." In addition, candidates like Eugene McCarthy and those of the U. S. Labor, American, Socialist Labor and American Independent parties would be on the ballot in a significant number of states. None would be eligible for public funding prior to the election—one of the criteria used in the Forums —and there seemed to be no valid baseline from which to pick and choose from the field of other contenders.

At the August press conference, Minow did state that the League would consider holding a separate debate for minor party candidates if it appeared, as the election season wore on, that they were waging campaigns "that engaged the interest of the American public." The idea was reconsidered on a number of occasions, and in September explorations were made as to possible locations and potential invitees but plans were dropped as it became clear that the other horses really wanted to run on the same track as the Republican and Democratic nominees. As anticipated, a series of challenges to the League and to the networks was mounted by Eugene McCarthy and others, directed both to the courts and to the Federal Communications Commission. Essentially, the prevailing opinions were that in their role as coverers of "bona fide" news events, the networks had no equal opportunity obligations, and that as a private organization, the League of Women Voters Education Fund could limit its debate invitations as it wished.

As an organization committed to opening up the electoral process, the League was never entirely comfortable with its third-party decision. It was well aware of the "loophole" offered by the FEC decision and, as some critics have charged, took advantage of it. Indeed, Lampl had been a participant in a series of meetings, convened by the Aspen Institute, where a variety of strategies to encourage more meaningful election coverage, including the successful Section 315 modification, had been discussed.

If the debates were to become a reality in 1976, the League had no other choice than the one it made. To invite every legally qualified candidate was a patent impossibility; to select one or two of the major "minor" contenders would have been more arbitrary and less defensible than the course it chose. The solution to the third-party dilemma was, and is, beyond the League's problem-solving abilities—it lies with Congress, the courts, and the Federal Election Commission.

The question of minority-party candidates was on the agenda for the August 3 steering committee meeting, but the bulk of time was devoted to working out a timetable for activities over the next thirty days. It was decided to send formal invitations to both candidates directly after the Republican convention—invitations that included a time and location for the first debate and suggested dates for the ensuing three. Tentative plans were made for the formation of a finance committee to assist in the solicitations underway and also for a committee to explore and refine the format suggestions outlined in the proposal. The committee also approved the idea of setting broad themes for each of the debates, specifically:

Debate 1   Domestic Affairs
Debate 2   Foreign Affairs
Debate 3   The Role of the Vice-Presidency
Debate 4   The Role of the Presidency

During the next two weeks, debate staff began looking at potential sites for the four debates—halls or theaters in different sections of the country with a relatively small seating capacity (800–1500) and with ancillary or adjacent facilities which could accommodate the candidates, the secret service, and the media. In line with the steering committee recommendation, a tentative hold was placed on the ballroom of the Chase Park Plaza Hotel in St. Louis for September 25, the League's suggested first debate date.

In July, Karayn and Lampl had attended the Democratic Convention to spread the debate gospel and, in addition, teams of volunteers from the New York City League had been stationed around the perimeter of Madison Square Garden collecting petition signatures from delegates, visitors, and passers-by.

Similar arrangements for signature-gathering were made for Kansas City; in addition, debate-boosting posters were to be carried on some of the buses assigned to state delegations. The Republican Convention team consisted of Clusen, Karayn, Hauser, and Betsy Dribben, public relations director for the League. As at the Democratic Convention, the idea was to talk debate to as many persons as possible—delegates and media. Arrangements were also made to hold a press conference on Thursday, August 19, to announce that formal invitations had been sent to both nominees.

The conference was held at 10 A.M. It was not the media event of the convention; about eleven reporters attended. The text of the telegram sent that morning to Carter and Ford was released. It read:

> In the spirit of free and open political discussions—discussions of issues vital to the future of the country—the '76 Presidential Debates, a project of the League of Women Voters Education Fund, is honored to invite you to participate in three appearances with [Gov. Carter] [The President].
>
> We are suggesting the first appearance take place Tuesday, September 28, at the Chase Park Plaza in St. Louis.
>
> The remaining two appearances are tentatively planned during the weeks of October 11 and October 25 in different regions of the nation. We are also suggesting an additional, or fourth, debate be scheduled the week of October 18 between the two vice-presidential candidates.
>
> Each of the four events is planned for one hour in the evening. We will invite radio and television networks to carry these events. Several of the networks have already expressed interest.
>
> Time is short. To facilitate planning, we urge you to designate a representative to meet with us as soon as possible to consult on the project in more detail.
>
> The '76 Presidential Debates, more than any other event during our Bicentennial year, could reaffirm our democratic institutions and revitalize voter interest. The League—which for 56 years has been involved in voter education—considers your participation to be in the highest national interest as we face an ever more complex future.

RUTH C. CLUSEN
Chairman, Education Fund

RITA E. HAUSER
NEWTON N. MINOW
CHARLS E. WALKER
Co-chairmen, Steering Committee

Although the League was aware that debates were being discussed among President Ford's political advisors, it, like the press, did not know that they had already become an integral part of his campaign plans nor, of course, that he intended to use his acceptance speech to challenge Carter.

In Plains, Governor Carter had prepared for release Friday morning a statement in which he planned to take the initiative and throw the debate gauntlet to Ford. The release embargo was quickly lifted following Ford's speech, and the country knew that, for the first time in sixteen years, there would be face-to-face meetings between the Republican and Democratic nominees.

The League was unquestionably instrumental in making the candidates focus on the question of debates. Without the preceding months of media and political contacts and pressure, it seems unlikely that there would have been the simultaneous peaking of interest and acceptance by both candidates. Undoubtedly, there would have been (and were) invitations by various groups or organizations for the candidates to meet under their auspices. The League's proposal, however, came early and persistently enough, so that each camp had ample opportunity to consider its value in developing campaign plans. It was presented as a package and had, as its sponsor, an organization whose prior voter-education credentials were of the highest.

While the candidates had agreed to debate, neither had agreed specifically to accept the League's invitation. Both, however, stated publicly that it was one of the options being considered. By Tuesday, August 24, each had appointed negotiating representatives to meet with the debate chairs, Walker, Minow, and Hauser, and Karayn, Clusen, and Lampl on August 26 at the Mayflower Hotel. Ford's representatives were Dean Burch, William Ruckelshaus, and Mike Duval. Carter's were Jody Powell, Gerry Rafshoon, and Barry Jagoda. Carter's people asked, and Ford's had no objection, that their delegation include Richard Moe to represent Walter Mondale.

Before the final arrangements for the first exploratory meeting had been made, CBS, on August 20, and NBC, on August 23, sent telegrams to the chairmen of the Senate and House Commerce Committees, the Communications Subcommittees, and ranking minority members, urging them immediately to initiate legislation which would suspend the equal-time provisions of Section 315. Both telegrams were pegged to the Carter/Ford debate statements and indicated that a waiver would give the networks the freedom to cover the election as they did in 1960.

Upon hearing about the telegrams, Karayn and Lampl met with Senator Pastore on Tuesday, August 24. Orally and via a written chronology, they traced the League's involvement in bringing to the surface the debate issue and their contacts with the candidates, including the arrangements for the first negotiating session in forty-eight hours. They also indicated that prior to President Ford's surprise announcement, the networks had indicated a willingness to cover the debates, if and when the League was successful.

They pointed out that on May 25, when debates were mainly a glimmer in the League's eye, ABC President Elton Rule, in a speech to ABC affiliates, stated: "Though we in television may not arrange debates on our own, we may . . . cover them as legitimate news events if they occur under the sponsorship of some other organizations. The League of Women Voters has offered to sponsor such debates. . . . ABC would be proud to present debates similar to those in 1960. We would be proud to cover the discussions envisioned by the League." On June 21, Herbert Schlosser, president of NBC, told his network affiliates that NBC would broadcast debates, if they were arranged by groups like the League of Women Voters.

Senator Pastore asked the two League representatives to appear before a Commerce Committee hearing that morning to repeat their story for the record and for the other members of the committee. During the hearing he stated: "At this juncture I don't believe it would be fair to take the ball out of the hands of the League of Women Voters, since they have already taken the initiative and made substantial efforts. . . . I am all for the suspension, but I wouldn't want the Congress to be in the awkward position of confusing the issues, muddying the waters, and possibly delaying or jeopardizing the debates from ever taking place."

ABC and PBS did not join the waiver efforts, which continued in the House and Senate until the final announcement of agreement by the candidates and the League.

Immediately after the Republican Convention, Karayn went to Aspen, Colorado, to meet with Douglass Cater to discuss, among other matters, refinements in the format proposal to be used during the negotiations. On August 17, a lengthy reaction paper was sent to all members of the steering committee and a meeting scheduled for August 26, just prior to the first meeting with the candidate representatives.

From the outset of the debate preparations, it seemed clear that the candidates and their advisors would, as they did in the 1960 network meetings, insist on a format and setting which matched their perceptions of what would be in their best interests. The history of the '60 debates had been pored over by Karayn, both in print and via interviews with many of the principals. As happened then, the idea of "pure" debate was rejected early in the game, on the grounds that it would result in too narrow a field for discussion. A number of alternatives had been proposed, and as August 26 rolled around, the consensus was for a sequence of journalist-posed questions, followed by a period in which the candidates would pose questions to each other. This concept seemed to have adherents on both political sides, as indicated in a memorandum Karayn prepared for the steering committee on August 24.

> Several recent statements by the candidates and their representatives have broadened our options to have a more flexible format for the debates. Both of the candidates appear to be willing to engage in real face-to-face encounters in which each questions the other directly. Jody Powell, on CBS News, Monday, August 23rd, said that Carter wanted less of a news conference format and more of a free exchange of views than between the candidates in 1960. Rogers Morton, on the same news show, said that he believes that the previous debates prevented real discussion between the candidates.

> This fits in with what I suggested at the first Steering Committee meeting: that we have a mix of questions and answer with a news panel, followed by the candidates questioning each other and closing statements.

I think we would find that just having the pure "Oregon debate" format would be disappointing and produce more heat than light. The proof of this is in the past. In the McCarthy-Goldwater debate set up by one of the networks, both men were overly polite and deferential. The Kennedy-Humphrey debate in the West Virginia primary in 1960 had the same result.

The candidates need the stimulation of incisive questions to get their juices flowing. A panel of questioners also will ensure that major issues are not overlooked. Candidates could go on for the whole hour without a focus on the issues and with too much attention to narrow emotional points. We should be more interested in substance than performance.

Format was the main topic of discussion at the August 26 steering committee meeting. Although the subject had been raised earlier, it had not been thoroughly explored by the full committee, and the suddenness of events had radically shortened the time available for discussion. There was a strong minority view that the League should retain as much flexibility as possible regarding format and should look for a somewhat experimental approach, in which each of the debates would have a somewhat different structure. Cater, in a memorandum, stressed the importance of leaning to an Oregon-style debate with as much extemporaneous give-and-take as possible. Theodore White outlined a sequence in which the first two debates would take place before a joint session of Congress with committee chairmen posing the questions for the candidates. For the third and fourth debates he suggested a university setting, followed by some historic site such as Cooper Union Hall. After about fifty minutes of discussion, the committee voted to go into the negotiations with the format pretty much as outlined in the Karayn memorandum.

Although the committee deliberations were limited, a considerable amount of work had already been expended on format considerations. Part of the debate strategy was to enter negotiations with a well-thought-out proposal, so as to have a firm jumping-off point for discussion. Given the available time and the pressure on all sides, to have presented an array of alternative formats for each debate might have irrevocably snarled the proceedings. In short, August 26 did not appear to be an auspicious time for experimentation.

The document that the League took to the negotiating session was a working paper—a starting point for discussions and one open to modifications from both sides. Essentially it called for three presidential debates and one vice-presidential debate, to be held during the weeks of September 27, October 11, October 25, and October 18, respectively.

LENGTH: 60 minutes.

FORMAT: Questions from a panel of journalists, no opening statements, four-minute closing statements. Questions would alternate from one candidate to another, with each able to respond to the other's answers. Follow-up questions would be permitted. For the last third of the debate candidates would question each other.

PANEL: Composed of a moderator plus three correspondents—one from print, one from broadcasting, and one from editorial, columnist, or magazine ranks.

THEMES: Domestic Policy. Foreign Policy. Role of Presidency. Role of Vice-
Presidency.

Debates would be held in different parts of the country and would have
an audience.

The Republican negotiators also had their "working paper"—a press conference by President Ford in Vail on August 24, in which he stated that he favored
four presidential debates of "at least 90 minutes," focusing first on national
security and then on domestic, foreign, and economic policy.

The meeting began at 2:40 on Thursday afternoon, August 26, and was
chaired by Charls Walker. Although there was no question about the seriousness with which both sides entered into the negotiations, there was, as would
be expected, considerable jockeying back and forth within the framework of
the proposals presented. The procedure in the first and second sessions was
basically to review the total package and then go over each component, bal-
ancing counterproposals until an agreement or compromise was worked out.

Although Senator Dole had followed his running mate's debate challenge
with one of his own, which Mondale promptly accepted, the first series of substantive exchanges occurred when it became apparent that the Republicans
were not prepared to state categorically that there would be a vice-presidential
debate. The question was left hanging until the second session, when both parties agreed that the vice-presidential arrangements would be worked out in a
separate series of meetings.

The League proposal for a live audience for the debates was troublesome
for both parties—each would have preferred the equivalent of a "studio" setting, in which the audience was cameramen, technicians, etc. Failing that, an
in-house audience composed solely of press would have been more acceptable.
As one participant put it, "An audience is superfluous to the event." The main
concern was audience reaction—both visual and vocal—which could affect
television viewers and which could also detract from the substance of the debates. Additionally, an audience lit for cameras might be distracting for the
candidates and cause them to "play to" the audience rather than each other.
The League pointed out that to eliminate an audience would be contrary to
League procedure for candidates' meetings and could also jeopardize the debates' standing as bona fide events. The question came up repeatedly in the two
sessions, and it was eventually determined that there would be an audience
composed equally of press and League members and their guests. It was also
agreed that the audience was not to appear on camera during the debates.

With only two hours alloted to the first negotiating session, none of the
parties expected final agreements to be worked out. Although the bulk of the
session was spent in circling around debate questions on the table—Ford's
ninety minutes and four debates versus Carter's preference for three hour-long
debates, as well as the subject matter for each debate—the meeting adjourned
with agreement on: the mix of questioners; the use of professional moderators;
no opening statements; up to three-minute closing statements; candidates to use
no notes; question sequences to include follow-up from journalists and response
by second candidate; September 23 as the date for the first debate.

A second meeting was set for 10:00 A.M., September 1, with arrangements for a two-hour lunch break, so that each party could consult its principals and/or review decisions still pending.

Within the opening half-hour the number of presidential debates had been set at three—an item that had involved considerable jockeying in the first session. Since four debates had been a Ford proposal, Carter's negotiators were more willing to trade in their sixty-minute length for the minimum of ninety minutes originally suggested in Ford's Vail statement.

The question of "themes" for each of the debates was not resolved until midway through the afternoon session. It was obvious that each side was focusing on the first debate as the one which would probably have the largest audience and the greatest impact on viewers. Throughout most of the discussion, Powell took the position that his side really didn't see any overwhelming need to limit the subject matter for any of the debates; the governor would be just as comfortable in a format with wide and free-ranging questions.

The Republican counter was generally that a completely unstructured line of questioning would blunt the educational value of the debates and result in a potpourri of impressions and responses. Naturally, Ruckelshaus and Burch kept returning to a first debate on foreign policy and, just as naturally, Powell rejected the suggestion. The trade-off on length, i.e. ninety minutes vs. sixty minutes, entered into the balance finally struck, when both sides agreed to the League proposal for the first encounter to deal with domestic issues. Once that agreement was reached, it was quickly determined that debate number two would deal with foreign policy, and that the final meeting would have no topical boundaries.

The structure versus no-structure split was apparent, also, whenever the subject of having the candidates question each other came up. Prior to the negotiations, both Powell and Carter had indicated they favored direct questioning. At the August 26 meeting, Powell reiterated his support but also allowed that the matter wasn't particularly high on his list of negotiating points. If it wasn't high for him, it was certainly low on the Republican side, and whenever the subject arose, one of the three would brush it aside and turn the group's attention to another matter under consideration. The result was the shelving of the issue in the first session.

The League believed that direct questioning would make for a more informative and interesting debate. Between the two negotiating meetings, Karayn brought up direct questioning with Burch, who had labeled the idea "a dud," since neither candidate would want to look as if he were "beating hell" out of the other. He also tried to revive the idea with Jagoda but his efforts to sell it were unsuccessful, and when the issue was raised again in the second session, mutual "cross-examination" was rejected once more.

The "mix" of journalists for each panel was determined early in the first session, as was the fact that the League would encourage the questioners to get together prior to each debate to construct a strong and nonrepetitive line of inquiry. There was, however, considerable discussion as to how the journalists would be selected. Obviously, the networks would not be picking their correspondents, and the candidates and the League rejected the 1960 mechanism of drawing names from among the pool reporters assigned to each candidate.

While neither side suggested that it wanted a hand in the final selection, each expressed concern about the caliber and fairness of the individuals chosen as well as a firm conviction that the moderator should remain a neutral figure throughout and should be a professional rather than a League person.

The issue was resolved when Hauser, who chaired the second session, suggested that the candidates present, for each debate, a list of fifteen journalists in each of the three media categories. It was also understood that the League would compile a master list of individuals knowledgeable in the area under discussion, and that the three rosters would be amalgamated and pared down by the League staff and chairs. The League also volunteered to inform the candidates about the final selection just prior to making the announcement public.

Other than arriving at a date for the first debate, there were no final decisions made on dates for the second, third, or vice-presidential debates other than to determine a general time frame—i.e., the weeks of October 4, 18, and 11. Both sides wanted to have the debates over by the week before the election, leaving a clear field for their own media plans and public appearances.

Pinning down the final days was less a matter of adjusting to the candidates' schedules than of shoe-horning into America's sports schedule—Monday night football, the World Series and play-offs.

Although the League had suggested and put a hold on the ballroom of the Chase Park Plaza Hotel in St. Louis for a September 28 debate, it did so more to have a talking point than out of any firm conviction that it should be the first debate site. As a result and as the date changed, the Chase was moved aside in favor of other suggestions. The first round of specific suggestions came from Ruckelshaus, who put forth the idea of using three of the presidential libraries—those of Truman, Eisenhower, and Johnson, each of which had small theaters. While Powell made no overt objection, he showed little enthusiasm for the idea and, in fact, the word "presidential" set off an extended discussion on the mode of address for each candidate. In an effort to offset the advantages of incumbency, the Carter people proposed that no title be used in introducing either man, e.g., either Mr. Ford and Mr. Carter or the candidate of the Republican and the candidate of the Democratic party.

Without much difficulty the group managed to narrow the site choices by quickly eliminating Plains, Grand Rapids, Atlanta, and Washington, D.C., leaving the rest of the country as possible hosts to the debates. Apparently, neither side had particularly strong convictions as to location, although the discussions led to a preference for a theater or theater-style facility. Among the suggestions were the Beaumont Theater in New York; Knox College, Galesburg, Illinois, the site of one of the Lincoln-Douglas debates; and the Walnut Street Theater in Philadelphia. Further exploration was left to the League staff, with the understanding that no final choices were to be made without on-site visits by the television consultants for each candidate—Bill Carruthers for President Ford and Jagoda for Governor Carter.

Although a great many details were left unresolved, there was enough understanding between the two sets of representatives to decide that, barring an emergency, no further full-fledged negotiating sessions were necessary. Both sides and the League reserved the option of coming back after each debate to propose changes in format, length, or whatever.

The last half hour was spent drawing up a statement for the press, in which both candidates accepted the League debate invitation, "subject to final agreement on all technical matters." The agreements reached in the seven hours of negotiation were generally operative throughout the entire course of the debates, and although two of them, panel selection and audience control, were the subject of considerable controversy, they provided a sound basis for subsequent dealings with the candidates and their representatives.

Except for a thirty-second shortening of the response to the panelist's questions in the last debate, no changes were made in the format. Karayn continued to push for direct exchanges between the candidates but to no avail. Without some firm understanding beforehand, it was impossible to make any major format changes after the first debate. The media "winner-loser" syndrome was fully operative, and any substantial modification would undoubtedly have been interpreted as a sign that one or the other candidate was unhappy enough about his prior performance to push for a change.

The "technical" details left for further discussion were considerable. In addition to dates and locations, they included agreement on the set, positioning of the candidates, negotiations with the networks, composition of the audience, arrangements for the vice-presidential debate, and a host of other items. As of September 1, the League had the debates, but following the FCC ruling barring union and corporate contributions it had no cash-on-hand with which to mount them. A decision was made to withdraw whatever monies were necessary from the Education Fund reserves and to launch, via direct mail and newspaper advertisements, a campaign for individual contributions. One fund-raising suggestion, which the League rejected, was to have on-air appeals made at the close of each televised debate. Initial estimates were that the four debates would cost between $250,000 and $280,000. The final tally was $322,000, and the LWVEF raised more than a quarter of a million dollars in contributions. Although there were a few large donors, i.e., $5,000 to $10,000, most of the contributions were in the $15 to $25 range.

The League had rented a four-room suite on 15th Street for the Presidential Forums, which had become the debate headquarters. At its peak, the debate staff consisted of fourteen people, supplemented by consultants and regular members of the League staff. The workload was divided into three general areas: production; press; and office back-up and research. Broad policy decisions were made by the three co-chairs, League president, and board, with Karayn and Lampl responsible for the day-to-day operating decisions.

On the production side, Karayn hired Jack Sameth, a WNET producer who had worked on the Nixon-Kennedy debate, to act as coordinator. Sameth and his assistant, Read Jackson, took over the task of getting an acceptable set in hand by September 23 and making the necessary arrangements within the theater. Because of a prior commitment, Sameth and Jackson were available only through the Philadelphia debate and were replaced in debates two and three by Mike Pengra and Audrey Rasmussen. Marilee Mossman was also involved in the production side of the debate arrangements. Bob Wightman was engaged to design the set and Fiorentino Associates the lighting plan.

Press responsibilities were split into two units. The job of distributing credentials and equipping and servicing press facilities at the debate sites was contracted out to the Washington, D.C., firm of Wagner and Baroody, while the flood of press inquiries was juggled by Ellen Herman at the debate office and Betsy Dribben at the League.

The office staff consisted of two administrative assistants, Gloria Coe and Carolyn Amundsen; a business manager, Gladys Scheer; a research coordinator, Pat Fox, who also handled arrangements for the panelists; and Susan Cantril, who worked with the Secret Service on security and credentials arrangements. Temporary typists and receptionists were hired as needed.

In addition to fund-raising, various members of the League staff were utilized in the debate effort. A full-time secretary, Jean Golub, was reassigned to the debate staff, and other secretarial help was used as needed. Nancy Thompson, from the public relations department, coordinated the activities of the large corps of League volunteers at each site who acted as ushers, and helped staff the press room and other debate offices.

The candidates' sensitivity about the composition of the live audience remained an active concern, at least until after the first debate passed without incident. The "public" tickets averaged about half of the seats available in each of the theaters. Half of these, some 90 to 100, were distributed by the Education Fund. The chairs had five tickets for each debate, and the members of the steering committee had two. The balance was parceled out to League special guests and staff members. The remaining "public" tickets were distributed by the local League, who made an allocation among its members and invited guests from the community at large. In addition, each of the candidates had twelve to fifteen seats at each debate.

The tickets were numbered sequentially, and the Secret Service insisted on having a complete list of invitees prior to each debate, as well as setting up security checks in each of the theater lobbies, where purses, parcels, briefcases, etc., were searched.

The announcement of the time and location for each debate brought in a flood of ticket requests from the general public as well as from individuals who had real or tenuous connections with the League or the principals involved. Because of the limited seating arrangements, none could be honored. The League was not the only recipient of the ticket heat—candidates and party chairmen were also subject to the same pressures. As a result, the League and the candidates agreed on another audience limitation—no elected officials. This spared all sides from having to pick-and-choose from the hundreds of party luminaries available in each area, and it also shielded the candidates from the potential embarrassment of having an unsympathetic public official singled out for pre- and/or post-debate lobby interviews.

The second round of candidate negotiations took place on-site—September 13 and 14, following the selection of the Walnut Street Theater and the drawing up of the design for the stage set to be used for the four debates. The Carter team consisted of Barry Jagoda, Gerry Rafshoon, and Bob Squire; Ford's was Bill Carruthers, Marke Goode, and Delon Smith; the League's was Karayn, Lampl, and Sameth. In order to assure uniformity in appearance of both candidates, the group developed the "belt-buckle" principle. Since Ford was 3½ inches taller than Carter, this meant that his lectern was built to intersect his torso some 2½ inches above his belt buckle and Carter's 1½ inches below the buckle point. The procedure was simplified by the fact that neither candidate opted for suspenders. There was relatively little disagreement on most of the issues on the agenda—basic lighting; type of microphones for the candidates; seating of the audience in the theater balcony; which candidate would be on which side of the stage; seating of the moderator and the questioners; placement of automatic timers, etc.

However, one session stretched out until 2:30 in the morning, as the two sides hammered out an agreement on the attitude of the candidates during the debate. While the Ford people had no basic objection to a chair being placed at each of the lecterns, they stated that it would not be used by Ford, who intended to stand for the full ninety minutes. Jagoda's position was that Carter intended to use the chair when he was not answering questions, and that one sitting and one standing candidate would be antithetical to the concept of uniformity that the two sides had agreed upon. The Ford side's riposte was that it didn't care what Carter planned to do, the president was going to stand. This "up" versus "down" discussion probably consumed more time than any other single point in the substantive or technical negotiations and necessitated a series of telephone calls to each of the principals. The final agreement boiled down to each candidate standing or sitting, as he chose.

During the same two-day period, the League also held a series of meetings with representatives of the three networks and PBS. A preliminary session had been held in New York on September 8, but this was the first time the networks had seen the completed set design and had the opportunity to discuss on-site production details. It is something of an understatement to say that the networks were chafing at their role as a "coverer" of the League's event, and the fact that the set virtually dictated where cameras would be placed did little to lessen their discomfort. As one television producer put it, "They built a television studio on stage." Although the networks had discussed pool coverage at the New York meeting and determined rotation, the issue was raised again in Philadelphia with formal requests from CBS and ABC for unilateral cameras in the theater.

The hottest issue, however, was the ban on cut-aways—the prohibition against shooting the audience while the debate was underway. All of the TV representatives felt that the agreement between the League and the candidates was an unacceptable infringement on their journalistic integrity and was, in fact, a form of censorship. The League, as indicated earlier, had agreed to the audience black-out as part of the negotiated package—the price paid for its insistence that the debates be conducted in front of a live audience.

At the Philadelphia meeting, Karayn and Lampl agreed to raise the matter again with the candidates' representatives, and a meeting was held on Wednesday evening, September 15. The networks' position was presented as well as their not so veiled threat of refusing to cover the debates if the ban remained in effect. The candidates, who were equally adamant, refused to budge and reminded the League that all decisions reached during the negotiating sessions were "joint" decisions.

At the request of the networks, the League convened another meeting on Saturday, September 18, to rehash the cut-away issue along with questions that had arisen, primarily from CBS's Dick Salant, about the selection of the panel

THE GREAT DEBATES

of journalists. Once again, the networks raised their strong objections to being denied the capability of showing the audience. The League's position as expressed by Minow was that as long as the candidates held firm, the League was obliged to hold firm and that it was up to the networks to decide whether or not the restrictions were so onerous that they could not cover the event.

The meeting started with ten network people—and ended with eight. About a third of the way through, the CBS delegation, Salant and Bob Chandler, left, following an exchange between Walker and Salant when Walker, after being interrupted for the third time, asked Salant to "Please, shut up." Salant refused to accept his apology and walked out, taking Chandler with him.

Before he left, Salant raised a number of questions about the panel selection, implying, if not directly charging, that the candidates had a say in who went on the panel and, in effect, had veto power. CBS, he said, could not cover an event where the normal journalistic standards were not being met. He questioned Clusen sharply on a statement she had made that the League had been in touch with the candidates within the last two days regarding the panel for the first debate.

There was an understanding between the League and the candidates that prior to the public announcement of the questioners they would be informed of the final selection, and this procedure was followed for each of the three debates. At no time did the candidates reject the League choices. The first panel had not been completed at the time of the September 18 meeting. Final selections had been made, but one newspaper journalist declined because of lack of television experience and a CBS correspondent refused to appear, presumably after checking with higher-ups in the network. Two other persons from CBS were asked to appear on the second and third presidential debates, and each turned down the offer.

For the first debate, the candidates hand-delivered to the League office their lists of fifteen individuals in each of three specified categories. The only persons from the League or debate staff who had access to the lists were Karayn, Lampl, and Clusen. A League list had also been prepared on the basis of personal knowledge of journalists who were experts in the topics slated for discussion, i.e., domestic and economic issues, and from the flood of letters and phone calls from news organizations recommending one of their staff people and from individuals recommending themselves or others.

The initial culling and weeding process was handled by Karayn and Lampl; the final selection was made in a discussion, usually a conference call, with the co-chairs and the three League principals. By the time of the final call, the list had been whittled down to eight or ten people. The group would then reach consensus on their first choices for questioners and moderator and, in case of turn-downs, indicate possible substitutes.

This was the procedure followed for all three debates. However, the candidates made fewer suggestions for debates two and three, and the proportion of League-generated names grew progressively larger. The idea of having lists had originated with the League, not the candidates, and, for each debate, there was duplication of names among the three lists. Since the journalists were selected from three separate media categories, picked according to their knowledge of the subject or subjects under discussion, and because the national press corps is a relatively small group, the overlaps were not surprising. Obviously, the narrowest choices were among television correspondents—choices reduced even further by the CBS boycott. As the debates progressed, the field also shrank, in line with the League policy of not picking two individuals from the same news organization. Thus, for example, once Jim Gannon of the *Wall Street Journal* had appeared on the first debate, other correspondents from the *Journal* were eliminated from consideration.

In retrospect, preparation of the candidate lists was probably an unnecessary exercise; however, they did provide a mechanism for determining a portion of the pool from which the questioners would be selected. To the League, at least, it seemed to be a more responsible method than the one used for the 1960 debates—letting the networks select their correspondents and picking the print journalists by lottery.

While the meeting dispelled some of the networks' doubts about the selection process, it did little to assuage their concerns about the audience black-out. If the candidates had agreed, the prohibition would have been lifted; as it was, the networks were left to decide whether the restriction warranted their electing not to cover the event. While the dispute was in the public eye, the League office received well over a hundred phone calls, letters, and telegrams from individuals expressing advice or opinions. Surprisingly, without exception, they favored the League/candidate position.

After the questions about the selection process and the audience had been aired, if not resolved, the final third of the meeting revolved about some still pending production questions. From the outset, the FCC definition of the media's role as "coverers" created a host of artificial and real barriers between the League and the networks. At times, particularly in the early stages of the debates, these were exacerbated by the network's frustration at being handed a series of faits accomplis. Attorneys on all sides kept busy, handing down interpretations of what might constitute "collaboration" between the event sponsor —the League—and the broadcast media.

For example, up until the 18th the networks had indicated that the pool probably should not provide audio-visual checks for the candidates on the day of the debate. The question was reintroduced in a discussion of the extent of technical cooperation permissible under the 315 modification. Although the go-ahead was not given at the meeting, the League was asked to make a request for audio-visual checks to the pool on the following Monday—it was granted.

Another reintroduced question concerned the arrangements for the house audio system in the Walnut Street Theater. Earlier, ABC, on the advice of counsel, had insisted that the League provide and operate the sound system for the theater as part of the separation of responsibilities. For technical reasons, the sound was brought up again on the 18th and the ground laid for the eventual agreement that ABC would operate the house system and bill the League for the debate-related costs. As it turned out, ABC wired all sound through their distribution amplifier in the theater. When the audio failed in Philadelphia, the League tried unsuccessfully to "recapture" the house system, so that the debate could continue in the theater. ABC was never able to find the failure within its own system. When, after twenty-seven minutes, the signal

THE GREAT DEBATES

was received that the audio was restored, no one on the League staff knew that it was back only for the television audience. The house system and the audio feeds to radio and the press room were still not operative. With the lesson of Philadelphia, the League maintained a back-up house system for each of the subsequent debates—an arrangement that didn't prevent another in-theater problem during the Williamsburg debate when, a few minutes before air time, NBC asked the audio person feeding both systems to make an adjustment in the sound levels, which cut amplification for a portion of the theater audience.

The September 18 meeting marked the last "confrontation" between the League and the networks—their grievances had been aired, as had the ground rules under which the League was operating. Thereafter, on-site arrangements were worked out by the League's production coordinator, Jack Sameth and subsequently Mike Pengra, with comparative ease and equanimity.

The first panel was announced on Monday, September 20, and at a pre-debate meeting it was suggested that the journalists might want to get together prior to the event to work out a comprehensive line of questions. The League wanted no part of the session but believed that prior consultation among the panelists would avoid repetition and help pinpoint the broad areas that should be covered under the topic assigned to the debate. Although the first set of questioners decided among themselves not to meet, each of the subsequent panels elected to hold predebate discussions on the questions to be pursued and who should do the pursuing.

As the final touches were being put on debate number one, the search was going on for a site for debate number two, which was to take place in less than two weeks, on October 6. Karayn's idea was, whenever possible, to hold the debates in a setting with some historical significance. For the second debate, on foreign policy, preliminary surveys singled out the War Memorial Theater in San Francisco, the location of many of the working meetings leading to the formation of the United Nations. The date and place had been cleared with the candidates, and both had built it into their campaign schedules. A post-Philadelphia visit by the League production staff and candidate and network representatives indicated that the War Memorial had a number of deficiencies—primarily, lack of an air-conditioning system and inadequate lighting facilities. The area was frantically combed for a suitable substitute in a search which revealed that, because of the usually mild climate, only a few of San Francisco's larger theaters had air-conditioning—essential for the debates because of the heat generated on and off stage by the camera lights. The final choice was the Palace of Fine Arts, also not air-conditioned, but where a large temporary unit could be installed and vented out over the stage area. As it turned out, San Francisco had an abnormal heat wave the week of the 6th, with daytime temperatures in the eighties, and while the candidates remained cool, the house audience sweltered.

For each of the debates, the project staff was deployed in shifts. The production crew—Pengra, Mossman and Rasmussen—would arrive at the site some five or six days prior to the debate to attend to all in-theater arrangements. They were followed closely by Susan Cantril, who worked with the Secret Service on the details of theater security and distributing credentials to all the individuals who had access to the site. Distribution of press credentials would begin some three days prior to the event, as would the work of coordinating the League volunteers who served as ushers and provided additional help in the debate offices and press rooms. With nine days separating the San Francisco and Houston debates, and a week between Houston and the third presidential debate, the logistics were sometimes overwhelming.

Time and the lack of assured funding were the dual clouds under which the debates were put together. In the three weeks between the conclusion of negotiations and the first debate, a staff had to be assembled, consultants hired, a set built, and logistics worked out for moving it from site to site, procedures instituted for audience selection, press credentials, and security. As indicated, working out a modus operandi with the networks consumed considerable time and energy. Through it all, the press maintained its voracious appetite for both substance and trivia—dates, sites, the names of the journalists, were all announced piecemeal, not to stretch out the story but because final decisions had not been made. For example, the negotiations for the vice-presidential debate started the week before the San Francisco debate, and final arrangements concerning length, format, and location were not worked out until after the second debate—six days before the vice-presidential contenders were scheduled to meet. It was a comparative luxury when the decision to hold the final debate in Williamsburg was made some three weeks before the actual date.

While the debates were being put together, the League development office began to raise the money to pay for them, and the League attorneys began the task of drawing up rebuttals to the petitions and suits filed by the excluded candidates.

As September 23 rolled around, all of the involved staff were juggling the logistics of the debate to follow, as well as dealing with the one at hand. The pre-planning done before the Philadelphia debate worked with surprisingly few hitches and, in the month that followed, refinements were made in virtually all the procedures. Efficiency increased with each debate as did the ability to spot potential trouble spots, and by Williamsburg what had been a unique project, with its own particular demands and problems, had become a relatively well-oiled operation.

The decision to hold the debates in four theaters spread around the country and with audiences present compounded the discomforts of the time and money squeeze. Everyone connected with the project recognized that it would have been infinitely simpler and less costly to have the debates originate from one location. The issue was raised on many occasions—by Karayn, by the co-chairs, and by others. The main reason for the geographic spreading of the debates was the League's prior history and experience in holding candidate meetings—for the debates to be bona fide events, it would mean doing what came naturally, holding them before an audience and in different parts of the country. Opinions from counsel differed as to whether a single location would have raised additional legal complications in terms of the FCC modification. Similar unanswered questions were raised as to whether the exclusion of an audience would jeopardize the status of the debates.

However, with or without the League's prior history, the debates were conceived, designed, and produced to be broadcast on national television. The League did not doubt, even during the heat of the pre-Philadelphia disagreements, that the networks could or would cover them. The League was also certain that, regardless of the complications, it wanted the debates to have some of the trimmings and flavor of actual candidate appearances.

Whether they were held in one location, in four locations, or in a television studio, it is doubtful that the format of the debates would have been too different from what was aired during September and October. The negotiators had made a conscious and firm decision that the candidates were going to appear in a familiar framework, responding to journalists' questions, not one in which the candidates would question each other. With more time prior to the first debate, that decision might have been open to modification, although Karayn's experience in pressing for candidate questioning suggests otherwise.

The League, too, had a conscious strategy, developed during the two months of predebate planning. It was to go into any negotiating session with a fully developed plan—as indicated, one that was open to modification but which provided a hard base on which to open discussions. It was a proposal which both sides had had ample time to consider during the July through August contacts—suddenly and radically to change the ground rules when the hope became a reality would have been confusing and, perhaps, self-defeating.

Charles Benton's telephone call to the Education Fund in September 1975 came hard on the heels of a trustees' meeting where there had been considerable discussion of the potential role and activities of the League during the presidential election year. Adopting a slogan of "Issues Not Images," the board had pressed for a combination of activities aimed at increasing voter knowledge about election issues. The Forums and the debates were a more than welcome addition to the League's agenda.

Without the debates as a vehicle and with Section 315 in place, the electorate would have had relatively little exposure to the candidates' stand on issues, and that exposure would have been through the candidate-controlled political advertising and the materials presented on nightly newscasts. The debates did present the electorate with more than four hours of unfiltered side-by-side responses to a broad range of questions.

An estimated 100 million Americans watched some or all of the debates and had the opportunity to make their own judgments about the candidates and their qualifications. There were no fireworks and few surprises in what they saw and heard, but that in itself is not surprising. Presidential campaigns are run by professionals whose job is to both protect and enhance their candidates. With "the whole world watching" it is something of a pipe-dream to expect off-the-cuff answers by individuals thoroughly exposed to the rigors of campaigning and the spotlight of public life.

If they accomplished nothing else, the 1976 debates will have done a service for future presidential debates by sweeping away some of the mythology that grew up around the 1960 encounters. The intervening years and the refusal of three prior sets of nominees to engage in debate dimmed memories and increased press and public expectations to unrealistic levels.

It is hoped that the 1976 debates broke a sixteen-year-old pattern and paved the way for candidate exchanges as an essential ingredient of future presidential elections. However, until and unless Section 315 is repealed or modified, television's role in providing comprehensive and creative coverage will be severely curtailed. The League, or another organization, can present debates, with varying formats, but the current communications law precludes a host of other approaches that would expand the electronic media's ability to inform the electorate about the positions and personalities of the men and women competing for public office.

It is not for the League to judge the effect of the debates on the 1976 elections or to tote up their weaknesses and strengths. From the moment the debates became a reality, the League knew that it would be open to criticism —some justified and some not. What was done was not perfect—nor could it have been. But what was done was according to the best judgment of those involved and according to the very real dictates of time and resources.

7.

Candidate Briefings

STUART EIZENSTAT for CARTER
and
MICHAEL RAOUL-DUVAL for FORD

EDITOR'S NOTE: Briefing of candidates in preparation for televised debates would seem to be a crucial consideration in overall campaign tactics. One would suppose that such briefings would have a high priority in debate preparations and that they would be linked to the political jockeying in negotiations between the two candidates' staffs. However, this kind of information is quite difficult to come by. We were unable to obtain briefing data for the Kennedy-Nixon 1960 debates. The oppportunity for investigating briefing activities for the 1976 debates came about when Michael Raoul-Duval, then special counsel to President Ford, wrote me to say that the 1962 book had been of great help to Ford's staff in negotiating the current debates and in preparing briefing materials. Subsequently, I was able to contact Stuart Eizenstat, who had briefed Governor Carter, and to interview Raoul-Duval. Each later responded to ten questions relating to briefing activities, Raoul-Duval by mail and Eizenstat in a taped interview. Their answers, given below, provide some insights into the briefing of presidential candidates for televised debates.

Stuart Eizenstat for Carter

1. *Which members of the campaign staff were actively involved in briefing the candidate for the 1976 presidential debates and what were their roles?*

The way we prepared our debate material is that the issue staff, of which I was the head, was responsible for preparing the briefing material, that was prepared in an average of perhaps two or three thick books for each debate. The president was then sent those, perhaps ten days before each debate. He would review them and make rather copious notes and comments, sometimes asking for additional material or clarifications. And then after that, and depending on what the topic was for the debate (I was always present), I would go down with a person on my staff, or persons on my staff. In addition, Jody Powell, Hamilton Jordan, and Charlie Kirbo were present at all of them. For the first debate, the people I just mentioned were there and I think that Jerry Jasinowski was also present, who is on my staff, and then we had a separate little meeting with Charlie Schultze, Larry Klein, and Joe Peckman, as I remember it, in

Plains, before the first debate. For the second debate in San Francisco, the same people were there, I think Jerry Rafshoon was also in the room and I think Pat Caddell was in the room in the hotel in San Francisco where we did the debriefing, Mr. Kirbo, Hamilton, Jody; in addition we brought in Congressman Les Aspen and Dr. Zbigniew Brzezinski, Les for the defense side, Zbig for the foreign policy side, because, as you remember, the second debate was on foreign policy. And then for the third debate, I think essentially was just staff without outsiders because it covered everything.

2. *What was the method (or methods) used for candidate briefing? Were any aids employed? Please describe a typical briefing session. Approximately, what percentage of the candidate's time, before the first debate and between the others, was devoted to debate briefing and preparations?*

In terms of oral briefing, and meeting before the first debate, we did have a meeting, but very little actual briefing in the way of practice if you notice, in fact none of that for the first debate. For the second debate we did throw a few questions out, to sort of get him warmed up, and I believe we did that for the third debate as well. In the second and third debate those sorts of model question and answer sessions would be done the morning of the debate. Then we'd let him rest in the afternoon and evening so that his mind wasn't cluttered. He, as he currently does as President, likes to work as much as possible by written memorandum, so he relied heavily on the written material that we had given him in those briefing books rather than relying mostly on oral or verbal give and take.

3. *What overall strategy guided the briefing sessions?*

Well, our intent in all the sessions was to make it clear that this was a person who first had a grasp on all the major issues. That was very important because as a challenger, as someone who had never held a federal office, it was important to convince people that he had a grasp of the issues. So it was important that he know a good deal of facts, a lot about programs, and the like. The second was a strategy of really trying to let him be himself, not programming an answer, letting him talk as naturally as possible. And third, and particularly in the second and third debates, to make sure he put then President Ford on the defensive by being assertive and direct. I think, at the beginning of the first debate, because he was facing the president, then Governor Carter was a little more tentative than he was after he got started. In fact, I think he, himself, said so and we felt that after the first half of the first debate that he clearly took the offensive and, if you will, won that part of the debate. Impressions are often made, however, on the first few minutes. That was one of the reasons we were concerned about the sound loss because we thought, clearly, the momentum had shifted after he got started and felt comfortable debating an incumbent president.

4. *How were the specific issues on which the candidate was briefed arrived at? How was it determined that certain questions on given issues might be asked during a debate?*

106   **THE GREAT DEBATES**

We, in our briefing material that we had sent him, sent him not only background material, but model questions and answers that we expected would be covered. In the two warm-up sessions before the second and third debate we threw a few of those out just to give him a flavor of how the questions might come out. But we tried to phrase the questions in that part of the briefing book in the way that we thought they would be asked, and on the topics which we thought would be covered. I think we had almost 100 percent success guessing which questions would be asked. We gave him a whole array of questions for each debate; it was fairly predictable as to which questions would be asked. Then we tried in the briefing material to give him a model answer in a well-organized fashion.

5. *What candidate strengths, advantages, or assets and what weaknesses, disadvantages, or liabilities guided the preparations for the debates?*

The only disadvantages that we thought we had was the fact that we were debating an incumbent president. Sometimes people have a sense that the president and the presidency are interchangeable and they almost resent somebody really debating hard with the president because they hold the presidency in such an aura that sometimes to be too pointed to the president is viewed as rude or whatever. That was a concern we had which I think was alleviated fairly quickly, but it was a concern we had. That's the only disadvantage that we saw other than the fact that, of course, President Ford had half the federal government working for him preparing him and he had been in public light in the federal arena for twenty-five years. The advantages we had were that we had a clearly more intelligent, articulate, photogenic, personable candidate, who was just a better candidate. We had the better person, a more outstanding person, a person who would make a more lasting impression. It was just a point of getting across the fact that Carter also had the depth and knowledge for the presidency.

6. *What was the perception of the opponent's ability and experience? Was this a factor in the briefing sessions?*

No, not a factor in the briefing sessions really so much as simply a recognition that President Ford's qualities, his main positive qualities, were that he was an honest person, would come across as an honest and forthright person, and that he would be well programmed when it comes to facts and figures. But again, the ultimate advantage that we thought we had was that we had the quicker man, the deeper man, a person who was more articulate, could use words right, and would come across as more youthful, forceful, and dynamic.

7. *Once the names of the panelists were known, was the candidate briefed as to the kinds of questions and the way questions might be asked?*

The way you phrase the question had no relationship to who the panelists were. We had given him, before we even knew that, the model questions and answers in the briefing material, and then ran through a few of the most likely questions before the second and third debates. But we didn't say, you know, ". . . so and so is likely to ask this question" because we had no way of really knowing.

8. *Was there any plan to handle truculent questioning?*

No, not any particular plan, we knew that the president (then Governor Carter) was very quick on his feet, and that he wouldn't have any trouble with a truculent question, and we didn't expect any from the panelists.

9. *Were there any discussions about the use or avoidance of certain words or names? And if so, were particular euphemisms considered?*

No. There was a question of how President Ford should be addressed, whether it was President Ford or Mr. Ford. I think, initially, it was determined to call him Mr. Ford. Then, I think, after the first debate, we decided to call him President Ford which was his title.

10. *Were there any discussions about candidate responsiveness to questions?*

Well, only that it was important to be responsive to the questions and make it clear that he was answering the question correctly.

Michael Raoul-Duval for Ford

1. *Which members of the campaign staff were actively involved in briefing the candidate for the 1976 presidential debates and what were their roles?*

The "campaign staff" had very little involvement in briefing President Ford in preparation for the 1976 debates. The president relied primarily on his substantive knowledge of the issues which, of course, was the result of a quarter century of experience in Congress, and over two years as president.

His normal economic, domestic and foreign policy briefing books were updated for the debates. Because this inevitably involved government policy, this task was coordinated by me at the White House.

Public opinion and campaign information was integrated into the president's briefing materials from three general sources. Doug Bailey and Bob Teeter developed "theme" material which provided guidance to the president on the potential campaign impact of various issues.

Our campaign committee provided in-depth research material on the positions and statements of Governor Carter. These were edited and organized by Dave Gergen.

Finally, the President was briefed on the television and staging aspects of the debates by Bill Carruthers.

2. *What was the method (or methods) used for candidate briefing? Were any aids employed? Please describe a typical briefing session. Approximately, what percentage of the candidate's time, before the first debate and between the others, was devoted to debate briefing and preparations?*

The president spent a relatively small amount of time preparing for the debates. The majority of the time that was spent in preparation went to reading the issue briefing books and the compilation of Governor Carter's positions and statements.

Of course some outside material was used. For example, the excellent studies on key national issues prepared by Dan Yankelovich's group were very helpful. [Editor's note: See chapter 4, p. 54.]

Some time was allocated—primarily before the first debate—to familiarizing the president with the physical set-up. A video TV camera was used for this purpose.

3. *What overall strategy guided the briefing sessions?*

Our guiding principle was not to tamper with the president's own style. We wanted the television viewer to see him the same way we saw him day-after-day in the Oval Office, and otherwise at work as president. We avoided trying to "create" a new TV image and instead tried to bring out his strength—which was an extraordinary understanding of the problems facing the nation and which solutions would work.

4. *How were the specific issues on which the candidate was briefed arrived at? How was it determined that certain questions on given issues might be asked during a debate?*

To the limited extent we attempted to anticipate specific questions which might be raised by the debate panel, we utilized the same procedures used to prepare for press conferences. In general, key newspaper, magazine, and TV reports were analyzed to determine recurring areas of attention.

5. *What candidate strengths, advantages, or assets and what weaknesses, disadvantages, or liabilities guided the preparations for the debates?*

President Ford's strength was his substantive grasp of the issues. His potential weakness was his lack of experience with television.

6. *What was the perception of the opponent's ability and experience? Was this a factor in the briefing sessions?*

We considered Governor Carter to be very effective in the television debate format, and this obviously affected our preparation. We did not, however, focus the briefings on our opponent except to analyze his statements on the issues.

7. *Once the names of the panelists were known, was the candidate briefed as to the kinds of questions and the way questions might be asked?*

In general we tried to anticipate the types of questions likely to be asked, but we did not go into any detail on the style or mannerism of the panel members.

8. *Was there any plan to handle truculent questioning?*
No.

9. *Were there any discussions about the use or avoidance of certain words or names? And if so, were particular euphemisms considered?*
No.

10. *Were there any discussions about candidate responsiveness to questions?*

We were anxious for a full and probing examination of each man's positions on the issues. That is why President Ford issued the debate challenge in the first place. We recognized that this was primarily the responsibility of the reporters on the panel. In order to facilitate their efforts to elicit specific and responsive answers, we insisted, during the debate negotiations, that follow-up questions be permitted.

8.

Production Diary of the Debates

HERBERT A. SELTZ and RICHARD D. YOAKAM

The Format Takes Shape

Finding a starting point for a production diary of the 1976 presidential and vice-presidential debates was not easy. Such grand schemes do not spring up full-blown at any one moment, and there was much preliminary activity that contributed to the evolution of the debates as they finally appeared on the air. Other parts of this book cover much of that pre-1976 legal and organizational activity which made it possible for the debates to take place. Our purpose is to examine, as we did in 1960, the influences and pressures that shaped the debates into TV and radio programs broadcast to millions of Americans in the fall of 1976.[1]

In September 1975 Jim Karayn had been hired by the League of Women Voters to produce a series of primary election forums to be televised on PBS. Serious thinking about the prospect of the League presenting presidential debates began in March 1976.[2] Karayn was named project director.

Karayn had spent twenty years in local and national television news and public affairs. He had been with NBC News and was bureau chief and producer for NET in Washington; in the early 1970s he was a founder and president of NPACT, the National Public Affairs Center for Television. In that capacity he had supervised the production of documentaries and special events coverage, including Watergate and impeachment hearings for PBS.

On April 26, Karayn, Ruth Clusen, president of the League of Women Voters, and Peggy Lampl, League executive director, met in New York with top executives of the three commercial television networks to discuss the possibility of holding presidential debates.[3] The meetings were brief and circumscribed by the political, legal, and regulatory constraints treated elsewhere in this book. The dialogue was strained. On May 5 at the League's annual convention in New York, Clusen announced that the League would sponsor the debates. In May and June the presidents of NBC and ABC endorsed the idea and agreed that their networks would carry the debates, if they occurred; CBS did not firmly commit itself to broadcasting the debates until the Monday before the first debate in Philadelphia in September. The League staff was still small, and money was thin. By early July the League was deeply committed to the debates. A steering committee made up of such national figures as Theodore H. White, Douglass

Cater, and others had been formed; former FCC chairman and present Chicago communications attorney Newton Minow, former Undersecretary of the Treasury Charls Walker, and New York attorney Rita Hauser were named co-chairs of the debates project.

Karayn had become, by his own admission, the leading student of the 1960 debates. He interviewed virtually everyone still alive who was connected with the Nixon-Kennedy confrontations. He had distilled out of that effort the basic ideas he felt were crucial to the success of the debates in 1976. More ideas would come later, and more problems would emerge, but Karayn's thinking in July and August clearly delineated the shape the debates were to take.

Karayn told the authors that the League had to try to make the debates more than prime-time, super-publicized, "Meet The Press" style events.[4] He was concerned that holding the debates at any cost might easily become the prevailing attitude, as it had in 1960. He referred to the authors' earlier conclusions regarding the 1960 debates:

> . . . the networks did not produce the programs—they had no choice concerning the talent, did not choose the time and place, date or script (format). The networks came out second best on the formats for the programs, but this, to them, was not as important as having the programs on the air.[5]

Karayn told us that at first he felt our statement was too strong, but that former CBS President Frank Stanton had agreed that it was not. He clearly understood that many of the problems the League would face would be the same problems that had confronted the networks in 1960. He felt it would be hard to innovate too much since it was in the framework of 1960 that the candidates were basing their thinking; it would be difficult to get them to agree to much that was radically different from the previous events.

Karayn and many others who would be close to the debates in 1976 had looked at the 1960 recordings, and had found the broadcasts stilted, formal, and as one observer put it, "antique in style, demeanor, audio, and everything else."[6] Karayn said that he wanted the debates this time to deal with the big issues facing the nation, that a major flaw of the 1960 debates had been that the questions tended to be too topical and controversial and were not aimed at getting responses on major issues. So, though he felt the candidates were "thinking '60," he wanted to try to develop a format that would give the American voters more information about the candidates than they could get from the evening TV news, the Sunday afternoon panel shows, political commercials, or reading newspapers and news magazines. Karayn had referred to the primary election forums as "voter comparative shopper's guides," and said he thought about the debates in the same way.[7]

The options talked about at the time included pure debate, but Karayn thought that would be dull viewing. He was intrigued by steering committee member Douglass Cater's strong support for the so-called Oregon debate format.[8] But again, he thought the candidates would resist radical change, although he said it might be possible to get them to try out a version of the Oregon format in the last debate.

Karayn had said repeatedly that he was against opening statements. He showed that the 1960 debate format allowed eight-minute opening statements, and four-minute closing statements, which took up approximately half of the program. He did think there might be closing statements to allow the candidates to summarize what they had said, and perhaps to respond to each other. As to time, Karayn wanted the debates to be sixty minutes long. At the first steering committee meeting it had been agreed that each debate would have a broad theme: the first would focus on domestic affairs; the second, on foreign affairs; the last, on the role of the presidency. Further, Karayn advocated limiting the number of issues taken up in each debate, and he continued to urge that throughout the debate period.

Karayn wanted a panel of newsmen and newswomen to ask the questions, but he thought the number should be reduced from four to three—one from broadcasting, one from print, and one to represent the editorial side of news magazines or newspapers.[9] The selection of the news panel had been a big problem in 1960, and it became a bigger problem in 1976. Karayn maintained that the selection of the questioners ought to be done by the League steering committee. But, he had learned that in 1960 Kennedy's press secretary, Pierre Salinger, had raised a ruckus about the lack of newspaper representation on the questioners' panel (which led to an elaborate lottery system and changes in the later panels). Karayn therefore devised a plan to have the League draw up a large list of reporters and then winnow it down. Those names would be shown to the candidates' representatives, and the League would then eliminate any persons to which either or both sides had strong objections. Karayn thought that that procedure would be diplomatically sound and that it would be acceptable to the candidates. Later, he would change his mind. Panel selection was to become a major issue with the broadcast networks, and a frustrating and time-consuming hassle for the project staff.

Karayn's background in television news and public affairs, of course, made him very aware of the other elements of such a huge undertaking, e.g., logistics and staging, and of the implications of televising the events. Later, there would be charges that the debates were staged for TV, but Karayn had said all along that the League had to be realistic about the needs of television—lighting, set design, positioning of the cameras and of the candidates.

The League of Women Voters had always had an audience at its candidate events, no matter where they had taken place, so an audience was part of the League's (and Karayn's) plan from the beginning. While it isn't always easy to fill the hall when the candidates are running for minor offices, in the case of presidential debates everyone wants to get in, and there is a huge press contingent as well. Karayn wanted to stage the debates in small auditoriums and in locations with nearby facilities to take care of the hundreds of reporters who would follow the events. How the audience would act was another problem. At the Forums, he said, the audience reaction had had an effect on the way the candidates responded.[10]

As to location, Karayn knew that the networks and the candidates would have to have a say. Candidate travel schedules could dictate some locations, as they had in 1960. The networks would be less concerned about locations (they were much more flexible technically in 1976 than in 1960), but coverage requirements would still demand close liaison. Finally, such matters as how to arrange the set, where people would stand or sit, and whether there would be reaction shots of one candidate while the other was speaking, and/or of the audience, would be matters the candidates would have to agree on in advance.

A remarkable amount of Karayn's summer planning survived to become the core of the 1976 debates. Douglass Cater pushed hard for the "Oregon debate" and wrote a long report, and a column about it in the *Washington Post*. The planners still wanted more give and take between the candidates. Karayn promoted the idea of having some panel questions and some face-to-face discussion. By August 24 Karayn was encouraged that this might be arranged, since Carter press secretary Jody Powell and Rogers Morton, GOP campaign chairman, had said so on a television news program.[11] Powell said Carter wanted less of a news conference format and more of a free exchange of views. Morton said he thought the 1960 debates had prevented real discussion between the candidates. But Karayn seems to have cooled on the "Oregon debate" idea. He told the steering committee he thought the questioner panel was needed to stimulate the candidates, and was also aware that past man-to-man and Oregon-style primary debates didn't generate any excitement.

The first negotiation session with the candidates' representatives took place in Washington, D.C., the afternoon of August 26 at the Mayflower Hotel, the site of some of the 1960 meetings. Earlier that day Karayn had met with members of the League steering committee for a final strategy session and had asked for some final guidance. He said, "I want to know if we have any other ground rules; is there a place where we will refuse to step across in terms of conditions. I want to know—in 1960 it was said by everybody who participated that they felt that the need to get the debates on television was so important that any kind of issue about content, format, number, dates, all of that, was so miniscule in comparison to having the debates." Karayn says that question was really never answered, except to say: "Jim, we want these debates, period, and I understood what that meant."[12]

Newton Minow emphasized that it was important to have a place and a time firmly in mind and to present them to the candidates' representatives as a certainty, at least for the first debate. So, the steering committee chose Tuesday, September 28, at the Chase Park Plaza Hotel in St. Louis. Karayn later commented: "We just picked a place, we wanted some place neutral, not Chicago because that was where the first debate had taken place in 1960. And, nobody ever goes to St. Louis for this, so why not St. Louis? We always assumed the place and date would change."[13]

Those attending the first negotiation session were: Karayn, Minow, Charls Walker, Rita Hauser, Ruth Clusen, and Peggy Lampl for the League; for Ford: presidential counsel Michael Raoul-Duval, former FCC chairman Dean Burch, and former attorney-general William Ruckelshaus; for Carter: press secretary Jody Powell, TV advisor Barry Jagoda, and campaign advisor Gerry Rafshoon. Observing for Democratic vice-presidential candidate Walter Mondale was his administrative assistant, Richard Moe. GOP vice-presidential candidate Robert Dole was not represented.

The League proposed the format for the first debate: one hour in length, no opening statements, questions from a panel of journalists, the last twenty or thirty minutes to include face-to-face discussion between the two candidates, closing statements. Limits on answers to questions and rebuttals would be 2:30 and 1:30, respectively.

The League also proposed that the project co-chairs, Minow, Walker, and Hauser, and League president Ruth Clusen handle the moderator's role through the four debates. That idea was turned down by the candidates' representatives, and it was agreed that moderators with professional experience would be chosen by the League.[14]

The League had suggested specific titles for each debate: no. 1: "America's Challenge at Home"; no. 2: "America's Goal in the World"; no. 3: "The Vice-presidential Debate"; no. 4: "Making Government Work, the Role of the Presidency."[15] The Carter people wanted the sessions to be open and freewheeling. They feared that Ford would be well briefed on a specific subject, and initially they held out for open discussion in all debates. This issue was not settled at the August 26 meeting.

Also discussed were the length of the debates and the dates on which they would occur. The Ford representatives wanted longer debates—ninety minutes —on the theory that Carter would not hold up as well as Ford during an extended period. They also wanted to start as early in September as possible. Karayn suggested a compromise from the League's one-hour proposal: that the debates last seventy-five minutes. That was rejected by both sides because it would assure instant analysis by the commentators, as the networks filled out the remaining fifteen minutes until the next normal program break.

The Ford people were still toying with the possibility of four presidential debates, instead of three, so a compromise was worked out. William Ruckelshaus said he would agree to three debates by the party ticket leaders, if the Carter side would be willing to start the debates earlier in September. Tentatively they agreed on September 23.

The issue of an audience was also discussed. The League had both historic and practical reasons for the presence of an audience, and it had been told by its lawyers that an audience would make the sessions "more legal" as bona fide news events. The candidates' representatives were wary that an audience's reactions might be disruptive. Then too, they feared that the candidates would play to the studio audience rather than to the much larger TV audience. This matter and many others were also left up in the air. What came out of the first negotiation session was a tentative agreement that there might be some debates. They agreed that if debates were held, at least the first one would be ninety minutes and would deal with domestic policy and the economy. They agreed that there would be an audience, but that television would not be allowed to take pictures of it. They agreed to meet again on September 1.

In the meantime, Karayn was concerned about the cool reception given to the proposal that the candidates question each other directly. He held several separate sessions with the candidates' representatives in the five days between the two meetings, to try to get them to agree to the concept, but he was not successful. At the September 1 negotiation session both candidates' groups firmly rejected the idea.

Also on September 1 the date of the first debate, September 23, was made firm. The other dates were still undecided, but it was agreed those could be worked out later, roughly in the weeks of October 3, 11, and 18. Neither side wanted to have a debate during the week before the election.

The sticky issue of how the questioner panel would be chosen had been on Karayn's mind since he first proposed that the candidates' representatives might have input into who might be considered. He had told the steering committee that he now thought the issue could be troublesome, and that instead of letting the candidates' representatives see the list of proposed panelists, the League should make its own decisions and announce them to the candidates.[16] But when the candidates' representatives heard that the League would select the panelists, they asked to be allowed to make suggestions. The candidates' representatives were told that they could suggest up to fifteen names in each of the three categories—print, broadcast, and magazine/wire services—for each debate. The League would then choose the three panelists from among those and other names, and would inform the candidates of the selection before inviting the panelists. To alter the League's decision, the candidates' representatives would have to show proof that a panelist was extremely biased in favor of the opposing candidate. Finally, all agreed not to discuss this arrangement with anyone else.

The negotiators did not agree on any of the sites, but they did decide the debates would not be held in hotel ballrooms or in Washington. Unresolved was a whole list of things: technical details, set design, whether the candidates would sit or stand, staging.[17]

On to Philly

The League of Women Voters has emphasized that the negotiations for the debates were handled in two meetings, as compared to the dozen or so before the 1960 debates. Of course, this view has a lot to do with how they defined a meeting. The League project group had many meetings and there was a lot of internal discussion about format. And, it is clear that the candidates' representatives and Jim Karayn had meetings and phone calls about the production of the debates even before the final agreements on September 1.[18]

The two men closest to the broadcast production for Carter and Ford, respectively, were Barry Jagoda and William Carruthers. Jagoda, thirty-three, had worked for NBC and CBS news in New York and Washington in the late sixties. He moved up to associate producer and producer with CBS, covering major news stories; pools, documentaries, instant specials, political campaigns, and election nights followed. In 1975 he became a partner in a media and production firm. In 1976 he joined the Carter campaign as television advisor. Carruthers, forty-six, had an extensive background in television entertainment production and direction. In 1956 he did "Soupy Sales" on ABC. "Ernie Kovacs" and "The Steve Allen Show" ensued, along with numerous game shows and entertainment specials. In 1969 he formed the Carruthers Company, based in Los Angeles. In 1970–71 he was special consultant to President Richard Nixon. After that he continued to produce game shows and entertainment specials such as "Sinatra, The Main Event" and "Daytime Emmys." In 1976 he became a campaign TV advisor to Gerald Ford.

According to Carruthers, Duval, Powell, and Jagoda were concerned that the League of Women Voters had little previous experience in television—the

Forums aside. Each camp feared that the other would have greater influence with the League in determining the shape and form of the debate broadcasts. Carruthers later said: "We kept bouncing it around, and there were dialogues between Jagoda and Duval and Duval and Jody Powell, making sure that no one was taking advantage of the other." Also, Carruthers said, he met with Karayn at the Executive Office Building and took a kind of father-figure stance with the League project director. Carruthers told Karayn to protect himself from the networks by hiring top-level consultants. He related the conversation in this way: "I said unless you protect yourself with a substantial staff of recognized TV people who have experience in this sort of thing, you're going to get your head handed to you by the networks. They're going to say, 'You're not capable of doing this on your own, and what business does the LWV have staging debates?' " Carruthers also relates that even before he met with Karayn, he had talked to Imero Fiorentino, a nationally known lighting-production consultant. Carruthers and Fiorentino had worked together on special events, including the Ford rally at Ann Arbor, Michigan, and the Republican national convention; for years before that, they had collaborated on entertainment specials and political telecasts.[19]

Carruthers says that he told Fiorentino he was concerned about how the debates would look on the air, and recommended that if Fiorentino were hired by the League of Women Voters, to avoid a possible conflict of interest, he should set up two separate groups within his company to handle Republican campaign assignments and the debates.[20] Carruthers says that a day or two after his conversation with Karayn, Karayn called back and said he had hired Fiorentino. He also hired Jack Sameth, one of three people involved in major roles in both the 1960 and 1976 debate broadcasts, to be the production coordinator.[21] Karayn says that Carruthers may have suggested the hiring of Fiorentino, but that he doesn't remember it specifically. Karayn met with Fiorentino and his vice-president, Bill Klages, September 8, while attending a meeting in New York.[22] At that time, the lighting consultants gave him a cost estimate for their work that was far higher than the League project budget had anticipated.

Fiorentino recalls telling Karayn the cost would be about $25,000, or $7,000 dollars per debate, and that Karayn responded that this was beyond his budget. Fiorentino and Klages went back to their New York office and decided they had to do the work for the League as a matter of prestige and competition. The following day they told Karayn they'd do the job without charge, if necessary. Karayn responded that such an arrangement would be illegal for the League, so they settled on a total charge of $7,500 plus expenses, in return for which the Fiorentino firm would be the lighting and production consultant and packager. Fiorentino suggested, and Karayn hired, Robert Wightman as the scenic designer.[23]

Karayn now had his "top-ranked team." Karayn says that Barry Jagoda questioned the hiring of Fiorentino because of his close relationship to Carruthers. But when challenged by Karayn to come up with anyone else as well known in the lighting-consultant business, Jagoda agreed he couldn't.[24]

In regard to the site for the first debate, the League had been talking about Philadelphia for some time. It was thought that the debate could take place in an historic shrine like Independence Hall or Carpenters Hall. But surveys of those spots showed them to be much too small: not more than a hundred people could have squeezed into Independence Hall, let alone the TV equipment.

Again, it was Carruthers who came up with the answer. Carruthers's secretary had suggested the Walnut Street Theater. Her father, William McGuinn, was a member of the theater's board of directors. Karayn, Sameth, and the League staff, along with Jagoda and Rafshoon for Carter, and Duval, Carruthers, and the White House security people for Ford, went to the theater on the seventh. Everyone liked it. Carruthers said he especially liked it because the stage was relatively small.

"It would," he said, "force the candidates closer together, and the closer they were, the better it would be for us."[25] Jagoda said it was fine with the Democrats. For a TV production, the theater had everything needed—good source and volume of power, a good house-lighting board, small but adequate dressing rooms and staff areas, convenient access to the Ben Franklin Hotel and press center two blocks away. It was settled.[26]

Two major aspects of the production of the first debate began the next day. Karayn and company went to New York to meet with the networks for the first time, and Sameth started rounding up his production team. Sameth contacted Fiorentino, Klages, and Wightman, and the set-building project was launched. At the same time, in Los Angeles, Carruthers was having his own company's designers sketch a set, based on his trip to the theater the previous day. Carruthers says he sent a copy of these plans to Fiorentino and discussed them with Karayn, but Karayn doesn't remember seeing them. Fiorentino is not certain that he saw them, and Wightman is sure he didn't.[27]

Carruthers's concept of the set was that it should compliment the president. He felt that Gerald Ford's height advantage over Carter (6 feet 1 inch compared to 5 feet 9½ inches) could be communicated to the viewer more dramatically if the debaters stood.

"In terms of directing the show," he said, "the guys who would be doing the shows for the various networks would be showing the two debaters in one shot, and there was no question about the fact that we would be showing the three to four inch advantage."[28]

Jagoda's concept was just the opposite. He envisioned something like the set for the ABC program "Issues and Answers": participants seated close to each other, relaxed, even casual. But at this point, it doesn't appear that he pushed very hard for this idea.

Karayn also fancied himself a set designer. He wanted the set to look somewhat like the one CBS designed for the first debate in 1960. This included seating the questioners with their backs to the audience, together with the moderator.[29] He also wanted a less conventional lectern.

These suggestions aside, it was Bob Wightman who designed the set that appeared on the stage September 23. Karayn's ideas reached Wightman through Sameth. Wightman says, "We [Sameth and Wightman] evolved this plan . . . where the panelists would be facing the candidates and there could be cameras literally in a 360 degree arrangement."

Although they knew there was going to be an audience, Wightman was asked to design a television set. Wightman said, "The debate was being staged in front of people, that was the premise. But the people . . . would be a tiny group in comparison with the television audience, so we were thinking about that television audience, and that, I'm sure, was what the League was thinking about."[30]

Cost and portability were also considerations. Wightman said the set had to be used for all the debates, and "they wanted an efficient set that would be able to travel well." He also said he was aware of budget limitations, "so we couldn't do just anything that came into our heads."

On the ninth Wightman and Sameth met at Fiorentino Associates. They talked over the project in general, and decided to look at furniture for the set. They went to the Manhattan showrooms of the Herman Miller Company. Wightman, Sameth, and Miller personnel spent some hours looking at various styles of chairs, stools, and modular desk units. They also considered some curved components as possible lecterns.

Wightman and Sameth picked out a 2 foot by 12 foot light oak desk unit from the company's "Action Office Line," two "Eames" engineering stools, and four "Ergon" management chairs. All six were covered with dark brown leather. The League had said it could not receive the furniture as a gift—the Miller Co. had suggested that—so they worked out a negotiated "token" charge of $1,000.[31]

On the eleventh, the design team went to Philadelphia, placed some chairs on the theater stage, and for the first time got a feeling for how the set might look there. It was Wightman's first view of the theater. It was also then that "the wall" was born. Sameth, looking into the house, realized that the candidates would be looking at the panel; behind them would be TV cameras, and behind those, the audience. So, he made a television decision—to build a wall, and since the wall would block the view of the audience, to move the audience to the balcony. He also worked out camera shooting patterns based on the 360 degree concept.

Back in New York, Wightman worked late into the night, and the next morning had designs, storyboards, and color samples for Sameth and his assistant Reed Jackson to look at. In less than twenty-four hours they would be back on the stage in Philadelphia to start a two-day series of unveilings for the candidates' representatives, the League, the pool, and the networks.[32]

The other major production process going on at the same time as the set design was the League's contacts with the networks and their pool. The idea that the events would be covered by a pool was part of Karayn's late-summer thinking. Pooling means that one or more of the television networks assembles a pool of equipment and personnel to provide common aural and visual coverage of a news event. The members split the cost on an equal share basis. Pools often cover entire proceedings "gavel-to-gavel," and subscribers to the pool can broadcast any or all of it. Pooling is used for political conventions and other major special events such as space trips. On top of the general pool coverage, each network usually has its own cameras and audio installations—"unilaterals." This makes it possible for an individual network to select shots from the pool and add its own pictures and sound at various points in the coverage.

On September eighth, Karayn and Sameth met with the networks for the first time. Attending were: for ABC, Wally Pfister, vice-president for special

118

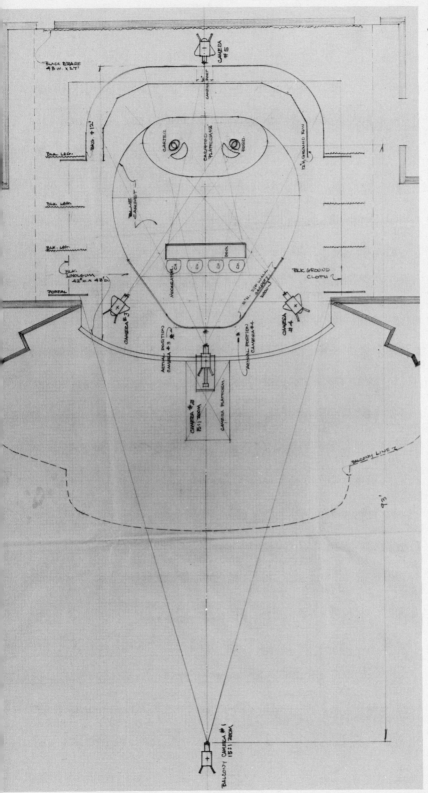

Designer Robert Wightman's original plan for the Philadelphia debate, complete with camera positions and fields of view. Several changes were made when the set was put up on the stage of the Walnut Street Theater. The principal close-up cameras, #3 and #4, were moved toward the center of the stage. Their actual positions are indicated by asterisks. The lecterns were moved closer together and forward on the platform; step units were placed at the front and sides of the riser; and the single camera in back (#5) was replaced by two vertically stacked cameras shooting the press panel through the test-tube-shaped camera portal. (*Courtesy of Robert Wightman*)

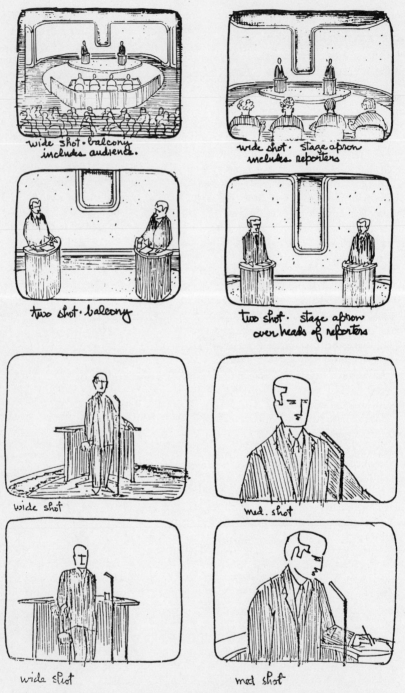

wide shot · balcony
includes audience.

wide shot · stage apron
includes reporters

two shot · balcony

two shot · stage apron
over heads of reporters

wide shot

med. shot

wide shot

med shot

TOP: Wightman's storyboard sketches of what the front shots from the balcony and the stage would look like. BOTTOM: Wightman's sketches for an alternative lectern design. Project director Jim Karayn had hoped that the set would incorporate a lectern that would not hide the candidates but would still provide support and a writing surface. Various designs were considered, but the candidates' representatives wanted, and got, a traditional lectern. (*Courtesy of Robert Wightman*)

events, and Elliot Bernstein, senior special events producer; for CBS, Bob Chandler, vice-president for special events, Sanford Socolow, Washington bureau chief, and Russ Bensley, executive producer for special events; for NBC, Robert Mulholland, executive vice-president of NBC News, Christie Basham, director of news operations, NBC Washington Bureau, Gordon Manning, vice-president for special events, and Paul Klein, vice-president for programming; for PBS, Wallace Westfeldt, director of news and public affairs and senior executive producer, WETA, Washington, and Gerald Slater, executive vice-president, WETA.

Karayn had convened the meeting to tell the network executives how the League of Women Voters was going to conduct the debates. He announced that the first one would be September 23 at the Walnut Street Theater in Philadelphia. The next three would be during specific weeks in October. The ninety-minute length was set only for the first debate. He explained that the debates were going to be news events. If the networks wanted to cover them, that was fine. If they didn't, that was okay too.[33]

The networks had been thinking they would have to pool at least some of the coverage.[34] Karayn suggested they form an internetwork unit to cover all four debates. They rejected that idea but did set up a pool. Midway through the meeting they asked the League group to leave the room, and the networks drew lots and worked out the PBS participation in the pool.

This was the first time in its history that the Public Broadcasting Service was to become a full partner (a voting/producing member) in a pool. Slater told the authors he had talked with PBS executives about this. Normally PBS had paid a 17 percent share of the costs when they took a program from the network pool. Slater's view was that it was important to pay the additional cost—another 8 percent—and to participate in the decisions. PBS also wanted to produce one of the debates.[35]

With just the four networks present, Slater announced PBS's interest in full partnership, and it was agreed upon. Westfeldt, who had had a long career with NBC before joining public broadcasting, later commented, "PBS as a full participant in the pool is a rare thing for two reasons: absence of money, and a general reluctance on the part of the commercial networks to believe or accept public broadcasting as an equal member in terms of its technical capabilities." Pfister says he suggested that each of the three commercial networks take one of the presidential debates, and that PBS do the vice-presidential one. Slater and Westfeldt agreed. Questioned about their technical capabilities, they assured the others they could handle the job. The draw gave ABC first choice, and Pfister chose the first debate. NBC drew second choice and picked the third debate. CBS took the remaining one.[36]

Because the networks and their pool were to be covering a "bona fide news event" to comply with the Section 315 exemption, they considered their relationship to the debates a very sticky matter. Concerned about their legal stance, they felt that the pool could not get involved in the staging or the arrangements for the debates. It could not in any way assume control of the event. Philadelphia pool producer Elliot Bernstein summed it up: "At any point, if we began to assume control of this event, our ability to cover it would be jeopardized. And so the original approach for the networks, and the original guidance that I got from my bosses—and my bosses were representatives of all four networks because we were a pool—was that we just go in, and whatever they do, we cover; and not produce this event in any way . . . we cover this as we would cover any other news event. We show up with our cameras and turn them on."[37]

Consequently, they told the League some of the things they would not do. Legally, they were not permitted to aid the League in any way, with communications devices, stage managing, timing, public address system, and the like. For example, Sameth was asked how he intended to use the timing devices that would tell the candidates the amount of time they had left. He said he thought they should be mounted on the cameras, as they had been in 1960. The networks replied, according to Sameth: "No, you won't, because we cannot allow your equipment to be mounted on our cameras; that would be an illegal no-no."[38]

To get around the problem of pool involvement in the event, and to provide more journalistic freedom for each network, CBS asked for unilateral cameras in the theater. They had sent producer David Buksbaum to scout the Walnut Street Theater early in the morning of the eighth. Based on their thinking at that time—that there would be no audience in the balcony—Chandler thought all the networks could put their own cameras in the balcony and direct their programs from those positions. There was also a suggestion by CBS that each network receive what are called "isolated feeds" from some of the pool cameras. This meant that instead of getting a mix of shots determined by the pool director, each network's director would select from those for his own broadcast.

This plan was not well received by the other networks. ABC's Pfister and NBC's Mulholland explained their views. "If we had a pool," Pfister said, "and we wanted to cut from one camera to another, and they were cutting their own program, they might miss our shot, or get a flash of our shot in theirs.[39] We could not be in a position of telling everyone moment-by-moment what shot we were going to take." Mulholland didn't like having all those cameras in the balcony. He said: "Even though the networks might have agreed to do that . . . then all the Philadelphia stations, all the newsreels, everybody else would have been in there . . . and ultimately the poor candidates would look up and they could have seen five, ten, maybe fifteen cameras sort of facing them, and they'd have no idea where to look."[40] It was in internetwork argument, and CBS lost.

Allowing unilateral cameras was an issue between the League and all of the networks, and Karayn ruled at the meeting that no unilateral cameras would be permitted in the house. There was objection to his rule.

Karayn also informed the networks for the first time that they could not take pictures of the audience. This caused a bigger uproar, and the networks raised what they believed—and still believe—to be an important journalistic issue. They said that coverage of the debates as a bona fide news event included their right to cover the audience. They inquired whether the candidates had made the decision. Karayn's response was: "We do not feel we've agreed to any condition that would inhibit TV coverage."[41] All the network people spoke vigorously about the principle.

The issue of televising the audience touched off a long and sometimes bitter controversy between the League and the networks. In a broader context, it bred suspicion on both sides that there were hidden agendas and motives. The League felt that the networks were raising issues like this out of pique at not producing the debates this time. The networks felt that the League was not being honest with them, and that the candidates had more to do with the planning of the debates than had been revealed. The networks wanted to know everything, they said, so they could at least tell their audience the ground rules. NBC pool producer Christie Basham summed it up in her reflections about the relationship between the League and the networks:

> We had a lot of semantic arguments with Jim Karayn at that time . . . what the League was doing because the candidates had asked for it, and if the candidates asked for it, wasn't the League in a sense agreeing with the candidates . . . everytime you would get up to that point where [the networks] would say, "Well, haven't the candidates set those rules?" No, they are our rules . . . it was a circle.

The "Four" Philadelphia Debates

There were not just four debates, there were seven, and four of them took place in and around Philadelphia. There was the growing debate over the journalistic freedom of the networks versus the League's own dictums as to how the debate would be staged and covered. There was a debate between the League and the network pool about how they would interface, and there were two Ford-Carter debates: the one on the stage before millions, and the other behind the scenes, where the Carter and Ford handlers haggled over just how the main event would be staged.

The action at the site started on Monday, September 13. At one o'clock Karayn had his first meeting with the candidates' representatives since the site survey on the seventh. On the theater stage, they looked at Wightman's plans and talked generally about the lecterns, the colors and physical aspects of the set, and the logistics of entering and leaving the stage.

Karayn met later in the afternoon with Elliot Bernstein. Bernstein says his first impressions of the theater were mild and general: "There was a stage, and there would be an event . . . the two candidates would be playing to the audience, and we would come in and set up our cameras somewhere in that orchestra."[42]

Karayn met again with the candidates' representatives, a marathon meeting which went on into the early hours of the next day. Ten or eleven hours were spent arguing over the most minute details of staging the first debate. Even today, some of the participants remain passionate about some of the events. At the center of the hostility was an unspoken suspicion that, somehow, one or the other side might gain an advantage that might just cost the election.

There was not much form to the meeting. Karayn served as moderator. The arguments surged back and forth. How would the candidates look? Would they sit or stand? What shape and height for the lecterns? Who would supply stand-ins for camera rehearsals, makeup, timing devices? Where would the candidates look? Should there be stools on the set?

Carruthers was adamant that Ford would stand during the whole event. Jagoda, on the other hand, kept suggesting different ways the debaters might sit down. He remembers saying, "Why don't we sit down and relax, and have the debate in that format? The Ford people responded, 'The President of the United States will stand up and address the American people.' . . . It was a very rigid notion."[43]

Carruthers recalls: "The big bone of contention was that Carter wanted to sit, and Jagoda started throwing out . . . late-night talk-show concepts. I said, hey look, Jimmy Carter can do anything he wants to. The President's going to stand at the lectern for ninety minutes; he doesn't want a chair, he doesn't want to sit down, he's coming to debate."[44]

Obviously, neither side would have agreed to allow one candidate to do one thing while the other did something else. Both sides phrased their argument "in the interests of uniformity."

They discussed the lecterns. Karayn had pushed for lecterns that wrapped around the candidates from behind, so that they could stand in front of them and lean or write on them. Since Carter is right-handed and Ford is left-handed, this would have worked. Jagoda claims he would have gone along with that arrangement, but Carruthers didn't like the idea and it was shoved aside.

They did reach agreement about the height of the lecterns. They decided to measure both candidates from the floor to their belt buckles and then split the difference. The distance turned out to be approximately forty-two inches. Carruthers and Jagoda were happy with the belt-buckle compromise, but they kept needling each other about the difference in the height of the two men. Jagoda says that he had looked at the recordings of the 1960 debates, and even though there was a similar height difference between John F. Kennedy and Richard Nixon, he didn't see it on the screen. "So I dropped my argument," he related. "But since I had seemed to be concerned about it, it was useful to continue to have that on the table as an issue. And at one point I said, what do you mean you have to equalize these lecterns . . . and someone made a facetious remark: 'Why don't we just cut a hole?' And then Carruthers, or one of those guys went out and said that Jagoda wants to put the President of the United States in a hole. That got on the news wires, and Jagoda recalls a day later his mother called him from his hometown and said: 'Why are you trying to put the president in a hole?' "[45]

Through all of this, the others involved sat around and listened. Karayn said, "I felt like John J. Anthony in a court of domestic relations." Bob Wightman made sketches of various kinds of lecterns, in case they were wanted. There was a lot of telephoning, or pretending to telephone higher-ups. Both Carruthers and Jagoda say the other telephoned. It was: "Well, if you don't believe me, I'll call my man, and we'll settle it." Or, the reverse of that: "Do you or don't you speak for your man?"[46] At about 3:00 A.M. the first Ford-Carter debate yawned to an end.

At ten the next morning all hands met on stage at the Walnut Street Theater for the unveiling of the set plans. Sameth had marked on the stage where the candidates would stand. There were tables and chairs where the panel would be. Copies of Wightman's plans, samples and colors of fabrics, and story-board sketches were handed out. Sameth made a formal presentation, while the network representatives, the pool team, the League staff, and the candidates' representatives looked on. The story-board sketches showed what the shots might look like if the nets put their cameras where Sameth thought they should. The plans also had the camera shots marked in.

First impressions varied considerably. The size and importance of "the wall" sank in. It was the first time the network people realized the extent to which the shape of the set and the wall were going to dictate the nature of the production.

Elliot Bernstein had been named the pool producer. At forty-two, Bernstein had spent twenty-three years in various aspects of commercial TV. While in college, he worked as a shipping clerk for Fox Movietone News. He had been with CBS as a film librarian, with UPI as a reporter-producer for the wire-service syndicated television newsreel, covering civil rights protests in the south. He had been Midwest bureau chief for ABC and news director of their television station in San Francisco. In 1971 he joined the ABC special events unit, covering space shots and two Nixon trips to Russia. On the second Nixon trip to Russia and on Ford's trip to China, Bernstein was the pool producer. He had also been pool producer for the Republican national convention the previous summer.

When Bernstein saw the set plans on September 14, his impressions were radically different from his view of the empty theater the day before. "They unveiled," he said, "what was in effect a television studio that they were going to install. This was not my understanding of the 315 exemption. My feeling of a news event is something that happens spontaneously . . . or something that is scheduled as an event. The only way this would be scheduled as an event is that it would be scheduled for the people in the room, and obviously the people in this room were being ignored."[47] After the debates were over, Bernstein broadened his impressions: "I felt, 'nobody is ever going to believe that this is not a network event.' Here was a television studio laid out on the stage. In order for the event to be staged successfully, it was obvious from the start that the League had designed and was conducting these debates for a television audience, and not as something that we show up to cover. . . . I'm not an attorney. And the reaction on the part of lots of us was that we were getting into a situation that could subject us to violations of Section 315 of the FCC code."[48]

Bernstein was not alone in his concern. CBS's Chandler said that when he saw the camera angles on the set plans, "I screamed bloody murder to Sameth and Karayn."[49] Wallace Westfeldt's response was: "I didn't think that PBS should participate if the rules were being set by others."[50] Some of the objections must have seemed gratuitous to Karayn. "Naturally we created a set. . . . I insisted that the set designer we used be somebody familiar with television. We were very cognizant that a horrendously large part of this whole audience would be viewers on television, and so it would be foolish, I thought, to create a set that was untelevisable. In that set plan, we even showed a position for cameras, which I guess diplomatically we should never have done."[51]

Karayn also says that part of the difficulty stemmed from the hands-off attitude of the networks. He remembers two instances. Once, he called a network to ask for prime-time fall sports and specials schedules and was told that the lawyers had advised them not to talk to the League about such things. Later, Karayn says, a network board chairman called him to complain about the scheduling of the first debate. Recalled Karayn, "That really annoyed me; when I was seeking information—not advice and not permission, but information—nobody on any of these networks would help me."

Karayn says: "If we had set up some kind of relationship, I would have talked with them. I would have maybe cut out that wall. The idiot thing about the wall is that it was never bitched about except in that one hour session . . . because the minute you pointed out to them that we were going to have cameras ringing the thing, they no more wanted to show the cameras in the background than anyone else."[52]

So, the second of the four debates in Philadelphia—the one between the networks and the League—had been joined. The networks and their pool were getting more nervous about their involvement in the event. They were also becoming more suspicious that there were hidden agreements between the League and the candidates. There was still some internal friction among the networks over the use of unilateral cameras.

They met again that day with Karayn in the hotel room where the candidates' representatives marathon had taken place the night before. The session wasn't nearly as long, but issues surfaced that were to echo through the following week, and beyond. These issues reveal quite clearly the core of misunderstanding and distrust between the League, as sponsors of the debates, and the networks, as pool producers and transmission belts of the events to the American public. The networks argued that journalistic principles were at stake. The League responded that it had made the rules and that the agreements between the candidates' and the League were not the networks' concern.

The question of unilateral cameras was settled quickly; CBS wasn't winning the argument with the other networks, and Karayn ended it by ruling once again against unilateral cameras inside the theater. There would be, and were, unilateral cameras in the lobbies and outside the debate sites, but none in the hall while the debates were on.

The networks again stated what they wouldn't do, so as to avoid charges of collusion in the staging of the broadcasts. At this point it was a long list. They would not put the timing devices on the cameras. Pool personnel would not even hold up cue cards for the candidates. They would not schedule time for the candidates to come in and check out the set and the microphones. They would not provide TV monitors in the house so the audience could see the TV broadcast while watching the live action. They would not provide feeds of pictures and sound to the press area in the hotel a block away. They would not provide feeds to the dressing rooms, or to the League command post in the theater. They voted down requests from the League to allow League personnel in the pool truck before or during the broadcast. They wouldn't allow Fiorentino or Klages to go into the pool truck to check out the lighting on the set. They would not provide communication circuits for members of the League project staff to use to communicate with each other and with the pool.[53]

Why this stiff-necked attitude? It goes back to the Section 315 exemption to allow coverage of the debates as bona fide news events. All of the networks were worried about becoming too deeply involved. And all had been talking to their legal staffs for guidance. Bob Chandler says the guidelines were understood:

The guidelines were simple. The exemption was based on the bona fide news event. . . . therefore the guideline was simply that our behavior, our conduct, had to be governed by what we normally did when covering a bona fide news event. Normally, when we cover a bona fide news event, we're not involved in the planning of the event; we're not involved in the staging of the event; we're not involved in the negotiations that lead to the event.

Once all those things are determined, we simply come in and cover the event. That was the whole basis for our comments. Every dispute . . . sprung from that basic premise.[54]

Karayn told the networks again that they could not take pictures of the audience during the debates. The issue had smouldered since the meeting on the eighth. It now burst into flame. It became such a major issue that for a time it appeared, at least on the surface, that the networks might not cover the debates. Statements were wired and phoned back and forth, the news media got wind of it. It blew up into a confrontation that brought the news executives face to face with the debate project's co-chairs.

While fussing about the audience shots, the networks picked up information about the agreement that had been made between the League and the candidates during the negotiations that the candidates would have a hand in suggesting names for the panel of questioners. If the candidates had a hand in deciding there would be no audience shots, and if they had a hand in picking the press panel, did this challenge the legitimacy of the debates? The networks said they wanted no part in negotiating the debates themselves, but they were now very interested in who had been involved. The face-off took place on Saturday, September 18, at the League headquarters in Washington. The array included Chandler and CBS news president Dick Salant. NBC sent a member of its Washington legal staff along with its representatives. The League entourage included Clusen, co-chairs Newton Minow and Charls Walker, and the other regulars.

Questions flew. The NBC attorney, Howard Monderer, said he thought the presence of an audience was a legal question; without an audience there might be doubts about whether it was a bona fide news event.

ABC's Pfister said that being prevented from taking pictures of the audience was the most important issue. He said it was the first time in his memory that television had been restricted on the pictures it could take, once it had been admitted to an event. He gave as examples the trips to China with Nixon and Ford, coverage of state meetings in Russia, and coverage of the House Judiciary Committee hearings.[55]

On the issue of whether or not the League had agreed to allow the candidates to help choose the questioners, the networks' hackles were sticking straight up. Salant, especially, wanted to know how this had come about. Walker and Minow explained. Walker reviewed the categories of questioners and also said they agreed that the questioners should be viewed as "fair" by both Ford and Carter. The final decision, he said, would always rest with the League. He also told the networks, and Minow concurred, that the League had agreed with the candidates' representatives that they would not discuss the selection process agreement with others.[56]

That upset Salant; he and Walker argued. Everyone agrees that Walker used the words "shut up." Some say it was as plain as: "Would you please shut up."[57] Others say it was milder than that. Whatever the specifics—there is no transcript—Salant thought he was told to shut up, and as Chandler tells it: "It was like somebody had shot a bullet at him." Walker tried to apologize, did apologize; but Salant refused him.

Salant grabbed his papers and stalked out, telling Chandler to come with him. From here on the incident contains elements of slapstick. The two walked down narrow corridors to get to the elevators, and there Salant discovered he had left his briefcase in the meeting room. Chandler went back and got it.

Salant told reporters waiting outside the League headquarters that CBS would have to consider whether or not it would carry the debates, given the offensive ground rules. The other network spokesmen joined Salant with statements opposing the ban on audience shots. Questioned by reporters, Ford advisor Duval said he could see no reason to change the agreement with the League, and he quoted from a letter that CBS president Arthur Taylor had sent to a congressional committee in August, in which Taylor had said a live audience might detract from the substance of the debates.[58] Carter advisor Barry Jagoda felt the decision remained entirely with the League.

Whatever the CBS threats not to cover the debates amounted to, Elliot Bernstein said that the first thing he saw when he arrived at the Walnut Street Theater the following Monday was a CBS remote truck—not even the pool equipment had yet arrived.

None of the other networks was as upset about the questioner issue as Salant. ABC's Pfister likened the setup to a news event staged by any organization: "If you say it's a news event, then the people staging the news event . . . have a right to pick whom they want as their panelists."

NBC's Mulholland said that the issues of the audience shots and the picking of the questioners added up to a broader issue: "We tried to get the League to understand that in pursuing its end . . . even with good intentions . . . it was trampling on the rights of other organizations or other principles. . . . That's what I think it really boiled down to and we lost."[59]

The networks asked that the audience-shots question be taken up by the League and the candidates again. Minow agreed, but it's not clear whether there actually was another review. The first debate was now five days away. While the networks left the impression they might not cover the debates, they were caught in a bind.

PFISTER: We were squeezed, and they had the cards . . . we had to cover it.[60]

CHANDLER: As much as our journalistic principles were offended . . . we knew deep in our hearts . . . that this was simply an event that couldn't be ignored, whether it was bona fide or not.[61]

MULHOLLAND: In our terms of what's a news event, a debate between an incumbent president and a challenger is a news event whether it happens in the street . . . in a theater . . . in one of our television studios, it's a news event.[62]

126   **THE GREAT DEBATES**

Meanwhile, the candidates prepared for the debates. Ford did more of this than Carter, and, in a more formal way. Lecterns and a questioners' panel table were set up in the family theater at the White House. Ford and his advisors met there four or five times prior to Philadelphia, and several times later. At these sessions, usually in the evening, the president practiced answers to questions posed by his staff. Portable video-tape equipment was used to record these rehearsals. They had two purposes. The first was to check on wardrobe, makeup, appropriate gestures and postures, and how the president would look. The second was to determine whether or not the briefing books prepared for the president were comprehensive enough. If he found he could not answer a question based on the material given him, more material was gathered.

Carruthers said that the sessions were useful because they made Ford more familiar with the physical setup and got him to polish his answers and presentation.[63] Duval told the authors that they usually ran forty-five minutes, and that afterward Ford and the others would review the video tapes, although Ford watched the tapes only for a few minutes.[64]

Carter did not rehearse in this way, but he did go over questions and answers in informal situations with his advisors in Plains, Georgia, and while campaigning. He did not use lectern, scenery, or cameras.[65]

The Show Goes On

Journalistic principles, grand strategies, postures, maneuverings for advantage, and insults aside, the debate on the twenty-third was to be produced by the network pool. Elliot Bernstein had that responsibility. For ten days he'd been submerged in what he later called "hocus-pocus," juggling the networks hands-off restrictions as well as the League's ground rules. "I was the funnel," he said. "If NBC had a problem or complaint with the League, they would call me, and I would call the League. If CBS called with a point of view about the audience shots, . . . I would relay that to the League.[66]

On Monday, September 20, Bernstein and his pool team arrived at the Walnut Street Theater and started to work with the lighting. Parking the pool truck was a problem: the Secret Service wanted it across the street, not next to the theater stage door. Bernstein went to the candidates' representatives—and the problem was solved.

The set arrived on Tuesday and the crew spent all day putting it up. The curved back wall was a series of flats covered with magnolia-white carpeting. It was 12 feet high, 36 feet long, and 14 feet deep. A neutral color was chosen because it could be tinted with set lights. The candidates would stand on a one-foot-high, carpeted, kidney-shaped riser, 19 feet wide and 9 feet deep. The carpet was a vivid blue.

After all the talk about sitting and standing, the lecterns came out in a traditional design. They were 42 inches high, covered with dark oak formica. The tops were semicircular, with an area cut out to hold a digital clock. There was a shelf under the top for water glasses. The crescent-shaped wall behind the press panel was 5 feet high and about 34 feet long, if fully extended. It was covered with a magnolia-white rug on the inside, and on the outside with the formica used on the lecterns. On the stage floor was a 50-foot square of black linoleum, with a blue oval rug design painted on it. The set wall behind the candidates had a test-tube-shaped camera port that hid two vertically stacked cameras for shots of the press panel. The chairs, desk unit, and stools picked out in New York were delivered and set in place. The original design for the set was a little fancier and costlier. A trim unit around the edges and top of the back wall had been planned as a three-dimensional moulding. To save money, painted masonite was used. The floor covering originally had been planned as a large ground cloth with a real rug on top of it.

The light plot was designed for television. Lighting consultant Imero Fiorentino observed: "It was no secret that television was going to cover the event . . . and we might as well light it sufficiently for television. Obviously, television lighting requires more light than stage lighting, so it would be foolish to spend money to light it with little instruments, and then on top of it put big instruments."[67] Fiorentino described his lighting approach as straightforward: "You could phone it in . . . it's very easy, but what's different is that one of the two men could be president. We chose to stay away from anything that approached great portraiture, because it's dangerous, it can kill you . . . we chose to play it a little safe and standard."

Fiorentino and Bill Klages discussed the plan, and Klages drew the plot. He employed the usual elements: key, back, side, fill, cross, and background lights. For fail-safe, there were back-up key lights on separate circuits.

Fiorentino said there was little difference in the lighting of the two candidates. "It was practically a mirror image, one side to the other. And there is a good reason for it. The two men look basically the same, physically, except for the hair. That's the only place there was a difference . . . in the intensity of the back light. There was a back light in each case . . . very dim and practically nonexistent for Ford; and the other was brighter because he has hair."[68]

The actual lighting in Philadelphia was up to Everett Melosh, who had held the same assignment in 1960. Melosh ran fresh cable to the lighting instruments, used the theater control board, and doubled up only the main key lights, as the plot had dictated. Additional lights were aimed into the house, to light the audience for the opening and closing shots.

It was time to be practical. With just two days to go, the timing devices were placed on two of the main cameras instead of on floor stands, which would have gotten in the way. The pool agreed to provide pictures and sound to various places within the theater and the League agreed to assume some of the cost. TV monitors were installed in the candidates' dressing rooms, in the League command post, and in the house. The League rented television sets and had them set up in the hotel press center.

There were still some sticky points. How would the pool communicate with the League and with those on the stage, and still maintain a hands-off attitude? It was decided that a private-line communication circuit would be run to the League command post, and a pool representative would be stationed there to relay communications in both directions. The pool installed its own stage manager, who could, of course, communicate with Bernstein.[69]

There was no communication between the pool and the moderator. The stage manager was installed at the last minute, not to do the traditional job of cuing people to start and stop, but to help the pool line up shots on the press

THE GREAT DEBATES

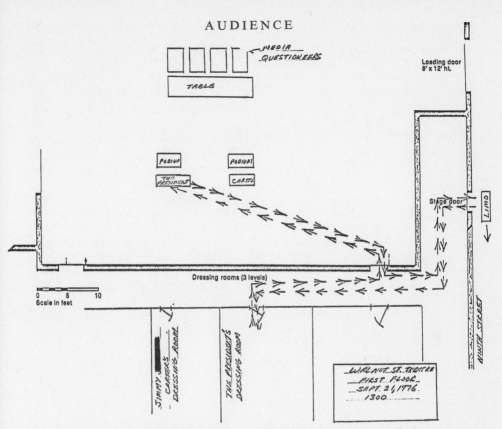

AUDIENCE

Nothing is left to chance. A page from the White House staff plan for Ford's trip to the Philadelphia debate showed the route he would take to his dressing room and to his place on the stage.

A couple of old hands at presidential-debate lighting. Everett Melosh (standing), the ABC lighting director for the Philadelphia debate, had performed that function for the third and fourth debates between Richard M. Nixon and John F. Kennedy in 1960. Imero Fiorentino (seated) had been a lighting consultant for Nixon in 1960; in 1976 the League of Women Voters hired his firm as lighting/production consultant and packager for the four debates. (*Courtesy of League of Women Voters*)

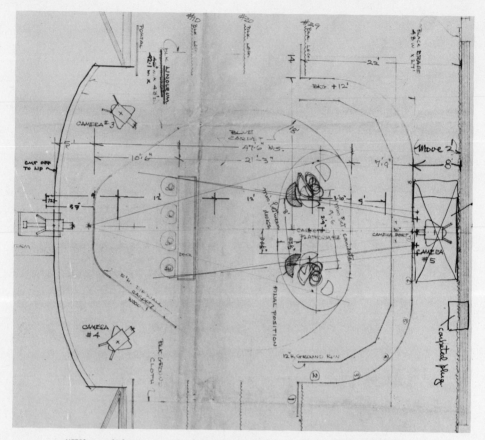

"Where did you say the lecterns should go?" A detail of Wightman's floor plan for the first debate reflected later adjustments in the placement of the lecterns and the rear cameras to allow better TV shots of the candidates and the questioners' panel. (*Courtesy of Robert Wightman*)

So that all could "hear." The PBS broadcast of each debate included a signer, who appeared in a lower corner of the TV screen so that the approximately fourteen million hearing-impaired Americans could follow the debates. (*Wide World Photos*)

panel. Since there were to be follow up questions, it was important for the pool director to know when they would occur. So, it was arranged that the panel members who wanted to ask follow up questions would signal with their hands.

Unlike most bona fide news events, there were rehearsals. In Philadelphia, students from a Temple University radio-TV class were recruited to act as the questioners and as Jimmy Carter. Bob Salica stood in for Carter. He told the authors he was a Republican but that he qualified to stand in for Carter because he was 5 feet 9 inches tall. John Kostic, not a student, stood in for Ford. He said Mark Goode of the White House staff had invited him. The rehearsals were long. The night before the debate they ran through the whole thing. Bernstein was very cautious about getting everything right—could they hear each other, which camera shots were the best, how to cut between the panelists?

The final rehearsal turned out to be time well spent. As the rehearsal went on, it became apparent that the panelists' stand-ins and the candidates' stand-ins couldn't hear each other. Bernstein took the problem to the League. Because of the restrictions, Bernstein was concerned that if his pool team worked out a solution, they would be participating in the event. But he pushed hard on the problem. The afternoon of the debate, when Carter and Ford came to the theater for what were called audio-visual (AV) checks, Bernstein sat down at the questioners' table and asked both Carter and Ford if they could hear him speaking. They said they were having difficulty. So, the pool bought two sets of speakers, and placed them on the stage floor behind the candidates and the panelists—a miniature public address system just for the participants.[70]

The set was also adjusted. The candidates' lecterns were moved about a foot and a half closer to the questioners and to each other. This had more to do with camera shots than with the hearing problem. Bernstein was concerned that the cross two-shots—those showing one candidate in the foreground with the other candidate in the background—had too much empty space in the middle.[71] Steps were added to the front and sides of the candidates' riser to make it easier for them to step on and off. There had been discussions earlier about widening the cut out in the back wall to accommodate two side-by-side cameras, but this was dropped in favor of stacking one camera over the other.

Early in the meetings between the pool and the League, the networks had said they would not provide the sound from the pool for the theater public address system. It was an unusual decision since, for practical reasons, television and radio networks customarily provide a feed of their sound to such house systems. Two separate amplification systems, competing with each other, can cause the screaming and howling known as "feedback." Karayn had agreed that the League would provide its own PA system for the audience, but he predicted to Sameth that the networks would change their minds.[72] And, in fact, they did: the pool sound from the stage was fed to loudspeakers facing the audience in the theater balcony.

The basic broadcast setup was the same at all four debate sites. At broadcast time, there were nine cameras in the theater—one a spare in case of failure. Two cameras were placed behind the set, one mounted above the other, to take pictures of the press panel and wide shots of the stage looking into the theater. There was a camera on each side of the set to take reaction shots of the candidates and side shots of the panel. Three cameras were positioned on the front apron of the stage. These were the main cameras, which took the head-on shots of the candidates. The eighth camera was high in the back of the theater, for wide shots of the stage and the opening and closing shots which included the audience.

The audio pickup was handled by ABC radio technicians and was standard for this kind of public affairs program. Each candidate wore two tiny microphones on a tie-clip. The wires from those microphones were run inside their clothing—down their pants legs—and were connected by cables to the audio mixers when Ford and Carter came on stage. The moderator and panelists used microphones (again, two for each) placed on the table in front of them.

A unique feature of the 1976 debates broadcast on PBS was the use of signers for the hearing-impaired. Nancy Kowalski and Mary Ann Royster repeated everything in sign language; they were shown in an oval insert in the lower portion of the television screen.

"Fine tuning" of the stage setup involved some minor re-positioning of the cameras. The original camera plot by Sameth was laid out with the understanding that each candidate would talk directly to a separate camera. These cameras were positioned at the sides of the questioners' panel and fairly wide apart—one aiming across the stage to Ford, the other across the stage to Carter. Bernstein, and the candidates' representatives, did not like this setup. Bernstein said that it would have had the candidates looking past the panel when they talked to the camera. So, he moved the candidates' cameras behind the panel closer to the center of the stage, making it easier for the candidates to talk either to the panel members or to the camera with a minimum of head movement.

The theater's star dressing rooms were immediately behind the stage.[73] Each had a gold plaque on the door bearing the autograph of the most famous person to have used it—Cornelia Otis Skinner on one door, Helen Hays on the other. Each was a two-room suite, with a bath. Ford's had two sinks, Carter's only one. A New York newspaper carried the headline: "President Leading Carter in Sinks, Two to One."[74] The dressing rooms were decorated by Gimbels department store. In Carter's suite, a large glass jar held peanuts. For Ford, a similar bowl held hard candies—or "boiled lollies," as an Australian journalist described them during a press tour.

The afternoon before the debate, the candidates and their handlers came to the theater to check things out. Carter walked to the building from a hotel two blocks away. Ford was driven there in the presidential limousine, with motorcycle escort ahead and Secret Service car and press buses behind. The candidates' representatives, Carruthers and Jagoda, had been in the pool truck to check out the lighting the night before, but they visited it again with Bernstein to take another look.

The off-white carpeted set wall was lit with both white and blue lights, so that the amount of blue—a color that complements flesh tones—could be adjusted. There was some disagreement. The Carter people, as they would throughout the debates, wanted the background to be less blue—or warmer, as they put it. The Ford handlers wanted it to be more blue. Imero Fiorentino now became "the mediator in the blue background division." As Fiorentino described it: "The blueness of the background changed all the time. Now, if there was anything that was of interest to the candidates' representatives, and befuddled me to death, it was the blue background, because one wanted a lot of blue, and one—God knows why—naturally didn't want it blue . . . that was one of the big challenges."[75] The background was the bluest in Philadelphia, but blue, bluer, discussions continued in San Francisco, Houston, and Williamsburg, and Fiorentino's act got better all the time.

Fiorentino told the authors that lighting wasn't his main usefulness to the League. He was intensely aware of the attention that air conditioning, makeup, and lighting had received in 1960. Fiorentino's professionalism was the League's insurance that problems encountered in the 1960 debates would not recur. "What does an Imme do? . . . Both of the candidates' reps knew me personally, they knew me by reputation. And I gave the thing they hired me for in the first place, and that was the easing of the pressure—being there."[76]

If blue was something for the candidates' representatives to chew on, the stools on the stage were something for them to gnash their teeth over. Back at the marathon nit-pick session between the League and the candidates' representatives, the question of sitting or standing had taken hours. It wasn't settled yet. Carruthers says that President Ford told him he didn't want the stool behind his lectern. At the audio-visual checkout, Carruthers introduced Jack Sameth to the president, and told him Ford wanted the stool removed.

Said Sameth: "I guess it was in the afterglow of meeting the president of the United States that I did say to a stagehand, 'Strike the president's stool.' I did it, not thinking of all those arguments and discussions about parity on the stage. . . . If Carter had a stool, the president had to have one. There was a large argument following that."[77] There certainly was. Jagoda walked onto the stage, found that the stool was missing, and raised the roof.[78] Karayn tried unsuccessfully to sooth him. Jagoda demanded that Carruthers be called back for an explanation. Carruthers says, "I got about thirteen phone calls in forty-five minutes."[79] Jagoda says he accused Carruthers of reneging on an agreement. Carruthers told Jagoda he just took his instructions from his boss. They shouted at each other and at Karayn: "How could the League be so treacherous?" Sameth tried to calm them by assuming the blame, but that didn't quiet matters. Jagoda demanded that the stool be put back, and Karayn told Carruthers to do so.

Carruthers relates that he went back to the theater before the debate. "There was nobody in the theater except a lonely stagehand. He told me he couldn't put the stool back because an hour ago the advisor to the president had ordered it taken off. I told him, 'I am the advisor to the president, and I'm asking you to put it back.' Well, he picked that stool up like it was the crown jewels of England, and placed it gently and carefully behind the lectern." The stool made one more move. Just before the debate, Ford signaled Carruthers to remove the stool. Carruthers picked it up and moved it back away from Ford, not off the riser, but near the center of almost every two-shot from the stage right camera throughout the debate.[80]

The order in which the candidates would speak was determined by a coin-flip the day before. It turned out that Carter would get the first question and Ford would go last for the closing statement. The flip also determined that the order would be reversed for the final debate in Williamsburg. (In San Francisco, they flipped again and there Carter won and went first.) The members of the questioners' panel drew lots to see who would ask the first question, and that task went to Frank Reynolds of ABC.[81]

Thirty minutes before the broadcast, PBS asked Bernstein to put up a picture of the stage from the back of the theater to be used in their pre-debate program. He did so, and Karayn objected. Karayn was under the impression that no pool video would be aired prior to the debate. Bernstein didn't remember any such agreement and went along with the PBS request.

In an age of transistors and digital electronics, the first debate was started with a procedure reminiscent of getting a small-town broadcast of a high-school football game on the air. Again, because of concerns over collusion, the stage manager could not cue moderator Ed Newman to start, and the pool refused to give the League any of their synchronized clocks.

Says Sameth: "I had to cue from an old clock the theater had hanging in the green room. I checked it out with the telephone time service, to find out how far off it was." Sameth couldn't talk to the pool truck, nor to Ed Newman, but he could talk to the timer in the wings offstage. Sitting next to Sameth was the pool assistant director, who could talk to the pool truck.

Sameth described what ensued: "I had to yell down 10-9-8 . . . looking at the clock in the green room . . . loud enough so that the pool could hear it over their intercom to the truck . . . and the timer repeated my countdown into her line to Ed Newman. By this unbelievable, nonprofessional way, Ed Newman did speak his first words exactly on time."[82]

The Audio Failure

The program began at 9:30 P.M. The candidates fielded the panel's questions, and their words and images went out to an audience of some 85 million persons in the United States. The theater audience listened quietly, as they had been instructed. Bernstein became concerned about how hot it might be on the stage. Jimmy Carter perspired noticeably, and Bernstein was on the intercom to Sameth with suggestions about boosting the air conditioning. Otherwise, everything was rolling along smoothly. Bernstein recalled: "The best moment was when Newman said 'We're running short of time and we're going to modify the format in order to get another sequence of questions in.' The feeling at that point was that everything had gone lovely, gone very well, and we had something to be proud of."

A few minutes after the best moment, one of the worst moments in the history of American broadcasting hit Bernstein and everyone else. At 10:51:05,[83] just as Jimmy Carter said:

Well, one of the very serious things that happened in our government
in recent years, and has continued up until now, is a breakdown in
the trust among our people, and, the . . .[84]

the sound failed.

There were several loud hums and pops. Carter's lips were moving, and for about 25 seconds he was seen to continue talking. Within 35 seconds he had

132   **THE GREAT DEBATES**

stopped. The screen showed both candidates frozen in their positions on the stage, the panel members in front of them. Various silent shots of the candidates and others continued for 27 minutes and 2 seconds.[85]

The sound from the stage microphones traveled to a small table offstage left, where two portable mixers and a sound technician controlled the levels. There were two microphones for each of the speakers. The cables for each mike went into a different mixer, i.e., Carter mike one went to mixer A, Carter mike two went to mixer B. This is standard backup procedure.

From the stage mixers, cables carried the sound to an audio booth in the rear of the theater where they were plugged into a distribution amplifier. From that distribution amplifier, the pool truck and all of the subscribers—radio and TV networks, independent stations, Voice of America, foreign broadcasters, and the house public address system—received their sound. From that point a subscriber, such as CBS-TV, would run a line to its nearby remote truck, and from there to the Philadelphia telephone company, which relayed it to New York for network distribution.[86]

On such occasions, it is not uncommon for the networks to be very cautious and to put in further backup systems of their own. In fact, CBS-TV had such a backup. They ran a separate line from the pool truck to their remote truck.[87]

With no sound coming from the theater, everyone involved picked up a telephone or a private line headphone and started calling everyone else. It was a nightmare. To one of the authors, stationed near the radio pool in the press center, it sounded like this:

"This is ABC New York, we've lost sound . . ."
"This is NBC New York, we're not getting sound . . ."
"This is CBS New York, we've lost sound . . ."

"Elliot, this is George Murray, what's going on . . ."
"I have no idea what's going on . . ."

In the audio booth, activity even more frantic was taking place. The sound engineers were checking everything. Phillip Levens, ABC director of TV operations, dashed from the pool truck to the booth. Or, tried to dash. It took him more than 5 minutes to cover about 250 feet. He had to go through several Secret Service check points, and people were milling around. He walked across the back of the stage to check first with the stage audio operator. He was assured that the trouble wasn't there. When he got to the booth, he had a pretty good idea where the trouble was, and he found the engineers taking the distribution amplifier apart.

Engineers checked each of the audio circuits, one at a time. With all twenty-four of them inspected and with no improvement, it was obvious that something common to the whole distribution system had failed. They thought it might have been the power supply, but checking that did not help. A backup battery power system showed an electrical overload. "It was obvious," Levens said, "that there was a short across the power supply. This process of elimination should have caught the thing within minutes, and repaired it. Why it didn't we'll never know, but it didn't. So then we started concentrating our efforts on finding another way to get the program going again."[88]

No one is sure just how long this process took. Elsewhere in the theater it must have seemed like years. The candidates were still standing at their places. Moderator Ed Newman told the authors: "Neither Carter nor Ford spoke to the other. I talked to them, over and over again, telling them what was going on, or what wasn't going on. They were very cooperative, and neither seemed to get upset by what was happening. I asked them if they wanted to sit down, but neither did."

Newman also said he was glad to find out that he couldn't talk to the broadcast audience either. "For a moment," he said, "I thought Carter's mike had failed, but I knew they had double mikes so that didn't make much sense. I thought my mike was still on, so I started to ad-lib something about how there had been a failure. I don't think I've ever been in a situation as sticky as that . . . because I immediately thought to myself, what in God's name am I going to talk about. I can't talk about what they've said . . . or review it . . . or evaluate it, since I'm the moderator and supposed to be impartial."

Off stage, Karayn and Sameth were worrying about how to get started again. They knew there would be critical legal questions raised if the debate were not finished because of the broadcast interruption. At the same time, they expected the sound to be restored at any minute. Karayn recalls moving back and forth between the command post and the stage. On stage, he told Newman that the debate would be finished even if the broadcast was not resumed. He talked to Bernstein in the pool truck and got into a row. "Jim began having a long and heated dialogue with me," Bernstein remembered. "He wanted to begin the debate for the people in the theater and said that we should turn our cameras off. I said, you do whatever you want, we are not going to turn these cameras off, if you want to resume the debate, resume the debate."[89]

Karayn later said: "The only thing I could have thought there was the embarrassment of seeing two presidential candidates with their lips moving, with a conversation going on, and questions being asked . . . the world seeing that there was no sound."[90]

According to Sameth, Karayn also asked for exteriors or wide shots during the period the candidates were standing mute on stage, "so that the candidates could mop their brows, or be at ease."[91] Bernstein says he doesn't recall that request, but does remember watching the separate network pictures in the pool truck, and noting that the networks were not using the pool pictures from the stage very much of the time. (They were showing pictures of their correspondents interviewing people in the lobby, analyzing the debate up to that point, and making dark jokes about the audio failure.) Karayn also wanted the theater PA system restored, so that the debate could continue at least there. He made several trips to talk to the on-stage audio man. He was told first that the PA could not be restored, and later, close to the time audio was restored, that the audio engineers would try to get it back for him.[92] Bernstein, outside in the truck, never realized that the PA system wasn't working.

In the balcony, League president Ruth Clusen was getting her share of advice. Witnesses say that Theodore White, a steering committee member, became very upset that Carter and Ford were just standing on the stage. He and others told Clusen she should do something about it. Says Clusen, "The gen-

"There's your camera, Mr. President." In Philadelphia during the audio-visual check ABC pool producer Elliot Bernstein (pointing) shows President Ford where to look. William Carruthers is at the left and Mark Goode is between him and the president. Facing Ford is ABC-TV director Richard Armstrong. (*Courtesy of William Carruthers*)

"Is that my camera, Mr. Jagoda?" Barry Jagoda and vice-presidential candidate Walter Mondale on the stage of the Alley Theater in Houston during the audio-visual check for the third debate. (*Courtesy of League of Women Voters*)

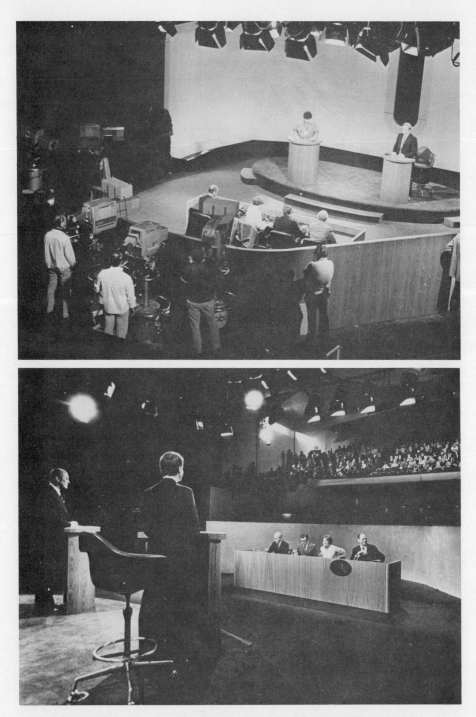

Two perspectives in Philadelphia. TOP: a rehearsal, with stand-ins for the candidates but with the real press panel, seen from the balcony of the Walnut Street Theater. (*Courtesy of League of Women Voters*) BOTTOM: a view of the candidates, press panel, cameras, and theater audience from backstage during the audio outage. The wall separating the set from the audience is clearly seen in both shots. (*Courtesy of William Carruthers*)

eral thrust of it was you can't leave those candidates standing there . . . call up, exert your leadership."

So she decided to approach the candidates' representatives about taking Ford and Carter offstage to wait it out. "When I went," she said, "it was like lemmings to the sea, they all followed me."[93]

Clusen, Minow, Walker, Rita Hauser, and perhaps others, went backstage, but the group found there really wasn't anything they could do but agree that the debates should continue as long as the candidates wanted them to. And they returned to their seats.

Backstage, the candidates' representatives were also wringing their hands. The candidates' campaign staffs met and worked out an agreement that when the debate resumed, Carter would finish his interrupted answer to a question about controlling U.S. intelligence agencies, and then both men would make closing statements.

There was a rule that the candidates' representatives could not be on the stage during the debates, but both Carruthers and Jagoda went to the wings and encouraged their man with hand signals and smiles. The two sides also discussed whether they would take Carter and Ford offstage and agreed they would not, unless there was no way to continue.

As the time dragged on, Carruthers and Rafshoon decided they ought to go out onto the set and explain to Ford and Carter what was happening and what was going to happen. As Carruthers relates it, Rafshoon was tying his tie in preparation for going on stage when the audio returned.[94]

The sound came back because the engineers simply twisted some wires together. In the audio booth in the back of the theater they took the wire from the stage mixer, and wrapped it together with a wire going to the pool truck, by-passing entirely the disabled distribution amplifier. They did this because CBS had run a backup line from its truck directly to the pool truck. In the radio pool, about 20 minutes into the failure, one of the authors heard:

"I understand CBS local has a unilateral audio line and is monitoring something in their truck. Yes. Well, tell them to feed it to New York. They say they will."

<blockquote>

CBS, New York: I only hear background noise.
   Voice: That's the noise in the hall,
      That's what we're hearing too.
      That's what you're supposed to hear . . .
      Do you hear Newman?
CBS, New York: Yes
   Voice: O.K. Well feed it out straight.
CBS, New York: Now, we've got it. All nets, do you get it?
    ABC: Yes.
    NBC: Yes.
    CBS: Yes.
   Voice: O.K., we're cuing Newman.

</blockquote>

Twisting those wires together got the sound to the pool truck, and from there, by way of the CBS backup line, to the CBS truck, and from there, to the telephone company and to New York. Levens said: "I'm not certain we even got the wires taped, I think we said, 'Don't touch it, it's working.' "[95]

The broadcast resumed at about the same time that the League had decided to continue the debate, broadcast or not, public address system or not.

None of the principals realized it had been 27 minutes. As Carruthers said: "We were frozen in time, we were suspended . . . there was nothing anybody could do."[96] Nerves were stretched tight after all this. Bernstein remembers getting into a shouting match with Karayn about pictures of the action on the stage after the debate ended. Bernstein said that Karayn got on an intercom line and told him to turn his cameras off. There had been an agreement that the pool would not take shots that might embarrass the candidates, such as someone pulling up a shirttail to take the microphones off. But they had also agreed that the cameras would follow incidents of editorial interest. Bernstein thought Karayn was violating that agreement. While they argued, Carter and Ford shook hands; the pool missed the shot, and the TV audience didn't get to see it. Karayn says it was not he who talked to Bernstein. Bernstein says it could have been Sameth—it was the end of a very long day.

Bernstein and the pool were now part of the debate story. He said there must have been at least fifty television people gathered around the truck. "I was so surrounded by television people," Bernstein recalls, "I was seriously trying to figure out a way to hook the van onto the cab and drive it back to New York."[97]

The next day network newscasters displayed the part that had failed—a shiny, foil-wrapped capacitor worth twenty-five cents. President Ford invited Bernstein and Pfister for coffee in the morning, and he told them he understood it wasn't their fault. Carter communicated with them, too. He told them that, coming from an engineering background, he knew how technical problems could develop.

"I was very depressed," Bernstein recalled. "For a couple of weeks after that I really felt awful. The meeting with the President was like taking two aspirin, I felt better for about two hours . . . but this is the American Broadcasting Company, the network of the Olympics . . . sending pictures back from the top of the Alps."[98]

Summary of First Debate

DATE: September 23, 1976, 9:30 P.M., EDT
PLACE: Walnut Street Theater, Philadelphia, Pennsylvania
PRODUCER: Pool—ABC, Elliot Bernstein
DIRECTOR: Richard "Ace" Armstrong, ABC
DESIGNER: Robert Wightman
LIGHTING: Fiorentino Associates/Everett Melosh, ABC
MAKEUP: For Carter, Joe Cranzano; for Ford, Harry Blake
TIMING: Production assistant Merrily Mossman operated the timers. Karayn made the decisions about adding to or cutting the questions sequences. Professional debate timers were on hand as neutral arbiters for any timing controversy.
TECHNICAL SUPERVISOR: Pool—Joe Debonis, ABC

PRODUCTION COORDINATOR FOR LEAGUE: Jack Sameth

MODERATOR: Edwin Newman, NBC

PANELISTS: Frank Reynolds, ABC; Elizabeth Drew, *New Yorker*; James Gannon, *Wall Street Journal*

FORMAT: Domestic and economic issues, 90 minutes. Answers to questions, up to three minutes. Answers to optional follow-up questions limited to two minutes. Comment by opposing candidate, limited to two minutes. Closing statements, limited to three minutes. Candidates could not use scripted comments or notes, but could take notes and refer to them during the debates.

PROGRAM ANALYSIS

OPENING: Pool (video only). Exterior, Walnut Street Theater Long shot of stage from balcony, candidates on set Carter left, Ford right—audience in lower foreground. Cut to closer two-shot of candidates on stage, press panel in lower foreground. Cut to two-shot, Carter in foreground. Cut to two-shot, Ford in foreground. Cut to four-shot from backstage camera showing press panel, zooms and pans to Newman. At 01:00, Newman speaks.

SHOTS: Armstrong used four basic one-shots; the tightest showed the candidates' shirt-collar points: Others ranged from the candidates' hands on top of the lectern, to the bottom of the candidates' coat lapels, to the top of the microphone tie-clip.

REACTIONS: There were side and front reaction shots, which tended to be loose. The side two-shots in particular revealed a great deal of empty center. The two-shot with Carter in the foreground usually showed Ford's stool in the center of the frame. There were also shots taken from the center front camera which showed some or all of the press panel in the foreground and the two candidates in the background. These were more like re-establishing shots, since they did not show facial expressions or reactions by the candidates. There were also one-shot reactions from the side cameras. These were loose; Carter often appeared ill at ease and looking straight ahead rather than at Ford.

COMMENTS: The director's cutting was conservative, slow paced, and reflected the restraint of the candidates. It was a rather formal and stiff 90 minutes. There were 11 reaction shots of Carter for a total of 2:20, and 13 of Ford for a total of 2:38.

CANDIDATES' TOTAL SPEAKING TIME: 71:53. Ford—37:14. Carter 34:39.

San Francisco

From the beginning, the League's intention had been to hold the debates at various sites around the country, at locations with some historic importance. Philadelphia had been a natural choice for the bicentennial year. San Francisco was selected for the second debate largely because the subject was to be foreign policy, and San Francisco had been the scene of the signing of the United Nations Charter in 1945. For a time the League considered holding the second debate in the building where the signing had taken place, the War Memorial Auditorium. Before the Philadelphia debate, Jack Sameth had gone to San Francisco to look at it. Sameth reported that there were serious lighting problems and that the site would be barely adequate. After a second inspection, by CBS pool producer Jack Kelly and Bill Klages, the War Memorial was ruled out.

Following the first debate Sameth left the League to return to his job as a producer for WNET, New York, and Mike Pengra, took his place as League production supervisor. Pengra, who had worked with Karayn previously, was brought in two days before the Philadelphia debate to observe that one, and to coordinate the rest. Pengra had been a producer-director of television films in commercial and educational broadcasting and for the USIA. He worked on political campaigns as a free-lance producer, and as a writer for television and film companies around Washington, D.C., and is now vice-president and co-owner of Eli Productions in the capital.

Pengra went to San Francisco almost immediately to look for a place to stage the second debate. It had been suggested that he look at a theater in the Palace of Fine Arts, a building originally constructed for the Panama-Pacific Exposition of 1915. Armored tanks had been stored in the building during World War II. In the 1950s it had been restored, and a theater had been constructed at one end of the long, cavernous, curved structure.

Pengra arrived in the middle of the night, and met with theater personnel in the early dawn hours. He was concerned that the theater was not air conditioned, but was told what all visitors to San Francisco are told: that the whole city is naturally air conditioned. Refreshing bay air was pumped inside the building at night, and it remained cool through the day. Pengra may have had some reservations about this civic salesmanship, but time was pressing, and on September 28 the Palace of Fine Arts theater was announced as the site for the second debate.[99]

The CBS pool producer was Jack Kelly. He had fifteen years with CBS behind him, about seven years as a producer. Like the others, Kelly's forte was special events. He had done major pool coverage for political conventions, space shots, overseas presidential trips, and the spring primary elections.

During the week, Kelly and the pool worried about parking and arranged for a light grid to be built and installed. But by the weekend before the debate new problems developed. The weather wasn't cooperating; an early fall warm front moved in and stayed. Now all that assurance that there was no need for air conditioning began to disappear. Pengra, Kelly, and Klages held a meeting on the stage seventy-two hours before Carter and Ford would face each other again, and they decided to put in air conditioning.

The stage at the Palace of Fine Arts is large, and the job of cooling it was a big one. Air-conditioning contractors were called in. One suggested renting the kind of air-conditioner used to cool off jet airplanes as they sit at airport gates. That turned out to be prohibitively expensive. Another suggested putting 10-ton units outside, and piping the cooler air onto the stage through flexible duct-work. That was expensive too, but San Francisco's mayor and public relations people came to the rescue, working out an arrangement to cover the cost, helped by a donation from a member of the Magnin department-store family.[100]

After the audio failure in Philadelphia, CBS was not about to have anything like it happen to them. Elaborate backup systems were installed for virtually every phase of the production. The audio had backups to the backup. CBS used two separate systems—mixers and separate distribution amplifiers—and backed them with a third. The League hired a San Francisco firm to run the public address system. In the event that all three of the broadcast sound setups failed, they had separate PA microphones ready to be rushed on stage for the candidates and the press panel.

The pool lighting director, Bill Schelling, used the basic Fiorentino plot, but with a few changes to get a little more modeling on the candidates' faces. The day before the debate, CBS had some problems with overheated dimmers. Spares were brought in, and the broadcast was not affected. Special precautions were taken to make sure there wouldn't be a power failure during the debates. The San Francisco power company could switch from one source to another, and CBS brought in a large portable generator that could handle everything except the air conditioning. They even practiced switching from city power to the generator three or four times.[101] CBS backed up the video switcher with one that could handle at least five of the nine cameras, in the outlandish event that the main one quit during the broadcast. To be quadruply sure, each network ran a separate audio line to the CBS pool truck, and CBS ordered a separate audio circuit from the pool truck all the way across the country to New York, in case the primary circuit failed.[102]

Kelly was apprehensive, but was glad he was the producer of the second debate and not the first. "Elliot [Bernstein] really went through a grinder," Kelly commented. "I was expecting to walk into another windmill, and I had the additional pressure of the loss of audio. . . . The relationship . . . between the League and the networks was awkward . . . but it went very smoothly. . . . I was really surprised every day that things went as well as they did. Part of the pressure came from the press: 'Is it going to go wrong again, are you going to lose audio, are you going to lose video . . . what are you doing differently from ABC?' " Recalled Kelly, "I spent more time answering questions on that remote than I've ever done before in my life. . . . Every time I turned around, somebody was asking the same question . . . 'What are you doing differently?' "[103]

Many problems had been solved in Philadelphia. The intercom and audio-video feed arrangements were the same, and there was no argument about them. The timing devices were mounted on the cameras as a matter of course. Stagehands hired by the League were there again to hold up cue cards if the electric timers went out.

There were two minor set changes. A small riser was placed under the chairs of the questioners' panel, so that the candidates would not have to look down as far to talk to the panel members, and thus could play to the cameras more easily. The candidates' riser was moved back one foot.

The low wall between the stage and the audience was still there. Besides, at the request and expense of the White House staff, a new wall, eight feet tall and about 100 feet long, was built across the back of the stage. Since the theater dressing rooms and office area were not separated from the stage, the wall was built to shut them off and block out noise.[104]

Getting the air conditioning in and working wasn't quite as easy. Two days before the debate, Pengra arranged for the system to be put in, and contractors dashed off to build it. The air-conditioning units were positioned outside the theater next to the wall. Large flexible ducts, looking like elephant trunks, wound their way onto the stage and the debate set, where they were suspended from the light grid and aimed at the lecterns.

Twenty-four hours before the debate, the system was running. There was no way to air-condition the whole theater, but, the contractors said, they could cool the area where the candidates would stand to between 60 and 70 degrees. Pengra said the contractors told him: "You can walk on stage tomorrow morning, and you're going to love it." But, Pengra couldn't sleep that night. Around 4:00 A.M. he got a call from a theater official, who said that he couldn't sleep either. He was on the stage with the air-conditioner running. He said the temperature was 75, with no lights on and no equipment running. Pengra went to the theater, and the two of them got a ladder and lowered the ducts six to eight feet. "It was just like a water hose," Pengra said. "By God it was cool, it went down to 67 just like that!" Later that day the ducts were adjusted so they wouldn't blow directly on the candidates. During the audio-visual check Pengra told Ford and Carter that if they got too warm during the debate they could just step a foot or so from behind their lecterns and stand under the main jets of cool air—like taking a shower.[105]

The day before there had been reheasals all afternoon with stand-ins on the set. Mark Brand of the Carter campaign staff took the governor's place, and Roger McPike, a San Francisco attorney and Republican worker, stood in for Ford. McPike "debated" well. He told the authors he did a lot of campaign speaking in the Bay area. He spoke knowledgeably about defense and foreign policy in answer to questions fired at him by stand-in panelists.

Kelly also had two sessions with the real panel of questioners. They came in around noon the day of the debate and returned about two hours before the debate to rehearse the opening of the program.

Because of the time difference the debate would go on the air at 6:30 P.M. San Francisco time. The candidates had come to the theater for the AV check that morning. Carter arrived at 10:45. He walked around the stage, shook hands with the crew, and was led over to the audio mixers, where CBS engineers solemnly explained the very carefully backed up system. Gerry Rafshoon and Carter went to his lectern, where they rehearsed various ways to stand and look at the Ford side of the stage.

Ford came to the theater after Carter had left. The president talked a bit, checked the location of his main camera, and told the press pool that these debates "were getting to be old stuff; I feel like a winner." Ford also practiced a few lectern gestures, including various positions for his hands on its top and sides. As he left, the crew members came around to shake his hand.

During the AV check, "blue" again became a controversial color. Jagoda and Rafshoon started the discussion by asking for no blue, just the white lights on the off-white set. Fiorentino talked them into some blue light, and he got Jagoda to agree that if the Ford people wanted more blue, he could raise it higher. When Bill Carruthers arrived with Ford, he immediately asked for more blue. So, Fiorentino turned it up. He'd found the middle range acceptable to both sides. He told the authors: "I went to each guy and I said, 'Remember the blue (or white) you saw that you didn't want . . . well, I didn't go that far. But, I went up a little bit from the blue (or white) that you did want. And, I'm doing the same for the other.' That made them very happy." "Of course," he added, "we're worrying about things that don't matter. . . . People tune

"If this one doesn't work, it's backed up by two others." During the audio-visual check in San Francisco Jimmy Carter is shown one of three CBS audio mixing systems by engineer Neal Weinstein. (*Courtesy of League of Women Voters*)

"It's always delightfully cool in San Francisco . . . ," especially if technicians work around the clock to install a temporary air-conditioning system. Cool air is pumped in through the flexible pipes hanging from the grid. (*Courtesy of League of Women Voters*)

"Dear Jimmy . . ." While standing in for her husband's opponent during President Ford's audio-visual check in Williamsburg, Betty Ford writes a note to Jimmy Carter. (*White House photo*)

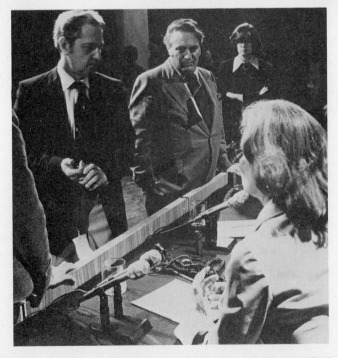

Making it happen in Williamsburg. NBC director Frank Slingland and debate project director Jim Karayn chat with moderator Barbara Walters. (*Courtesy of League of Women Voters*)

their sets all over the place. My mother said the backdrop was green in Phila-delphia. I didn't have the heart to ask her what the faces looked like."[106]

Shortly before 6:30 P.M., the temperature was about 85 degrees where the audience was; it was cooler on the stage with the air conditioning.

The candidates' dressing rooms had been decorated with different but equal furniture and fittings gathered from ten San Francisco firms. There were potted palms and citrus trees, chrysanthemums, glass-topped tables, rattan chairs, and carved elephant benches. A press release from a San Francisco public relations firm said the objective was a "come-right-in, non-decorated look."

The program got on the air, and the debate started in a much more pro-fessional manner. This time, the separation of League and pool was almost wiped out. Pengra got the countdown from the pool truck, where they knew exactly what time it was. It was relayed to the timer, and she cued the mod-erator. It was almost like twentieth-century television.

Summary of Second Debate

DATE: October 6, 1976, 9:30 P.M., EDT

PLACE: Palace of Fine Arts, San Francisco

PRODUCER: Pool—CBS, Jack Kelly

DIRECTOR: Arthur Bloom, CBS

LIGHTING: Fiorentino Associates, Bill Schelling, CBS

DESIGNER, MAKEUP; TIMING: Same as for first debate

TECHNICAL SUPERVISOR: Pool—Brooks Graham, CBS

PRODUCTION COORDINATOR: Mike Pengra, League of Women Voters

MODERATOR: Pauline Frederick, NPR

PANELISTS: Richard Valeriani, NBC; Henry Trewhitt, *Baltimore Sun*; Max Frankel, *New York Times*

FORMAT: Foreign and defense issues, 90 minutes. Timing, rules, rotation, clos-ing statements—same as first debate.

PROGRAM ANALYSIS

OPENING: Pool (video only)

Exterior, outside Palace of Fine Arts, reflecting pond in foreground. Cut to long shot of stage from back of theater showing empty seats in center frame. Cut to side shot of panel, Frankel in foreground. Cut to stage right two-shot, Ford in foreground. Cut to center camera two-shot, panel in foreground. Cut to medium shot of Pauline Frederick.

SHOTS: Bloom used both wider and tighter one-shots than were used in the first debate. The tightest showed just the top of the candidates' necktie knots.

REACTIONS: Bloom took more one-shot reaction shots of Carter and Ford, and they were tighter. The side two-shots were tight with little empty space in the center of the frame. The tightest side two-shot usually occurred when Carter was seated on his stool. Re-establishing shots from the front included either two or four members of the panel in the foreground.

COMMENT: Bloom worked for relationship shots from both the front and back of the stage, showing the candidate with a panel member asking a question. He also took single shots of the candidates while they were listening to the questions. He used slow zooms both in and out while the candidates were answering.

Like Don Hewitt, CBS director sixteen years earlier, Bloom took a free-wheeling approach. His shooting and cutting matched the more lively, and at times, heated, second debate. He re-positioned his side cameras during the broadcast to trim and tighten two-shots. There were 27 reaction shots of Carter for a total of 2:31, and 29 of Ford for 2:35.

CANDIDATES' TOTAL SPEAKING TIME: 73:26. Ford—36:32. Carter—36:54.

Houston: The Vice-Presidential Candidates on Stage

The one truly new element in the 1976 debates was the debate between the vice-presidential candidates. Long before the League's negotiations with the candidates, it had been a solid conviction of some League executives that there should be a meeting between the number two men on each side. The reasoning was sound: three vice-presidents had become president since 1945. It became something of a special project for League executive director Peggy Lampl. "It was," she said, "my suggestion. I said one day at a meeting, 'We ought to have a vice-presidential debate, given the recent history.' The reception at the beginning in the steering committee was an overwhelming bore. But we just plugged away. The candidates had no confidence in it, but I think both sides grew to assume that it would happen, and that actual negotiations would be left to the vice-presidential candidates."[107]

There does not seem to have been any serious objection to a vice-presidential debate at the general negotiation sessions with the Ford and Carter representatives in late August. It is clear that the Democrats were more favorable to the idea than the Republicans, although they did not press the point very hard.[108] The Republicans, including vice-presidential candidate Robert Dole, almost ridiculed the idea during the debates period, and criticized it roundly after the elections. On the campaign trail Dole had frequently said that the voters were more interested in going to Friday night high-school football games than in listening to the vice-presidential candidates debate. He frequently referred to the event as the "Doyle and Mundale" debates, suggesting that many people didn't even know the names of the candidates. On the day of the debate, Dole said he would rather have had the four or five days' preparation time to spend campaigning.

After it was over, Raoul-Duval said the vice-presidential debate had been a very bad idea. Duval told the authors: "It never should have occurred. We didn't want to come right out and say it; we would have been accused of being unfair and not playing the game. It was unrealistic; they were not going to talk issues, so it was a question of who was better at using the TV medium. It's back in a dark corner somewhere, where I hope it will disappear and people will forget about it."[109]

It wasn't as easy to put together as the rather casual assumption the League made in its invitation to Ford and Carter. When the debates were set up, the vice-presidential candidates were not issued a personal invitation. Jim Karayn said that the invitation went to the presidential candidates only, "because we knew, obviously, they [the vice-presidential candidates] could not accept without getting it from the boss."[110] Peggy Lampl said the veep negotiations were more difficult than those involving the top of the ticket. The length of the debate, the subject matter, the site, were all topics for discussion. Karayn's first idea was to hold it in the Midwest, because both men were from the area. He later suggested that both the vice-presidential debate and the last presidential debate be held in Williamsburg, Virginia, to save money and time. But in a conference call between Karayn and the two men's aides, the idea of taking it to Atlanta came up. Dole's side strongly favored debating in the South. The Mondale staff was at first suspicious that carrying the debate into Carter's home territory was a Republican political ploy, but they warmed to the plan. A survey trip to Atlanta was made, but no theater was available.[111]

Senator Dole's people suggested changing the set. They were concerned that Senator Dole would not be able to stand and write for a long period because of his damaged arm. Dole's representatives also suggested that the vice-presidential candidates be seated to distinguish this debate from the presidential ones. Karayn was receptive to simple changes that didn't involve new construction: the vice-presidential candidates could debate in front of a black curtain or choose different furniture, if they wished.

Regarding the format, the Dole people had suggested an unstructured one-hour period, with answers limited to one minute; the Mondale side wanted a session of 90 minutes and longer answers. The Democrats also urged organization of the questions into topic areas. Karayn continued to advocate a face-to-face format, as he had throughout the debates period.

A compromise finally evolved. The debate was set for 75 minutes. Answers were limited to two-and-a-half minutes, with the first respondent to have one minute for rebuttal. Opening and closing statements were to be two and three minutes, respectively. The debating period was to be divided equally among three areas: domestic issues, foreign issues, and questions on any subject. New York Senator Jacob Javits, an advisor to Dole, made two contributions to the agreement. He suggested that the VP debate be held in Houston, Texas, and he convinced the negotiators that it would be all right to have it on Friday, October 15, which was the end of Sukkoth, a Jewish holiday.[112] It had taken ten days to settle the arrangements.

In Houston, the League chose the Alley Theater, one of the country's first resident professional theaters. Built in 1968, it had all the advantages of a modern house, among them, an arena with a thrust stage and plenty of lighting control. In addition, a main power company distribution point was located under the building.

The set, trucked in from California, had to be modified to fit on the Alley stage. The walls were compressed on the sides, and the questioners' panel was moved about four feet closer to the candidates. The painted linoleum floor-covering was no longer usable, after being put down and taken up twice. So, the stage floor was painted black.

The Alley Theater provided an intimacy for the audience that the other debate sites didn't have. Even though the wall was still in the way, the steep rake of the house seats put the audience much closer to the action.

The other unique aspect of the Houston broadcast was that the production for the pool was done by the Public Broadcasting Service. It was the first time PBS had produced for a national network pool. As a network, PBS had no central headquarters production center. A staff and equipment had to be pulled together from stations that were part of the network. WNET, New York, and WETA, Washington, provided the operators and supervisors. The equipment was rented from public station WGBY, Springfield, Massachusetts, and from Continental Television, a New Jersey-based firm. The two remote trucks had been used before to originate PBS's "Live from Lincoln Center" broadcasts.

Wallace Westfeldt had been assigned as the pool producer. He had come to public television in January 1976 after fifteen years with NBC News as a reporter and producer. Much of his time had been spent on the "Huntley-Brinkley Report" and "NBC Nightly News." He became director of news and public affairs and senior executive producer at WETA, Washington.

To Westfeldt, forming a production team and doing the broadcast as a PBS pool effort were among the most interesting aspects of his assignment. Westfeldt wanted to see if it could be done by putting together a composite crew from New York and Washington. Lighting installation was simple. PBS used the house system with a portable backup dimmer unit. A special PA system was brought in, and the audio setup was given an extensive back up similar to that used in San Francisco. There were no serious technical problems in getting ready for the debate. Still, PBS wasn't taking any chances. Cables were carefully waterproofed the day before the debate. Director Bob Wynn staged disaster drills in anticipation of every conceivable audio and video problem.

Rehearsals were held the day of the debate, but they were much shorter than previously. During the AV checks with the vice-presidential candidates, Mondale and his staff arrived first. There was a lot of joking and informal talk. Mondale said he had played tennis that morning. Mondale and Barry Jagoda worked for a time on eye contact with the cameras. There was some practice with answers to questions, but Mondale seemed impatient with this and it was cut short after he said, "That's enough," several times.

The Dole group had technical and staging questions. A severe wound during World War II had rendered Senator Dole's right arm almost useless. To accommodate him, the senator's lectern was raised about two inches and turned toward the center of the stage and Mondale.[113] This allowed Dole to lean on the podium with his left arm and to support his right arm with his left hand. Dole used this stance frequently throughout his campaign.

For the first time, a member of the candidate's family was involved in the AV check. Elizabeth Dole had accompanied her husband to the theater. Dole asked if he would be able to see the audience during the debate, fearing that it might be a distraction. He was told he would not see them, and the house lights were lowered. But, he still seemed concerned about it, so Mrs. Dole went out into the house, and more lights were turned off. The senator looked at Mrs. Dole for awhile and seemed satisfied that the problem had been solved. Dole did not practice questions and answers. When the press pool came in, Mrs. Dole posed with him for still pictures. The lighting adjustments regarding "blue" were minimal this time. Westfeldt says Jagoda wanted the set wall made bluer, but there wasn't the long colloquy about it that had taken place elsewhere. At the start of the program, cuing had become very simplified. As in any broadcast, the stage director cued moderator Jim Hoge, and the program began.

On the air, and in the theater the Houston debate was the most trouble-free. Summing it up, Westfeldt said: "It was really sort of cut and dried . . . it's fun to do live programs: the adrenalin flows."

Summary of Third Debate

DATE: October 15, 1976, 9:30 P.M., EDT
PLACE: Alley Theater, Houston, Texas
PRODUCER: Pool—PBS, Wallace Westfeldt
DIRECTOR: Bob Wynn, freelance
LIGHTING: Fiorentino Associates; Stan Alpert, Paul Siatta for pool
DESIGNER, TIMING, PRODUCTION COORDINATOR: same as in San Francisco
MAKEUP: Tom Ellingwood for Dole, Joe Cranzano for Mondale
TECHNICAL SUPERVISOR: Pool, Mal Albaum, WNET
MODERATOR: James Hoge, *Chicago Sun-Times*
PANELISTS: Hal Bruno, *Newsweek*; Marilyn Berger, NBC; Walter Mears, Associated Press.
FORMAT: Domestic, foreign, 75 minutes. Opening statements of two minutes. Questioning: answers from candidate A up to 2:30; response from candidate B, up to 2:30; rebuttal from candidate A up to 1:00. Closing statements, up to 3:00. Rules same as for presidential debates.
PROGRAM ANALYSIS
OPENING: Pool (video only). Long shot—balcony; audience and stage. Two-shot, stage right, Mondale in foreground. Panel, stage left. Long shot—balcony, zooming toward stage. Medium shot—moderator.
SHOTS: Wynn's approach was to start wide and work in tighter throughout the debate. At the beginning he used loose one-shots showing the top of the lectern or below. Both candidates used a lot of hand and arm gestures. There were no shots tighter than tie-clip until near the end of the debate, and the only tight closeups—tie knot—came during the closing statements.
REACTIONS: Many reaction shots came from the center stage camera, and included both candidates and two or three panel members, and sometimes even the moderator. Some were so wide they might be better described as re-establishing shots. Wynn also used a side two-shot showing much of Dole's back in the foreground and Mondale in the background. During one Mondale speech, Wynn took three reaction shots of Dole. He took one one-shot reaction during the entire debate: Dole for three seconds.
COMMENTS: Both candidates took extensive notes during the debate, and this action showed in the side two-shots. While most were past the speaker into the reactor in the background, Wynn frequently reversed this pattern by showing the reactor in the foreground and the speaker in the background: usually Dole was speaking. There were a couple of camera problems. In the one-shots on Dole, Wynn would start wide and zoom into a tighter shot, but on Mondale, Wynn used two cameras to get to the tight shot by starting to zoom in, cutting away to something else, like a wide shot from the center camera, then cutting back to a tighter shot. It appeared to the authors that the lens on Mondale's main camera was sticking in one part of its zoom range.

During Dole's closing statement, his main camera developed trouble, so Dole's statement was shot by another camera, which made him seem to be looking off to the left.

CANDIDATES' TOTAL SPEAKING TIME: 66:12. Dole—33:01. Mondale—33:11.

Williamsburg

In 1776 five students at the College of William and Mary met in the Raleigh Tavern in Williamsburg, Virginia, and formed Phi Beta Kappa, as they wrote, to "search out and dispell the clouds of falsehood by debating without reserve the issues of the day." In 1976, Phi Beta Kappa Hall, on the campus of William and Mary, appeared to be just the right size and shape to accommodate Carter and Ford in their last encounter, on October 22. The League opened negotiations with the college. A performance of Gilbert and Sullivan's *The Sorcerer* was rescheduled, and the arrangements were made.

William and Mary students quickly launched debate-related projects. Dorms competed to make the best banner welcoming "Gerry and Jimmy." The students threw a wine and cheese party and a volleyball game for the Secret Service and receptions for the technicians and the foreign press. They invited TV correspondents, producers, and members of the candidates' staffs to speak to classes. The state-owned liquor store laid in more supplies. A faculty member commented that the debates had little to do with the college at all, that beating Michigan at football would do more for William and Mary.[114]

A big closed-circuit television screen was installed in the eleven-thousand seat fieldhouse, and the basketball team was moved out. Phi Beta Kappa Hall received a four-thousand-dollar face lift, including new carpeting and a gilded sign on the facade. Student volunteers oiled the seats so they wouldn't squeak during the debate.

As this euphoric atmosphere grew, NBC moved in its equipment. The set was unloaded and put up for the last time, and preprogram lighting began. The set needed some retouching, but there were no serious problems. A complete lighting setup and control board were installed. As had been done since Philadelphia, the audio was doubled up and backed up. This time NBC controlled the audio from the pool truck rather than in the theater.

A bit of a scare developed when the pool and debates people learned about the sometimes erratic habits of the local power supply. No one seems to have mentioned this during the earlier site surveys, but\a couple of days before the debate NBC was told that there were sometimes power failures in the city. The NBC pool brought in a second and separate power system and actually operated from it, with the local power as a backup.[115]

The pool producer for the fourth debate was Christie Basham, another veteran of NBC. Basham had started as a production assistant in the NBC Washington bureau nineteen years earlier. She had been film-assignment editor for the network for nine years and Washington producer for "NBC Nightly News" for three years. Before the pool assignment, she had been Washington director of news operations for NBC, and she had been pool chairman on President Ford's trip to Helsinki in 1975. She had observed all three previous debates.

The atmosphere at the AV check for this debate was noticeably more tense than it had been at any of the previous events, especially on the Carter side. It

THE GREAT DEBATES

was later explained to the authors that the tension was caused mainly by the closeness of the election, eleven days away. The Carter group came on the stage all business. Carter walked right to his lectern and launched into a series of real answers to real questions put to him by his staff—about unemployment and tax reform, priorities if elected, keeping promises made during the campaign, the Arab boycott, and foreign policy. That caused a serious problem. The pictures and audio of the AV check were not supposed to be seen or heard anywhere but in the pool truck. Somehow, the sound was distributed elsewhere, including the press center at the Williamsburg Lodge.

The Carter supporters learned what had happened almost immediately, and they became very upset. Jagoda said, "I didn't want to see a wire story saying, 'Carter said in rehearsal today this, that and the other.' That becomes part of the news generating process. . . . It might have been on the evening news that night."[116] NBC quickly cut off the sound and spent the next few hours calling everyone who might have received it to tell them that it was not to be used.[117]

Fiorentino told the authors, "There was much more tension today, lots of nit-picking; all business and really tense people, it was 1960 for the first time."

In contrast Ford came in laughing and joking. Mrs. Ford was with him. They shook hands and posed for pictures with League executives. Betty Ford stood behind Carter's lectern. The president sat down on the controversial stool. Betty Ford took out a piece of paper and started to write on it.

Ford: "What are you doing, writing a note to Jimmy?"

Mrs. Ford: "Yes, I am."

After Mrs. Ford had left, press secretary Ron Nessen released the note to the press. She had wished Carter good luck, and added: "I happen to have a favorite, my husband, President Ford . . ."[118]

Ford did not have a rehearsal.

The only problem that developed the day of the debate was with the PA system in the theater. There was feedback from time to time during the afternoon, and adjustments were made. But the problem continued during the debate; the audience in Phi Beta Kappa Hall had trouble hearing the candidates.

NBC controlled the broadcast audio from the pool truck and also supplied a feed to the house PA. The League, as it had done twice before, hired a local sound company to provide the PA system for the theater audience. There was a separate mini-PA system on the stage, as there had been at the other three debates, feeding the sound from the questioners and the candidates into small speakers placed inside the candidates' lecterns and on the floor close to the press panel. This is called a mix-minus system.

There is disagreement about what caused the PA problem in Phi Beta Kappa Hall. The League accused NBC of cutting off the sound to the PA. NBC says it did not do that. NBC did tell the house PA operator that he would have to run his system at a low level. During the debate, the pool and the PA operator worked together to lower the PA each time one questioner—Bob Maynard—talked. The feedback that bothered the pool on the afternoon of the debate and caused the low-level PA that evening could have come from two sources: the house PA or the mix-minus on the stage. One or both, turned up too high or out of balance, could have caused the problem. During the ninety minutes that the debate was on the air, no one involved—producer, director, audio technician, or PA operator—was aware of the problem. They all say they learned about it after the debate or in the next morning's papers. The broadcast audience could hear everything, the people in the theater could not.[119]

After all the talk about format changes, there was one for the final debate, and it was minor. The time for answers to questions was reduced by thirty seconds. Everything else remained the same.

Frank Slingland of NBC Washington had directed the second 1960 debate. Sixteen years later he was in Williamsburg for the final 1976 event. He told the authors he hadn't wanted to do it again. "In 1960," he said, "we had to show each and every shot to the candidates' representatives. In Senator Kennedy's case, it was his brother, and Bill Wilson and Leonard Reinsch . . . and in Nixon's case, Ted Rogers and a couple of his people. Each and every shot was shown . . . and they were critical of backgrounds, of one lens being softer than another lens, of one side of the set being lighter than the other."[120]

Slingland had watched the previous three 1976 debates and thought that the directors had felt restricted, their shooting conservative. He agreed to take the job, but decided to take a more freewheeling approach.

For the first set of questions and answers Basham and Slingland had agreed on a series of more or less matched shot sequences. That done, Slingland turned to Basham and said, "Look, I hope you're not expecting me to do any equal sequencing of shots from now on. . . . We're going to be on our own and we are going to be taking what looks good. I got the answer: 'Go ahead, it's yours, keep it coming.' " In the end Slingland enjoyed it.

The much discussed and often rejected face-to-face confrontation between the candidates might have happened at Williamsburg, if Jim Karayn had made a different decision about timing near the end of the debate. The questioners had agreed among themselves that when the time came to shorten the questions and answers, they were going to relinquish their time and ask Carter and Ford if they had questions for each other. Karayn didn't know about this and instructed moderator Barbara Walters to proceed with two more rounds of regular length. The "plot" failed.[121]

There was only one tense moment that echoed the trouble in Philadelphia a month earlier. About twenty minutes into the debate a piece of cardboard that had been taped above a camera lens to shield it from the lights came loose and dropped over the lens. That camera happened to be on the air. Everyone jumped. Slingland cut to another camera immediately. Even though the incident took just a split second, another network called the NBC truck to ask what had happened. Bob Mulholland said: "I aged ten years in that one second." Most people who watched the debate didn't even notice it.[122]

Summary of Fourth Debate

DATE: October 22, 1976. 9:30 P.M., EDT

PLACE: Phi Beta Kappa Hall, College of William and Mary, Williamsburg, Virginia

PRODUCER: Pool—NBC, Christie Basham

DIRECTOR: Frank Slingland, NBC

LIGHTING: Fiorentino Associates; Marvin Purbaugh, NBC

DESIGNER, TIMING, PRODUCTION COORDINATOR: same as in San Francisco

MAKEUP: Same as in Philadelphia

TECHNICAL SUPERVISOR: Pool—Don Pike, NBC

MODERATOR: Barbara Walters, ABC

PANELISTS: Joseph Kraft, syndicated columnist; Jack Nelson, *Los Angeles Times*; Robert Maynard, *Washington Post*.

FORMAT: Open topics ninety minutes. Questions, answer 2:30, followup question, answer, 2:00. Response, 2:00. Closing statements, 3:00. During the debate the length of the closing statements was expanded to 4 minutes to balance out the time remaining. Rules: same as before.

PROGRAM ANALYSIS

OPENING: (Pool video only) Wide shot, balcony, Stage left two-shot, Ford in foreground. Medium shot, balcony camera, both men at lecterns. Backstage camera, Ford left, Carter right, press panel center, audience in background. Medium shot, moderator.

SHOTS: Slingland used a wide variety of one-shots ranging from a loose shot of Ford that included the entire top and some of the base of the lectern to what were the tightest one-shots of the entire debate series—closeups which did not include even the tie-knots. He did quite a bit of one-to-one cutting during the same speech, from lectern top to tie-bar; or the reverse, from tight closeups to medium shots to show the candidates writing notes.

REACTIONS: Slingland introduced some different reaction shots and shooting patterns. Once, when Ford was speaking, he put in two reverse angle two-shots. He also used a shot that started as a one-shot of the candidate speaking, and then zoomed back to include the other candidate listening or taking notes. He also used the balcony camera to get a high angle shot of the candidates listening to questions.

COMMENTS: There were 15 reaction shots of Carter for a total of 4:00, and six of Ford for a total of 1:40. The apparent imbalance in reaction shots is deceiving. With the exception of two one-shot reactions of Carter, both candidates were always in the picture. Slingland must have seen more motivation to cut away from Ford than from Carter. There were no one-shot reaction shots of Ford.

CANDIDATES' TOTAL SPEAKING TIME: 70:08. Ford—38:57, Carter—31:11. (Carter passed or gave very brief answers to several rebuttal questions.)

Conclusions

The League of Women Voters, American public opinion, and the major-party candidates wanted the 1976 debates. The only obstacle to broadcasting them was Section 315 of the FCC code. The American radio-TV networks, and some independent stations, covered the debates as bona fide news events. League sponsorship gave the broadcasters a path around Section 315, and the candidates, a transmission belt to virtually every American voter.

Of the parties in this tripartite arrangement, the candidates had the most control. The League was committed to sponsoring the debates. The networks, despite their legal and journalistic doubts and fears, could not have avoided them—all three became, to a greater or lesser extent, prisoners of the process.

The League packaged and produced the debates for television and got the consent of the candidates on most matters. The format, the dates, sites, staging, and method of selecting the questioners were worked out between the League and the candidates.

The candidates' representatives worked hard for their principals on both substantive and picayune issues. They made numerous moves aimed at gaining a real or imagined advantage, but they never pushed them to the point of foreclosure.

Foreclosure—refusal to broadcast the events—was never an option for the networks. It is inconceivable that the Republican and Democratic candidates for the presidency could have appeared together anywhere without network coverage.

The League of Women Voters. The League was somewhat idealistic about its role, influenced by the organization's tradition of nonpartisan voter service. It put together a highly competent and tough staff that got the job done under severe time limitations. Regarding the format, the League ended up with most of what it said it wanted in its early planning. One major desire was not achieved—they were never able to get the candidates to engage in face-to-face discussion. Most of the other elements—including the controversial choice of questioners and audience shots—were League positions even before they were agreed to by the candidates.

As far as the authors were able to find out—and we pursued it vigorously —there were no vetoes of panelists by the candidates. To this day there are rumors. There are journalists who believe they were blackballed by one side or the other. And, there are journalists who think the candidates had a hand in the selection. The candidates' representatives say they did not want to see the proposed lists, or to put themselves into a veto position. They say, and the League officials agree—and have said so publicly—that there were informal discussions about possible panel members before they were chosen. All agree that there were no panels on which all of the names suggested by the candidates' representatives appeared. Finally, at least once, and perhaps twice, the candidates' representatives were not informed of the makeup of a panel before the names were announced to the news media.

The League should have taken the network's advice and hired an audio consultant for the four debates to do what Imero Fiorentino did with the lighting and the set, and to pay particular attention to the public address systems in the theaters.

Jim Karayn played the key role as organizer and leader of the debates project, working with a small staff to bring off what many, including network executives, thought could never happen.

As sensitive as the selection of questioners was, Karayn could have saved himself and the League a lot of grief by being more candid with the networks, and more sensitive to their concern about the audience shots. It was almost deceitful that the television viewer got only the most fleeting impression that there was an audience in the theaters. There seems to be little foundation for the League's fear that the networks would have misused shots of the audience during the debates. Given the importance of the events, conservative production and journalistic values would have prevailed.

The Networks. To protect their legal positions and professional standards, the networks waged a sometimes egocentric, but mostly very serious rearguard action. While they recognized clearly that Section 315 precluded them from being involved in the planning of the events, they also feared that agreements between the League and the candidates—particularly in regard to the picking of questioners and the ban on shots of the audience—would compromise their legal and journalistic positions. Because of their apprehension, the networks took steps to protect themselves—at least in the beginning—by setting complex hands-off procedures, which made the production of the broadcasts awkward.

The broadcasts presented by the networks' pool were, with one major exception, flawless. In the authors' view, the complicated procedures taken by the networks to head off potential legal problems may well have contributed, at least indirectly, to the Philadelphia audio failure. The list of things the networks said they couldn't do made the first production by the pool more complicated. If the "can't dos" hadn't been there, or if they had been minimized from the start, the ABC pool producer would have had more time to devote to the details of the broadcast and might have caught the weak link in its audio system. Since the "can't dos" were largely disregarded in the later debates, we wonder, even in view of Section 315, why they were necessary at all.

The essence of "hands-off," or what Elliot Bernstein called "hocus-pocus," may be in an item from the September 17 pool minutes relating to the AV checks for the candidates. It reads: "Members agree that pool will not schedule anything for candidates, but will not turn its back if candidates appeared while pool was working."

It is clear to the authors that ABC played the long odds with their audio setup, and lost. When a part failed, the whole system failed. That could have happened to anybody. What ABC did not do was provide an alternate system to fall back on. Improvising a way to restore the sound, under frantic pressure, took too long.

In the debate series there were two instances in which the broadcasts themselves seemed to reflect the awkward atmosphere of the whole situation.

In Houston there was an obvious chance for audience reaction shots when the theater audience laughed at some of Senator Dole's remarks. A director, operating freely, might have considered taking a shot of the audience if there was enough reaction to make it a significant part of the story. To do that, he would have had to have a camera aimed at the audience, and sufficient light. Because of the no-shot rule, neither was available at that moment. To have faithfully reported the whole story of that debate, the director should have had the option of shooting the audience.

In Philadelphia during the audio breakdown, the pool and the networks could have covered it. The networks had reporters and cameras in the theater, in the lobby and outside the building. When the failure occurred, the network anchor persons—Cronkite, Reasoner-Smith, and Brinkley, who were in studios in New York, were relaying fragmentary and sometimes erroneous information. Brinkley twice announced the debate was over. The correspondents in the lobby —whose job was to get reaction after the debate—had even less hard information, and said so. Outside the theater there were cameras and reporters all over, particularly around the stage door. But, during the sound failure, the only outside coverage to get on the air were brief CBS and NBC interviews with Mrs. Carter. Inside, the pool cameras remained on wide shots of the stage. They did not show close-ups of the candidates waiting it out, or Ed Newman's attempts to communicate with Ford and Carter, or the technicians working to get things started again, or the audience.

The networks thus chose not to cover a sub-event. When they became a part of the story, they didn't cover themselves.

The Candidates' Representatives. The candidates' television advisors, particularly those representing Gerald Ford, got what they wanted. The Ford people were methodical and persistent. They had the power and resources of the White House, and they used them. In the negotiations, the Republicans were aggressive. They had firm ideas about how the programs should look—Ford should look presidential, thus he would stand up to debate, there should be a panel to fire questions, and the programs should be ninety minutes so that Ford could demonstrate his experience. At the same time they felt style was more important than substance—that audiences have a short memory for issues, and would see the debates primarily as a beauty contest.

The Carter representatives protested at length about the stiffness and formality of what the Republicans were proposing and supporting. They say they wanted an informal, seated, "talk-show" format—which was more suited to Carter's style—but they seem to have been doing more reacting than proposing, and they did not push as hard. They believed Carter could also handle the more formal atmosphere, and may have accepted that in the end as less of a risk than what they first proposed.

Both sides knew that the candidates' representatives controlled the events, so when they were in agreement, there was little chance of other outcome. Both used control as strategy in the negotiating sessions.

News Events? In 1960, because Section 315 was suspended for the debates between Nixon and Kennedy, everything seen and heard, from the moderator's "good evening" to his "good night" sixty minutes later, was identical on all the networks. This time, because the networks were covering a bona fide news event under Section 315, each devised its own broadcast around the pooled report. Each covered the debates as part of its overall election campaign coverage.

There is no doubt that the 1976 debates were bona fide news events. They could have been held anywhere—even, as one pool producer said, on an aircraft carrier in the Pacific with the Mormon Tabernacle Choir—and they would have been news events.

Contrasts? There is much to contrast between the two sets of debates sixteen years apart. The vice-presidential candidates debated, and a new kid on the block, PBS, took its place with the commercial networks as a full-fledged member of the pool producing club. The programs were in color this time. Technology had advanced—the worries of the 1960s about soft zoom lens and camera tubes that didn't match had disappeared. Huge boom microphones were replaced by fingernail-sized mikes worn on tie-clips. There was an audience this time, because the League of Women Voters had always had an audience at its political events. Besides, the League believed that the presence of an audience was related to the legality of the broadcasts. In 1960 the debates took place in studios; in 1976 they were held in theaters. For the Kennedy-Nixon debates, there were four different sets, the creations of network designers. For the Carter-Ford debates there was only one set, the design of which was similar in some respects to several of the 1960 sets.

Lessons? Some lessons were learned in the sixteen years. Makeup, which made headlines in 1960, was not an issue in 1976. Both candidates used their own professional makeup artists. While there was still some discussion about lighting, it was minimal, compared to the adding and matching of lighting instruments, the discussions of shadows and intensity, that went on in 1960. In 1976 an outside consultant oversaw consistent and trouble-free lighting throughout the programs. Reaction shots were a big issue in 1960. Candidates' representatives and relatives were in the control rooms during the broadcasts and put pressure on the directors regarding the use of reaction shots. This time reaction shots were accepted as a normal part of coverage, and the candidates' representatives were kept away.

With time and distance, the issues discussed above may seem trivial. This may be, but at the time, and in the atmosphere of a close race for the presidency, the staging of part of that race, and the coverage of it, became an all-consuming matter. Much of the time and energy spent on "looking professional," "sitting or standing," or "cutting the risks" obscured the true purpose of the debates.

The League resisted the idea that any other organization could do the job, although the candidates claim that they had plenty of offers from other organizations to present one or more debates. The League said it was "the only game in town." And that is precisely the difficulty with this sort of arrangement. The debates, as they came to the air, were truly the "only game in town." They provided a sanitized, risk-free environment for the candidates and an artificial forum for the voters. The League's objective of true face-to-face confrontations was ruled out by the candidates, because it was risky.

The major influence on the 1976 debates was Section 315, not what the League would have thought best, or what the networks might have wanted to do. It is significant that Jim Karayn said at the outset that the 1976 debates would resemble the 1960 ones. Given the amount of influence the candidates had in 1960, and again in 1976, plus Section 315, this had to be the case.

The participants became trapped within the process. Each agreement and commitment, fully accepted or not, was shaped by the dynamics of the inevitable big event. The 1976 debates broadcasts turned out as they did because the presidential candidates were, as in 1960, clients to be served. The League of Women Voters played the role of intermediary. They could influence the final shape and form of the debates only to the extent that the candidates would agree to their plans. In the negotiations between the League and the candidates, the networks could have no control. When the time came for the broadcasts, the League and the networks produced events tailored by and for the candidates. The League accomplished its goal of presenting debates, but at a price.

The networks were shackled by the legal situation. Accustomed to being producers, they were uncomfortable as conduits. The three-way arrangement between the candidates, the League, and the networks facilitated the 1976 debates, but, as in 1960, debates at any cost did not best serve the American public.

In 1980, or four, or eight, or sixteen years from then, if there are debate broadcasts, it is likely that they will resemble the debates of 1976 and 1960. Before debates can become more useful to the voter, Section 315 must be repealed and a way must be found to reduce the candidates' influence.

NOTES

1. The authors shared equally in both the research and the writing of this study, which was supported by a grant from the Office of Research and Graduate Development, Indiana University, Bloomington, and funds raised by Sidney Kraus.

Much of the material was obtained by personal observation and interviews at the time of the debates in Philadelphia, San Francisco, Houston, and Williamsburg, and with many of the program principals from November 1976 to May 1977. The authors acknowledge that the debates were also carried by radio, but this study deals almost entirely with TV.

2. Interview with Peggy Lampl, executive secretary, League of Women Voters, March 15, 1977.

3. Interviews with Lampl; Wally Pfister, vice-president, ABC News; Robert Mulholland, executive vice-president, NBC News; Richard Salant, president, CBS News, February 13–14, 1977.

4. The authors first interviewed Karayn before the second debate in San Francisco and in person and by phone on November 29, 1976; March 16, 1977; March 21, 1977; April 18, 1977; April 20, 1977; April 31, 1977; and May 1, 1977.

5. See Sidney Kraus, ed., *The Great Debates, Kennedy v. Nixon, 1960* (Bloomington: Indiana University Press, 1962), chapter 5.

6. Interview with Bill Carruthers, President Ford's TV advisor, March 18, 1977.

7. Karayn interviewed in the *New York Daily News*, April 28, 1976.

8. See "The Oregon Plan of Debating," *Quarterly Journal of Speech*, XII (April 1926) pp. 176–80.

9. Interview with Karayn.

10. Interview with Karayn.

11. "CBS Morning News," August 23, 1976.

12. Presidential Debates Debriefing, Crystal City Marriott, November 26, 1976; interviews with Karayn.

13. Theodore White suggested the first one be held before a joint session of the Congress with House and Senate committee members asking the questions.

14. Interview with Karayn.

15. The League had actually thought there might be five debates, four for the presidential candidates, but time considerations cut the number from five to four.

16. Interview with Karayn.

17. Karayn interviews; also interviews with Michael Raoul-Duval, presidential counsel, March 15, 1977, and Barry Jagoda, special assistant to President Carter, March 16, 1977.

18. Interviews with Karayn, Jagoda, and Bill Carruthers.

19. Interviews with Imero Fiorentino, LWV lighting consultant, January 27, 1977. Fiorentino's firm also worked for the Democrats during the 1976 campaign.

20. Interview with Carruthers. While members of the Fiorentino firm worked for the Republicans during the debates period, Fiorentino did not. He told Carruthers that he would not personally light anything until after the debates. Near the end of the campaign Fiorentino formed a separate group to handle the Ford "media blitz" regional telecasts hosted by Joe Garagiola.

21. The other two were Everett Melosh, ABC lighting director, and Frank Slingland, NBC director.

22. Interviews with Karayn.

23. Interview with Fiorentino.

24. Interview with Karayn.

25. Interview with Carruthers.

26. At each debate the League paid the theater rental for the day of the debate, the pool paid for the setup days.

27. Interviews with Karayn, Carruthers, and Robert Wightman, debates set designer, January 26, 1977.

28. It did not show up in the television pictures because in the shots from the front of the stage the candidates were eight feet apart, and in the side shots, the camera next to Ford had been raised considerably to compensate for his height.

29. Karayn, Marriott debriefing. In 1960 the moderator was seated with the candidates on the set during the first and second debates. The Nixon-Kennedy set most like Wightman's was the ABC set for the fourth debate designed by George Corrin.

30. Interview with Wightman.

31. Interview with the Justin Thompson, regional manager, Herman Miller Co., February 7, 1977. After the debates, Miller bought the furniture back for a thousand dollars, and donated it to the Smithsonian Institution.

32. Interview with LWV production coordinator Jack Sameth, February 5, 1977.

33. Interviews with Karayn, Pfister, Mulholland, Sameth, and Robert Chandler, vice-president, CBS News, February 14, 1977.

34. Interview with Pfister. Before going to the meeting with Karayn, executives of the commercial networks had met in Mulholland's office to discuss this.

35. Interview with Gerald Slater, executive vice-president, WETA, Washington, D.C., March 24, 1977.

36. Interview with Pfister.

37. Elliot Bernstein, ABC pool producer, Marriott debriefing.

38. Interview with Sameth.

39. Interview with Pfister; Bernstein memo to Pfister, September 17, 1976.

40. Interview with Mulholland.

41. Direct quote from Pfister's notes on September 8, 1976, meeting, and interview with Pfister.

42. Interview with Elliot Bernstein, January 26, 1977.

43. Interview with Jagoda.

44. Interview with Carruthers.

45. Interview with Jagoda.

46. Carruthers's version, backed by Karayn and Lampl, is that they took a dinner break sometime around 10:00 P.M. with the agreement each side would make some calls to try to break the "sit-stand-how-will-they-look" logjam.

47. Interview with Bernstein.

48. Bernstein, Marriott debriefing.

49. Interview with Chandler.

50. Interview with Wallace Westfeldt, senior executive producer, WETA, Washington, D.C., March 14, 1977.

51. Karayn, Marriott debriefing.

52. Interview with Karayn.

53. Interview with Sameth.

54. Interview with Chandler.

55. Interviews with Pfister, Salant.

56. Pfister's notes of the September 18, 1977, meeting at the League headquarters in Washington. At the November 29, 1976, Marriott debriefing Raoul-Duval asked League president Ruth Clusen if the agreement was no longer operative, before he

would talk about it. She said it was not operative. All League and candidate sources interviewed confirmed that the agreement was as Walker explained it to the networks.

57. Chandler, Marriott debriefing.
58. *Washington Star/News*, September 19, 1976.
59. Interview with Mulholland.
60. Interview with Pfister.
61. Chandler, Marriott debriefing.
62. Interview with Mulholland.
63. Interview with Carruthers.
64. Interview with Michael Raoul-Duval, March 15, 1977.
65. Interview with Jagoda.
66. Interview with Bernstein.
67. Interview with Fiorentino.
68. Interview with Fiorentino.
69. Interviews with Bernstein, Sameth.
70. Interviews with Bernstein, Sameth.
71. Interviews with Bernstein, Sameth.
72. Interview with Karayn. The pool minutes of September 17 show the networks suggested the League hire an audio consultant. The pool minutes of September 20 show the networks still consulting their lawyers on the propriety of doing the audio themselves, and laying off some of the cost to the League.
73. In 1960 the dressing rooms were a big, expensive item. ABC actually built identical cottages within a New York studio to accommodate Kennedy and Nixon.
74. *New York Post*, September 23, 1976.
75. Interview with Fiorentino.
76. Interview with Fiorentino.
77. Interview with Sameth.
78. Interview with Jagoda.
79. Interview with Carruthers.
80. This version of the story is mainly from Carruthers, but Karayn and Jagoda confirm many of the details.
81. Interview with Edwin Newman, February 15, 1977.
82. Interview with Sameth.
83. ABC master control log, September 23, 1976.
84. Verbatim transcript, first debate.
85. There are various estimates of the exact length of the audio failure. The authors are using the ABC New York master control log which reads: "lost audio for 25 minutes, 55 seconds from 10:51:05 to 11:17:00 (all nets, ABC pool). Trouble due to blown main distribution aud. amp. in theater in Philadelphia."

There are time discrepancies between the network trouble reports. NBC's says the audio was lost from 10:50:46 to 11:18:00. CBS's says the gap went from 10:50:48 until approximately 11:20. PBS reported the loss from 10:51 to 11:19.

Viewers also got different impressions of the outage length, because none of the networks rejoined the debate at precisely the same moment. PBS missed all of Carter's 11-second finish to his interrupted answer, and had to take an off-air pickup to get any of the remaining sound since its link to Washington was never restored. ABC rejoined earliest—viewers of that network heard and saw Newman testing his microphones and asking: "Are we back on the air?" From the time the sound failed until Newman said: "Ladies and gentlemen, it is not necessary to tell . . ." was 27 minutes 2 seconds.

86. The PBS signal was sent to its Washington headquarters for distribution from there.
87. Phillip Levens, director of TV operations for ABC, says the pool offered backup to all networks, but only CBS took it.

88. Interview with Phillip Levens, January 27, 1977.

89. Interview with Bernstein, and Marriott debriefing.

90. Karayn, Marriott debriefing.

91. Interview with Sameth.

92. Interview with Karayn. Persons in the theater heard intermittent remarks from the PA during the outage.

93. Ruth Clusen, Marriott debriefing, November 30, 1976.

94. Interview with Carruthers.

95. Network and telephone company sources told the authors there were other audio circuits available. One ran directly from the pool truck to the telephone company. Another, installed for CBS News feeds, ran from backstage to the CBS remote truck. There are conflicting views concerning the involvement of these lines in the restoration of the sound. In any event, none had anything to do with the problem in the distribution amplifier.

96. Interview with Carruthers.

97. Bernstein, Marriott debriefing.

98. Interview with Bernstein.

99. Interview with Michael Pengra, LWV production coordinator, March 16, 1977.

100. Interviews with Pengra, Lampl.

101. Interview with Bill Schelling, CBS pool lighting director, February 24, 1977.

102. Interviews with Pengra, Chandler; also interview with CBS pool producer Jack Kelly, January 26, 1977.

103. Interview with Kelly.

104. Interview with Pengra.

105. Interview with Pengra.

106. Interview with Imero Fiorentino in the Palace of Fine Arts theater, October 6, 1976.

107. Interviews with Lampl.

108. Interview with Jagoda.

109. Interview with Raoul-Duval.

110. Karayn, Marriott debriefing.

111. Interview with Karayn. Karayn also tried to meet with the candidates' representatives in Atlanta to discuss format changes for the last presidential debate. But the Ford camp didn't show up, and Democratic support for changes evaporated.

112. Interview with Karayn.

113. Interview with Westfeldt.

114. *Chronicle of Higher Education*, November 1, 1976; *The Flat Hat*, special debate issue, October 22, 1976.

115. Interview with Don Pike, NBC pool technical supervisor, April 11, 1977.

116. Interview with Jagoda at Phi Beta Kappa Hall, Williamsburg, Va., October 22, 1976.

117. Interview with Mulholland. NBC's embargo efforts apparently were successful.

118. *New York Times*, October 23, 1976.

119. Interviews with Lampl, Basham, Pengra; and interviews with Sam Sambataro, NBC pool audio supervisor, and Oliver Midgett, Jr., Audio International Inc., Norfolk, Virginia.

120. Interview with Frank Slingland, NBC pool director, April 6, 1977. Also see *The Great Debates, Kennedy vs. Nixon, 1960*, chapter 5.

121. Jack Nelson, *Los Angeles Times*, NBC Forum, Washington, D.C., March 5, 1977.

122. Interview with Mulholland.

9.

Making the Least of It?
Television Coverage of the Audio Gap

GLADYS ENGEL LANG and KURT LANG
with the assistance of JOHN STENSRUD

The news media, especially television, have been charged repeatedly with sensationalism. It is said that they emphasize the unusual and dramatic at the expense of the normal and the routine, so that significant issues may fail to get the coverage they deserve. Still, there are times when the opposite occurs: a development with real dramatic potential, touching on problematic issues, is effectively routinized. This, as we shall document, is what happened during the audio breakdown that interrupted the first television debate between Gerald Ford and Jimmy Carter. Throughout this twenty-seven minute gap, when the two candidates intermittently appeared on the screen but could not be heard— if they said anything—all three networks consistently underplayed the unique and dramatic elements in the situation. A "reality" of high drama was, as a result, made to seem ordinary.

With the debates long over, the gap may appear to be only a fortuitous incident that everyone involved would sooner forget. It was at the time quite extraordinary, however, insofar as it presented each news staff with a variety of operational problems. These problems centered on the basic question of how long it would take to restore the sound, or *if* it could be restored, and whether the debate would, indeed, resume. The three news staffs had a primary responsibility to keep the audience informed but, lacking full information themselves, they were largely dependent on their own assumptions about what had gone wrong and what was likely to happen. These assumptions, in turn, influenced the way each network programmed the "wait." Other influences included the news staffs' conceptions of the news event they were to cover, what other responsibilities and restrictions they recognized, and their usual operating procedures for contingencies of this sort.

It is our contention, based on detailed examination of broadcast content,[1] that the three networks, by underplaying the dramatic, unusual, and unprecedented aspects of the situation, converted an incident that could have given rise to prolonged and vituperative controversy to one that did not become a serious issue. To document this contention, we present information on the treatment given to the likelihood that the debate had ended; to recapitulation and "instant analysis" of the debate up to the time the sound went dead; to

158

what the candidates were doing during the gap; to the possibility of a "conspiracy" or "dirty tricks"; to the diagnosis of the technical failure and of the effort to restore sound; and to the issue of whether the debate should have continued despite the broadcast failure.

Had the Debate Ended?

At approximately 9:50:50 P.M.[2] September 23, as the first televised Ford-Carter debate was nearing its end, the audio transmission failed. For twenty seconds, people in some 38 million households tuned in heard nothing, though the debate appeared to be going on. Carter, who was speaking, soon lapsed into silence, and the debate did not resume until twenty-seven minutes later.[3]

Up to the audio breakdown, the three networks were transmitting the debate through a pooled audio-visual feed, for which ABC was responsible. They broke away shortly thereafter, each providing special coverage from both its network news headquarters in New York and its portable units outside the Walnut Street Theater hall.

The basic question, the answer to which would surely influence the viewer's decision to stay with or tune out the broadcast, was whether and when the debate would continue. The idea that the three networks might have supplied different "answers" was suggested in the course of an "experiment" involving groups in separate lecture halls viewing on different channels. Research staffs were to distribute questionnaires as soon as the debate ended. In the CBS room, they began giving them out almost immediately after Walter Cronkite came on the screen; those in the NBC hall delayed awhile; and those in charge of the ABC group waited until just minutes before the sound came back on.

To check whether these differences in distribution time reflected different information given out by the three networks, we coded all statements by the news staffs about debate continuance as to whether they indicated or implied that the audio, and presumably the debate, would surely return, whether they were noncommittal, or whether they put the possibility of resumption into serious doubt. An example of *positive* prediction is a statement, like that made by Harry Reasoner of ABC at 9:51:10 (also audible on NBC), that "the pool broadcasters in Philadelphia have *temporarily* lost the audio [and] *will* fix it as soon as possible." An example of a *neutral* statement is: "Now the stage manager is trying to indicate *whether or not* they'll be able to go back on the air." The phrase, "*if* they do get the audio reestablished," suggests at least the possibility that the debate may not continue and is therefore considered *negative*.

The tabulation of these predictions (Table 1) confirms that ABC was the network most insistent that the debate would continue. Its only pessimistic

Table 1: Predictions of Whether the Debate Would Resume

Network	Positive	Neutral	Negative	Total	% Positive
ABC	7	3	1	11	64
NBC	4	5	1	10	40
CBS	2	2	3	7	28

note was struck just forty seconds before full sound returned from inside the theater, as Reasoner ventured that "there may be a situation shortly in which they declare the situation at an end."

On NBC, David Brinkley, in the anchor position, and Douglas Kiker, reporting from the theater lobby, were both voluble but mainly noncommittal. Predominating during most of the coverage were neutral statements like "they are *trying* to restore" and they "*hope* to have it fixed." Then, three minutes before the end of the gap, Brinkley flatly declared (as Carter could be seen getting up from his chair), "I gather that the debate is over. Is that right? The League of Women Voters has decided not to go ahead with any more of the debate. It's now eleven fifteen in the East . . . the debate is over and that is it."

Cronkite, on CBS, less than ninety seconds after the sound went dead, was the first of the anchormen to voice the possibility that the audio might not be restored in time for further debate. A few minutes later, resuming a recap of the debate he had already begun, he began by saying that "*very probably* this first meeting is over." He went on to speak of the debate in the past definite tense ("all of you who *watched* this debate"). Statements on all networks toward the end of the gap reported discussions in the hall about whether or not to declare an end to the encounter, but only NBC had formally declared it over. A viewer on CBS might nevertheless have received this impression, inasmuch as Cronkite began his review of the debate almost immediately, while NBC waited for about five minutes and ABC until about nine minutes had passed.

Additional clues came from background voices, sometimes identified for the viewer, and other noises occasionally transmitted over the air. Such sound was usually taken as a sign that the audio was about to be restored. On three of the four such occasions on ABC, newsmen took them as evidence the debate was about to resume. NBC and CBS made similar interpretations but picked up such noises less often.

Finally, the candidates still standing at their lecterns served as a reminder that the debate, at least officially, was not yet over. The networks differed in both the amount of time they showed the pool picture of the men waiting and how prominently they displayed it on the home screen. All carried the pool picture, in a split screen arrangement, most of the time they broadcast from the studio. Since NBC spent more time interviewing from the theater lobby (see Table 2), it kept the candidates on view the least amount of time; ABC, interviewing the least amount of time, let the viewers see Carter and Ford more of the time. Both NBC and ABC shared the screen about equally between anchormen and the pool picture, but on CBS, since the pool used no close-up shots, the candidates were small figures, indeed, in a corner of the TV monitor.

Instant Analysis: Recapping the Unfinished Debate

The main points of interest during the gap—which would keep the audience tuned in—were why the debate was so unexpectedly interrupted and whether and when it would continue. The television news organizations covering the debate could hardly keep silent and simply transmit the pool picture while waiting for the sound or for a resolution of the situation. Thus, once it was evident that the interruption was more than momentary, they had to decide what they should be covering; also, they had to be mindful of their responsibilities and the possible restrictions the nature of the event placed on their freedom of action. Cutting away entirely was precluded by the lack of information on what was happening, by the importance invested in the occasion, and by the fact they had geared their resources for instant wrap-up and analysis. The only alternative was to provide filler material fitting the tone of a presidential debate without intruding on the event in a way that might appear to favor one candidate or that might affect the outcome.

The extent to which all three networks stuck to conventional reporting is understandable: if the debate resumed, anything said during this interim was likely to become mixed in the viewer's mind with the debate itself. This could lay the networks open to charges of interference, of "instant analysis"—Agnew's favorite target, not just immediately after the event but while it was going on. Prevented by prior agreement from showing audience reactions to the debaters, the networks had to be sure not to substitute the assessments of their commentators for those of the audience. This problem was most acute in connection with any "who did better" evaluation.

All initially treated the interruption as temporary, but bit by bit, as time passed, the news organizations went over to the kind of commentary and analysis prepared for post-debate broadcasts. There were three ways to proceed: authoritative commentary, usually by the anchorman; pooling of information between reporters at the same or different locations; and interviews with members of the candidates' staffs. It is easier to keep control of content and tone in solo commentary, through internal balance, than in discussion. Newsmen exercise some control over the content of interviews by the persons they select, by the questions they ask, and by their ability to terminate the interview. But interviews are more risky than an anchorman or several reporters talking among themselves.

As Table 2 shows, CBS relied most heavily on the commentary of its anchorman, Cronkite; NBC spent most time in interviews; on ABC the pooling of information predominated.

ABC did, of course, enjoy one resource not available to the others. It had direct access to the pool and to its reporter in a glass booth overlooking the inside of the theater. Time could be spent in conversation between the anchormen and the unseen ABC "inside man." Both the availability of personnel inside the theater and the expectation that those in charge of the pool arrange-

Table 2: Time Allocations

	ABC	NBC	CBS
Time into "gap" at beginning of			
debate recap	9'	6'	2'
first interview	18'30"	9'50"	8'
Percent of time spent in			
solo commentary	13	50	76
discussion	72	4	0
interviews	15	46	24
	100	100	100

ment might provide some authoritative information may explain why ABC was the last to begin any recap of the debate. This began only when Howard K. Smith, moderator of the first Kennedy-Nixon debate in 1960, joined Reasoner on the screen to offer his view of the debate.

From then on, ABC, notwithstanding its optimism about debate resumption, showed the least hesitation in making explicit assessments of the debate, of the candidates' performances, and of the outcome of the debate. Its newsmen also displayed far more levity than did those on CBS or NBC. Reasoner and Smith concurred that the candidates had stuck to issues and facts, so much so that it may have been hard to follow their arguments. This observation was followed by a very personal evaluation of the strongest point scored by Ford and of "the nearest thing to a low level of debate" attained by Carter. Their discussion was interspersed with phrases such as "*I* really prefer" and "*I* think" and with judgments acknowledged by Smith to be "highly subjective."

The ABC interviews came late and took up the least time. Bill Wordum talked first to Robert Strauss, a Democrat, for two minutes twenty seconds and then to Ron Nessen, a Republican, for one minute forty seconds. Wordum was about to interview Mary Louise Smith, a Republican, when the debate resumed. A reasonable balance was certainly maintained.

Interview questions largely sought to elicit claims of "victory" from the two candidates' spokesmen. Most questions were phrased as if the debate were over —e.g., "How do you feel the debate *went?*" When Strauss, who had already been interviewed on NBC and CBS, refrained from claiming a victory before the debate was officially over by calling "the people the big winner" and stating that both debaters had done well, Wordum pressed him to indicate if he would "score one clearly for Carter in [his] column." Strauss finally acquiesced, "Score one clearly." To put the coverage back into balance, the reporter then turned to Nessen: "We have just heard from Chairman Strauss, who feels both candidates performed very well indeed. But in his column, not surprisingly, he says he thinks score one for Jimmy Carter. How do you feel?" And Nessen, as he had already insisted in answering other network reporters, said Ford "won by a clear margin."

ABC was the only network to "score" the debate and compare it with 1960, but the score was said to be very close. Reasoner explained:

> We had twelve questions and twelve answers and then twelve follow-ups (except for the last one) and then twelve rebuttals, and I tried to keep score, and I really tried to be objective as a boxing referee would do in a twelve round fight. . . . I figured up on a point system of five points per round for each contestant, just on debating, just how they made their points and how well they looked. It came out to 33 points in twelve rounds for Jimmy Carter and 32 points for Gerald Ford.

Howard K. Smith agreed it was very close but "in 1960 I carried out just such a score and gave Nixon 18.5 points to Kennedy's 18 points."

Compared to ABC, the CBS wrap-up, which began within the first two minutes, was less evaluative and contained nothing meant to be funny. Most of the recap, characterized by a judicious avoidance of opinionated statement, was an account of the issues covered; no new issues were said to have been injected into the campaign. Also, Cronkite characterized the debate as "a very lively discussion" and "a little more of a debate than anticipated." He spoke of "sharp exchanges," with the debaters "dignified but striking back." Both men were reported to have stuck to the issues.

In its interviews, CBS did indeed solicit partisan judgments. It could do this without loss of "objectivity"; its six interviews—more than either NBC or ABC had—were neatly balanced between Ford stalwarts and three Carter backers. Time was also closely divided. The Democrats had an even three minutes and the Republicans twenty seconds more.

Six questions invited direct comparisons between candidates' performances but were accompanied by reminders that the debate was not officially over: "What do you think *so far* is his strongest and weakest answer?" "How would you assess the president's performance *so* far?" "[Tell me] how the debate went *up to the point that we were all cut off*." Neither Strauss nor Nessen, the first two to be interviewed, claimed victory, nor were they pressed by Leslie Stahl, the interviewer, to do so. Her follow-up probes sought to pin down certain elements in each candidate's performance. For example, Strauss was asked, "Did either candidate look particularly nervous or ill-at-ease?" (To many viewers, Carter seemed somewhat nervous at the start, sweating as Nixon had in his first debate, and hesitant in his speech.)

Later this cautious approach seems to have been abandoned. When Stahl came on camera with Jody Powell, she said to Cronkite and the audience, "You'll be very surprised to know that he thinks Carter won." Still later, when a CBS reporter was interviewing Mrs. Carter, who kept reiterating her hope that the debate would go on, he made the victory statement for her and the not-surprised audience: "Actually you thought he won, I'm sure."

NBC, through Brinkley, began to review the debate about five minutes into the gap, calling it "a very lively debate . . . very tough at times, even rough . . . both heavy on facts." On first hearing from Douglas Kiker that a technical problem had arisen, Brinkley remarked, "You don't have a screwdriver and a pair of pliers on you, do you?" But except for this "lapse," he held his wry humor in check. He also maintained a studied neutrality during the recap of the debate, always careful to state, when perhaps seeming to express an opinion, that he was not doing so. For example:

> Much of the argument was about what new programs might be put into effect in the federal establishment in the next presidential term . . . what they will cost . . . who's going to do the tax-paying in the next four years . . . the rich? . . . the middle class? . . . If not them, who? . . . I must say, *without offering any opinion about winners or losers*, that question was not fully answered. Perhaps some of the audience might be left unsatisfied on that score.

This concern about avoiding even the appearance of taking sides was in evidence even after Brinkley began what he expected to be a wrap-up statement following the erroneous report that the debate was over. Summing NBC's coverage, he stressed its neutrality, "We have heard from some prominent Democrats and some prominent Republicans, each of whom thought his side won and gave his reasons why."

The tone of these interviews, on which NBC relied more heavily than did its competitors, was less formal than the studied neutrality maintained in the anchor booth. Kiker put the standard question to Ford's press secretary this way: "What's your impression? How do you think *your guy* did so far?" He easily elicited from Nessen a claim of victory but was unable to get a similar statement from Strauss, the Democratic national chairman, even though, like Wordum on ABC, he tried to put the words in Strauss's mouth: "You're obviously saying that you think Jimmy Carter won this debate." Strauss reiterated that both had handled their questions well.

The first NBC interviews began about two minutes later than the first on CBS and covered, with one exception, the same people. However, NBC was less successful in equalizing time, spending three minutes fifty seconds with the two Republicans but more than twice that time with the three Democrats. The discrepancy comes from an exchange between Jody Powell and Kiker, which was allowed to go on for five minutes, presumably as NBC waited for definite word about ending the debate. What finally terminated the Powell interview was the announcement by Brinkley, premature as it turned out, that "the debate is over."

Kiker was an aggressive interviewer, willing to challenge party spokesmen with provocative statements like, "I know you're going to say that he [Carter] was as cool as a cucumber." This approach, together with the considerable length of interviews, gave both political camps greater opportunity to promote imagery and to counter any adverse impressions. Although Strauss and Nessen were able to make the same points (Strauss, that Ford "looked programmed," and that Carter was the "more responsive," and Nessen, that the president demonstrated his experience, knowledge, and ability) on all networks, Kiker specifically invited Ford's national campaign manager to refute the "programming" imagery disseminated in the press: "Any surprises tonight? Did things go pretty well according to game plan? Did the questions you brainstormed come up?"

The same technique is illustrated by the following interchange with Jody Powell:

> KIKER: [Carter] was pretty tough on President Ford. . . . He said if Ford was going to blame him for the Democratic Congress that he [Ford] ought to be blamed for being part of Watergate . . .

> POWELL: I think you've misquoted him there, as sometimes happens. He said that if the unjust charge was made that he was responsible for all the actions of the Democratic Congress, which he had never been a part of, then, perhaps it would be—nothing but a bit of tongue in cheek—appropriate to ask President Ford to accept responsibility for the previous administration. He did not at all say he was part of Watergate.

NBC was the only network to raise issues that might have come up in the debate but did not. In this same interview with Powell, Kiker made a passing reference to the *Playboy* interview. And a couple of minutes later, after NBC declared the debate over, Cathy Mackin got Rosalynn Carter to comment not only on the *Playboy* issue but also on her efforts to iron out with Mrs. John-

THE GREAT DEBATES

son, Carter's criticism of the former president. In this way, NBC's questions injected issues into the unfinished debate that the debate panel had decided not to pursue.

Faint Echoes of Watergate

The first Ford-Carter debate may well be remembered for its twenty-seven minute gap long after the words have been forgotten. One would think that there was a far more dramatic story in the breakdown than in what the candidates had already said. What aspects of this drama received attention during the gap?

The sound went dead just as Carter was addressing the touchy issue of intelligence agencies and legislation required for protection against such excesses as had recently been exposed. Viewers could see his lips move, as he continued to speak. What was he saying that was suddenly and unexpectedly covered by a curtain of silence? It is hard to recall now that we have the official explanation for the audio failure the dramatic impact of the sudden fadeout of Carter's voice. It would have been natural for some among the millions in the audience to joke about some kind of conspiracy—the "dirty tricks" of Watergate or intervention by the CIA! Carter himself is alleged to have quipped while on stage,[4] "Mr. Kelley [the FBI Director] may not have liked what I was saying," a remark that was neither transmitted over the air nor reported by broadcasters *during* the gap.

To have allowed suspicions of sabotage to spread would have further shaken the trust in the political process and the government's concern for individual rights, which had already received such jolts during Watergate. This placed some constraint on the coverage of the gap. As long as there was no evidence of conspiracy, to dwell on the possibility could only reactivate the old anxieties and further demoralize the nation. It must be remembered that in the sixties, the media were charged with helping to spread rumors by reporting them during their coverage of protest demonstrations and ghetto riots.

Although there was no jamming of telephone lines by people concerned about "foul play" or "sinister forces," ABC and NBC acted immediately to allay such suspicions. They issued categorical denials of the possibility of sabotage at a time when they themselves had no way of being certain. Just after the sound went off, Harry Reasoner assured the audience that this was "*not* a conspiracy" against Carter or Ford; his words coming through the pool could also be heard on NBC, when Douglas Kiker shortly thereafter repeated Reasoner's calming message, "It is *not* a conspiracy" directly from the theater lobby.

CBS, on the other hand, gave no sign that they were aware people might suspect Watergate had surfaced again. By not referring to this possibility, they dealt with the suspicion of possible sabotage by ignoring it.

NBC pursued the question in an interview with Jody Powell, who was asked by Kiker if he knew why the mikes went off:

> I asked that [said Kiker] because it's been my experience in a situation like this that there's always a theory held by a lot of people that there was a conspiracy to cut 'em off. We have no proof of that. It was just simply a technical foul-up as far as we can determine. Isn't it correct?

Powell agreed that "not only do you have no proof of this but nobody has brought up the subject that I know of, have they?" To which Kiker then replied, "Not as far as I know."

ABC dealt with this theory even more often than NBC but mostly by making it seem foolish. Early banter between Reasoner and Smith contained guarded and vague references to the possibility of "conspiracy," for instance, saying the debate could not finish "in spite of the fact that security measures were tight." When they did refer to the fact that Carter was about to answer a question about security agencies, any suspicion of a "dirty trick" was immediately sloughed off with a joke:

> I doubt that Eugene McCarthy or Lester Maddox or the other minority parties that wanted to be there tonight have been able to engineer this. . . . I doubt that . . . the American Telegraph and Telephone Company which handles the lines and things like this want to do it.

All this went on even though nobody, during those twenty-seven minutes, had any firm evidence that the fiasco stemmed from a simple mechanical failure. Nevertheless, all three networks, each in its own way, chose not to pursue the story—the one by ignoring the possibility, the other seeking disconfirmation, and the third by making the possibility seem ridiculous. In each case, sensational aspects remained unexploited.[5]

Technology on Trial: TV the Main Loser?

The interruption of the presidential debate by technical failure was in its way a disaster, akin to electricity blackouts, in that it threw cold water on the myth of technological invulnerability. Even the networks acknowledged in news programs the kind of fiasco the gap had been—"the media's longest public pause for technical difficulties," or, as other pundits put it, the biggest loser was neither Carter nor Ford but American electronics.

Here, there was a real story to report. First of all, everyone was interested in *what* had happened, that is, the specific cause of the breakdown at such a dramatic moment in the debate. Then there was the issue of locating responsibility for the technical failure. Who was to blame? Was there anything about the specific arrangements for broadcasting these debates that increased the chance that something like a disruption of sound would occur?

One issue at stake was the much heralded dependability of electronic communication, from which the networks derive a good deal of prestige. They were not about to let themselves become scapegoats. All went out of the way to explain their lack of control and the unusual handicaps under which they were laboring—handicaps which also explained their inability to give the public more information about what was going on. The extent to which newsmen felt hampered is evident in two interviews, both by Kiker of NBC. Having earlier explained he was "isolated in a corridor," Kiker approached Ron Nessen to ask about what was going on and whether he [Nessen] had any "contingency plan." Nessen snapped back, "No, I think you're supposed to be the one with a contingency plan."

Later, there was this exchange between Kiker and Powell:

POWELL: Perhaps it [the audio failure] shows . . . that everybody makes mistakes every now and then.

KIKER: Even the networks?

POWELL: That's right. . . . I wouldn't want to criticize the networks, of course.

The most vulnerable and the likely scapegoat was ABC, which was responsible for the pooled transmission. Yet the reporters on that network never referred to its special stake in the rapid restoration of sound. Instead the audience received, early into the gap, a reminder from Reasoner that the debate was under the auspices of the League of Women Voters. The networks were not running the show, and when they did run it in 1960, they had not had this kind of problem, said Howard K. Smith, who didn't "like to cast aspersions but . . ."

Also, references to the dependability of technology, to how often such failures occur, were most frequent on ABC. At the beginning the seriousness was played down as not so unusual but, as time passed, the emphasis shifted and the myth of technological infallibility was debunked but in a jocular tone. Four times during the first five minutes, the "*gremlins* that affect *all* electronic journalism" were invoked. The audience was also told that "anybody who has worked in radio or television for a period of years has run into this." Meanwhile, Victor Ratner, the ABC correspondent inside the theater, enumerated some of the difficulties in preparing "this historic old building" for the broadcast, told of the additional cables that had to be brought in, and how "gremlins" had been at work in the preparation all along. Reasoner's reflection on "the frail magic of electronic journalism" stirred Ratner to allow that phone calls to the moon might be easier than getting a debate out of the Walnut Street Theater.

Being responsible for the pool also gave ABC an advantage, namely having a reporter in the hall with whom the news staff could communicate. Despite his isolation in a glassed-in booth, the chance that he could provide further clarification of the situation probably accounts for the fact that ABC stayed with the pool picture as long as it did. But the advantage was not very great, since ABC was subject to the same restrictions as the other networks. Under the agreement with the League, there could be no audience reaction shots. Consequently, though the networks had reporters within the audience, no video equipment or direct communication link was available. Strict security measures barred news teams deployed in the lobby for interviews from entering the hall even in this emergency, whose newsworthiness was apparent. They were unable to cover that story.

The reason for this lack of information on the nature of the technical failure was given at least five times by CBS. Thus, Walter Cronkite pointed out: "One of our problems with a pooled feed . . . is that the communications sometimes are not quite as direct as they would be if each network was handling its own broadcasting." Leslie Stahl, in the lobby, also commented on this predicament, adding a new dimension: "I'm standing outside the hall . . . wearing a tag that says LOBBY ONLY. I'm not allowed to go inside, so I haven't information about the technical problems."

NBC was not as explicit but managed to air its irritation, as in the verbal jousts with Carter and Ford representatives already mentioned. Similarly, on ABC, Reasoner, trying to interpret noises through the pool feed, remarked on his inability to hear what was being said on stage, though less in irritation than in bewilderment:

> It's somewhat unusual because frequently you would be able to hear what they are saying by a direct communication line even though it's not going out over the broadcast lines. But in this case nobody seems to know what they are saying.

The complaint was, "We have some people [in the audience] and I [Reasoner] can't even speak to them to ask what's going on."

A good deal was known, however, even though the precise cause of the breakdown—the blowing of a condenser or capacitor in one of the amplifiers in the booth of the radio sound engineer—was not determined until early next morning. Thus, by 9:57, six minutes after the sound went dead, it had been determined that the location of the trouble was inside the theater. Half-way into the gap—by about 10:04—plans for an alternative sound distribution system had been formulated, and work was underway. Somewhere between 10:11 and 10:13 the makeshift system was tested, but this information apparently was not conveyed to network news personnel.

At just about the time engineers had located the failure in the distribution system inside the hall, at 9:56:40, Harry Reasoner was saying on ABC: "A guess from what we can hear [from the theater] and the way it looks[6] is that it is not a general breakdown in Philadelphia . . . something . . . to do with the microphones of the two candidates." And, Ratner, inside the hall, reported there had been some discussion about bringing in an additional microphone just to get the broadcast going:

> There is a great deal of gesturing going on amongst the technicians on stage, but it's difficult for me within this glassed-in area to hear what they are gesturing about. . . . There's still no sign of action down there on the stage . . . except that a lot of people are undoubtedly tearing their hair out in the technical booths which are the nerve center of these broadcasts.

At this time, the news staff apparently had not yet garnered any information about the location of the problem or plans underway to restore sound.

On NBC there was a similar lack of information. Its standard bulletin was "We don't know what happened." By the time the trouble had been tracked to the inside audio booth, NBC was reporting, "The problem . . . is in the technical truck—undoubtedly—outside the auditorium." By the time technicians were at work bypassing the audio booth in the theater, David Brinkley was saying, "We still don't know what's wrong. Whatever it is, it is not in our audio. . . . It's in the sound coming from the rostrum there." And it was when the bypass was already being tested that Brinkley announced the debate over, still informing viewers that "the problem is somewhere inside the hall, on or around the podium and that's all we know, which is not a great deal." Even as late as 10:17, just before the debate resumed, NBC was still saying:

THE GREAT DEBATES

All we know . . . is that it's somewhere between the microphones clipped to their neckties and the network truck outside the hall. Beyond that I can't go because I don't know. *I don't think anybody knows at the moment.*

First reports on CBS focused on the lack of success in determining the nature of the technical difficulties, as when they announced at 10:00, "The television pool which has been handling this broadcast has still not been able to determine the reason for the interruption." Though CBS indicated that it could not relay any information that the pool did not have, post-debate news reports[7] indicate that ABC technicians did know by this time that the trouble was in the distribution system within the hall and had conveyed that information to those in charge of the pool coverage. Problems in attaining information were mentioned again several times before Cronkite was at last able to tell the audience:

> The TV pool still has not been able to tell specifically what is wrong . . . [*it*] seems to be in a couple of amplifiers, as they call them, in their sound system. They're trying to get them fixed so that we can carry on here tonight.

By 10:13:40 the audience was assured that the debate would resume "no matter how long it takes to get the two amplifiers [fixed] that the pool network ABC says is giving us the trouble." Neither the information about the amplifiers nor that the debate would resume, which CBS must have obtained from ABC as the alternate distribution system was being tested, was transmitted by ABC to its own viewers.

Although the story of what was being done to get the debate back on the air was dramatic and suspenseful, no network seems to have made any effort to cover it for the viewing public. If their news personnel and cameras could not get into the theater, Jim Karayn who directed the debate for the League pointed out, they could have focused on the ABC control truck outside. They could have stood there "saying, at least, we don't know what the trouble is."[8] Some engineers were later to argue that the "system was rigged improperly . . . like the old kind of Christmas tree lights. When one blew, they all blew."[9] On the other side, ABC would claim that the same distribution system had proved reliable under more difficult situations, as during the Montreal Olympic Games, and nobody had any reason to anticipate problems.

There must have been a good news story in the way ABC engineers in the audio booth tried to locate the specific trouble and laid their plans for bypassing the booth. The first plan was to get the audio back to the ABC control truck and let the networks pick it up from there. Later, it was decided to make use of an extra backup CBS had run from its own mobile unit into the ABC pool truck so the audio could be delivered on to New York, via CBS's circuits, and thence via telephone company lines to the networks and stations. Philip Levens, director of ABC's television operations in Philadelphia, has been quoted as saying that this was done within twenty to twenty-two minutes, with tests of the new linkup, using crowd noises, made in the remaining five or six minutes.

None of the networks reported from the ABC control truck. Nor did they try putting authorities (like Levens) on the air to tell what they knew about salvage attempts. Not that, as Karayn cautioned, "they should have gone inside the ABC truck . . . I'm sure you'd have had to bleep out half the conversation going on there."[10]

The Candidates as Prisoners of Television

In her reporter's notebook, Elizabeth Drew, one of the four questioners for this debate, wrote: "This has to be the greatest electronic foul-up of all time. The President and the would-be President are like prisoners behind their lecterns."[11] Never certain when the sound might go on, they were afraid to be caught unawares. One careless gesture, word, or movement caught and blown up over TV could destroy a carefully contrived image of presidentiality.

Wasn't there something unusual and dramatic about these two men of power immobilized by television and for twenty-seven minutes at its mercy? This captivity was partly of their own choosing. Each campaign staff was anxious to have its candidate deliver his carefully prepared closing statement. Ford's staff, especially, was counting heavily on a favorable audience response, and much effort had gone not only into the wording of the statement but also into preparation for its delivery. Parts of that final speech would be used for short video commercials during the campaign and it would be part of Ford's last appeal on election eve. But the candidates were prisoners of TV also because, with the cameras almost constantly on them, they could be seen on one network or the other for most of the gap.

Yet television did little to satisfy whatever curiosity viewers may have had about the personal drama in this situation. The pool employed no close-ups, and its picture occupied less than full screen. This afforded the audience little opportunity to scrutinize facial expressions or body movements and to form any idea of the two men's responses to the situation. Nor did the picture show what, if any, interaction occurred between them during this enforced wait.

The commentary supplied little information to supplement the picture. News personnel said little either about the candidates' personal plight or about what was happening on the stage. CBS reported at 10:07:20 that "the president and Governor Carter are still at the podium." NBC did little more. Twice it pointed out that President Ford and Governor Carter were on the rostrum "waiting," thus telling the viewers what they could see for themselves. ABC newsman Vic Ratner was able to tell the audience a bit more, given his vantage point inside the theater. Soon after the wait began, he reported that Carter and Ford had been unaware that the audio was lost until they looked at an off-stage monitor which showed that the broadcast had come to a halt. Their cue evidently was the unexplained ripple of laughter in the audience, under strict orders not to respond demonstrably to any statement by the candidates. Only on ABC did one hear Ed Newman, the moderator, thanking both Ford and Carter "for their *patience* and *understanding*" and Carter's response, "Thank you, thank you for the kind words." Later ABC viewers were to hear from the man in the glass booth that Jimmy Carter was "sitting with his hands folded, President Ford wiping his brow, and both of them getting a little warm under those lights." That Ford wiped his brow had not been visible on the screen. Thereafter, as on the other networks, it was "just a case of *waiting. . . .*"

170   THE GREAT DEBATES

The networks might have conveyed that the audience in the hall was paying attention to the stage. Only later that evening during the post-debate CBS special did one learn from Roger Mudd, a reporter in the theater audience, that the audience applauded twice—when Carter sat down and when the two men wiped their brows during the audio break. Judging by later news comment, the audience was intently watching for any cues to Carter's and Ford's feelings. Elizabeth Drew said Ford and Carter just stood there silently—except, one surmises, for the quip by Carter previously noted. Frank Reynolds, another reporter on the panel, said that the two men never looked at each other, while Drew said that they glanced at each other furtively but only when assured the cameras weren't on them. On one occasion, about fifteen minutes into the gap, the monitor showed Ford looking at Carter, but most of the time, Reynolds said, Ford stood there "like a rock—refusing to sit down—trying to project a strong leader image."[12]

Was it not noteworthy that the candidates did not "exchange one word of commiseration" though, as Reynolds surmised in a follow-up program, "they must have been seething." Newman later speculated that being "in a pickle together" may have made the two men more friendly. To others, like NBC's John Chancellor, who had not been in the hall, both Carter and Ford looked like people "who'd had their pockets picked," so that, if there was camaraderie, it was because they had been through a disaster.

The story possibilities are not endless, but there was something to be noted about the personal drama of the two caught up in the silence. Of this drama, only those in the hall were fully aware. Viewers received little indication from either picture or commentary during the gap that anything worth reporting was going on.

Debates in Jeopardy

Perhaps the least commented on and potentially most important aspect of the audio failure was the possible threat it posed to the continuation of the debate series. Two more presidential debates and one vice-presidential debate were planned. What made these debates problematical were the grounds for a Federal Communications Commission ruling that exempted them from the equal-time provision of the law. The exemption rested on a semifiction: that they were ostensibly *not* arranged by a broadcaster but were an independent event before a live audience in attendance, without regard for whether or not it was to be broadcast. The debate was set up by the League of Women Voters Education Fund. Though patently designed for television, the network staffs had no control over the arrangements. They had to abide by the fiction that they were reporting a bona fide news event and were not involved in any way in a production staged for a television audience.

The fiction clearly implied that the debate would take place even if television or radio did not cover it. Therefore, the debate should have continued when the sound went off. However, for technical reasons, it could not go on. The internal public address system was tied in with the audio broadcast signal. This was a customary means of preventing feedback and static over the air. On this occasion, the League had not provided its own PA system (it would do so in the succeeding debates). If there had been such a backup system, the sound could have been amplified in the hall, irrespective of what went over the air. Instead, the television coverage of the first debate, an event that allegedly would have occurred without nationwide coverage, put a stop to the event it was meant to cover.

Most alarming was the argument that without a live debate, there no longer was a bona fide news story and the network coverage was no longer exempt from the equal-time requirement. With continued coverage of the silenced debate, the delicate compromise by which the debates had been arranged became vulnerable to new challenges from minority candidates and civil libertarians who, from the beginning, had decried the FCC ruling.

If this was a real possibility, then there was good reason either to prevent the technical breakdown from causing the paradox or not to alert the critics. Jim Karayn, who, as project director, had labored long and hard to make the debates a reality, was aware of the possible legal complication. He tried, unsuccessfully, to get the PA system back from ABC so that the debate could resume without television coverage. We do not know how many others recognized the sudden vulnerability of the broadcast compromise. At least, nothing was said on the air about this development. As time went on, there was a rumor to the effect that the League might call a halt to the debate. The networks obviously could not do this and still maintain the semifiction that they were only transmitting the debate. Apparently, no network considered cutting its coverage of the event.

The implications of the incident for future debates subsequently got some airing in the press. Representative Lionel Van Deerlin of California, chairman of the House Communications Subcommittee, was quoted as saying that this "made a mockery" of the FCC interpretation of the debates exemption. FCC Commissioner Abbott Washburn was reported as thinking that most Americans would agree that the event was a bona fide news event and "a very major one."[13] That the television audience was kept in ignorance of this slumbering issue probably helped keep it from growing into a major controversy after the first debate. As it turned out, no serious attempt to stop further debates materialized.

Discussion

This analysis of the news coverage during the audio outage reveals differences in style and emphases among networks. Yet none of these differences, noted in the text, overshadows the fundamental similarity in the way the three news teams acted to meet this crisis. Their response was influenced, first, by the fact that they had geared their schedules and deployed their resources towards providing a post-debate analysis. Producers fell back on these plans when they were unexpectedly confronted with an interruption. They did not cover the story of the gap itself. Thus, they did not convey any of the tenseness that must have been experienced by those caught up in the failure—from the presidential candidates on the stage all the way down to the most subordinate technician. During the entire gap, the pool camera provided practically no close-ups of Ford and Carter; nor did it give any idea, through picture, sound, or commentary, of what must have been a frantic effort to restore the audio.

News personnel appeared caught in a situation not of their own making.

Thus, the most pervasive theme in the coverage was the breakdown in internal communication, over and above the actual interruption of sound from the hall. Commentators repeatedly alluded to the way the pooled audio feed prevented them from obtaining the information needed to clarify the situation. Perhaps the fact that they went out of their way to explain to the viewing audience the seriousness of the handicap under which they were operating was also intended to forestall any criticism.

It seems significant that the big story of the breakdown was about television itself. Each aspect of that story touched on certain broader issues of television's responsibility to the public. Thus, there was no reason to dwell on the possibility of sabotage or censorship, and, appropriately, the networks did not do so. Nor was there, for whatever reason, any mention of how the candidates themselves, along with the video pool, were contributing to their entrapment. We have noted the various ways in which each network maintained a stance of objectivity in recapping, through commentary and interviews, the unfinished debate.

The one aspect of the story that was never specifically mentioned or even vaguely alluded to throughout the gap was the threat posed by the interruption for the precariously maintained fiction that allowed the debate to be held in the first place. Did network news personnel judge this not to be a bona fide news story, or did they feel constrained not to mention it? Certainly, the challenge from the minor parties and ACLU to the arrangements was still very much alive and therefore part of the story of the breakdown. But to treat this issue during the gap would have been to give it the widest possible exposure. One can argue that this was not the time or the place to air it, but the direct bearing the interruption had on the semifiction under which the debate was being held made it a hard issue to ignore. But then television, like other industries, is perhaps more concerned about dramatizing its own public role than in covering and dealing with some of the dilemmas that arise from its presence.

NOTES

1. Videotapes used for analysis were made available from the Educational Communications Center at Stony Brook and the Television News Archives at Vanderbilt University. Full transcripts were prepared from these tapes by John Stensrud, who also carried out preliminary content analyses under the guidance of the authors. This paper is an elaboration of a presentation at a conference on the Ford-Carter debates at the Annenberg School of Communication, Philadelphia, arranged and chaired by Robert Meadows and Marilyn Jackson-Beeck, May 20, 1977.

2. All time references in the text are to Central Standard Time.

3. Immediately after the debate, the gap was referred to as 28 minutes. By October 4, 1976, *Broadcasting* was calling it exactly 26 minutes, beginning at 10:51:05 EST and resuming at 11:17:05. How long the gap was is a matter of definition. If the gap is defined as a "media event," it is measured as the number of minutes networks were cut off from the sound coming from the Walnut Street Theater. The "gap" defined this way varies by networks: ABC—26 minutes 10 seconds; CBS—27 minutes 50 seconds; NBC—27 minutes 30 seconds. If the "gap" is defined in terms of the debate as the "event," then our best count is that 28 minutes 10 seconds

elapsed from the point at which Carter was last heard speaking to the point at which he concluded the last sentence of his rebuttal to Ford. We compromise by calling it a "27-minute gap."

4. Elizabeth Drew, "A Reporter in Washington, D.C.," *New Yorker*, January 10, 1977, p. 56.

5. The style by which ABC converted "bad news" into "happy news" is further illustrated by its reporting of the gap on network news the following evening. Responding to a reporter's query about whether he thought a Republican had pulled the plug, Governor Carter was seen replying, "Well, I thought maybe the FBI didn't like what I was saying." And, in his final note to the news, Harry Reasoner had this comment: "There were, you might imagine, a good many witty remarks about last night's 28-minute audio failure, ranging from the man who asked, 'Who let Rosemary Woods into the control room?' to the alleged case of one commentator who went twenty-one minutes without noticing those fellows weren't talking anymore. . . . It may not have been the best part of the debate but I think that there was one general unspoken feeling: *Wasn't it nice for a change to have some sort of national disaster which was funny?*"

6. Ratner reported the stage managers and/or technicians were on stage. They could not be seen on TV.

7. For instance, *Broadcasting*, October 4, 1976, p. 28.

8. Ibid., p. 28.

9. ABC network news, September 24, 1976.

10. *Broadcasting*, October 4, 1976, p. 28. We have relied heavily in this account of what was being done to restore sound on the articles that appeared in this issue of the magazine as well as on personal discussion at the Annenberg Conference on the Ford-Carter Debates with Jim Karayn.

11. Drew, *New Yorker*, January 10, 1977.

12. This and other quotes in this section are from network post-debate specials and were taken directly from videotapes made available to us by the Educational Communications Center at Stony Brook.

13. *Broadcasting*, October 4, 1976.

10.

The Good But Not Great Nondebates:
Some Random Personal Notes

RICHARD S. SALANT

That there has been so much discussion, analysis, and debate about the 1976 confrontations between Gerald Ford and Jimmy Carter, and between Fritz Mondale and Robert Dole, is healthy. They were an important part of the 1976 presidential campaign.

But there is a consensus that they could have been better, that more could have been done to make it possible for voters to vote on an informed basis, and that there is still much to be done. Only by focusing on the past—as those who are contributing to this book are doing—can we come closer to achieving the ultimate objective of an informed voting citizenry in the future.

At the threshold, I note my discomfort with the title of this book. It is convenient, dramatic—and inaccurate. They were not debates any more than the Kennedy/Nixon events in 1960 were debates. They were joint interviews, with journalists comprising the interviewing panel and setting the specific agenda. Nor, whatever they were, were they great. They contributed a good deal to public knowledge and voter perceptions. They may have had a considerable influence on the outcome of the election—I will leave that question to the consideration of others. But they were imperfect. Useful, yes. In basic format, worth preserving. Good, yes. But not quite great. That these events were not debates is not the reason that I believe that they were imperfect. Certain consequences, which I shall discuss below, flow from the fact that they were joint press interviews rather than debates. And true debates *are* desirable. But so are joint press interviews.

Nor do I regard it as a flaw—or at least as a flaw which is curable by whatever organization might be putting these appearances together—that the candidates often were not responsive, but simply used questions as a trigger for sometimes interesting but often irrelevant previously prepared statements which, on more than one instance, were simply repetitions of excerpts from earlier campaign speeches. A poor, disappointing or unenlightening interview may be the fault of the format, or it may be the fault of the interviewers. But most often, where professional and very able journalists are the interviewers, as they were in this case, the fault may lie with the interviewees—as I think, by and large, it did here. An interviewer, no matter how skilled, may sometimes not be able to elicit relevant, much less brilliant, responses. To a considerable

175

extent, as every reporter knows, it is the interview subject who has the ultimate control, especially in a "live" interview, where editing is impossible and interviewee filibustering, tempting. Interviewees—and especially political candidates and even more especially presidential political candidates—can be brought to interviews but in general, no matter what the skills of the journalist, they cannot be *made* to be responsive, enlightening, or relevant if they are determined not to be so. The journalists can do, and in the 1976 presidential joint appearances did do, their best. If the candidates slipped and slid and hedged and were unresponsive and took refuge in prepared mini-speeches, that in itself should have been significant and enlightening to the viewer and the listener because it was one measure of the nature of the candidates. The viewer and the listener could then make up his or her own mind on what this meant in deciding for whom —if anybody—he or she should vote.

It may have been a flaw that these were not true debates, but not a flaw about which the League of Women Voters could have done anything. Just as in 1960 we at CBS sought true debates and failed because Kennedy and Nixon would not agree to them, so, I am told by the League of Women Voters representatives, the League also vigorously pressed for direct interchanges between the candidates. The candidates, they tell me, refused. And so the League of Women Voters, like anybody else trying to put events like this together, was faced with one of the ultimate questions: "If the candidates don't do it my way, should it not be done at all?" There are surely some arrangements insisted upon by the candidates which are so undesirable that compromise should be ruled out and the project should be abandoned. But just as I believe that the networks were right in 1960 in going forward with the format which prevailed then, rather than insisting on debates or nothing, so I believe that the League was right in settling for a basic format which the candidates were willing to accept.

On this issue, the question is whether, failing agreement by the candidates on direct confrontation, it would have better served the public interest and the democratic process that there should have been nothing. In various public appearances—before journalism students, before community leaders—I have put this question and asked for a show of hands. The overwhelming majority voted that it was better to have what we had than to have nothing at all. I agree.

Neither, in my view, was it a flaw that the events might have been dull. These events are not entertainments; they should not be designed to be entertainments; and the desire to be entertaining or titillating or dramatic should neither control nor influence the format. That serious journalists and critics should so frequently measure these events for their nonboredom factor condemns the journalists and critics and their values more than it condemns the event or the format of the event. The League of Women Voters and its representatives, who played so important a role in devising the format for these events, are to be congratulated, not condemned, for resisting the importunities of the critics (and one of its own chief advisors who, after the first debate, advocated shortening the events to sixty or seventy-five minutes, and otherwise changing the format to increase viewer interest) who gave too high a priority to audience circulation and show-business values. On this issue, John Leonard (*New York Times*, October 24, 1976) said it right:

THE GREAT DEBATES

The complaint that the televised debates between the candidates are boring is itself boring. One tires of people who sit around twirling their knobs, fiddling with themselves as though they were stereo consoles, mood synthesizers: I'm turned off. Who says that politics or politicians are supposed to turn you on? In a presidential election year, you ought at the very least to be at a low hum without any outside help at all: it is the normal respiration of intelligence.

Inevitably with the attention—entirely appropriate—that has focused on the "debates"—there has been a silly season, characterized by truly remarkable overstatement by normally sensible observers. Thus, Richard D. Heffner, (*Los Angeles Times*, October 6, 1976) wrote in a piece entitled "Watergate Mentality Slops Over Into Debates":

> It will be a sad spectacle on television tonight, for no matter who 'wins' the second debate . . . , every American who approves of the encounters will be a loser . . .
> Approve of the debates or not, one can hardly deny that this year they are the product of gross expediency—the essence of Watergate. . . .
> For who can deny that the essence of public morality and of the law—the majesty of this great nation—was subverted two weeks ago, will be subverted tonight and twice again before October is out. . . .
> And what is worse is that, precisely in the spirit of Watergate—take what we want to take, do what we want to do, just so long as we can get away with it and don't get caught—too many of us are cheering these events . . . We deserve better of ourselves. . . . What a triumph of expediency over principle! What a blatant assault upon due process, and ultimately upon our national well-being! Tocqueville would weep.

Mr. Heffner is one of the leading students of Tocqueville—he is one of the few who know that if you leave out his first name, you must leave out the "de." That, alone, entitled Heffner's views to respect. But I am presumptuous; I do not for a moment believe that Alexis de Tocqueville would have shed a tear —or even looked unhappy.

It must take some time before the *Los Angeles Times* gets to the desks of the *New York Times*, for Russell Baker, seventeen days later, on October 23, provided the East coast echo:

> If the Ford-Carter debates did not violate the law, they certainly made a farce of it. The cream of the jest is that very few people, despite the resurgent reverence for law supposedly born of the Watergate affair, seemed to care. . . .
> The squire of San Clemente may feel a justifiable twinge of cynicism at seeing so many of last year's righteous souls fallen into a conspiracy worthy of a flim-flam gang. . . .
> It was a splendid illustration of the most uplifted minds in the nation laboring to violate the spirit of law while adhering to the letter.

What these condemnations were about was that minority candidates had been excluded by the League of Women Voters from the joint appearances and that the League had been able to do so because the Federal Communications Commission, in a decision upheld by a split ruling (2-1) by the Court of Appeals for the District of Columbia, had reversed a long-standing holding that such "debates" or joint appearances, even if under the complete control and auspices of an independent, outside, nonbroadcasting organization, were not exempt from Section 315 of the Communications Act—the provision which requires equal opportunities for all candidates, no matter how obscure, for the same office.

There is a valid question whether the FCC and a majority of the Court of Appeals were correct. Perhaps indeed, strategically we in broadcast journalism would have been better off if the FCC had stuck to its earlier rulings and so would have aborted these events. That would have dramatized the inflexibility and negative effect of Section 315 and would have placed us, so hobbled in our journalistic responsibilities by Section 315, in a better strategic position than we now are to obtain legislative relief from that egregious provision.

But it seems to me to be melodramatically overstating the matter to equate all this with Watergate and the Watergate mentality. Heffner and Baker seem to be suggesting that the Aspen Institute should never have asked for the FCC's reconsideration of its earlier ruling that such "debates" under outside independent auspices fell within Section 315—a suggestion no more sensible than would be a suggestion that the NAACP and others should have waited for a constitutional amendment to eliminate the old Supreme Court "separate but equal" rulings rather than asking for a reconsideration of those cases. And we never would have had the *Brown* v. *Board of Education* decision.

The Messrs. Heffner and Baker also seem to condemn the League for going forward after the FCC and the Court of Appeals had made the decision that these events were exempt from Section 315. They appear to insist that *if* the League nevertheless went ahead and arranged the events, the networks should have ignored them, and that the League, the candidates, and the networks having failed to boycott, the public should have shut them out, and not looked or listened. And so all of us should go hide our heads in San Clemente.

The Heffner/Baker contentions are classic examples of destroying a case by overstatement. The "debates" were not symptoms of Watergate corruption— nor were the FCC and Court of Appeals decisions which made them possible. The decisions may have been mistaken but they were hardly corrupt, literally or spiritually. At worst, they reminded us that, like so many administrative and judicial decisions before them, bad law (here Section 315) often makes bad decisions.

A related contention is that these joint appearances were somehow inherently defective and immoral, and should not have been exempt from Section 315, because they were not true "news events" since they were intended for the television audience, and would not have gone forward if they were not broadcast. The proponents of this argument see the proof of their argument in the fact that the "debate" between the two candidates was halted when, during the first such event at Philadelphia, there was an audio failure and the proceedings were halted for twenty-seven minutes until the sound was restored.

Of course, the League intended these for television. And it is entirely reasonable to assume that Messrs. Ford and Carter would not have taken so much time out of their campaigns to participate just for the benefit of a relative handful of people in the auditorium. But the argument proves too much. There are a great many news events—probably a large majority—press conferences, demonstrations, fishing in ponds, political conventions, hijackings and kidnappings, etc., etc., ad infinitum, which are, in one way or another and to a greater or lesser extent, designed to be seen by the television audience or read about by newspaper readers. If the press were to ignore all happenings which are not in one way or another designed for the evening news broadcasts, or the morning papers, or the attention of reporters or editors, the press would pretty much have to confine itself to the reporting of blizzards, droughts, fires, tornadoes, earthquakes, and the eruption of volcanos.

By any sensible standards, these were news events and were no less so just because they probably would not have taken place if they had not been broadcast.

Nor do I believe that, while I had some basic disagreements with some of the arrangements which the League made or imposed (see below), there was anything inherently wrong with the fact that these events were under the auspices of the League—or, conversely, that these events were flawed merely because they were not under the sole auspices of the networks. In respect of format or other basic arrangements, I am not at all sure that we—the network news organizations—could have done significantly better than the League. *Perhaps* we might have been a little more sophisticated. *Perhaps* we would have bargained a little harder. *Perhaps* the set would have looked a little less like the village thermometer showing how well the local United Fund drive was doing. *Perhaps* we would not have given in to some of the candidates' demands so quickly because at least in some respects the networks might have had a little more clout (even that is arguable since it may well be that presidential candidates might find it more difficult to disagree with, and pull out of, an event under the auspices of so prestigious, unassailable, and formidable a public service organization as the League of Women Voters than one under the auspices of the mean, male-dominated, big old networks).

But, I find nothing wrong with the mere fact of having such events under the auspices of a responsible outside organization, nor do the networks have any God-given right to be the only ones to arrange such events. Indeed, it is somewhat easier for us networks to have somebody else do it—if the format displeases, or somebody has to be left off the panel, or a wrong choice of panelists is made, we could always—and legitimately—lay it on the League and disclaim responsibility. There are a lot of headaches and indeed, as the League has discovered to its sorrow, a lot of costs that can be avoided by having someone else do it. As we at CBS made clear to the congressional committees, we were willing to have the League go forward, and we would have gone forward with the League and the broadcasts, even if Section 315 were repealed, so that these events could have been under our auspices.

And so in the future, even if Section 315 should be repealed so that debates and joint appearances could be under broadcasters' auspices, it is not only possible but entirely probable that we would still cover and broadcast such events, given reasonably sensible basic arrangements, under outside auspices—including League auspices.

To the extent that they partake of press conference characteristics, as these events did, we would hope that the sponsoring organization, whether it be the League or anybody else, would not only turn to able lawyers and lobbyists, as the League did in choosing its debate committee, but that there would also be a greater representation of those who are intimately familiar with journalism. Indeed, if the League of Women Voters or some similar organization goes forward in the future, perhaps it would do so in conjunction and cooperation with journalistic organizations—such as the wire services; or the Society of Professional Journalists, Sigma Delta Chi; or the American Society of Newspaper Editors; or the American Newspaper Publishers Association. I suspect that the League itself, and its advisors, might welcome this: Its advisory committee and other representatives, during the period when these events were being developed, turned to us for advice which we had to refuse because our lawyers said that any participation in the arrangements—even advice—would cost the events their exemption under Section 315.

But there was nothing inherently wrong about the fact that these "debates" were arranged by the League, which is owed a large debt for its immense contributions and without which they would not have been held. Conversely, I would emphasize, there is nothing inherently right about a policy which would permit *only* the networks to play this role.

At least philosophically, the exclusion of all but the Democratic and Republican candidates presents the most difficult issue. But I do not see that, as a practical matter or as a matter of realistic recognition of things as they are, the League had very much choice on this issue, any more than we networks would have had very much choice had we been the producers.

Like it or not, this is currently, and long has been, essentially and normally a two-party system. It is not the function of the League, or the networks, to distort reality by pretending otherwise. Less than two percent of the voters voted for minority presidential candidates. Gene McCarthy received 751,728 votes; Roger MacBride, of the Libertarian Party, came fourth with 172,750 votes; Lester Maddox was fifth with 170,780 votes—and so on down the list among those who were on the ballots in any state, to 6,022 votes for Frank Ziedler of the Socialist Party.

It would simply have been a practical impossibility for these events to have gone forward in 1976 with the inclusion of *all* the minority candidates who, when one considers that even those who are eligible for nothing more than write-ins in the states which permit such write-ins, would have had to be considered. The contest was in fact between the Republican and Democratic candidates, and all the political philosophy about whether this ought to be seems to me irrelevant. Judgments must be made and the line must be drawn somewhere. It is impractical to have a half-dozen or a dozen or twenty or forty candidates all participate—enlightenment would have been overriden by abstract political philosophy. In fact, it is difficult to believe that either of the two major candidates would have participated at all. And who can blame them?

That is not to say that there may not be circumstances in the future, as there have been in the past, where sensible judgments might not be justified in insisting that one or more third-party candidates should be permitted to participate. Surely it would have been an egregious blunder to have gone forward with only the Democratic and Republican candidates participating when, for example, Theodore Roosevelt was the candidate of the Bull Moose party in 1912; or Robert LaFollette was running in 1924 as the Progressive party candidate; or George Wallace was running in 1968.

But computers and automatic formulas cannot substitute for hard judgments. And again there is always the bottom-line question: Is it more sensible, is it more clearly in the public interest and in accordance with the objective of voter understanding and enlightenment, to go forward with only the major party candidates than it is to have nothing at all? I think the answer is clear—it is "yes." It is no more sensible or realistic to insist on the inclusion of all minor candidates, or even some, in such debates or panels as a price of their going forward than it is to command that newspapers—or even their "battle pages"—treat all qualified candidates equally as the price of any coverage at all.

I do not mean to suggest that there should not be some *other* arrangements which would give some of the minority candidates more than was provided for them in 1976—or in 1960. There are indeed some candidates—perhaps McCarthy, MacBride, Maddox, for example—who were entitled to less than participation in the events but more than it was possible to give them. But under Section 315, there is no room for any selection at all so far as the broadcaster is concerned. At one point during the campaign, the vice-chairman of the Federal Elections Commission estimated that there were over twenty parties with presidential candidates and an additional seventy presidential candidates without political party designation.

And so it was not practical, under the strictures of Section 315, for the networks to provide any additional special coverage of those who might have been "major" minority candidates. The dilemmas which networks faced during the 1976 presidential election was that, because of Section 315, the only opportunities for minority candidate appearances on the networks were, for all practical purposes, either the "debates" or such exempt regularly scheduled hard news broadcasts (for example, the "Evening News") and regularly scheduled interview broadcasts (for example, "Face The Nation"). And on these, normal news judgment must prevail—and that judgment inevitably was that the contest was between Ford and Carter. We could not provide broadcast exposure for the minority candidates on any *special* broadcasts, since those were not exempt. If we put the "major" third-party candidates on, we would have no choice, under Section 315, but to put the entire roster on. And so special appearances—presentations of special interviews, or opportunity for a direct presentation outside of regularly scheduled hard news and interview broadcasts—were for all practical purposes precluded. Were it not for this obstacle presented by the intractability of Section 315, we might well have had some special broadcasts involving the more important minor candidates. But substantially greater exposure on our hard news and interview broadcasts was not warranted, since there it is basically news judgment which must prevail and I would guess that proportionately, we gave the "major" minority candidates as much attention as responsible newspapers did.

And so, though the issue is not free from difficulty, and the complaint that the way the League broadcasts developed did not do full justice to the more important minor candidates is understandable, it does not seem to me that the answer lay in trying to shoehorn them into the League broadcasts which, as noted, probably never would have taken place if the League had insisted that McCarthy, Maddox, MacBride and Anderson—or any of them—had to be added. The fault lay not with the League or the absence of such candidates from the broadcasts. That we as broadcasters did no more for these minority candidates was due to the unyielding nature of Section 315.

Up to this point, I have noted that I have no basic quarrel with the 1976 joint presidential appearances as such. But, as is altogether too well known, I did have serious (and excessively noisy) reservations about two aspects of the procedures which were finally adopted by the League. One, and most important, was the participation—whatever it was—by the candidates in the process of selection of the panelists. Second was the insistence by the League, apparently in turn at the insistence of the candidates, that although an audience was present at these events, broadcasters were flatly forbidden to show the audience during the appearances. Each of these presented very serious issues of journalistic principle.

As for the role which the candidates played in the process of selection of panelists, I have difficulty because although we broadcast these events, we were, by law, divorced from them completely. And so, to this day, I am not at all sure just what role the candidates and their representatives played in the process of selection. We did not even know that they played any role until it was disclosed to us by a League representative at a cocktail party virtually on the eve of the first debate. When I sought—without appropriate diplomacy and with excessive persistence—the details at a meeting with the League of Women Voters, I was told that this was none of my business and that the League had a right to do it any way that it chose and that our only choice—and a Hobson's choice it was—was to broadcast them or not to broadcast them. When I pursued the matter, I was further told that the details were "confidential." One of the members of the committee charged with the arrangements for the League of Women Voters said in response to one of my questions that he did not know whether a potential panelist was dropped because of objections by one of the candidates or the other. I was assured that the candidates had no "veto power" but, to me, this left a large area of how much weight the League might have given to the candidates' reactions to the lists. We had been told by one or the other candidate's camps that there were lists "floating around" and that in at least one case, there were strong objections by one candidate to a name which appeared on the list and that name subsequently disappeared from the list. I was assured by the League of Women Voters at that meeting that as early as September 1, the League had publicly stated that the panelists would be picked "in consultation with the candidates," and I was told that there was a transcript of the press conference at which a League of Women Voters representative had so stated this. When I asked at that meeting for a copy of the transcript, I was told it was in another building. When I later asked again for the transcript, I was finally told that there was no transcript and perhaps such a statement had not been made after all. I was told at that meeting that the League had decided from the outset that it was proper for the candidates to have some input in the selection because it was important that the panelists must be viewed as "fair" by both candidates—and that in order to assure the

182

candidates of such fairness, they would be given the right to submit a list of up to forty-five names for each event.

On September 17, just before that meeting with the League representatives, the president of the League had confirmed in a television interview—for the first time to my knowledge—that the panelists were chosen "in consultation" between the League and the candidates: that "it was part of the agreement that we would tell them [the candidates] our choices before we told the public" and that such prior notification was *primarily* a courtesy" (italics mine); that the League had not yet been faced with the problem of an objection by either of the candidates to any of the proposed panelists, but if such objections should occur, "we'll cross that bridge when we come to it"; and that on the question of selection of panelists "we're in consultation with them [the candidates] as it goes along."

And so I am left with uneasiness concerning the process of selection— but no truly hard first-hand knowledge. I frankly do not know with certainty precisely what the process was. The fact is that the journalists serving as moderators and panelists were first rate. I have no reason to believe that had we at CBS News selected the moderators or the panelists, we would have done any better.

But the principle remains. It is simply the principle, which has always been basic at CBS News, as it must be in any responsible news organization, that we lose our integrity, our independence, and our journalistic prerogatives if we share with the interview subjects the selection of those who are to interview them. As the written CBS News Standards state: "The subject of an interview shall have no voice in the selection of the interviewer, nor, in any news coverage, should the subject of the coverage have any voice in the selection of the correspondent assigned to cover him/her on the story."

It was to vindicate this important policy that I stated at the outset that there are consequences which flow from the fact that these were not debates but were joint press interviews. Once the format of a press interview was adopted, then, as a matter of basic journalistic policy, the candidates or their representatives should have had no input—whatever it was—in the selection process. The result may well have been precisely the same. But once that principle is abandoned, it demeans the journalistic process.

In my view, the principle is a critical one. We at CBS News will continue to insist on it.

So too, a journalistic principle is involved in the second issue—the prohibition against reflecting by camera or by microphone the fact, as indeed it was the fact, that there *was* an audience present. (Ultimately, the League did take the position that they would abandon this restriction if the candidates agreed, but the candidates did not.) It is a long established and important journalistic principle that those who arrange an event cannot properly tell the journalists who are covering the event where to focus their attention—what to cover and what not to cover. The managers of political conventions, the sponsors of a press interview, demonstrators—almost everybody involved as subjects when there are cameras and microphones present—are often eager to control just where the cameras and microphones are pointed and what the public will hear and see—and more important what they will not hear and see. But a reporter cannot permit such a delegation to outside parties—particularly to outside parties who are managers of, or major participants in, the event.

Once the audience was there, it became part of the event and as a matter of journalistic policy, we as journalists cannot accept the direction of those who put on, or participate in, the event.

This made us second-class members of the press. Print reporters were subject to no such restrictions and they took advantage, as they had every right and obligation to do, of their freedom. And so, James Wooten (*New York Times*, October 23, 1976) was free to write, the day after the October 22 Williamsburg debate:

> There was more to the television debate here tonight than met the camera's eye.
>
> On the screens in millions of American living rooms, Jimmy Carter and President Ford seemed to stand alone and aloof across a soft gray room from four distant panelists. But in Phi Beta Kappa Hall on the campus of the College of William and Mary, the two men were at the core of a living, breathing, sneezing, coughing, giggling, yawning, widening circle of humanity that stretched from the eight cameramen stationed around them to the not-so-very-important people in the last row of the curving balcony.
>
> They were all an invisible and thus—for most of America—an irrelevant part of the third, final and perhaps the most crucial of the nationally televised meetings between Mr. Carter and Mr. Ford.
>
> Because their staffs had insisted that cameras could not show anyone other than the six participants, much of the essence of the moment was lost to most voters' eyes.
>
> When Mr. Ford, for instance, forgot—or avoided mentioning—the name of Earl Warren, the late Chief Justice of the United States, titters of amusement rippled through the audience.

Good, legitimate reporting—which told the *New York Times* readers something about the character of the event. Television could have shown that directly—sight and sound. Radio can reflect the sound of the event. Each can do this first hand. The restriction forbade us to do that which radio and television do best: Permitting the public to see and hear for itself, without having to be told about it second-hand by a reporter, no matter how skilled.

It is no valid argument to urge that we could not be trusted—that we might have shown an untypical member of the audience sleeping, or drowsing. Of course, reporters can always distort an event by focusing on the distracting and the untypical. But under our system of a free press, the remedy for bad reporting is *not* to forbid reporting at all.

That, precisely, was the principle involved. The chances are that we would have remained focused on the candidates and the panelists and that there would have been only fleeting and minimal focus on the audience which was present. But the choice has to be the journalists'—ours; it cannot be the dictates of the managers of the event or the participants in it. If it is the latter and not the former, we become public address systems—passive transmitters of handouts and not journalists. Once, for reasons of its own, the League decided that an audience should be present, it was wrong as a matter of principle to require,

184

as the price of coverage, that we pretend that there was no audience present.

And so, on balance, I think much of the criticism of these "debates" was misplaced. The quarrel whether some other format would have been more useful misses the point. For it is my view that too much attention has been paid to the particular format and its details. But too much attention has been paid for a simple reason—that was all that there was to which to pay attention.

To me the central point is that no single format can possibly do all the things that it would be desirable to do to give the voter fuller understanding of the character and nature of the candidates—what manner of people they are, where they came from, what they have done, and where they stand. It is true that joint press conferences like the League events get in the way of candidates' direct exchange of views, and tend to make the panelists and their questions intrusive and perhaps distracting. It is true that direct debates between the candidates may place too high a premium on quickness, on glibness, on off-the-cuff reactions—on skills which may or may not be important in evaluating candidates.

The short of it is, however, that no single format can do all the things that are demanded of it. The real answer, I am persuaded, is that it must be made possible, during a presidential election campaign, to use the *full* range of formats, each of which can supplement the others, each of which can compensate for the shortcomings of the others. Only if such a full range is permissible, and is utilized, can we come closer to the full information which the voter, by listening to radio and watching television, should have.

It is for this reason that, repeatedly over the years, CBS has suggested to the congressional committees and to others that there should be a package or a mix of broadcasts starting with a half-hour for each of the major candidates directly to present his or her own case in his or her own way, and ending with a half-hour summary at the end of the campaign for each candidate. And in between there should be such joint press conferences as those held in 1976; *and* Oregon-type debates; *and* one-on-one in-depth interviews with each of the major candidates; *and* a documentary about each candidate, tracing the candidate's origins, record, and what he or she has said and has not said, what he or she has done and has not done.

With that kind of mix, we would not engage in endless discussion about the details of events like those sponsored by the League, because together, such a variety of broadcasts would make the whole greater than the sum of the parts. The League events would be only one of the games in town—and not the only one.

But—and I point this out reluctantly because our motives are suspect—this kind of mix of candidate broadcasts, which I believe to be the true answer to what broadcasting can do and should do, is possible only with the repeal of Section 315. Except for the "outside auspices" exemption by interpretation (which indeed can be reinterpreted out of existence by a future FCC), none of these formats is practical so long as Section 315 remains. It is not feasible to do one-on-one interviews with all of the dozens of candidates who might be eligible. It is not feasible to have debates among a dozen or more candidates. It is not feasible to devote an hour to an in-depth interview with all the potential candidates.

As long as Section 315 is on the books and all that can be worked out is what the League of Women Voters was able to work out, we are settling for only a few slices instead of the whole loaf. The slices are good; they are nutritious; they are far, far better than starving to death. But the American voters—the democratic process itself—deserve the whole which repeal of Section 315 would make possible and which CBS News is ready, willing, and eager to provide.

EDITOR'S NOTE: This chapter was prepared and completed long before publication in the spring of 1979 of the *Report of the Twentieth Century Fund Task Force on Televised Debates*. The *Report* advocates presidential debates every four years under the sponsorship of "a nonprofit, nonpartisan citizen group devoted to citizen education and participation," and specifically excludes broadcasters (networks) as sponsors. The only one of the sixteen members of the task force issuing the *Report* who dissented from that exclusion was William Small, vice-president, CBS News. Small wrote, "As the only veteran of broadcast journalism on the Task Force, I feel compelled to dissent, not because I am opposed to the League of Women Voters sponsoring debates, but because I am opposed to the specific exclusion of broadcasters from such sponsorship." Mr. Salant, who moved to NBC after retirement from CBS, agrees with Small and would have commented specifically about the exclusionary statement, had the *Report* been issued in time for this publication.

11.

Grilling the Pols: Q & A at the Debates

LOUIS T. MILIC

The debates of 1976 were treated in the press and in some television commentaries as if they were a written, rehearsed, and played program rather than a live event in which anything could happen—and twice did—such as the twenty-minute loss of audio in the first debate and the surprising view of the Soviet domination in Eastern Europe by Gerald Ford in the second. Curiously, what did not attract much interest or comment was the undeniable fact that what the candidates had to say was greatly dependent upon a different set of players, the panelists/questioners. These determined (more or less) what topics the candidates could speak about and what they could not speak about. This was in sharp contrast to the Lincoln-Douglas debates, in which the principals decided for themselves what issues they would present to the public in their seven encounters before the 1858 senatorial election. As it happened, they spoke mainly about slavery. Even the deliberately restricted format specified for the presidential debates of 1976 allowed for a degree of unpredictability very unusual in television and relatively unusual in staged political campaign events. This unpredictability is due in great measure to the linguistic properties of two types of utterances (questions and answers) with which every speaker of a language is acquainted but which have only recently been studied with care by linguists. Rhetoricians, of course, have known about questions for ages. Because politicians are professional rhetors and journalists are professional inquisitors, the debates in fact provided, for those who could observe it, the spectacle of a fascinating linguistic struggle between natural antagonists.

These debates consisted almost entirely of the asking of questions by selected panelists and answering by the candidates. Although inevitably when politicians are involved, questions are not always answered conscientiously, this is not simply the result of carelessness. So the moderator of the third debate (Barbara Walters) led off with the following statement:

> Questioners will alternate questions between the candidates. A candidate has up to 2½ minutes to answer the questions. The other candidate has up to two minutes to respond. If necessary, a questioner may ask a follow-up question for further clarification, and in that case the candidate has up to two minutes to respond. As was initially agreed to by both candidates, the answer should be responsive to the particular question.[1]

The last sentence deserves notice in that it actually raises the issue of responsiveness, and implies that the answers in previous debates were nonresponsive and that the candidates had acknowledged this. The vocabulary used to describe the exchange should be noted: *questioner, answer, respond, clarification.* The hoped-for scenario is something like this: a questioner asks a question of the candidate, who answers as responsively as possible; then the other candidate responds; if clarification is needed, the questioner may ask a follow-up question and the candidate responds. It is normal to answer a question, but does it make sense to respond to an answer? The word *respond* in Walters's statement is used to mean *comment* as well as *answer. Respond* is a verb with a wider range than *answer*, which is explicitly limited to the linguistic result achieved by a question. To respond can mean to answer but it can also mean to exhibit nonverbal behavior (e.g., with a dirty look). So the response allowed for in the ground rules may be a statement incorporating an alternative to the answer provided by the other candidates, or indignation, even outrage. The complexity of this vocabulary reflects the complexity of the linguistic/semantic aspects of the exchange itself.

Every reporter knows how difficult it is to ask "good" questions, questions that elicit good answers, i.e., that reveal something about the person questioned, clarify the issues, produce an unexpected reaction. The surfeit of such interviewers' questions as "How did you feel when you (won the lottery, were lost at sea, saw your dog run over, ate 200 pancakes)?" emphasizes both the need for the training of television reporters in this art and the difficulty of the entire matter. The success of some television interviewers (e.g., Mike Wallace) and the effectiveness of some White House press corps reporters suggests that the asking of serious questions is a matter requiring forethought, knowledge, and an understanding of language.[2]

The avoidance of direct questions by politicians is well known and was most dramatically publicized during some of the exchanges between members of the press corps and former President Nixon on the subject of Watergate. The rambling evasiveness that characterized most of his replies led to hostile, aggressive, quasi-judicial cross-examination by reporters in a spectacle which, for all that it was unattractive, reflected a democracy's willingness to subject its highest official to the ordeal of questioning.

That questioning is an ordeal is demonstrated by how infrequently those who do not have to answer questions are willing to do so. In debate two, Jimmy Carter raised this point explicitly: "We have also seen Mr. Ford exclude himself from access to the public. He hasn't had a *tough cross-examination-type* press conference in over 30 days. One press conference he had without sound."[3] The forms of democracy impose questions by the press on members of the government and by the courts on those who come before them either as defendants or witnesses. In many cultures, the asking of questions, especially of elders, superiors, and strangers, is discourteous or deliberately hostile. To mitigate the appearance of discourtesy when the asking of questions is essential, various linguistic subterfuges are resorted to, such as the use of the third person (e.g., "Does the general wish to review the troops?").

Although questions are sometimes used in polite discourse as a way of expressing disagreement, an onus attaches to questions. To question someone's honor, his motives, or ability is to assert that they are tainted or deficient. A question is often less a means of eliciting information than the application of pressure to another to accept a statement made in question form or to reveal information he wishes to keep concealed. Thus the "taking of the Fifth" before congressional committees is in fact, if not in law, a self-incriminating procedure. The compulsion to answer under whatever sanction is a proceeding not too far removed from the application of judicial torture (one of the original meanings of the Latin *quaestio*, the ancestor of our word *question*), or what used to be called the "third degree."

Socially, therefore, questioning involves numerous implications unrelated to the simple exchange of an item of information between someone who wants it and someone who has it. Linguistically, questions are complicated transformations of statements. As a result of long practice with language, any native speaker can tell when he is being asked a question, even though it may come in a variety of types: WH questions (beginning with words like *who, which*), inversion questions ("Did he go?"), tag questions ("He went, didn't he?"), intonation questions ("He went?"), indirect questions ("I ask you whether you saw him leave."). The last is common in the law courts, as is the leading question ("Now did you say that you saw the person leave by the side door of the building at 8:35 P.M., carrying a heavy parcel containing several calculators and typewriters . . ."). The rhetorical question, popular in speeches from the hustings, is of course not a question at all, but an attempt to elicit agreement from an audience. It is second nature with politicians.

Since what is natural to politicians is often a source of discomfort and even suspicion to the voting citizen, it seems worthwhile to examine the details of question and answer as these took place during the three presidential debates, to discover if possible what actually happened and to assess the moral and rhetorical quality of the contributions made by both panelists and candidates.

A close examination of the linguistic substance of the three debates reveals an immediate patterning in the answers. Basically, answers may be satisfactory or unsatisfactory. That is, in the present context, questions are nominally directed for one single purpose: to extract a statement that reveals the position of a candidate on a given issue, so that the voter may determine whether he wishes to support a candidate with such a view. A satisfactory answer is one that permits the described intellectual process to take place. An unsatisfactory answer is one that does not.

The satisfactory category may be refined, however. An answer can be *direct* (short, to the point) or merely *responsive* (in the sense that an answer can be constructed from the materials of the response). The unsatisfactory category can be similarly subdivided into *nonresponsive* answers which furnish an opportunity for a speech, for image-building, or for placing the opponent in a difficult position; and responses that *evade* the question and sometimes proceed by digression in another direction. An example of each kind follows.

Direct Response
[As to which constitutional amendments he would work hard for if he were president]

CARTER: I would not work hard to support any of those. We've always had, I think, a lot of constitutional amendments proposed, but the passage of them has been fairly slow . . . (III-10)[4]

Responsive
[As to new legislation for controlling agencies like the FBI]
FORD: You are familiar, of course, with the fact that I am the first President in 30 years who has reorganized the intelligence agencies in the Federal Government: the C.I.A., the Defense Intelligence Agency, the National Security Agency and others.

We've done that by executive order. And I think we've tightened it up; we've straightened out their problems that developed over the last few years.

It doesn't seem to me that it's needed or necessary to have legislation in this particular regard. I have recommended to the Congress, however—I'm sure you're familiar with this—legislation that would make it very proper, and in the right way, that the Attorney General could go in and get the right for wiretapping under security cases.

This was an effort that was made by the Attorney General and myself, working with the Congress. But even in this area, where I think new legislation would be justified, the Congress has not responded. So I feel in that case, as well as in the reorganization of the intelligence agencies, as I've done, we have to do it by executive order. (I-22)

Nonresponsive
[As to achievements of his administration on behalf of minorities and programs for future progress]
FORD: Let me say at the outset, I'm very proud of the record of this administration. In the Cabinet I have one of the outstanding, I think, administrators as the Secretary of Transportation, Bill Coleman.

You're familiar, I'm sure, with the recognition given in the Air Force to General James, and there was just approved a three-star admiral, the first in the history of the United States Navy, so we are giving full recognition to individuals of quality in the Ford administration in positions of great responsibility.

In addition, the Department of Justice is fully enforcing, and enforcing effectively, the Voting Rights Act, the legislation that involves jobs, housing for minorities, not only blacks but all others. The Department of HUD is enforcing the new legislation that outlaws, that takes care of redlining.

What we're doing is saying that there are opportunities, business opportunities, educational opportunities, responsibilities where people with talent, black or any other minority, can fully qualify. The Office of Minority Business in the Department of Commerce has made available more money in trying to help black businessmen or other minority businessmen than any other administration since the office was established. The Office of Small Business, under Mr. Kobelinski, has a very massive program trying to help the black community. The individual who wants to start a business or expand his business as a black businessman is able to borrow, either directly

190

or with guaranteed loans. I believe that on the record that this administration has been responsive and we have carried out the law to the letter and I am proud of the record. (III-9)

Evasive-Digressive
[As to his concept of the national interest and the role of the U.S. in the world]

CARTER: Well, I'm not going to name my Cabinet before I get elected. I've got a little ways to go before I start doing that.

But I have an adequate background, I believe. I am a graduate of the United States Naval Academy, the first military graduate since Eisenhower. I have served as the Governor of Georgia and have traveled extensively in foreign countries and South America, Central America, Europe, the Middle East and in Japan.

I've traveled the last 21 months among the people of this country. I've talked to them and I've listened. And I've seen at first hand, in a very vivid way, the deep hurt that's come to this country in the aftermath of Vietnam and Cambodia, Chile and Pakistan, and Angola and Watergate, the C.I.A. revelations.

What we were formerly so proud of the strength of our country, its moral integrity, the representation in foreign affairs of what our people or what our Constitution stands for—has been gone. And in the secrecy that has surrounded our foreign policy in the last few years, the American and the Congress have been excluded.

I believe I know what this country ought to be.

I've been one who's loved my nation as many Americans do, and I believe that there's no limit placed on what we can be in the future, if we can harness the tremendous resources, militarily, economically, and the stature of our people, the meaning of the Constitution, in the future.

Every time we've made a serious mistake in foreign affairs, it's been because the American people have been excluded from the process.

If we can just tap the intelligence and ability, the sound common sense and the good judgment of the American people, we can once again have a foreign policy that will make us proud instead of ashamed.

And I'm not going to exclude the American people from that process in the future, as Mr. Ford and Kissinger have done.

This is what it takes to have a sound foreign policy—strong at home, strong defense, permanent commitments—not betray the principles of our country and involve the American people and the Congress in the shaping of our foreign policy.

Every time Mr. Ford speaks from a position of secrecy in negotiations and in secret treaties that have been pursued and achieved in supporting dictatorships, in ignoring human rights, we are weak and the rest of the world knows it.

So these are the ways that we can restore the strength of our country, and they don't require long experience in foreign policy. Nobody has that except a President who has served a long time or a Secretary of State.

But my background, my experience, my knowledge of the people of this country, my commitment to our principles that don't change

—those are the best bases to correct the horrible mistakes of this Administration and restore our own country to a position of leadership in the world. (II-3)

To understand why Ford's answer to III-9 is nonresponsive, one must recall that he was asked about the achievements of his administration on behalf of minorities and of his plans for the future. His answer cited: the naming of one black to a cabinet position, and the promotion of black senior officers in the armed forces to advanced general and flag rank; enforcing existing legislation; and the availability of money to black businessmen. No other minorities are mentioned and no future plans are offered. But even the half of the question that was dealt with was not answered responsively, as the appointment of a Cabinet officer, the promotion of officers, or the enforcing of laws do not constitute achievements.

Carter's answer to II-3 does not deal with the question. It discourses on his qualifications for conducting foreign policy, the difficulties of the nation, his love for it, his plans for an "open" foreign policy, the administration's "mistakes." The answer *evades* the question by means of a digression. A sophisticated professional could infer even from these responses the positions of the candidates: i.e., that Ford's policy toward minorities is highly conservative, which is why he has no achievements or plans to speak of, and that Carter's concept of the national interest is so like Ford's that he could not differentiate them, or he did not wish to present it and therefore was obligated to evade the question. But for the voting citizen, the answers are unsatisfactory because they are uninformative.

Determining the adequacy of an answer is a matter which requires a deeper investigation than is possible here and which renders naive the supposition that a debate will truly inform the citizenry about the views of the candidates. The main difficulty is in identifying the answer, a process requiring intense but instant analysis.

Consider the lead question of the last debate, roughly paraphrased as "What sacrifices are you going to ask the American people to make to realize your objectives?" (III-1) The simplest kind of answer would begin with a recognizable restatement of the question, e.g., "I would ask the American people to sacrifice comfort and affluence," or "To realize my objectives, I would ask for the following sacrifices." In these formulations the key terms emphasize and organize the listener's intake. He can tell what sacrifices are expected of him. Even an answer which is a paraphrase of the original question, using synonyms in place of key terms, can be interpreted easily, if the structure is adequate or recognizable: "To balance the budget (or cut inflation), I would maintain unemployment and avoid a tax cut," or "I would ask the people to give up certain luxuries to help the economy." But once beyond these lexical or structural guideposts, the listener is bound to have a problem in dealing with a response like the following (ellipses and italics mine):

> The American people . . . will be called upon to make *those sacrifices* to preserve the peace . . . we will have to maintain a [sic] adequate military capability . . . we will have to add a few billion dollars to our defense appropriations to . . . have adequate strategic forces.

This simplified first chunk of Ford's answer shows more clearly the failure to follow any standard response formula than the complete original does. The key phrase *those sacrifices* is a red herring in that it appears to refer to something already mentioned, which cannot be the case since this is the beginning of the answer. Ford continues:

> The American people will be called upon to tighten their belts a bit in meeting some of the problems we face domestically.

Either in expansion or illustration of this statement he argues that

> America can[not] go on a big spending spree with a whole lot of new programs that would add significantly to the federal budget.

With such restraint, a tax cut for "middle-income people" would be possible, and he concludes:

> And then with the economy that would be generated from a restraint on spending and a tax reduction . . . the American people would be willing to make those sacrifices . . .

It is manifest that most listeners—as opposed to those examining a transcribed text—would have been at a loss to list the sacrifices required by Ford but would have vaguely felt that he had answered the question because of his use of the term *sacrifices* on two occasions, one at the beginning, one at the end. The original questioner attempted to clarify the answer by the following compact summary question:

> Doesn't your policy really imply that we're going to have to have a fairly high rate of unemployment over a fairly long time, that growth is going to be fairly slow, and that we're not going to be able to do very much in the next four or five years to meet the basic agenda of our national needs in the cities, in health, in transit and a whole lot of things like that, aren't those the real costs? (III-1b)

Ford's answer to this consisted of a reference to the large amount already spent on human needs and to the possibility of a tax reduction as well as of a solution to the problems of the economy and the city. In substance, the second response was a denial that any sacrifices would be called for. Rhetorically, however, it presented such positively toned terms as *tax reduction* and *solution to problems*.

Carter's response to the same question (not a comment on Ford's answer) consisted of a summary of the sacrifices demanded by his opponent along with a promise to demand less himself. This latter, however, was accompanied by a reference to the 1973 oil embargo and the patriotic spirit elicited by Nixon's demand for national solidarity, including a pseudo-quotation attributed to numberless citizens: "I want to make a sacrifice for my country." The actual references to inflation, welfare, and tax reform are sandwiched between the first reference to embargo patriotism and a closing one:

> But I think a balanced approach, with everybody being part of it, and a striving for unselfishness could help as it did in 1973 to let people sacrifice for their own country. I know I'm ready for it. I think the American people are too.

In other words, great sacrifices will not be required, but the people are willing to make them.

Upon careful study, these two answers reveal a fundamental nonresponsiveness, and unwillingness of the candidates to commit themselves audibly to a specific list of sacrifices, which is after all understandable. Ford's reply is essentially a speech about his program. Carter's more effective but equally unresponsive answer is rhetorically dramatic in calling up the oil embargo, the gasoline shortage, the imaginary display of willingness to sacrifice, and the quotations from eager citizens.

An analysis of all the answers given to the sixty-four questions asked during the three debates (counting all follow-up questions but leaving out responses to answers and final statements) reveals the pattern of adequacy shown in Table 1.

Table 1: Adequacy of Answers, Debates I-III

Category	I Carter	Ford	II Carter	Ford	III Carter	Ford	Summary Carter	Ford
Direct response	1	1	4	4	2	1	7	6
Responsive	2	5	1	4	6	5	9	14
Satisfactory (Subtotal)	3	6	5	8	8	6	16	20
Nonresponsive	5	4	2	2	1	2	8	8
Evasive/Digressive	3	1	3	1	1	3	7	5
Unsatisfactory (Subtotal)	8	5	5	3	2	5	15	13
TOTAL	11	11	10	11	10	11	31	33

It was generally agreed during the campaign that the first debate favored Ford, the second Carter, and the third neither one. It is interesting to observe from the tables that Ford was more responsive than his opponent in the first two debates and less so only in the third (though his totals remained higher), while Carter increased his responsiveness slowly throughout. To say that there is a relation between "winning" and adequate answers would be to go beyond the data. To some extent, responsiveness itself is not perceived, but what is substituted for it may well be. Evidently Ford's gaffe about Eastern Europe was not palliated by being part of a responsive answer to a question about detente. The perceived effect of responsiveness on the electorate is a question of a different sort, which may be derived perhaps from some of the survey data in other parts of this book. The actual effect of responsive answers may ultimately not be knowable and may therefore be speculated about. The nature of an answer, however, is subject to a variety of forces, of which perhaps the most important is the question itself and how it is framed.

Questions, as has been noted above, may in the abstract be of several distinct types. In practice, especially in such an event as a televised debate, questions are likely to be influenced by a variety of factors: the intellect and articulateness of the questioners, their willingness to be blunt and direct, the subject

matter, the context. Thus they often fail to conform to the paradigm. A study
of the sixty-four questions that were actually asked reveals that few of them
fall into very clearcut categories. Eight types in fact seem to emerge:

1. *The yes/no question*: "Did I understand you to say, sir, that the Russians
   are not using Eastern Europe as their own sphere of influence in occupying
   most of the countries there and making sure with their troops that it's a
   Communist zone, whereas on our side of line the Italians and the French
   are still flirting with . . ." (II-4b)
2. *The what-which-who question* (WH): ". . . And which of the ones that I
   listed—that is balanced budgets, school busing, school prayer, abortion, gun
   control—which of those would you really work hard to support if you were
   President?" (III-10)
3. *The multiple question*: ". . . Would you say that your views are compatible
   with those of Chairman Arthur Burns. And if not, would you seek his resignation if you are elected?"
4. *The reference question*: a long statement followed by a question in itself
   without meaning except by reference, used only by Elizabeth Drew of the
   New Yorker: "So how do you say that you're going to be able to do these
   things and balance the budget?" (I-6)
5. *The leading question*: "You would . . . withhold arms from Iran and Saudi
   Arabia even if the risk was an oil embargo and if they should be securing
   those arms from somewhere else?" (II-5b)
6. *The alternatives question*: "Isn't it a fact that you're not really talking about
   fewer Federal employees or less Government spending but rather that you
   are talking about reshaping the Federal Government, not making it smaller?"
   (I-9)
7. *The "why" question*: "Since Gen. Brown's comments have caused this country embarrassment in the past, why is he still this nation's leading military
   officer?" (III-8)
8. *The "how" question*: "How specifically . . . are you going to bring the
   American people into the decision-making process in foreign policy?" (II-3b)

This classification, though based on the data, is at times difficult to apply,
since the form of the question can mask its own nature, as in this example:
"When do the needs of the cities and our own needs and those of other backward and even more needy countries and societies around the world take precedence over some of our military spending? Ever?" (II-7b) Despite its form, this
is a yes-no question. The yes-no question above (1, II-4b) actually asks "Do
you really believe . . .?" Similarly, other questions require interpretation; some
apparently multiple questions merely repeat the same item by paraphrasing;
some multiple questions consist of two or three related questions, usually of
different types. A glance at Tables 2–5 will show that the yes-no question is
both the most common (41%) and the most effective in eliciting satisfactory
answers (65%). The second most numerous (multiple: 19%) received satisfactory answers only half the time. The same is true for the third in order
(WH: 9%). The worst is the type that offers alternatives and the reference
type. The "how" question shows no instance of allowing unsatisfactory answers

Table 2: Question Type and Answers Elicited, Debate I

Question Type	No.	Direct Response	Responsive	Nonresponsive	Evasive/Digressive
Yes/No	7	1	3	3	
WH	0				
Multiple	3		1	1	1
Reference	2			2	
Leading	2	1		1	
Alternatives	4			2	2
Why	1				1
How	3		3		
	22				

Table 3: Question Type and Answers Elicited, Debate II

Question Type	No.	Direct Response	Responsive	Nonresponsive	Evasive/Digressive
Yes/No	13	4	4	3	2
WH	0				
Multiple	5	2	1	1	1
Reference	0				
Leading	1	1			
Alternatives	1				1
Why	0				
How	1	1			
	21				

and the leading question was unsurprisingly effective in preventing all-out evasion.

It can be seen in Tables 2–4 that each panel of questioners had its own patterns of preference. The team for debate II vastly preferred yes-no questions (62% of those they asked), completely ignoring three types. The group for debate III sought specificity with WH and yes-no questions. In terms of effectiveness at extracting satisfactory answers, the third team was the best (Table 6). But it can be noted that effectiveness steadily increased as, presumably, questioners profited from their predecessors' errors and learned to pin down their quarry.

The jump in effectiveness between debates I and II is most meaningful. The second team had seen the candidates in action and had an idea of how to block retreat, stymie defenses, and somehow get past the barrier of language. But there is a limit to what can be learned even from experience, as many of the questions asked by these experienced journalists expressed a longing for information instead of constituting a device for securing the statement of an opinion or a position. The weight of experience lay with the candidates, who had been asked thousands of questions of this kind under every possible circumstance, whereas the examiners were, by comparison, green. The candidates answered the questions satisfactorily whenever they wished (50–60% of the time: Table 6) and could not be compelled to do so more often, given the ground rules of

Table 4: Question Type and Answers Elicited, Debate III

Question Type	No.	Direct Response	Responsive	Nonresponsive	Evasive/Digressive
Yes/No	6	2	3		1
WH	6	1	2	1	2
Multiple	4		2	1	1
Reference	0				
Leading	2		1	1	
Alternatives	0				
Why	3		3		
How	0				
	21				

Table 5: Questions and Answers by Type, Summary

Question Type	Direct Response	Responsive	Nonresponsive	Evasive/Digressive	Total
Yes/No	7	10	6	3	26
WH	1	2	1	2	6
Multiple	2	4	3	3	12
Reference			2		2
Leading	2	1	2		5
Alternatives			2	3	5
Why		3		1	4
How	1	3			4
TOTAL	13	23	16	12	64

Table 6: Effectiveness by Debate Team

	Newman (I)	Frederick (II)	Walters (III)
Satisfactory answers	41%	62%	67%
Unsatisfactory answers	59%	38%	33%

the occasion. At a genuine press conference (the proto-model for these debates), the hard questions cannot be escaped, as Nixon learned, when everyone in the room had the same question and the follow-up questions sequenced without letup or mercy. Both candidates were aware how well the debate format protected them from the "tough cross-examination-type press conference" (II-4) —indeed they had insisted on it. Of course these generalizations about the debates should not blind us to the fact that, though the principals remained constant, the debates were three separate events, held in different places, at three different moments in the campaign, and were staffed by completely different panelists and moderators. Team I, fearing a charge of collusion, strictly avoided a planning meeting. Perhaps building on that experience, teams II and III met and conferred, the former merely to plan general strategies and define areas, the latter to determine which questions would actually be asked and by whom.[5] It is probable that this planning played a part in the rise of effectiveness in the

Table 7: Length of Questions and Answers, Debates I–III

Debate & Question No.	Questioner	QUESTION Type	QUESTION Length	ANSWER Type	ANSWER Length	Candidate
Debate I						
1	Reynolds	How	15	Responsive	81	Carter
2	Reynolds	Yes/No	7	Nonresponsive	20	Carter
3	Gannon	Yes/No	14	Nonresponsive	53	Ford
4	Gannon	Yes/No	7	Responsive	34	Ford
5	Drew	Reference	19	Nonresponsive	40	Carter
6	Drew	Reference	14	Nonresponsive	44	Carter
7	Reynolds	Yes/No	19	Responsive	41	Ford
8	Reynolds	Leading	6	Direct Response	11	Ford
9	Gannon	Alternatives	13	Nonresponsive	68	Carter
10	Gannon	Alternatives	9	Evasive/Digressive	63	Carter
11	Drew	How	21	Responsive	60	Ford
12	Drew	Alternatives	7	Evasive/Digressive	35	Ford
13	Reynolds	Why	15	Evasive/Digressive	74	Carter
14	Reynolds	Yes/No	3	Direct Response	44	Carter
15	Gannon	Alternatives	15	Nonresponsive	51	Ford
16	Gannon	Yes/No	13	Nonresponsive	37	Ford
17	Drew	How	13	Responsive	75	Carter
18	Drew	Multiple	17	Nonresponsive	29	Carter
19	Reynolds	Leading	30	Nonresponsive	53	Ford
20	Reynolds	Multiple	10	Responsive	38	Ford
21	Gannon	Multiple	14	Evasive/Digressive	45	Carter
22	Drew	Yes/No	17	Responsive	38	Ford

Debate II

	Questioner	Question Type		Response Type		Answer
1	Frankel	Yes/No	20	Nonresponsive	69	Carter
2	Trewhitt	Multiple	18	Direct Response	71	Ford
3	Valeriani	Multiple	21	Evasive/Digressive	84	Carter
3b	Valeriani	How	4	Direct Response	43	Carter
4	Frankel	Yes/No	25	Responsive	61	Ford
4b	Frankel	Yes/No	9	Responsive	21	Ford
5	Trewhitt	Yes/No	17	Evasive/Digressive	82	Carter
5b	Trewhitt	Leading	9	Direct Response	12	Carter
6	Valeriani	Multiple	14	Responsive	35	Ford
6b	Valeriani	Yes/No	2	Direct Response	10	Ford
7	Frankel	Alternatives	18	Evasive/Digressive	76	Carter
7b	Frankel	Yes/No	10	Responsive	24	Carter
8	Trewhitt	Multiple	18	Nonresponsive	58	Ford
8b	Trewhitt	Yes/No	15	Evasive/Digressive	25	Ford
9	Valeriani	Yes/No	10	Nonresponsive	54	Carter
10	Frankel	Yes/No	34	Responsive	64	Ford
10b	Frankel	Yes/No	10	Nonresponsive	42	Ford
11	Trewhitt	Yes/No	9	Direct Response	35	Carter
12	Valeriani	Multiple	11	Direct Response	47	Ford
13	Frankel	Yes/No	5	Direct Response	31	Carter
14	Trewhitt	Yes/No	6	Direct Response	13	Ford

Table 7 (continued)

Debate & Question No.	Questioner	QUESTION Type	QUESTION Length	ANSWER Type	ANSWER Length	Candidate
Debate III						
1	Kraft	WH	17	Evasive/Digressive	42	Ford
1b	Kraft	Leading	11	Nonresponsive	37	Ford
2	Maynard	Yes/No	13	Responsive	65	Carter
3	Nelson	Multiple	19	Responsive	42	Ford
3b	Nelson	Yes/No	12	Evasive/Digressive	14	Ford
4	Kraft	Multiple	20	Responsive	38	Carter
4b	Kraft	Yes/No	4	Direct Response	1	Carter
5	Maynard	Why	15	Responsive	34	Ford
6	Nelson	Yes/No	18	Responsive	63	Carter
7	Kraft	Leading	25	Responsive	50	Ford
8	Maynard	WH	11	Responsive	76	Carter
9	Nelson	Multiple	16	Nonresponsive	44	Ford
10	Kraft	WH	17	Direct Response	29	Carter
11	Maynard	Why	13	Responsive	34	Ford
11b	Maynard	Yes/No	17	Direct Response	16	Ford
12	Nelson	WH	15	Evasive/Digressive	63	Carter
12b	Nelson	WH	7	Responsive	14	Carter
12c	Nelson	WH	1	Nonresponsive	25	Carter
13	Kraft	Yes/No	10	Responsive	43	Ford
13b	Kraft	Multiple	13	Evasive/Digressive	38	Ford
14	Maynard	Why	11	Responsive	70	Carter

Numbers represent lines used in the newspaper transcript of the Debates. (*New York Times* for I & II, *New Orleans Times-Picayune* for III.) For conversion into number of words, multiply by 6.5.

Table 8: Summary of Length of Questions and Answers by Panelists and Candidates

Questioner	Number Asked	Average	Total Lines	Questions	Number Asked	Average	Total Lines
Debate I				Debate III			
Reynolds	8	13.1	105	Kraft	8	14.6	117
Gannon	7	12.1	85	Maynard	6	13.3	80
Drew	7	15.4	108	Nelson	7	12.6	88
Team I	22	13.5	298	Team III	21	13.6	285
Answers				Answers			
Carter	11	53	583	Carter	10	44	444
Ford	11	41	451	Ford	11	36	394
Debate II							
Frankel	8	16.4	131				
Trewhitt	7	13.1	92				
Valeriani	6	10.3	62				
Team II	21	13.6	285				
Answers							
Carter	10	51	510				
Ford	11	41	451				

CARTER vs. FORD, 1976

201

questioning, or at any rate the increase in adequacy of the answers in the last two debates. Of course, the types of questions asked also changed, as noted above, in the direction of those more likely to elicit satisfactory answers. There was a constant effort, initiated or supported by the League of Women Voters, to make the questions shorter in the last two debates. Several members of the last two panels felt they had achieved this goal but the figures suggest otherwise (Table 7).

The average length of a question in each debate was almost exactly the same. Of course, the ground rules changed slightly. In I, each panelist asked a question and a follow-up for each of the first three rounds. The panelists in II and III had agreed to ask follow-ups only when they felt these were needed. Thus there were more primary questions in II and III and fewer follow-ups. Table 8 reveals some individual peculiarities: Richard Valeriani was the most laconic of the panelists and Max Frankel substantially the most expansive, on the average. Carter spoke 25% longer than Ford, overall, in each debate. The answers, naturally enough, were longer than the questions: about three and a half times. Not only the type of question influenced adequacy of the answer. Each panelist did as much research before the debate he or she participated in as time allowed (usually five days) and arrived with a list of questions which were reduced to between nine and twenty-five by the time the theater of operations was entered. Most questions were in the form of notes, *aides-mémoire*, jottings, phrasings. Several wrote out their questions verbatim, though they might adapt them to the immediate context. Perhaps unsurprisingly, one of the latter received 100 percent-satisfactory answers (Table 9). Hardly any one of the panelists had a very accurate idea of his or her own effectiveness, and some expressed surprise when informed of the computed scores.

Table 9: Effectiveness of Question, by Adequacy of Answers

	No. of Answers	Direct Response	Responsive	Non-Responsive	Evasive/ Digressive	Raw Score[1]	Effectiveness Index[2] (%)
Gannon	7		1	4	2	−5	14
Reynolds	8	2	3	2	1	+2	63
Drew	7		3	3	1	−1	43
Frankel	8	1	4	2	1	+2	63
Trewhitt	7	4		1	2	+1	67
Valeriani	7	3	1	1	2	+1	67
Kraft	8	2	3	1	2	+2	63
Maynard	6	1	5			+6	100
Nelson	7		3	2	2	−1	43

1. Computed by subtracting unsatisfactory from satisfactory answers.
2. Computed by dividing satisfactory answers by total questions.

There was a wide range of satisfaction with one's own performance but a general feeling of dissatisfaction with the adequacy of answers. Although several panelists were apparently writing (or had agreed to write) impressions of their experience,[6] few had reviewed transcripts or viewed videotapes or had a very definite memory of what took place on the linguistic plane. But that is where

THE GREAT DEBATES

the solution to the mystery lies, the mystery being formulated in this question: given the opportunity to make clear to the entire electorate how they differed on a wide range of issues, why did the candidates not grasp it firmly and say clearly where they stood?

We know that both Ford and Carter can answer questions clearly, directly, informatively, and candidly. Both did so in interviews, and Carter has notably done so in his press conferences since he assumed the Presidency, and with some *éclat* in the telephone call-in of March 5, 1977. It is possible to conjecture that they did not always do so during the debates because of stage fright, nervousness, or lack of sleep, but this is improbable. Anyone who survives a campaign for president will not be rendered incapable of answering questions clearly by participation in a television debate. One must seek elsewhere—in politics—for an understanding, specifically in the interface between language and politics which the debate situation crystallizes.

It is highly probable that the debaters would answer questions satisfactorily when it was in their interest to do so, when, that is, it would cost no votes, alienate no supporters, enhance one's image as a candid and forceful campaigner, and possibly place the opponent in an unfavorable light. In debate I two such questions were asked, one of each man. Frank Reynolds asked about the contrast between Ford's pardon of former president Nixon and his unwillingness to grant amnesty to draft resisters. The answer involved Ford in a two-paragraph defense of the pardon, which led to this follow-up:

Q: I take it then, sir, that you . . . are not going to reconsider and think about the 90,000 who are still abroad. Have they not been penalized enough—many of them been there for years?

FORD: Well, Mr. Carter has indicated that he would give a blanket pardon to all draft evaders. I do not agree with that point of view. I gave in September of 1974 an opportunity for all draft evaders, all deserters, to come in voluntarily, clear their record by earning an opportunity to restore their good citizenship. I think we gave them a good opportunity—I don't think we should go any further.

In the context of the standard of the debates, this was a brief and direct answer. Obviously Ford wanted to get clear of a discussion of the Nixon pardon as quickly as possible. Moreover, his supporters and the Reagan voters demanded a hard line on amnesty. He could not hope to gather any votes by vacillating, but he could lose some. So he took his position while offering the unattractive alternative to his opponent. Carter, in his comment on the answer, took five paragraphs to free himself and did so only by shifting to a consideration of our criminal justice system.

Carter got an opportunity to retaliate later on in the same debate on a question by the same panelist about energy:

Q: Governor . . . would you require mandatory conservation efforts to try to conserve fuel?

CARTER: Yes, I would. Some of the things that can be done about this is a change in the rate structure of electric power companies.

We now encourage people to waste electricity, and by giving the lowest rate to the biggest users. We don't do anything to cut down on peak load requirements. We don't have an adequate requirement for the insulation of homes, for the efficiency of automobiles—and whenever the automobile manufacturers come forward and say they can't meet the amendments that Congress has put forth, this Republican Administration has delayed the implementation dates.

In addition to that, we ought to have a shift toward the use of coal, particularly in the Appalachian regions where the coal is located, a lot of very high quality, low-carbon coal, low sulfur coal is there, it's where our employment is needed. This would help a great deal.

Because the administration had no firm energy policy, Carter could afford to be specific. No one objects to fuel conservation as long as the details are abstract and fuel rationing, for example, is not mentioned. The public cheerfully accepts the possibility that auto makers may be under pressure to meet conservation standards. And the reference to coal, Appalachia, and jobs is bound to be attractive to some listeners and unpalatable only to a very few. Ford's comment revealed his problem, as he felt compelled to claim that he *did have* an energy policy and that he had recommended increased coal production, solar energy research and the like, the whole punctuated by a large number of figures.

The contrast between the unsatisfactory answers presented earlier and the pointed answers just cited suggests that any general conclusion that the debaters always tried to answer questions evasively would be simplistic and unjustified. A more accurate appraisal would require the consideration of other factors.

As a basis for the assessment of the candor and responsiveness of Ford and Carter, it may be reasonable to wonder how the Kennedy-Nixon debates score on some of the same points. It would also be reasonable to expect progress, given that the former served as model to the latter and that accounts of the former served as breviaries to the aides of the candidates in 1976. The four 1960 debates comprised 42 questions, whereas the three later ones covered 50 (without follow-ups), or 64 altogether. In the first debate of the 1960 series the two candidates each answered five questions. All five of Nixon's answers were unsatisfactory, while only two of Kennedy's were. In the fourth debate, in which each candidate answered three questions, all three of Kennedy's answers were satisfactory and only one of Nixon's was. Thus, Kennedy's adequacy score was 6 in 8 in the first and last debates, whereas Nixon's was 1 in 8. The general range of questions was essentially the same.

Since Kennedy's victory was paper-thin and since studies of the debates show that the result over the four occasions was a tie,[7] it cannot be claimed that the adequacy of answers was a major factor. A deeper analysis might turn up the particulars which influenced the voters, but it is more likely that we would discover only the effects of image at first (Nixon's makeup), corrected by the American passion for the underdog, the economic realities, and the religious and political loyalties that constitute and determine the electorate.

Whether or not adequate answers in televised debates help to elect a candidate, it is certain that candidates believe that "mistakes" can be very dangerous. Indeed it has long been part of the wisdom—call it cynicism—of political observers that politics demands dissimulation. Machiavelli needs no citation but Frank H. Kent, contemporary of Coolidge and Hoover, is also instructive:

> The fact is that unless proficiency in using language to conceal both thought and belief is acquired, anything like genuine and sustained political progress is out of the question. Absolute sincerity and a successful political career are utterly incongruous and impossible. . . . It is possible for a man to be wholly sincere—and a few are—after his election, but not while he is in process of being elected, not while he is appealing to the people. . . . No man thus engaged, who fully and frankly expressed his real convictions, made manifest exactly the way he felt and thought on public matters, could possibly be elected to any considerable office in the United States. . . .
>
> This sounds like a cheap piece of cynicism. It is, however, said in no supercilious sense nor with the least desire to seem smart and superior, contemptuous of the collective intelligence of the American voters, or scornful of the popular comprehension. On the contrary the proposition that the American people as a whole cannot stand complete sincerity in politics and that any man who told them the unvarnished truth about the issues, about himself, about his opponent, about his campaign, would unquestionably be politically destroyed, is laid down in all seriousness. . . .
>
> It is all very nice for the campaign orators to talk about having "faith in the intelligence of the American people" and it sounds and reads well to pay tribute to their supposed ability to govern themselves and "to decide rightly." There is no purpose here to speak with disdain of the democratic scheme of government. . . . The cold fact is that in present-day politics when the American people decide an issue rightly it is an accident and not because of either an unerring instinct for the right or a clear comprehension of the facts, because they have neither.[8]

The implication of this view is that our best hope is to nominate candidates of such quality that the ineptness of the voters cannot ruin the Republic. Another view is that the primary process should select candidates likely to be responsive to questions.[9] George Seldes, in reflecting on the 1960 debates, considers a variety of future ground rules designed to promote good exchanges between the candidates, but one of his major fears is the possibility that a "TV personality" rather than a good candidate would be nominated.[10] Many have been concerned about the fact that these debates were not debates in that the speakers did not address each other.[11] It appears naive today to suppose that there is any chance of returning to the rhetorical tradition of the nineteenth century. Our political speakers (as the transcripts mercilessly betray) no longer have the ability to organize and deliver a *speech* of more than five minutes, although they often do ramble on for longer than that.

The disappointment with the format, the tinkering with the form, length, and subject matter of the questions, are all in a sense irrelevant. The language and practical rhetoric provide an experienced political campaigner with the resources to answer any form of question with any degree of adequacy. Elizabeth Drew's determined efforts to pin down Carter (I-5,6) as to how he could accomplish his program and balance the budget were ultimately unsuccessful, and it is hardly likely that one percent of viewers realized what had taken place. On the other hand, even though Henry Trewhitt asked a yes-no question about a grain embargo to the Soviet Union to secure human rights, Carter had no difficulty rephrasing the question in the "direct" part of his answer, so that the embargo resulted only from a "crisis," and then moving fast to a general discussion of Arab oil embargoes, past and future. No system acceptable to the candidates could be devised that would prevail against the candidate's devotion to his hope for success, a more seductive mistress than truth.

In sum, we are likely to continue to have debates similar in kind to these. Beyond a desire to select the best possible questioners, I would recommend no changes except possibly to allow the audience to express itself (if there is one on hand) and to advise the participants to avoid glaring at each other. No damage is done by a display of courtesy. The possible inclusion of a random citizen in each panel might give a valuable impression of republican independence, especially if such a tribune of the people were entitled to break in when he thought an answer to be unsatisfactory. For national security reasons, some questions should be considered improper, and the right to refuse to answer should be allowed. It is an axiom we cannot dispute that the dissemination of the views of the candidates (even distorted by their political necessities) must be a gain for democracy. Someone listening is bound to learn something useful. But it would be worthless trying to legislate responsiveness—it cannot be done because language won't permit it. We should note, however, that the two elections following upon debates have been among the closest in our history. I interpret that as meaning that the debates emphasize the similarity of the views of the candidates. It will ultimately be up to them to make the effort to be distinguishable.

Appendix: Topics Covered in the Debates

Debate	Questioner	Question No.	Topic
I	Reynolds	1–2	Priorities, income policy (Carter)
	Gannon	3–4	Budget, taxes (Ford)
	Drew	5–6	New budget priorities, budget balance (Carter)
	Reynolds	7–8	Draft resisters' pardon (Ford)
	Gannon	9–10	Federal bureaucracy reform (Carter)
	Drew	11–12	New programs vs. cost (Ford)
	Reynolds	13–14	Safety of nuclear energy, energy conservation (Carter)
	Gannon	15–16	Public service jobs (Ford)
	Drew	17–18	Tax relief (Carter)
	Reynolds	19–20	Government ethics, getting along with Democratic Congress (Ford)
	Gannon	21	Arthur Burns (Carter)
	Drew	22	FBI oversight (Ford)
			Topics Covered: 10
II	Frankel	1	Republican record (Carter)
	Trewhitt	2	Cold war tendency (Ford)
	Valeriani	3–3b	Role of U.S. in world, open decision making (Carter)
	Frankel	4–4b	Detente, Soviet hegemony (Ford)
	Trewhitt	5–5b	Human rights, oil embargo (Carter)
	Valeriani	6–6b	Relations with Peking (Ford)
	Frankel	7–7b	Defense and priorities (Carter)
	Trewhitt	8–8b	SALT, cruise missile (Ford)
	Valeriani	9	U.S. strength (Carter)
	Frankel	10–10b	International morality (Ford)
	Trewhitt	11	Panama (Carter)
	Valeriani	12	Mayaguez (Ford)
	Frankel	13	Arab boycott of Israel (Carter)
	Trewhitt	14	Negotiations with Vietnam (Ford)
			Topics Covered: 17
III	Kraft	1–1b	Sacrifices and costs to achieve program (Ford)
	Maynard	2	Level of campaign (Carter)
	Nelson	3–3b	Watergate (Ford)
	Kraft	4–4b	Yugoslavia and foreign policy (Carter)
	Maynard	5	General Brown (Ford)
	Nelson	6	Ability of associates (Carter)
	Kraft	7	Conservation record (Ford)
	Maynard	8	Urban goals (Carter)
	Nelson	9	Civil rights (Ford)
	Kraft	10	Constitutional amendments (Carter)
	Maynard	11–11b	Gun control (Ford)
	Nelson	12a,b,c	Supreme Court appointments (Carter)
	Kraft	13–13b	Economic record (Ford)
	Maynard	14	Loss of Carter's lead (Carter)
			Topics Covered: 14

NOTES

1. Compare moderator James Hoge's introductory remarks to the vice-presidential debate in Houston (October 15, 1976) on the same subject: "I should mention at this point that I will intervene if a candidate is not addressing the question which has been posed to him." But it should be noted that he did not act on his warning.

2. In a series of telephone interviews held between March 24 and April 4, 1977, with all but one (Richard Valeriani) of the panelists, it was found that all the panelists had spent a great deal of their available time thinking up topics for questions and that five had written their questions out and some of these had made a number of drafts of each question.

3. Carter's comment to Ford's answer to Question 4b (see Appendix).

4. Question codes consist of two numerals: a roman, indicating the presidential debate (I, Philadelphia; II, San Francisco; III, Williamsburg), and an arabic, indicating the question. The vice-presidential debate is not considered. The Appendix gives a complete index to the questions, questioners, and topics.

5. From individual telephone interviews. See note 2.

6. James P. Gannon (I), describing his experience as a selected panelist prior to the debate, wrote an article in his newspaper, the *Wall Street Journal*, September 27, 1976. Jack Nelson (III), Washington Bureau Chief for the *Los Angeles Times*, reflected on his experience on October 25, 1976, specifically mentioning several questions he had planned to ask but did not have time for and the agreement made among the members of team III to ask each candidate what question he might have for the other.

7. Elihu Katz and Jacob J. Feldman, "The Debates in the Light of Research: A Survey of Surveys," in *The Great Debates*, ed. Sidney Kraus (Bloomington: Indiana University Press, 1962), p. 195.

8. *Political Behavior* (New York: William Morrow, 1928), pp. 74–76.

9. Sidney Kraus, ed., "Presidential Debates De-Briefing, Tuesday, November 30, 1976," statement by Sig Mickelson.

10. Kraus, *The Great Debates*, pp. 167–69.

11. E.g., J. Jeffery Auer, in Kraus, p. 147.

12.

Presidential Debates:
A Plan for the Future

JIM KARAYN

On the night of August 19, 1976, in Kansas City, Gerald Ford, accepting his party's nomination for president, challenged Jimmy Carter to a series of nationwide debates. "I'm ready, I'm eager," he said, "to go before the American people and debate the real issues face to face with Jimmy Carter." The challenge was right at the top of his address, fastened there in last-minute rewrites, and the convention hall went wild. After months of campaigning in search of delegates and in defense of his tenuous leadership over a divided party, Ford's sudden challenge was a welcome battle cry to the assembled troops. Debating his rival, it seemed, would be the ultimate test of presidential mettle—the title fight after nearly a year of sparring and preliminary bouts.

Not to be upstaged by the Ford challenge, Jody Powell, Carter's top advisor, insisted that the Democratic candidate had also planned to call for direct debates and that on the very day of Ford's speech a similar dare was being prepared for transmission from Plains, Georgia, to the Republican convention hall halfway across the country. As fate would have it—Powell reflected later—the ditto machine at Carter headquarters broke down, and the message never reached its appointed destination.

In reality, and regardless of how history will record who challenged whom, neither candidate's intention to debate the issues was supported by a concrete plan on his part. Neither candidate, until August 19, had actually committed himself, his campaign, his party, or the electorate to such face-to-face encounters. In both camps, there was hesitation in breaking the sixteen-year embargo on presidential debates. "Going before the American people," as Ford put it, meant live television, and that was risky business. Most political observers still thought that in 1960 Kennedy's good luck in drawing the lead-off spot for his opening statement had given him a decided edge over Nixon throughout the confrontations. In 1976, careful arrangements would have to be made to insure balanced views of both candidates and less dependence on the outcome of a lucky draw.

On the morning before Ford's address, at 8:00 A.M., ten hours after the Republican nominee had been selected, I telegraphed a message to both party headquarters simultaneously. It formally invited the candidates to participate in a series of debates sponsored by the League of Women Voters Education Fund. It had been written and rewritten many times by the debates negotiating team composed of the League's president Ruth Clusen; executive director Peggy Lampl; co-chairs Rita Hauser, Newton Minow, Charls Walker; and myself. The final draft contained specific details which, we knew, would inevitably change in the weeks to come. The invitation gave the number of debates—three presidential and one vice-presidential; their length—one hour; and the date and place of the first encounter—Tuesday, September 28, at the Chase Park Plaza in St. Louis. In the absence of any tangible proposals from the candidates or their parties, we were especially intent on spelling out the details of our approach to the debates, and even if the exact format would be the product of many modifications, this telegram of August 19 from the League would serve as a practical basis for all subsequent talks. Expressing the League's hope that the debates "could reaffirm our democratic institutions and revitalize voter interest . . . as we face an evermore more complex future," the telegram emphasized the urgency of the matter—"time is short; to facilitate planning, we urge you to designate a representative to meet with us as soon as possible to consult on the project in more detail."

Later that morning, at the Muehlebach Hotel in Kansas City, Clusen, Hauser, and I held a press conference to disclose the contents of the invitation and to create, we hoped, an attentive and supportive ambience for the debates. Eleven reporters showed up. Copies of the telegram were received with the same enthusiasm as for religious tracts passed out on a street corner. At that moment, just ten weeks from election day, it seemed that relatively few people —including the press, the networks, and the campaign staffs—were willing to take our project seriously. Even now, in Kansas City, despite all the League's efforts since early spring, widespread indifference and skepticism toward presidential debates lingered. They were dispelled only when Ford's challenge made the idea of his debating his rival a climactic reality. Suddenly, on that night of August 19, the debates became serious business, and the expectation that they would clarify all issues and solve voters' dilemmas was feverishly high. Suddenly, too, the League became the center of public and media attention.

Clearly, staging the debates was risky business, with different parties involved, each with its own formula, each wary of foul play, and each knowing that compromises would be the only way to pull off the debates in the long run. Unfortunately, the long run was not so very long. Compressed into those thirty-five days was the production work of a six- to nine-month operation. It still seems incredible to me, looking back, that so much ground could have been covered in so little time. Apart from the vital support of League members, we began this phase of work with a full-time staff of just three people. In the month ahead, another thirty would be recruited. In store for us, at the top of the improvised agenda, were two major meetings with the candidates' staffs, and at least a half dozen more with the networks. In these sessions, the overall format of the debates would be worked out: the duration of each encounter (finally agreed upon as ninety minutes); the topical issues; the kind of panels to be assembled; the questioning procedure; the follow-up questioning procedure;

210

the candidates' summations, and so on. A variety of technical, logistical problems could be resolved only in consultation with network specialists. There were questions about camera angles and stage settings. Arrangements for outside media coverage of the events had to be made. Locations and auditoriums across the country had to be scouted carefully. The press and the public had to be informed daily of new developments. And, most importantly, panels of questioners had to be assembled.

An Agenda of Events

The sudden shifts encountered in the course of a campaign are not conducive to the kind of calm, reasonable planning that presidential debates require. For something as serious and as vitally significant to the entire nation as the debates, it is foolhardy to risk their careful implementation to last-minute deadlines. Moreover, for the entire electorate to get the full benefit of its political process during an election year, and to be fully cognizant of presidential debates—not with breathless anxiety or anticipation, but with collected calm—as an integral part of that process, it is necessary to begin thinking now about their future. Whether we limit our focus to presidential elections or envision potential debates at a lower level as well—senatorial, congressional, and gubernatorial races—the need is the same: to create a broad framework, in scope and in time, which allows for the careful planning of such debates. What I am proposing is an *Agenda of Events*, a formal schedule of campaign activities among candidates, not exclusively confined to a series of face-to-face encounters or debates.

In January of an election year, such an Agenda would commit all Republican and Democratic candidates running for the presidency and vice-presidency to participate in a specific timetable of events, if they received their party's nomination. That way the bargaining and negotiating with candidates for their participation in debates would not have to wait until after the party conventions, or until the candidates had decided whether or not such debates might be personally beneficial.

What I am suggesting is that presidential (and vice-presidential) debates be mandatory and that they automatically become a part of the American political process for the benefit of the American voter. If the candidates know this from the start, it should work no hardship on those who finally win the nominations. In fact, mandatory debates would serve the candidates well, even an incumbent president, without minimizing the enormous assistance they would give the challenger.

Infusing the election year with a carefully laid out plan for debates should help not only the candidates but the media and the electorate as well, given the assumption that we will continue to have federally funded presidential and vice-presidential campaigns. Too often overlooked by campaign observers was the fact that the Federal Election Campaign Act made 1976 the first year in the nation's history that the primaries and the general election were federally funded. Federal funding regulations accounted for the debates taking on an even larger role than they normally might have. As candidate Jimmy Carter said to one reporter, they became "the surrogate campaign." Because funds to each candidate were trimmed to $21.8 million in 1976, many traditional campaign enterprises—from political rallies and countrywide swings to store-front headquarters in every city—had to be curtailed or even eliminated.

In the future the costs of traveling from coast to coast as frequently and as freely as candidates have been used to will become prohibitive. At the same time, the need for candidates to reach diverse voter blocks and growing numbers of independent or noncommitted voters will probably not diminish. Knowing that their campaigns are being fueled by taxpayers' money, candidates may feel pressure to become more visible and more accountable to the public concerning national issues and their respective political stands. To break through the impasse of these conflicting conditions, candidates may become less skeptical, less hesitant, about committing themselves to debates and political forums on television. Such a commitment recognizes that in a mass society, particularly in America today, political facts and events are *real* only to the extent that public opinion coalesces around them. To paraphrase the French political scientist, Jacques Ellul, it is the mass media, and television in particular, that create public opinion and translate raw political data into the images and symbols that best suit the public's needs. The medium is politics, and we must be increasingly prepared to define its best uses and form. Such a commitment, however, is not intended to supplant the grass-roots features of campaigning, the public appearances, the handshakes, and all the ritualistic routines—as few as they may be under federal funding—that are normally crammed into a candidate's search for votes. Nor is it meant to predetermine the course of any candidate's campaign. Rather, the Agenda of Events, once adhered to by all parties involved, will make certain that issues and personalities must be examined at close range, at a specific time and in a specific way, thus complementing or enhancing each one's regular campaign activities.

The League's Experience

One important lesson drawn from the League's project is that if the format, schedule, and final details of the debates are left to the later stages of a campaign year, the candidates and their representatives become too involved in the decision-making process. They will expect the debates or any other planned events to fit tightly into their own campaign timetables, rather than the other way around. Guarding themselves against any unnecessary risks while attempting to maximize self-exposure may add undue strain to any stage of negotiations. Even though such negotiations will continue to play an important role throughout the campaign year by providing flexibility and room for changes in the Agenda—among candidates, networks, and sponsors or funding representatives—most basic components should be worked out, agreed upon, and ready to implement before there are nominees. Armed with concrete plans at the beginning of the election year, and operating within a supportive national framework, future organizers of the debates will be able to reduce greatly the uncertainties at the beginning and the precipitous rush of last-minute work that characterized the League's experience.

It is ironic that in the months before August 19, the League had carefully laid out a plan to seek public support for the debates. We were well aware that before we could hope for nationally televised confrontations, we had to generate public fervor. After sixteen years of no debates, politicians, broadcasters, the press, and the general public had come to assume that such televised encounters were virtually impossible in this country. Since the Kennedy-Nixon confrontations in 1960, a web of legal barriers, political indifference, and general apathy had relegated presidential debates to limbo.

The League's dogged determination to promote the debates was a gamble. Our chances for success were predicated on the existence of four conditions unique to the 1976 campaign. First, there was a widespread feeling across the country, particularly in this Bicentennial election year and after a decade of political scandals and Watergate, that people wanted to know more about their elected representatives, that they favored debates, and that public pressure could in fact be harnessed to make the candidates commit themselves. Second, there were no legal or legislative grounds that the candidates, especially the incumbent, could use to get out of debates. An FCC ruling in the fall of 1975 had made it possible to circumvent the so-called equal-time provision of the Communications Act (Section 315). Non-broadcast groups could stage political debates, and radio and television could cover them without threat of penalty. Third, the Democratic nominee, who by late April appeared to be Carter, would need all the public exposure that debates offered. Fourth, and the most significant, was the position of the incumbent president. Not having been elected by the people, Gerald Ford would have to struggle to secure the nomination of his party, while persistently running twenty to thirty popularity points behind his yet-to-be-named opponent, who would be the nominee of a party twice the size of Ford's.

Equipped with this rationale, the League decided to undertake the project. I suggested to Clusen and Lampl that we inform the networks of our plans before announcing the decision to the 145,000 members of the League at their biennial convention on May 6, 1976, in New York. Meetings with the heads of the networks were consequently arranged for April 26 in New York.

We wanted to find out exactly where the networks stood on the issue of televised debates, and if there would be a conflict of interest with the League's plans. To each of the three network representatives the same questions were asked: Is there any chance that you might go ahead on your own and do the debates? Might you seek a waiver of 315 as you did with success sixteen years before for the Nixon-Kennedy coverage? Each responded negatively to both questions, emphatically, without a margin of doubt.

Following those meetings, we realized that if the League did not proceed immediately, it would be quite likely that yet another presidential election would take place without televised debates. We began immediately to build our national campaign for public support. In May, we had little besides the time to conceptualize, to fix strategies, and to draw important lessons from 1960.

Our efforts were concentrated in five areas. First, endorsements were sought from a cross-section of national groups—political, civic, professional, business, and labor. These groups were urged to support the idea of presidential debates as a vehicle to better inform the electorate and to help the League itself obtain their sponsorship. Second, a major, nationwide petition drive was launched by League members throughout its local chapters in search of four million signatures. This represented an important attempt to enlist grass-roots backing for the debates. It was hoped that such a drive would convince the candidates of the significance of the debates—and of the League's seriousness in promoting them. Third, an editorial campaign in the daily press was mounted. By mid-summer, virtually every important newspaper across the country had drawn its readers' attention to debates and the need for them. Fourth, a series of polls was commissioned through George Gallup, Jr., who was a member of the League's steering committee. In July, just after the Democratic Convention, one such poll showed that 7 out of 10 persons wanted the debates and thought that they would be a good way to bring the presidential campaign into sharper focus.

Finally, there was work to be done with the candidates themselves. Throughout May, June, and July, the debates project staff, the national co-chairs, and members of the steering committee met with staff and advisors of Carter, Reagan, and Ford, to try to persuade them that participation in debates would be advantageous to each candidate. There was especially little encouragement at this level, where the League needed the most support and where some clout could have forced serious talks and decisions before the last minute. As it was, Ronald Reagan became the only candidate who actually committed himself to the idea of debates. The others hedged their bets throughout the primaries, willing to consider the idea only if they needed to, while the League was forced to operate in an atmosphere of doubt and uncertainty. Even if the two Republican contenders could not officially commit themselves until one got the nomination, a prior pledge to debate would have enabled the League to put its planning and strategy phase into action much earlier. As it was, following the Ford challenge, there were two short negotiating sessions on August 26 and September 1, with the first debate only three weeks later. It would have been almost impossible to schedule the first encounter any earlier, even though it was quite late in the campaign.

Begin Events Early

As we look to 1980, an important element of the proposed Agenda is that the scheduled events should begin early in September, perhaps even the Wednesday or Thursday of Labor Day week. There are several reasons for this. First of all, the debates are likely to get voters interested in the candidates and the campaign earlier. This was one of the important effects of the debates in 1976. A surprisingly large number of American voters were still undecided. To a large extent, their verdicts depended on the debates and the visceral feelings which they projected. The debates were meant to bring the campaign down to earth, into every home, and into the realm of personal, electoral response. As such, the presidential campaign became a more immediate concern to every voter. Unfortunately, this happened at the eleventh hour with hardly enough time for voters to reflect carefully on the depth of issues and positions. Yet, the debates may have contributed to refuting widespread predictions of a national turnout well below 50 percent of eligible voters. The final figure of 53 percent was considered a good showing, given the general apathetic mood across the nation. It would have probably been much higher if state registration laws, which generally set cutoff dates at the beginning of September, had been changed to accommodate latecomers. In Wisconsin, for example, where this general rule does not apply, voters may register on election day; the turnout there was 65.5 percent.

A second reason to begin the events on the Agenda earlier is that there would be less anxiety—on the part of the candidates, the press, and the public —about their sudden-death significance, and also about the effect of blunders, slip-ups, revealing disclosures, and theatrics. The superficial aspects of the debates or encounters should become less momentous to voters if they are stretched out over a longer period, if there is room to move and time enough to correct errors and false meanings. Ultimately, a combination of advanced scheduling—to be mapped out by January of the election year—with debates starting early will eliminate the risk of too many surprises, feverish expectations, and the on-again-off-again faltering that threatened the Ford-Carter debates until the very last minute.

The Makeup of the Agenda

What events should the proposed Agenda include? Principally, debates, in one form or another. Direct confrontation between candidates—even with questioners in the middle—produces the drama and the excitement that intrigues the nation, and the world. However, the debates should be prefaced with half-hour solo appearances by the candidates, back to back, on television and radio the week of Labor Day. As substitutes for opening statements in the debates, these solo appearances would provide a basis for future questioning of the candidates. They would also give the public a brief but comprehensive summary of what the candidates have to offer, why they are seeking the presidency, what they see as the major national issues, and how they intend to attack them. Their views, policy stands, and hopes for America in the four years to come would set the stage for the subsequent face-to-face encounters between the candidates. With all of their limitations and under any conditions or any format, debates bring the two candidates together; they attract enormous audiences; and they get to the candidates' stand on the issues, even if the statements are not as deep or as detailed as we might want.

The experience of 1976 revealed the sheer number of people that the debates reach. The Nielsen index found that about 90 percent of all households were tuned in, which translates into 100–120 million viewers. No other campaign activity created that kind of audience and captured such wide national interest. Even if candidates were to mount special, multimillion-dollar television specials, or a supersophisticated commercial blitz, they could not hope to capture the large audience that is ready to watch direct debates on real issues. There is virtually no other way to reach so many people, so immediately, with such forceful campaign content, in an election year. The sense of confrontation is there. The index also showed that most people watched each encounter until the end, and that audiences did not drop significantly from debate to debate. This was in sharp contrast to 1960.

The debates of 1976 also served the indispensable purpose of bringing both candidates together. The settings were not of their choosing, the questions not of their making. Together, on neutral ground, they forced voters to size up the opposition. The contest for victory between these two men and the parties they represented and the issues they stood for went to the very heart of our nation's democratic process. It was a balanced look, with both candidates reacting to the same set of challenging circumstances.

The televised confrontations gave viewers a chance to hear different positions and policy choices on such specific issues as defense cuts, amnesty, national health insurance, aid to distressed cities, and environmental protection. Even though a voter may have been committed to the ideas and personality of his or her preferred candidate, the mere setting of the debates—the equal exposure of opposing views—compelled each voter to become aware of the other side's stand. For so many independent and uncommitted voters this exposure may have made the difference between voting and not voting on election day. For the candidates themselves, the confrontation meant that, in their own heads and in their own words, they were forced to become knowledgeable, coherent, and in persuasive command of issues to an extent well beyond any single speech or interview or even any debate on the local level. Without the instantaneous, coast-to-coast audience that television creates, the same two candidates, debating in Biloxi, Mississippi, one day, and Chicago, Illinois, the next, might contradict themselves a hundred times without worry. Not here. Built into the setting of these televised encounters was a strong sense of accountability and comprehensive expertise on the candidates' part.

The Number of Debates

In the future, I cannot imagine more than three or four presidential debates. Any more might generate a backlash effect by the electorate and keep the candidates from participating in the more traditional forms of campaigning. I would also strongly suggest that vice-presidential debates continue—no more than two.

The debates should be evenly spaced between the nine or ten weeks between Labor Day and election day. The first presidential debates should follow the week after Labor Day and the "opening statements" of the two candidates. The last debate should definitely be the week before the election, although candidates will resist in order to have that week clear for their individual campaign activities.

As part of the Agenda, mid-way through the debates there should be individual interviews with each of the candidates. This would be especially helpful in correcting errors, clarifying obscure points, or just emphasizing key statements made during the actual debate. Voters would be helped by watching candidates defend their positions and answer fresh questions in a calmer, reflective manner. In 1976, such a one-on-one interview with Gerald Ford after the second debate might have clarified what he meant regarding "freedom" in Eastern Europe.

Another event on the Agenda might be a set of encounters with key advisors—the chief economic, domestic, and foreign policy advisors—of each of the candidates. During any presidential campaign these advisors are a vital part of the candidate's image and policymaking activities. To most people, they are unknown or, at best, faceless names in campaign news. Yet, if the man they work for becomes president, their roles will be enhanced and upgraded; cabinet positions or White House staff assignments will likely follow. Seeing them and listening to their specialized views, even if they reiterate the candidate's positions, would serve to familiarize voters with the team behind the captain.

216

The Debate Format

When surveyed soon after the last Ford-Carter debate, seven out of ten respondents said they would like to see presidential debates again in the next election. When asked what kind of changes they would like to see in future formats, most people favored the kind of direct exchange between candidates that had been so studiously avoided in the past. Perhaps, there is still hope for some kind of compromise by 1980. While I think it is very important that a series of formal questions from a moderator or panel initially set the framework of each debate, at some point during the encounters time could be parceled out just for the candidates: "Now that you've heard each other's views and policy stands, would you like to question your opponent on any of the issues that have been raised here tonight?" There was a place in each of the Ford-Carter debates for such an open-ended question directed to both candidates, but neither would agree to any direct questioning despite published utterances to the contrary. During the first negotiations, the League proposed that a portion of each debate be devoted to direct questioning between candidates. After each presidential debate, we again proposed a format change, but each time the candidates' representatives would not discuss the matter.

In 1960, when the issue of direct exchange between candidates was raised, both candidates' representatives felt that in such a situation, before live cameras, the two candidates would treat each other in a highly deferential manner. One Nixon aide feared that they would be "too polite," and that any attempt to achieve real discussion of issues—or just to make the debates a real debating situation—would be overruled by the candidates' own desires to promote images rather than controversies. By 1976, nothing much had changed. Strategists and pollsters in both camps measured the raw data to determine, for every debate setup, what could be gained and what would be risked. Their results showed that when either candidate attacked the other in a very tough, direct way— through print or broadcast media—the "attacker" was hurt more than the "attackee." They called it the backlash effect.

Another important aspect of the format for debates is the composition of questioners. A carefully assembled panel must insure that all questions are sharp, to the point, without pretense. One problem in attempting to select members that are experts on economic issues, or foreign affairs, or environmental problems, or any other policy-making field, is that they may use the forum of debates to expound their own theories or take on authoritative roles. Another problem is that many experts or peer-group figures are committed to a set of policies or a specific candidate by the time the debates take place. Finally, it does not always follow that a historian or an economist, as well versed on the issues as he or she may be, will produce good, incisive questioning. This is a skill that befits journalists more than any other group. Nevertheless, in terms of exploring new styles and formats, some consideration should be given to a panel of broader representation.

Debates for Minority Candidates

Another item that must be considered for future presidential debates is the question of third-party and independent candidates. I think that there should be one or two debates for the minority candidates, depending on how many are considered "viable."

Deciding exactly who is a "viable" candidate, and who is not, is a delicate and difficult problem. In 1976, for instance, there were over a hundred candidates for president legitimately registered with the Federal Election Commission at the time the debates began.

In discussing minority candidates, one cannot ignore Section 315 of the Communications Act—the equal-time provision. I am for its permanent repeal in terms of presidential and vice-presidential races, and possibly across the entire political spectrum, including senate, congressional, gubernatorial, and local races. I think that any flagrant abuses by any broadcaster would be caught by public interest groups. The mere fear of license revocation would keep political broadcast coverage balanced.

Summary of the Agenda

The Agenda of Events should thus be a carefully planned group of political activities that would augment the campaign and serve the electorate in a logical step-by-step manner. To summarize, these would be the major events in the nine- to ten-week period from Labor Day to election day:

Week 1 Back-to-back addresses by the two candidates.
Week 2 Presidential debate 1.
Week 4 Presidential debate 2.
Week 5 Individual interviews with the presidential candidates.
Week 6 Vice-presidential debate.
Week 7 Presidential debate 3.
Week 8 Minority candidates' debate.
       Appearances by candidates' advisors.
Last week before election—Presidential debate 4.

Obviously, there will be many suggestions about how best to handle debates. Although the Agenda may appear too structured, I would not propose any concept that was inflexible. Other summary points to be made are that debates would have a format guaranteeing some direct exchange between the candidates and that the Agenda should be announced in January of the election year. Finally, Section 315 should be repealed.

A National Debate Commission

How can we establish such an Agenda and ensure that there will be debates in future presidential races? I am strongly in favor of the creation of a special national commission to carry out the Agenda of Events, as I have outlined here. The importance of an institution that has the clout and the conviction to oblige candidates to debate cannot be underestimated, particularly in the wake of 1976. In the League's experience, the real threshold between attitudes of indifference and skepticism and of eager anticipation toward the debates was August 19, the date of Ford's challenge. The months of background mobilization and work on the part of the League might have come to naught had one of the candidates not seized upon the idea of debates as a desirable means to his campaign ends. Without the clout of a national debate commission, therefore, any future debate may be jeopardized by the candidates themselves.

The national debate commission, as I envision it, would be chartered by Congress and comprised of representatives from wide-ranging civic groups, political associations, broadcasters, business and labor officials, other interest groups and organizations such as the League, and individuals familiar with the negotiation and production aspects of the debates. The commission must remain autonomous, free from any political meddling, and its purse funded directly by Congress or by the Federal Election Commission. Such money would cover the costs of organizing and setting up the debates and any other events on the Agenda.

If there is to be a debate fever in this country, I would hope it reaches down to nonpresidential races. For every presidential/vice-presidential election in this country, there are hundreds at other levels of government. In congressional and other local elections, the commission's role of establishing a viable framework for debates, of formulating guidelines to be followed by candidates and broadcasters, of rallying public enthusiasm, of fixing schedules and determining appropriate formats, would be tremendously valuable in revitalizing our nation's political campaign process at the grass roots. Here is where the most work needs to be done and where the commission, as an institutional promoter of greater dialogue between candidates and the electorate, can be most effective.

I am firmly convinced that the best interests of America's voting public are at stake in this discussion of an Agenda of Events, a national commission, and a framework for careful planning. In our age of growing voter apathy and less-than-candid political campaign activities, the possibility of direct, established communicative links between candidates and the public is not to be overlooked. In our age of weakening party affiliations and fuzzy definitions of issues, candidates, and their policies, the real benefits of televised debates are immense.

Beyond the domestic scenario, there is the international impact of these debates. The 1976 presidential debates were broadcast in over 100 countries. An exact audience count was impossible, but it was estimated that over 150 million persons outside the United States saw each of the presidential debates. It is hoped that those who witnessed these historic events viewed them as a demonstration of American democracy at its best.

Part II

Effects of the Debates

13.

Uses and Effects of the 1976 Debates: An Overview of Empirical Studies

DAVID O. SEARS and STEVEN H. CHAFFEE

The body of research on the Ford-Carter debates can, surveyed as a whole, tell us a great deal both about those particular confrontations and about the present state of social research on political mass communication. It is often said of presidential debates that their political meaning depends on the interpretation made of them by the press. Similarly, our understanding of the role played in the campaign by debates depends on the interpretations made by the research community. In this paper we undertake the task of reviewing the many empirical studies built around the Ford-Carter debates. As will be seen, the conclusions researchers reached from these studies were different in several important respects from the wisdom that had emerged from studies of the 1960 Kennedy-Nixon debates. Some of these differences are doubtless due to the shifting character of the electorate and to the differing campaigns of 1960 and 1976. Some other differences can be traced to changes in the ideas and techniques that guide social research.

There are several obvious similarities between the 1960 and 1976 elections, including the closeness of the result and the fact that the eventual victor in each case had been a comparatively unknown Democrat. But some longer-term historical changes are worth noting too. One is that television emerged in the 1960s as the principal source of news for most Americans, and correlatively the principal medium of campaigning for presidential candidates.[1] A second important trend has been the steady decline in the importance of political parties in determining the vote. The percentage of voters who hold allegiance to either of the two major parties has been dwindling for several decades, and there has been a corresponding increase in the importance of political "issues" as a predictor of voting behavior.[2] Whereas the 1960 debates mainly gave voters an opportunity to examine the personal attributes ("images") of the candidates, in 1976 there was more reason to expect the content of the debates to engage the attention of the audience, because fewer people saw their political interests as clustered in the general policy thrust of one party.

The standard question asked about mass communication in 1960 had to do with the direct effect of a persuasive message on the opinions and behaviors of the audience. This kind of effect was seen as seriously limited by resistance within the voter based on party identification and other predispositions, and by selective patterns of exposure and attention to tendentious media presentations.[3] Two notable shifts in the theoretical context of media studies have since occurred. One is the flowering of studies of the "uses and gratifications" functions that media content can serve for people. Increasingly, since a seminal study by Katz, Gurevitch, and Haas published in 1973, researchers have given attention to the ways media messages are used, and effects are evaluated relative to the use that is sought by the receiver rather than by the outcome intended by the sender.[4] A second and related development has been a growing tendency to define communication effects in terms of information gained rather than attitudes (or behaviors) changed.[5] This is particularly the case where the news media are concerned, since their primary goal is ostensibly the provision of knowledge on which the people can base informed democratic decisions.

The Ford-Carter debates took place mainly because each candidate thought he had a better chance of winning the election if he debated. According to a key Ford strategist, the debates were seen as almost the only means for overtaking Carter, who held about a twenty-point lead in the polls before the Republican Convention.[6] Ford needed something that would stir up the voters if he was to win enough of them over by election day. Carter's strategic view of the debates was predicated on the assumption that they would, as the research from 1960 suggested, serve mainly to reinforce those voters leaning toward the Democratic candidate and convince them to vote for him.[7] By late summer Carter's lead had begun to dwindle and his advisers considered many of the "probable" Carter votes to be soft, that is, easily susceptible to a Republican media blitz.[8] So the debates were seen as a method of putting the challenger on a par with the incumbent president in the most visible events of the fall campaign; this should minimize further erosion of Carter's vote. Each strategy was correct to a degree: Ford gained some ground on Carter during the early debates period, but not quite enough to overtake him.

While the candidates approached the debates with predatory designs, there was a third interest involved as well. The League of Women Voters agreed to stage the debates as a service to the electorate, to aid in the general enlightenment of the vote. This democratic perspective is more consonant with the trends discussed above: a less partisan and more issue-oriented electorate relying on television to inform it, and a research community attuned to the informational needs of the mass-media audience. As in 1960, a strictly bipartisan debate format was used, with each candidate expected to answer each question posed and allotted an equal amount of time to do so. Unlike almost any other mechanism for presentation of political information during a campaign—consider such alternatives as advertisements, speeches, conventions, campaign-trail "news"— the debates are designed to break through the barriers induced by narrow partisan appeals and to reach potential voters who might otherwise pay little attention to the glittering array of symbols each candidate employs in the quest for support.

The terms of battle in the Ford-Carter debates were set by the political context of the day, and the location of the two candidates in it. Each had emerged from a series of bitterly contested party primaries, largely because he had projected an image of rectitude and decency that contrasted with the shabby recent past, the Vietnam-Watergate era, in which public esteem for the presi-

224   THE GREAT DEBATES

dency had declined so markedly.[9] Each had fended off rivals from the outer extremes—Ford from the right and Carter from both left and right—to win the nomination. Carter was vulnerable on the charge of being "fuzzy on the issues," while Ford had the task of defending a domestic economic policy that was not very popular; each relished the opportunity to attack the other on weak points like these.[10] Ford issued the challenge to debate in accepting his nomination at the Republican convention; this was barely five weeks before the first debate was held on September 23. Politicians are accustomed to acting on such short notice, but social science is not.

Research in the Heat of the Debates

Katz and Feldman entitled their summary of the 1960 studies "The Debates in the Light of Research."[11] They likened the researchers' procedures to the operation of a firehouse, as if research teams are constantly on call awaiting an opportunity for study to present itself. This is not really the case, of course, and it testifies to the resourcefulness of the field that so many research teams were able to suspend their other activities in order to organize debates studies on the spur of the moment. (This pressure was exacerbated by the fact that the timing coincided with the beginning of the academic year in the universities where most of these researchers teach.) Some three dozen studies are represented in our review here, and even this is surely not a complete inventory. Additional studies continue to appear, and there is potentially no end to them because many of the data sets have been archived and will remain subject to secondary analysis and reinterpretation. A full listing of the studies we will refer to here appears at the end of this chapter, alphabetized by first author and numbered; for brevity's sake our references to these studies will be by number.

Some of the research reviewed here is based on nationwide samples (see 36, 37), and some of them have been analyzed beyond simple descriptions of marginal percentages (20, 31, 33). There is also one statewide sample (15, 16). But the most common form of study is the local survey conducted within a limited community, often with student interviewers. Many of these were panels of as many as five waves (5, 13) or four (15, 16, 41). Two-wave panels with interviews before and after a specific debate were especially popular (2, 3, 7, 8, 26, 29, 35). Table 1 summarizes the sampling and interviewing designs of the thirty-two audience studies. This total effort yields a very rich body of information about changes that went on in the electorate during the debates period, representing more than 26,000 interviews with more than 16,000 U.S. citizens.

Getting studies into the field on short notice entailed some sacrifices. Except for a few commercial polls (33, 36) those studies with predebate interviews were limited to small or local samples. The larger samples in Table 1 are found mostly in projects that delayed fieldwork until the later debates (2, 17), including some where a small panel was interviewed early and then augmented with a larger sample later (for example, 29). Samples of students also tended to be larger (10, 21, 27), and were sometimes used for experimentation (27, 28, 34, 43). Several studies analyzed the content of the debates and the related media coverage rather than audience reactions (4, 18, 22, 23, 30) or in addition to them (6, 29, 31). And there is at least one article examining the reaction to the debates in another country (14).

Table 1: Sampling Designs of Audience Studies

Study No.	Sampled Population	Before Debates	After D1	After D2	After VP	After D3	After Election	Panel N (waves)
General Population Samples:								
33	National	758	758					758 (2)
20	National	411	411					411 (2)
36	National	2,000	na	300		2,000		
31	National	na	na	na	na	na	2,875	
15, 16	Wisconsin	164	164			164	164	164 (4)
Local Community Samples:								
35	Akron	400	312					234 (2)
7	Cedar Rapids	149	149				149	149 (3)
13	Cleveland	388	157		120	75	298	352 (2)
44	San Francisco	397	193			170	182	na
5	Syracuse	104	297	256	427	233		
8	Cincinnati	480	618			760		480 (2)*
3	Cheyenne, students	427	427					427 (2)
41	Philadelphia (student acquaintances)	203	203	113		113		113 (4)
25	Philadelphia	200				132		132 (2)
6	3 sites	125				126	128	
19	Evanston	21	(21 "October")				21	21 (3)
29	Madison	97			353		323	95 (3) 323 (2)
2	Lansing, Athens				466	466		466 (2)
24	Cleveland ethnic					771		
17	Buffalo					326		
26	New Haven			99	99			99 (2)
38	Palo Alto					383		
14	Netherlands					319		
Student Samples:								
21	adolescents	561; 130	129	124		125		508 (2)
34	students	195	195					195 (2)*
43	students	218	195					195 (2)*
28	students	127	195					127 (2)*
27	students	308; 386						*
9	students	150	150	150		150		150 (4)
11	students	na	na					35 (2)
39	"convenience"	91	91	91	91	91		91 (5)
10	students		260	263		263		263 (4)

*Experimental design

THE GREAT DEBATES

Theoretical Expectations

What general expectations might we have about the impact of political mass communications delivered during the fall (post-Labor Day) phase of an American presidential campaign? A series of conditions generally obtain that permit some fairly clear predictions: (1) Many voters possess strong predispositions with regard to the relevant attitude objects—party identification, general liberalism or conservatism, issue preferences, and prior attitudes toward the candidates. Many, if not most, voters will already have made an irrevocable candidate choice. (2) Relative to these predispositions, the informational input from the usual campaign communication is rather weak. The volume of exposure is low (due to lack of interest and hence small audience, weak attention, brevity of message, etc.); its content will tend to be favorable but not decisive.[12] (3) The processing of such comparatively simple affective preferences as are involved in political attitudes is heavily dominated by consistency pressures, so that new information often is assimilated according to the person's predispositions. (4) The normal cognitive processing mechanisms brought to bear on such communications are far from awesome, usually involving sporadic attention, minimal learning and poor memory, skimpy cognitive organization, the use of simpleminded and distorting heuristics, and so on.

Given these standard preconditions, the best baseline prediction is that single communications would be interpreted within the framework of existing affective predispositions, and consequently that they would mainly reinforce such prior preferences. Hence, only communications delivered quite early in the campaign (before candidate preferences have built up very strongly) or those with intrinsically very powerful persuasive content would have much widespread impact on voter affect toward the main attitude objects of the campaign.

Presidential debates add some novel elements that modify these expectations somewhat. Debates seem to be much more attractive media events than are the usual one-sided partisan communications in that they are likely to draw much larger audiences. The adversarial nature of debates may, however, affect how the information is processed. Sears, Freedman, and O'Connor[13] have argued that anticipating debates polarizes strongly committed partisans, as they prepare to cheer their hero and boo the villain. This would promote still further polarization along predispositional lines. But less-committed persons, by their reasoning, would become more open to influence because they anticipate being able to make a clear comparison of the alternatives and a fully informed choice. Finally, following the "positivity" principle, debates should involve competing appeals that are intrinsically nearly offsetting, given the careful selection process involved in picking the presidential candidates and preparing them for the performance.

The earliest of a series of debates might have some lasting partisan advantage to one candidate if there is some widely perceived superiority in his or her performance. This would accrue because of the large audience, and the mild "openness" encouraged in the uncommitted by the debate format. But even the earliest debate would mainly reinforce and stabilize the preferences of committed partisans. And later debates ought to stabilize voters' attitudes in approximately their predebate positions, unless something radically embarrassing happens to one candidate or the other.

The Voters' Expectations

By far the most common reason voters gave for watching the debates was, "To see how the candidates stand on issues." In one study this goal received a mean rating of 2.85 on a 3-point scale (the next highest among 11 means was only 2.57); in another it ranked first of 17 items, with a rating of 3.44 on a 4-point scale (29, 44). It was rated highest of all reasons by a sample of adolescents (21), and was cited by 40 percent in a fourth study, by far the reason most often given (5). Learning about the candidates as personalities was secondary to issue information, but it too was important. In one sample 90 percent said that learning the candidates' issue stands was "very important," while 75 percent said that so was judging what they were like as people (35). Other studies produced similar results (5, 29).

More generally, voters said they felt the debates could help them decide whom to vote for. Many felt the choice was a difficult one and they were (at least initially) underinformed for it (35, 37). In one study, 71 percent said before the first debate that they had too little information to make a choice between Ford and Carter, 69 percent wanted help in deciding, and 65 percent thought it at least "somewhat likely" that the debates would help them (35). Help in deciding how to vote also ranked high on lists of uses and gratifications in other studies (21, 29). It was seen as particularly important by voters who felt underinformed (r = .23) or that the choice was difficult (r = .33), and most of those who wanted guidance also expected to be influenced by the debates (r = .55) (35). It is not clear whether this emphasis is a normal one or mostly due to the relatively unknown quality of Carter, and even of Ford.

There were of course other reasons for watching. An important one was keeping up with the campaign and otherwise doing one's civic duty (29, 44). Another was the less socially desirable admission that there simply wasn't much else to watch on TV at the time; 21 percent mentioned this as a reason for watching the last debate in one sample (5). Simple "spectator" gratifications, such as enjoying the excitement of the election race, tended to be ranked very low as reasons for tuning in the debates (29). We will return later to this contrast between the voters' stated needs for information and their apparent disregard of more entertainment-oriented aspects of the debates.

Debate Content

The general conclusion that emerges from several content analyses is that the debates themselves were heavily issue-oriented, but the subsequent coverage of them was decidedly less so. The interrogating reporters spent 92 percent of their time on issues, and the candidates responded with issue-related comments either 77 or 80 percent of the time, depending on the analysis (29, 31). The other content categories had to do with demographics, personalities, parties, and group references. Two studies report evidence that the candidates were not overly constrained by the format of the debates, helping to shape their content, and being able to express their general policy divergences in them (4, 23). The various content analyses generally agree that economic issues dominated the first debate and foreign policy the second, with the final debate being more of a mixture, economic issues again leading such elements as the government's credibility and foreign affairs (6, 29, 30, 35). Table 2 presents a composite summary of the content of the three Ford-Carter debates, based on three studies (6, 29, 31).

The heavy issue focus of the debates was largely ignored, however, in the subsequent coverage by television, radio, newspapers, and magazines. All studies agreed that there was less than 40 percent issue content in the post-debate coverage; this means less than half the issue focus of the debates themselves. In covering the crucial first debate, issue content was given only 22 percent of the space in a national sample of newspapers, and only 16 percent of network TV news time. Across all debates, issue coverage was estimated at 37 percent for both newspapers and TV news, at 39 percent for *Time* and 36 percent for *Newsweek* (23, 31).

Instead of their overt content, news reports of the debates were preoccupied with "who won" and generally with the competitive, horse-race aspect. For example, 17 percent of newspaper space and 10 percent of TV news time dealt with the question of which candidate had won a debate. An additional 41 percent and 42 percent, respectively, of each medium's coverage was given over to statements about the performances of the candidates, the personalities and competence levels they projected, and the impact the debate would have on their campaigns (31). *Newsweek* spent one-third of its debate space, and *Time* one-fifth, on preparation, style, studio, and rules (23). In short, the media covered the debates much as they did any other campaign event, by focusing more on the "hoopla," media-event aspects of them than as a vehicle for trans-

Table 2. Issue Content of the Presidential Debates

	D1	D2	D3
Economic			
Taxes	****	0	*
State of Economy	**	**	***
Unemployment	***	*	***
Inflation	*	0	**
Other Domestic			
Size of gov't., budget	****	*	*
HEW	***	*	***
Social Issues			
Crime	*	0	**
Race, busing	0	0	**
Abortion	0	0	*
Environment/Energy	***	*	**
Credibility/trust gov't.	***	***	****
Foreign policy	0	****	***

**** = 18% +.   *** = 8–12%.   ** = 4–6%.   * = 1–3%.   0 = not mentioned
Sources: 6, 29, 31

mitting the candidates' positions on the issues. In this sense the media coverage did not address the self-reported needs of the voters.

The strong issue emphasis was not preserved in the press reports, but the *relative* emphases among the issues were. For example, 37 percent of the first debate was devoted to economic issues; press reports also mentioned economic issues more than any others, although this amounted to only 14 percent of all coverage in the newspapers and 5 percent on TV (31). Across the three Ford-Carter debates, foreign affairs and economics ranked 1–2 among issue topics in all three bodies of content—debates, newspapers, TV—but they constituted more than twice as much of the debates themselves as of the subsequent press coverage, in percentage terms (12).

Exposure to the Debates

A Seemingly Massive Audience. One clear fact about the debates is that almost all voters had at least minimal direct exposure to them. At least one debate reached 83 percent of the public nationwide, according to post-election data (31), and the Nielsen ratings estimated that 89 percent of households were tuned in to at least one (37). Local surveys reached estimates of 88 percent (29) and 91 percent (5) viewer exposure. Viewing of any single debate was of course less widespread. And, as in 1960, people were more likely to watch the earlier debates. About 70 percent watched some part of the first and/or second debates, more than 60 percent the final debate, and a little less than 50 percent the Dole-Mondale debate, according to the most representative samples interviewed by the most professional personnel (Table 3).

Table 3. Percentages Reporting Exposure to Any Part of Each Debate

Sample	D1	D2	VP	D3	Restrictions	(Source)
National (AP)	71	71		64	None	(37)
National (Roper)	72	65	48		None	(37)
National (Harris)	71				None	(37)
National (Gallup)	67	70		69	Registered voters	(37)
National (MOR)	89				Registered voters	(33)
National (Nielsen)	72	65	50	60	Households	(37)
Wisconsin	66	59	36	62	4-wave panel; phone	(15)
Madison (age 27+)	84	71	50	54	phone	(29)
Madison (under 27)	75	69	31	44	phone	(29)
Syracuse	78	60	58	56	phone, registered voters	(5)
Athens	84			54	2-wave panel	(2)
Lansing	81			63	2-wave panel	(2)
Akron	75				2-wave panel	
Illinois State U.	63	46		35	3-wave panel, students	(10)
New Haven			50		2-wave, screened for prior debate viewing	(26)
Cedar Rapids	88	87	74	54	3-wave panel, voters	(7)
Median across all studies	75	67	50	56		

THE GREAT DEBATES

Yet this seeming massiveness of the audience may give a misleading picture of audience attention. For one thing, a much smaller audience was present at all debates. Nielsen suggests 42 percent of the households tuned in to all three presidential debates (37), and a Syracuse survey found just 28 percent watched all four (5). Additionally, attention tended to be partial and sporadic for any given debate; relatively few watched all the way through from start to finish. The exact percentage who watched "all" of any single debate is difficult to estimate. Questions about amount of viewing a given debate were asked mainly in the panel surveys (2, 15, 29), which themselves overestimated debate viewing (due to attrition of less politically interested respondents over repeated interviews, and perhaps to the stimulating effects of earlier interviewing). Correcting for this bias, each of the presidential debates was probably seen in its entirety by about 25 percent of the population, while considerably fewer watched the full vice-presidential debate (see also 7, 26; even this may be something of an overestimate, given the social desirability of reporting full viewing).

Exposure to media coverage of the debates followed an analogous pattern, with very high reports of "any" exposure but much lower figures when significant forms of attention were asked about. For example, one study found that 97 percent were exposed either to the first debate or to some communication about it within 48 hours (7), and others found that 60 to 70 percent were exposed to some media interpretations of the debates (2, 10, 12). Across all the debates, one study found that 61 percent had "heard about" the debates on radio or TV (10). But some such exposure, at least at a superficial level, was practically inescapable given the heavy attention the media accorded the debates. A more sensible indicator of meaningful attention might be the 20 percent who read any columns or editorials or the 29 percent who read any news stories analyzing the third debate. Similarly, 38 percent heard at least one radio story, and 28 percent at least one TV story; and from 6 to 15 percent heard or read at least three stories in any medium (2).

Estimates of interpersonal discussion are hard to evaluate because of imprecise measurement. For example, in three studies about 80 percent reported some discussion of the first debate (7, 10, 27); a fourth gives a similar estimate, but adds that only 42 percent had discussed the debate more than "very little" (12). Both discussion and exposure to poll results on "who won" seem to have been rather high for the first two debates and to have dropped appreciably thereafter (2, 27, 40).

So the frequently cited estimate from 1960 that 90 percent of the public watches presidential debates implies a universality of exposure that does not bear up under close scrutiny. At most, about a fourth of the electorate followed the debates quite closely, another fourth paid them little or no attention, and the remaining half watched some part (but not all) of some (but not all) of the debates. Similarly some post-debate media and interpersonal communication reached healthy majorities of adults. But most of it was probably superficial, consisting (at least for the media) mainly of summary judgments about the debaters' performances and "who won."

Redundancy of debate exposure. One important consideration in evaluating the debates is to assess the extent to which they were redundant with the rest of the campaign. There is evidence of considerable redundancy in that those who watched the debates were also the people most likely to be exposed to the more usual run of campaign news (40). This redundancy manifests itself empirically in the correlations between debate exposure and other variables. First of all, viewing of the several debates and of post-debate media analysis were fairly strongly intercorrelated. For example, the amount of viewing of debate 1 was highly correlated ($r = .67$) with viewing of debate 2 (24), and the correlation for the first and final debates was $r = .33$ (2). Watching the debates and exposure to subsequent TV analyses were correlated $r = .41$ (2). Debate viewing was also fairly strongly related to other indicators of campaign exposure: reading other campaign news in the newspaper (gamma $= .44$), exposure to national TV news (gamma $= .25$; r ranging from .19 to .37 across five different samples), and reading national news in the newspaper (gamma $= .25$ and .26, $r = .40$ and .41) according to various studies (2, 7, 24, 26, 29). Debate viewers saw all media as influencing them (17).

The crucial underlying factor in debate exposure seems to have been general political involvement, rather than habitual exposure to television and newspapers. Debate exposure was quite strongly related to measures of political interest, discussion, and participation. The more educated also seem to have been more likely to watch the debates (see also 35). The important role of interest in the campaign is nicely illustrated by the impact of an experimental attempt to increase exposure to the first debate (8). One group was told in advance that "we'd really appreciate it if you could watch the debate" and told they would be reinterviewed; their households were called again just before the debate "to encourage everyone to watch." In comparison with a control group, this treatment significantly increased both the frequency and intensity of watching the debate. More important for our point, the other predictors—for example, campaign involvement and education—retained their separate significant effects. Campaign involvement remained a stronger predictor than the experimental treatment.

Table 4. Correlations of Debate Exposure with Other Variables

Source	Media use		Political behavior			Demographic			
	TV	News-paper	Discus-sion	Interest	Partici-pation	Educa-tion	SES	Age	Sex*
(29 young)	−.12		.30	.34	.19	.30	.06	.19	.13
(29 older)	−.20		.27	.40	.20	.20	.19	.21	.03
(7)			.33	.36	.44	.32	.25	.09	.06
(2)				.27		.08	.12	.25	.08
(8)				.27		.16		.18	
(24)	.11	.15				.11	.14		
(17)	.09	.18	.09						
(26)**	.02			.10	.26	.07	.18	.00	.14
(12)			.16				.27		

*Positive coefficient indicates females watched debates more than males.
**Coefficients from this source are gammas; all others in this table indicate Pearson r.

THE GREAT DEBATES

Table 4 shows the strength of relationships, across eight different studies, between media use, political and demographic variables, and viewing of the debates. The variables in Table 4 enabled investigators to account for fairly impressive percentages of variance in debate viewing: $R^2 = .34$ for young voters and $R^2 = .39$ for older (29), and in another study $R^2 = .45$ (7). It is important to note, though, that most demographic factors other than education did not account for significant increments of variance (for example, home state, age, sex); nor did most measures of "uses and gratifications" sought from the media; nor most measures of political partisanship. Nor were normal media use habits terribly important; people who normally watch television a great deal were no more likely than others to see the debates, and the relationships are nearly as weak for other media.

In short, the main predictors of debate exposure were interest in politics generally, and in this campaign in particular, including indicators of other forms of exposure to the campaign. In that sense debate exposure was at least partly redundant with other means of exposure to the campaign.

Issues: Salience and Position Clarification

One of the major manifest functions of a presidential campaign is to communicate to voters the candidates' positions on the important issues of the day. The voters are expected to base their choices partly on their approval of these positions—and do so, to some extent, as shown in the voluminous "issue-voting" literature.[14] The reporters assigned to question the candidates during the debates clearly felt this was their mandate, as indicated by their intense issue focus documented earlier. The candidates' responses were also heavily issue-oriented. And the voters said they most wanted to learn about the issues from the debates. Were they successful in facilitating the communication of candidates' issue positions? In some ways no, but in several important ways they were.

Agenda-Setting. A much-studied topic in recent years has been the impact of public communication in determining the issues or topics that people think are important.[15] Did the debates help set the issue agenda for the campaign by diverting voters' attention from some issues to others? The studies converge on a negative answer and point up a notable exception to it—Ford's East Europe comment. To assess the agenda-setting impact of the debates, it is necessary to correlate the issue emphases in the debates with changes from predebate to postdebate in the topics people think are important.

There is surprisingly little evidence on predebate voter preoccupations, but what there is indicates heavy emphasis on the state of the economy (inflation, unemployment) and perhaps on the size of government (6, 23, 27, 29).

The emphases of the first two debates included several topics that were not major public concerns (energy, credibility), and the correlations between the content of these debates and the public agenda were zero or even negative (6). There was a strong positive correlation (rho $= .49$) for the final debate. This seems, however, to have come about because the candidates addressed themselves to the voters' concerns rather than to changing those concerns: the perceived-importance ratings of eight issues were highly correlated from before to after the debates, and none changed significantly (29). Also, whether the person had watched the debates did not affect the relative salience of any issue. A study of five issues, and the last debate, similarly failed to find any evidence of impact on the public agenda (2). In another test a topic that was not heavily debated (inflation) was found to increase in importance relative to three heavily debated issues (6). Over time, debate content correlated more strongly with predebate public agendas than with post-debate agendas (29).

Two findings stand as exceptions to all this evidence of nonimpact. There seems to have been a temporary rise in salience of the topics discussed in each debate, but then a fairly rapid regression soon after to long-term baselines that had existed before the debate. This conclusion is buttressed by evidence that comments about foreign policy were most likely to be made by people interviewed immediately after the second debate, and comments about domestic policy immediately after the first and the third (31). A second impact was the "issue" of Ford's statement that East European Communist governments were autonomous. Much was made of this by Carter and in the press, and it was long remembered. In one sample that was heavy with East European ties, 80 percent had heard of Ford's comment; debate viewers were especially likely to cite it as a reason for their vote (24, 31). But this event was simply an incident, not an issue that arose because it was emphasized in the debates (it wasn't) and which then rose to a position of high importance on the public agenda (it didn't). Rather, it was a valence issue specifically attached to Ford, not a position issue on which the candidates ultimately differed.

Despite the current interest in agenda-setting by the media, there was in retrospect no strong reason to expect this kind of impact from the debates. No study has shown that either candidate introduced any new policy issues or positions in the debates; the voters seem to have been searching for the candidates' positions on issues, not for issues themselves; and the debates amounted to only a handful of events late in a year of long and intense campaigning. We should point out in accepting the hypothesis of no effect in this instance that the studies on which we must rely are not methodologically terribly persuasive. The sample size is quite limited in some cases (6, 29); there are ceiling-effect problems in two others (2, 24); and another lacks a good predebate baseline (23). At the same time, several of these studies have been contributed by investigators who have been able to demonstrate agenda-setting media effects in other situations; the fact that they concur in finding no such impact here strengthens the case for that inference.[16]

Learning Issue Positions. Did the debates succeed in clarifying for the public such differences as existed between the candidates on the issues debated? Three main designs were used to address this key question. The most appropriate was probably a panel pre and post a given debate, comparing its viewers to nonviewers (10, 27, 28). Other studies simply used panels pre and post a debate (3, 5, 15, 29, 33) or assessed the cumulative impact of debate-watching across the entire campaign (25, 31). Let us first consider the pre-post designs.

Most of the research focused on the first debate, and it is here that we find the most evidence that the voters found the issue-oriented information they said they wanted from the debates. One issue heavily emphasized in the first debate concerned unemployment and jobs. Carter favored providing federal programs to reduce unemployment more than Ford, who was seen as more in favor of providing private-sector jobs. And that debate appears to have definitely clarified the candidates' positions on this topic: the perceived difference between them on unemployment policy increased by 29 percent among viewers in one study (27); in two other studies the increases were 26 percent (33) and 17 percent (5) among all respondents. Not all the evidence was positive. For example, two studies found no differential impact on this issue, one reporting no change except for a drop in the "don't know" responses regarding Carter's position (15) and the other finding that viewers increasingly perceived both candidates as equally committed to reducing unemployment (10). But in all, it appears that the first debate did create a good deal of issue-position learning on unemployment, an issue that had ranked high on the public's predebate agenda of important problems.

The candidates' differences on several other issues were also clarified somewhat by the first debate. There was a marked increase (from 50 to 75 percent) in the proportion perceiving that Carter favored governmental reorganization, while Ford held constant at 20 percent (5). With respect to governmental spending, only Republicans saw Ford as more tight-fisted after the debate than before (28). A small item in the debates (albeit a large one in the minds of many researchers) was amnesty for Vietnam war draft-evaders. Several studies showed strong clarification effects on this topic (3, 10, 27); nationally, there was a 17 percent increase in the perception that Carter supported amnesty and a 20 percent increase on Ford's opposition to it (34). Tax reform, a very visible debate topic, was affected only in that both candidates were seen as more committed to it after the first debate than before (5, 10). There was a growing difference perceived on "taxing the middle class," however (27).

Perceived candidate differences did not increase on topics that weren't discussed in the first debate, which constitute a de facto "control condition." Among the issues in this category were cutting defense spending (10, 15); the B-1 bomber project (5); busing to achieve school integration (28); gun control (5); and the previously volatile issue of abortion (5, 10, 15, 28, 29), which seems to have become progressively less important as a determinant of the vote as the debates went on without stressing it (15). Perceived candidate positions on national health insurance did not change either (10, 27, 28) although some respondents perceived it as having been emphasized in the debate (27). So the main changes from before to after the first debate were limited to topics that were in fact debated, principally unemployment, governmental reorganization, and amnesty.

The main residues of the second debate were Ford's East Europe comment and some modest impact on perceptions of military-spending policies (10). Otherwise, there is no clear documentation of position-clarification effects of any of the later debates. Viewing of the vice-presidential debate did not, by itself, increase familiarity with the positions held by Dole and Mondale (26).

Post-debate media interpretations contributed little to issue clarification, which is not surprising since as we have noted they dealt mostly with matters other than the issue positions expressed in the debates. Of seventeen issues asked about in one study, only on one (the environment) did the post-debate analyses have any apparent effect, and that was to reduce perceived differences between the candidates (27). But the press's post-mortems did contribute significantly to accuracy about the vice-presidential candidates for both viewers and non-viewers; this may have been due to lesser attention to that debate and less pre-debate information about the candidates (26).

The other main methodology was to determine at the end of the debate period whether viewers cumulatively had clearer perceptions of the candidates' positions than nonviewers, controlling on other relevant variables. The stronger version of this might be termed a "recognition" test, since respondents were asked to respond to explicitly mentioned issues. This cumulative method also encourages the conclusion that the debates increased perceptions of issue differences. In one national sample, debate viewing was associated with sharper perceived differences between the two parties on a composite issue scale combining unemployment, size of government, inflation, and military spending. This finding held up even after education, political attentiveness, partisan strength, and media exposure were controlled (31). A similar finding was reported in one local survey of knowledge of the candidates' positions, with education and campaign involvement controlled (25). On the question of federal job programs, post-election data indicate a small but significant residual effect of the debates when education and strength of partisanship are controlled (31).

A number of other cumulative-impact studies found only weak effects on specific issues, however. One found a small effect on perception of Carter's position but none for Ford's (25), while a second could detect no significant effect (29). There were also small cumulative effects for some issues (governmental reorganization, B-1 bomber) but not for others (Ford's position on the constitutional amendment against abortion) when other variables were controlled statistically (29). Another study found that for only one of four issues (handgun registration) was knowledge of issue positions statistically associated with viewing of the specific debate in which it surfaced (25). And a student panel study concluded that the debates "made the candidates appear more alike" when differences were summed across nine issues (9).

Another version of the cumulative-impact method used a "recall" technique, and here the evidence of impact is less impressive. When asked in open-ended questions after the election what they recalled from the debates, most people expressed only global impressions rather than specific issue content (31). Only 16 percent remembered an issue item for Carter; and while 28 percent recalled a Ford issue, three-fifths of these recollections were of the peripheral East Europe comment. The predominant post-election memories from the debates had to do with the candidates' performances (about one-third of all responses), general competence (15 percent), and "personality" (17 percent) (31).

Issues need not be treated individually, since many policies are subsumed under two long-standing dimensions of political orientation— party identification and liberalism-conservatism. The studies provide little evidence that the debates contributed to an understanding of party differences. One argues that, for college students at least, perceptions of the candidates' party identification was unaffected because it was clear before the debates began (10). Another raises the possibility that the debates focus so much on the individual candidates that they may draw attention away from the long-term political differences that define the American party structure (12). On the question of ideology, however, the debates may well have had some cumulative impact. Ford came to be seen as

236

more conservative after the first debate, and Carter as more liberal after the second (5). Post-election data suggest both these effects for the first debate, although causality is difficult to infer with eleven other variables included in the regression equation (7).

In summary, then, the debates to some degree met the expectation that voters would learn where the candidates stood. The debates did not set any new agenda, but they did summarize the main ongoing themes of the campaign in a way that gave their audience a clearer picture of the differences between the candidates on several key domestic questions. The clearest evidence of learning came from short-term panel studies of specific debates. They indicate that the first debate, in particular, informed voters about the candidates' major domestic positions. The other debates had less discernible effects. Media coverage of the debates added little to issue perceptions because it focused more on the process and outcome of the debates than upon what was said. The high redundancy between debate viewing and other forms of exposure to campaign information made it quite difficult to isolate specific inputs from studies of cumulative effects. Apparently the issue-recognition measures had a lower threshold than did open-ended recall questions, as there was some modest cumulative effect on the former but none on the latter. In any event, all impacts were fairly short-lived, leaving little cognitive residue after the election, and they paralleled the effects of other campaign information sources that were available even had there been no debates.

Who Won?

The most commonly asked question in the surveys was, as in 1960, which candidate people perceived as having won each debate. There is a remarkable consensus in the answers: Ford, Carter, Mondale, and Carter, in order of debate. Table 5 summarizes the data in terms of percentage differences between those who thought Carter had won and those who gave the decision to Ford. Carter was seen as having benefited most by the series of debates; a national poll taken just before the election found 36 percent believed Carter had done better in the debates "overall," compared with 23 percent for Ford (37).

While it is impressive that so many different surveys arrived at the same general outcome, the percentages make it clear that these judgments were far from universal. Indeed the average split was about 38 to 31 for the winner, so large minorities thought the "loser" had won (37). From this one might glean the picture of a mostly ambiguous reality tilted only slightly, in each case, in one direction or the other. If so, we might expect large numbers of people feeling the debates were too even to yield a real "winner." But that was not the case. People were generally willing to view this ambiguous reality as yielding a winner. The percent saying "don't know" or "draw" or "neither" varied from 16 to 41 percent in the national surveys of the three presidential debates, with a median of 30 percent (37). The solid majority chose sides.

These winner-loser judgments were heavily affected by predebate preference for each of the three debates: people tended to see the candidate they had preferred before the debate as the winner, as shown in Table 6. Among Carter voters, for example, 65 percent saw him as having won the second debate; and 62 percent of them also felt he had won the first debate and only 5 percent

Table 5. Who Won? Advantage to Carter–Mondale

	D1	D2	VP	D3	(Source)
National Surveys					
Roper	−8%	+10%		+11%	(37)
Harris	−9	+24			(37)
Gallup	−13	+23		+5	(37)
AP	−2	+3		−3	(37)
Yankelovich				+7	(37)
Local Surveys					
Wisconsin	−23	+26	+31	+5	(15)
Madison (young)	−19	+39	+22	+16	(29)
Madison (older)	−27	+40	+33	+8	(29)
Students (Illinois St. U.)	−37	+15		−12	(10)
Cedar Rapids	−23				(7)
Syracuse	−23	+28	+11	+7	(5)
Students (SUNY-SB)	−10				(27)
New Haven	−18	+33			(1)
Cheyenne	−16				(3)
Students (U. of Wyoming)	−17				(3)
Philadelphia	−4	+35		+18	(41)
Median	−16	+26	+27	+7	

NOTE: entry is the percentage feeling Carter–Mondale won, minus the percentage feeling Ford–Dole won.

thought he had lost, despite the fact that all fifteen of our surveys showed he had come out behind on balance (see Table 5). Similarly, 70 percent of Ford's supporters agreed with the majority view that he had won the first debate, but 56 and 60 percent of them also thought he had won the second and third, respectively, when the consensus said he had lost. The organizing power of prior preference is also indicated by the fact that undecided voters were much less likely to see a clear winner than partisans were. The first and third debates were judged to be draws by 47 percent of the undecideds, and the second by 42 percent.

As might be expected, the major partisan predispositions that produce candidate preference were also good predictors of the winner-loser judgment. The voter's party identification was correlated from $r = .24$ to $r = .38$ with party of the perceived winner of each debate; for a summary index across these debates the figure was $r = .37$ for younger voters (aged 26 and below) and $r = .49$ for older voters (29), and other studies reported similar findings (3, 10, 26, 39). Correlations with political ideology measures were only slightly smaller. There is also some evidence that these long-term predispositions were more important than candidate preferences in predicting how people judged the winners of the first and vice-presidential debates, in which the candidates were not so well known (10, 26, 40).

Does this mean that there was no "real" winner of each debate? No, there is evidence of consensus above and beyond these partisan selectivities. Despite the strongly partisan reactions to the question of who won, there are some

THE GREAT DEBATES

marginal differences that account for the consistency across surveys shown in Table 5. There definitely was a net perception that Ford won the first debate and Carter the second; these were also the most-watched debates, and the ones that told voters the most about the issue differences that they had expressed interest in. Even the partisans show some agreement with the overall judgments. Among Carter voters 32 percent admitted Ford won the first debate, but only 10 percent thought he had won the second; with Ford voters just 5 percent gave Carter the first debate, but 16 percent the second. The undecideds' judgments also tended to reflect the majority views: 28–25 Ford in the first debate, 33–25 Carter in the second, and 33–20 Carter in the final encounter.

A good bit of this consensus appears not to have been based on "reality," however; that is, it was not based on the viewers' direct perceptions of the debates. Rather, the news media quickly established a consensual answer to the question of which candidate had won a debate, partly through immediate reporting of poll results. This in turn guided public responses to that question, as if it were the "correct" answer, and eventually it became so. Two examples of this press influence over "who won" emerge from studies of the first two debates that compared impressions of the winner immediately after the debate to responses on the following days, after the press interpretations had been broadcast and published. In the case of the first debate, when the media declared Ford the "winner," Carter had a 42–24 edge in a sample of students responding as soon as they had seen the debate. However, Ford was judged a 41–20 winner by a similar sample interviewed in the succeeding days (27). Similarly, Ford's

Table 6. "Who Won?" as a Function of Prior Preference: National Surveys

Prior Preference		Who Won?		
		Carter	Draw	Ford
Debate 1[1]				
	Carter	62	6	32 = 100
	Undecided	25	47	28 = 100
	Ford	5	25	70 = 100
	Total	32	34	34
Debate 2[2]				
	Carter	65	25	10 = 100
	Undecided	33	42	25 = 100
	Total	16	28	56 = 100
		40	30	30
Debate 3[2]				
	Carter	62	29	9 = 100
	Undecided	33	47	20 = 100
	Ford	12	28	60 = 100
	Total	40	31	29

1. SOURCE: AP poll immediately before and after debate. See *Ann Arbor News,* September 24, 1976, p. 1 (n = 1065).

2. SOURCE: PBS/Roper polls done at conclusion of debates and in the three days before.

edge grew from 8 percent near the end of the debate to 16 percent ten days later, and from 4 to 33 percent in a month, if we compare data from other studies (36, 41).

Carter was declared the "winner" of the second debate. Ford's pollsters found that "individuals interviewed immediately after the second debate thought that Ford had narrowly won the debate, but by the evening of the day after the debate, Carter had become the overwhelming "winner," as post-debate commentary (including a press conference by Ford) had focused attention on Ford's East Europe comment (42). Other findings support this conclusion; Carter's initial lead among Democrats was 33 percent for debate two, but a few weeks later it was up to 54 percent (41). The actual impact of these media judgments on voters' attitudes seems to operate only in the immediate debate aftermath. By the end of October press analysis exposure accounted for only 2 percent of the variance in judging the debates' winners, while 26 percent could be attributed to party identification and ideology (29). The percentage judging the first debate a "draw" rose from 30 to 52 percent in the ten days afterward (36).

So the perception of a winner is determined mostly by information other than the direct experience of watching a debate itself. Prior preferences seem to have guided immediate judgments very heavily, and the post-debate media interpretations subsequently swayed voters away from this immediate partisan division. Watching the debates themselves added very little variance to the judgment of who won ($R^2 = 6$ percent or less) beyond that explained by predispositions. Whether the initial reaction is more "real" than that based on subsequent media handling of the question is a moot point. Both immediate journalism and eventual history will record the outcomes shown in Table 5 as results of the debates even though they might not have come about had events been stopped with the finish of each debate proper.

Candidate Images and the Vote: Limited Effects

When a politician asks "who won," he is thinking about votes won or lost and of changes in evaluations of the candidates. These affective changes are the bottom line in the political marketplace. They are not, as a rule, for the public or the sponsors of debates (other than politicians), as we have already noted. In those eyes, debates are held to enlighten, not to direct, the decisions voters make. Nevertheless, the point of an election campaign is to select an officeholder. Accordingly, debate effects on that choice was clearly a central question for most researchers.

There was a certain amount of turnover in candidate evaluations and vote intentions in the fall campaign; they were not completely static. According to one national panel, 13 percent switched from one candidate to the other, and nearly one-third showed some change on a seven-point vote intention scale in the two weeks surrounding the first debate (20). Various studies estimated that from one-fourth to more than one-half of their respondents changed their evaluations on one or more image attributes (10, 25, 33). Nevertheless, the net evaluations of the candidates and net vote intentions remained highly constant through the debate period. There was a major slippage in Carter's vote margin before the first debate, and this continued to a lesser extent in that debate's immediate aftermath. During the rest of the campaign there was very little change in favor of either candidate. The same was true of candidate images. In one panel the mean composite image score for each candidate varied by less than 0.2 of its standard deviation over four waves (41); other studies reported similar stability (12, 15). The question is, what part did the debates play in inducing this degree of internal turnover—and overall stability—in attitudes toward the candidates?

Voting Intentions. As with the learning of issue positions, there is no one simple way to assess the debates' impact on voting intentions. One approach looks at fluctuations in the margin between the candidates across the period of the debates. Several panel studies found that Ford's prospects improved in the period surrounding the first debate (which he "won" in the limited sense described above). One national survey found that 13 percent changed candidates from before to after the first debate with Ford doing better (20); in Wisconsin, Carter's lead slipped from 9 percent down to 3 percent after the first debate (15); Ford's lead in a Republican region grew from 8 percent to 17 percent (5). The problem with ascribing these changes to the debate is that none of the studies attempted to relate debate viewing directly to the changes. In effect they present the same picture as the cross-sectional national surveys mentioned earlier: some Ford advantage during the period surrounding the first debate.

The retrospective studies tried to estimate the impact of exposure to the debates, as opposed to other determinants of the vote, on the basis of post-election measures. By this standard, the debates do not seem to have had any significant impact on the vote. Panel data show that the overriding factor in the final vote decision was predebate candidate preference. For example, 56 percent of the variance in the final vote in one study was accounted for by vote intentions measured before the debates; all other variables added another 16 percent (29); all intra-campaign attitude changes and debate-related variables together accounted for but 9 percent of the variance in another (10); and in a third the tau-betas between debate viewing and vote intention varied from .04 to .07 for the three debates (25). One suggestive finding is that in the Wisconsin panel predebate vote intention predicted the eventual vote most strongly among non-viewers; those who watched the debates regularly were the *most* likely to modify their initial candidate preferences and to make their final decisions after completion of the debates (15).

A third way to assess impact is simply to ask voters what *they* thought affected their votes (though this technique collides with the more general problem that people may be quite imperfect reporters of the causes of their behavior and attitudes; see Nisbett and Wilson, 1977). By this standard, the debates were often seen as having some influence, but rarely perceived as decisive. In national surveys only about 3 percent said they had changed their votes because of the debates (32, 38). The statement "impressed me during the debates" ranked only tenth on a list of reasons for the vote, cited by 13 percent of Carter's supporters and 7 percent of Ford's (32). But influence estimates were somewhat greater with less-demanding questions. In one survey 16 percent said the debates had been "very important," and in another 27 percent said the first debate had at least "some influence" on their preference (7, 38).

Many voters expected this first adversary confrontation to help them choose between the candidates and there is evidence that it did. In one study 38 percent of Ford voters became more certain, 13 percent less certain; for Carter voters, 37 percent more certain, 8 percent less (27). Other studies report that the first debate reduced the number of "no preference" and "leaners," and increased the number voting for each candidate (15); that 41 percent said their decision was made easier, and only 13 percent more difficult (35); and that more respondents moved to a candidate preference than to "both," "neither," or "don't know," on 16 of 19 indicators (33). In short, the debates seem to have played only a minor role in voters' vote choices. But they did clarify more often than they confused. And voters at least *felt* they helped somewhat, even if they did not feel the debates to be indispensable.

Overall Candidate Evaluations. Other studies tested the impact of the debates on overall evaluations of the candidates rather than on preferences between them. There were again two kinds of studies—those that examined candidate evaluations or preferences immediately after a debate, and those that relied on retrospective data collected at (or after) election time. The immediate effects on candidate evaluation were moderately strong, and predictable from our earlier evidence on "who won." One study plotted evaluations of the candidates by day of interview (31). Both candidates' ratings simultaneously moved sharply away from neutral over a period of two to four days after each debate. Ford's rating was helped by the first debate, Carter's by the last two. Other studies of immediate impact obtained similar, if more complex, findings. The first debate consistently seemed to make viewers more positive toward Ford (5, 10, 23, 41), with changes in evaluations of Carter varying from much more positive to somewhat more negative (5, 10, 41). The second debate seems to have made both Carter's and Ford's evaluations slightly more favorable, though the findings are not completely consistent across samples, and the third debate was clearly favorable to Carter but not for Ford (5, 10, 41). The vice-presidential debate plainly boosted Mondale's esteem without harming Dole very much (5, 26).

But these changes in candidate evaluation seem to have been either temporary, too slight to pick up retrospectively, or so multiply determined that they cannot be attributed solely to the debates. A considerable variety of studies found no residual impact of debate viewing on net evaluations of or preferences between the candidates, when tested retrospectively from election-day or post-election surveys. In general, such studies found highly significant effects of predebate evaluations of the candidates and weak or nonsignificant effects of debate viewing (7, 13, 15, 25).

Candidate Image. Many studies also considered voters' perceptions of more specific candidate attributes. Surprisingly little evidence of debate impact is found for specific "image" traits (though they are often thought to be most malleable through telegenic performances). Ford's own polling firm found strong gains for him on one trait ("good speaker") and some improvement on two others ("decisive" and "strong"), but none on six other traits (33). Two other national surveys (31, 32) were unable to find any evidence of debate impact despite examining a number of traits with different methodologies; this also tended to be the experience with local samples (for example, 9). Table 7 gives a more comprehensive account, displaying the specific results from the relevant studies. It is not strictly appropriate to make simple totals, because each study used varying numbers of traits, each debate was not represented

Table 7: Debate Impact on Specific Evaluative Traits

Attribute	Advantage to Carter				No Advantage				Advantage to Ford			
	D1	D2	D3	Overall	D1	D2	D3	Overall	D1	D2	D3	Overall
Good speaker					(16)			(16)	(34)			
Debate performance									(27)			
Effective campaigner									(31)			
Leadership					(16)			(16)				
					(32)	(32)	(32)					
					(13)			(33)				(29)
Capable									(3)			
Competent					(33)							
Decisive					(35)				(33)			
Strength					(41)	(41)	(41)		(33)			
					(16)			(16)				
					(3)							
Intelligence		(41)		(13)	(33)		(41)		(41)			
									(3)			
					(32)	(32)						
Wise		(41)					(41)		(41)			
Informed					(33)							
					(34)							
Trustworthy	(41)	(41)		(25)	(35)	(41)						
					(33)							
					(27)							
Honesty	(27)				(16)			(16)				
					(33)							
					(29)	(29)						
					(3)							
Straightforward					(27)							
Empathy/concern	(35)			(13)	(32)	(32)	(32)					(29)
	(28)				(33)							
Experience	(34)				(41)	(41)	(41)					(13)
					(28)			(25)				

NOTE: entries refer to the study in which the finding was reported. Where analysis summed across a period covering more than one debate, the result is shown in the "Overall" column.

equally, and tests of statistical significance were not reported in every case. But a crude tally shows that by far the majority of the traits exhibit no change. Ford's gains were apparently limited to the first debate and to attributes that might be characterized as "presidential presence." Carter registered a few improvements in more personal traits. But the overall picture is definitely one of stability, not change. Perhaps most important, neither candidate seems to have *lost* ground on any specific attribute, although there were some fluctuations in overall evaluations (see above).

Issue Proximity. The same general imperviousness to change holds for the distances voters subjectively perceived between their own and the candidates' positions on issues. The first debate improved Ford's margin in being seen as better at handling foreign affairs, from 22 to 31 percent, and he made lesser gains on maintaining a strong defense (9 percent) and holding down inflation (6 percent); on four other issues the changes were trivial (33). Another national study found that the last two debates seemed to change nothing; the percentage agreeing more with Ford or Carter on five issues varied by no more than 3 percent from one debate to the next (32). Retrospective studies also showed very little impact of debate viewing. The strongest predictor of postdebate issue agreement was predebate issue agreement (10). And debate watching did not affect the impression that Carter was "fuzzy on the issues" even though the percentage who answered "don't know" on Carter's issue stands declined considerably from before to after the first debate (15).

It is not possible to make unequivocal assessments of impact in the flow of an ongoing presidential campaign. Nevertheless, the various methodologies used here converge on a common finding: there was little lasting impact of the debates on evaluations of the candidates, preferences between them, or perceptions of the candidates' attributes. Each debate yielded some temporary benefit to the candidate who was the consensus "winner," but this advantage seemed to dissipate fairly quickly. Thus the effects of the debates in the major potential areas of affective impact are described rather well by the "limited effects model."

Reinforcement

Affective Bonding. Many voters felt ill-informed before the debates; the first debate arrived when their preferences and impressions were not yet especially resistant to change. Yet it seems to have created little net change. So we might look for evidence that the first debate strengthened predispositions and the relationships between them. (Later debates may have come too late to do much more than provide additional support for that structure.)

The immediate effect of the first debate was indeed a strongly reinforcing one, in terms of both overall candidate evaluations and judgments of specific traits. For example, the first debate's immediate effect was to move each set of partisans toward their own candidates on each of nine general traits (27). The polarization of both candidates' images across Ford and Carter supporters (that is, the gap between the two partisan camps in their evaluations of the candidates) was largest right after the first debate (19, 41). Attitude changes following the later debates were much smaller and not particularly in the direction of further polarization (2, 10).

More generally, the information flowing from the debates appears to have promoted higher levels of consistency among voters' party identifications, candidate evaluations, issue positions, and vote intentions (8, 15, 31). In particular, both candidate evaluations and issue proximity became more closely related to vote intentions thereafter. Issue proximity was most correlated with change in vote intentions among those highly exposed to the debates and was in fact a stronger predictor than party identification among these voters. Viewing the electorate as a whole, these several affective strands seem to have been "bonded" together by the information flowing from the debates. The first debate appears to have accounted for most of this "bonding" between predispositional variables and the issues and images of the campaign; regression analyses yielded only slightly higher R^2 values after the final debate than they had after the first (10).

Cognitive Structure. Such increased affective consistency as "bonding" might be expected to be accompanied by parallel cognitive changes concerning the candidates. Were voters more informed about the candidates, in terms of having more detailed information about them, more differentiated impressions of them, or more coherently structured impressions? One national study showed a considerable increase in the *number* of open-ended responses about each candidate in interviews done between the first and second debates; there was then a more modest increase between the next two debates (31). It appears that the voters acquired some added information about the candidates from the first debate. Regarding Carter, these particularly concerned competence and trust; they had no special focus for Ford (31). There is evidence that this rise in candidate information was most marked among the least-informed voters, which suggests that these voters were oriented to the debates mainly in terms of the global question of post-Watergate honesty, and were especially unsure of the less-known Carter. A study of the vice-presidential debates (26) is important because of the comparative lack of prior knowledge about the candidates. Predebate factor analysis of trait ratings revealed two factors in impressions of both Mondale and Dole. In the case of Mondale the correlation between these two factors diminished after the debate (from .31 to .21), and the two dimensions became somewhat more clearly separated conceptually (focusing on integrity and competence, rather than being slightly different versions of overall evaluation). This increased differentiation of Mondale's image was especially marked for viewers of the debate. The proportion of variance accounted for by a single general evaluative factor dropped from 46 to 30 percent for viewers but did not change for nonviewers; the correlation between the two factors (oblique rotation) dropped from .32 to .14 for viewers, and it too was unchanged for nonviewers. Viewing the debate appeared to have an opposite (if any) effect on impressions of Dole, increasing the power of a general evaluative factor. But the point is that viewing the debate did affect the organization of these impressions.

Debate Discussion. The first debate stimulated a good bit of talk, even among people who rarely talk about politics. In one sample two-thirds of those who generally talk about politics less than once a week discussed that debate (7); the two later debates stimulated significantly less interpersonal discussion (41). Post-debate interpersonal contacts clearly tended to reinforce the respondent's predebate preferences. First of all, predebate preferences were quite strongly related to the preference of the discussion partner ($r = .45$, as opposed to $r = .05$ for the preference of the newspaper read) (2). Such post-debate discussions enhanced the image of one's own candidate and diminished that of his opponent, and it affected the vote beyond the effects of predebate preference and judgments of the "winner," suggesting it had an independent reinforcing effect (16).

Some Instances of Affective Impact

However, it is too simple to write off the debates' affective impact in such stark terms. Around the edges of this overall reinforcement and crystallization there is evidence of certain modest systematic attitude changes in specific areas. These effects are important to note, even though they may not have been so massive as to have proven decisive in determining the election's winner.

The "Winner" Verdict

We noted earlier that the verdict of a "winner" was the main attitudinal residue of the debates and that this was particularly true for the first debate. This verdict seems to have played some role in promoting image changes at least immediately after the debate. The net candidate evaluations swung to the winner much more right after each debate than would be expected from the relatively narrow immediate "victories" each had won (31). And in one panel study the "winner" perception varied concomitantly with image changes following the first debate (41). Another study showed that Ford's image was affected more by "winner" verdicts after the first debate than by the later ones; Carter's image was affected about equally each time (10). The "winner" judgment also seems to have affected vote intention. It was highly correlated with vote intention ($r = .58$) in one study, which is consistent with the finding that people tended to perceive that their man had won (29). When included in a general regression equation, "winner" perceptions also made an independent contribution (4.5 percent of the variance) to the vote decision, although the lion's share of the variance (56 percent) was due to predebate vote preference (29). In another study (41) those who saw no clear winners in the debates judged them as less useful (though in this case there was no relationship between debate verdict and vote change). These effects of the "winner" verdict on image change contrast with the minimal effects we have noted of debate viewing or of exposure to post-debate analyses; neither by itself had a significant effect. Apparently the debates and subsequent analyses affected the vote only insofar as they created perceptions of "the winner."

First Debate Improved Ford's Image

We have already reviewed some evidence that Ford's image and vote situation, in particular, were helped somewhat by the first debate. The first debate primarily improved Ford's image as a public speaker, though, affecting it in a markedly debate-specific manner rather than generalizing broadly throughout a wide roster of character traits. Relative to Carter, he was seen as a better speaker, stronger, and more competent in foreign affairs than before the debate.

It appears, however, that most of Ford's advantage derived from the post-debate media analysis verdict that he was "the winner," rather than from any dramatic superiority he had manifested during the debate itself. Consistent with the data presented earlier on "who won," Ford's image was helped by the media analysis of the first debate. Attending to post-debate broadcasts produced a significant improvement in Ford's image among Ford partisans (7), and in another study (27) post-debate reports worked for Ford and against Carter on almost every one of seventeen trait items. An experiment showed a long series of positive trait changes for Carter at the end of the debate and no changes in Ford's image; a week later, though, the Carter gains had disappeared, while a comparably broad set of positive image changes had occurred for Ford (28). In another study (less precise because it spans at least the first two debates), exposure to post-debate analyses increased the perception of Carter as "fuzzy on the issues" (29), and exposure to newspaper analysis moved voters toward Ford (10).

The advantage to the "winner" of each debate was generally not long-lasting. Ford's first-debate advantage may have not been entirely transient, however. Carter's lead in the vote became narrower, and thereafter seems to have stabilized. We can at least speculate that the first debate crystallized the previously wavering "natural" latent support for Ford by reinforcing predispositions that had been temporarily questioned due to Watergate, the Nixon pardon, and the Reagan primary challenge.

"East Europe"

Ford's East European gaffe had an important negative impact on his foreign-policy image after the second debate (31). The salience of foreign policy was so low, though, that the net advantage to Carter of that second debate was an average of only .045 favorable comments per voter. In a post-election survey of urban ethnic voters, awareness of and reaction to the comment were not related to the vote although "importance" of it was, especially for Democrats who had defected to Nixon (24). Available data do not allow a precise assessment of its effects, especially of its use as a rationalization for attitude changes that had other determinants.

Mondale

There was also significant attitude change as a consequence of the vice-presidential debate, where Mondale scored a personal triumph. His popularity, competence, and trait evaluation all improved following the debate, and more so among viewers than nonviewers. Dole's image underwent no such change (26). This indirectly underscores the time-honored principle that campaign events are more likely to affect images of those vying for lesser offices than those of presidential candidates.

Weak Initial Attitudes

It is an obvious point, but important to document, that weak initial attitudes changed most. This is clearest in immediate post-debate image changes. After the first debate there was much greater change among those with no (or wavering) predebate vote choices (33). In a rather careful panel study of the first debate the principal predictors of post-debate change were lack of initial image differentiation and low partisanship (20). The same held for the vice-presidential debate, which created image change toward Mondale among viewers with weak initial preferences but not among nonviewers or those with strong initial preferences (26). Yet it is not certain that the debates had major *long-term* persuasive impact even on the weakly committed or undecided; debate viewing did not correlate with the vote even in these groups, in a retrospective analysis (10).

Voters with no strong initial partisan preference, yet heavily exposed to the debates, may have been more common in 1976 than studies of earlier elections would have led us to expect. According to the University of Michigan's Center for Political Studies, almost half the voters decided after the conventions, whereas usually only about a third do. This can be partly attributed to the historical decline of party identification (12) and partly to unfamiliarity with both Ford and Carter. In the Wisconsin sample, voters who made up their minds during the debates period outnumbered both the precommitted partisan voters and the "late deciders" who still did not have a firm voting decision just before the election. Importantly, in three samples voters who decided during the debates phase were less partisan, paid closer attention to the debates, and were rather knowledgeable in comparison with the earlier and later groups of deciders.[17] And a substantial minority of voters made significant use of the issue information provided by the debates in coming to their voting decisions (12). This conclusion is quite different from that reached in 1960; only future elections can tell us whether it was peculiar to 1976 or a manifestation of the changing character of the electorate.

Latent Functions for the Political System

Like the research community at large, we have been concerned here mainly with the debates as a source of possible information and vote guidance to the individual voter. But quite apart from that individual level of analysis, we can assess certain contributions of the debates to the American political system as a whole.[18] At least three kinds of evidence bearing on system-level factors can be found in the 1976 studies: the political socialization of pre-adults, the legitimization of institutions, and the international credibility of an incoming (and practically unknown) president of the most powerful nation in the world.

Political Socialization

A critical ingredient in the maintenance of the system is the successful recruitment of new participants to the political process by means of political socialization. And it appears that the debates did help to attract children's attention and interest to politics. The most direct evidence on political socialization comes from a panel study of sixth-, ninth-, and twelfth-grade students in a small midwestern town (21). Viewing of the debates was the strongest predictor of these youngsters' interest in politics at the end of the campaign, other than the predebate level of interest in politics. Discussion of the debates was another important contributor to increases in interest, at least for the older age groups. The findings were weaker for two other criterion measures of socialization, perceived political efficacy and strength of partisanship; only among the younger students was debate viewing or discussion a significant predictor of them. Debates viewing was a stronger predictor of the socialization variables than were measures of normal public affairs use of television and newspapers, in seven of nine comparisons.

Legitimization

Another important area of system attitudes is perceived legitimacy, both of the institutions of national government and of the particular authorities in power. This was the specific focus of one panel analysis (16). The debates did seem to contribute to a modestly improved evaluation of the institutions of national government. There were significant improvements from before the debates to after the election in the "confidence" ratings given to three of four governmental institutions: the presidency, the Congress, and the federal government (but not the Supreme Court). When these four measures were summed, the overall gains were significantly correlated with debates viewing (beta = .14 when predebate ratings were controlled in regression analysis), and with attention to post-debate press analysis.

Legitimacy can also inhere in evaluations at the "authorities" level of government; presumably it increases with more positive evaluations of *both* presidential candidates. Katz and Feldman concluded that the 1960 debates did increase citizen support for the system by improving the public's evaluations of both Nixon and Kennedy.[19] And the 1976 debates appear to have done something of the same kind. The net effect of the small individual changes in candidate evaluation cited earlier was a general shift toward more favorable impressions of both Carter and Ford, especially after the first debate. One consequence of this is that both generally were rated favorably on measures of specific attributes, such as being intelligent, honest, sincere, competent, trustworthy, etc. Even after the first debate both candidates were evaluated favorably, on balance (32, 34); the same is true for the vice-presidential candidates (26). But these gains occurred mainly among each candidate's supporters (16). As for the candidate the person did not vote for, his evaluation did not change on the average, across the campaign period. This net outcome masks an interaction of some note: among independent voters the debates did enhance evaluations of the other candidate, but this was canceled by negative effects among strong partisans (16). So overall there is some support for the hypothesis that the debates might have the latent systemic effect of increasing citizen support for the new government. But neither with respect to the broad institutions of the government nor with specific support for the new administration is the evidence very complete or compelling.

International Credibility

The third latent systemic function relates to the role of the U.S. vis-à-vis other national systems in international politics, and specifically to the perceptions held of the American president as a worthy world leader. When, as in 1976, there is a transfer of power from one leadership team to another, these attributes of intersystemic stability are thought to be of particular concern. The American political system is generally regarded as possessing a very high capacity for maintaining its essential continuity during periods of political change. The question for us here is whether any contribution to that general pattern can be traced to the Ford–Carter debates. The producer of the debates reports that they were seen in more than 100 countries, and in at least one the ruler was so impressed that he ordered that nation's three political parties to hold a debate.[20] While this may not exactly catch the spirit of democracy American-style, the debates provided a very palpable image of U.S. electoral processes and leaders in action, one that might significantly influence world opinion. Unfortunately we have only the thinnest of evidence on this point, from a single survey conducted after the debates (but before the election) in the Netherlands. In this sample 31 percent had watched at least one of the debates. When asked who they would have voted for in the American election, those who had watched the debates were much more likely to have a preference (74 percent, against 49 percent among nonviewers) and were less likely to prefer the more familiar incumbent president (14). Ford had a 44–30 edge among the viewers, but a whopping 36–13 advantage with the nonviewers. Even among conservatives Carter got much more support from the viewers; Ford had less support among liberals who had watched the debates than those who had not. Lacking a pre-debate baseline, we cannot be confident that these differences represent changes resulting from the debates. But they are at least consistent with the proposition that exposure to debates can engender confidence in new potential national leaders and an understanding of the general thrust of American political deci-sions.

Voters' Evaluations of the Debates

As we noted earlier, the voters held rather high expectations for the Ford–Carter debates. Several studies found that their overall evaluations after the debates were extremely favorable. In various samples, 78 percent thought after the first debate that they were a "good idea" (31); 93 percent thought the first debate had been "worth seeing" (27); and more than 75 percent of those who had watched the vice-presidential debate were "glad" they had (26). Another survey found a strong correlation ($r = .43$) between the number of debates watched and the perception that they had been "informative" (17). The first debate was rated positively in all four format items asked about in one study: give-and-take, fairness of moderator, fairness of questions, and difficulty of questions (27). At the most general level, then, the debates were clearly ap-proved.

The debates did disappoint voters' more specific expectations though. "Learn-ing about issues" had been the debates' most important anticipated use. As we have seen, some learning did occur. But the voters felt quite a bit of frustration in this area. Only 14 percent in a Roper poll considered the first two "very informative" (36). A panel study found those debates falling shorter of expec-tations for information than on all but one of eleven other uses/gratifications tested; television news was rated as considerably more helpful than debates for learning about candidates' issue stands (29). Only 21 percent of another sample said they had learned something new of importance about issue stands from the first debate (35). The same kind of disappointment was registered with regard to learning about the candidates as people. They fell well short of expectations for helping to "judge the personal qualities of the candidates"; 60 percent said it was at best "somewhat difficult" to get a true picture of the candidates; and among younger voters the debates were rated less helpful for this purpose than was television news, newspapers, or magazines (29). In another survey only 16 percent rated them "very revealing," while 44 percent said they had been "not revealing" or said "don't know" (36).

Additionally, many voters apparently expected the debates to simplify and clarify their vote decisions. The opportunity for direct comparison ought, it seemed, to indicate a clear-cut choice. In this they were also somewhat let down. One study showed the first debate rated lower on "whether to vote" and "how to vote" than any of the other ten dimensions asked about (27). The undecided voters largely remained so: 23 percent more rated the debate "poor" than "good" on "how to vote." More than in any other way, the debates fell short of

THE GREAT DEBATES

prior expectation in helping the voter to make up his or her mind how to vote (29). In late October 58 percent of a national sample said the debates were not at all or not very important, or they were unsure or hadn't watched (37). "Utility" of the debates declined after the first debate (7), and later most people in one sample even felt separate interviews would have been preferable to debates (29). On the other hand, 41 percent said the debates made their vote decision easier, 13 percent harder (1).

Finally, the debates were generally seen as more boring than expected. They were rated very positively on "appeal" before they began, but lost a full point on a seven-point scale and ended up just above a neutral rating after the first debate (7). Roper (36) found only 17 percent rating them as "very interesting," as against 41 percent "somewhat interesting" and 35 percent "rather dull." Paradoxically, the most satisfied debate watchers were those who watched to enjoy the excitement of the race or to use what they learned in political discussions (as indicated by high correlations between gratifications sought and helpfulness perceived). These were, it should be noted, the least common reasons for watching (29). Similarly, people who changed differed most from nonchangers in "enjoying the excitement of the debates," and less in watching the debates to learn about personal qualities or issue stands (38). Perhaps many voters, normally not very interested in politics, had inordinately high expectations about the entertainment value of the debates, then were disappointed, and tuned out. Election buffs may have found them much more to their satisfaction.

It appears that the post-debate media analyses made voters more negative about the debates and the candidates. The strongest evidence on this point comes from the comparison of college students immediately after viewing the first debate and those who were interviewed following the press interpretations (27). There were large drops from the first to the second set of interviews in saying the debate was "worth seeing" (-16 percent), helpful in deciding how to vote (-34 percent), and rating of the format (-13 percent in the net "good" minus "poor"). We have no systematic content analysis of the media interpretations that would explain this delayed disillusionment with the debates, but a common ploy was to deride them as "not-so-great debates" and to point out such flaws as the 26-minute gap. Press publicity had probably contributed to higher than reasonable expectations in advance; the audience was quite positive about most aspects of the first debate at the time they saw it; but later criticisms eroded this high evaluation and were probably incorporated into the responses to later interviews in which so much disappointment was registered.

Simplification

The debates were highly complex as communication stimuli. The overt verbal content was laden with statistics and technicalities far from the direct experience of the ordinary voter. The candidates scarcely touched on the simpleminded slogans and symbolic issues that had been so prominent in the politics of the previous decade—crime, racism, rioting, bra-burners, "The System," abortion, hippies, "The War," drugs, and so forth. Nevertheless, the voters coded this welter of information in very simple terms, along one or two general evaluative dimensions (26). Certain judgmental labels clung to the candidates even in the face of contravening evidence: Ford's detractors had him tagged as "unintelligent" despite his obvious fund of knowledge, and Carter remained "fuzzy on the issues" even after his positions became as well understood as Ford's, after the first debate (12). Voters' recall of debate content (retrospective after the election) showed three main topics: debate performance, general candidate evaluations (competence and personality), and Ford's East Europe fluff (32). Most of those who switched to Carter couldn't remember anything either man said in the just-concluded second debate—not even the East Europe comment—according to a small survey in New Haven (1). So voters tended to simplify the cognitive content down to bare bones, and presumably interpreted it evaluatively in ways that maximized consistency with prior attitudes.

Sensitive social scientists were able to describe the debaters' extraverbal communicative acts in highly discriminating terms: fluency, body language, eye contact, use of statistics, metaphors and imagery used by the candidates (18, 22, 30). But these subtleties seemed largely lost on the viewers, since they reacted in about the same way to the debates as did people with no visual exposure. For example, whether the debates were watched on TV or listened to on the radio made no difference in judgments of the winner or in impact on candidate image, according to one study (35). Most studies found relatively little difference between viewers and nonviewers; that is, between those who got information firsthand and those who got it secondhand.

Similarly, although detailed coding by social scientists showed considerable detailing of issue positions (30, 31), it was mainly global evaluations that remained with voters in the end. Despite their many fascinating specifics, the debates testify to people's ability to assimilate details in simplified evaluative processes that are not likely to disturb their initial judgments much.

Summary

To do justice to the many studies of them, we have intermingled in our review evidence on both the effects (on voters) and the uses (by voters) of the 1976 debates. Some researchers chose to examine effects and in general found them limited although not quite so limited as in prior political communication studies. Others, taking more of a consumer's-eye-view, concentrated on the uses people hoped to make of the debates and the extent to which these expectations were realized. The debates proved less helpful than anticipated, but there was evidence of some important learning of political information for at least that minority of voters who are called "issue-oriented." Many of the studies mixed these two orientations, of course. One writer's effect is another's use, and often both perspectives are lumped under the elastic catch-all label of "functions." The limitedness of effects and the usefulness of the debate content for voters who felt a need for it are major findings worth reviewing here.

Limited Effects

Much prior research (usually summarized as the "limited-effects model") suggests that media events have relatively little impact late in a presidential campaign. The post-Labor Day campaign context is ordinarily one with (1) strong affective predispositions (especially party identification and many already-established candidate preferences), (2) weak informational input (generally small audiences, poor attention, brief messages), and (3) processing dominated by strains toward affective consistency and rather unimpressive, simple-minded cognitive faculties.

Presidential debates, however, are extraordinary events. Most obviously, the 1976 debates (like those in 1960) differed most from ordinary political communications by (4) attracting almost all voters to at least some minimal direct exposure to the candidates, due both to full network coverage and to the intrinsic attractions of exciting direct confrontation. And in general they offered (5) approximately equal or offsetting appeals by highly qualified, experienced, attractive, well-prepared contestants. Approximately equivalent appeals, even when information-rich (or perhaps especially when information-rich), are generally thought to reinforce and strengthen whatever partisan preferences already exist.[21]

Hence, despite the expanded exposure, debates would be expected mainly to reinforce both the standing party allegiances and the candidate preferences built up over the many prior months of campaigning, primary elections, and conventions. The genuinely uncommitted voter might, of course, well be influenced to choose sides by a superior performance by one candidate. The unusually heavy flow of information in the first debate should, however, mold and solidify preferences enough so that later debates would mainly serve to reinforce post-first-debate intentions.

In 1976 the debates did indeed encounter substantial prior preference. Although only about 55 percent of the voters felt they had definite preferences before the debates (15, 31), most people were leaning toward a candidate. The debates did not in fact constitute any very powerful magnetic pull to one side or the other. In each case the viewers were quite evenly divided in assigning a "winner" and a "loser"—dividing mostly along partisan lines. The uncommitted were quite evenly divided in judging the winners. And most people viewed them only sporadically, watching some of the debates, later recalling rather little from them. Only about a quarter of the public could be described as truly "attentive." So despite the massive potential created by the debates, actual informational input was still weak.

As expected, then, vote intentions seemed not to be affected very much, nor were overall candidate evaluations, nor perceptions of the candidates' specific traits. Candidate evaluations changed in the "winner's" favor in each case, but apparently only briefly, soon regressing to predebate baselines. Rather, the debates (especially the first one) helped to "bond" together the voter's several affects: candidate evaluations, comparative perceptions of candidates' issue positions and one's own, and prior vote intentions. Party identification and prior candidate preferences turned out, as usual, to dominate all other variables in determining judgments of debate performance, candidate evaluations in general, and the final vote.

Around the edges of this dominant reinforcement-and-crystallization there also were some significant instances of attitude change. People with weak initial preferences tended to be most affected. The "winner" verdict tended to enhance the image of the winner, even if the effect only lasted a few days. Ford in particular seems to have been helped by the first debate, and Mondale may have won some points in the vice-presidential debate. Carter's weak initial performance and Ford's East Europe blunder did hurt, though apparently more because of the media aftermath than because of immediate voter reactions.

Nevertheless, Ford gained only a small amount of ground as a consequence of the first debate, and that may have simply represented the reassurance of wavering latent supporters (that is, another reinforcement effect). Similarly, in "winning" the remaining debates, the Carter/Mondale ticket simply held on to its previous slim margin. These "victories" may well have been due more to press interpretations that stressed they had "won" than to impressions they made on voters during the debates themselves. The lasting impact of the debates and press analyses was far less than their immediate influence on people's thinking, and few voters later cited the debates as a decisive factor in their decisions. Over time, specifics tended to be lost and people recalled the debates mainly in general evaluative terms; the best-remembered item, Ford's East Europe comment, was at most a minor factor. Conversions were rare; very few switched from one candidate to the other.

Issue Learning

On the other side of the coin, the debates proved helpful to undecided voters who were more interested in specific issues than in party affiliations and who paid close attention to the debates. These were presumably the kinds of people for whom the debates were staged, and there seem to have been more of them in 1976 than in previous elections (at least since campaign research began in the 1940s). The historical decline of partisanship and the concomitant rise of issue voting, coupled with the unusually high incidence of undecidedness, made the Ford–Carter choice a natural setting for debates. Most voters said they were watching to learn about issues, and the debates did turn out to be markedly issue-oriented—in terms of both the questions asked by reporters and the candidates' responses. The issues at stake were not, to be sure, novel. No new agenda of campaign issues emerged from the debates. Rather, the candidates used the debates to reiterate their established positions on major policy questions. There is convincing evidence that the debates served to convey these positions to voters who had been previously unfamiliar with them. This learning was particularly marked for the first debate and the domestic issues emphasized in it.

We cannot be certain that the debates were essential for this kind of learning; in the absence of debates, interested voters might well have found approximately the same issue-position information elsewhere. Debate watching was redundant to exposure to other sources of campaign information. Moreover, it was hard to detect traces of debate inputs after the election, either in recognition or recall tests of information. But during the campaign, and especially around the time of the first debate, there was a significant jump in familiarity with the candidates' positions that seems closely connected with the content of the debate.

Moreover, at least one study identified a group of voters who were heavily exposed to the debates and who made the vote decisions during the campaign. This group also displayed a high level of issue-voting.[22] There is supportive evidence that voters became progressively more certain of their choices, not less, as the debates occurred. This was not true of those who neglected to watch the debates (15). If the historical trend toward declining partisanship continues, such outcomes might become even more common. If increasing numbers of voters wait until the fall campaign to make up their minds, the potential utility of debates for the electorate will increase in the future.

Conclusions

What does all this research imply regarding the long-range policy question of the value of debates as an institution in American presidential elections? The debates can be evaluated as more or less beneficial from various points of view. Chief among them, of course, is the view of the candidates, since in the absence of compelling legislation the staging of future debates will be a matter of negotiation between the competing campaign organizations.

A superficial analysis would lead to the conclusion that Ford benefited most in 1976. He gained ground as a consequence of the first debate, and that was the only one that had much net impact. But this *net* effect was small, while the *total* effect may have been rather large. That is, a goodly number of vote decisions seem to have been affected by the debates, but overall they tended to break close to 50–50. Carter, having been ahead before the debates, could well have won the election simply by not losing the debates by very much. And of course Carter did win the election, which is the singular goal of any candidate, and the end toward which the debates constituted part of the means.

In a "normal vote" election, people vote approximately in accord with their enduring political values rather than on the basis of an unusually appealing candidate or a single salient current event.[23] Debates assure a heavy flow of information and clear perceptions of the candidates and their positions. We doubt that it is a coincidence that the two campaigns with televised debates, those of 1960 and 1976, came closer to being "normal vote" elections than any others in recent history. The information flow stimulated by debates tends to be translated by voters into evaluations that coincide with prior political dispositions. They perceive their party's candidate as having "won," and they discuss the outcome with like-minded people. Although those who label their predispositions "Democrat" are a far more diffuse group than are the Republicans, there are considerably more Democrats.[24] So the net effect of cumulative mass reinforcement stimulated by heavy information flow is probably to benefit the Democratic candidate.

If debates operate to encourage a "normal vote" outcome, aligned with major predispositional factors, they should also force fleeting and extraneous factors into a correspondingly minor role. In the 1976 studies, for example, home-state loyalties did not turn out to be especially important (5), nor did Ford's East Europe gaffe end up hurting him appreciably (24). In 1960 the debates may have reduced the religious issue, which had previously implied a virtual blackball of Roman Catholic candidates, to little more than another significant group loyalty.[25] Such potentially volatile items as the abortion controversy, Carter's *Playboy* interview, and Ford's pardoning of Nixon were not totally inconsequential in 1976. But they do not seem to have held the public prominence of what now seem like minor, isolated events from debate-less campaigns: Goldwater's defoliation comments in 1964; Romney's "brainwashing," Muskie's tears, and Humphrey's hecklers in 1968; and McGovern's mishandling of Senator Eagleton's history in 1972. Would debates have eroded the already narrow and centrifugal appeal of George Wallace in 1968? Did they, indeed, undercut the minority campaigns of Maddox and McCarthy in 1976? While we can only speculate, the most informed speculation would be that debates in effect provide the major party candidates with insurance against some fluke event upsetting their campaign plans.

In evaluating debates as a generic institution in American politics, we should point out some of the things they do not do—but which detractors of debates have suggested they might. They do not provide either candidate with an opportunity to destroy his opponent with a lucky "knockout punch" on television. Instead, voter interpretations tend to break almost evenly, being heavily colored by prior political allegiances. The debates do not give an edge to the candidate with the more personable on-camera "image." Instead they bring issues to the fore and call up party loyalties; image-voting is strongest among those who do not watch debates (15). They do not narrow the base of political discourse by focusing on a few "safe" issues. There was no evidence of agenda control via the 1976 debates. They do not function to reduce the importance of political parties. Rather, latent allegiances to the two major parties are reinforced by the debates. They do not trivialize politics in the manner of much television news, which seems to be replacing newspapers and magazines as the main news source for most Americans.[26] The debates themselves contained more issue content than any of the media covering them, including print media.

Political theorists, who see elections as a mechanism for orderly transition and for the legitimation of both the political system and the government that is elected, should be pleased with the contribution made by the debates. Viewing of the 1976 debates was associated with increased support for national governmental institutions in that brief fall period (16), and they helped build support at home and, less certainly, abroad for the incoming Carter. Like John Kennedy in 1960, a hitherto little-known Democrat was with the help of televised debates turned into a credible national leader in less than a year's time. And Ford recovered some of the respectability the Republican party had lost as a consequence of Watergate. Rather than one candidate benefitting at the expense of the other, there came to be greater respect for both. Young people, a social category that had become notably estranged from standard politics in the previous decade, were attracted by the debates so that their interest grew and there was some evidence of strengthened senses of efficacy and partisanship. In general, while the research is scanty and the findings statistically modest, a variety of indicators converge on the conclusion that the political system at large was positively served by the debates.

At the individual level, the voters seem to have profited by the debates too, though perhaps in ways they were not fully aware of. Their more self-conscious, expressed expectations concerned "cool," cognitive, information-acquisition opportunities. Many said they anticipated making their voting decisions on the basis of issue information provided by the debates. These expectations were unrealistic and doomed to some level of frustration and disappointment. People did not pay as close attention as they might have thought they would; the content was often complicated without seeming controversial; the candidates did not seem appreciably different as persons or as exponents of particular policies. Extensive learning and cool, rational decision-making is not the usual outcome of watching television. The tendency of voters (and especially of the news media) to downgrade the debates afterward was perhaps an inevitable product of overly high expectations. The voters seem to have been unaware of the amount they had learned from the debates and of how this had strengthened their very tentative predebate voting intentions.

Less talked about were "hot," affective anticipations. Although it was not so socially desirable to say so, some voters gave evidence of seeking drama, excitement, argument, confrontation, clash, and conflict in the debates. This would certainly seem to be the more likely motivation for the heavy viewing by those voters who had already decided how they would vote before the debates began. This factor would account for the huge but not especially attentive audience. Those who watched the debates only sporadically were the most likely to vote on the basis of party allegiances (15). Watching for excitement and something to talk about were the goals for which people later expressed the least disappointment (29). Even while they were watching for these extra-political reasons, though, it is likely that the precommitted voters were strengthening their vote choices by adding information that they interpreted as supportive in a consistent package of attitudes. Again, few voters could have been aware of such a subtle effect of the debates on their thinking.

Of all the latent effects of the debates, perhaps the most unfortunate was the reaction they elicited from the news media. Critics of the press's intervention and influence in political processes can find ammunition aplenty in these studies. People's perceptions of "who won" each debate were not only heavily colored by media interpretations, but the very preoccupation with "who won" was a product of the way the press structured its interpretations of the debates. Judging the winner was often given as a reason for watching (29, 44); it was the context in which the press placed each debate in advance; and then it was the principal focus of post-debate coverage. Major news organizations ran instant polls after each debate to determine who had won—and little else (37). Small wonder that so much long-term recall concerned "debate performance" (32), since that was the single feature of the debates that the press served to impress upon people.

The horse-race paradigm is not peculiar to debates, of course. It is the conventional organizing structure that American journalism, increasingly constrained toward "objectivity," applies to all political contests. Reporters, bored with hearing the same speeches over and over again, emphasize instead the "contest" aspects of the campaign rather than repeat the same issue positions as the candidate states them in town after town.[27] Not only do the debates sound like more of the same, they take the play away from the press, which responds negatively to them. It is notable that viewers liked the debates and the candidates a lot better right after the first debate than they did the next day, following the media analyses (27). The press's reactions also seem to have confused people, making them less sure of their choices and convincing them that the candidates were ambiguous.

In defense of the news media, it should be noted that they went to extensive (and expensive) lengths to gather hard empirical data on public reactions to the debates; several of the studies we have relied on here were based on surveys by journalistic organizations (20, 33, 36). And perhaps the reporters may be forgiven for their preoccupation with the horse-race aspect of the debates; they, after all, had heard what the candidates had to say many times, even if most other people had not. At any rate, the impact of the press analyses appears to have been short-lived and did not make an appreciable difference in the final electoral result.

We do not expect all future U.S. presidential elections to feature debates. Those that do are likely to have several things in common: a tight race, with at least one candidate who is not well known; an electorate in which a significant minority is undecided at the beginning of the fall campaign; and a final vote based on broad policy issues rather than personalities and transient factors, leaving most citizens reasonably satisfied with their government and with the American method of transferring power.

NOTES

1. For general discussions of the role of mass media in political campaigns, see S. Kraus and D. Davis, *The effects of mass communication on political behavior* (University Park: Pennsylvania State University Press, 1976); S. Chaffee (ed.), *Political communication: issues and strategies for research* (Beverly Hills: Sage Publications, 1975); D. O. Sears and R. Whitney, "Political persuasion" in I. Pool, W. Schramm, F. Frey, N. Maccoby & E. Parker (eds.) *Handbook of communication* (Chicago: Rand McNally, 1973).

2. N. Nie, S. Verba & J. Petrocik, *The changing American voter* (Cambridge: Harvard University Press, 1976).

3. J. Klapper, *The effects of mass communications* (Glencoe: Free Press, 1960).

4. E. Katz, M. Gurevitch & H. Haas, "On the use of mass media for important things," *American Sociological Review* 38: 161–84 (1973); J. Blumler & E. Katz (eds.), *The uses of mass communications* (Beverly Hills: Sage Publications, 1974), especially J. McLeod & L. Becker, "Testing the validity of gratification measures through political effects analysis," pp. 137–66.

5. L. Becker, M. McCombs & J. McLeod, "The development of political cognitions," in Chaffee, *Political Communication* (n. 1).

6. R. Cheney, "The 1976 presidential debates: a Republican perspective," in A. Ranney (ed.), *The past and future of presidential debates* (Washington, D.C.: American Enterprise Institute for Policy Research, 1979).

7. S. Kraus (ed.), *The great debates* (Bloomington: Indiana University Press, 1962).

8. S. Lesher with P. Caddell & G. Rafshoon, "Did the debates help Jimmy Carter?", in Ranney (n. 6).

9. See for example J. Dennis & C. Webster, "Children's images of the president and of government in 1962 and 1974," *American Politics Quarterly*, 3: 386–405 (1975).

10. See Cheney (n. 6) and Lesher et al. (n. 8).

11. In Kraus, (n. 7).

12. Persuasive appeals delivered by experienced, carefully selected communicators should be intrinsically quite impressive. Moreover, candidates for high office normally present themselves in a manner that draws predominantly positive evaluations, as reflected in "the positivity bias" toward public figures. See D. O. Sears, "Positivity biases in evaluations of public figures," presented to American Psychological Assn.,

Washington, D.C., 1976. Even so, any one-shot appeal is unlikely by itself to make a major enduring impression.

13. D. O. Sears, J. L. Freedman, and E. F. O'Connor, Jr. The effects of anticipated debate and commitment on the polarization of audience opinion, *Public Opinion Quarterly*, 28: 615–27 (1964).

14. For example see J. H. Kessel, Comment, *American Political Science Review*, 66: 459–65 (1972); A. H. Miller, W. E. Miller, A. S. Raine, & T. A. Brown, A majority party in disarray: Policy polarization in the 1972 election, *The American Political Science Review*, 70: 753–78 (1976).

15. See Becker, McCombs & McLeod (n. 5) for a summary of agenda-setting studies.

16. McCombs (6) co-authored the first agenda-setting study; McLeod (29) and Becker (6) co-authored the first test using a different methodology. M. McCombs and D. Shaw, "The agenda-setting function of the media," *Public Opinion Quarterly* 36: 176–87 (1972). J. McLeod, L. Becker & J. Byrnes, "Another look at the agenda-setting function of the press," *Communication Research* 1: 131–66 (1974).

17. S. H. Chaffee, and S. Y. Choe, "Time of decision and media use during the Ford–Carter campaign," *Public Opinion Quarterly*, in press.

18. D. Easton, *A systems analysis of political life* (New York: Wiley, 1965).

19. Katz and Feldman, (n. 11).

20. J. Karayn, "Presidential debates: a plan for the future," presented to American Enterprise Institute symposium on the debates, Washington, D.C., October 1977. See also chapter 12.

21. P. Converse, "Information flow and the stability of partisan attitudes," *Public Opinion Quarterly*, 26: 578–99 (1962). D. O. Sears, J. Freedman & E. O'Conner, "The effects of anticipated debate and commitment on the polarization of audience opinion," *Public Opinion Quarterly* 28: 615–27 (1964).

22. Chaffee, S. H. & Dennis, J., "Presidential debates: an empirical assessment." Paper prepared for the American Enterprise Institute for Public Policy Research, October, 1977. S. Chaffee and S. Y. Choe. "Time of decision," (n. 17).

23. P. Converse, "The concept of a normal vote," in A. Campbell, P. Converse, W. Miller & D. Stokes, *Elections and the political order* (New York: Wiley, 1966), pp. 7–39.

24. A. Miller, W. Miller, A. Raine & T. Brown, "A majority party in disarray: policy polarization in the 1972 election," *American Political Science Review*, 70: 753–78 (1976).

25. P. Converse, A. Campbell, W. Miller & D. Stokes, "Stability and change in 1960: a reinstating election," *American Political Science Review*, 55: 269–80 (1961).

26. T. E. Patterson, & R. D. McClure, *The unseeing eye* (New York: G. P. Putnam's Sons, 1976).

27. T. Crouse, *The boys on the bus.* (New York: Random House, 1973).

REFERENCES

1. Abelson, R. P. Poll analysis. Yale University, 1977.

*2. Atkin, C. K., J. Hocking, and S. McDermott. Home-state voter response and secondary media coverage (in this volume).

* Abridged versions of these papers appear in this volume. References in this chapter are to the original versions and therefore occasionally refer to data not appearing in this volume.

3. Baker, K., and O. Walter. The 1976 presidential debate and political behavior in Wyoming. Delivered to the Western Social Science Assn., Denver, April 1977.

4. Bechtolt, W. E., J. Hilyard, and C. R. Bybee. Agenda control in the 1976 debates: a content analysis. *Journalism Quarterly*, 54: 674–81 (1977).

5. Becker, L. B., R. E. Cobbey, and I. A. Sobowale. Onondaga County and the 1976 presidential elections: a report on voter reactions to the debates.

*6. Becker, L. B., D. Weaver, D. Graber, and M. McCombs. Influence on public agendas (in this volume).

*7. Becker, S. L., R. Pepper, L. A. Wenner, and J. K. Kim. Information flow and the shaping of meanings (in this volume).

8. Bishop, G. F., R. E. Oldendick, and A. J. Tuchfarber. The presidential debates as a device for increasing the "rationality" of electoral behavior: effects and implications. Presented to the Annenberg conference on the debates, Philadelphia, May 1977. In G. Bishop, R. G. Meadow, M. Jackson-Beeck (eds.). *The presidential debates of 1976: perspectives and promise.* New York: Praeger, 1978.

9. Bowes, J. E., and H. Strentz. Candidate images: stereotyping and the 1976 debates. Presented to the International Communication Assn., Chicago, April 1978.

10. Cantrall, W. R. The impact of the 1976 presidential debates on a student population. Illinois State University, 1977.

11. Casey, G., and M. Fitzgerald. Candidate images and the 1976 presidential debates. Presented to the Midwest Assn. for Public Opinion Research, Chicago, October 1977.

12. Chaffee, S. H., and J. Dennis. Presidential debates: an empirical assessment. In A. Ranney (ed.). *The past and future of presidential debates.* Washington, D.C.: American Enterprise Institute, 1979.

*13. Davis, D. K. Influence on vote decisions (in this volume).

14. DeBock, H. The influence of the Ford–Carter debates on the Dutch television audience. Netherlands Broadcasting Foundation, October 1977.

*15. Dennis, J., S. H. Chaffee, and S. Y. Choe. Impact on partisan, image, and issue voting (in this volume).

16. Dennis, J., and S. Chaffee. Legitimation in the 1976 presidential election. Presented to American Political Science Assn., Washington, D.C., September 1977. *Communication Research*, 5: 371–94 (1978).

17. Gantz, W., and C. Petrie. The politics of non-exposure: a comparison of viewers and non-viewers of the 1976 presidential debates. State University of New York at Buffalo, 1977.

18. Goldhaber, G. M., J. K. Frye, D. T. Porter, and M. P. Yates. The image of the candidates: a communication analysis of the Ford/Carter debates I, II, and III. State University of New York at Buffalo, 1976.

19. Graber, D., and Y. Y. Kim. The 1976 presidential debates and patterns of political learning. Presented to Assn. for Education in Journalism, Madison, Wisconsin, August 1977.

20. Hagner, P. R., and J. Orman. A panel study of the impact of the first 1976 presidential debate: media-events, "rootless voters" and campaign learning. Presented to American Political Science Assn., Washington, D.C., September 1977.

*21. Hawkins, R. P., S. Pingree, K. A. Smith, and W. E. Bechtolt. Adolescents' responses to issues and images (in this volume).

22. Jackson-Beeck, M., and R. Meadow. Content analysis of presidential debates as communication events. Presented to Assn. for Education in Journalism, Madison, Wis., August 1977.

23. Jackson-Beeck, M., and R. Meadow. Issue evolution: parameters in presidential debate and public perceptions. Presented to Midwest Assn. for Public Opinion Research, Chicago, October 1977.

THE GREAT DEBATES

*24. Jeffres, L. W., and K. K. Hur. Impact of ethnic issues on ethnic voters (in this volume).

25. Joslyn, R. A. Voter belief and attitude change and the 1976 debates. Temple University, 1977.

26. Kinder, D. R., W. Denney, and R. Wagner. Media impact on candidate image: exploring the generality of the law of minimal consequences. Presented to American Assn. for Public Opinion Research, Buck Hills Falls, Pa., May 1977.

*27. Lang, G. E., and K. Lang. Immediate and mediated responses: reaction to the first debate (in this volume).

28. Lupfer, M. B. An experimental study of the first Carter–Ford debate. Memphis State University, 1977.

*29. McLeod, J. M., J. Durall, D. Ziemke, and C. Bybee. Reactions of young and older voters: expanding the context of effects (in this volume).

30. Meadow, R. G., and M. Jackson-Beeck. A comparative perspective on television debates: issue evolution in 1960 and 1976. In G. Bishop, R. G. Meadow, M. Jackson-Beeck (eds.) (8).

*31. Miller, A. H., and M. MacKuen. Informing the electorate: a national study (in this volume).

32. Mitofsky, W. J. 1976 presidential debate effects: a hit or a myth. Presented to American Political Science Assn., Washington, D.C., September 1977.

33. Morrison, A. J., F. Steeper, and S. Greendale. The first 1976 presidential debate: the voters win. Presented to American Assn. for Public Opinion Research, Buck Hills Falls, Pa., May 1977.

34. Neuman, W. R. The visual impact of presidential television: a study of the first Ford–Carter debate. Yale University, 1977.

*35. O'Keefe, G., and H. Mendelsohn. Media influences and their anticipation (in this volume).

36. PBS/Roper polls press releases. WNET/13, New York City, 1976.

*37. Robinson, J. The polls (in this volume).

38. Rogers, E. M., D. Dozier, and D. Barton. Changes in candidate images as a result of the debates. Stanford University, 1977.

39. Rotzoll, K., and S. Tinkham. A Ford/Carter panel study from a Sherifian perspective. University of Illinois, 1977.

40. Sears, D. O. The debates in the light of research: an overview of the effects. Presented to American Political Science Assn., Washington, D.C., September 1977.

*41. Simons, H. W., and K. Leibowitz. Shifts in candidate images (in this volume).

42. Steeper, F. T. Public response to Gerald Ford's statements on Eastern Europe in the second debate. In Bishop, Meadow, and Jackson-Beeck (eds.) (8).

43. Wald, K. D., and M. Lupfer. The presidential debate as a civics lesson. Memphis State University, 1977.

44. Zukin, C. Personal communication. Ohio State University, 1977.

14.

The Polls

JOHN P. ROBINSON

There were far more polls taken in connection with the 1976 debates than the 1960 debates. While this chapter deals mainly with the large national polls, several other state and local polls were conducted and many of them are reported in other chapters in this section.

For the most part, we will draw on national polls taken by large, well-known organizations—Gallup, Roper, Harris, Yankelovich, CBS–New York Times, the Associated Press, and, although not thought of often as a polling organization, the A. C. Nielsen Company. Data from these polls will be used to answer three basic questions. What percentage of the electorate saw each debate? Who did they think won each debate? How did the voting intentions of the public appear to be affected after each debate?

1. Who Watched the Debates?

Table 1 shows the estimates of the percentage of the population that watched the debates. The A. C. Nielsen organization estimated that almost 90 percent of the sets in their sample were tuned to at least one of the debates, and 42 percent of all households were tuned to all three debates. Their estimates of the average number of debates partially or wholly seen was 2.2 out of 3. Nielsen estimated that nearly 20 percent of teenagers and 10 percent of younger children watched the debates.

The Nielsen data (gathered by mechanical recorders attached to TV sets rather than based on surveys of individual respondents) on viewing for each debate match up remarkably well with the survey data from Roper and Harris; and, for the first debate, from the Associated Press and Gallup as well. All five sources show over two-thirds of the populace watching the first debate. While Nielsen and Roper show a 6-to-7 percent audience decline for the second debate and AP and Nielsen a further 7-to-10 percent decline for the third, the Gallup data show larger audiences viewing the second and third debates than the first debate. This may be because the Gallup sample was of registered voters only, and voters would have been more interested in the debates than persons not registered.

The Table 1 data refer, of course, only to people who viewed any portion of the debate. The Nielsen data of viewing per average minute are at least 20 percent lower than the Table 1 figures, indicating a considerable amount of tuning out (and tuning in) of the debates. The Nielsen data also show a de-

Table 1: Viewing of Debates (in percentage)

	Debate 1 Sept. 23, 1977 Philadelphia	Debate 2 Oct. 6, 1977 San Francisco	Debate 3 Oct. 22, 1977 Williamsburg	Any Debate
Nielsen households	72.5	65.3	59.7	88.6
Roper	72	65	NA*	
Harris	71	NA*	NA*	
Associated Press	71	71	64	
Gallup**	67	70	69	
AVERAGE	71	68	64	

*Data not available
**Registered voters only

cline in average minute viewing across the time of the debate that ranges from 57.6 percent viewing on an average minute between 9:30 and 10:00 P.M. to 55.9 percent between 10 and 10:30 P.M. and 52.7 percent between 10:30 and 11 P.M. in debate 1, for example. Some observers have suggested this decline indicates discontent with the debates. Nonetheless, a decline of roughly 5 percent (from 57.6 to 52.7) is much less than occurs for usual entertainment programs between 9:30 and 11 P.M. on a typical weekday (when a TV event such as the debates is not televised). By this standard the debates did relatively well in holding the television audience (the proportion of viewers who turned to non-debate channels is not provided by the Nielsen data).

The Roper surveys indicate an important decline in debate interest over time, in line with the decline in audience size noted in Table 1. While 53 percent of those interviewed planned to watch the first debate and 52 percent the second debate, only 41 percent planned to watch the third. Prior to the third debate, Roper found only 17 percent saying they were "very interesting" (compared to 35 percent "rather dull"), 16 percent "very revealing" (44 percent "not revealing"), and 14 percent "very informative" (41 percent, "uninformative"). At the same time interest in the election itself rose, from 43 percent who claimed to be "very interested" prior to debates 1 and 2, to 48 percent prior to debate 3.

Nielsen indicates a 50-percent viewing rate for the Dole–Mondale debate, and Roper records a 48-percent rate.

2. Who Did People Think Won the Debates?

Table 2 shows, on the whole, that voters interpreted the debates as pretty much a stand-off in terms of who won. Substantial numbers of viewers (from 16 percent to 41 percent) thought each of the debates was a draw or could not otherwise identify a clear winner.

Nonetheless, the pattern of who emerged victorious from each debate was quite uniform across the four survey sources, and these tend to match press interpretations of candidate performance in each debate. Thus, respondents in all four surveys in debate 1 saw Ford's performance as superior, but the average

Table 2: Debate Winner (in percentage)

		Debate 1 Sept. 23, 1977	Debate 2 Oct. 6, 1977	Debate 3 Oct. 22, 1977
Roper	Carter	31	40	40
	Ford	39	30	29
	Other	30	30	31
		100 (N < 500)	100 (N < 300)	100 (N < 800)
Harris	Carter	31	54	NA* 33)
(Yankelovich)	Ford	40	30	NA* 26 } **
	Other	29	16	NA* 41)
		100 (N = 1516)	100 (N = 1503)	NA* (100)
Gallup	Carter	25	50	32
	Ford	38	27	27
	Other	37	23	41
		100	100	100
AP	Carter	32	38	33
	Ford	34	35	36
	Other	34	27	31
		100	100	100 (N = 1027)
Summary				
Carter–Ford:	Roper	− 8	+10	+11
	Harris	− 9	+24	+ 7
	Gallup	−13	+23	+ 5
	AP	− 2	+ 3	− 3
	AVERAGE	− 8	+15	+ 5

*Data not available from Harris
**Data from Yankelovich survey

margin of superiority of 8 percent was less than that attributed to Carter in debate 2 (average 15 percent). Debate 3 went to Carter, but by a smaller margin than either debate 1 or 2, and the Associated Press poll actually showed Ford slightly ahead; it was noted by AP, however, that the result was well within sampling error and that the sample was "relatively older and more Republican than registered voters as a whole."

Overall, then, the public scored Carter doing twice as well in debates 2 and 3 (+15 and +5) as Ford (+8) did in debate 1, in terms of the slight advantage that the candidates had in the debates. The Table 2 results are reinforced by the results of an NBC poll of 1600 adults taken on October 28 in which 36 percent felt that Carter did better "overall" in the debates compared to 23 percent who felt that Ford did better and 41 percent who said it was a draw or who were unsure who had won (Carter had a 31–22 edge when the question was asked after the second debate). Nonetheless, Carter's overall edge was not clearly reflected in voting intentions.

3. What Was the Relation between Debate Performance and Aggregate Vote Intentions?

This question is addressed in Table 3, where the evidence is more equivocal than in Tables 1 and 2.

Most debate interpretation has centered on the tremendous gap Ford closed between Carter and himself after the first debate. Some of the data in Table 3 call this interpretation into question, particularly the Associated Press predebate poll taken closest to the day of the debate. On that date, the poll showed Carter with only a 4.3 percent edge over Ford—a lead that dwindled to 2.0 percent after the debates. Nonetheless, the most widely cited data by Gallup—showing a 15 percent Carter lead—were obtained in late August, and it is clear that Ford had made significant inroads into Carter's margin in the early part of September. The widest September margin for Carter noted on the polls in late September is 11 percent, and the actual predebate margin may have been less than that.

Nonetheless, it still appears from Table 3 that Ford gained more of the vote after debate 1 than Carter did after debates 2 and 3, even though his margin of victory in debate 1 (as reflected in Table 2) was not as high as Carter's in debate 2 and a little higher than Carter's edge in debate 3. As in 1960, then, the first debate appears to have been the crucial one in terms of affecting vote intentions.

Most of these poll results need further elaboration by party affiliation across time to locate the impact of the debates. The poll taken by CBS and the *New York Times* did provide such a breakout from its rather large sample (N > 2500). This survey showed remarkable similarity between September 4 and election day in terms of the voting intentions of Republican and Democratic party identifiers—the biggest difference is 4 percent. The figures are also similar across time for independents, but they do show a 9 percent increase for Ford (made up of 5 percent from undecideds and 4 percent from Carter supporters). The CBS-*Times* surveys were not conducted after each debate, but the substantial Ford gain in late October noted in Table 3 suggests that Ford made most of these gains among independents *after* the second debate.

Other Observations

After the second debate, Harris noted increasing uneasiness about Carter's lack of experience and his avoidance of issues, as well as increasing confidence in Ford's leadership, especially in the area of foreign affairs.

Gallup notes the return of Reagan voters to Ford after the first debate. While only 2-to-3 percent of all voters mentioned the debates as their reason for voting for the candidate, the debates (and associated reactions) were the most often cited reasons for switching to Ford or Carter during the campaign. Carter's foreign affairs image rose much more than Ford's after the debates. Personality stereotypes seem to prevail: Ford—experienced, decisive, consistent, dull, and business-oriented; Carter—inexperienced, indecisive, intelligent, religious, and supportive of the poor and the working class.

Table 3: Voting Intentions (in percentage)

		Before Debate 1	After Debate 1	After Debate 2	After Debate 3	Pre-Election Day
Roper	Carter	46	40	43	NA*	47
	Ford	29	36	33	NA*	43
	Other	25	24	25	NA*	10
		100	100	100		100
		(Sept. 4)	(Sept. 21)			
Harris	Carter	49	46	44 / 45	45	46
	Ford	38	39	40 / 42	44	45
	Other	13	15	16 / 13	11	9
		100	100	100 / 100	100	100
		(Late Aug.)			(N = 2981)	
Gallup	Carter	52	49	48	49	46
	Ford	37	43	42	44	47
	Other	11	9	10	7	7
		100	100	100	100	100
		(Aug. 20–30)				
AP	Carter	45	47 / 46	49	—	
	Ford	41	45 / 43	45	—	
	Other	14	8 / 11	6	—	
		100	100 / 100	100		
		(Sept. 22)				

THE GREAT DEBATES

CBS–NY Times					
Carter	47	NA*	48	NA*	46
Ford	36	NA*	37	NA*	40
Other	17	NA*	15	NA*	14
	100		100		100
	(Sept. 4)				

Summary

Carter–Ford:					
Roper	+14	+4	+10	NA*	+4
Harris	+11	+7	+4	+1	+1
Gallup	+15	+6	+6	+5	−1
AP	+4	+2	+4	—	NA*
CBS–NY Times	+11	NA*	+11	NA*	+6
AVERAGE	+11	+5	+7	+3	+3

*Data not available

Conclusions

Almost 90 percent of the electorate watched at least one of the debates, with the first one attracting the largest audience. Although most viewers described the debates as dull and uninformative, viewing rates remained high during the debates.

When the poll results on the winner of the debates were averaged, Ford emerged as the winner of the first debate, Carter as a much bigger winner of the second, and Carter as a slight winner of the third.

While Ford clearly cut into Carter's lead across the time of the debates, the link of this shift to debate performance is quite difficult to document. The most detailed study of voting shifts by party affiliation indicates almost no aggregate shift between early September and election day among Democrats and Republicans. While the notable shift to Ford occurred in late October, Carter managed to do better in the only debate held during that time period.

Although a Gallup poll after the election indicated that less than 2 percent of voters cited the debates as affecting their votes, a much larger percentage of vote-*changers* cited the debates as the most influential factor in their vote.

An NBC poll of October 28 found that only 16 percent of viewers described the debates as "very important" in helping voters make up their minds and 26 percent as "somewhat important," compared to 48 percent who considered them "not very" or "not at all important" (10 percent who were unsure or didn't watch). Nonetheless, 63 percent said they would like to see TV debates become a regular part of the campaign, compared to thirty percent who took a negative view and 7 percent who were unsure.

REFERENCES

Associated Press Releases. September 24, October 7, and October 23, 1976.

New York Times. Sunday, October 31, 1976, p. 1.

NTI Bulletin. Northbrook, Ill.: A. C. Nielsen Company, November 5, 1976.

The Gallup Opinion Index (Report 137). Princeton, N.J.: American Institute of Public Opinion, December 1976.

The Harris Survey. Chicago, Ill.: *Chicago Tribune.* Releases 76:80, 76:87, and 76:88.

WNET Press Releases. New York: WNET, Channel 13, September 17 and 23; October 1, 6, 20, and 22; November 1 and 5, 1976.

15.

Informing the Electorate:
A National Study

ARTHUR H. MILLER and MICHAEL MAcKUEN

Introduction

Normative political theory suggests that the democratic citizen is interested in politics and that he or she votes on the basis of well-informed evaluations of the issues and competing candidates (Berelson, 1954). Early electoral research challenged these theoretical assumptions by demonstrating that the average citizen was not particularly interested in or well-informed about politics, and that the vote was strongly influenced by long-standing party loyalties (Campbell et al., 1960). Early research on the flow of information from the mass media to the voters also demonstrated a lack of direct effects of communications on support for a particular candidate (Lazarsfeld, Berelson, and Gaudet, 1948). Apparently, strong partisan predispositions, a tendency toward selective perception, and the relatively high personal costs of information-seeking in a pre-TV period greatly limited the effectiveness of mass communications in altering electoral choices. The conclusion inferred from these studies was that mass communication does not change political attitudes. If they have any effect at all, media outputs primarily reinforce political predispositions (Klapper, 1960).

A more recent review questions the limited-effects model, and studies searching for media effects have criticized the earlier work for utilizing inadequate research designs that too narrowly focused on direct effects, attitude change, and the vote (Kraus and Davis, 1976; O'Keefe, 1975). Attention has shifted from focusing entirely on attitudes or "summary evaluations of objects" to investigations of how the media may effect "cognitions" or stored information about political objects and the salience of these objects for the public (Robinson, 1972; Clarke and Kline, 1974; Palmgreen, Kline, and Clarke, 1974; and Palmgreen, 1975). Although the media may have limited effects on directly shifting political evaluations or on the vote decision, according to these studies, they do increase information-holding and the salience of various issues and political objects.

Because the presidential debates were a widely viewed media event, the 1976 presidential election provides a unique opportunity for studying the possible effects of the media on the level and type of information about the candidates

269

available to voters. Voting behavior research has recently demonstrated that candidate attributes and voter evaluations of the candidates have become increasingly important factors determining the outcome of presidential elections, while the impact of partisan predispositions has weakened (Kirkpatrick, Lyons, and Fitzgerald, 1975). The growing literature on candidate images has begun to explore the dimensions of public perceptions of candidates (Nimmo and Savage, 1976; Miller and Miller, 1976). Yet, this literature has given limited consideration to measuring the external inputs affecting the evaluations, thus emphasizing a theory that stresses perceptual predispositions. When the impact that information sources, such as the media, could possibly have on candidate evaluations are considered, the research often relies on very limited studies or experiments lacking generalizability and evidence of enduring effects.

Given the limitations in previous research, this study will investigate public cognitions and evaluations of the 1976 presidential candidates, how these assessments were influenced by the media output originating with the three presidential debates, and how media outputs interact with attitudinal predispositions to affect cognitions of candidate attributes and affective orientations toward each candidate. Following the promising trends in current media research, the emphasis will be on the relationship between media usage and information holding. In general, we will want to know if watching the presidential debates increased the information available to citizens about the candidates. Did watching the debates affect the perception of differences or similarities between the candidates? What beliefs about the candidates endured as a result of having watched the debates, and how did these cognitions compare with the content of the media? Did information obtained from the debates provide a unique contribution to the citizen's understanding of the candidates that was independent of other media sources such as newspapers and TV news? Finally, we will want to learn if the information obtained from the media had any impact on evaluations of the candidates. Although the relationship between media outputs and the vote is not discussed, we demonstrate that the debates, and the media more generally, did influence public cognitions and, to a lesser extent, evaluations of the candidates and thereby did affect the qualitative nature of the 1976 presidential election.

Data

The data employed in the analysis derives from two different sources. The Center for Political Studies 1976 national presidential election survey of 2,875 adult citizens serves as the principal data source.[1] It included a series of structured and open-ended questions designed to measure reactions to the presidential debates, plus items measuring both newspaper and TV usage habits, as well as the usual extensive complement of political attitude questions.

Content data obtained from newspaper and TV coverage of the debates forms the second set of data. The media content was manually coded from articles about the debates appearing on the front pages of twenty newspapers and from the audio portion of debate stories reported on the national TV news during the three days following each of the presidential debates.[2] The newspapers had been selected from the cities and towns of the survey sample places so as to represent the national press and so that the content data could be merged with the survey data from respondents who read any of the twenty newspapers.

The Debate Watchers

The 1976 presidential debates provided citizens with an opportunity to obtain information about the candidates with a minimal expenditure of personal time and effort. The fact that both candidates appeared simultaneously on television—the most accessible and least demanding media—during "prime time," when most people are relatively free of other obligations, and at repeated intervals over the course of the campaign meant that most of the adult population could use the debates as an information source for learning about the candidates.

The debates were more extensively used as an information source in 1976 than were other media sources, but obviously not everyone was equally interested in watching them. Debate exposure is only weakly associated with demographic characteristics, but among the noteworthy differences is a variation in initial viewing versus sustained interest among racial and age groups and by education level. While almost equal proportions of blacks and whites reported watching *all* of the debates (24 percent and 29 percent respectively), almost one-third of the black respondents but only sixteen percent of the white failed to watch any of the debates. Similarly, grade school and college-educated individuals differed only in the proportion watching none of the debates (see Table 1); the proportions watching three or four debates were again almost identical. Apparently college-educated respondents were slightly more motivated to watch the debates, but the sustained interest in following the debates was almost as high for all education levels. The relationship between age and debate viewing (also displayed in Table 1), on the other hand, reveals little age-related variation in initial debate interest but clear differences in sustained interest. Older individuals were much more likely than younger people to have a sustained interest.

Thus, while initial interest in the debates varied by race and level of education, with whites and the more highly educated showing more interest than blacks and the less well educated, there was no difference in initial interest across age groups. But sustained interest, which is related to age, does not vary by race or level of education. Although these differences are interesting, the lack of a strong relationship between any demographic characteristics and debate watching leads us to the conclusion that the debates were equally utilized as an information source by all groups in society.

Individual political interest and involvement proved to be stronger factors affecting debate watching than did demographic characteristics. Political attention, an index that combined interest in following politics and public affairs with a measure of political knowledge,[3] as well as strength of partisan identification were moderately related to debate exposure (see Table 1). Strong partisans and people who are highly attentive to politics were not only more interested in the debates but they demonstrated far more sustained interest than did Independents or the least attentive respondents.

CARTER vs. FORD, 1976   271

Table 1: Debate Exposure by Demographic Characteristics and Aspects of Political Involvement

Number of Debates Watched	Education			Age			Party Strength			Political Attention		
	Grade School	High School	College	18–29	30–49	50+	Strong Identi-fication	Weak Identi-fication	Inde-pendents	Low	Medium	High
4	31	25	32	33	50	73	40	25	24	8	25	39
3	16	18	19	31	38	35	22	18	12	9	14	24
2	21	24	28	58	57	39	19	27	27	21	28	23
1	7	13	11	33	20	15	7	12	14	18	12	7
0	25	20	10	40	29	31	12	17	23	40	17	6

Candidate Salience

Describing who watched the debates and how frequently they watched is a relatively simple task; determining whether the debates had any effect on information holding is substantially more difficult. Part of the difficulty arises from the problem of operationalizing the concept of information holding.[4] We have chosen to treat the concept in two ways, first by use of responses to open-ended questions asking the respondent to evaluate each candidate, and second with structured questions that measure perceived policy differences between the two candidates and between the two major political parties. The former operational measure, which is used for the major part of the analysis, indicates how salient various cognitions about the candidates are for the mass public. There is no attempt made to determine if these cognitions are accurate in any textbook meaning of the word "knowledge." Rather, we are interested in knowing what the respondent thinks are the "important" aspects of the candidates and how salient these features are for individuals with varying levels of exposure to the debates and other media inputs. The second operational definition of information, namely the perception of policy differences between the two candidates or between the two major parties, comes somewhat closer to a textbook definition of knowledge in that the perceptions can in principle be compared with some objective criteria or population value.

Demonstrating that watching the debates increased the public's level of information about the candidates requires evidence both of shifts over time and of a relationship between knowledge about the candidates and debate exposure. Given all the media coverage of the primaries and the nominating conventions, one could of course assume that by the time of the debates, nothing further remained to be learned about the candidates. Nevertheless, respondents interviewed after the debates made more numerous statements about what they liked or disliked about each of the candidates[5] than individuals interviewed before the debates (see Fig. 1). Furthermore, this apparent increase in information holding occurred at all levels of political attentiveness, suggesting that despite

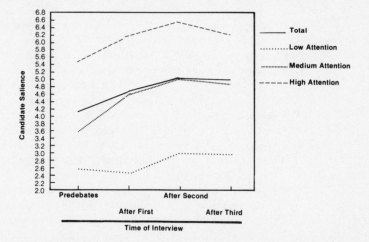

Fig. 1: Candidate Salience Over Time by Level of Political Attention

their occurrence late in the campaign the debates either provided the electorate, including even the best-informed, with some new information about the candidates or refreshed their memory.

A similar analysis of candidate salience over the course of the campaign period for each of the previous SRC/CPS presidential election studies (starting with 1952) adds confirming evidence of a possible impact of the debates. When the preelection interviewing period is divided into four equal time intervals and candidate salience is measured across these time points, the 1960 election is the only other case that reveals a systematic increase in salience.[6] Furthermore, public awareness of the candidates attained a higher level in the two elections preceded by debates than in those having none. Clearly, the increase in candidate salience over the course of the campaign could be the result of events other than the debates, but the data of Figure 1 and the comparison with salience in previous elections strongly suggest that the debates may have helped to stimulate public awareness of the candidates.

Disaggregating the open-ended comments about the candidates into several subcomponents of the candidate image, as established by past research (Miller and Miller, 1976), reveals sharper increases in salience for certain components than for others, and it provides a clearer sense of the cognitions that the voters had of each candidate. The average number of statements made about each candidate have been grouped into the several components and are presented in Table 2. The first candidate component, labeled "reliability," includes comments about responsibility, decisiveness, and stability. The second deals with "leadership" and is characterized by comments about the candidate as inspiring, communicative, warm, and likeable. "Traits" include comments that focus on the candidate's personal attributes: age, regional origin, health, and other demographic features. "Competence" incorporates comments about the candidate's experience and ability. The final candidate component deals with "trust" and focuses on the candidate's honesty and integrity. The remaining entries in the table are comments that make either partisan or group references or that focus on issues.

The size of the average number of statements incorporated by each component in Table 2 indicates the relative importance of that component in the overall cognitions citizens had about the candidates. Putting aside the partisan and issue components, it is quite evident from Table 2 that people thought about Ford primarily in terms of competence and trust, whereas competence, trust, and personal traits underlay their thinking about Carter.

Following the debates, change in the frequency of comments included by the various components suggests a possible debate effect on the public's cognitions of the candidates. References to competence, particularly about Ford, showed the most systematic and sharpest increases following the debates. The preponderance of these comments about Carter were negative, whereas those about Ford were positive, thereby suggesting that perhaps his participation in the debates helped Ford to establish the image of a competent and effective leader. Shifts in the frequency of issue comments about both Carter and Ford also suggest a debate effect. Statements about domestic policies increased after the first and third debates, both of which focused heavily on domestic problems. Comments about foreign policy also increased substantially after the second

Table 2: Candidate Image Components by Time of Interview

Image Components	CARTER				FORD			
	Predebates	After First	After Second	After Third	Predebates	After First	After Second	After Third
Candidate Components:								
Reliability	.237	.280	.273	.254	.168	.201	.203	.203
Leadership	.113	.115	.130	.154	.110	.131	.126	.159
Demographic Traits	.353	.353	.363	.250	.088	.097	.095	.081
Competence	.294	.385	.376	.475	.522	.598	.735	.783
Trust	.304	.372	.353	.360	.383	.414	.445	.409
Issue Components:								
Domestic Policy	.265	.287	.258	.285	.208	.259	.233	.249
Foreign Policy	.055	.060	.117	.078	.116	.135	.215	.149
Partisan Components:								
Party and Group References	.431	.474	.567	.532	.351	.377	.395	.382
TOTAL	2.052	2.326	2.437	2.388	1.946	2.212	2.447	2.415

NOTE: Cell entries give the average number of comments about each component given by a respondent interviewed during the indicated period. The positive and negative statements about each candidate were combined to obtain a total measure of salience. The maximum number of statements allowed per candidate was ten. The total represents the average number of responses given by individuals for a particular interview period and is simply the sum of the values in the relevant column.

debate, thus suggesting that the debates may have provided the public with some information relating the candidates and issues.[7]

The data of Figure 1 and Table 2 indicate that there were systematic increases in information about the candidates that correspond to the occurrence of the debates. Without a panel study it cannot be conclusively established that watching the debates caused this increase in candidate salience; however, disregarding change over time, the cross-section data do show a clear and moderately strong positive relationship between candidate salience and debate exposure (see Fig. 2). The more debates that were watched, the more information the re-

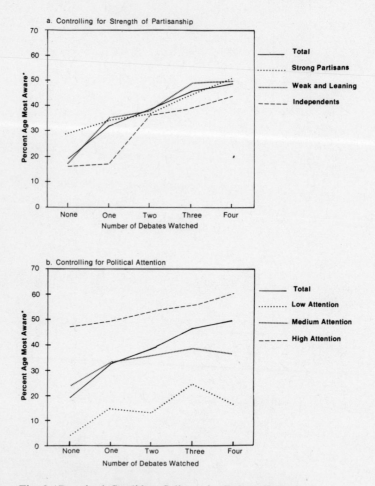

Fig. 2: Perceived Candidate Salience by Debate Exposure

*The "most aware" were defined as those who made three or more comments about *each* of the candidates when asked what they liked and disliked about them. This subset of respondents is roughly 38 percent of the *total* sample.

THE GREAT DEBATES

spondent had about the candidates. As can be seen from Figure 2, the respondent's level of political attention affected the overall degree of information that respondents had about the candidates. Not surprisingly, highly attentive individuals knew considerably more about the candidates than did the least attentive. Yet, regardless of these presumably more enduring differences in information levels, watching the debates was associated with higher levels of information about the candidates. Similarly, controlling on strength of party identification, which was only weakly related with candidate salience, did not reduce the relationship between debate exposure and level of information.

The possibility exists, however, that the zero-order relationships observed between candidate salience and debate exposure are simply the spurious reflection of either education or other media outputs such as TV news and newspapers. A multivariate analysis regressing candidate salience on debate exposure, exposure to national TV news, and frequency of reading about national politics in newspapers was therefore conducted to determine the unique effects of the debates.[8] Given the expectation that individuals who were better educated or more politically involved would generally have more to say about politics than the less well educated or least involved, the effects of education and strength of partisanship on candidate salience were first partialed out.[9] The regressions were then performed on the residuals for the total sample, as well as for the three subgroups defined by level of political attentiveness.

The results of the multivariate analysis (see Table 3) provide strong confirming evidence indicating that the debates had a significant independent effect on the electorate's cognitions of the 1976 presidential candidates. Not only was this effect independent of other media inputs but it was surprisingly strong given that the impact of long-term determinants of political cognitions—education, partisanship, *and* political attentiveness—had already been removed before calculating the regression equations. The more debates that were watched the more information the individual citizen had about the candidates, and this was true despite other information that might have been gained from reading the newspaper or watching the national TV news. The effect of the debates was greatest for the least politically attentive individuals. The effect of newspaper exposure on information holding, on the contrary, was greatest for the highly attentive and barely significant for the least attentive. Clearly, those who were very inter-

Table 3: Regression Equation Predicting Candidate Salience After Partialing on Education and Strength of Partisanship

| | Candidate Salience | Political Attention | | |
	Total	Low	Medium	High
Newspaper	.46*	.14	.26	.43
TV	−.01	.10	−.03	−.11
Debates	.35	.41	.27	.22
R	.345	.305	.205	.195
R²	.119	.093	.042	.038

*Table entries are unstandardized regression coefficients.

ested and knowledgeable about politics were obtaining most of their political information by reading the newspaper. Yet, even for them debate exposure was related to candidate salience. The national TV news, however, apparently provided little political information for any of the respondents, in confirmation of the 1972 Patterson and McClure (1976) finding that TV news conveyed little information about the substance of the candidates and issues.

In sum, we have documented systematic shifts in political cognitions that correspond to the occurrence of the presidential debates. The analysis has also revealed a significant and substantial relationship between debate exposure and candidate salience. Even after controlling for other media inputs, the debates apparently had some effect on raising the level of salient cognitions that the electorate had about the candidates. Alternatively, for some viewers the debates may not have provided "new" information; rather, they may have served to refresh their memory about something they had learned earlier or they may have stimulated the viewer to be more sensitive to information about the candidates that was available from a variety of sources including personal conversations, spot commercials, or party literature. Regardless of the process by which information about the candidates became connected with debate exposure, the data strongly suggest that the debates were events that led to higher levels of knowledge about the candidates.

Perceived Candidate and Party Differences

While the preceding analysis suggests that watching the debates increased information holding, it is not clear that this led to any cognition of differences between the candidates. Yet this is a particularly important concern because if voters are to cast their ballots for their preferred candidate, the candidate must project real differences and the public must be able to perceive this difference between them, regardless of whether it is a partisan, policy, personality, or performance difference. It is important, therefore, to determine if watching the debates was related to perceptions of differences between candidates or parties.

Two policy-related indexes were computed to serve as measures of perceived candidate and partisan "differences." The candidate measure indicated the difference that respondents perceived in the policies that Ford and Carter would pursue in dealing with the question of government responsibility for providing jobs and a good standard of living for everyone.[10] The perceived party differences index measured beliefs about how differently Democrats and Republicans would handle inflation, unemployment, the size of government, and military spending.[11] The public not only perceived significant policy differences between the candidates and the parties, but these perceived differences were found to be somewhat related to debate exposure. The more debates watched the clearer was the difference perceived to exist between the position that Ford and Carter took on the jobs issue; with Carter perceived as favoring a policy of government action to provide jobs and Ford perceived as favoring a policy that left individuals to deal with unemployment on their own. Similarly, those who watched more debates perceived greater policy differences between Democrats and Republicans. Perceived candidate and partisan differences were not, however, as strongly related to debate exposure as was candidate salience. Strength of partisanship and political attention had a definite impact on the relationship between

278

perceived differences and debate exposure. Among the highly attentive and strong partisans the relationship was somewhat weak, but the relationship remained quite significant among the less-involved respondents.

Although the effect of debate exposure on perceived candidate and party differences is considerably weaker than that found with candidate salience, the relationships remained significant in a multivariate analysis similar to the earlier one. The regression coefficients again indicated that the effect of debates, relative to the impact of newspapers, was stronger among those who were less attentive. The low overall multiple correlations revealed the overwhelming impact that education, strength of partisanship, and political attentiveness have on perceived differences. Partialing out the impact of these factors leaves relatively little variance for media inputs to explain, thus it was surprising that debate exposure and newspaper reading had any effect at all on these political perceptions.

One possible explanation for the considerably smaller impact of newspapers relative to the debates is that the media rarely presented information about the candidates in a fashion that conveyed clear differences. The coding of newspaper content revealed that only 22 percent of the substantive topics coded were reported in a fashion that indicated any differences between the candidates. The degree of candidate differences conveyed by the newspaper articles varied by topic reported, with considerably more difference suggested when the topic was an economic issue (45 percent of the topics conveyed a difference) and a partisan reference (41 percent), than when other topics were covered. Either the candidates did not differ on various policies and candidate characteristics or the media were not reporting them. The debates, on the other hand, offered a forum where both candidates were together at the same time, and this apparently did provide the viewing public with some information about their differences. Moreover, the relationship between debate exposure and perceived candidate differences adds further support to the earlier conclusion that the debates heightened public awareness of the candidates.

Content of Debate Information

The enduring cognitions that debate viewers had of the candidate's debate participation can be more completely described from responses to open-ended questions that focused on the debates. When asked in the post-election interview what they remembered from the debates about each candidate, a large proportion of respondents—28 percent when discussing Ford and 36 percent when asked about Carter—mentioned the overall debate performance of the candidates. Indeed, nearly half of all comments about the debates focused on either the candidates' competence or their debate performance. Comments about Carter, in particular, stressed debate performance, whereas competence was referred to more frequently when discussing Ford. References to various candidate personality characteristics were also quite prevalent in the recollections of the debates (17 percent for both Ford and Carter). Policy- and issue-related comments were substantially less frequently mentioned. Yet, after setting aside the rather large number of responses about Ford's East European gaffe (17 percent), issues formed the fifth most prevalent category of responses about Ford (only 11 percent) and the third most frequent about Carter (23 percent). Carter's Southern origin, his smile, and some demographic traits were also mentioned more frequently than were similar characteristics associated with Ford.

Generally, recollections of the debates did not vary by level of political attention, but some noteworthy differences did appear. Somewhat unexpectedly, highly attentive individuals were more likely than the least attentive to mention the candidates' debate performance (28 percent versus 24 percent for Ford; 41 percent versus 32 percent for Carter). Apparently these highly informed individuals, who rely heavily on the print media for their political information, had learned something from watching the debates that they could not obtain from newspapers—how the candidates acted and behaved under the debate conditions.

A similarly interesting, and again perhaps unexpected, pattern of responses occurred with respect to issue references. The least politically attentive viewers mentioned issues, particularly economic issues and primarily in reference to Carter (11 percent versus 8 percent), more frequently than did the highly attentive respondents. These differences suggest that the less-involved respondents were more sensitive than the highly attentive to learning about certain issues that were addressed in the debates. They were either (1) more concerned about these problems and thus watched the debates to learn how the candidates would deal with them, or (2) because of their sensitivity and interest in a particular issue, that issue was the aspect of the debates that was most manifest for them at the time of the interview, or (3) they had little prior knowledge about Carter's economic views and were, therefore, receptive to new information conveyed by the debates. Whatever the explanation, the pattern of results for the economic issues is quite consistent with that found in the earlier analysis of perceived candidate differences.

The sensitivity explanation would appear to be supported by the proportion of responses about Ford's statement on Eastern Europe that is found for the highly attentive (19 percent) relative to the least attentive (8 percent). Other studies[12] have demonstrated that most debate viewers were not immediately aware of Ford's gaffe, thus the knowledge had to be acquired after the debate. Respondents who were generally well informed about politics may be expected to be more interested in foreign affairs and more attentive to the various media sources that provided information about the statement and, therefore, more likely to make comments about the statement when reporting recollections of the debates. The data suggest that, in this case, having watched the debates most likely stimulated an interest in learning more about the East European statement rather than directly providing information that made the viewer aware of the implications of the statement.

To what extent are these recollections of the debates a reflection of the debate content or the newspaper and television coverage of the debates? A very rough estimate of this correspondence was ascertained by comparing recollections with a content analysis. We found a sharp difference between the debate content and the debate-related content that appeared in newspapers and TV news during the three days following each debate. The substantive focus of the debates was on issues—with economics and other domestic problems, including lack of trust in government and political scandals, receiving the greatest attention from the candidates. But neither respondent recollections of the debate nor media coverage simply reflected the substance of the debate.[13] Issues were, however, a relatively more important aspect of the media's coverage than they were of respondent recollections. Excluding references to Ford's statement about Eastern Europe, somewhat more than one-quarter of all media coverage of the debates focused on issues; whereas, depending on which candidate was being discussed, only 11 and 16 percent of the respondents mentioned issues when reporting what they recalled about the debates. A relatively substantial proportion of media coverage was also devoted to how the candidates had performed in the debates (17 percent of newspaper coverage; 13 percent of TV coverage) and to candidate competence (8 percent newspaper coverage; 10 percent TV coverage). Newspapers devoted more coverage (17 percent) than did television (10 percent) to a discussion of who won the debates and to the potential impact of the debate outcome on the general campaign (10 percent versus 8 percent). TV coverage, by contrast, placed relatively more emphasis on candidate personalities than did the print media (11 percent versus 6 percent).

Generally there appears to be a rough correspondence between the media content and respondent recollections. Those aspects of the debates that viewers remembered most readily—candidate performance, competence, and personality—were also quite prevalent in the media coverage of the debates. While this descriptive analysis cannot establish any causal connection linking information holding and media outputs, it does indicate that there was no obvious discrepancy between respondent recollections and the content provided by the media source. The comparison of debate and media content with respondent recollections demonstrates, however, that the public does not necessarily translate policy-related information into enduring issue knowledge. While the candidates addressed the issues in the debates, the public was more concerned with an assessment of general performance and competence. The public's concern basically reflected the emphasis of the media, but even the media coverage of the debates gave more attention to the issues than the voters did. If the 1976 campaign was "issueless," it was not because the candidates avoided substantive topics but because there were apparently no burning issues that captured the concern of the public.

Evaluative Effects of Debate Exposure

We have shown that the debates had a distinctive and measurable contribution toward increasing the electorate's information level, and we have explored the content of this information for both the public and the media. The next task is an attempt to assess the directional impact of this information flow; that is, did the debates produce an increase or a decrease in the public's evaluation of either candidate? Clearly there need not necessarily be a valence effect as the increased information stemming from the debates may be evenhanded, leaving the electorate in much the same position, though better informed, from which to make the choice between the two candidates. On the other hand, it is plausible to suppose that one candidate might have performed so well that the debates would have prompted the public to give him an unequivocal endorsement. We shall see that the empirical evidence is more supportive of the former than the latter conclusion.

The valenced image of the candidates, that is, how positively or negatively the public viewed Ford and Carter, can be assessed by subtracting the average number of negative comments made about a candidate from the average positive remarks on each of the eight candidate components. The summary data for respondents interviewed after the first debates had been broadcast are presented in Table 4. The average person made .097 positive and .162 negative comments about Carter's reliability. Thus the first entry is straightforwardly .097 − .162 = −.065, indicating a preponderance of negative comments. Looking down the columns, one sees immediately that Carter's affiliation with his party and social groups were his most obvious asset, while evaluations of Ford were predominantly negative on these points. On the other hand, Ford was favorably evaluated because of his perceived ability to do the job—his competence. A caricature of the election as a contest between an incumbent president and a majority-party challenger would not be contradicted by these data.

Table 4: Net Candidate Images

	Carter*	Ford*	Net Ford Advantage†
Reliability	−.065	.035	.100
Leadership	.040	−.006	−.046
Demographic Traits	.067	.017	−.050
Competence	−.042	.236	.278
Trust	.009	−.008	−.017
Political Affiliation	.159	−.192	−.351
Domestic Policy	.071	−.037	−.108
Foreign Policy	−.023	−.023	.000
All Components	.216	.022	−.194

*Table entries in this column represent the average number of positive comments minus the average number of negative comments made about the candidate on each component of the image.
†This column is simply the Ford column entry minus the Carter column entry. A positive value represents a Ford advantage, a negative value indicates a Carter advantage.

More significant for our purposes, though, is the relative similarity between the evaluative content of the two images. We see that both candidates were viewed positively, though Ford's total merely edges past the neutral point. The net advantage, however, goes to Carter, with the average respondent saying .194 more good things about him than about Ford. Historically this is the smallest difference between two presidential candidates in the last quarter-century (Miller, 1977). It also suggests the relative importance of even small shifts in evaluation which may have been caused by the debates.

One way to investigate the debates' impact would be to look at changes in evaluations people had after they viewed each performance. But our data, because they are not gathered with a panel design before and after each debate, are not suitable for addressing questions of immediate change. What we can do, however, is to look for enduring effects that may be seen if the interviewing period is divided into time segments corresponding to the debates. Yet, even with this approach there is no clear theoretical expectation of which particular debate should have an effect on any particular dimension of candidate evaluations. However, when we look at the single case of foreign policy, where we can explicitly expect a specific change after the second debate, we find it (see Table 5). Normally a president in office may be expected to benefit from his association with the nation's foreign policy, and such was the case going into the second debate. But after Ford's Eastern Europe gaffe, the president's foreign-policy image declined so dramatically that the novice Democratic challenger actually ended up with a net advantage.

The effect that the debates may have had on candidate evaluations, independent of other media inputs, can more generally be determined by applying a regression model similar to that used earlier to study the effects of the debates on information holding. Unfortunately, a considerably more complicated model

Table 5: Net Candidate Images on Foreign Policy Over Time

	Carter*	Ford*	Net Ford Advantage†
Before First Debate	−.011	.022	.033
After First Debate	−.031	−.006	.025
After Second Debate	−.018	−.038	−.020
After Third Debate	−.016	−.032	−.016

*Each number represents the average number of positive comments minus the average number of negative comments made about the candidate.
†This column is simply the value in the Ford column minus the entry in the Carter column. A positive number represents a Ford advantage, a negative value indicates a Carter advantage.

is implied when investigating evaluations. The inferences we drew about information gain were dependent on the proposition that we had effectively controlled for the most plausible of spurious relationships, which is to say the obvious effects of a respondent's education, partisan involvement, and political attentiveness, on his ability and inclination to offer comments to the interviewer. When investigating evaluations, we would have to contend with a substantially larger and more complex set of potentially confounding relationships[14] if we were to follow our earlier analysis approach. Instead of trying to eliminate statistically all plausible spuriousness, we shall assume that any excluded variables will have operated in roughly the same way over the period of our survey. If this is true, and no compelling counterargument is apparent, then the relationships observed for the debate period may be compared with those evident before the debates began. Both sets of relations should be equally affected by exogenous factors; thus the difference between the relationships ought to be a true indication of something having happened during the debate period.

Figure 3 graphically depicts the idealized operation of the model that underlies this mode of analysis. It also represents a positive relationship between debate exposure (measured in the post-election survey) and evaluation of Ford's

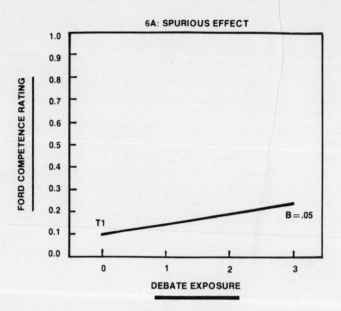

6A: SPURIOUS EFFECT

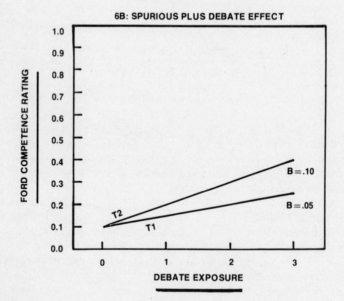

6B: SPURIOUS PLUS DEBATE EFFECT

THE GREAT DEBATES

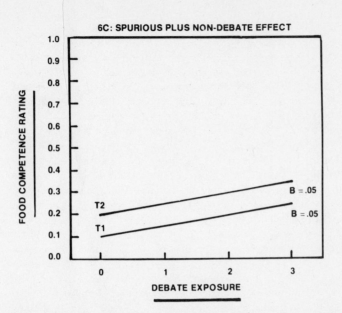

Fig. 3: Hypothetical Models of Relations between Candidate Evaluations and Debate Exposure

competence measured *before* the start of the debates. This is obviously a spurious relationship because no one could have seen a debate at that time. Now let us suppose that Ford's composed manner and general performance during the debates gave a positive boost to his image of competence. Selective perception aside, we would expect that those most highly exposed to the debates would also be most likely to pick up this information and, given that it is unidirectionally positive, it should produce most positive ratings. Those who were not exposed would evidence no change (insofar as they saw nothing of the performance), and those in between would show a middling increase in proportion to their exposure (see Fig. 3). These systematic changes in ratings would result in an algebraically *stronger* relationship, that is, a larger regression coefficient, between debate exposure and evaluations, and the difference between the coefficients which represent the predebate and post-debate relations can be said to reflect the extent to which changes in evaluations were due to the channeling of information through the debates (or due to the sensitizing effects of debate involvement).

If, on the other hand, positive information about Ford had passed through other channels unrelated to debate exposure, both the noninvolved and the highly involved would pick up the same information and change their evaluations similarly. Figure 3 represents the relationship that would result in this hypothetical case. The relationship between exposure and evaluation remains the same, that is, the regression coefficients for the relationships, since they represent the *slope* of the line, will be identical; thus the difference between the regression coefficients for the two time points will be zero. Although there may have been a massive shift in evaluations (a fact which will be indicated by an increase in the regression constant), the impetus was not attributable to the debates and our analysis procedure will properly inform us of that fact. The relative size of the predebate and post-debate regression coefficients will, therefore, be isomorphic with the process we postulate.[15] If the debates had an effect on the public's evaluation of the candidates there will be a significant difference between the pre- and the post-debate regression coefficients.

Turning from hypothetical models to the actual change data illustrated in Table 6, we note the meagerness of debate effects.[16] Clearly, the fact that information was transmitted through the debates had only a marginal impact on the public's evaluation of the candidates' images. The pre- and post-debate regression coefficients are generally quite similar in magnitude, and the differences do not approach any standard level of significance, thus indicating that debate exposure had relatively little enduring influence on whether the candidates were positively or negatively evaluated. The differences between coefficients for newspaper and television exposure (not shown) are also negligible and statistically insignificant.

These results are in keeping with what we know about the persuasive effects of political communications. Generally people who are most highly exposed to or most able to understand political information are those with the highest level of previous knowledge and the most heavily weighted predispositions. The persons more susceptible to media influence are those who are least likely to grasp the substance of the communications. To the extent that this model describes the 1976 situation, we would expect a strong impact only if the information passing through each source was dramatic and uniform in direction, favoring one candidate over the other. The possibility of debate impact was less fraught with these predispositional impediments to communication because the element of self-selection in exposure does not seem to have been as strong as, say, for newspaper reading. On the other hand, the net advantage of the debate performance for either candidate, that is, the directional uniformity of the debate-related information, was generally mixed, according to the election study data. Neither candidate dominated the other. Of course, we would expect an impact for all media sources only if the news at the time consistently favored one candidate over the other, a condition which apparently did not exist during the last six weeks of the campaign. Thus we do observe minimal effects, and yet we cannot infer that the debates, or other media, are incapable of having a profound impact.

The proposition that the effects of the debates were distorted by viewers' predispositions is susceptible to test. Table 7 demonstrates the extent to which the respondents' partisan orientation colored the information they received from the three media channels. In the case of a debate impact the coefficients most clearly suggest a pattern of reinforcement, where exposure reinforces the partisans' positive image of their own candidate and heightens their distaste for the opposition. Moreover, the impact is proportional to the strength of their partisanship. A reinforcement pattern, however, was less evident for television viewing and nonexistent for newspaper reading. This evidence is in accord with our understanding of the most plausible models of perceptual distortion. The bias effect of predispositions, while varying in direct proportion with an indi-

286   THE GREAT DEBATES

Table 6: Regression Coefficients and Differences Indicating Enduring Effects of Debate Exposure on Candidate Images

	Carter			Ford		
	Predebates*	Post-Debates*	Difference†	Predebates*	Post-Debates*	Difference†
Reliability	−.047	−.011	.036	.008	−.005	−.013
Leadership	−.023	−.003	.020	.012	−.002	−.014
Demographic Traits	.019	.005	−.014	−.011	−.006	.005
Competence	−.033	−.018	.015	.026	.038	.012
Trust	.007	.033	.026	.043	.009	−.034
Political Affiliation	.051	.004	−.047	.007	.009	.002
Domestic Policy	.014	.016	.002	−.014	.008	.022
Foreign Policy	.009	.007	−.002	.023	.011	−.012
TOTAL	−.003	.033	.036	.095	.061	−.034

*These figures are the unstandardized regression coefficients (note that they are from two different populations) associated with the debates when candidate evaluations on each component and total image (controlled for partisanship, education, and income) are regressed on newspapers, television, and debate exposure.
†These are the difference between the pre- and post-debate coefficients.

Table 7: Enduring Effects of Media and Debate Exposure on Candidate
Evaluations by Partisan Predisposition Controlling for Education

| | Carter Image* | | | |
	Strong Democrats	Other Democrats**	Other Republicans**	Strong Republicans
Newspapers	.136†	.121	.048	.053
Television	.185	−.001	−.472	−.360
Debates	.286	.192	−.076	−.415

| | Ford Image* | | | |
	Strong Democrats	Other Democrats**	Other Republicans**	Strong Republicans
Newspapers	−.070	−.116	−.144	.072
Television	−1.328	−.104	.856	.431
Debates	−.547	−.289	.254	.834

*The dependent variable is the number of positive comments minus negative comments about each candidate. Here the control is on education to maintain sample stability, obviously not on partisanship as in Table 8.

†These are the differences between the regression coefficients before and after the debates.

**This category includes both partisans who are weak identifiers and independents who lean toward the party indicated.

vidual's predispositions, ought to vary *inversely* with the relative strength and persistence of the information signal. An individual's perceptual mechanisms will easily dominate weak and ambiguous signals, while clear and frequently repeated information will make its way into the recipients' cognitions. The data suggest that information transmitted by the newspapers is less susceptible to this sort of perceptual distortion than that passed by the fleeting images of the television screen.

Thus we are left with an indication of minimal long-term debate impact on candidate evaluations, with virtually all potential effect absorbed by the viewers' perceptual predispositions. This result provokes the obvious conclusion that the debates did not alter the election outcome. On the other hand, we have ignored the possibility that viewer evaluations of the candidates may have been altered in the short run by the debate performances, only to be changed again by subsequent campaign events.

Investigating the possibility that the debates had some short-term effect on how individuals evaluated the candidates, however, requires over-time data gathered frequently enough to assess day-by-day shifts in attitudes. Although the interviews from our study were not conducted so as to produce a representative national sample for any given day, the daily samples can provide a crude indication of short-term reactions if they are adjusted for the obvious sampling fluctuations in variables that would affect our results. In this case we have controlled these fluctuations by regressing candidate evaluation on partisanship (direction and strength), education, and income (as a measure of social status), and then analyzing the residuals. The ensuing data series of daily samples now represents an indicator of how the candidates were rated every day during the last six weeks of the campaign.[17]

A close inspection of the daily time series of candidate evaluations among debate watchers (see Figure 4) suggests that there was short-term movement of the images after each of the debates and that the popular assessment of the winners and losers is reflected by the data. Carter did poorly in the first encounter, but followed with positive performances in the subsequent debates. Ford helped his cause in the first and third debates, but slipped rather badly in the second. Most important, it is apparent that the effect of any debate lasted only a few days.

A more formal estimate for the magnitude and endurance of the debate impact on candidate ratings was derived from a mathematical model that describes the over-time causal effect of one variable on another.[18] The resulting

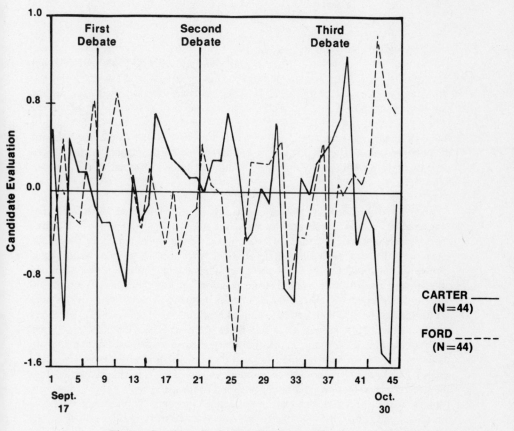

Fig. 4: Candidate Evaluation for Debate Watchers During Campaign Period

CARTER vs. FORD, 1976   289

estimates for the total impact of each debate are presented in Table 8. The pattern is as expected, and it simply quantifies what we have already summarized above. Recalling that the difference between the candidates for the entire sample was only .194, we see that each of the debates had a marked influence on how the public perceived the candidates. Yet, we are also able to estimate the endurance of this impact, and it seems that the total effect of each of the debates had run its course in about two days after the event.

Table 8: Short-Term Effects of Debates on Candidate Evaluation

	Carter*	Ford*
First Debate	− .205	.507
Second Debate	.459	− .283
Third Debate	.772	.679

*Each number represents the total net shift (in numbers of comments) that may be attributed to the debates during the duration of their impact. A negative value reflects a decrease in favorable evaluations, positive values represent an increase in favorable ratings.

Thus we are left with the strong impression that the debates were just one set of many events that took place during the campaign and that also affected the public's evaluations of the candidates. It is clear from the evidence that the electorate was moved by the candidate performances during their face-to-face confrontations, but it is equally clear that people then reacted very quickly to subsequent events which also affected their evaluations of the candidates. In terms of campaign events, the public's memory is just not very long. It is not at all surprising, therefore, that in a cumulative sense the debate performances did not make an enduring contribution to the election outcome.

Conclusion

The 1976 presidential debates produced a better-informed electorate than would have existed if the debates had not been held. Watching the debates increased the level of manifest information that all citizens had about the candidates regardless of their education, political involvement, or general information-seeking habits. The analysis presented above could not, however, demonstrate how much of the apparent information increase was the result of the voter's gaining new knowledge directly from the debates rather than the debates refreshing the voter's memory of specific knowledge learned earlier or stimulating the viewer to subsequently learn more about the candidate. Nor did the analysis establish how long the information persisted past the election; although data not presented here do indicate that the information gains were still evident at the time of the post-election interview (on the average, six weeks after the preelection interview). Despite these limitations, the major conclusion that is quite strongly supported by the evidence is that those individuals who watched the debates exhibited a heightened political awareness at exactly the time when political information is crucial—shortly before an election. In this respect democracy was well served, for without the debates a significant proportion of the electorate would have remained relatively uninformed about the candidates.

The information obtained from the debates and their subsequent media coverage was largely focused on candidate competence, performance, and personality attributes rather than on issues. Yet, some increase in issue- and policy-relevant information can be linked to the debates. Evidence was found for a significant relationship between debate exposure and the perception that the candidates would pursue quite different policies determining the government's role in guaranteeing that every citizen has a job and a good standard of living. An increase in issue- or policy-related information should not, however, be the sole criterion for judging the merit of the debates. Candidate competence and performance are equally important factors, for they can suggest to the voter how a particular candidate might operate once in office. It is not clear that debate performance reflects on the candidate's fitness for the presidency any less than information on a candidate's issue position indicates what policies will be pursued by the candidate once elected. Furthermore, what a president does for the country is determined not only by the types of policies the administration pursues, but also by the character of the individual who occupies the Oval Office. Indeed, the numerous scandals of the Nixon administration have served to emphasize the importance of candidate characteristics such as honesty, trustworthiness, competence, and reliability—candidate attributes that proved to be important determinants of the 1976 vote (Miller, 1977). If the vote decision is being affected by these factors, the electorate should be informed of the differences that exist between the candidates so they can make a more carefully considered choice. Apparently the debate forum provided some information about the differences.

The effects of the debates on the public's evaluations of the candidates are more difficult to summarize. On the one hand, we were able to identify a sizable short-term impact, but apparently the viewer's response was only transitory. Our analysis of enduring impact revealed very little change in candidate assessment that could be attributed to debate exposure, with the obvious conclusion that the debates had little direct influence on the election outcome. On the other hand, the evidence on reinforcement suggests that partisans who tuned into the debates came away with more positive images of their own candidate and less favorable ones of the opponent. It seems, then, that the debates did not affect the election in the way one might normally think, which is to say that neither candidate was able to dominate his opponent so completely as to make a uniformly favorable and long-lasting impression on the public. The impact may have been more indirect in that, having reinforced partisans' predispositions to view positively their party's candidate, the debates may have helped Carter to maintain his Democratic majority and thus win an election that was heavily determined by partisan loyalty.

Normatively the 1976 debates appeared to serve democratic goals quite well. They provided a forum that was apparently not biased in favor of either the incumbent or the challenger, and at the same time they served to inform the public and stimulate political awareness of the candidates who represented their electoral options.

NOTES

1. The CPS 1976 national presidential survey was made possible by grant #SOC 7613562 from the National Science Foundation. Starting in mid-September, respondents were interviewed before the election and again immediately after it. The pre-election sample was randomly divided into halves; the first half was interviewed during the first part of the interview period, and the second half was interviewed during the latter part. This design allowed us to divide the sample for analysis purposes by time of the presidential debates without any loss of representativeness. The use of various demographic controls, such as education, partisanship, and political attentiveness, in the analysis has also added stability to the sample estimates. These control variables "smoothe out" some of the fluctuations in the sample that arise because of who is available to be interviewed during particular periods of the interviewing phase.

The 1976 sample is comprised of roughly 2,250 respondents. Some of them represent both a cross-section and a panel sample element; thus, weights of 1.5 had to be used to attain a representative cross-section sample. The software we were employing to do the statistical computations could not handle decimal weights, so we used integer weights of 2 and 3. The resulting weighted N is 5734 rather than the 2870 we would have obtained with decimal weights. The use of integer weights has, of course, no effect on the analysis, but the reader should be aware of the fact that the real N is roughly half the number of cases that are reported in the data displays throughout the report.

2. Each paragraph of newspaper coverage was coded for up to six substantive topics. Topics were then weighted inversely by the number of topics appearing in each paragraph so as to obtain an accurate representation of the amount of coverage given to each topic. National TV news transcripts were obtained from the Vanderbilt Archives and coded in the same fashion, except that the coverage was divided into time segments rather than paragraphs.

We had no funding for gathering the media content; thus, our effort was limited to the twenty selected newspapers and the national television news on the three days after each debate. A small amount of CPS overhead funds were provided by Warren E. Miller to aid in the collection of the media content. If other funding becomes available in the future, this project will be extended to incorporate more newspapers and TV broadcasts over a longer period of the campaign.

3. In order to get a measure of how attentive a person was to politics, which would have an effect on his or her use of the media besides simple exposure, we employed two separate measures. The first item ascertained how closely the respondent said he or she normally followed government and public affairs even when there was no election. We wanted to correct the measure, though, with a reality test. We assumed that anyone who was generally attentive could tell us which party controlled Congress both before and after the election. Thus, we scored the respondents on their ability to correctly answer these two basic-knowledge questions. Those 40 percent who followed politics most or some of the time *and* correctly identified the Democratic majorities were coded high on attentiveness. Those who followed public affairs only now and then or hardly at all *and* could not answer either Congress question were coded low on attentiveness. Added to this category were a small number who hardly ever followed politics and gave only one correct informational response (presumably guessed) to bring the low total to 20 percent.

4. Information holding can be defined in several ways. We are using a count of the number of responses given to a series of open-ended questions about the presi-

dential candidates. This approach is similar to the message discrimination work of Clarke and Kline and Palmgreen, Kline, and Clarke (see References).

5. Four specific questions were used here, two about each candidate. Respondents were asked, "Is there anything in particular about (Mr. Carter/Mr. Ford) that might make you want to vote *for* him? Is there anything in particular about (Mr. Carter/Mr. Ford) that might make you want to vote against him?" Up to five responses were coded for each question.

6. Candidate salience, that is, the average number of open-ended comments per candidate, for five previous election (1968 data were not available) campaigns divided into four two-week segments is presented below:

Candidate Salience by Time Segment
within Interview Period

Year	T_1	T_2	T_3	T_4
1952	1.90	1.87	1.85	1.92
1956	1.93	1.90	2.06	1.99
1960	1.93	1.97	2.18	2.16
1964	1.92	2.14	2.12	2.00
1972	1.90	1.94	1.88	2.02
1976	1.85	2.02	2.22	2.20

It should be noted that the 1976 analysis is not exactly identical to the one done for earlier studies because the 1976 time points divide the interviewing period into segments determined by when the debates actually occurred rather than into four equal periods. This should not affect the comparisons.

The 1976 values given here differ from those presented in Table 1 because only three open-ended responses per person were available for the cross-time comparisons, whereas the 1976 analysis used five responses. Again, this should not affect the conclusions to be drawn from the analysis since the treatment of the data is comparable across time.

7. These analyses cannot demonstrate the duration of any effect that the debates may have had on either providing new information or increasing the sensitivity of the voter to certain aspects of the candidates and the campaign. The systematic fluctuation in references to the issues following the debates does suggest, however, that issue-related cognitions are more subject to short-term influences than are personality-related cognitions. This further suggests the possibility that the impact of the debates and other media on issue information would be less enduring than comparable effects on personality or partisan-related cognitions.

8. The media exposure variables reflect how often the respondent read about national politics in newspapers and how frequently he or she tuned into the network evening news programs. Thus, we have a direct measure of information exposure and do not have to rely on the dubious inference that newspaper readers and television viewers are necessarily exposed to political content. In an analysis not reported here we found these items to better reflect normal information-gathering habits than the campaign exposure items we might have used. Using the steady state measures, we are able to attribute the full impact of the debates to the debate-involvement variable: any increased media exposure due to the debate involvement will, at least theoretically, be picked up by the debate variable itself.

Our overall strategy was to use as exogenous variables only those which might *not* be expected to vary because of the debate phenomenon or other campaign-oriented activity. Thus, we use habitual media exposure, political attentiveness, education, and partisanship rather than campaign attentiveness, interest in the campaign, and ratings of the candidates. We do not, then, estimate the potential nonrecursive relationships that might be expected to develop among these variables during the course of the campaign, but instead use estimators of the relationships between conceptual variables at equilibrium.

9. It turns out that education and partisan strength have a positive relationship with information holding. In order to get a purer assessment of the media information impact, we wanted to remove the steady state effects of articulation and partisanship that could not be attributed to debate watching. We first regressed the information-holding measure in the two steady state variables for those cases interviewed before the debates started. Using these empirically determined effects, we predicted the level of salience for the post-debate sample and subtracted the predicted score from the actual score. Thus, a positive score (residual) would ensue if the respondent held more information than would be expected from his or her education and partisanship, a negative score if one held less.

10. The perceived candidate-difference index was calculated as the absolute difference between where respondents placed Ford and Carter on a seven-point issue scale. Respondents were presented with a scale on which one end indicated that the "government should see to it that every person has a job and a good standard of living," while the opposite end indicated that the "government should just let each person get ahead on his own."

11. The perceived party-difference index incorporated five policy questions that dealt with inflation, unemployment, defense spending, and the size of the federal government. Respondents were asked whether the policy would be handled better by Democrats, by Republicans, or about the same by both. Believing that the policy would be handled better by either of the parties was coded 1 and the number of 1's were then added over the five items. The resulting index ranges from zero to five; zero means no difference perceived between the parties and five indicates the maximum degree of perceived difference.

12. One particularly interesting study demonstrated that individuals interviewed immediately after the second debate thought that Ford had narrowly won the debate, but by the evening of the day after the debate, Carter had become the overwhelming winner. The early interviews showed no awareness of Ford having goofed, whereas by the later interviews respondents had indeed become aware of Ford's misstatement. See Fredrick Steeper, "Effects of the Second Presidential Debates," presented at the 1977 American Association for Public Opinion Research Conference, Buck Hill Falls, Pennsylvania, May 19–22, 1977.

13. Recalculating the "total" percentages of Table 5 for newspaper and TV coverage, but including only those substantive categories that received significant (more than 1 or 2 percent of the total time) attention in the debates, indicates that newspapers did a better job of reflecting debate content than TV news did. The recalculated percentages are as follows:

| | Media Coverage | | |
Topic	Debates	Newspaper	TV News
Competence	4.1%	16.3%	18.5%
Personality	5.1	12.2	20.4
Previous record	9.3	6.1	5.6
Economics	21.6	20.4	9.2
Other domestic	16.5	12.2	7.4
Foreign issues	22.7	22.4	24.1
Government trust	11.3	6.1	5.6
Group preferences	4.1	2.0	5.6
Partisan preferences	5.2	2.0	3.7

THE GREAT DEBATES

Both newspaper and TV coverage of the debates overstate the attention given to competence and personality in the debates, and TV grossly understates the debate emphasis on economic and domestic issues.

14. Such a web of relationships would have to include the respondent's social economic status, the intensity of his or her policy and ideology orientations, the orientation to different personality qualities, and of course the direction of his or her partisanship predisposition. In effect, we would have to "control" for the entire matrix of variables which go into one's electoral choice, a task to be shunned by any sensible data analyst. Our limited attempts at control are more directly designed to ensure sampling stability over time.

15. Our estimates of change due to information channel may be conservatively biased because of our having aggregated all interviews taken after the first debate into one time point. Clearly those respondents contacted early during this debate period could have only watched one debate. If the effects of the debates were cumulative, then these people's evaluation response would only partially reflect the total response we would have observed had we interviewed them later. For this reason, we have considered using only the respondents interviewed during the latest periods of the campaign. The results for these alternative comparisons are the same as those for the analysis shown here, and, wishing to base our analysis on as large an N as possible (to minimize the error of the regression estimators) and to minimize any possible sampling bias associated with time of interview, we have used the entire set of respondents interviewed during the debate period.

16. The dependent variable here is the number of positive comments minus the negative comments made by each respondent about each candidate for the specific image component as well as the overall total. The evaluation measure was then regressed on partisanship (direction and strength), education, and income, in order to eliminate the most obvious of spurious effects and to keep the estimated coefficients as free as possible from the sampling fluctuations associated with interview time. The differences between pre- and post-debate coefficients here are very small, and due to the sampling estimates of the regression estimators, many of the true values could in fact be zero, hence the notation of statistical insignificance. Yet, because of the purely random fluctuations of sampling error there is some probability that any true difference may be twice as large as the value obtained. While there is a possibility that sampling error may produce some incorrect conclusions about the size of the coefficients, it should be noted that these are maximum-likelihood estimates, which is to say that they are the best estimates of the true parameters that can be made with the data at hand.

17. The individual data points represent the evaluation means (corrected for partisanship, education, and income) for those interviewed each day who also watched three or four debates. The noticeably erratic shifts from any given day to the next are more likely reflections of conventional sampling error (the daily "samples" are on the order of twenty-five cases) than true changes. However, each daily point is our "best" estimate of the actual value, and the overall pattern is likely to give an accurate picture of public reactions. In this same vein it should be noted that the sample sizes for the first and last few days are very small and that the dramatic shifts during the closing days of the campaign may be more apparent than real.

One would expect less systematic reactions to the debates from those who did not pay much attention. Thus, we have concentrated our analysis on the highly exposed, and the data of Figure 7 were computed from respondents who watched all the presidential debates (or at least three out of the set of four). Time plots similar to those in Figure 7 for the nonwatchers reveal no clear consistent and direct impacts.

In addition, we are talking about the effects aside from perceptual distortion in that our data are controlled for partisanship. Thus, the debates may indeed have had the long-term *reinforcement* impact suggested in Table 9, and the effects would not show up in this short-term analysis.

18. A first-order linear filter, which represents the impact of the debates as an exponential decline over time (with the largest impact coming directly the day after the telecast), yields an estimation equation of the form:
$$Y_t = a + bX_{t-1} + cY_{t-1} + U_t,$$
where the public's evaluation (Y_t) is a function of the debates (represented by X_{t-1}) and the "stored" impact of the debates (Y_{t-1}) and all other campaign events (U_t). We determined that Y_t was a function of the disturbances of the form $Y_t = gY_{t-1} + U_t$ (an ARMA [1, 0] noise model), a fortunate happenstance which enabled us to use a weighted least-squares procedure to estimate the parameters.

Due to the large amount of sampling error in our daily mean estimates, and because our estimation strategy is only a first cousin to more sophisticated methods, one ought to treat the impact estimates as only approximations. In the same sense our estimates of duration, 1.75 and 2.68 days, ought to be treated only as indications of the transciency of impact.

REFERENCES

Berelson, B. R., P. F. Lazarsfeld, and W. N. McPhee. *Voting.* Chicago: University of Chicago Press, 1954.

Campbell, A., P. E. Converse, W. E. Miller, and D. E. Stokes. *The American Voter.* New York: Wiley, 1960.

Clarke, P. and F. G. Kline. "Media Effects Reconsidered: Some New Strategies for Communication Research." *Communication Research,* 1 (1974), pp. 224–40.

Hibbs, D. A. "On Analyzing the Effects of Policy Intervention: Box-Jenkins and Box-Tiao vs. Structural Equation Models," in D. R. Heise (ed.), *Sociological Methodology 1977.* San Francisco: Jossey-Bass, 1977.

Kirkpatrick, S. A., W. Lyons, and M. A. Fitzgerald. "Candidates, Parties and Issues in the American Electorate: Two Decades of Change." *American Politics Quarterly,* 3 (July 1975), pp. 247–83.

Klapper, J. *The Effects of Mass Communications.* New York: Glencoe Free Press, 1960.

Kraus, S. and D. K. Davis. *The Effects of Mass Communication on Political Behavior.* University Park, Pa.: Pennsylvania State University Press, 1976.

Lazarsfeld, P. F., B. R. Berelson, and H. Gaudet. *The People's Choice.* New York: Columbia University Press, 1948.

Miller, A. H. "The Majority Party Reunited?: A Summary Comparison of the 1972 and 1976 Elections," in J. Fishel (ed.), *Parties and Elections in an Anti-Party Age.* Bloomington, Ind.: Indiana University Press, 1977.

Miller, A. H. and W. E. Miller. "Ideology in the 1972 Election: Myth or Reality." *American Political Science Review,* 70 (September 1976), pp. 832–49.

Nimmo, D. and R. Savage. *Candidates and Their Images.* Pacific Palisades, Calif.: Goodyear Publishing Company, 1976.

O'Keefe, G. "Political Campaigns and Mass Communication Research," in S. H. Chaffee (ed.), *Political Communication.* Beverly Hills: Sage, 1975, pp. 129–64.

Palmgreen, P. *Mass Communication and Political Knowledge: The Effects of Political Level and Mass Media Coverage on Political Learning.* Ph.D. diss., University of Michigan, 1975.

Palmgreen, P., F. G. Kline, and P. Clarke. "Message Discrimination and Information Holding About Political Affairs." Paper presented to the International Communication Association, New Orleans, April 1974.

Patterson, T. E. and R. D. McClure. *The Unseeing Eye.* New York: Putnam, 1976.

Robinson, J. P. "Mass Communication and Information Diffusion," in F. G. Kline and P. J. Tichenor (eds.), *Current Perspectives in Mass Communication Research.* Beverly Hills: Sage, 1972, pp. 71–93.

Robinson, M. J. and K. A. McPherson. "The Early Presidential Campaign on Network Television: Accuracy and Imbalance in the Evening News." Unpublished manuscript.

Steeper, F. "Effects of the Second Presidential Debate." Paper presented at the American Association for Public Opinion Research, Buck Hill Falls, Pa., 1977.

16.

Immediate and Mediated Responses: First Debate

GLADYS ENGEL LANG and KURT LANG

Though almost three decades have passed since Hovland's experiment using army orientation films first made us aware of sleeper effects,[1] few studies of mass communications in the public opinion process have been informed by this concept. The distinction between the direct impact of a communication immediately after exposure and its more delayed effects nevertheless remains crucial. The exact meanings of a communication are not always evident in the initial encounter with its text but take time to evolve. First impressions are often modified when checked out against supplementary information, including the reactions of significant others and of credible mass media sources.

What is true for a particular communication item (like a video commercial) will be equally, and perhaps even more, true of a significant communication event (like a televised presidential debate), which invariably elicits a flood of communications, some distinctly partisan and meant to influence reactions. Others, mainly from the journalistic fraternity, provide contextual (and sometimes corrective) information as well as interpretive comment.

Especially visible in connection with press coverage is the ever more common rush toward a definitive public judgment of the event, the "instant news analysis," which the Nixon–Agnew administration attacked as a media plot to neutralize potential political gains from major appearances on television. But another form of "instant analysis" has by now become something of a science. In election year 1976, newspapers and politicians joined forces with pollsters to employ the newest technology to shorten the time lag between an event and an authoritative measure of the public response to that event.

The televised Ford–Carter debates were no exception. When, during the first encounter on September 23, 1976, the sound went dead, network newsmen immediately began to elicit evaluations of performance from partisan spokesmen, even though the debate had not yet officially terminated. Not long after the two candidates had made their final statements, TV reporters jumped in with their own judgments. All these early appraisals seemed to agree on one point, namely that neither had gained a clear advantage over his adversary. To be sure, two polls whose results were broadcast that evening (one by Roper, the other by the Associated Press) gave Ford a *slight* edge, but a *New York Times* headline two days later still read "Debate Viewed as a Draw by Experts in Both

298

Parties" and cited polls to support this view. Yet a Gallup poll published the following week showed Ford to be the "victor" by a thirteen-point margin, and the judgment based on a poll conducted on Long Island by *Newsday* was that "Ford's success in the debate seems conclusive." Recapitulations at the end of the three debates unanimously gave the first debate to Ford.

Whatever one's predilections lead one to believe, no one so far has been able to supply any really hard evidence that the reporting of such results swings votes.[2] Nevertheless, such information is definitely not ignored. Many members of the electorate are as interested as party strategists in what the polls report about the relative standing of the candidates. This is not only because the public sees the campaign as a "race" but also because a candidate's popularity represents a real political asset, which can help him shape policy and persuade a reluctant Congress. Similarly, how well a candidate does in a debate has something to do with the kind of image—as leader, as wise statesman, as "man of the people"—each is trying to project.

This rush to judgment by the media on the 1976 presidential debates afforded an opportunity to assess the extent to which the initial impact was contaminated by other political communications, especially the news commentary on the debates and on "who won." Does the quick verdict become assimilated into how viewers of the debate remember it? If the direct and immediate impact of the first debate differed from its delayed effect, as we shall try to document, this raises the question about the point in time most suitable for measuring public reaction so as to pin down definitively the debate "effect": before viewers have learned the judgments of others or after a lag sufficient for a collective definition to develop?

Description of the Study

We used a before-and-after design with two exposure conditions. All "before" questionnaires were filled out either on the day of the first debate or on the day before. Items covered what respondents were looking for, what each candidate stood for, media exposure to past and current political events, interest in the campaign and in voting, and political preferences.

Our subjects were students on the Stony Brook, New York, campus, nearly all of them undergraduates and first-time voters.[3] In a way, the study is a cross between laboratory and field experiments. One group—some of whom had completed the predebate questionnaire earlier, some completing it while waiting for the program to start—viewed the first debate under "controlled" conditions in one of three adjoining lecture halls.[4] Interaction could not be altogether prevented but was held to a minimum. Their "after" questionnaires were completed during the twenty-seven-minute gap. The other group, having first filled out the predebate questionnaire in a classroom, viewed the debate in whatever setting was available—at home, in their college dormitory, or wherever they happened to be. Since they had time to discuss the debate and to be exposed to press commentary between the time they watched the debate and the time they completed their "after" questionnaires four to seven days following the debate, their responses are considered "contaminated." Indeed, over 90 percent in the latter group said that they discussed the debates, over 80 percent that they had learned what the polls said about who "won," and 75 percent that they had read about the debates in the newspaper or news magazines. Analysis contrasts the responses of 308 students who viewed in the lecture hall and gave their reactions immediately after with responses of 386 students who viewed elsewhere and gave their reactions after some delay.[5] Those who did not view or who saw only clips on TV news are eliminated from the analysis presented here.

Questionnaires were distributed in thirteen sociology, political science, and communication classes, most of them at the introductory level, so that all majors were represented among those answering. We also publicized the public viewing of the debate and urged students to come early enough to complete our questionnaires beforehand.

Though random assignment was not possible, the two groups are subsamples of the same student population; they are surprisingly well matched on such variables as age, declared academic major, interest in the campaign, mass media exposure, intention to vote, and measures of political efficacy and cynicism. The one exception is candidate preference. The contaminated exposure group contains more who favored or, if they had not yet definitely made up their minds, were leaning toward Ford and fewer who described themselves as either totally undecided or against both candidates.[6] Consequently, all comparisons of the amount of change under the two exposure conditions are given separately for the supporters of Ford, of Carter, and of all others.

Evaluations of the First Debate

"Was the debate worth seeing?" Overwhelming majorities replied affirmatively. Supporters of either Ford or Carter were somewhat more enthusiastic than those with no distinct preference. However, responses in the week following the debate, while still favorable, had become somewhat less favorable. Only 77 percent in the contaminated group said yes, versus 93 percent in the group questioned immediately after the debate. The difference persisted across candidate preference. What was it about the debate that elicited this initial favorable response and what elements were the first to erode? Respondents were asked to rate as good, fair, or poor certain aspects of the debate format, what it revealed about the candidates and their stand on issues, and how useful it was in making up one's mind about whether and how to vote. These ratings are summarized in Table 1, where the scores represent the proportion rating the debate "good" minus the proportion rating it "poor." Thus, a positive rating indicates the degree to which the balance of evaluation was better than "fair," a negative rating the degree to which it fell below this minimum standard.

As to format, the moderator, Edwin Newman, received the highest marks for his fairness. Respondents also generally approved the questions, which they judged fair and reasonably difficult. But there was less certainty that the debate afforded opportunity to observe a direct give-and-take between the candidates; here the average rating was only "fair." In line with this, we find the debates rated higher on showing where Ford and Carter stood on issues than on the spontaneity of their replies. They were considered even less revealing of what the candidates "were really like." To some extent these ratings follow partisan lines, and those who had expressed no preference for either candidate before the debate tended to be somewhat less approving, though not consistently so.

300

Table 1: Rating* of Debate as Help in Assessing Candidates and of Debate Format by Voter Preference and Exposure

	Ford			Carter			Neither			Total		
	Immediate	Mediated	Change	Immediate	Mediated	Change	Immediate	Mediated	Change	Immediate	Mediated	Change
Format												
Give-and-take of debate	9	8	−1	10	−32	−42	1	−13	−14	4	−21	−25
Fairness of questions	62	64	+2	76	59	−17	69	60	−9	71	63	−8
Fairness on part of moderator	88	67	−21	78	72	−6	59	72	+13	77	70	−7
Difficulty of questions	59	47	−12	61	38	−23	37	32	−5	55	40	−15
Mean rating	37	34	−3	45	20	−25	28	17	−11	35	22	−13
Candidates												
What Ford is really like	20	13	−7	20	−3	−23	−9	−5	+4	13	2	−11
What Carter is really like	7	8	+1	32	1	−31	−6	−10	−4	29	1	−28
Ford's stand on issues	56	53	−3	55	24	−31	19	16	−3	41	32	−9
Carter's stand on issues	16	11	−5	59	20	−39	24	0	−24	46	14	−32
Spontaneity of Ford's replies	42	49	+7	16	3	−13	29	19	−10	24	20	−4
Spontaneity of Carter's replies	12	23	+11	41	19	−22	36	2	−34	25	20	−5
Help in Deciding												
Whether to vote	1	−15	−16	+10	−31	−41	−20	−34	−14	−2	−27	−25
How to vote	−3	−22	−19	+5	−44	−49	−23	−44	−21	−3	−37	−34
N =	(60)	(115)		(164)	(198)		(66)	(61)		(290)	(374)	

*Percent rating "good" minus percent rating "poor." A negative "change" means a downgrading, a positive one an improvement between the two exposure conditions.

Overall, the debate was judged least helpful in deciding whether and how to vote. And here again, those leaning toward either Ford or Carter evaluated the debate somewhat more favorably than those who preferred neither. A disproportionate number within this undecided and/or antagonistic group had already indicated before the debate that they neither expected nor would be looking for help in making their vote decisions.

In the *controlled-exposure group*, where responses were obtained immediately after the debate, there were no marked differences in the assessments of the debate format by Ford and Carter supporters. That Ford supporters rated the "fairness" of the moderator somewhat higher while Carter supporters thought reporters' questions somewhat fairer hardly seems significant. It is significant, however, that respondents, asked what the debate revealed about each candidate, split pretty much along partisan lines. Each camp more often saw the debate as showing what its own man was "really like," informing them where he stood on issues, and revealing the spontaneity with which he answered questions. On all these points, Carter supporters tended to rate the debate higher for what it revealed about Ford than Ford supporters rated it with regard to Carter. Yet, despite the greater influence partisan preferences appear to have had on perceptions of Ford supporters, Carter supporters actually saw the debate doing somewhat more for Carter than Ford partisans saw it doing for Ford. Those preferring neither candidate were generally most negative in assessing both the debate format and what it revealed.

These differences are also reflected in immediate reactions to the debate as a help in deciding whether and how to vote. On both counts, Carter's followers were most inclined to rate the debate better than "fair"; the net approval of help on whether to vote or not was +10, for how to vote +5. The comparable figures for Ford's following were +1 and −3 respectively, while reactions among the "neither-group" were distinctly negative.

Mediated evaluations obtained during the following week—that is, in the *delayed-response group*—were distinctly lower on nearly all counts than in the controlled-exposure group. The slippage was far greater among persons who, before the debate, had preferred Carter and whose initial reactions had apparently been most favorable than among those who had preferred Ford. Between the two exposure conditions, the relative position of Ford and Carter supporters on many measures was, indeed, reversed.

The change measure in Table 1 is the simple arithmetic difference between ratings of the controlled- and contaminated-exposure groups with the sign reversed, so that a negative number indicates a downgrading, a positive one an upgrading in approval of the particular aspect of the debate. Most downgraded by Carter supporters was "helping determine *how* to vote"—a loss of 49 points. Next, by amount of slippage, were: the give-and-take between the candidates (42), *whether* to vote (41), and Carter's issues stand (39). Moreover, Carter slipped more than Ford in the eyes of his own followers, whose vision of the debate became blurred in other respects as well. They were less sure they had learned what either Ford or Carter was really like or where each stood on issues, and they were less likely to consider the questions posed by reporters as "difficult" or answers as particularly revealing. The most serious slippage among Ford supporters was with respect to the moderator, whom Ford supporters

302   **THE GREAT DEBATES**

responding immediately had given unusually high ratings. Among Carter supporters judgments of Newman remained relatively stable.

Downgrading of the debate among persons leaning toward neither candidate was limited by the comparatively low rating given the debate format and its usefulness under the controlled-exposure condition. Yet comparisons between candidates point to a slippage in Carter imagery parallel to that which he apparently experienced among his own following. Carter "lost" more than Ford on spontaneity (-34 versus -10), on clarifying where he stood (-24 versus -3), and revealing what he was really like (-4 versus $+4$).

The Debate Performance

The question that arises is whether the candidates' performance in the debate had anything to do with this delayed downgrading of the debate, especially among those not supporting Ford. Respondents were asked before the debate, "Who do you expect to come out best in the first debate—Carter or Ford?" The follow-up question—"Who do you think came out best in the first debate?"— allowed respondents to indicate, if they wished, that "both did equally well" or "both did equally poorly."

A majority had expected Carter to "win" the debate, but the verdict went to Ford by 37 to 27. Once again there is a sharp contrast between those responding immediately and those responding during the week following. The controlled-exposure group gave the debate to Carter by roughly a seven-to-four margin, and those who saw no clear winner said both had done well twice as often as they said both had done poorly. The judgments in the contaminated-exposure group went in the opposite direction, with Ford leading Carter, by roughly the same margin, and those seeing a tie becoming somewhat less charitable and more critical of both.

The difference between the two exposure conditions persists when we look separately at responses of Ford and Carter supporters. It is not, in other words, a consequence of the different political complexions of the two groups. The immediately-after verdict splits very much along partisan lines, but Carter clearly did better among persons partial to neither debater. However, those with no preference who responded after several days' delay were equally clear in believing Ford had done better; the judgments of Carter supporters were far more evenly divided though still favoring their own candidate; while more Ford partisans thought Ford had won. The percentage of Carter supporters who thought he had done better dropped from 59 to 28 percent; among those with no preference, the drop was from 43 to 15 percent. The last group, in particular, was distinctly more inclined to say that both men had performed poorly.

Nor is this rather striking contrast between exposure conditions accounted for by differences in predebate expectations. An almost identical 64 percent in the immediate-response group and 62 percent in the delayed-response group expected Carter to win. Nearly two-thirds of all perceptions about who did better were concordant with prior expectations. But expectations of a Carter win were more often confirmed in the controlled-exposure condition; pro-Ford expectations in the contaminated condition. Furthermore, the Carter confirmation rate drops somewhat more between the two conditions than the Ford confirmation rate rises. Ford's gains were greatest among those who had expected him to do better all along, and Carter's losses concentrated among those who before the debate had expected Ford to lose. We are observing shift and not just erosion.

Candidate Imagery

Our pre-questionnaire included an adjective list culled from the media coverage of the campaign, with respondents asked to indicate for each whether it did or did not describe the candidates. The list was repeated on the post-questionnaire. These responses are summarized in Table 2. The "before" column shows how the followers of Ford and Carter rated their own candidate on each adjective relative to the other candidate. The values represent differences, not actual ratings of the candidates. That is to say, they indicate the extent to which each candidate was perceived by his own supporters as having a *distinctive* image: the smaller the difference (that is, the lower the value) next to a descriptor, the more similar do the candidates appear within the particular constituency. Whether this is because both candidates have equally high or low ratings is not shown. A positive sign in the "before" columns denotes that respondents are more ready to attribute the particular trait to the candidate they favor than to his opponent. This is usually the case for traits judged positively. When partisans more often pin a label on the other candidate, the characterization usually has negative undertones.

There is, of course, nothing absolute about this tendency. On some labels the consensus cuts across partisan lines. Even before the first debate, Carter and Ford supporters alike considered Ford the clumsier, the more conservative, and the more predictable; Carter was seen as the more religious, liberal, vague, and opportunistic of the two. Ford had higher standing as an administrator, but Carter was believed to be better at debating. On ten other descriptors, perceptions of the candidates were distinctly partisan. Before the debate, the favored candidate consistently had the edge on honesty, intelligence, knowledgeability, presidential appearance, sincerity, and trustworthiness, but Ford supporters seemed to have had none of the doubts that apparently plagued Carter's following about their own candidate's evasiveness and vagueness relative to his opponent.

The shift columns are to be viewed in an analogous fashion. A positive shift indicates that the trait was seen as applying more clearly to the preferred candidate relative to the other after the debate than before; a negative shift indicates a movement in the opposite direction. When viewed in the controlled condition, the first debate tended to accentuate partisan perceptions. Carter generally did better among his potential constituency than Ford did among his. The only descriptor on which he clearly lost ground relative to Ford was on presidential appearance. Although the measure shown does not discriminate between gains due to one's candidate's positive projection or his opponent's deficiency, that Ford managed to cash in on his incumbency is clear from other evidence. Ford's gains are generally less consistent than Carter's, but he did apparently manage to persuade his following that he could match Carter in debating skill, while the latter merely maintained the advantage his supporters gave him from the beginning.

304

Table 2: Candidate Perceptions Before and After First Debate by Preference and Exposure

	Prefer Ford				Prefer Carter			
	Difference Before	Shift		Gain or Loss	Difference Before	Shift		Gain or Loss
		Immediate	Mediated			Immediate	Mediated	
Partisan Traits								
Corrupt	−.13	−.05	−.02	+.03	−.31	+.04	+.20	+.16*
Evasive	−.49	−.26	−.45	−.19	−.02	−.37	−.04	+.33†
Genuine	+.48	−.26	−.08	+.18	+.22	+.40	+.24	−.16
Honest	+.41	−.07	−.02	+.05	+.24	+.28	+.13	−.15
Intelligent	+.06	+.07	+.09	+.02	+.48	+.21	+.03	−.18†
Knowledgeable	+.18	+.19	+.27	+.12	+.27	+.03	−.14	−.17
Presidential	+.67	+.32	+.28	−.04	+.36	−.16	−.40	−.24*
Sincere	+.53	−.32	−.17	+.15	+.21	+.38	+.22	−.16
Trustworthy	+.45	−.17	−.05	+.12	+.26	+.04	+.01	−.03
All Partisan				−.08				−1.58†
Competence								
Experienced Administrator	+.68	+.19	+.40	+.21	−.08	+.30	+.01	−.29†
Good Debater	−.04	+.26	+.49	+.23	+.40	+.04	−.41	−.45**
Combined				+.45†				−.74**
Ford Traits								
Clumsy	+.62	−.49	−.49	00	−1.00	+.60	+.55	−.05
Conservative	+.64	+.25	+.23	−.02	−.68	−.44	−.61	−.17
Predictable	+.44	−.49	−.14	+.35*	−.38	−.04	−.25	−.29
Carter Traits								
Liberal	−.49	−.04	−.49	−.45†	+.65	+.27	+.17	−.10
Opportunistic	−.38	+.02	−.11	−.13	+.20	+.02	−.01	−.03
Religious	−.41	+.12	−.06	−.18	+.64	−.27	−.03	+.24†
Vague	−.60	−.05	−.36	−.31	+.07	−.25	−.08	+.17

*p ≤ .05   †p ≤ .01   **p ≤ .001

Yet insofar as our main analytic problem here is to differentiate between contaminated and controlled exposure, the critical columns for this purpose are those labeled "gain or loss." They summarize the difference between the shifts under the two exposure conditions. For example, in both exposure groups, Ford supporters had come to see Ford as even less evasive relative to Carter than they had before the debate. Among Carter supporters, shifts on evasiveness are smaller but tend to favor Carter, because Ford also appeared to be evasive. Most important, time elapsed since viewing changed perceptions of Ford supporters on this trait much less ($-.19$) than those of Carterites ($+.33$), thereby once again putting their candidate in a position close to parity with Ford. Since evasiveness is a negative trait, the net shift among these viewers went against Carter.

The pattern of gains and losses resembles that previously observed for evaluations of the debate. The difference between the immediate and the mediated response is almost invariably in the same direction, regardless of partisan preferences; that is, a gain for Ford among his following goes with a loss for Carter among those leaning toward him before the debate. Ford, who had gained very little in the controlled-exposure condition, managed to improve his standing vis-à-vis Carter where exposure was contaminated. His gains among his own followers between the two conditions were on being a "good debater," genuine, sincere, knowledgeable, and trustworthy; his "losses" were on being vague and evasive. On presidential bearing and honesty, there was no change, but Ford's admirers had scored him high on these traits before the debate.

While the image of Ford improved within his own constituency, Carter lost ground with his. Persons responding days after the debate gave him relatively lower ratings on being a "good debater," an "experienced administrator," presidential, intelligent, knowledgeable, sincere, genuine, and honest; "gains" on being evasive, vague, and corrupt were, in fact, political losses.

Respondents were also asked which traits had been highlighted by the debate. Most often mentioned was Ford's conservatism; Carter's liberal views also ranked high, being cited by slightly over one-third of the respondents. But in the week after the debate, it was among the Ford supporters that the conception of ideological differences between the candidates was sharpened: Ford held his own on being the more conservative and gained 45 points as being the less liberal. Gains Carter scored on being the less liberal within his own group were smaller, and on liberalism he actually suffered a loss relative to Ford.

Issues

In the main the debate highlighted candidate differences on issues students had chosen before the debate as important in making up their minds (Table 3). An exception was the candidates' stand on amnesty for draft evaders, but 65 percent of the respondents had been aware of differences on this issue beforehand, and it had not ranked particularly high as a vote determining factor. Respondents were very much aware of differences on four other issues highlighted by the debate—level of government spending, unemployment, the tax burden on the middle classes, and inflation—which were considered important for one's vote, and these differences were further accentuated by the debate.

On the other hand, abortion, an issue where a majority saw significant differences between the candidates, did not surface in the first debate, and no noticeable changes in perceptions followed. On abortion, as on five other issues —equal rights for minorities, farm subsidies, church–state relations, marijuana, and aid to Israel—there was a slight decline in the number perceiving significant differences, probably because the issue was not discussed, not because the two candidates sounded so much alike. Among the issues *not* highlighted, invasion of privacy was the only one with a modest but unexplained increase of differences, which cannot be attributed to the debate.

Table 3: Perceptions of Issues, Differences between Candidates, and Issues Highlighted in First Debate by Exposure (in percentage)

Issues (in order of declining importance)†	Significant Difference Before	Decrease in Number Who Saw Differences between Candidates after Debate		Issues Highlighted in Debate	
		Immediate	Mediated	Immediate	Mediated
Unemployment	52	29	28	81	79
Inflation	58	23	19	60	60
Tax on Middle Class	49	25	24	74	71
Federal Aid to Education	44	21	18	48	41
Environment	34	32	4	32	4
Government Spending	70	19	15	88	86
Rights for Minorities	30	0	−4	10	12
Invasions of Privacy	21	10	12	*	5
Military Outlays	62	−7	11	16	50
Urban Aid	59	3	11	35	40
Nat'l Health Insurance	48	3	9	30	29
Abortion	53	−10	6	1	10
Draft Amnesty	65	24	21	92	83
Aid to Israel	39	−11	−10	*	5
Church–State	22	−13	−8	0	3
Marijuana	30	−9	−3	0	1
Farm Subsidies	45	−11	5	8	23

*less than .5 percent
†Importance = percentage who said the stand taken by either candidate would be important in making up their mind.

On issues, we find noticeably less differences between the two exposure conditions than we found on performance and candidate imagery. The biggest difference occurred with regard to protection of the environment, one of the more salient issues but one where only a minority had seen a significant difference between the two candidates before the debate. The debate seems to have enhanced perceptions of a difference among the controlled-exposure group, but any such change appears to have been dissipated within the week following, when few people acknowledged that the debate highlighted this difference. Those who cared about the environment may have been scrutinizing the debate for clues about the candidates' stand on this issue, but the lack of emphasis in the post-debate commentary helped condemn it to oblivion.

With regard to military spending, constitutional amendment on abortion, and farm subsidies, the trend is the other way around. An initial decrease in perceived differences immediately after the debate is followed by a recovery beyond the original level. Although the recovery is accompanied by an increase in the number who "saw" the difference highlighted in the debate, the fact that only 16, 1, and 8 percent, respectively, of the controlled-exposure group made this connection speaks against the debate as a direct influence. The increase in perceived difference is probably attributable to commentary and other communications about the debate.

Landslide and Underdog Perceptions

The contrast between the immediate impact of the debate and the mediated responses obtained after several days delay point to the attenuation of some short-run effects. There was, as we observed, a general downgrading of the debate: less approval of its format, of its usefulness, and of the information it provided. Also, evaluations of the relative performance of the two candidates differed. Within the controlled-exposure group, Carter was perceived as the winner; for those responding in the week following, he had become the loser. During the same interval, Carter's personal image also suffered some erosion, but there was little change in the number perceiving significant differences between the candidates on those issues highlighted by the first debate.

Were these changes translatable into a movement of votes that almost gained Ford the election? Did the support for Carter soften as a result?

Obviously, one would not expect many changes in vote intention in so short a span of time, and the large majority with a preference before the debate, no matter how weak, did not switch or waver. The dominant change, if it is a change, was in the direction of reinforcement; that is, persons became "more certain" and "more eager" to vote rather than the reverse (Table 4). Also, a considerable number of crystallizations occurred among those initially unwilling to state a preference between the two major candidates. Here Carter gained slightly more than Ford. But comparison of the two exposure conditions suggests once again that some of the Carter gains immediately following the debate may have eroded. The erosion, however subtle, manifests itself in a number of ways. First, there are the actual changes in preference. Those responding immediately less often switched away from Carter or wavered in their preference for the Georgia governor than those responding during the week after. Also, crystallization among those initially behind neither candidate favored Carter in the immediate-response group and Ford in the delayed condition. Second, among Carter supporters the net increase in both certainty of preference and eagerness to vote was greater than among the Ford constituency; days later changes favored Ford. Whatever losses Ford seems to have suffered immediately after the debate were recouped.

These findings must nevertheless be qualified. The changes observed are perceptions and preferences, not definite vote intention, and the sample is atypi-

THE GREAT DEBATES

Table 4: Changes in Vote Preference, Certainty, and Eagerness to Vote
After First Debate by Exposure and Initial Preference (in percentage)

	Ford		Carter		Neither	
	Immediate	Mediated	Immediate	Mediated	Immediate	Mediated
No Change	70	78	80	76	55	58
Wavered*	16	10	9	11		
Switched	14	12	11	13		
Crystallized						
Ford					11	26
Carter					35	16
	(58)	(114)	(168)	(203)	(66)	(62)
More Certain	38	22	37	22	27	13
No Change	49	71	55	59	56	75
Less Certain	13	7	8	19	17	13
	(61)	(117)	(170)	(202)	(70)	(63)
More Eager to Vote	42	22	39	21	32	14
No Change	42	70	54	59	58	72
Less Eager	16	8	7	20	10	14
	(50)†	(98)†	(148)†	(179)†	(31)†	(43)†

*Now "undecided"
†Eligible to vote only

cal even though a student population without long-standing political loyalties and civic commitments may be an unusually sensitive indicator of shifting sentiment. In addition, there is an underlying consistency about all the data together. They indicate a gradually developing feeling that Carter, unlike John F. Kennedy in 1960, had not scored heavily and that, regardless of one's personal reaction, Ford had therefore improved his chances for election by the debate. Respondents were very much aware that Ford had trailed badly in the polls. In response to a direct question, more respondents pinned the underdog label on Ford (29 percent) than on Carter (17 percent); the rest had no clear perception of either. Among those responding immediately after the debate, there was a slight but insignificant increase in underdog perceptions of Ford. The contaminated-exposure group was as likely to think of Carter as of Ford as underdog. This label is, of course, related to a person's expectation of who would win in November. By and large the followers of each candidate considered his prospects better than his opponent's. Therefore, those with no candidate preference before the debate provide the best indications of changing perceptions. Within this group, there was a sharp contrast between those responding immediately after and those responding some days later. A clear majority in the controlled-exposure group expected Carter to win; in the contaminated-exposure group this expectation was reversed.

Implications

There are several alternative explanations for our findings. The question here is: which accords most closely with the data presented? A first explanation relates to the *nature of the two exposure conditions*. Unless experimental contamination is ruled out as a cause of variation, no other explanation has any credence.

All persons who filled out questionnaires distributed during the twenty-seven-minute sound gap had witnessed this first debate from its beginning. We can be less certain about exposure to the debate among those responding later —we had to rely on their self-reports. Only those saying they watched the debate "live" were included. Of these, 84 percent had definitely seen the beginning of the debate and 79 percent indicated they had kept watching during the gap. However, even when responses of those who did not see *both* the beginning and the gap are omitted from the analysis, the contrast between the immediate and mediated response group remains.

Still, the difference in reaction may be a function of viewing in a group versus viewing as individuals.[7] For students in the lecture hall, the debate was a spectacle luring people from their dorms and digs to a public "happening"; for those watching the debate under other conditions, viewing was a far more routine event. While we cannot completely ignore the possible influence of the viewing situation, we nevertheless discount its significance for several reasons. First, we were able to minimize interaction among the lecture hall audience, so much so that any group effect was probably weaker than that found among those viewing in the residence halls (where one-third of the later-response group watched). It is also probable that most of those viewing at home also viewed in groups and so were subject to group effects. Given these conditions, in what direction might group viewing influence response? Possibly, those at the public viewing might have come prepared for more of a spectacle and thus have been more susceptible to disappointment than those whose viewing was more routine. But we have no evidence that the two groups differed in what they wanted to see or expected to see.

A second line of explanation focuses on *erosion over time*. If erosion were a matter of mere forgetting, any initial effect of the debate would wear off. Both candidates would soon revert to their predebate standing. But this is not what happened. Some of the initial gains, namely Ford's, were selectively reinforced between the two conditions. It was the candidates' personal images and evaluations of their performance, which are less subject to "forgetting" than overall impressions, which changed more in favor of Ford than perceptions of how the two had differed on some particular issue during the debate.

Third, differences over time might be explained as a *strain toward cognitive consistency* to redress a short-run imbalance between partisan preferences and perceptions of the candidates created by the debate. This is to say, as the week wore on, the perceptions of Carter by Carter's following should have become more favorable, and Ford should also have been defined more positively by his potential supporters. Yet our findings provide no evidence that the short-run effect of viewing was to increase imbalance. Immediate changes in candidate perceptions were by and large along partisan lines, with an increase in consistency translated into greater certainty about one's preference and greater eagerness to vote. What remains unexplained is the one-sided difference between the controlled and contaminated conditions, with cognitions of Carter supporters becoming less, not more, consistent with time.

Specifically political factors suggest still a fourth line of explanation. Carter's support among college students had been generally diagnosed as "soft." Our own subjects were no exception. Yet, inasmuch as the proportion of "certain" relative to that of "undecided but learning toward" was the same for Carter as for Ford, supporters of both seemed equally open to persuasive influence from the debate, except that pro-Republican pressure on "contaminateds," who apparently moved in a more Republican milieu, may have been greater than pressure on those within or hovering about the Carter camp. In this way, an initial response favorable to Carter could have been neutralized by competitive campaign influences. This explanation can satisfactorily account for certain changes in imagery but *not* for other attitudinal shifts, such as downgrading the debate as useful in arriving at a decision on voting. It is plausible only if we make the additional assumption that what persons "saw" or "learned from" the debate was effectively counteracted by communications to which persons were exposed in the week following.

This brings us to the fifth explanation, the one that seems most satisfactory to us. *The contaminated group must have been influenced by communications about the debate to which no one in the controlled-exposure condition could possibly have been exposed.* The collective definition of the debate—the way it emerged in the public mind—did not depend solely on what each viewer had experienced by himself or herself in intimate communion with the TV set. Rather, it developed over time by way of a process in which each person's impressions were constantly tested against those of others, including interpretative and analytic commentaries offered by authoritative mass media sources. Impressions gained directly from the debate were accordingly modified and elaborated. Those that diverged too much from this consensus enjoyed little support and, consequently, were likely to fade until they were no longer expressed. Persons within the controlled-exposure condition had given their evaluations without the benefit of any such give-and-take.

Taken together, our findings suggest that most respondents were aware of the drift in sentiment. There was a feeling that Carter was slipping and that Ford, who was rapidly closing the gap, could no longer be considered the underdog. The awareness that the debate contributed to this shift was pronounced in the contaminated-exposure group. As yet, no bandwagon for Ford was about to roll, but the belief that the debate had improved Ford's chances was gaining ground. Such "landslide" perceptions apparently had their origin in media reports.

Less than systematic analysis of media debate coverage supports this contention. One recurrent theme, largely based on polls but also expressed as private estimates, was that Ford had "won" the first debate. This view predominated among the delayed-response group but not those responding directly. The difference could be designated a "polling effect" but is more correctly a reflection of the overall image conveyed by the media. A second theme casts doubts on the efficacy of the debate as a campaign device. Before the debate, both electronic and print press invoked the image of Kennedy skillfully using this format to turn the tide against Nixon. By contrast Carter had failed dismally. His "failure" as a debate performer spilled over to other aspects of his image. Negative evaluations dampened enthusiasm not only for the candidate but for the debate as conducted. Unfavorable comparisons to 1960 were common even though the 1976 series had lasted longer, involved more penetrating questioning of the candidates, and forced them to stick closer to the point than Kennedy and Nixon had.

The comparison between the more positive response immediately after the debate and the more negative delayed response suggests that if Carter was judged wanting, this was mostly against the background of high expectations shaped by the relevant past. The press did its part by deploring the lackluster performance of both Carter and Ford, suggesting that how either man handled himself was irrelevant to his ability to meet the requirement of office, and thereby inadvertently helping Ford exploit the advantage of his incumbency. But which candidate gained more from the debate and why is hardly the point. What matters is that the impact of the 1976 debates cannot be assessed without taking full cognizance of the context provided by other and less dramatic communications.

NOTES

1. See C. Hovland, A. A. Lumsdaine, and F. D. Sheffield (1949). The sleeper effect represents delayed conversion and has been used to refer to "coming around" to the communicator's point of view after a period of time. See also W. R. Catton, Jr. (1960), pp. 348–54, and C. Hovland, I. L. Janis, and H. H. Kelley (1953), pp. 19–55.

2. For a good summary of the evidence on polling effects see H. Mendelsohn and I. Crespi (1970), pp. 17–25. A discussion of less direct effects of published poll results on voter behavior is in K. and G. E. Lang (1968).

3. Faculty members who were of invaluable assistance in distributing these questionnaires include Susan Chambre, Tom Jukam, William Linehan, Norman Luttweg, Kristen Monroe, Norman Prusslin, Sasha Weitman, and Gerald Zeitz. Our thanks.

4. Special mention is due Richard Carlson and Richard DeSimone, staff members of Stony Brook's Educational Communications Center who made both the viewing and taping of the debates possible. Carl Roberts, a graduate student in sociology, joined us both in drawing up the questionnaire and in preparing the data for computer analysis. Other students Robert Stevenson, Robin Landberg, and Merilee Newman provided invaluable help with the coding.

5. This paper reports only one aspect of the study which was originally designed to help understand more about so-called political apathy and alienation among young voters. A third brief questionnaire was distributed after the last debate. The need to protect anonymity made it difficult to recontact respondents not originally contacted in classrooms. Still, we have 428 persons filling out three questionnaires, 393 only the first and second, 60 only the first and third, 216 only the pre-questionnaire, 125 only the second, and 79 only the final.

6. This probably reflects the higher proportion of commuting students who viewed the debate at home. Long Island (Nassau and Suffolk counties) is still disproportionately Republican.

7. Experimental studies contrasting the differential effects of viewing in large assembled groups, small informal groups, and alone are hard to come by. Research on the social context of exposure to communications is concisely summarized in W. Weiss (1969), p. 85.

REFERENCES

Catton, W. R., Jr. "Changing Cognitive Structure as a Basis for the Sleeper Effect." *Social Forces*, 1960 (38).

Hovland, C., I. L. Janis, and H. H. Kelley. *Communication and Persuasion*. New Haven, Conn.: Yale University Press, 1953.

Hovland, C., A. A. Lumsdaine, and F. D. Sheffield. *Experiments on Mass Communication*. Princeton, N.J.: Princeton University Press, 1949.

Lang, K. and G. E. Lang. *Voting and Nonvoting*. Boston: Blaisdell, 1968.

Mendelsohn, H. and I. Crespi. *Polls, Television, and the New Politics*. Scranton, Pa.: Chandler Publishing, 1970.

Weiss, W. "Effects of the Mass Media of Communication" in G. Lindzey and E. Arson, *The Handbook of Social Psychology*, Vol. V (2nd ed.). Reading, Mass.: Addison-Wesley Publishing, 1969.

17.

Impact on Partisan, Image, and Issue Voting

JACK DENNIS, STEVEN H. CHAFFEE, and SUN YUEL CHOE

A notable recent trend in American voting behavior has been the marked decline in identification with a political party as a determinant of the vote. During the turbulent late 1960s, specific issue positions replaced party ties as the strongest predictor in voting research (Nie, Verba, and Petrocik, 1976; Brody and Page, 1972; Page and Brody, 1972; Boyd, 1972; Kessel, 1972; Pomper, 1972; and RePass, 1971). To be sure, partisanship still has considerable explanatory power, but it is no longer the overwhelming single factor that it was through the 1950s. This is due in part to the fact that fewer people identify with any political party today; it also reflects a lessened probability that those who retain a partisan self-image will vote on that basis (Dennis, 1975). Since both of these tendencies are especially marked in the youngest voters, we should expect the decline in the explanatory importance of partisanship to continue (Nie et al., 1976).

This steady diminution of the salience of partisanship opens up some interesting research opportunities for students of the role of mass communication in American electoral politics. The earliest voter surveys in the 1940s had found that partisan predispositions greatly overshadowed policy issues and news events in determining voter reactions to presidential campaigns (Lazarsfeld, Berelson, and Gaudet, 1944; Berelson, Lazarsfeld, and McPhee, 1954). The subsequent decline of partisan loyalty invites a reexamination of the potential impact of the mass media on the voting decision. In mass communication the dominant phenomenon of the intervening quarter-century since the early voting studies has, of course, been the emergence of television. A new major mass medium has the potential to transform the electoral decision process in significant ways. If we are in an era of greater issue voting, as at least the 1972 election studies suggest we might be (Miller, Miller, Raine, and Brown, 1975), one should consider such questions as whether our present-day media raise issues to a central position in campaign discourse (even when the candidates or parties fail to do so); whether the media convey more substantive issue content than voters would otherwise receive; the extent to which different media transmit (or distort) the issue positions of each party or candidate; and how the media set the political agenda by making some issues more salient than others. At the same time, given

314

television's highly personalized presentation of public affairs, the "image" of each candidate in the mind of the voter also commends itself to study. During the era in which issue voting has overtaken party voting, it appears that voting on the basis of candidate personalities has remained at approximately the same level of importance (Nie et al., 1976).

What we are raising is the broad proposition that the news media may well have taken on, in an era of dwindling partisanship and growing issue-consciousness, new electoral functions that go well beyond the very circumscribed role ascribed to them in the earlier "limited effects model" (Klapper, 1960). Political conditions have changed sufficiently to provide the *opportunity* for a considerably greater impact of mass communication on the vote than the traditional formulation would suggest (Chaffee, 1975; Kraus and Davis, 1976).

It is a widely accepted generalization that political mass communication mostly results not in conversion but in *reinforcement*—a term that is often all too loosely defined. Reinforcement is sometimes used to describe cases where a person's mildly partisan stand becomes a more extreme one, or a tentative decision evolves into a firm one. The label "mere reinforcement" is applied to cases where, following exposure to argumentative material, there is no evidence of change in the person's position.

In this paper, we will employ a more empirical, multivariate conception of reinforcement, which we can tentatively call *bonding*. Extensive political information of a bipartisan variety, reaching a large and heterogeneous audience via the mass media, should have the general effect of bonding together the many elements that contribute to the voting decision. This would manifest itself empirically in a strengthening of the correlations between the vote and such predictors as socioeconomic status, party, ideology, policy issues, and candidate images. Which of these factors becomes dominant depends on the character of the media presentation and of the person receiving it.

The debates phase of the 1976 presidential campaign lent itself particularly well to the study of these factors. The debates provided a rich collection of political information via television, at a time when both presidential candidates were finding it difficult to attract strong support. Their huge national audience included many voters who were waiting to see what the candidates said and did before committing themselves to firm voting decisions.

For the voter who lacked a partisan basis for voting, the debates could provide both "issue" and "image" cues to guide his or her decision. And for the partisan voter they offered an opportunity to assess one's party's choice against one's own political evaluations.

Design

Our study was set in the state of Wisconsin, one of the most crucial states in the 1976 election. Telephone interviewing, with sampling based on area codes, prefixes, and four random digits, was used throughout the study.[1] The first wave of interviewing was completed just before the first debate (T_1: September 17–23). Those who agreed to be reinterviewed were called again, between the first and second debates (T_2: September 24–October 6). Two more waves of reinterviewing followed, one after completion of the four debates but before the election (T_3: October 23–November 1), and the final wave after the election

(T_4: November 3–29). Across these four waves, there was a continuing panel of N = 164 respondents who were interviewed all four times. In this paper we will report results based only on those 164 respondents for whom we have a full set of data. To judge from the election results, this was a highly representative sample: 49.6 percent reported voting for Carter, and 48.9 percent for Ford, while the corresponding Wisconsin actual vote figures were 49.4 percent and 47.8 percent. For the main variables—vote intention, party identification, issue positions, candidate images, debate viewing, and other attention to the campaign —measures were repeated in each wave (T_1–T_3) that were as nearly identical in wording as was practicable. Some of these were also asked in the post-election (T_4) wave.

Vote intention was measured on an eleven-point scale in the T_1–T_3 waves, ranging from a score of 1 for those sure to vote for Carter, up to 11 for those certain they would vote for Ford. (Intermediate points on this scale indicated a feeling that there was "some chance" or a "good chance" the voter might switch, or "undecided" or "undecided but leaning.") All other scales were scored in the same direction (high scores favorable to Ford) so that positive correlations would indicate consistency among measures. Personal image questions were measured on five-point scales, with the following items asked of each candidate in each wave: honesty and integrity, strength and decisiveness, friendliness and pleasantness, capacity for effective leadership of the government, clarity on the issues, and ability to inspire confidence as a speaker. Five-point scales were also used to measure the respondent's own position and the positions ascribed to Ford and Carter on each of four issues: unemployment, tax reform, abortion, and defense spending (see Table 1). The distances of each candidate from the respondent were calculated, and then the absolute difference between these two scores was used in data analysis. Ideological differences were calculated in the same way, using the distances of each candidate from the respondent on a five-point "liberal-conservative" scale. Party identification was measured on a five-point continuum, with "independent" in the middle, "strong" Democrats and Republicans at the extremes, and "weak" identifiers and "leaning" independents grouped together at the intermediate points. An index of socioeconomic status was constructed from measures of education (years), income, and occupational prestige (Featherman, Sobel, and Dickens, 1975).

Findings
Viewing and Judging

Since our overall goal is to assess the impact of the debates on the audience, a preliminary but critical question is how large that audience was. We found rather high levels of viewing overall. A solid majority of our respondents were exposed to all or part of the three debates between Ford and Carter, the lowest figure being 59 percent for the second debate. About 36 percent also saw the Mondale–Dole vice-presidential debate. At the same time there was a sizable minority of the population who did not watch the debates at all. They, plus those who watched only portions of the debates, or only one or two, give us a basis for comparing respondents in terms of the *extent* of debate exposure.

When asked after the debates which candidate the voter felt had "won," the most common response to each debate was to judge it as a tie. Among those

316   THE GREAT DEBATES

respondents who did perceive a winner, the majority believed that Ford won the first debate (37 percent–14 percent), Carter the second (46–20), Mondale the third (48–17), and Ford the final debate (29–24). It is clear that neither candidate scored an all-out, crushing victory over his opponent as far as Wisconsin voters were concerned.

Vote Decisions

The major potential impact of the debates that we are concerned with here is on the vote decision. The first question is whether the voting intentions of our respondents changed during the course of the study. Carter enjoyed his greatest margin of support—53 percent to 44 percent—prior to the debates. After the first debate, which Ford was popularly judged to have won, he had made up most of this ground on Carter, whose lead shrank to 3 percentage points (50–47). Ford's surge was not sustained throughout the debates period, however; Carter held a 51–48 lead after the final debate, and finally managed to capture Wisconsin's electoral votes by less than two percentage points. While we found only one case of switching from one candidate to the other, our respondents did not hurry into firm voting decisions. Only about 30 percent were certain how they would vote before the debates and never wavered. At T_1 only 55 percent had a preference between the candidates. At T_2 this rose to 63 percent, and then to 70 percent after the debates (T_3). Finally at T_4, 83 percent of them said they had cast a ballot on election day. So, even though the net Carter–Ford difference was changing only slightly, there were many vote decisions being made during the debates period.

Ford and Carter gained nearly equal increments of support from each time-point to the next; there were similarly equal decrements in both the "leaning" and the "not voting/no preference" categories over time. From the perspective of potential impact of the debates, these aggregate findings are encouraging, even though it is by no means clear that any of the trends we found can be attributed to the debates as distinct from other campaign stimuli and events. While a sizable degree of voter doubt still remained after the debates, this doubt had declined markedly from the level that existed before the debates.[2] And the very bipartisan pattern of decision-making, with about equal numbers shifting in each direction, is worth noting in view of the rigorously bipartisan character of the debates themselves.

Parties, Issues, and Images

We theorized that a number of psychological factors would provide links between the debates and the vote. These include partisan (and ideological) self-identification, personal images of the candidates, and perceived proximity to the candidates on current issues. These variables did not change significantly over time during our study, but there remains room for variation in their respective degrees of association with the vote, at different times and among different groups.

With identical measures at three time-points, we were able to make separate estimates of measurement reliability, and the stability of each of the variables measured (Heise, 1969). The only scales that were not highly stable were the comparative evaluations of the two candidates' speaking ability (.56), and the issue distance scores on tax reform (.60) and defense spending (.65). Reliability of measurement was highest for party identification (.94), moderate for liberal-conservative ideology (.64) and image items (.67 to .82), and a bit lower for three of the four issue distance measures (.56 to .70). The last finding is not surprising, since three different scores are involved in calculating the issue distances. The volatile abortion issue, on which the sample respondents tended to have extreme opinions, is the only one that could be accurately characterized as unreliable (.28).

The high stability of our image and issue measures is a discouraging finding, insofar as the hypothesis that the debates might directly modify these elements of the vote decision is concerned. Our results are unlike those of the 1960 debates studies, where some important mean changes in the images of Kennedy and Nixon were found (Tannenbaum et al., 1962). On the other hand, there were some (stable) differences between Carter and Ford. For example, Ford was consistently described as clearer in his positions on issues, and he also had an advantage in perceived strength and decisiveness; Carter's issue positions—notably on unemployment and tax reform—were closer to those of the average voter.

Bonding

Our main theoretical expectation was not, however, that the debates would dramatically alter candidate images or issue differences, but that they would strengthen the relationships between these factors and the vote. In various research literatures, this general process may be part of what is meant by such terms as "crystallization," "reduction of dissonance," or "reinforcement." But our hypothesis of *bonding* is a bit more positive in character, a process through which the voter is able to connect the various influences on her/his thoughts and feelings about the candidates and to develop an integrated, affirmative behavior: the vote.

Figures 1 and 2 provide a picture of the bonding process over the course of our study, as represented by the correlations at each time-point of each image item (Fig. 1) and issue item (Fig. 2), with the vote intention at that time. The most important fact in each figure is that these correlations gradually increased from T_1 to T_3, whereas the correlation between party identification and the vote did not (see Fig. 2).

More specifically, perceived leadership was a very strong correlate, particularly after the first debate. But as Figure 1 shows, all of the image items grew in the strength of their relationship to the vote intention from T_1 to T_3. The bonding between image perceptions and the vote was at its peak just prior to election day. Similarly for issues, it is clear in Figure 2 that two topics that were discussed in the first debate, unemployment and the tax system, jumped sharply from T_1 to T_2 in their association with vote intention. Defense, a major topic in later debates, shows a gradual increase in importance from T_1 to T_3. Abortion, a divisive issue that was avoided in the debates, remained a weak predictor of vote intention throughout the fall.

We can also distinguish between candidate attributes that are relevant to one's capacity to perform as president versus personality characteristics that have little to do with competence for high office. The substantive issues for

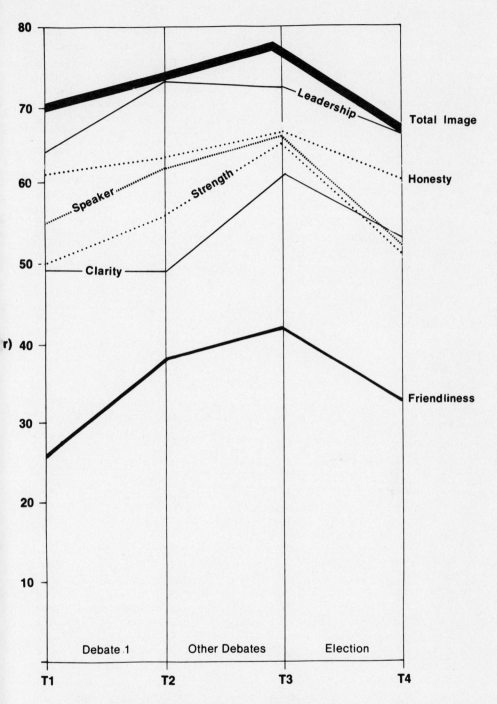

Fig. 1: Synchronous Zero-Order Correlation between T_1 Image Difference Score and T_1 Vote Intention Score (N = 164)

CARTER vs. FORD, 1976   319

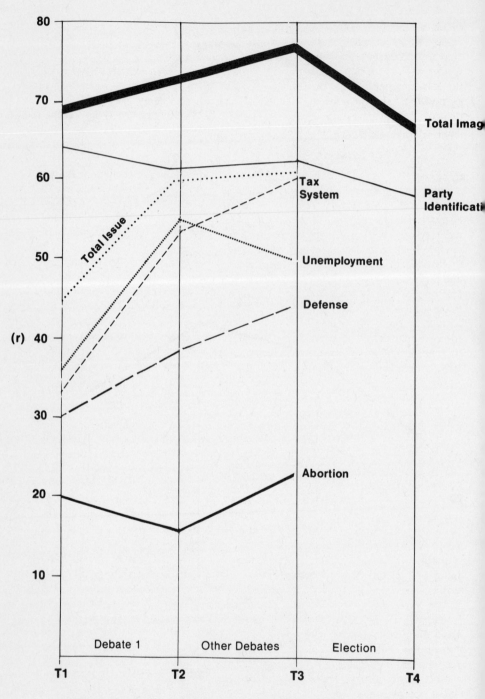

Fig. 2: Synchronous Zero-Order Correlation between T_1 Issue Difference Score and T_1 Vote Intention Score (N = 164)

THE GREAT DEBATES

which presidential leadership is important—unemployment, taxation, and defense—all increased in importance from T_1 to T_3, as did the competence-relevant attributes of leadership, and strength and decisiveness. The weakest predictors of the vote throughout the preelection period were friendliness (probably the least competence-relevant image measure in our questionnaire) and clarity of positions and speaking ability. Perhaps the most surprising finding in the light of this comparison is the importance of the "honesty and integrity" of the candidate. Previous research had not led us to expect this attribute to loom especially large, but it seems to have been a highly salient one in the post-Watergate context.

The debates period was also associated with greater differentiation among issues. Economic issues (tax reform, unemployment) were always at the top in this (limited) competition among our measures. But the gap between them and abortion became considerably greater during the debate period. Economic issues were, of course, the ones given greatest attention in the debates; they were also among those of greatest salience to the general population.[3]

If we compare (in Fig. 2) the relative association of total image, total issues, and party identification, we see at all stages of the contest that image differences are the most highly associated with intended vote. But one should bear in mind that we measured only four issues from a much larger universe of policy questions that people were concerned about; and one of these (abortion) turned out to be of relatively low general salience. Had we included a more extensive list of issue measures, the total issue index might well have equaled or exceeded both images and party identification as a correlate of the vote.

Bonding and Debate Exposure

Table 1 takes a different approach to the analysis of specific image and issue items. Here the sample has been broken down into the low, medium, and high exposure groups based on the extent to which people said they had watched the four debates. Since the image and issue item scores were quite stable over time, for this analysis we have summed each respondent's scores across the four waves. These summed item scores are then correlated with the *change* in vote from the person's T_1 voting intention to the actual (T_4) vote. These changes in vote during the period of the debates are associated with some items more strongly than with others, but the differences also depend on the extent to which the person was exposed to the debates.

The total image difference perceived between the candidates is associated more with changes in the low-exposure group than is the case among those who watched the debates. Further, every image item shows a decrease in correlation as one moves from the low- to the high-exposure group (Table 1). This finding is contrary to the belief that the debates are mainly image-enhancing events. Issue differences, on the other hand, are important primarily in the high-exposure group. Party identification has its greatest apparent T_1–T_4 impact in the medium-exposure category, while ideological differences are more important in the other two groups—those who watched the debates regularly and those who didn't watch them at all.

Since we are dealing in Table 1 exclusively with vote decisions that were made after our T_1 interviews, and since none of the predictor variables changed

Table 1: Correlations between Image/Issue Differences and Vote Changes, by Exposure to the Debates

	Correlation Between Summed Difference Score* and Vote Change from T_1 to T_4		
	Low Exposure (Nonviewers) (N = 35)	Medium Exposure (Occasional Viewers) (N = 65)	High Exposure (Regular Viewers) (N = 64)
Image Differences			
Honesty/Integrity	.42	.25	.29
Strength/Decisiveness	.31	.25	.11
Friendly/Pleasant	.22	.22	.12
Leadership capacity	.36	.29	.26
Clarity of positions on issues	.34	.24	.14
Inspires confidence as a speaker	.41	.24	.24
Total Image Difference	.42	.29	.23
Issue Differences			
Government action to increase employment	.05	.28	.32
Change tax system so high-income people pay more	.11	.08	.25
Legalized abortions	−.03	.21	.04
Government spending for defense and military	.25	−.06	.38
Total Issue Difference	.16	.16	.31
Ideological Difference	.36	.04	.29
Party Identification	.08	.37	.10

*All scales are scored so that a positive correlation coefficient indicates that the person is voting in a direction consistent with the listed item. At T_1, "vote" refers to the respondent's stated voting intention; at T_4 it refers to the actual vote the respondent reported having cast.

appreciably during this period, the coefficients in this table can reasonably be interpreted as indicating the extent of latent bonding of each factor. For example, the large coefficient for party identification in the medium-exposure group means that these respondents eventually made decisions that tended to be quite consistent with their partisan predispositions, while those in the other two groups did not. Those who did not watch the debates made their decisions mainly on the basis of the images they held of the candidates, while those who watched the debates regularly tended to resolve their indecision on the basis of issue content. Put a slightly different way, we could describe the regular debate-watcher as an attentive listener seeking information that would link one candidate or the other to the position the voter holds on certain issues. The occasional debate-watchers, on the other hand, are looking for cues that will satisfy them that their party's candidate is of sufficient quality to merit a vote; one need not listen

THE GREAT DEBATES

to every detail of every debate to gain this assurance. The nonwatchers get neither kind of information. Their decisions are made on the basis of global ideology rather than specific issues, and candidate images (especially honesty and integrity) rather than party connections.

In terms of specific issues, those persons most heavily exposed to the debates show the strongest relationships between vote change and the issues of unemployment, tax reform, and defense spending—but relatively little for the perceived issue difference on abortion. Unlike the low- and medium-exposure groups, those with high exposure consistently associate the issues that were actually debated with their vote decisions. This encourages the inference that the debates facilitated issue-based voting for those who were watching attentively with issue concerns in mind.

A Causal Model of Voter Decision-Making

Our final analysis introduces controls for other important sources of variation, in a recursive path model (see Fig. 3) of presumably important influences on the vote across the several stages of the campaign. First, we assume that some structural influences on one's vote predate the campaign. Political party identification, for example, was a feeling acquired long before the fall 1976 campaign. One's socioeconomic status had also been determined at an earlier time. These exogenous influences were unlikely to change during the brief time span of our study.

Next in temporal order, perceived ideological differences between the candidates relative to one's own general ideology would seem to influence both initial voting intentions and other, later variables in the decision-making process. Then, as the debates take place, we assume that perceptions of specific image and issue differences between the candidates (in relation to oneself) are clarified and made salient; subsequently they help to determine one's final voting choice. These influences on the vote are themselves in our sequential model influenced by the preceding variables in the causal sequence.

What we do not include in this theoretical model is debate exposure, which is not normally a part of vote-decision processes. We are assuming that a somewhat modified empirical model is needed for each exposure group. Our key hypothesis is that there should be a larger effect of post-debates issue differences on the vote for highly exposed respondents than for those who were less exposed to political issue information via the debates. By contrast, we hypothesize that the strongest direct influences on the vote for the less-exposed groups would be images, early vote intentions, and preexisting party identification.

To estimate the coefficients for the various paths in this recursive model, we have used structural equations and solved these equations using multiple linear regression computations (Duncan, 1975). We have also decomposed the effects of each early variable in our model into direct effects on later variables, plus indirect effects that operate via intervening variables (Alwin and Hauser, 1975; Finney, 1972). Table 2 summarizes the results of several analyses, showing the direct and total effects of each prior variable on each subsequent one—with debate exposure both controlled and uncontrolled.[4] First, let us consider the overall direct effects, without the debates as a factor. The theoretical variable of most central concern in our hypotheses is issue differences. For the total sample there

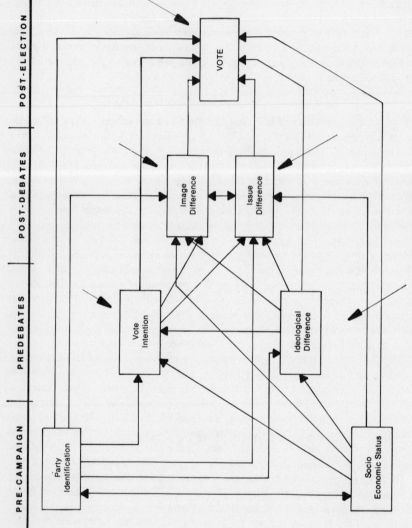

Fig. 3: Direct Effects on the Vote

THE GREAT DEBATES

was no significant effect of issues on the vote when other influences were controlled ($\beta = .10$). Candidate image was of considerably greater consequence ($\beta = .28$) in explaining the vote—even when the major predictor, T_1 vote intention ($\beta = .41$), was controlled.

The total-sample analysis in Table 2 gives us a good deal of additional information about the determinants of the vote in our path model. Perhaps the most surprising is that socioeconomic status had very little impact on the vote decision process when other variables were controlled ($\beta = .06$).

The other exogenous variable in our model, party identification, was a major factor, as previous research had led us to expect. It had large direct effects on the early endogenous variables of ideological difference ($\beta = .39$) and Time-1 vote intention ($\beta = .59$), plus large indirect effects (via the latter) on issue and image perceptions, and on the vote. Our decomposition of the indirect and direct effects (not shown) indicates that the effect of party identification on the vote had for the most part already occurred before the debates began; there was, however, some remaining direct effect ($\beta = .15$) during the period of our study.

The person's predebates vote intention was the best single predictor of the eventual vote ($\beta = .41$), as might be expected. It also had a strong influence on candidate images ($\beta = .57$), and to some extent this connection provided an indirect path to the eventual vote. The initial vote intention predicted issue differences with the candidates ($\beta = .36$) about as well as ideology did ($\beta = .35$).

These overall results tell us nothing about the debates, however. Had we entered exposure to the debates into the model as an additional predictor variable, it would not have produced any significant paths. Debate-watching, a bipartisan behavior, did not enter into any strong zero-order correlations with the directional partisan variables in our path model. To examine the impact of the debates, therefore, we turn to analyses of the subsamples partitioned on the extent of exposure to the debates, and we retest our model on each separately. The results appear in the righthand portion of Table 2.

It is most useful to compare a given coefficient from one exposure group to the next. For example, the stability of the vote is greatest in the low-exposure group ($\beta = .63$), and least in the high-exposure group ($\beta = .30$). While consistent with our general hypothesis that the debates would influence vote decision-making, this result is unlike the conventional conclusion in political mass communication research. Ordinarily it is thought that people who are heavily exposed to public affairs via mass media are relatively impervious to influence by that information, because their preexisting political knowledge and partisan commitment levels have been very high (Pool, 1963).

Probably the most important comparison for our purposes is the direct effect of issue differences on the final vote, when all of the other variables in our model are controlled. This coefficient was $\beta = -.12$ for the low-exposure sample, $\beta = .04$ for the medium-exposure group, but a rather strong $\beta = .31$ among the high-exposure voters. In this third group, issue differences constituted the strongest single direct predictor of the vote. Put another way, the bonding of issues and the vote was most prominent among those who were most fully exposed to the debates.

In the same vein there were nontrivial indirect effects (not shown) of T_1 vote intention (and to a lesser extent of ideology) via issue differences in the

Table 2: Summary of Regression Analyses of Vote Decision-Making Model, by Exposure to Debates

Dependent Variable	Predetermined Variable	Total Sample (N = 164)		Low Exposure (N = 35)		Medium Exposure (N = 65)		High Exposure (N = 64)	
		Direct effect	Total effect	Direct effect	Total effect	Direct effect	Total effect	Direct effect	Total effect
Ideological difference	Party ID	.39***	.39	.14	.14	.35**	.35	.54***	.54
	SES	−.04	−.04	−.22	−.22	−.06	−.06	.06	.06
		$R^2 = .148$		$R^2 = .048$		$R^2 = .114$		$R^2 = .292$	
T_1 Vote intention	Party ID	.59***	.63	.49***	.51	.57***	.62	.67***	.72
	SES	.12	.11	.28	.25	.05	.04	.16	.17
	Ideology	.11	.11	.12	.12	.13	.13	.09	.09
		$R^2 = .427$		$R^2 = .421$		$R^2 = .408$		$R^2 = .520$	
Issue difference	Party ID	.10	.46	.43**	.58	−.07	.37	.08	.53
	SES	−.04	−.01	−.30	−.33	.19*	.18	−.02	.07
	Ideology	.35***	.39	.35*	.37	.47***	.52	.28*	.32
	T_1 Vote intention	.36***	.36	.19	.19	.45***	.45	.41**	.41
		$R^2 = .418$		$R^2 = .479$		$R^2 = .562$		$R^2 = .426$	
Candidate images	Party ID	.03	.46	−.05	.29	.16	.56	−.03	.49
	SES	−.09	−.03	−.25	−.12	−.08	−.07	−.03	.08
	Ideology	.20**	.26	.15	.23	.16	.23	.24*	.29
	T_1 Vote intention	.57***	.57	.63**	.63	.55***	.55	.55***	.55
		$R^2 = .453$		$R^2 = .361$		$R^2 = .527$		$R^2 = .440$	
Final vote	Party ID	.15*	.60	.12	.50	.27**	.67	.06	.61
	SES	.06	.09	−.08	.04	.09	.10	.01	.10
	Ideology	.04	.19	.16	.27	−.10	.04	.11	.30
	T_1 Vote intention	.41***	.61	.63***	.83	.41***	.59	.30*	.55
	Issue difference	.10	.10	−.12	−.12	.04	.04	.31**	.31
	Candidate images	.28***	.28	.35*	.35	.28**	.28	.22*	.22
		$R^2 = .685$		$R^2 = .790$		$R^2 = .730$		$R^2 = .687$	

Note: Direct effects entries are standardized regression coefficients (beta). Total effects include direct effects plus indirect effects (not shown in table) through intervening variables in the model.
$*p < .05$, $**p < .01$, $***p < .001$

326

THE GREAT DEBATES

high-exposure sample. This does not hold for either of the other two groups. We might well conclude that issues, while they did not contribute heavily to the vote decision for the full range of citizens in our sample, were central to the vote decision among those who watched all of the debates.

A contrasting picture emerges with candidate images, which steadily decline in importance to the vote decision as one moves from the low- to the high-exposure subsamples in Table 2. The direct effect of image drops from .35 to .28 to .22 (and the indirect effect of T_1 vote intention via images, not shown, drops from .22 to .16 to .12) as we compare these subsamples. Combining these findings with those (above) for issues, we are inclined to infer that a major effect of the debates was to enable voters to substitute issue-based decisions for image-based voting.

As our uncontrolled analyses had suggested, party-based voting is primarily a characteristic of the medium-exposure subsample. The direct effect of party identification on the final vote, with T_1 vote intention and other intervening factors controlled, is $\beta = .27$ among this group of voters, a figure that puts it approximately on a par with candidate images as an apparent influence. Party identification is not significant in either the low- or high-exposure group, however, so that in general it does not emerge as a dominant influence on the vote decisions made during the debates period. Partisan predispositions had already exercised most of their impact (indirectly, through T_1 vote intention) before the debates occurred. The latent importance of party identification in the medium-exposure group suggests that those voters attended to the debates only enough to assure themselves that their party's candidate was worthy of their vote. By contrast, the low-exposure group changed in vote intention relatively little during the debates period, and in those cases where it did change the personal images of the candidates were the main factor. The high-exposure group was quite distinct in being influenced rather little by either party or image factors, and instead it underwent considerable change in vote intention on the basis of issue considerations.

Discussion and Conclusions

We have attempted to evaluate the impact of attention to the debates against the background of long-term historical changes occurring within the American electorate. We are especially intrigued by the recent upsurge of issue-voting and are impressed by the potential of the debates for enhancing this tendency.

From the viewpoint of democratic theory, debates can serve the useful function of informing voters about the likely policies of the contending candidates. In an ideal sense, debate information should serve to increase the citizen's capacity for rational voting. If debates are to serve this demanding purpose, they should penetrate at least in part into a realm where rational electoral decisions become possible and information costs are lowered (Downs, 1957; Key, 1966; Shapiro, 1969; Riker and Ordeshook, 1968; Davis, Hinich, and Ordeshook, 1970). This seems to have happened with the 1976 debates, partly because of the capacity of television to reach such a broad audience.

The part played by debates in vote decisions can be expressed in terms of an analogy to chemistry. Potentially, the elements of voting decisions—party identification, candidate images, and issue positions—can be bonded to the vote in a molecular manner. Which of them will become most closely attached to the vote depends on the environment in which this bonding process takes place. Candidate debates function as a *catalyst*. While they do not enter directly into the decision in a determinative way, they add information to the environment in which the bonding of other elements takes place. This modification of the environment makes it more likely that issue content will become closely bonded to the vote. In the absence of this catalyst, voters instead attach their votes to their partisan predispositions or to their perceptions of the candidates' personalities.

All three kinds of bonding are instances of "reinforcement," but our central point in this paper is that it is important which of the three kinds of elements is most reinforced by becoming bonded to the vote decision. Our evidence points to the conclusion that the debates are most useful for issue-oriented voters. While we do not yet understand this phenomenon fully, we can see even in this modest study that debate exposure led to a bonding of the vote with candidate issue differences as well as other political perceptions. This kind of outcome is assumed in the Jeffersonian exposition of democratic theory which says that voters ought to be informed about the issues when they decide who should serve them in the highest office of the land.

NOTES

1. We wish to acknowledge the financial assistance of the Research Committee of the Graduate School, University of Wisconsin, Madison; the Vilas Estate Trust; the National Science Foundation; the American Enterprise Institute for Public Policy Research; and Sidney Kraus for his funds from diverse sources to aid studies of the impact of the debates. The Wisconsin Survey Research Laboratory also deserves special thanks for collecting, coding, and preparing the data for analysis. The thoughtful collaboration of Jack M. McLeod throughout the project has been essential. We have benefited from the advice of Leonard Berkowitz on questionnaire construction, and of Halliman Winsborough and M. Mark Miller on data analysis. And we are grateful for assistance in processing the data to Claire Knoche, Terry O'Rear, Karen Stray-Gundersen, and Donna Wilson.

2. Gallup showed that by October 22–25, around 37 percent of Ford and Carter supporters still did not know for sure that they would end up voting for their chosen candidate. For data on the usual time of decision, see Flanigan and Zingale (1975). Unfortunately, we do not have very well-established norms available to determine whether the decline in doubt during the debates period exceeds what would have been expected in that period if there had been no debates.

3. *The Gallup Opinion Index*, No. 135 (October 1976), p. 10.

4. The complete results, including unstandardized as well as standardized coefficients, are available on request from the authors.

REFERENCES

Alwin, D. F. and R. M. Hauser. "The Decomposition of Effects in Path Analysis." *American Sociological Review*. Vol. 49, February 1975, pp. 37–47.

Berelson, B. L., P. F. Lazarsfeld, and W. N. McPhee. *Voting*. Chicago: University of Chicago, 1954.

Boyd, R. W. "Popular Control of Public Policy: A Normal Vote Analysis of the 1968 Election." *American Political Science Review*. Vol. 66, June 1972, pp. 429–49.

Brody, R. A. and B. I. Page. "Comment: The Assessment of Policy Voting." *American Political Science Review*. Vol. 66, June 1972, pp. 450–58.

Chaffee, S. H. (ed.) *Political Communication*. Beverly Hills: Sage, 1975.

Davis, O., M. Hinich, and P. Ordeshook. "An Expository Development of a Mathematical Model of the Electoral Process." *American Political Science Review*. Vol. 64, June 1970, pp. 426–48.

Dennis, J. "Trends in Public Support for the American Party System." *British Journal of Political Science*. Vol. 5, 1975, pp. 187–230.

Downs, A. *An Economic Theory of Democracy*. New York: Harper & Row, 1957.

Duncan, O. D. *Introduction to Structural Equation Models*. New York: Academic Press, 1975.

Featherman, D. L., M. Sobel, and D. Dickens. "A Manual for Coding Occupations and Industries into Detailed 1970 Categories and a Listing of 1970-Basis Duncan Socioeconomic and NORC Prestige Score." Working Paper #75–1. Madison, Wisc.: University of Wisconsin, 1975.

"Final Survey: It's Too Close to Call." *The Harris Survey*. November 2, 1976.

Finney, J. M. "Indirect Effects in Path Analysis." *Sociological Methods and Research*. Vol. 1, November 1972, pp. 175–86.

Flanigan, W. and N. Zingale. *Political Behavior of the American Electorate*. Boston: Allyn and Bacon, 1975.

Heise, D. R. "Separating Reliability and Stability in Test-Retest Correlation." *American Political Science Review*. Vol. 34, February 1969, pp. 93–101.

Kessel, J. H. "Comment: The Issues in Issue Voting." *American Political Science Review*. Vol. 66, June 1972, pp. 459–65.

Key, V. O., Jr. *The Responsible Electorate: Rationality in Presidential Voting, 1936–1960*. Cambridge: Harvard University Press, 1966.

Klapper, J. T. *The Effects of Mass Communication: An Analysis of Research on the Effectiveness and Limitations of Mass Media in Influencing the Opinions, Values and Behavior of Their Audiences*. New York: Free Press, 1960.

Kraus, S. and D. Davis. *The Effects of Mass Communication on Political Behavior*. University Park, Pa.: Pennsylvania State University Press, 1976.

Lazarsfeld, P. F., B. R. Berelson, and H. Gaudet. *The People's Choice*. New York: Columbia University Press, 1944.

Miller, A. H., W. E. Miller, A. S. Raine, and T. A. Brown. "A Majority Party in Disarray: Policy Polarization in the 1972 Election." *American Political Science Review*. Vol. 70, September 1976, pp. 753–78.

Nie, N. H., S. Verba, and J. R. Petrocik. *The Changing American Voter*. Cambridge: Harvard University Press, 1976.

Page, B. I. and R. A. Brody. "The Policy Voting and the Electoral Process: The Vietnam War Issue." *American Political Science Review*. Vol. 56, September 1972, pp. 979–95.

Pomper, G. M. "From Confusion to Clarity: Issues and the American Voter, 1956–68." *American Political Science Review*. Vol. 66, June 1972, pp. 415–28.

Pool, I. "The Effect of Communication on Voting Behavior," in W. Schramm (ed.), *The Science of Human Communication*. New York: Basic Books, 1963.

RePass, D. "Issue Salience and Party Choice." *American Political Science Review*. Vol. 65, June 1971, pp. 389–400.

Riker, W. H. and P. C. Ordeshook. "A Theory of the Calculus of Voting." *American Political Science Review*. Vol. 62, March 1968, pp. 25–42.

Shapiro, M. J. "Rational Political Man: A Synthesis of Economic and Social Psychological Perspectives." *American Political Science Review*. Vol. 63, December 1969, pp. 1106–1119.

Tannenbaum, P., B. Greenberg, and F. Silverman. "Candidate Images," in S. Kraus (ed.), *The Great Debates*. Bloomington, Ind.: Indiana University Press, 1962, pp. 271–88.

18.

Influence on Vote Decisions

DENNIS K. DAVIS

Previous research suggests that the presidential debates constitute an unusual and important form of political communication. The debates attract the interest and attention of most voters regardless of their party affiliation or social status. Selective exposure may be minimized. A significant minority of the public reports that their choice is influenced by the debates.

Role of Mass Media in Election Campaigns

In previous studies (Kraus and Davis, 1975; Davis, 1977) we have discussed a strategy for locating mass media effects. We have developed the view that mass media will be most effective when routine patterns of communication behavior are disrupted.

We have argued that it will be possible to locate significant communication effects if research is directed toward examining those situations in which routine communication behaviors have been disrupted. Reports of what we have termed "critical events" can be expected to break through the social and psychological barriers created by selectivity processes. Individuals who would otherwise ignore political messages, misunderstand them, or quickly forget them may respond very differently to critical event reports. Elsewhere (Kraus and Davis, 1975) we have described events which might be categorized as critical. We believe that it may be appropriate to regard the debates as a type of critical event, especially for those persons who are undecided in their vote choice or who have experienced difficulty in making their vote decision.

But how can such effects be detected? It would be unrealistic to expect that debate viewing alone will directly influence voting choices.

A more viable strategy for evaluating the influence of the debates may be to examine the manner in which the debates intervene in vote decision-making during the course of the election campaign. If we knew which variables were most important in this decision process, we could examine the relationship of debate viewing to these variables and assess the role of the debates in the process.

Until recently, the most extensive data-based discussions of vote decision-making were to be found in research conducted by Lazarsfeld, Berelson, and Gaudet (1948) and Berelson, Lazarsfeld, and McPhee (1954). Most of the evidence in these studies supports the conclusion that political communication behavior has a minimal influence during elections because such behavior is so constrained by selectivity processes.

This view of vote decision-making has been the predominant model for evaluating communication effects for more than two decades (Kraus and Davis, 1976, pp. 48–54). Two recent studies suggest that a major revision of this model may be necessary.

Nie, Verba, and Petrocik (1976) review two decades of survey data collected by the Survey Research Center at the University of Michigan. They develop and support the view that American voters increasingly make their choices of candidates based on perceptions of candidate issue positions. They argue that voters are more knowledgeable about issues and more consistent in their own stands on issues (pp. 148–50). They maintain that issue evaluations have become an important basis for vote decisions (pp. 164–73). While these researchers devote much of their attention to issue voting, they also note that evaluation of the personal attributes of candidates continues to play a significant role in vote choice (pp. 166–71).

The researchers argue that they have demonstrated that the vote decision-making process has changed significantly but they admit that panel data will be necessary to provide a conclusive, direct test of their views.

Mendelsohn and O'Keefe (1976) provide additional perspective on the role played by social structural, psychological, and communication variables in the vote decision process. Their research was based on a 1972 election study of a panel of more than 600 voters in Summit County (Akron, Ohio). Structural variables were found to constrain the vote decision process somewhat. However, a large defection of Democrats to Nixon and to other Republican candidates occurred despite party affiliation (pp. 95–97). Nixon found modest support even among voter groups that traditionally voted solidly Democrat such as blue-collar workers and low social status individuals. McGovern was forced to struggle to hold the votes of groups that previously could be counted on to give overwhelming support to Democratic candidates.

The researchers found some evidence of issue voting. In particular, voter positions on social welfare and the war were likely to predict vote choice (pp. 103–105).

The researchers found evidence that vote decisions were also based on candidate attribute evaluations.

One intriguing and potentially disturbing finding in this study was the inability of the researchers to explain the vote choice of late deciders (those who decided after July 1972). These voters constituted more than 20 percent of the panel (141 out of 618). Issue agreement and attribute perceptions could explain only 17 percent of the variation in vote choice in this group (pp. 118–23). The authors suggest that these voters tended to be indifferent to the 1972 campaign. Thus, persons who decided late and presumably had the opportunity to deliberate their decision longer did not take advantage of this opportunity. Instead, these voters appear to have been less politically responsible than those who decided earlier. The lack of co-variation between their issue agreement, attribute perceptions, and vote choice may be evidence of an irrational, indifferent vote decision.

The authors differentiate another group of voters who merit attention (pp. 61–65). More than 22 percent of the voters indicated that they were having a hard time making a vote decision. These voters became more perplexed as the campaign went on. However, the authors speculate that such voters may have occasionally turned to the media for aid. The authors believe that a very different model of the vote decision process may be necessary to account for the vote choices of this group. The mass media may play a greater role for this group than for any other in their vote decision.

A Model of the Vote Decision Process

A theoretical model of the vote decision process can be derived from the research we have just reviewed. Two crucial sets of variables in this model will be issue agreement and attribute perceptions. We can expect that these variables will be highly related to vote choice. It is important to observe the changes in these two sets of variables over the course of the election campaign. It is necessary to determine whether significant *shifts* in issue agreement and in attribute perceptions occur during the course of the campaign.

But how important are such shifts in explaining vote choices? If the early voting studies are correct, these shifts should result in little more than an elaboration of the stereotypes of candidates held prior to the campaign. These initial stereotypes should be the best predictors of voting behavior, and the shifts that occur during the campaign should add little to their explanatory power. On the other hand, if the campaign is to have a significant influence on vote choices, this influence ought to be reflected in shifts in perceptions. These shifts in turn should provide a significant explanation of the variance in vote choice. Our strategy will be to explore the links between political communication behavior (especially debate viewing) and changes in perceptions of the candidates.[1]

We created a model of the vote decision process (see Tables 1–3 for a list of variables included). This model has five stages. Variables in each successive stage are expected to be causally related to variables in all preceding stages. However, the best direct predictors of variables in later stages are expected to be the variables contained in the immediately preceding stage. Social structural variables are included in stage one. These variables are conceptualized as providing broad constraints on the vote decision process, but their direct influence on vote choice is expected to be minimal. In stage two, three sets of predictor variables are included. These are routine political communication behaviors, initial (prior to the campaign) perceptions of candidate attributes, and initial agreement with candidate stands on issues. These variables are likely to constrain later communication activity (such as debate viewing), especially if selectivity processes are operating. Persons who engage in little communication or only selective communication during the course of the election campaign and who have initially well-developed and highly polarized (in the direction of one of the two candidates) perceptions of attributes or issue stands can be expected to vote in accordance with their early preconceptions. Persons who communicate frequently during the campaign and who begin with vague or inconsistent perceptions of the candidates can be expected to develop perceptions during the campaign which guide their vote choice.

In stage three, we have included two types of debate variables: exposure to the debates and anticipated uses of the debates. These variables are expected to intervene in the vote decision process. As we have indicated earlier, if the debates were a critical event they should disrupt routine political communication patterns and result in redefinition of initial perceptions of the candidates. Stage four includes the shifts in perceptions of candidate attributes and issue stands that have taken place over the course of the campaign. These shifts are expected to be directly related to vote choice in stage five.

This model could prove useful in evaluating the influence of the debates. It should be noted at the outset that the model is likely to provide conservative estimates of debate effects. In evaluating it we will statistically control for all variables included in earlier stages of the model as we look for debate effects. Thus, we will be assessing the ability of the debates to intervene significantly in the vote decision process and to create effects that cannot be predicted from a knowledge of social structural variables, routine communication behaviors, and initial perceptions of candidates. The model will also allow us to assess whether the debates simply functioned to reinforce initial preconceptions. By comparing the relative strength of these two sets of effects (that is, significant intervention versus reinforcement), we hope to produce a comprehensive evaluation of debate influence.

Data Collection

Data were collected that permit evaluation of this model during the past election campaign in Cleveland, Ohio, by several researchers associated with the Communication Research Center at Cleveland State University.[2] A random sample of 388 Cleveland-area voters was contacted by telephone prior to the start of the debates to form a panel to be used in assessing the influence of the debates. The sample was drawn by randomly choosing 500 numbers using a random digit dialing technique. Three attempts were made to reach each number selected. A private, commercial market-research firm, Marketing Research of Cleveland, completed all telephone interviews. On the first wave, 388 voters were contacted during the ten days preceding the first debate. Our efforts to create a panel from these 388 voters met with modest success.

One hundred and fifty-seven persons were contacted after the first debate, 120 after the vice-presidential debate, and 75 after the last presidential debate. In all, 352 of the original 388 persons were contacted after one of the three debates we surveyed. After the election our last wave of interviews reached 298 of the 352 persons who had been recontacted. Over the course of the campaign we had an attrition rate of approximately 23 percent. Our panel members tended to be older and better educated than the general population in Cleveland.

These persons may be above-average voters, but it seems reasonable to believe that they represent the bulk of persons who actually vote. Nevertheless, it should be noted that the models we have evaluated may be less applicable to less-educated and more politically apathetic voters.

Measurement of Variables/Creation of Scales

Questionnaire items were used to measure all variables. Debate exposure and use were measured with items that asked for self-reports. In addition to being asked whether debates had been observed firsthand, respondents were asked whether they had read newspaper accounts, watched TV reports, or talked to others about the debates. Debate use items were developed using examples of media uses and gratification items used by Blumler and McQuail (1968). Items used in our analysis included questions on whether respondents anticipated making the following uses of the debates: to determine candidate issue stands, to judge personality attributes, to judge honesty, to help make their vote decision, to provide arguments useful in defending their vote choice to others.

Debate exposure and use were high for our respondents. This is consistent with the interpretation that our respondents may be above average in their motivation to participate in politics. This was a group that looked forward to the debates and expected to make use of them.

Routine communication behaviors were measured using standard items. Behaviors measured included use of newspapers for political campaign news, watching of network news programs, talking about the political campaign with others, and opinion leadership on political campaign topics. The following demographic items were measured: sex, age, education, and political party affiliation.

The two key variables measured in our survey were perceptions of candidates' attributes and perceptions of agreement with candidates' positions on the issues. In each wave of the survey, respondents were asked which of the two candidates best exemplified each of seven personality attributes: most experienced, most honest, most intelligent, most likeable as a man, most qualified as an administrator, most concerned with needs of the average person, and strongest leader. Major shifts occurred on nearly every attribute, ranging from 34.4 percent shifting their perceptions of experience to 57 percent shifting perceptions of intelligence. Voter perceptions of the candidates changed greatly during the campaign. Yet it was not clear whether either candidate benefited more from these shifts. Carter appears to have a slight edge on more attributes, though Ford has a clear lead on others. How were these shifts related to vote choices? To what extent were they influenced by communication behavior during the campaign? These are questions our analysis will seek to answer.

We created two measures of initial polarization of attribute perceptions. If a respondent chose Carter as best exemplifying an attribute, he or she was given a score of 1 on a Carter polarization scale. A similar score was created for Ford attribute polarization. Scores on both scales could range from 0 to 7. Persons who said "don't know" or "no difference" in making an attribute evaluation were scored a zero for that attribute.

Our most difficult scaling problem lay in creating a summary score that would give the greatest weight to major changes in attribute perceptions. We created a scoring procedure that would give less weight to minor shifts and more weight to shifts we believed represented major deviations from previously held perceptions. For example, if someone consistently favored a candidate twice and then changed his or her choice in a third interview, this change was given a high weight. On the other hand, if someone twice said "don't know" and then named a candidate in the third interview, this shift was of less importance and given less weight.

Issue stand perceptions were measured using items that asked respondents to identify which of the candidates most favored or opposed each of the following issues: creation of a national health care program, busing to achieve racial balance, creation of public works jobs, and passage of a Constitutional amendment to ban abortions. These issue stand perceptions were matched with each voter's own stands on these issues. An overall agreement score was created. If a voter perceived Carter as most in favor of an issue which the voter also favored, he or she received a score of +1 on issue agreement. If the voter did not favor this issue position, he or she was given a score of −1. This scoring procedure was reversed for Ford (score of −1 for issue agreement with Ford and +1 for issue disagreement). Issue agreement scores were summed across all four issues, creating a total score whch ranged from −4 to +4. Issue agreement scores were calculated for respondents for both wave one and wave five. Unfortunately, in calculating the wave five score, the respondent's wave one report of his or her own issue position had to be used as an estimate of the wave five position because no measure of the wave five position was made. This may not be a serious problem because the four issues used in this study were much discussed before the campaign. However, if significant changes did occur in a respondent's own issue positions, our estimates of wave five issue agreement will be inaccurate.

Data Analysis Results

Regression analysis was used to evaluate the vote decision model proposed above. Variables from each stage in the model were entered in successive sets using a step-wise procedure. In this way the predictive power of variables contained in each stage could be assessed. Also, if variables in later stages attenuated relationships initially found, this attenuation could be noted. Two regression analyses were done with the 1976 election vote as the dependent variable. One included the entire sample and the other included only those persons who said that they were undecided about whom to vote for prior to the debates or who said that they were having a hard time deciding whom to vote for (N = 219).

Table 1 reports the results for the entire sample. Several findings should be noted in this table. Neither shifts in issue perception nor shifts in issue agreement initially are very useful in predicting vote choice. A conservative estimate of explained variance is only 2 percent. The addition of the debate variables does not add much to the explanation. Only two beta weights are significant. Persons who expected to assess candidate issue stands shifted toward Ford (−.12). Persons who expected to assess the honesty of the candidates shifted toward Carter (.17). Neither of these relationships is strong, and both are attenuated by the addition of variables in later stages. The explanation of variance jumps sharply after communication behaviors and initial perceptions of candidates are added (from 2 percent to 54 percent). Initial polarization of candidate attribute perceptions appears to account for much of this addition to explained variance. The addition of the demographic variables adds only 4 percent to the variance explanation. Interestingly, when initial candidate perceptions are controlled for, all of the routine communication behaviors emerge as significant predictors (using an F-test) even though some zero order correlations are quite

336   **THE GREAT DEBATES**

small. Newspaper reading and opinion leadership predict a Ford vote, while TV viewing and talking about the campaign predict a Carter vote. Reading of newspaper analyses of the debates emerges as the sole significant debate variable and predicts a Ford vote.

These findings suggest that early-formed conceptions of the candidates were the most powerful predictors of how individuals would vote. Consistent with this finding is the fact that 90 percent of those who had made vote choices before the debates voted for the candidates they initially favored. It is likely that most voters engaged in considerable selectivity and that most communication behavior simply reinforced early views held about the candidates.

A somewhat different picture emerges from the findings for the undecided/ hard deciders reported in Table 1. Shifts in attribute perceptions and issue agreement initially explain 15 percent of the variance in vote choice. This proportion increases as other sets of predictors are added. The debate variables do not explain much of the variation in vote choice. Only one is significant after all of the predictor variables have been added. Persons who expected to assess the honesty of the candidates tended to vote for Ford ($-.12$). Again all of the routine communication behaviors emerge as significant predictors, but this time they are much stronger while early conceptions of the candidates are much weaker predictors. As before, newspaper reading and opinion leadership predict a Ford vote, and TV viewing and talking about the campaign predict a Carter vote.

These findings suggest that those who were initially undecided or who had difficulty making their decision experienced important changes in their perceptions of the candidates during the campaign. Communication behavior is also likely to be important in arriving at a vote choice. On the other hand, early conceptions of the candidates appear to play only a minor role in vote choice.

Tables 2 and 3 report the result of regression analyses in which shifts in attributes perceptions and shifts in agreement with candidate issue stands are used as dependent variables. The purpose in conducting these analyses was to assess indirect effects of variables in stages three to five. While the debates may not have had a direct impact on voting choice, they may have indirectly influenced such choices by producing changes in issue agreement and attribute perceptions.

The debate variables are not strong predictors of shifts in either attribute perception or issue agreement for the entire sample. Tables 2 and 3 indicate that only four variables have predictive power. Persons who talked about the debates tended to develop attribute perceptions favorable to Ford (though this relationship is attenuated by the addition of variables in later stages). Persons who expected to use the debates to assess the honesty of the candidates tended to develop attribute perceptions favorable to Carter. Persons who talked about the debates tended to shift toward greater agreement with Ford on the issues.

Two of the routine communication behaviors are significant predictors. Reading newspaper stories tended to result in development of attribute perceptions favorable to Carter, while talking about the campaign tended to result in development of favorable perceptions of Ford. It should be noted that these effects are in the opposite direction of the effects that these variables showed in relationship to voting choice. Newspaper reading predicted a Ford vote, while talking about the campaign predicted a Carter vote. The existence of

CARTER vs. FORD, 1976   337

Table 1: Regression Analyses for the Entire Sample and for Undecided/ Hard Deciders Using 1976 Vote Choice as the Dependent Variable[1]

Independent Variables	Entire Sample					Undecided/Hard Deciders				
	Zero-Order Correlations	Stage 4	Stage 3+4	Stage 2+3+4	Stage 1 to 4	Zero-Order Correlations	Stage 4	Stage 3+4	Stage 2+3+4	Stage 1 to 4
Stage 4										
1) Changes in attribute perception[2]	.18	.18*	.16*	.35*	.36*	.39*	.40*	.37*	.62*	.69*
2) Changes in issue agreement[3]	.04	.05	.02	.17*	.17*	.09	.13	.10	.19*	.23*
Stage 3										
1) Debate viewing	.03		.07	.06	.06	.06		.09	.06	.08
2) Newspaper analysis	−.08		−.07	−.09*	−.08*	−.16		−.13	−.08	−.03
3) TV analysis	−.02		.01	.04	.03	−.04		.03	.09	.06
4) Debate talking	−.04		−.04	.01	.03	.00		.04	−.03	−.03
Debate Uses										
1) To make decisions	.01		−.01	.01	.02	.03		−.01	.01	.04
2) For issue stands	−.08		−.12	−.04	−.02	.01		.00	.04	.08
3) For personality	.00		−.05	.01	.00	.02		−.01	.05	−.01
4) To assess honesty	.19		.17*	.01	−.02	.19		.10	−.06	−.12*
5) For arguments	.10		.08	.01	.01	.07		.04	−.02	.02
Stage 2										
Communication Behaviors										
1) Newspaper	−.09			−.07	−.10*	−.07			−.27*	−.36*
2) TV network news	.11			.14*	.15*	.12			.27*	.26*
3) Campaign talking	.05			.13*	.13*	.11			.26	.27*
4) Opinion leadership	.00			−.08*	−.08*	.00			−.15	−.17*

CARTER vs. FORD, 1976

	(1)	(2)	(3)	(4)	(5)	(6)	(7)	(8)
Initial Perceptions								
1) Attribute polarization for Ford	-.60		-.43*	-.42*	-.43		-.28	-.27*
2) Attribute polarization for Carter	.47		.26*	.23*	.25		.28	.30*
3) Issue agreement (+ agree Carter/ − agree Ford)	.45		.23*	.18*	.31		.22	.20*
Social Structural Variables								
1) Age	.00		.08*		.00		.24*	
2) Education	-.21		.01		-.05		.04	
3) Sex (2 = female)	-.05		-.11*		-.14		-.22*	
4) Democrat	.33		.13*		.15		.14*	
5) Republican	-.38		-.12*		-.20		-.15*	
R^2	.04	.09	.60	.64	.17	.20	.60	.70
Adjusted R^2†	.02	.02	.54	.58	.15	.08	.49	.59

[1] Vote choice scored as Carter = 2, Ford = 1.

[2] + is change toward Carter; − is change toward Ford.

[3] + is change toward agreement with Carter; − is change toward agreement with Ford.

*Beta weights significant at the .05 level.

†Adjusted R^2 is a conservative estimate of R^2 which incorporates an adjustment.

Table 2: Regression Analyses for the Entire Sample and for Undecided/Hard Deciders Using Changes in Issue Agreement as the Dependent Variable[1]

Independent Variables	Entire Sample					Undecided/Hard Deciders				
	Zero-Order Correlations	Stage 4	Stage 3+4	Stage 2+3+4	Stage 1 to 4	Zero-Order Correlations	Stage 4	Stage 3+4	Stage 2+3+4	Stage 1 to 4
Stage 4										
1) Changes in attribute perception	−.07	−.07	−.07	.00	−.03	−.10	−.10	−.12	.06	.04
Stage 3										
1) Debate viewing	−.02		.04	.01	.02	−.03		.04	.02	.03
2) Newspaper analysis	−.07		−.05	−.03	−.02	−.13		−.14	−.07	−.07
3) TV analysis	.00		.02	.01	.02	.05		.09	.01	.02
4) Debate talking	−.13		−.16*	−.11*	−.09*	−.16		−.17*	−.07	−.07
Debate Uses										
1) To make decisions	.06		.07	.01	.01	.01		.04	.02	.00
2) For issue stands	−.04		−.07	−.05	−.06	−.08		−.09	−.04	−.06
3) For personality	−.03		−.05	−.10*	−.10	.03		−.01	−.03	−.01
4) To assess honesty	.09		.10	.09	.06	.05		.04	−.03	−.04
5) For arguments	.05		.05	.08	.08	.12		.13	.19*	.17*
Stage 2										
Communication Behaviors										
1) Newspaper	−.12			−.07	−.04	−.21			−.16*	−.13
2) TV network news	.01			.05	.05	.03			.10	.10
3) Campaign talking	−.05			−.02	.01	−.09			.00	.01
4) Opinion leadership	−.07			−.03	−.01	−.11			−.06	−.04

THE GREAT DEBATES

	(1)	(2)	(3)	(4)	(5)	(6)
Initial Perceptions						
1) Attribute polarization for Ford	.05	−.05	−.05	.08	.01	.00
2) Attribute polarization for Carter	−.03	.15*	.10	.05	.19*	.17
3) Issue agreement	−.43	−.52*	−.54*	−.45*	−.49*	−.49*
R²		.05			.09	.01
Adjusted R²		.00			.00	.00
Stage 1						
1) Age	−.06		−.08	−.08	−.11	
2) Education	−.10		−.09	−.09	−.08	
3) Sex	.13		.08	.14	.08	
4) Democrat	.06		.09	.03	.03	
5) Republican	.02		.00	.02	.03	
R²	.00	.27	.33	.33	.31	.33
Adjusted R²	.00	.17	.08	.08	.13	.08

[1]Issue agreement change scored as 1 to 4 = change toward Carter; −1 to −4 = change toward Ford.
*Beta weights significant at the .05 level using an F-Test.

Table 3: Regression Analyses for the Entire Sample and for Undecided/Hard Deciders Using Changes in Attribute Perceptions as the Dependent Variable

Independent Variables	Entire Sample					Undecided/Hard Deciders				
	Zero-Order Correlations	Stage 4	Stage 3+4	Stage 2+3+4	Stage 1 to 4	Zero-Order Correlations	Stage 4	Stage 3+4	Stage 2+3+4	Stage 1 to 4
Stage 4										
1) Changes in issue agreement	−.07	−.07	−.10	.00	−.03	−.10	−.10	−.11	.06	.03
Stage 3										
1) Debate viewing	−.03		.04	.04	.05	−.02		.09	.09	.10
2) Newspaper analysis	−.08		−.04	−.02	−.02	−.11		−.08	−.09	−.11
3) TV analysis	−.09		−.06	−.02	−.01	−.18		−.16*	−.07	−.08
4) Debate talking	−.11		−.12*	−.07	−.07	−.06		−.06	.00	.06
Debate Uses										
1) To make decisions	.09		.04	.04	.01	.09		.06	.03	.04
2) For issue stands	.10		.05	.02	.01	.01		.02	.00	.00
3) For personality	.09		.04	.05	.07	−.01		−.07	−.03	.03
4) To assess honesty	.19		.18*	.22*	.22*	.25		.27*	.29*	.30*
5) For arguments	.03		−.03	.00	.00	.01		−.05	−.01	−.02
Stage 2										
Communication Behaviors										
1) Newspaper	.01			.09	.12	.06			.26*	.34*
2) TV network news	−.06			−.09	−.08	−.23			−.25*	−.16*
3) Campaign talking	−.24			−.19*	−.18*	−.22			−.20*	−.22*
4) Opinion leadership	.12			.08	.09	.17			.14*	.11

CARTER vs. FORD, 1976

Initial Perceptions							
1) Attribute polarization for Ford		.10	.02	.01	-.10	-.10	-.13
2) Attribute polarization for Carter		-.30	-.40*	-.42*	-.30	-.39*	-.44*
3) Issue agreement		.07	.24*	.22*	.14	.19*	.18*
Stage 1							
1) Age	-.03			-.12*	-.19		-.30*
2) Education	-.07			-.03	-.05		-.02
3) Sex	.11			.06	.02		-.01
4) Democrat	.04			.02	.03		-.04
5) Republican	-.04			-.02	-.05		.00
R^2	.00	.07	.26	.28	.12	.39	.45
Adjusted R^2	.00	.01	.17	.16	.00	.23	.25

*Beta weights significant at the .05 level using an F-Test.

343

these opposing effects may explain why the zero order correlations of these communication behaviors with voting are relatively low, especially in the case of the undecided/hard deciders.

One finding in Table 2 is particularly striking. There is a high negative beta weight for the relationship between the extent to which attribute perceptions were initially polarized toward Carter and shifts in attribute perceptions. This relationship indicates that those who were initially polarized toward Carter tended to show major shifts toward Ford. This was not true of persons who started out polarized toward Ford. These relationships indicate that attitudes did not tend to become polarized toward either of the candidates as the campaign went on. In fact, for those who initially favored Carter strongly, the campaign appears to have produced many shifts favorable to Ford. Those who began with very positive perceptions of Ford's attributes tended to retain these perceptions but they did not strengthen them. These findings suggest that the campaign served to develop "balanced" perceptions of both candidates and thus legitimize both of them as worthy contenders for the presidency.

One interesting finding is that initial perceived agreement with a candidate's stand on issues resulted in the development of more favorable attribute perceptions of that candidate (beta weight of .22). But polarized perceptions of a candidate's attributes did not result in significant increases in issue agreement (though beta weights are in the appropriate directions—negative for Ford and positive for Carter).

The model clearly fails to account for shifts in perceived agreement with candidate's stands on issues. The modest amount of variance which is accounted for is explained almost entirely by perceived agreement before the debates. Since the shift in perceived agreement was created by subtracting initial agreement from agreement after the election, this common variance is an artifact of the method used. Consideration must be given in future models for the inclusion of more variables that might explain shifts in issue agreement.

The addition of the debate variables appears to account for modest amounts of variance in attribute perception shifts and shifts in issue agreement. However, a conservative estimate of explained variance indicates that the ordinary R^2 may be overestimating the size of explained variance. Four variables stand out as significant predictors. Two of the four were also found to be predictors for the entire sample, though the beta weights for the sample as a whole were not as large. Again, talking about the debates results in the increased agreement with Ford's stand on the issues. Persons who expected to assess the honesty of the candidates developed attribute perceptions favorable to Carter. Persons who watched analyses of the debates on TV tended to develop attribute perceptions favorable to Ford. Persons who expected to obtain arguments from the debates useful to them in defending their vote choice tended to develop issue stands in agreement with Carter.

Communication behaviors are again significant predictors of shifts in attribute perceptions, and the beta weights are considerably stronger than those found for the entire sample. Newspaper reading predicted the development of attribute perceptions favorable to Carter. Watching TV news and talking to others predicted the development of attribute perceptions favorable to Ford.

Again, these effects are the opposite of the effects which these communication behaviors were found to have on vote choice.

Polarization of attribute perceptions before the debates was found to be related to development of attribute perceptions favorable to Ford. This indicates that persons polarized toward Ford tended to increase their polarization while those polarized toward Carter tended to develop favorable views of Ford. Initial agreement with a candidate's issue positions was related to later development of attribute perceptions favorable to that candidate. An almost significant beta weight was found for the relationship between initial polarization of attribute perceptions toward Carter and later shifts toward issue agreement with Carter.

The only strong relationship found for demographic variables was the one between age and shifts in attribute perceptions. This strong negative relationship suggests that older persons tended to develop more favorable perceptions of Ford.

Conclusions

It is possible to draw several theoretical and substantive conclusions from the findings reported above. Our major theoretical conclusion is that we have developed a model that is moderately successful in conceptualizing the vote decision process. The model explains almost 60 percent of the variance in vote choice. The model has enabled us to isolate some potential media effects which would have been ignored by a more conventional strategy. The model seems to be especially suited to explaining vote choice among persons who are undecided about their vote choice just prior to the campaign or who express concern about the difficulty of the vote choice they are facing. For these persons the model suggests that routine communication behaviors may play a major role in initiating changes in perceptions of candidates' attributes, which in turn affect their vote decision. Some direct influence on vote choice is also indicated. Surprisingly, the direct and indirect effects of the routine communication behaviors are in opposition. We could provide no simple explanation for these effects but hope to conduct future analyses which may account for them.

The perspective on the role of the mass media in the 1976 election campaign which emerges from these findings is quite complex. Use of the debates for differing purposes has opposing effects. Neither candidate benefited consistently or substantially from the debates. However, there is a trend in the data that favors Carter. Most of the debate uses were related to development of favorable attribute perceptions of Carter. The direct and indirect effects of debate viewing were favorable to Carter though neither was statistically significant. In the case of newspaper analyses of the debates and to a lesser extent television analyses, there is evidence of media influence favorable to Ford. One might speculate that Ford's "win" in the first debate was magnified by newspaper accounts especially for those persons who failed to watch later debates. Both candidates appear to have benefited equally from the influence the debates had on issue agreement. Newspaper analyses were most beneficial to Ford; talking about the debates produced issue agreement with Carter. Among the undecided/hard deciders, those who expected to use the debates as a source of arguments to defend their views tended to move toward issue agreement with

Carter. These opposing communication effects are best viewed as serving to legitimate both candidates—especially Ford, who was viewed negatively by a predominately Democratic Cleveland electorate.

One additional effect of the debates found in analyses could not be reported here but is worthy of note. The debates were more likely than other forms of mass communication to encourage changes in attribute perceptions. This was something we had hypothesized would occur if the debates functioned as critical events. Using newspapers to follow the campaign and watching TV news tended to reduce the likelihood of changes in attribute perceptions. Interestingly, reading or viewing analyses of the debates also reduced the likelihood of changes. But direct viewing of the debates was linked to attribute changes in the undecided/hard deciders group.

This research provides evidence for the view that the mass media have a larger role than simply reinforcing early perceptions of political candidates. Media use is related to significant changes in perception of candidates' issue stands and personal attributes. It can serve to legitimate candidates who are relatively unknown. Special communication events like the debates may produce effects that differ greatly from effects produced by routine communication behavior. Mass media appear to be especially important for persons who are undecided before a campaign begins or who express difficulty in making a decision. The media use behavior of such persons is more likely to predict changes in perceptions of candidates or vote choices. Future research is necessary to provide an understanding of these media effects. Much additional research will be necessary to provide an adequate explanation of the role played by mass media in the vote decision process.

NOTES

1. I gratefully acknowledge the assistance of Sidney Kraus and Dr. John Robinson in the design and execution of this study. Support for this research was provided by the Communication Research Center of Cleveland State University and by funds raised by Kraus.

2. Sidney Kraus and John Robinson participated with the author in the design and execution of this research.

REFERENCES

Berelson, B., P. F. Lazarsfeld, and W. McPhee. *Voting: A Study of Opinion Formation in a Presidential Campaign.* Chicago: University of Chicago Press, 1954.

Blumler, J. G., and D. McQuail. *Television in Politics: Its Uses and Influence.* Chicago: University of Chicago Press, 1969.

Davis, D. K. "Assessing the Role of Mass Communication in Social Processes." *Communication Research.* Vol. 4, No. 1 (January 1977), pp. 23–34.

Kraus, S., and D. K. Davis. "Critical Events Analysis" in *Political Communication: Issues and Strategies for Research.* S. H. Chaffee (ed.). Beverly Hills, Calif.: Sage Publications, 1975.

Kraus, S., and D. K. Davis. *The Effects of Mass Communication on Political Behavior.* University Park, Pa.: Pennsylvania State University Press, 1976.

Lazarsfeld, P. F., B. Berelson, and H. Gaudet. *The People's Choice: How the Voter Makes up his Mind in a Presidential Campaign.* New York: Duell, Sloan and Pearce, 1944.

Mendelsohn, H., and G. J. O'Keefe. *The People Choose a President: Influences on Voter Decision Making.* New York: Praeger, 1976.

Nie, N. H., S. Verba, and J. R. Petrocik. *The Changing American Voter.* Cambridge, Mass.: Harvard University Press, 1976.

CARTER vs. FORD, 1976

19.

Reactions of Young and Older Voters: Expanding the Context of Effects

JACK M. McLEOD, JEAN A. DURALL,
DEAN A. ZIEMKE, and CARL R. BYBEE

Answers to the question, "Did the presidential debates affect the 1976 election?" will depend on answers to two prior questions: what "effects" are we talking about, and what "debate stimuli" are we examining?

Identifying Debate Effects

A broad approach to debate effects includes a variety of potential indicators of change: information about candidates and issues; attitudes on issues and perceptions of candidates' stands on issues; salience of various issues; level of interpersonal communication; interest in the campaign; and dozens of other possibilities. All these factors may have subsequent impact on vote outcome or could be considered as worthy effects in themselves. Effects in this broader view might also include long-term changes, for example, in the political socialization of children or in the strengthening of abstract political system values such as trust and efficacy that eroded during the Vietnam and Watergate periods.

Specifying Debate Stimuli

One obvious measure of debate stimuli is the summation of the individuals' level of viewing or listening to each of the debates. Debate impact is then tested by examining the relationship between the level of debate exposure and the effect variables. There are several reasons, however, why debate exposure may not be such a simple causal stimulus: 1) the debates were only one among many sources of campaign information; 2) the debates constitute considerably more complex stimuli than is implied by a simple measure of debate watching; and 3) the impact of the debates may come not only through the content of the debates but also indirectly through their stimulation of social processes.

The debates were only one among many sources of campaign information, and are best understood if we can ascertain what functions were served or what segments of the population were reached more adequately by the debates than by the more customary sources of information. Descriptions of who watched the debates most and how well the audience members felt the debates served their various needs require that we evaluate them in a comparative mode by contrasting them to alternative information sources within various population segments.

The potential sources of debate impact did not end when the telecasts ended. To the extent that people discussed the debates with other people and read or listened to analyses of the debates, these subsequent actions could be considered additional sources of influence. Similarly, audience members' evaluations of who won and how helpful the debates were could be included as part of a complex debate stimulus.

Debate impact may have come not only from the content of the debates but also from the stimulation value they generate; this implies the need for studying debate impact as part of a social process. The usual conception of media impact asserts that some attribute of message content (for example, the superior performance of either Ford or Carter) acts *directly* and immediately on the individual audience member. Alternatively, the debates could have an impact on the vote *indirectly* if the social processes affected one or the other party differentially. Democratic presidential candidates have lost as often as they have won since 1948 in large part because their adherents are more erratic in turning out to vote. In the 1976 election there may have been more Democratic identifiers who are unstable in their interest and allegiances. The fact that President Ford was the better-known incumbent implies too that Governor Carter had more potential for gain from the debates. This formulation of effort, of course, requires evidence that debate watching leads to gain in loyalty among the adherents of both major parties.

We saw the debates as highly salient and dramatic events whose impact could be best understood by contrasting them to existing flows of information. Their presentation of both candidates on the same program made them distinctive from partisan performances like party conventions and media advertising. Unlike the daily coverages of the campaign, the debates were to become focused media events that were salient enough to stimulate interpersonal discussion and newsworthy enough to generate news summaries and interpretations in the media.

Study Design

In mid-September, about a week before the first debate, ten-minute telephone interviews were conducted with 97 eligible voters in Madison, Wisconsin.[1] Topics covered issue and image perceptions and vote preferences along with other questions serving as predebate control measures. During the last two weeks of October, those contacted by phone were among 353 respondents completing hour-long personal interviews that straddled the fourth debate. Since the major focus of the larger research program was on younger people's political communication behavior, persons under twenty-seven years old were selected at twice their actual proportion. As a result, the younger and older voters have been kept separate in cross-section analyses. In the weeks following the November election, short telephone interviews were taken with 323 respondents. An additional data base is made up of 133 respondents who were interviewed both during the 1974 Congressional election and in this round. This panel provides the basis for long-term changes in political values and for time-one measures of other effect criteria not included in the pre-debate telephone interview.

Results

Our supposition that the debates were a series of highly salient events is substantiated by our data. The proportion of those who viewed at least some of any given debate ranged from 84 percent of older viewers for the first debate to the 31 percent of young voters who watched the vice-presidential debate. Only 12 percent of both our samples failed to see or listen to any of the four debates, and less than twice that proportion saw the entirety of all four debates. We also found an expected decline in viewing across the three presidential debates and an average of about 10 percent higher watching among older voters. There appears to be no lack of variance for the crucial measure of debate viewing used in the effect analyses.

Who watched the debates? Our first major research problem was to identify factors leading to debate watching and to compare those antecedents with those associated with alternative sources of campaign information. An index of debate watching was formed by adding the level of viewing (four-point scale) across the first three debates. The fourth debate was not included because almost one-third of the interviews were conducted before that debate. For purposes of contrast, two alternative types of campaign information sources were examined: campaign news exposure and partisan exposure. Campaign news exposure, the seeking and use of relatively unbiased sources of campaign information, was measured by summing three questions: recall of news stories from the campaign; desire to read two League of Women Voters pamphlets; and time spent watching election night returns. Partisan exposure, the seeking and use of partisan information, was constructed from three items: recall of campaign advertisements; desire to read partisan pamphlets; and time spent viewing favored party convention. Our general expectation was that the antecedents of debate watching would be more similar to those of campaign news exposure than to those predicting partisan exposure. Debate exposure was seen as less a political act and less specifically motivated than the other formats; to a greater extent it should be a function of demographic characteristics and usual entertainment media behavior. As shown in Table 1, twenty-five variables, grouped into five blocks, were used to identify format antecedents. The zero order correlations defy interpretation in that more than half the coefficients are statistically significant. This is clarified by the sequential introduction of the five blocks in regression analyses shown in the right half of the table (Kerlinger and Pedhazur, 1973).

The four demographic variables predict debate viewing better than the other two sources, although in no case is the individual beta significant. Interestingly, education does not predict campaign news exposure and is negatively related to partisan exposure among older voters when other variables are controlled for. Our expectation that debate watching is less a function of political orientations and behavior is also upheld in the added variance comparisons. While political variables tend to be stronger predictors of campaign news and partisan exposure, among older respondents these relationships tended to disappear after media and other variables were brought into the analysis.

The mass media add significant amounts of variance beyond the demographic and political variables in each of the six comparisons (Table 1). Our

350

prior expectation that entertainment as well as public affairs media exposure would determine debate watching is clearly not found. In fact high entertainment viewing among the older sample was associated with *lower* levels of debate watching.

Eleven items were used to measure the motives people have for paying attention to presidential campaigns (Blumler and McQuail, 1969; Blumler and Katz, 1974). For each, the respondent was asked whether the given item applied to him/her a lot, a little, or not at all. On the basis of correlations among the eleven items, five groups were formed. As shown in Table 1, these five gratification patterns tend to show lower standardized regression coefficients (betas) for debate watching than for the other two sources. This supports our prediction that debate watching would be relatively low in specific motivation. The contest pattern (judge personal qualities, judge which candidate will win, enjoy the excitement of the election race) especially predicts partisan exposure, and among older respondents it is the single strongest predictor of campaign news exposure.

What emerges then for debate watching is not a picture of strong equalitarian viewing that is likely to act to even out the participation of the more active and less active members of the electorate. Previous public affairs media activity strongly predicts to high levels of debate use. Entertainment viewing may even have acted as a deterrent among older voters. At the same time, debate watching does not seem to have been a highly political act nor does it seem to be very specifically motivated. From that vantage point, it gives promise to produce effects not found under more partisan conditions and with motivation that could deter such effects.

Were the debates helpful? Eleven items were used to measure the reasons the persons had for following the campaign. These same questions were used to determine how helpful the debates had been. The debates were seen as relatively helpful in determining the issue positions of candidates, what they would do if elected, their personal qualities, and their weak points (not shown in tables). They were judged as less helpful in enabling the person to make up his/her mind, in judging the election winner, and in providing excitement. Perceptions of debate helpfulness have potentially important implications for future public broadcast policy if it can be shown that they aided not only the most avid election campaign followers but also those less likely to be reached by standard print and broadcast news sources. To examine this issue, we first divided our sample into high and low users of public affairs content in newspapers and on television. We then looked at means of perceived helpfulness of the debates at three levels of debate exposure (nonviewers were excluded). In these data analyses (not shown in our tables), we found those younger respondents who infrequently used public affairs content were almost as satisfied by the debates as the heavy users were. Their average level of helpfulness was only .04 less than the heavy public affairs users across the eleven items. Differences between high and low public affairs viewers in the older sample were somewhat greater (but still not significantly different), averaging .15. In general, however, we can say that the debates were not highly redundant to customary media sources in terms of perceived helpfulness.

Table 1: Zero-Order Correlations and Standardized Regression Coefficients of Antecedent Variables and Use of Various Sources of Information during the Campaign by Age of Respondent

	Zero-Order Correlations						Beta Coefficients					
	Debate Watching		Campaign News Exposure		Partisan Exposure		Debate Watching		Campaign News Exposure		Partisan Exposure	
Antecedent Variable	Young	Older	Young	Older	Young	Older	Young	Older	Young	Older	Young	Older
Demographic												
Sex (high = female)	-.13c	.03	-.13c	.13c	-.06	.16b	-.05	.03	-.11	.12c	-.02	.03
Age	.19a	.21a	.13c	-.02	.00	.27a	-.04	.11	.00	-.14c	-.16c	.07
Family social class	.06	.19b	.14c	.03	.08	.04	-.03	.13c	.14c	-.05	.00	-.01
Education	.30a	.20b	.25a	.15c	.12c	-.13c	.15	.04	.01	.08	.06	-.18b
Political												
General interest in politics	.34a	.40a	.37a	.43a	.32a	.35a	.08	.11	.10	.09	.13	.07
Efficacy	.12c	.14c	.09	.16b	.17b	.21a	.04	.00	-.04	.01	.00	.06
Party affiliation (high = Dem.)	.01	-.07	.02	.21a	-.03	-.04	-.01	-.16b	-.05	.09	-.10	-.08
Partisanship	.11	.14c	.18b	.21a	.32a	.08	.04	.06	.09	.03	.20a	-.01
Importance of personal qualities	.04	-.03	.04	-.06	.05	.02	.01	.03	.04	-.01	.02	.00
Issue salience	-.03	.10	-.01	.26a	.01	.30a	-.16b	-.06	-.12c	-.02	-.11	.02
Political activity	.19a	.20b	.22a	.13c	.16b	.12	.03	.05	.08	-.01	.12c	.00
Interest in third parties	-.09	-.16b	.00	-.06	-.13c	.00	-.05	-.11	.03	-.04	-.10	.02
Mass Media												
Public affairs newspaper reading	.40a	.41a	.43a	.41a	.29a	.35a	.22b	.17c	.20b	.12	.13	.10
Public affairs television viewing	.37a	.26a	.31a	.26a	.31a	.52a	.21a	.27a	.15c	.21b	.13c	.42a
Public affairs magazine reading	.05	.22a	.15b	.19b	.07	.16b	-.09	.14c	.05	.02	.01	.20a
Entertainment newspaper reading	-.12	-.20b	-.07	.14c	.10	.13c	-.09	-.03	.03	.05	.09	-.04
Entertainment television viewing	-.15b	-.01	-.16b	-.13c	.07	.04	.03	-.25a	-.07	-.11	.09	-.18b
Entertainment magazine reading	.16b	-.04	.09	-.02	.10	-.02	.12c	.04	.05	.10	.06	.07

THE GREAT DEBATES

Gratifications Sought											
Informational	.17b	.17b	.21a	.36a	.25a	.36a	.02	.01	.12c	.10	.14c	.18b
Contest	.25a	.23a	.25a	.42a	.37a	.34a	.07	.14	.06	.30a	.23a	.23a
Communication	.14c	.13c	.08	.30a	.06	.23a	.09	-.05	-.08	-.06	-.11	-.01
Candidates' strong points	-.04	.20b	.09	.38a	.17b	.37a	-.01	.02	.08	.14	.04	-.10
Candidates' weak points	.11	.15c	.14c	.36a	.14c	.13c	-.06	.02	.00	-.06	-.05	.01
Interpersonal Communication												
Political discussion	.30a	.27a	.33a	.41a	.22a	.28a	.09	-.04	.10	.11	.01	.02
Homogeneity of family/friends	.09	.20b	.08	.24a	.08	.10	.01	.07	.05	.05	.02	-.02
Added variance accounted for:												
Demographic (first block)							.10a	.15a	.09a	.06c	.03	.09a
Political							.09a	.14a	.13a	.22a	.19a	.18a
Mass Media							.12a	.09a	.08b	.08b	.09a	.17a
Gratifications sought							.02	.01	.03	.11a	.06a	.07a
Interpersonal Communication							.01	.00	.01	.01	.00	.00
Total variance accounted for:							.34a	.39a	.34a	.47a	.37a	.50a

Note: Number of respondents is 192 for young and 161 for older respondents. Significance at the .10 level is indicated by the letter c, at the .05 level by the letter b, and at the .01 level by the letter a. Coefficients in the first six columns are zero-order associations without control for any other antecedent variable. Beta coefficients in the last six columns of the table indicate the standardized relationships after all other antecedent variables are controlled. Variances in the lower portion of the table indicate the additional variance accounted for by the indicated block of variables over and above the amount accounted for by all previous blocks of variables.

CARTER vs. FORD, 1976

Another comparison with other information sources was made possible by the repetition of two helpfulness items (personal qualities and candidates' stands on issues) for five other sources: television news, newspaper news, magazines, television ads, and campaign brochures and literature. The results (not shown in tables) revealed that the debates were moderate in their helpfulness. In all cases, television news was seen as considerably more useful in terms of mean ratings, while magazines, television ads, and campaign materials were given considerably lower ratings. Newspaper news had a more variable position in having the highest ratings on issue positions but much lower in personal qualities.

Before consigning the debates to a role as merely a supplement to television news and the newspaper, we should keep several things in mind. First, the debates were seen as helpful by those not reached by these other sources. Second, the amount of time devoted to the debates was only a small fraction of the attention given the presidential campaign by these standard sources. That is, given the relatively short time devoted to the debates, it is perhaps remarkable that the debate helpfulness ratings were not that much lower than those for the other sources. Finally, the debates were rated considerably higher than three other sources. Their dominance over television advertising is especially noteworthy in that considerable influence has been attributed to this source recently (Patterson and McClure, 1976).

Who won the debates? We found a substantial plurality in both age groups who judged Ford to be the winner of the first debate and Carter to emerge the victor in the second and last debates (not shown in tables). Although almost half the younger respondents were unable to say who won the vice-presidential debate, Mondale is clearly the choice over Dole by those who were able to make a judgment. Previous party and candidate assessments played a substantial role in making these judgments about who won; however further analyses revealed that the perceptions were not overwhelmingly partisan. Even Democrats agreed Ford won the first debate, and Republicans correspondingly awarded Carter the second and final encounters.

What political consequences did the debates have? We concentrated on two types of intervening conditions that might affect vote preferences: shifts in cognitions about issue positions and image characteristics of the candidates. Other effect variables were examined in less detail.

1. Issues and Agenda-Setting

According to the agenda-setting hypothesis, those watching the debates most should increase their salience ratings on issues most frequently mentioned in the debates (McLeod et al., 1974). The results for our pre-post panel (n = 97) are presented in Table 2. For each issue the prior predebate level of salience was controlled first along with age as the initial block of variables introduced into the regression analysis. The level of debate watching, summed across the first three debates, was then introduced as the second block. Its standardized regression coefficient, or beta weight, is indicated in Table 2. Its final beta weight is also shown.

If the agenda-setting hypothesis holds, there should be a strong positive relationship between debate watching and increases in the salience ratings of the most frequently mentioned issues in the debates: unemployment, tax reform, and bureaucracy in government (Bechtolt et al., 1978). The data in Table 2 give little support to this hypothesis. None of the beta coefficients for debate watching on the most-discussed issues is statistically significant, and only tax reform shows a coefficient (.13) beyond negligible levels. The agenda-setting hypothesis was tested more formally by computing a Spearman rank-order correlation coefficient between the frequency of mention of each of our eight issues in the debates and the beta coefficients of these issues ranked from the most positive to the most negative. Again, no support was found for agenda-setting. Neither the correlation before controlling for other debate variables ($r_s = +.11$) nor the correlation after control ($r_s = -.30$) supports the agenda-setting formulation (data not shown in tables).

Analyses of the four other debate variables also gave little support to the agenda-setting hypothesis. Of the thirty-two comparisons (4 variables times 8 issues) of salience changes, only three reach the .10 level (Table 2). In terms of rank-order correlation, attention paid to the debates corresponded most closely to content frequency ($r_s = +.59$), closely followed by debate evaluation ($r_s = +.47$). The other two measures give little support (discussion, $r_s = +.25$; analysis, $r_s = -.20$). The results overall are not impressive.

No specific agenda-setting predictions could be made for perceiving the debate winners. It appears to operate largely through those seeing Carter–Mondale as winning tending to increase salience on all issues and particularly on unemployment, bureaucracy, and foreign policy. All three tended to be issues important to the Carter campaign, and, therefore, a plausible alternative explanation is that voters supporting Carter before the debates used them to adjust their saliences toward issues stressed by their candidate.

2. Changes in Issue Positions

Each respondent's position on four specific issues was obtained along with his/her perceptions of each of the candidates' stands on these issues. Analyses of debate watching and changes in the four specific issues indicate some surprising findings (Table 2). Most of the debate viewing effect occurs on the abortion issue that was discussed for less than two minutes in one debate. Those watching more of the debates tended to retain their own predebate position on abortion and to hold to their previous perception of Carter's position. They also tended to become more accurate in perceiving Ford as supporting a Constitutional amendment. In total, half the variance in issue positions accounted for by debate watching occurs on the respondents' own position, with slightly more of the remainder involving shifting perceptions of Ford's position than of Carter's. This seems to contradict the common wisdom of selective perception that asserts that respondents bring perceptions of their candidate's positions into line with their own.

Other debate variables subsequent to watching seem to affect the federal jobs program issue more than other issues. Discussion appears to produce a shift toward support of such programs, while the following of the debate analyses in the media is associated with lessening of endorsement. Those paying close attention to the debates as well as those attending to the media analyses tended to become more accurate in perceiving Ford as being opposed to job programs. The following of post-debate analyses was also connected to accuracy in cor-

Table 2: Changes in Issue Salience and Issue Positions After the Debates: Standardized Regression Coefficients of Debate Watching and other Debate Variables (Pre-Post debate panel)

| | Debate Watching | | Other debate variables: | | | | |
	Before Control	After Control	Attention	Discussion	Analysis	Evaluation	Debate Winner
Salience of Issues							
Unemployment	−.01	−.14	−.01	.15	.03	.06	.36[a]
Tax Reform	.13	.13	−.07	.07	−.05	.15	.08
Bureaucracy in government	.02	−.02	.08	.00	−.17[c]	.12	.19[b]
Crime	−.03	.00	.01	−.09	−.13	.19[b]	.05
Inflation	.10	.06	−.03	.04	.14	−.02	.09
Defense spending	.08	.08	−.05	−.04	.10	−.05	.11
Abortion	−.12	.00	−.26[a]	.10	−.10	.10	.09
National health care	.10	.11	−.10	.02	.06	−.01	.16[c]
Total of 8 issues	.06	.09	−.17	.09	−.04	.11	.30[a]
Foreign policy (post-debate only)	.17	.20	−.18	.12	.08	−.07	.21[b]
Position on Issues							
Federal job programs							
Respondent	−.07	−.13	.08	.17[b]	−.20[a]	.08	.04
Perception of Ford	−.10	.10	−.26[b]	.05	−.27[a]	.14	−.10
Perception of Carter	.03	−.11	.10	.07	.14	.06	.09
Abortion amendment							
Respondent	−.24[b]	−.25[b]	.10	−.01	−.19[c]	.10	−.07
Perception of Ford	.19[c]	.27[b]	−.06	.05	−.12	−.17	.02
Perception of Carter	−.22[b]	−.16	−.08	−.10	.03	.11	−.11

THE GREAT DEBATES

Build B-1 bomber							
Respondent	−.02	.03	.08	−.22^b	.01	−.08	−.18^e
Perception of Ford	.13	−.01	.18	.10	.06	−.12	.11
Perception of Carter	−.03	.00	.00	−.08	−.03	.05	−.06
Reorganize federal government							
Respondent	.21^e	.18	.10	.06	−.09	−.09	−.04
Perception of Ford	−.11	−.06	−.03	−.01	−.07	.12	−.17^e
Perception of Carter	.04	−.03	−.01	.01	.23^b	.00	.14
Issue Proximity (High = closer to Carter)	.05	.00	.05	.17^e	−.01	.00	.22^b

Note: Number of respondents is 97. Beta coefficients shown for Debate Watching Before Control are those obtained with controls for predebate levels of the row variable and age but before controls for other debate variables have been introduced. Debate Watching After Control indicates the beta after all of the other seven predictor variables have been controlled. Debate Winner is scored with those perceiving Carter–Mondale winning as high. A positive beta coefficient indicated increased salience or agreement with the row variable; a negative one signifies decreasing salience or disagreement. No predebate measure of foreign policy salience was available. Significance is indicated by the letter c at the .10 level, by b at the .05 level, and by a at the .01 level.

rectly associating Carter with promises to reorganize the federal government. Finally, discussion again played a role in moving the respondent's own position in a less conservative direction by strengthening opposition to construction of the B-1 bomber. The direction of these shifts may be a function of discussion in the liberal climate of opinion in the sample city; studies conducted in a conservative area might produce opposite partisan results for discussion.

Assessments of who won the debates have relatively slight impact on specific issue positions and perceptions, but when the effects are summed across the three cognitions and four issues in our Issue Proximity measure there is a significant relationship between perceiving Carter–Mondale as winning and moving closer to Carter or away from Ford (Table 2). The selective interpretation explanation was tested in our sub-analyses by controlling for predebate presidential vote preference (data not in tables). In this case the control reduced the relationship between perceptions of debate winning and issue positions markedly. Prior Carter voters apparently made judgments of winning the debates and shifted issue positions and perceptions as part of the same process late in the campaign. The only other debate variable to show any connection with issue proximity was discussion, which tended to produce a closer issue connection to Carter.

3. Changes in Images

Apparently debate watching per se had little to do with image shift on the five characteristics studied (Table 3). None of the variances accounted for by debate watching prior to the introduction of other debate variables is significant, and only one regression coefficient is at the .10 level, where the heavy watchers tended to become less likely to attribute a sense of humor to Carter.

Among the other debate variables, the level of attention bears little relationship to image changes in Table 3. Discussion hurt Ford in lowering perceptions of his leadership qualities, while following analyses of the debates tended to be related to seeing him as less honest and straightforward and having less of a sense of humor. To a greater degree, following media accounts of the debates seemed to reinforce the perception that Carter was fuzzy on the issues. Finally, respondents who felt the debates had been helpful to them tended to show increasingly favorable ratings of Carter while showing little change in assessing Ford's image.

Perceptions of debate winning appear to be the key debate variables in accounting for shifts in candidate image (Table 3). Those perceiving Carter as winning the debates were more likely than others to see Ford as less honest and straightforward, less capable of leadership, more fuzzy on issues, and less concerned with the average citizen. They tended to see Carter as more honest and concerned and were less likely to lower their estimates of his sense of humor and his leadership qualities. In general, seeing Carter as the winner was related to holding a less favorable image of Ford and maintaining or enhancing the impression of Carter. Our critical variable of Image Favorability difference (Carter favorability minus Ford favorability) is strongly tied to the judgment of who won the debates. Our sub-analyses (not shown in tables) indicate that prior levels of presidential preference and party affiliation account for some of the image change, but that the winner-image shift relationships remain signifi-

358

cant. Selective interpretation of the debates, then, is not the whole story of changing images. Less biased interpretation of the debates may be functionally related to shifting candidate images.

4. Other Effect Variables

Table 3 shows the relationship of debate variables to twelve other effect variables. Discussion of the debates shows a tendency to reduce the likelihood of voting, while perceiving Carter as the winner was associated with an increase in vote intention. On the other hand, debate discussion shows a strong association with discussion of other aspects of the election campaign. Campaign interest increased among those paying most attention to the debates and those seeing Carter–Mondale as debate winners. Debate-winning perceptions also seemed to generalize to heightened levels of general political interest along with debate discussion. Debate discussion also is associated with increases in gratifications sought, as is a favorable evaluation of the debates.

The only effect associated with the final beta weight of debate watching is the viewing of election night media coverage (Table 3). When introduced into the regression analysis model *before* other debate variables, debate watching is also associated with heightened campaign interest, gratifications sought, election discussion, and perceptions of being influenced by the debates, but all these seem to operate indirectly through other debate variables as evidenced by the negligible betas present *after* the other debate variables are introduced.

Perceptions of debate winning again play a role in changes in the second group of effect variables in Table 3. Those seeing Carter as winning increased their probability of voting, their campaign interest, and general political interest. They were more likely than others to watch the election returns and to perceive Carter as winning and gaining in support late in the campaign. Once again we controlled for predebate presidential vote preference in our sub-analyses (not shown in tables) in order to test the alternative selective interpretation explanation that the changes are due to pro-Carter people using the debates to bolster their voting commitment. As was the case in all other sub-analyses except for issue positions, the controls for voting preference do not seriously weaken the debate winner variable's predictive power.

In Feeling Thermometer questions respondents were asked to indicate their evaluations of various political figures and institutions on a scale ranging from 0 to 100. Since these measures were not included in the predebate telephone interviews, prior presidential vote preference was used in the initial block of controls for Table 3. Again we see debate watching per se has little impact, but the level of attention was associated with favorable evaluations of both Ford and Dole. Following debate media analyses was connected to low evaluations of Ford. Perceiving the debates as helpful seemed to be associated with favorable candidate evaluations and particularly with Carter and Dole. Finally, perceiving the debate winner as Carter was significantly related to all thermometer ratings in a consistent way.

5. Presidential Vote Preference

Two debate variables are significantly related to changes in vote preference (Table 3). The more respondents discussed the debates and the more they per-

Table 3: Changes in Candidate Image and Political Variables After the Debates: Standardized Regression Coefficients of Debate Watching and other Debate Variables (Pre-Post Debate Panel)

		Debate Watching		Other debate variables:				
		Before Control	After Control	Attention	Discussion	Analysis	Evaluation	Debate Winner
Image Characteristics								
Honest and straight-forward	Ford	-.10	-.02	-.01	-.06	-.14[c]	.09	-.21[a]
	Carter	.08	-.03	.11	-.05	.09	.19[b]	.15[c]
Sense of humor	Ford	-.03	-.04	.08	.09	-.15[c]	-.10	.00
	Carter	-.12	-.23[c]	.10	-.04	.00	.14	.24[b]
Capable of effective leadership	Ford	-.09	-.11	.07	-.18[b]	.10	.10	-.16[b]
	Carter	.13	.01	.11	-.09	.08	.15[c]	.25[a]
Fuzzy on the issues	Ford	-.01	-.08	.02	.07	-.02	.08	.29[a]
	Carter	-.10	-.18	.03	.00	.25[b]	-.05	-.07
Little concern for the average citizen	Ford	.08	.10	-.09	.15	-.11	.03	.23[b]
	Carter	.03	.00	.12	.06	-.02	-.19[c]	-.21[b]
Image favorability	Ford	-.05	-.03	.04	-.09	-.03	-.02	-.20[a]
	Carter	.09	.07	-.02	-.11	-.02	.20[b]	.26[a]
Political and Other								
Probability of voting		.05	.10	-.08	-.19[c]	.03	.16	.19[b]
Election discussion		.17[c]	.00	.08	.42[a]	.07	.08	.05
Interest in campaign*		.25[b]	.02	.26[b]	.10	.15	-.05	.20[b]
General political interest*		.09	-.01	-.01	.31[a]	.13	-.10	.18[b]
Gratifications sought		.18[b]	-.01	.09	.20[b]	.12	.35[a]	.03
Watched election returns*		.26[b]	.26[b]	-.06	-.02	.10	.13	.21[b]
Perceived influence of debate*		.18[c]	-.01	-.02	.15	.28[b]	-.01	.01

Feeling Thermometer							
Ford	−.05	−.11	.22ᵃ	−.07	−.19ᵃ	.08	−.27ᵃ
Carter	−.05	−.13	.08	−.06	.01	.21ᵃ	.25ᵃ
Dole	−.04	−.16	.27ᵃ	−.10	−.11	.16ᵇ	−.25ᵃ
Mondale	.09	.01	.00	.03	.14	.13	.24ᵇ
Presidential Vote Preference							
(high = Carter)	.03	.00	−.02	.15ᵇ	−.04	.06	.30ᵃ

Note: Number of respondents is 97. Beta coefficients shown for *Debate Watching Before Control* are those obtained with controls for predebate levels of the row variable and age but before controls for other debate variables have been introduced. *Debate Watching After Control* indicates the beta after all of the other seven predictor variables have been controlled. *Debate Winner* is scored with those perceiving Carter-Mondale winning as high. An asterisk * indicates no direct predebate measure was available. For these variables, predebate levels of following the campaign in the media and campaign discussion were used as surrogates of prior levels. Significance is indicated by the letter *c* at the .10 level, by *b* at the .05 level, and by *a* at the .01 level.

ceived Carter as winning, the more likely they were to shift their vote preferences toward him. A more complete vote preference model is shown in Table 4, where both predebate and post-debate measures of our earlier Issue Proximity and Image Favorability variables are included in the analysis. Predebate vote preference accounts for 56 percent of the variance in post-debate vote preference. Both predebate issue proximity and image favorability start out with strong zero-order correlations with post-debate vote preference, but their influence is sharply altered by the introduction of later variables in the model. Issue proximity goes to near zero in the final analysis and the beta coefficient of image favorability becomes significantly negative with the introduction of its post-debate counterpart.

Table 4: Changes in Presidential Voter Preference After the Debates: Standardized Regression Coefficients of Debate and Political Variables (Pre-Post Debate Panel)

	Post-debate Zero-order Correlation Coefficient	Standardized Regression Coefficients	Additional Variance Accounted for by Block
Predebate Political Variables			
Presidential vote preference	.75[a]	.46[a]	(.561)[a]
Issue proximity	.58[a]	.05	
Image favorability	.58[a]	−.27[b]	(.044)[a]
Debate Variables			
Debate watching	.12	−.02	(.000)
Debate attention	.06	−.03	
Debate discussion	.40[a]	.13[c]	
Debate analysis	.02	−.05	
Debate evaluation	.11	.01	(.012)
Debate winner	.58[a]	.16[b]	(.045)[a]
Post-debate Political Variables			
Issue proximity	.65[a]	.16[c]	
Image favorability	.72[a]	.37[a]	(.057)[a]
Total Variance Accounted For			
			(.718)[a]

Note: Number of respondents is 97. Significance of the individual zero-order correlation and beta coefficient at the .10 level is indicated by the letter *c*, at the .05 level by *b*, and at the .01 level by *a*.

The two debate variables that start with strong zero-order relationships to post-debate vote preference are reduced considerably in strength but are not eliminated by the addition of the other control variables. Debate discussion drops to a probability level of .07 and estimation of the winner becomes .05. Decline in the latter variable comes mainly after the introduction of post-debate issue and image variables, indicating indirect as well as direct paths to vote-preference changes. The best single predictor of vote-preference change after all other variables are controlled is image favorability, with issue proximity predicting very slightly less than debate-winner perception. There are some problems of multicollinearity created by the strong correlations between image favorability and issue proximity (.56 pre-debate, .69 post-debate), but at least provisionally we can attribute a stronger role to image shift. The major point of our analysis is, however, that debate variables other than debate watching also seem to play a role in producing vote preference changes.

6. Long-Term Effects

The 1974 and 1976 means of comparable variables were examined (not shown in tables). As expected, the 133 panel respondents had higher stated probabilities of voting in the recent presidential election than they did in the congressional elections two years earlier. There is also a slight rightward shift in political position and a surprising decline in general political interest. Political trust showed a significant gain from what may have been a low point in the Watergate period around 1974. The thermometer rating of Ford showed a significant decline over the two-year period, while that of Mondale, then a presidential hopeful, remained unchanged. The Republican party gained significantly during the two-year period, and the ratings of the Democratic party moved downward but not to a significant degree.

In the first set of comparisons in Table 5, debate watching accounts for a significant proportion of change in campaign participation over 1974 levels, but the nonsignificant beta after control indicates that watching operates largely through two other debate variables: discussion and use of media analyses. While discussion appears to be tied to increased participation, it is surprisingly associated with a decreasing likelihood of voting. The vote probability finding for discussion replicates the finding for the pre-post panel, as does a tendency for those seeing Carter as winner to report a high probability of voting. The earlier panel finding that both debate discussion and perceiving Carter as the winner are associated with a Carter vote preference are replicated in the 1974–76 panel. In the long-term panel, too, there is a tendency for those following media analyses of the debates to express a preference for Ford after the debates.

There is some evidence that the debate effects may have spread to party affiliation (Table 5). Changes toward Democratic party affiliation (or away from Republican affiliation) are related to both debate discussion and judging Carter as the winner; however, close attention to the debates is associated with movement toward Republican affiliation. Political position, on the other hand, is predicted only by evaluation where those finding the debates most useful were more likely to move toward moderate or conservative positions. Partisanship, the strength of party affiliation regardless of direction, showed a positive connection with both debate watching and discussion and a trend to less strong identification among those paying close attention and following the media accounts of the debates. Debate watching and discussion also are related to heightened political interest. Finally, there appears to be a connection between finding the debates helpful and increasing levels of both political trust and efficacy.

The last set of comparisons of thermometer ratings from 1974 to 1976 shows that with respect to Ford and to Mondale the initial marginal effects of debate watching are nullified when other debate variables are introduced. Debate discussion tended to produce higher ratings of Mondale and lower ones for

Table 5: Changes in Political Orientations and Behavior from October 1974 to Post-Debate 1976: Regression Coefficients of Debate Watching and Other Debate Variables (Long-Term Panel)

| | Debate Watching | | Other debate variables: | | | | |
	Before Control	After Control	Attention	Discussion	Analysis	Evaluation	Debate Winner
Campaign Behavior							
Campaign participation	.19[b]	.03	.06	.23[a]	.15[c]	−.02	.10
Vote probability	.03	.05	.00	−.20[a]	.02	.06	.15[c]
Presidential vote preference	.15[c]	.00	.03	.24[a]	−.14[c]	−.02	.42[a]
General Political Behavior							
Party affiliation (Dem.)	.10	.09	−.14[c]	.16[b]	.02	.00	.15[b]
Political position (left)	.08	−.02	.10	.06	.10	−.18[b]	.10
Partisanship	.13[c]	.17[c]	−.20[b]	.22[a]	−.15[c]	.10	.06
General political interest	.30[a]	.16[c]	.12	.18[b]	.06	.04	.03
Political trust	−.06	.01	−.11	−.01	−.03	.23[a]	−.12
Political efficacy	.06	.06	−.05	−.05	.03	.20[b]	.02
Feeling Thermometer							
Ford	−.13[c]	−.01	.03	−.16[b]	−.05	.02	−.32[a]
Mondale	.17[c]	−.01	.01	.23[a]	.01	.03	.40[a]
Republican party	−.12	−.01	−.08	−.09	.05	.11	−.27[a]
Democratic party	.02	−.02	−.16[c]	.16[b]	.04	.19[b]	.11

Note: Number of respondents is 133. Beta coefficients shown for Debate Watching Before Control are those obtained with controls for 1974 levels of the row variable and age but before controls for other debate variables have been introduced. Debate Watching After Control indicates the beta after all of the other seven predictor variables have been controlled. Debate Winner is scored with those perceiving Carter-Mondale winning as high. Prior level for presidential vote preference is 1972 presidential vote as reported in 1974. Significance is indicated by the letter *c* at the .10 level, by *b* at the .05 level, and by *a* at the .01 level.

Ford. Assessments of debate winners were again consistent with the changes in the feeling thermometer ratings. Perceiving Carter–Mondale as debate winners was associated with lower Ford ratings. The increase in Republican party ratings was also associated with perceiving Ford–Dole as debate winners, but perceptions of winning did not markedly affect Democratic party ratings. Those discussing the debates and those finding them helpful tended to maintain or enhance ratings of the Democratic party, while there was also a tendency for those paying close attention to lower such ratings. In general, it appears that the other debate variables and perceptions of who won had marked impact on the 1974–76 panel as well as on those participating in the pre-post longitudinal study.

Conclusions

The strategy adopted in this research was to use very broad definitions of both debate stimuli and possible debate effects. For the evaluation of possible effects, this meant examining not only the direct impact on changes in presidential vote preference but also the indirect consequences on the election outcome through shifts on issues and images as well as using other political behavior as criteria.

Four basic research questions were examined: Who watched the debates? Were they helpful to the public? Who was seen as winning them? and What were their political consequences?

The first question is relevant to the issue of whether the debates added anything to the electoral process that was not already there in existing electoral information sources. It is apparent that the debates reached a considerably broader audience than did competing sources like the political conventions, interview shows, and perhaps even the standard evening news coverage of the campaign. There was some evidence that the debates attracted the less politicized and less specifically motivated people more than did competing news and partisan sources. On the other hand, the results made it clear that the debates should not be thought of as a kind of equalitarian forum. They were watched most by those already heavily exposed to the campaign through usual media sources.

How helpful the debates were thought to be varied considerably by the criterion used, although the average level of approval was fairly high. The perceptions of helpfulness also varied by what the person was seeking and how much time was spent in watching the debates. In comparison with other campaign information sources, the debates were seen as intermediate: less helpful than television news and newspapers, more useful than magazines, television advertising, and campaign literature.

The question of who won the debates must be answered in relation to which of the four debates is being considered. Our sample, despite having a much higher proportion of Democrats than Republicans, tended to see Ford winning the first debate and Carter the second and fourth. Mondale was given a clear edge in the third. More important, partisan political affiliations were not so strong as to overwhelm these perceptions.

The role of debate watching in political effects per se seems to be of lesser importance than those of other aspects of debate behavior. The effect of debate watching on political behavior tended to disappear when the other debate variables were introduced. Its main function, therefore, was to focus attention, promote discussion, and induce the following of media analyses. Only in shifting positions and perceptions on the abortion issue and in stimulating general political interest and partisanship does debate watching appear to have had direct impact.

Among other debate variables, level of attention had a major indirect impact among younger voters through greater likelihood of seeing Carter as winning the debate. Those paying close attention also became more aware of Ford's opposition to the job programs, and increased their ratings of Ford and Dole while moving away from the Democratic party. Debate discussion effects formed a strong pattern of increasing support for Carter, a pattern tied to shifts of the respondent's own position toward that of Carter on two issues and to a decline in Ford's leadership image. In both panels, discussion was associated with an increasing intention to vote for Carter. Following media analyses of the debates appeared to play an informative rather than a partisan role. It was associated with more accurate perceptions on at least two issues. Seeing the debates as being helpful was associated with increasingly favorable evaluations of candidates and political institutions generally. This suggests the debates may have symbolic value for strengthening confidence in the political system.

The strongest relationships to effect variables were found for the perception of debate winners variable. Those seeing Carter–Mondale as winning the debates tended to become more issue-conscious and particularly to increase their salience on pro-Carter issues. They tended to move closer to Carter on issue positions, but this was partly due to those who were for Carter prior to the debates moving their own issue positions into line with their chosen candidate. They developed images more favorable to Carter and less favorable to Ford, independently of their previous vote preference. Not surprisingly, they revealed vote preference shifts toward Carter that were at least partly independent of their issue and image changes. Seeing Carter as winner had other consequences as well. They became more involved in the campaign and showed increased affinity with the Democratic party. Perceptions of winning, then, seemed to have played a critical role in the election, at least among the sample studied here.

Taken generally across the six debate variables, the effects of this study depart substantially from common-sense notions of exposure leading directly to effects or the alternative of partisan selective processes preventing such change. The effects found were most often indirect through debate watching acting to stimulate social processes and cognitive reactions. Rather than working positively in developing favorable attitudes, they seemed most potent in retarding the slippage of Carter's image that was taking place among those less stimulated by the debates. Finding weak points among the candidates seemed more likely than strengthening positive feelings. The lack of evidence for agenda-setting and the relative weakness of selective perception and interpretation as alternative explanations represent differences from both traditional and more recent approaches to political communication research. Finally, the effects shown for debate variables influencing accuracy on issues and stimulating more enduring political value orientations serve as reminders that debate impact was not necessarily confined to changing presidential voting.

NOTE

1. The present study is the last phase of a larger research program on Communication and the Young Voter begun in 1972 and funded by a grant from the John and Mary R. Markle Foundation to the first author. For greater elaboration of differential effects within age and education categories, see McLeod, et al., "The 1976 Presidential Debates as Forms of Political Communication," a paper presented to the Association for Education in Journalism, Madison, 1977. Our thanks go to Jane Brown, Sun Yuel Choe, Ron Faber, William Luetscher, Karen Schirle, Alan K. O. Tan, and Donna Wilson, who conducted the pre-debate telephone interviews along with the last three authors. We also thank the fifty-seven members of the Communication Research Methods course who did the personal interviews in October. The samples represent disproportionate stratified systematic probability samples of voting list addresses in the city of Madison.

REFERENCES

Bechtolt, W. E., J. Hilyard, and C. R. Bybee. "Agenda Control in the 1976 Debates: Content Analysis." *Journalism Quarterly.* Vol. 55 (1978), pp. 672–79.

Blumler, J. G., and E. Katz (eds.). *The Uses of Mass Communication,* Vol. 3. Beverly Hills: Sage Publications, 1974.

Blumler, J. G., and D. McQuail. *Television in Politics.* Chicago: University of Chicago Press, 1969.

Kerlinger, F. N., and E. J. Pedhazur. *Multiple Regression in Behavioral Science.* New York: Holt, Rinehart & Winston, 1973.

McLeod, J. M., L. B. Becker, and J. E. Byrnes. "Another Look at the Agenda-Setting Function of the Press." *Communication Research,* Vol. 1 (1974), pp. 131–66.

Patterson, T. E., and R. D. McClure. *The Unseeing Eye: The Myth of Television Power in National Elections.* New York: Putnam, 1976.

20.

Adolescents' Responses to Issues and Images

ROBERT P. HAWKINS, SUZANNE PINGREE, KIM A. SMITH, and WARREN E. BECHTOLT, JR.

Childhood and adolescence are periods during which children learn about political processes, form affective relationships with political parties and figures, and are exposed to campaign and news events. Election campaigns, then, are an excellent time for children to accelerate their learning about the political system, and the evidence so far indicates that they do (Chaffee et al., 1970). In particular, the debates of the 1976 campaign may even have been especially important for children who watched them, because the relatively issue-oriented content of the debates was quite different from what they might otherwise absorb.

In discussing socialization to politics during political campaigns in general and during the 1976 campaign with its debates in particular, we may find it useful to distinguish, as much of the political socialization literature does, between at least two aspects of political socialization: attachment to the system and partisan attitudes (Easton and Dennis, 1969; Sears, 1975a). While admittedly plagued with measurement problems, this distinction seems especially important for understanding the effects of the debates. With their strongly partisan but two-sided content, debate viewing and political socialization should relate very differently for these two classes of dependent variables.

Attachment to the Development of the Political System

Studies of political socialization carried out in the 1950s and early 1960s suggested that much of later socialization derived from an initially positive conception of politics and government centered around the image of the "benevolent leader" (Greenstein, 1965; Hess and Torney, 1967). As the child gradually distinguished other roles and levels of government and distinguished between roles and the fallible humans who fill them, there was naturally some attrition of this positive attitude toward government.

Subsequent studies, however, have placed important qualifications on this picture, suggesting that the strong positive affect associated with the "benevolent leader" may have been in part an artifact of the social class, nation, and historical period tested (Sears, 1975a). For example, the head of state is *not* the central political figure for children in all countries; disadvantaged social classes and ethnic groups often see leaders as fallible or even malevolent; and presidents since

Eisenhower and Kennedy have generally been much less idealized. Even if attachment to and involvement in the political system cannot be assumed to flow from early positive affect, such attachment (or its lack) remains a key political socialization outcome.

We see several basic reasons to hypothesize a direct, linear relationship between debate viewing (and discussion of the debates as a surrogate source of exposure) and a variety of attachment variables, among them political efficacy, interest in politics, and strength of partisan affiliation. First, debate viewing (or discussion) is itself a form of political participation that might be expected to generalize to other aspects of attachment. Second, by focusing on the images and issues of *both* candidates, the content of the debates may have served to make the nature of the American political system more salient. Finally, that same content, with its far greater than usual discussion of issues, may have provided an opportunity to form a relatively rich set of cognitions around which attachment attitudes could organize.

Development of Partisan Attitudes

In contrast to the direct relationship for attachment variables, the relationship of debate viewing to partisan political socialization must necessarily be more complicated. The development and elaboration of partisan attitudes and predispositions are of course an equally important part of political socialization in any society where partisan competition is part of the political process, although there is still considerable argument about how much early attitudes persist or influence adult attitudes (Sears, 1975b).

With age, children and adolescents are more able to state a party affiliation and this affiliation becomes more stable (Vaillancourt, 1973). But partisan political socialization is not merely a matter of party affiliation. For example, even young children in fifth and sixth grades can make other affective judgments (for example, of individual politicians) that are consistent with their party preference. From these and similar findings one can abstract the notion that progress in political socialization of partisan attitudes may be a result of an increasing integration and interrelatedness of a range of partisan attitudes and affiliations that occur at least in part because of cognitive-developmental advances.

The consistency (or strength of association) of party affiliation, vote preference, image attitudes, and issue perceptions can of course be used to track advances in this aspect of political socialization across ages, but it is also quite appropriate for the study of debate effects as well. Because the debates presented two opposing candidates, each trying to look as attractive and to be as forceful and persuasive as possible, direct effects of debate viewing on image or issue perceptions must be considered highly unlikely. Even if one candidate had clearly run away with the debates, selective perception by followers of the opposing candidate would tend to obscure such an effect. More realistically, because both candidates were fairly cautious and neither was clearly the victor, watching the debates probably had quite opposite effects on different people. The identical exchange could easily have benefited both Ford and Carter by reinforcing their supporters' views. Thus, one would expect the campaign in general and the debates in particular to provide both the raw material and the impetus for increased bonding of a variety of partisan attitudes. If debate viewing, taken as a contingent condition, is associated with greater bonding, then we would again have some justification for arguing that the debates had an important effect on political socialization.

Debate Viewing and Discussion

We will also examine several other points. First, since debate viewing and discussion of the debates are of interest in their own right, we will try to identify predictors of these two variables.

Second, those who ordinarily use the mass media for public affairs information should have been more likely to view the debates and (to a lesser extent) to discuss them.

Just as we predicted that debate viewing would be directly related to subsequent attachment, prior levels of attachment variables should predict debate viewing and discussion. Professed interest in politics, knowledge of politics and government, and strong party affiliation should lead to debate viewing and discussion, unless, once again, the debates were an event that could not be ignored by those uninterested in or affiliated with partisan politics.

Age and Debate Impact

Finally, if the 1976 debates can be considered political socialization events, the research reported earlier about age-related changes in bonding and attachment variables suggests we examine any debate effects in interaction with age. In doing so, however, one can easily argue either of two opposing interaction hypotheses. First, because younger adolescents are less involved in politics, studies of the involvement-effects relationship suggest that they may be the ones most affected by the debates (Patterson, McClure; Rothschild, Ray). Likewise, one could argue that because younger adolescents' knowledge and attitudes are still under construction and not well integrated, they might be more susceptible to new information and persuasive messages (Hawkins). On the other hand, older children might be better able to understand the issues raised in the debates, and such understanding may well be a prerequisite for any sort of effects.

Method
Design

The design used in this study represents an attempt to obtain the advantages of a panel design while avoiding the problem of reactive measurements when respondents are interviewed several times. All respondents were pretested one week before the first debate on a very short list of general political process variables. The sample was then randomly divided into four groups, each of which responded to a much longer questionnaire at later times.

With this design we can examine and control for changes in predispositional variables and look for both individual and cumulative effects of the debates with relatively little fear of effects of prior testing. However, there is always the very real possibility that campaign events other than the debates are responsible for differences. Thus, while the design gives us some assurance that any differences found between groups are truly changes in political orientations, we will have to turn to multiple regression to approach these changes as effects of the debates.

THE GREAT DEBATES

The sample was drawn from a rapidly growing community of 7,000 about twenty miles from Madison. All four of the city's wards have given substantial margins to the Democratic ticket in the last three presidential elections. The gubernatorial races have been closer, but the city as a whole has also gone Democratic recently.

All sixth-, ninth-, and twelfth-graders in the city school system were invited to participate in the study. Some twelfth-graders declined to participate, so they make up only 22 percent of the total sample of 561. The sixth- and ninth-grade samples are almost exactly divided between males and females, but the twelfth-grade females outnumbered males by three to two. Attrition due primarily to absences at the scheduled second testing reduced the final sample to 508.

Procedures

One week before the first presidential debate, students responded to brief self-administered questionnaires in large-group settings. After this pretest, students were randomly assigned to be retested at one of four times: the day before the first debate, or the day after the first, second, or third presidential debates. Random assignment was not completely successful. Significant differences were found in reported political party affiliation of the groups (x^2 significant at .025 level)—too many Republicans in the first group, too few Republicans in the third group, and too few undecideds in the second group.

Measures

Many of the measures used here need little or no explanation. Two sets of variables, however, are slightly less commonplace. Candidates' images were assessed by ten five-point semantic differential scales, which were then factor analyzed. A single factor solution was obtained which explained 50 percent to 60 percent of the total variance. Factor scores for each respondent were calculated to provide summary evaluation of each candidate's image.

Children's perceptions of the candidates' stands on the issues were measured by placing the candidates, five issues (tax reform, limiting abortion, big government, unemployment, and cutting defense) and "me" in all twenty-eight possible paired comparisons. Children rated each pair on a five-point scale ranging from "very much alike" to "very much different." For the analyses reported here, we were interested not in the absolute distance of each candidate from "me" and the issues, but the difference in distance between the two candidates. Thus, for each issue one candidate's distance from that issue was subtracted from the other to produce an index of their perceived difference. The scales thus formed ranged from "−4" to "+4," with positive scores indicating Ford was closer to the issue and negative scores indicating Carter was closer.

Results[1]
Political Characteristics of Sample

We found that these adolescents were overwhelmingly for Carter initially (50 percent to Ford's 25 percent, 8 percent for others, and only 17 percent undecided). There was also a solid, if less-marked dominance by Democrats (31 percent to 19 percent GOP, with 15 percent independent). Not surprisingly for adolescents so early in the campaign, 32 percent of the sample said they did not know what their party was. These patterns were fairly similar for each age group, although twelfth-graders were somewhat less sure of their party and considerably less sure of their vote preference. At first glance, this may seem to contradict usual notions of decreasing instability and "don't know" responses with age, but even our youngest respondents may be past the age of extreme political ignorance and the oldest group may be taking a more serious and cautious decision-making approach to the campaign.

Bearing in mind the moderate grade by time of measurement sample sizes and the disparities in the random assignment, party identification seemed fairly stable during the campaign. However, there are some apparent shifts in proportions that indicated some variability as well. For example, fewer sixth-graders called themselves Republicans after the second debate (T3) and more responded "don't know," even though this group may have had somewhat more Republicans than average at the pretest. There are also very few independents among sixth-graders at the end of the campaign.

For ninth-graders, there seemed to be a shift from Republican to Democrat after the first debate, with gradual recovery toward parity through the rest of the campaign. If anything, the trend is even more pronounced for twelfth-graders, although their smaller sample size makes it difficult to interpret the percentages too closely. In addition, while we know that too few of those initially undecided were assigned to T2, there still seemed to be a slight trend toward an increasing number of undecided responses during the campaign—quite the opposite of the greater understanding of and identification with parties one might predict. While this could be an undetected randomization artifact, an alternative explanation examined in more detail later is that presidential campaigns are much more about candidates than about parties.

Sixth-graders' vote intention remained fairly steady through the campaign, except that Carter lost some support to Ford and the "undecided" categories after the first debate. With ninth-graders Ford gained support after the first and final debates, but the second debate seems to have helped Carter. Twelfth-graders favored Ford before the first debate, but then reversed to favor Carter; however, Carter's advantage dwindled with further debates. In addition, the proportion of undecided twelfth-graders seems to have increased during the campaign.

Attachment to the Political System

Turning from partisan characteristics to two variables indexing attachment to the system, we found contrasting trends across the campaign for different age groups. Sixth-graders became more interested in politics and perhaps felt somewhat more efficacious as well. Both ninth- and twelfth-graders became less interested in politics and ninth-graders felt less political efficacy, especially at the end of the campaign. Twelfth-graders felt more efficacious after the first two debates, but dropped most of the way back to predebate levels after the final debate.

Summing up adolescents' general political responses to the campaign, the two partisan responses (party and candidate) are not wholly fixed but are certainly more stable than not, especially for candidate preference. The shifts that do seem to occur appear reversible and thus may well be reactions to discrete campaign events such as the debates. The two attachment variables (interest and efficacy), in contrast, seem to show larger and more durable shifts that may be reactions to the campaign as a whole.

Viewing and Perceptions of the Debates

Nearly 60 percent of the sample planned to watch the debates, and subsequent analyses confirmed that a majority did in fact report at least some viewing. While variances are quite large because of a small number of adolescents who watched entire broadcasts and a somewhat larger group who watched none at all, our sample averaged about fifteen to twenty minutes viewing per debate. And while it is difficult to be sure of debate-to-debate comparisons, sixth-graders may have watched slightly more of the later debates, while twelfth-graders watched considerably less after the first debate.

The debates were not a central topic of conversation; a majority reported discussing the debates with family and friends either "none" or "not too much." The three age groups reported peak amounts of discussion at different times during the campaign, but all three were clearly talking less about the debates at the end of the campaign than they had earlier.

Looking at adolescents' estimates of who won the first debate, one is struck first by the prediction the day before (T1) of a Carter victory by sixth- and ninth-graders, with the opposite prediction by twelfth-graders. After the first debate and in recalling it after the second, sixth- and ninth-graders believed the first debate much more even. By the final debate, sixth-graders seemed to reinterpret the first debate as a Carter victory, while twelfth-graders became even more convinced it was a Ford victory.

All three grades saw the second debate as a Carter victory, and this perception seems to have strengthened with time for sixth- and ninth-graders, but weakened for twelfth-graders. All three groups again saw the final debate as another Carter victory. And all the adolescents predicted a Mondale victory in the vice-presidential debate but afterward believed Dole had won.

These findings suggest that the adolescents were quite sensitive to the outcomes of the debates, either through actual viewing, discussion with others, or news summaries. Furthermore, there are strong indications of partisan influence on both prediction and recollection.

Respondents' reasons for watching and avoiding the debates were assessed. Overall, an interest in the issues of the campaign and a partisan response to the debates were more important than situational reasons for viewing or avoiding the debates. Furthermore, dividing the sample into those who watched some of the debates and those who did not located differences on some of these gratifications and not on others. First, situational reasons for viewing the debates seemed to have relatively little impact, in that they were no more important for viewers than for nonviewers. Second, partisan reasons for viewing did not distinguish viewers and nonviewers among sixth- and twelfth-graders, but ninth-grade viewers found these gratifications relatively more important than non-viewers. Reasons for avoiding the debates were quite reasonably more important for ninth- and twelfth-grade nonviewers, although not for sixth-graders. And an interest in the issues as a reason for watching was more important for viewers than nonviewers at all three grade levels.

Partisan Attitudes

Some issues were more clearly identified with the candidates than others For ninth- and twelfth-graders, Ford seemed closer to "unemployment" and "big government—red tape" than Carter. In a perfectly sensible contrast, Carter was generally seen as closer to "cutting defense." While these are clearly disadvantages for Ford, one could argue that they result from averaging the selective perceptions of a pro-Carter sample, as further demonstrated by the closeness of Carter to "me."

However, "limiting abortion" and "tax reform," two other issues that could be selectively perceived, did not seem more closely associated with one candidate than the other. If anything, "tax reform" may have been perceived as Ford's issue, despite its strong positive connotations, the pro-Carter sample, and Carter's own efforts to make it "his" issue. Based on these overall perceived differences, we tentatively concluded that "cutting defense," "big government," and "unemployment" were perceived as campaign issues that one can use to distinguish between the candidates.

The differences among issue means may be too small and unreliable for strong conclusions about trends across the campaign. However, ninth- and twelfth-graders' perception of a Carter advantage on these three issues seemed to fade by the final measurement, much later than the changes in party and vote preference.

Mean image factor scores were calculated separately for each candidate and thus cannot be used to compare the two candidates. However, Carter was perceived as more presidential in terms of the raw scales from which these factor scores were constructed. In terms of the factor scores, the campaign apparently improved Ford's image for sixth- and ninth-graders, although not for twelfth; Carter's image declined for sixth- and twelfth-graders, but not for ninth. Furthermore, these changes seemed tied to particular times during the campaign, perhaps reflecting candidate performance in the debates: judging by image scores, the first and third debates were beneficial to Ford and harmful to Carter; Carter was better off before all the debates and after the second one.

Bonding of Partisan Attitudes

The bonding hypothesis states that with increasing age and during an election campaign, partisan variables such as party identification, candidate preference, and perceptions of images and issue stands should become more highly correlated, especially for debate viewers. In such a multivariate situation, however, it is convenient to use one variable as the criterion and look at bonding of all the others with it. We decided to base our choice of a criterion on an empirical test.

We examined test-retest correlations of vote preference and party affiliation for different age or time-of-measurement groups and separately for debate viewers and nonviewers. The test-retest correlations for party averaged about .40, while those for vote preference (a three-point index with undecided responses placed between Carter and Ford choices) averaged about .65. Furthermore, while the correlation coefficient decreased for party as the time interval increased, little or no attrition was present for vote intention. These findings tended to confirm our suspicions that even in adolescence one's attachment to a specific candidate is a more central partisan predisposition than party affiliation itself; thus we used vote preference as our primary criterion variable for the bonding tests that follow.

As a first test of the bonding hypothesis, we examined bonding to party affiliation and perceived candidate images for debate viewers and nonviewers in each age group. Vote preference and party affiliation seemed to become more associated with age, and are more bonded for debate viewers than for nonviewers among sixth- and ninth-graders. Either debate viewing helped tie the two together at younger ages than would otherwise be the case, or else debate viewing was related to some other political socialization variable (presumably from the attachment group) responsible for the correlation.

In contrast, the correlations between a candidate's image and vote intention *decreased* with age: twelfth-graders seemed much more able to evaluate the candidates independently of who they would vote for. Once again, these relationships are stronger for debate viewers than nonviewers; but the overall downward trend with age helped eliminate one competing third variable hypothesis. If debate viewers tended to be those who are more advanced on age-related political socialization acquisitions and processes, debate viewers of a given age might have been expected to behave more like older adolescents than their nonviewing counterparts, and this explanation was difficult to refute for the party-vote correlations. However, since vote and candidate image became less associated with age, the larger correlations for debate viewers were more plausibly explained in terms of an effect of the debates.

Differences between the candidates are also worth noting, although explanations are necessarily more tenuous. Vote intention was more strongly related to Carter's image for sixth-graders but to Ford's image for twelfth-graders, suggesting several possible explanations. First, Ford's two years as president may have provided a relatively complete and stable image, while Carter's appearance as a national figure was much more recent. Second, Ford's position carried significance for both partisans and nonpartisans, while Carter's exposure was entirely as a candidate. Finally, Carter's image or personality was much more a campaign issue than Ford's, and this too could account for the accentuated age-trend for Carter.

We also examined the same correlations, but for different times of measurement during the campaign instead of age groups. Unfortunately, a full age by time of measurement by viewing division would have required an even larger sample. Trends here were much less pronounced, but it appeared that bonding may have decreased slightly for Ford's image, while increasing slightly for Carter's over the campaign. The correlation between vote preference and party appeared to have undergone vast fluctuations during the campaign. However, a check on the pretest correlations for the four groups suggested that the very low correlations after the second debate were a randomization artifact for that group—their pretest correlation was much lower than the other groups' as well.

Including the pretest correlations, however, allowed for two separate tests of bonding effects during the campaign. For one thing, the party-vote correlation was generally stronger during the campaign than before, especially for those groups tested near the end of the campaign. This suggested that something about the campaign helped these adolescents integrate at least their party and candidate choices. Determining whether the debates were in part responsible is more difficult. While debate viewers are more bonded than nonviewers, viewing the debates seemed to have made the most difference at the first debate for party-vote correlation and at the second for vote-image correlations. Immediately after the final debate near the end of the campaign, nonviewers seemed to catch up for both party and image variables. In other words, any effects of the debates on these facets of bonding happened early in the campaign and appeared to wash out later.

We also examined comparable correlations between vote preference and perceived issue differences between the candidates for debate viewers and nonviewers in each of the three age groups. Apparently, Unemployment and Big Government—Red Tape were seen as bad things associated with the opposing candidate, while Tax Reform, Cutting Defense, and Limiting Abortion were seen as good things more associated with one's own candidate. And for all issues except Cutting Defense (which ninth-graders inexplicably associated with the opposing candidate), increasing maturity was associated with greater ability to relate one's candidate choice and one's perceptions of the candidates' stands on issues. In fact, sixth- and sometimes even ninth-graders often seemed not to understand the issues. For example, Tax Reform may simply be understood as Taxes for many sixth-graders, since they associated this issue weakly with the opposing candidate instead of their own.

Differences between debate viewers and nonviewers were not consistently illuminating. Correlations for Unemployment, Red Tape and Tax Reform were stronger for twelfth-grade viewers than nonviewers, but the trend was sometimes reversed for younger adolescents. In contrast, however, Cutting Defense was more strongly related to candidate preference for nonviewers. Perhaps the most convincing finding for debate effects is the *lack* of difference for Limiting Abortion, because it was the only one of these issues studiously avoided during the debates.

Evidence for increased bonding during the campaign was far weaker than for increases with age. In fact, while there were some variations with time, it was very difficult to call any of them trends toward increased bonding. Combining all three age groups produced far smaller correlations than those for the twelfth grade alone, making trends harder to spot and evaluate. The reversals mentioned above by sixth-graders further obscure the picture. Given these problems with the correlations between vote preference and issue perceptions, we should probably say that our sample was not large enough to look for debate-related bonding over the campaign.

When we examined the correlations for the twelfth grade alone without separating viewers and nonviewers we gained some insights into changes in this facet of bonding over the campaign. In general, the correlations between perceived issue differences between the candidates and vote preference decreased during the campaign, a trend similar to that for candidate images. In other words, there was evidence that adolescents were responding with relatively little knowledge at the beginning of the campaign and could only assume that their candidate held their favored position on an issue or had uniformly desirable attributes. Later on, presumably with more information, their perceptions of their own and the opposite candidate were more mixed and presumably more accurate.

However, in contrast to perceptions of images, where the decrease in bonding was fairly monotonic, there were some marked deviations for perceptions of issue stands. Limiting Abortions was an issue avoided by both candidates throughout the campaign, and so we found a very slight decrease in correlation that we may tentatively regard as a baseline against which to compare other trends. The correlation of vote preference with Cutting Defense decreased rapidly, as if it were a salient issue claimed by both candidates. However, the correlations with the three other issues showed occasional reversals of the overall trend, as if the debates or other news identified a candidate more clearly with an issue. Tax Reform was seen as one's own candidate's issue immediately after the second debate (T3), possibly as a lagged effect of the first debate on domestic issues and subsequent news coverage of positions. Likewise, Big Government became more strongly associated with the opposite candidate, with the same lag after its discussion in the first debate. And Unemployment returned to be strongly associated with the opposing candidate only after the final debate, in which it was a major topic of discussion.

Socialization to the Political System

We approached this issue through a path model, which included antecedents of debate viewing and discussion and then possible effects of these two variables on such attachment variables as interest in politics, strength of party affiliation, and political efficacy. The antecedent variables were the pretest measures of public affairs media use (for example, "How many days a week do you watch the news on television?"), which we assumed reflected long-standing communication habits. These were thought to be related (although not necessarily causally) to a second group of variables, three pretest measures of political attachment. These three variables were placed after media use since our theory was, after all, about changes in these variables. From these two sets of variables we expected to predict both watching the debates and discussion of them.

From there, these three groups of variables were expected to predict changes in the attachment variables as measured during the campaign. Basically, we expected to find debate viewing and discussion adding small increments to the attachment variables, with all the other variables controlled for, but we also thought that the antecedents to viewing and discussion would account for a substantial part of their variance, so that we could then argue that these antecedents were also acting through viewing and discussion in addition to their own small direct effects.

Finally, given the three age groups of the sample, it would seem obvious for grade to be the prior variable for the whole path model. Instead, we chose to calculate the model separately for each grade, because we wished to look for greater or lesser effects of the other variables depending on age. This will, however, place us in the position of comparing the significance levels of path coefficients and will require some caution.

Table 1 presents the path coefficients for the left-hand portion of the model, in which debate viewing and discussion are the criterion variables. We found use of the mass media for public affairs information to be generally a good predictor of knowledge about politics but not of strength of party affiliation. Pretest interest in politics, however, was associated only with public affairs television use and not at all with use of newspapers.

Television news viewing also predicted debate viewing itself (although not significantly for ninth-graders), while newspaper reading was not significantly related. Twelfth-graders knowledgeable about politics at the pretest were more likely to view the debates; the relationship was much weaker for younger adolescents. Those more attached to a political party viewed the debates more at all three grades, although the relationship was statistically significant only for ninth-graders. And interest in politics led clearly to debate viewing only for ninth-graders. Overall, considerably more of the variance in debate viewing was more explainable for twelfth-graders than for the younger adolescents, but even this 21 percent is not overwhelming and leaves a great deal of debate viewing unexplained.

The percentage of variance explained in discussion of the debates was much smaller for ninth- and twelfth-graders, and there was considerable grade-to-grade fluctuation in predictor variables. Watching television news led to discussion for sixth- and perhaps twelfth-graders, but not for ninth-graders, whose discussions of the debates seemed independent of everything except their pretest interest in politics, which was also a predictor for twelfth-graders. Phrased from a different point of view, discussion of the debates did not follow from television news viewing for ninth-graders, just as it was not strongly predicted by pretest interest in politics for sixth-graders. And overall, discussion of the debates, even more than viewing them, seemed to stem from something other than those media use and political attachment variables.

Table 2 shows the full set of paths from the left-hand side of the model to the three criterion political attachment variables. Quite naturally, strength of political partisanship was well predicted by its prestest measurement, but for twelfth-graders it also followed from political knowledge. Even controlling for pretest partisanship, those more knowledgeable weakened their strength of party affiliation (that is, they moved to "leaning" or "independent"). While knowledge was not a predictor for sixth- or ninth-graders, sixth-graders were made more strongly partisan by discussion of the debates, even though discussion was not predicted (or even slightly negatively related) to pretest partisanship. Thus, it seemed that talking about the debates with family or friends did affect sixth-graders' political attachments, perhaps by providing additional information helping them discover just what party they favored.

378

Table 1: Direct Effects of General Political Orientations and Public Affairs Mass Media Use on Time Spent Viewing the Debates and Discussing Politics

Dependent Variable	Predetermined Variable	Direct Effects		
		6th Graders N = 193	9th Graders N = 197	12th Graders N = 118
	Public Affairs TV Use (X1)	—	—	—
	Public Affairs Newspaper Use (X2)	—	—	—
	X1 by X2 Correlation	.292	.315	.155
Political Knowledge (X3)	X1	.10	.20a	.28a
	X2	.22a	−.09	.28a
	R² =	.070	.036	.044
Partisanship Strength: Time 1 (X4)	X1	.05	−.01	.13
	X2	.11	−.12	.15
	R² =	.017	.016	.060
Political Interest: Time 1 (X5)	X1	.24a	.14b	.24a
	X2	.06	.10	.10
	R² =	.069	.040	.076
Debate Viewing (X6)	X1	.18b	.10	.25a
	X2	−.03	.12	.12
	X3	.13	.13	.25a
	X4	.13	.16b	.15
	X5	.12	.20a	.07
	R² =	.115	.137	.208
Debate Discussion (X7)	X1	.25a	.00	.18
	X2	.12	.04	.13
	X3	.05	.09	.08
	X4	−.10	.02	.06
	X5	.10	.19a	.19b
	R² =	.127	.050	.134

*Note: Entries are standardized regression coefficients. R^2 = variance explained by that set of paths.
[a]$p < .01$ [b]$p < .05$

Interest in politics was also strongly predicted by its pretest levels, although it was much more stable for sixth-graders than for older adolescents. Beyond that, watching the debates also increased interest in politics despite an overall trend toward decreased interest for ninth- and twelfth-graders. In addition, discussion of the debates also fostered interest, but this time only for ninth-graders.

Table 2: Direct Effects of Antecedent Variables on Political Efficacy, Political Interest, and Strength of Partisanship in the Path Model for 6th, 9th, and 12th Graders,

Dependent Variable	Predetermined Variable	Direct Effects		
		6th N = 193	9th N = 197	12th N = 118
Partisanship Strength (T2)	Public Affairs TV Use (X1)	−.07	−.04	.11
	Public Affairs Newspaper Use (X2)	−.03	−.02	−.02
	Political Knowledge (X3)	−.03	.10	−.22[b]
	Partisanship Strength T1 (X4)	.45[a]	.54[a]	.62[a]
	Political Interest T1 (X5)	−.01	.05	.15
	Debate Viewing (X6)	.14	−.08	.15
	Debate Discussion (X7)	.30[a]	.08	.03
	$R^2 =$	.309	.310	.488
Political Interest (T2)	Public Affairs TV Use (X1)	−.01	.14	.08
	Public Affairs Newspaper Use (X2)	.09	−.01	.03
	Political Knowledge (X3)	.10	.02	.00
	Partisanship Strength T1 (X4)	.10	.13	−.08
	Political Interest T1 (X5)	.41[a]	.27[a]	.29[a]
	Debate Viewing (X6)	.19[a]	.18[b]	.18
	Debate Discussion (X7)	.03	.30[a]	.11
	$R^2 =$	.330	.375	.226
Political Efficacy	Public Affairs TV Use (X1)	.04	.06	.18
	Public Affairs Newspaper Use (X2)	−.10	−.01	.14
	Political Knowledge (X3)	.19[a]	.13	.20[b]
	Partisanship Strength T1 (X4)	−.13	.02	.03
	Political Interest T1 (X5)	.12	.00	−.06
	Debate Viewing (X6)	.16[b]	.13	−.17
	Debate Discussion (X7)	.02	.14	.02
	$R^2 =$	.101	.080	.092

Note: Entries are standardized regression coefficients. R^2 = variance explained by that set of paths.
[a] $p < .01$ [b] $p < .05$

Finally, political efficacy was examined, even though campaign effects on this more general aspect of political attachment might be expected to be somewhat delayed. Not surprisingly, pretest political knowledge was associated with efficacy, possibly in part because pretest efficacy was not measured. What was surprising was that debate viewing was related to higher levels of efficacy for sixth- and ninth-graders, but to lower levels for twelfth-graders. Unfortunately, interpretation of this relationship as an effect of the debates must remain tenuous because efficacy was not measured at the pretest. Still, the case was strengthened somewhat since both political knowledge and interest in politics are included as controls and the stronger relationship for the youngest adolescents was consistent with previous research on the efficacy-damaging effects of Watergate.

Discussion

Beginning with the notion that election campaigns might well be times of accelerated political socialization, we first hypothesized that the debates between Carter and Ford in the 1976 campaign might serve as particularly salient and influential socialization stimuli. The debates provided an opportunity to gain relatively detailed comparative information about the candidates—information that would ordinarily require more active search.

Given this assumption about the opportunity provided by the debates, we predicted that debate viewing would allow increased integration or "bonding" of partisan attitudes—those involving evaluation of opposing candidates or parties. In addition, we predicted that debate viewing would lead to changes in the other main category of political socialization outcomes—attachment to the political system.

The amount that adolescents watched the debates was a function of strength of party affiliation (an Attachment variable) and, for sixth- and twelfth-graders, of general television news viewing. Ninth-graders, in contrast, watched the debates out of an overall interest in politics, and the more knowledgeable adolescents, especially at twelfth grade, were more likely to watch the debates. Taking account of the division between prior media use variables and attachment variables, sixth-graders came to the debates more out of their prior media use habits while ninth-graders came more because of their levels of attachment to the political system, and twelfth-graders came equally for the two reasons.

Discussing the debates with family and friends was somewhat less predictable than debate viewing, but once again it was a function of previous public affairs media use for the youngest adolescents, of an attachment variable (interest) for ninth-graders, and of both for those adolescents nearly old enough to vote. However, even for twelfth-graders these predictors do not account for a large part of the variance in debate viewing and discussion, leading us to conclude that perhaps the unique character of the debates themselves overrode the more usual limitations on attention to political media events (Blumler and McLeod, 1974).

Whatever led these adolescents to attend to the debates, our main hypotheses were about the effects of those debates on two aspects of political socialization. For the first of these, bonding of partisan attitudes and perceptions, we did find greater bonding for debate viewers than nonviewers. Specifically, debate viewing appeared to help sixth- and ninth-graders tie together their candidate preference, their party preference, and their perceptions of candidate images. For bonding of candidate preference to perceptions of candidates' stands on the issues, debate viewing strengthened this tie only for twelfth-graders, and it seems that younger children were too confused about the issues to make use of issue content in the debates. Thus, younger adolescents evidently used the debates for information about candidate party and image, while older adolescents gained information about candidate issue stands.

The debates also affected various aspects of adolescents' attachment to the political system. While debate viewing did little to solidify strength of party affiliation, discussion of the debates (presumably more selective) was an important predictor for the youngest adolescents. The debates did increase interest in politics, even though ninth- and twelfth-graders as a whole became *less* interested in politics during the campaign, a finding reminiscent of Blumler and McLeod's results with first-time voters in the 1970 election. However, while they found voters seemingly "turned off" by the initial party broadcasts, something else about the campaign was at fault here, because those who did watch the debates professed greater interest. Discussion of the debates was again clearly not simply a surrogate for debate viewing, since it produced increased interest among ninth-graders, but not among sixth- or twelfth-graders.

Debate viewing also appeared to have weak effects on political efficacy, a characteristic of attachment that should be fairly stable and relatively less affected by specific events such as a campaign. As one might expect because of their lesser experience with political campaigns, sixth-graders' own feelings of efficacy seemed somewhat more affected by the debates than were ninth-graders', but the real surprise comes from the reversed sign for twelfth-graders. While the coefficient is not significantly different from zero for the smaller twelfth-grade sample, it is very different both from those of the two younger groups and from the twelfth-graders' own coefficient for interest. These high school seniors became *both* more interested in politics and more cynical of them after viewing the debates, a result that could have very different implications for their future political participation depending on which of the two is more stable and more influential.

These variations in effects from age group to age group do not consistently fit either of the competing hypotheses we advanced: the impact of the debates was sometimes greater on the younger groups and sometimes greater on the older, depending on the particular dependent variable under consideration. Obviously, arguing greater or lesser effects with increasing age was too simplistic. The debates, like nearly all other media presentations, were complex and rich events, and different people were able to make use of and/or resist different parts of that richness. These findings suggest that a more direct approach along these lines, such as examination of effects for adolescents approaching the debates with different gratifications in mind, will yield further interesting results.

The main point of these findings, however, has to do with the classic direct effects question: did the presidential debates between Gerald Ford and Jimmy Carter directly affect not simply attention or incidental learning, but political socialization processes themselves? While we realize the limitations of our methodology and the variables used, our answer is yes.

382   **THE GREAT DEBATES**

NOTE

1. A number of tables detailing means and percentages and figures illustrating differences in correlations between subgroups have been omitted because of space considerations in this volume. They may be obtained by writing author Hawkins.

REFERENCES

Blumler, J., and J. M. McLeod. "Communication and Voter Turnout in Great Britain," in Leggatt, T. (ed.), *Sociological Theory and Survey Research*. London: Sage Publications, 1974.

Chaffee, S. H., L. S. Ward, and L. P. Tipton. "Mass Communication and Political Socialization." *Journalism Quarterly*, 47 (Winter 1970), pp. 647–59.

Easton, D., and J. Dennis. *Children in the Political System: Origins of Political Legitimacy*. New York: McGraw-Hill, 1969.

Greenstein, F. *Children and Politics*. New Haven: Yale University Press, 1965.

Hawkins, R. P., S. Pingree, and D. F. Roberts. "Watergate and Political Socialization: The Inescapable Event." *American Politics Quarterly*, 3 (October 1975), pp. 406–22.

Hess, R. D., and J. V. Torney. *The Development of Political Attitudes in Children*. Chicago: Aldine, 1967.

Patterson, T. E., and R. D. McClure. "Political Advertising: Voter Reaction." Paper presented at annual meeting of the American Association for Public Opinion Research, Asheville, N.C., May 1973.

Rothschild, M., and M. Ray. "Involvement and Political Advertising Effect: An Exploratory Experiment." *Communication Research*, 1, (1974), pp. 264–87.

Sears, D. O. "Political Socialization," in Greenstein, F., and N. W. Polsby (eds.), *The Handbook of Political Science*, Reading, Mass.: Addison-Wesley, 1975a.

Sears, D. O. *Political Attitudes Through the Life Cycle*. San Francisco: W. H. Freeman, 1975b.

Vaillancourt, P. M. "Stability of Children's Survey Responses." *Public Opinion Quarterly*, 37 (1973), pp. 373–87.

21.

Information Flow and the
Shaping of Meanings

SAMUEL L. BECKER, ROBERT PEPPER,
LAWRENCE A. WENNER, and JIN KEON KIM

Questions about information flow and the construction of meanings are basic to an understanding of political communication. These are important questions not only to communication theorists but also to persons interested in discovering ways to develop a better-informed electorate. The 1976 debates between presidential candidates James Earl Carter and Gerald Ford and between their running mates were events that injected major new elements into the flow of information.

The subject of this study is the question of how the debates interacted with other factors to affect exposure of people to political information and, in turn, to affect people's constructions or reconstructions of meaning for political concepts. Specifically, we were concerned with two major questions:

1. How did the various characteristics of voters combine to affect their exposure to different forms of the debate story?
2. How did exposure to the various forms of the debate story combine to affect the construction or reconstruction of the "meaning" of Gerald Ford, of Jimmy Carter, and of the idea of presidential debates itself?

The importance of voters' perceptions of political candidates and of the election process, as exemplified in this case by voters' perceptions of the debates, is often overlooked by those who consider the role of communication in an election. This communication serves more vital functions than simply aiding voters in their decisions about which levers to pull in the voting booth. Two of the most important are the legitimizing of the candidate who wins and the legitimizing of the election process itself. It is our hypothesis that communication plays a key role in bringing about and maintaining acceptance of the electoral process and of the new office holder. The major focus in this study is on factors that explain exposure to and perceptions of the presidential debates and on the effect of that exposure on voter images of the candidates.

There is some theoretical basis and research evidence to support the belief that certain voter characteristics affect exposure to new political information. However, there is no good theoretical basis or research evidence to give one confidence in predictions about the relationships among these factors or their relative weights in affecting exposure to different kinds of political information. Hence, ours and other efforts to understand these relationships and relative influences are clearly exploratory.

One of the major issues is whether sources of political information differ in usage and in their impact on meaning construction. Voters have little direct exposure to most political events. The television version of the debates was necessarily different in some respects from the newspaper versions and both were different from the versions created in interpersonal communication. Did these differences result in different effects or were these sources essentially redundant? Our probes are intended to explore this question also.

Method

Data for this study were gathered in a panel survey of three waves of face-to-face interviews with a stratified random sample of 149 potential voters age 18 and older in Cedar Rapids, Iowa. Initial interviews were conducted on September 11, 1976. The second wave of interviews took place on September 25, two days after the first debate. The third and final wave was conducted on November 6, four days after the general election.

The major questions of the study were answered with a series of hierarchical regression analyses in which variables were entered into the analyses by blocks, ordered according to assumptions about the relationship among them (Cohen & Cohen, 1975; Kerlinger & Pedhazur, 1973).

Results
Exposure

Though the audience of voters for the live broadcasts of the presidential debates declined somewhat from one debate to the next, it remained surprisingly high. Some or all of the first debate was seen by 87.9 percent of our sample of voters, the second debate by 87.2 percent, and the final debate between Carter and Ford by 73.8 percent. The debate between the vice-presidential candidates drew far less attention; it was seen or heard by 54.4 percent of the sample.

Of those exposed to the first debate broadcast, 90.1 percent saw it on television, 3.8 percent heard it on radio, and 6.1 percent reported that they were exposed to some of both. For the second two presidential debates taken together, those same results were approximated; the exposure of 89.9 percent was through television, 4.3 percent was through radio, and 5.8 percent was through both media.

All of the voters who watched or listened to the debates, of course, did not sit through them in their entirety. Not only did the first debate attract a larger audience, but those who watched tended to watch longer; 88.5 percent of those exposed watched over a half hour. On the other hand, not only did the vice-presidential debate have the smallest audience, but its audience tended to drift away more quickly; only 70.4 percent of those exposed viewed or listened more than thirty minutes.

There was also a great deal of exposure to the first debate other than simply viewing or listening to the live broadcast; within the first two days after the event, 77.2 percent of our sample reported exposure to a story about the debate on a newscast, 21.5 percent reported hearing or seeing other material about the debate on some broadcast, 55.7 percent said they listened to some of the network commentators immediately following the debate, and 82.6 percent read about it in a newspaper. All but 20.8 percent of our sample also reported talking to other people about the debate within those first two days following the event. Only 2.7 percent of these voters reported exposure neither to the live broadcast nor to any other communication about the debate within that 48-hour period. If we considered all four debates, instead of merely the first one, only 4.5 percent failed to see or hear at least some portion of them live. It is important to note that not a single voter that we found saw or heard a debate without also getting supplementary information from some other person, from a newspaper, or from broadcasting.

Our sample agreed with most observers around the country that Ford "won" the first debate: 32.2 percent gave the decision to Ford, 9.4 percent gave it to Carter, 40.3 percent believed it was a draw, and 18.1 percent indicated they had no opinion. Our respondents who talked with other people about the debate reported that their views were roughly similar.

Predicting Exposure to the Debates

A series of hierarchical regression analyses were used as an aid in examining the factors influencing exposure to the debates. A separate regression was done using each of five dependent measures of debate exposure: (1) a measure of the total amount of exposure to the live debate broadcasts, (2) the amount of newspaper reading about the first debate in the two days following the event, which we assumed was somewhat indicative of the relative amount of reading about each of the debates, (3) the number of people one talked with about the first debate, which, again, we assumed was an approximation of interpersonal communication about all of the debates, (4) exposure to newscast items, commentators, and other radio and television broadcasts about the debates, not including the live broadcasts, and (5) total exposure to the first debate, which was the sum of the last three measures plus amount of viewing or listening to the live debate broadcast after each measure was normalized.

As Table 1 shows, of the five different dependent measures of exposure, these six sets of independent variables best predict total exposure to information about the first debate ($R = .67$). We believe that this finding is consistent with our assumption that there is a great deal of redundancy and, hence, a high degree of interchangeability among the different sources of information about a major event such as the debates because this was the one dependent measure that gave equal weight to the various kinds of information about the debates, from viewing of the first debate as it went on to talking about the debate with other people. To put this another way, the most stable and important kind of exposure is the amount of exposure to increments of information in the environment rather than amount of exposure to any particular medium or form of the message about the event.

Though the total set of independent variables predicted exposure to debate information in various media about equally well, the individual variables varied widely in their importance for predicting these different kinds of exposure. For both exposure to the live debates via broadcasting and other exposure to debate information via radio or television, habitual viewing of television news was the best single predictor, according to the significance tests of the standard beta weights. Age and the tendency to avoid broadcast political news, not to use that news for conversation, and not to use it as para-social interaction were the major predictors of exposure to the live debates (Wenner, 1977).

Not using broadcast news as an aid in conversation was also a major predictor of newspaper reading about the first debate. The other major predictor of exposure to debate information from newspapers was the habit of news magazine reading and, to a lesser extent, newspaper reading. Education was also a predictor of reading about the debate.

The best single predictor of talking to a variety of other people about the debate was the number of one's usual political activities (Milbrath, 1965). Again, the inclination to watch political news was important, along with the inclination to use political news selectively.

For total exposure to the story of the first debate from all sources, the best predictors were habitual use of television newscasts and news magazines, and the inclination to watch political news. Education, interest in this particular campaign, and normal level of political activity were also important.

Another and probably more important way of looking at the power of these variables to predict exposure is in terms of our blocks of predictor variables, rather than in terms of single variables. As the bottom of Table 1 shows, our model of the hierarchy of influences fit the data reasonably well, especially for explaining total exposure to the first debate story, total exposure to the four live debates, and reading about the debate. The demographic and habitual news media use variables account for the bulk of the variance, with the other blocks —involvement with the present campaign, general political involvement, and political efficacy/cynicism (Campbell et al., 1954, 187–98; Agger et al., 1961) —in descending order of importance. The major break in that pattern is for the news uses and gratifications block. It accounts for much more variance than some of the blocks above it in the hierarchy.

Impact of the Debates

Following the first debate, over a fourth of the respondents (26.9 percent) said that the debate had had some effect on their decision about whom they favored. Reasons cited were widely scattered but tended to indicate a gain for Ford. Following the election, a slightly larger percentage (32.2 percent) indicated that the debates had affected their preference for one candidate over the other. A slightly larger percentage of Carter voters (25 percent) than of Ford voters (23 percent) thought the debates had influenced them. That difference, however, was not significant.

One of the most striking signs of the impact of the presidential debates was the way they stimulated political talk. Before the first debate, our voters were asked how often they talked politics with friends or members of their family. Almost a fourth of the sample responded that they usually talk politics less than once a week; a third of these said that they never talk about politics. Yet, within two days of the first Carter–Ford debate, two-thirds of these respondents said that they had talked to other people about the debate; more than 11 percent said that they had talked to three or more other people. The debate stimulated almost as much talk among those who seldom talk about politics as it did among

Table 1: Simple and Multiple Correlations and Beta Weights for Predictors of Debate Exposure

	Total Debate 1 Exposure			Total Live Debate Exposure			Reading About Debate			Talking About Debate			Non-live RTV Information on Debate		
	r	R	Beta	r	R	Beta	r	R	Beta	r	R	Beta	r	R	Beta
Education	.32[c]	.32	.14[a]	.05	.05	.03	.28[c]	.28	.15[a]	.24[c]	.24	.10	.21[c]	.21	.12
SES	.25[c]	.35	.05	−.02	.07	−.14	.22[c]	.31	−.01	.13	.25	−.02	.13	.22	.04
Age	.09	.37	.10	.22[c]	.25	.17[a]	.16[b]	.37	.12	−.12	.26	.01	.04	.23	.04
Sex	−.06	.38	.00	−.12	.27	−.09	−.04	.37	.02	−.11	.30	−.08	.00	.23	.23
TV News Use	.22[c]	.45	.18[b]	.35[c]	.40	.25[c]	.04	.37	−.02	.04	.32	.05	.21[b]	.33	.22[b]
Radio News Use	.08	.46	.05	.18[b]	.43	.09	.09	.39	.08	−.10	.33	−.09	.15	.36	.11
Newspaper Use	.20[b]	.47	−.04	.10	.43	−.08	.34[c]	.45	.17[a]	−.02	.33	−.09	.11	.36	−.08
News Magazine Use	.39[c]	.52	.17[b]	.21[c]	.13	.46	.38[c]	.50	.20[b]	.22[c]	.36	.07	.22[c]	.38	.10
Political Talk	.33[c]	.54	.10	.21[c]	.46	.12	.28[c]	.52	.13	.17[b]	.37	−.04	.22[c]	.39	.08
Interest in Campaign	.36[c]	.58	.18[a]	.17	.47	.05	.28[c]	.53	.12	.19[b]	.41	.08	.26[c]	.43	.24[b]
Care about Outcome	.16	.59	−.08	.10	.47	.02	.14	.53	.05	.12	.41	−.08	.01	.45	−.16
Strength of Leaning	.12	.59	.06	.01	.48	−.01	.10	.53	.01	.09	.41	.05	.04	.45	.43
Political Activity	.44[c]	.60	.17[a]	.21[c]	.49	.11	.33[c]	.53	.07	.36[c]	.46	.23[b]	.24[c]	.45	.08
Strength of Partisanship	.03	.60	−.09	−.01	.49	−.06	.05	.54	−.08	−.02	.46	−.12	−.02	.46	−.08
Strength of Con-Lib Beliefs	.17[b]	.61	−.05	−.01	.50	−.13	.09	.54	−.07	.19[b]	.46	.02	.05	.46	−.08
Political Cynicism	−.12	.62	−.12	.00	.50	−.03	.21	.54	.03	−.12	.47	−.11	−.17[b]	.49	−.19[b]
Political Efficacy	.30[c]	.62	.05	.11	.50	−.02	.21[c]	.55	.06	.22[c]	.48	.03	.20[b]	.49	.01

Use News Broadcasts for:															
Avoidance	−.41c	.65	−.18b	−.30c	.55	−.21b	−.20b	.55	.01	−.29c	.49	−.18a	−.28c	.51	−.08
Conversation	−.03	.66	−.12	−.14	.56	−.15a	−.10	.58	−.20b	.15	.51	.13	−.05	.52	−.11
Para-Social Interaction	−.13	.66	−.04	−.11	.58	−.16a	−.14	.58	−.03	−.08	.51	.01	−.02	.52	−.02
Surveillance	−.12	.67	−.12	.02	.58	−.03	−.13	.59	−.12	−.10	.51	−.04	−.08	.53	−.13
Entertainment	−.07	.67	.02	.02b	.58	.03	−.13	.59	−.06	.04	.52	.11	−.09	.53	−.03
Selectivity	.04	.67	.08	−.05	.58	−.04	−.04	.59	.04	.18b	.53	.15a	−.01	.53	.05
Variance Accounted for by Each Block															
Demographic Variables	.143c			.071b			.138c			.091c			.055		
Habitual News Media Use	.151c			.144c			.131c			.048			.098c		
Involvement with Present Campaign	.048b			.014			.014			.027			.050b		
General Political Involvement	.025			.023			.013			.047a			.010		
Political Efficacy/Cynicism	.017			.001			.002			.013			.041a		
News Uses and Gratifications	.065b			.083b			.051			.057			.038		
Total Variance Accounted For	.450c			.337c			.350c			.283c			.282c		

c = significant at p < .01
b = significant at p < .05
a = significant at p < .10

CARTER vs. FORD, 1976

those who often do. Even of those who had earlier said they "never" talk about politics, 69.2 percent discussed the first debate with one or more persons within that two-day period.

Debate Impact on Candidate Image

In order to facilitate the comparison of the candidates' images by Ford and Carter voters, we used a measure of image factor scores which was constant over the three waves. The method of computing these scores was determined on the basis of six factor analyses. During each wave the respondent was asked to indicate his or her opinion of "presidential candidate Gerald Ford" and then of "presidential candidate Jimmy Carter" on each of nineteen semantic differential scales. A separate factor analysis was done of the ratings of each candidate at each of the three interview times. The factors which held up consistently across the six factor analyses (that is, across both time and candidates) were used as the dependent variables for purposes of the present study. These factors were ability, style, poise, and conservatism.

Surprisingly, since a major issue of the campaign was Carter's "fuzziness," we found that the average shift in the image of the two candidates differed little. The greatest image shift during the course of the campaign was on the perception of Ford's poise; Ford voters as well as Carter voters steadily and substantially lowered their rating of Ford on this dimension. There were no other major shifts among Carter voters, except the drop in their perceptions of Carter's poise after the first debate, though that perception became more positive by the time the election was over. Ford voters, on the other hand, during the course of the campaign became much more positive about Ford's ability and conservatism and somewhat more positive about his style, while becoming much more negative about Carter's ability, style, and conservatism.

In order to examine the debate story's influences on these four image dimensions of presidential candidates Ford and Carter at time 3, we used a series of hierarchical regression analyses which controlled for the time 1 image score on the factor we were interested in at time 3. We attempted to isolate the unique debate story factors which most influenced the change in the rating of the candidates from time 1 to time 3. Separate analyses were run on Ford and Carter voters, using as the dependent variables the four Ford and the four Carter image factor scores at time 3. The hierarchical model specified the time 1 image as the first block entered in the analysis, so that it served essentially as a covariate. It should be noted that the first five blocks entered after the time 1 image score follow a temporal sequence. The last block represents habitual news communication behaviors of each voter, which, while not unique to the debate story, provide additional information about the debates and consequently should influence the perceived image of the candidates at time 3.

We will summarize the analyses by considering one image factor at a time. For each factor we will first examine Ford voter images of the candidates, followed by those of Carter voters (see Table 2).

Candidate Ability. For both Ford and Carter voters, as expected, the perception of candidate ability at time 1 accounted for more variance in the time 3 image than any other block or variable.

Table 2: Beta Weights for Predictors of Candidate Image

	Ability Image				Style Image				Poise Image				Conservative/Liberal Image			
	Ford Voters		Carter Voters		Ford Voters		Carter Voters		Ford Voters		Carter Voters		Ford Voters		Carter Voters	
	F*	C†	F	C	F	C	F	C	F	C	F	C	F	C	F	C
Time 1 Ability	.53c	.51c	.69c	.49c	.59c	.62c	.69c	.59c	.27b	.42c	.48c	.58c	.31b	.53c	.50c	.22b
Viewing Presidential Debate 1	.02	−.02	−.04	.02	−.05	.03	.03	.13	−.14	−.11	.19	−.08	.18	−.20	.24a	−.20
Post-Debate 1 Reading	.10	−.08	.19	.00	−.08	.06	.11	−.06	−.26b	−.06	.08	−.02	.10	−.08	−.15	.08
Post-Debate 1 Talk	.06	−.01	−.06	−.25	.05	.20a	.10	−.33b	−.13	.01	−.18	−.15	−.02	−.01	−.12	.19
Post-Debate 1 Broadcast	.28b	.12	.05	.13	.10	.01	.16	.16	−.12	.14	.07	−.09	−.06	.16	.08	.05
Viewing Presidential Debate 2	.00	.21	.10	−.13	−.11	.19a	.05	−.16	.02	.14	.15	−.24a	.19	−.07	−.12	.01
Viewing Vice-Presidential Debate	.08	.16	.11	−.21	.25b	.06	.00	−.09	.28b	.04	.02	−.11	−.14	−.02	.11	−.01
Viewing Presidential Debate 3	−.38c	−.38c	−.06	.02	−.08	−.34c	−.08	.06	.07	−.03	−.22b	.19	−.08	.07	.07	.32b
TV News Viewing	.12	−.22b	−.04	.17	.08	.02	−.06	.09	.01	−.10	−.26b	.09	.12	−.10	−.15	.09
Radio News Listening	.03	−.08	.20a	−.21a	−.02	−.10	.23b	−.10	.18	.02	.26b	.01	−.12	−.04	.02	−.13
Newspaper Reading	−.26b	−.04	−.15b	−.06	−.02	−.09	.01	−.03	.16	−.23a	−.07	−.04	−.16	.14	.01	−.25b
News Magazine Reading	−.01	.00	−.07	.01	−.01	−.11	−.05	−.07	.28b	.02	.08	−.07	.04	−.01	.11	−.08
Talk before Voting	−.08	.23b	−.22a	.07	.17	.16	−.18	.18	.11	−.03	−.04	−.01	.13	−.10	.34b	−.58c

*Ford
†Carter

c = significant at p < .01
b = significant at p < .05
a = significant at p < .10

For Ford voters, the second most important variable in explaining the time 3 ability image of both candidates was amount of viewing of the last presidential debate: for both candidates, increased viewing led to a decrease in perceived ability, although Ford's image decreased less than that of Carter. The variable which next best explains an increase in Ford voters' image of their candidate's ability is the amount of exposure to radio/television commentary or news about the confrontation following the first debate. Finally, the last variable which contributed significantly to a more negative image of Ford's ability by his voters was a large amount of newspaper reading. As for Ford voters' perception of Carter's image, more frequent conversation about the election in the week before voting was linked to a significant increase in perception of Carter's ability at time 3. Finally, Carter's ability rating deteriorated with an increase in television news viewing for Ford voters.

After accounting for time 1 perception of candidate ability, preelection talk by Carter voters most significantly contributed to their image of Ford's ability; the more they talked, the more negative their perception of Ford's ability. Likewise, Carter voter perceptions of Carter's ability were negatively correlated to the amount of talking about the first debate. Interestingly, the next most significant variable for Carter voters' image of both candidates was the amount of radio news listening. As radio listening increased, these voters perceived Ford's ability more positively and Carter's ability more negatively.

Candidate Style. Once again, time 1 perception of candidate style accounted for the greatest amount of variance in the time 3 image. Following this in importance, viewing of the debates contributed significantly to Ford voters' perceptions of candidates' style. Viewing of the vice-presidential debate was positively correlated with Ford voters' image of their candidate. As was the case with the ability image, high viewing of the last presidential debate contributed negatively to the image of Carter's style by Ford voters. As talking about the election increased, Ford voter image of Ford style also increased. In contrast, amount of talk immediately following the first debate was related to a more positive perception of Carter's style by these voters.

After controlling for the time 1 image, we found that amount of radio news listening accounted for the most variance in Carter voter image of Ford's style: as with perceived ability, increasing amounts of radio news listening led to a more positive image of Ford. Carter's perceived style, on the other hand, decreased as the amount of talk about the first debate increased. Talking about the election in the week before voting was the next most significant variable in explaining Carter voters' perceptions of candidate style at time 3. As in the case of the ability image, a great amount of talking before the election led to a negative image of Ford's style and a positive image of Carter's style.

Candidate Poise. In contrast to the first two candidate image factors, the time 1 perception of candidate poise is not consistently the best predictor of the time 3 image. For Ford voters' image of Ford's poise, reading of news magazines accounts for the greatest amount of variance—more reading is associated with a positive score on this factor. In order of importance, the variables best explaining time 3 image of Ford poise are viewing of the vice-presidential debate, the time 1 poise image, and reading about the first presidential debate.

The first two are positively correlated with the time 3 image, while the third led to a decrease in Ford's poise image. For Ford voters' perceptions of Carter's poise, the time 1 score accounted for the most variance in the time 3 score. Next in importance is newspaper reading, which is negatively correlated with Carter's poise image among Ford voters.

As opposed to the Ford voters, the time 1 image score accounts for the most variance in the time 3 score for Carter voters' image of both candidates' poise. Carter voter image of Ford poise is negatively tied to television news viewing and positively related to radio news listening. Carter voter image of Carter poise is next best explained by viewing of the second and third presidential debates: amount of viewing of the second debate is significantly related to a negative image shift, but there is a trend in the opposite direction for viewing of the third debate.

Candidate Conservatism–Liberalism. As was the case with the poise factor, the image of candidate conservatism at time 3 is not consistently best explained by the rating of that image at time 1. For Ford voters, however, the time 1 scores do best explain the time 3 image. On the question of candidate conservatism the data suggest a trend that viewing of the first and second presidential debates by Ford voters led to an increasingly conservative image of Ford and a more liberal image of Carter. The perception of Ford's conservatism by Carter voters at time 3 is best explained by their impression at time 1. The only other variable significant in explaining Carter voters' tendency to rate Ford as more conservative was amount of talking about the election before voting. Similarly, this variable accounted for the greatest amount of variance in Carter voters' image on this factor for their own candidate: the more Carter voters talked about the election, the more liberal they perceived their candidate to be. In contrast, the next most important variable indicated that the more Carter voters watched the last debate, the more conservative they perceived their candidate. On the other hand, amount of newspaper reading was positively related to Carter's liberal image. The final significant variable, accounting for Carter's time 3 image by his voters, was the time 1 image of his conservative–liberal position.

Impact of Debate Exposure on the Press for Consistency

In planning this study we assumed that exposure to the debates—especially viewing or listening to the live debates—would increase the press for consistency between one's perceptions of Carter and one's perceptions of Ford. Hence, we hypothesized that the time 1–time 2 changes in Carter's image and time 1–time 2 changes in Ford's image would be negatively related and that the negative relationship would be greater the more exposed one was to the debates. We hypothesized the same thing for the time 1–time 3 changes, with total viewing of the four debates as the intervening variable. However, not only did we find that amount of exposure was not associated with the press for consistency in either case, but we found no press for consistency. Though voters' images of Carter and Ford were negatively correlated at each of our three interviewing times, *changes* in these images tended to be *positively* correlated. As a voter became more positive (or negative) toward one candidate, he or she tended to become more positive (or negative) toward the other.

Perceptions of the Debates

Since both the acceptance by the public of the legitimacy of the election process and the probability of debates between presidential candidates in future years are undoubtedly affected by public opinion about the value of the debates, we were interested in that opinion and the way in which exposure to the debates affected it. Our measure for this purpose was a set of ten scales on which respondents indicated their reaction to the concept "Broadcast Debates between the Two Major Presidential Candidates." From responses to these scales, four factor scores were computed: debate utility, appeal, issue stress, and personality emphasis.

Interestingly, amount of exposure to the debates did not seem to affect perceptions of the debates even though such perceptions changed significantly during the course of the campaign. From the hierarchical regression analyses no clear pattern emerged from which we could infer the precise ways in which exposure to the debate story and other information about the campaign affected those perceptions.

We should note in passing that we found consistent and positive relationships between voter perceptions of the utility and appeal of the debates and the ability and style of both Ford and Carter. These correlations between candidate and debate factor scores ranged generally in the .20 to .40 range, suggesting that one's expectations and perceptions of such debates depend in fair part upon one's perceptions of the quality of the candidates.

Discussion

The results of this study support the idea that the debates served a stimulative function, especially the stimulation of political talk. The striking increase in such talk reported just before and after the initial Ford–Carter debate suggests that at least one of the important effects of presidential debates is to enhance the opportunities for interpersonal influence.

Probably more important, though, are the related inferences that can be made about the factors that cause voters to expose themselves to important political news, such as the debates, in different kinds of ways. As Table 1 demonstrates, a voter's usual medium for news was generally the best, or one of the best, predictors of the amount of debate information he or she sought from any particular medium. The major debate variable that did not work this way was the amount that a voter talked about the debates. Though one's usual frequency of political talk was a significant predictor, other variables such as one's level of political activity in the past, education, and interest in the campaign were stronger predictors.

The other important inference is that we are unlikely to be able to isolate the impact of the live debate broadcasts, since they resounded so strongly through almost all possible channels of communication. Virtually all persons who were exposed to those original broadcasts were buffeted by the echoes as

394   **THE GREAT DEBATES**

well; even those who missed the original could not totally escape the debate story without difficulty.

Overall, habitual media use played a larger role in explaining exposure to the debate story than any of our other sets of variables, with demographic variables (education, socioeconomic status, and age) and the uses and gratifications people normally seek from television news explaining most of the remainder. It should also be noted, of course, that all of these variables together accounted for somewhat less than half of the variance in exposure to the debates. A great deal of the variability in such exposure remains to be explained.

Though the images of the presidential candidates that voters had by the time the election campaign was over were best predicted by the images these voters had at the start of the campaign, as we expected, exposure to the unfolding debate story during the campaign clearly affected them, but apparently in ways specific to these particular candidates rather than in ways that might be generalizable to other candidates in future presidential debates. That is to say, there is no general pattern that we can discern which appears to be independent of particular candidate and particular debate or source of debate information.

The analysis pointed out the importance of voters' interpersonal discussion about the campaign. Talking about the first debate in the days immediately following its broadcast was important in voters' forming of perceptions of Carter's ability and style: the more Carter voters talked about the first debate, the less positive they rated Carter's ability and style at time 3. Post-debate discussion had the opposite effect on Ford voters; that is, the more they talked, the more positive their perceptions of Carter's style. This finding tends to support the tendency for regression to middle positions: as Ford voters became more familiar with Carter through the debate and post-debate discussion, the less apprehensive they became about the Democratic candidate. Carter voters similarly became less enthusiastic about their candidate following his performance in the first debate.

More important than this post-debate talk was talking about the election during the week before voting. The more Ford voters talked during this time, the more positively they rated Carter's ability and Ford's style. For Carter voters, the more they talked during this week, the lower they rated Ford on ability and style but the higher they rated Carter's style. In addition, increased talk by Carter voters also led to a more conservative view of Ford and a more liberal view of Carter. These findings support a press for consistency through maximizing the difference between their candidate (Carter) and his opponent (Ford). The strongest explanation for these findings is that people tend to talk politics with people holding similar political beliefs. In addition, it supports the notion that partisans tend to seek reinforcement when they are uncertain about their party's candidate, in this case supporting Carter who was relatively unknown and who was accused of being vague on the issues.

Perceptions of the presidential debates became somewhat more negative during the course of the 1976 campaign, but the evidence suggests that variance in the amount of exposure that a voter had to the live debates or to other information about the debates had little detectable effect on that negative movement. It should be noted, though, that the decreasing enthusiasm for the debates was not severe. Overall, when the election was over, voters were still somewhat positive about the utility and appeal of presidential debates, and they remained somewhat concerned about insufficient stress on issues and too much stress on candidate personalities in the debates.

We found some evidence that the particular characteristics of each candidate interacted with the particular characteristics of each source from which information was obtained, so that each source helped or hurt each candidate a bit on some particular dimension. However, overall we found no consistent advantages for either candidate from any one source.

Perhaps most important of all, the heavy exposure to information about the presidential candidates, stimulated directly and indirectly by the debates, along with the fair degree of satisfaction with the debates that we found probably resulted in a certain degree of commitment to the election process and to the candidate selected through that process. Carter voters maintained an image of Ford that was somewhat positive on ability, style, and poise: while Ford voters maintained an image of Carter that was somewhat positive on those same qualities. The only factor on which there was sharp divergence in the perceptions of the two candidates was the conservative–liberal factor, though the two groups of voters agreed more in their ratings of the two candidates on this factor than on any of the others. Both groups perceived Ford to be toward the conservative end of the continuum and Carter to be toward the liberal end.

One of the most positive findings in this study is that the debates stimulated exposure to various kinds of communication about the campaign without, at the same time, causing voters to balance their increasing support for their own candidate by becoming more negative toward the opposing candidate. Thus, they increased the potential for legitimation of the candidate ultimately elected. We should note, of course, that this result in the 1976 campaign may have been due to the fact that sharp differences between the candidates apparently were not perceived by voters. Whether results will be quite different in future years if we have more contrasting candidates is unanswerable at this time. That question and the question of the particular characteristics of candidates which interact with various sources of information about debates between the candidates to shape the perceptions or "meanings" of those candidates should be prominent on the research agendas of mass-communication scholars.

REFERENCES

Agger, R. E., M. N. Goldstein, and S. A. Pearl. "Political Cynicism: Measurement and Meaning." *Journal of Politics*, 23 (1961), pp. 477–506.

Campbell, A., G. Gurin, and W. E. Miller. *The Voter Decides*. Evanston, Ill.: Row Peterson, 1954.

Cohen, J., and P. Cohen. *Applied Multiple Regression/Correlation Analysis for the Behavioral Sciences*. Hillsdale, N.J.: L. Erlbaum Assoc., Publishers, 1975.

Kerlinger, F. N., and E. J. Pedhazur. *Multiple Regression in Behavioral Research*. New York: Holt, Rinehart & Winston, 1973.

Milbrath, L. *Political Participation*. Chicago: Rand McNally, 1965.
Wenner, L. A. "Use and Avoidance of Network Television News Coverage." Unpublished Ph.D. diss., University of Iowa, 1977.

22.

Shifts in Candidate Images

HERBERT W. SIMONS and KENNETH LEIBOWITZ

Presented herein is a summary of findings from a four-wave panel survey that focused on debate-related shifts in candidate images.[1] Modeled after Tannenbaum, Greenberg, and Silverman's study of "Candidate Images," as reported in *The Great Debates* (1962), the survey yielded semantic differential data on images of the principal candidates as future presidents, and on images of the ideal president. These data allowed for scale-by-scale comparisons between candidates and across time periods (T_1 through T_4) and also provided the basis for rough comparisons between Tannenbaum et al.'s Kennedy–Nixon profile and our sample's image profiles. In presenting findings we will concentrate on shifts across time rather than on differences among respondents or objects of judgment at any one time; the former are of greater theoretical interest and should be less sensitive to the demographic and political makeup of our sample.

Besides comparing image profiles, the study investigated relationships among candidate images, judgments of who won the debates, and voting intentions. Our general hypothesis was that shifts in images would be paralleled by shifts in the other variables, thus reflecting indirectly the influence of the debates.

Method
Sample

The respondents were Philadelphia-area residents who had been contacted in their homes by trained student interviewers from Temple University just before the first presidential debate and just after each of the three debates.

From an original sample of over 250 persons, usable data across all four waves were obtained from only 113 respondents. The high rate of attrition was due to a variety of factors: loss of interest, lateness, apparent carelessness in responding, missing questionnaire pages, and failure of some interviewers to return questionnaires.

The final sample was representative neither of the voting population nor even of our original sample, yet it was considered adequate given our interest in shifts in scores and relationships among variables. Our final group tended to be somewhat older and better educated, leaned heavily toward Carter and toward Democrats generally, and included more registered voters than in the original sample.

Seven semantic differential scales (Foolish–Wise, Unfair–Fair, Inexperienced–Experienced, Weak–Strong, Colorless–Colorful, Conservative–Liberal, and Passive–Active) were taken directly from the Tannenbaum et al. study, and an additional scale, Cold–Warm, was changed from Tannenbaum et al.'s more ambiguous Cool–Warm. To these eight adjective pairs were added five others that seemed especially appropriate in this election contest (Deceptive–Open, Unattractive–Attractive, Negative–Positive, Irreligious–Religious, and Unintelligent–Intelligent).

Results

This section first compares shifts in candidate images; then it reports on relationships among candidate images, judgments of who won the debates, voting intentions, and findings bearing on the exposure variables.

Shifts in Candidate Images

The image profiles of Ford and Carter are graphically portrayed in Figures 1 and 2 alongside mean Ideal President (IP) ratings at T_1 on the same semantic differential scales. Caution is urged in using the data to compare candidates at any one time period, because Carter's generally more favorable ratings may simply have been a function of the biases manifested in the sample. More to the point of this paper in any case is how the candidates' images changed over the course of the debates.

As is apparent from Figure 1, Ford consistently lost after debate 2 the ground he had gained after debate 1, but his image improved on virtually all scale items once again after debate 3. Thus, to take an item on which there were quite dramatic shifts (the .001 significance level was used throughout), Ford appeared significantly wiser following the first debate, more foolish following the second debate, and somewhat wiser again after the final debate (the last-named shift was not significant). Since Ford's competence as president had consistently been called into question, these shifts are important, and they are paralleled by similar shifts on the intelligence dimension, especially from T_2 to T_3. When it is noted that Ford also appeared somewhat weaker, colder, and more deceptive at T_3, the second debate must be counted as a clear defeat for him in image terms, one that upset a pattern of gradual image improvement.

Although Carter had been billed by the media as the more uncertain quantity in this election contest, his image ratings remained relatively stable across time (indeed, no shifts were statistically significant). And, whereas mean shifts for Ford were extremely consistent from one time period to the next, Carter's image declined on some items while improving on others.

The overall pattern of shifts in image (D^2) for each candidate was analyzed. D^2 is a composite measure of overall "distance" in semantic space between two profiles (the higher the score, the greater the distance). In our case it was clearly advisable to array image profile data on a single evaluative dimension by computing D^2 differences between Future President ratings for each candidate at each time period and Ideal President ratings. This not only elimi-

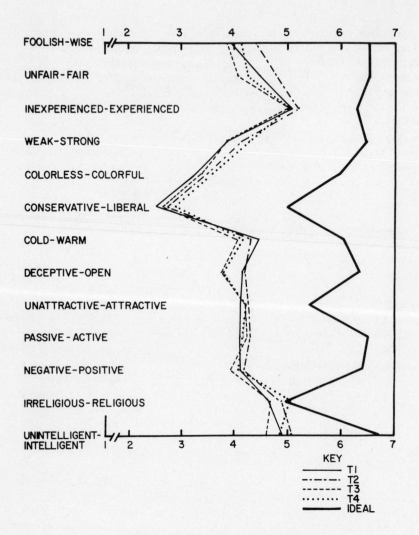

Fig. 1: Ford as Future President

nated the need to treat Future President factor clusters separately but also provided the basis for comparing shifts in candidate images with other variables.

As per Osgood, Suci, and Tannenbaum's (1969) recommendation, Wilcoxon matched-pairs signed-ranks tests were used to compare D^2 scores. Consistent with our scale-by-scale analyses of image data, Ford's overall image rose significantly, fell significantly, and then rose slightly. Parallel shifts occurred in Carter's image, but these were of considerably smaller magnitude (all were nonsignificant). As expected, given our mostly Democratic sample, Carter's composite image was consistently more favorable than Ford's over the length of the study. Neither candidate's image improved significantly between the first testing and the last although both gained slightly—Ford more than Carter.

THE GREAT DEBATES

The data summarized thus far provide the basis for rough comparisons between our sample and Tannenbaum et al.'s sample of University of Wisconsin married-student-housing residents. Although we are unable to offer statistical comparisons, there appear to be marked similarities between the two samples in terms of IP ratings. For the seven directly comparable items, only responses on the Colorless-Colorful dimension differed by more than .3 points (from 5.4 in 1960 to 5.9 in 1976).

Even more remarkably, there were great similarities between the Kennedy–Carter profiles and the Nixon–Ford profiles. By comparison to all other image attributes, inexperience was the major liability for both Democrats; experience was the chief asset of both Republicans. Least liked in Nixon and Ford was

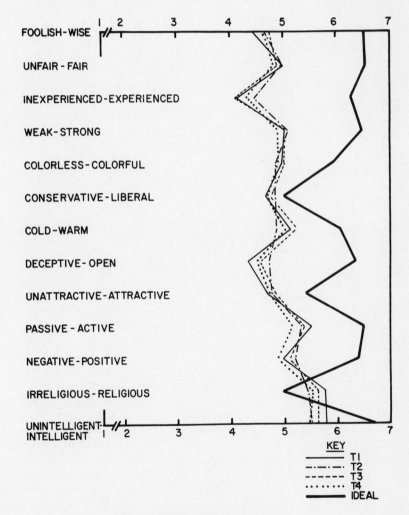

Fig. 2: Carter as Future President

Table 1: Means for Ford and Carter as Future President*

| | Ford | | | | Carter | | | |
| | Mean | | | | Mean | | | |
	T_1	T_2	T_3	T_4	T_1	T_2	T_3	T_4
Foolish–Wise	3.95	4.42	3.87	4.15	4.43	4.67	4.73	4.66
Unfair–Fair	4.49	4.29	4.09	4.29	5.00	4.99	4.91	4.84
Inexperienced–Experienced	5.09	5.21	5.06	5.08	4.14	4.46	4.13	4.29
Weak–Strong	3.86	4.16	3.86	4.27	5.03	5.06	5.05	4.87
Colorless–Colorful	3.27	3.50	3.40	3.55	4.98	4.86	5.01	4.89
Conservative–Liberal	2.57	2.76	2.66	2.90	4.66	4.83	4.78	4.70
Cold–Warm	4.45	4.33	4.05	4.16	5.12	4.87	5.22	5.09
Deceptive–Open	4.16	4.19	3.79	4.00	4.33	4.74	4.57	4.56
Unattractive–Attractive	4.13	4.25	4.20	4.22	4.69	4.79	4.84	4.75
Passive–Active	4.11	4.34	4.23	4.14	5.50	5.32	5.35	5.16
Negative–Positive	4.10	4.15	3.93	4.09	4.98	5.20	5.12	4.84
Irreligious–Religious	4.64	4.90	4.66	5.00	5.77	5.43	5.61	5.54
Unintelligent–Intelligent	4.89	5.04	4.61	4.88	5.79	5.51	5.60	5.48

Concept					
Ford-IP	Mean	9.63	9.13	9.74	9.39
	(SD)	3.82	4.01	3.86	3.99
Carter-IP	Mean	7.80	7.48	7.75	7.62
	(SD)	3.17	3.41	3.38	3.36

*Standard deviations ranged from 1.18 to 1.98. Only three t-tests of differences between mean values were significant at the .001 level (see text).

their apparent conservatism; most liked in Kennedy and Carter was their appearance of being highly active.

There were some notable differences as well. Tannenbaum et al.'s sample perceived both Kennedy and Nixon much more favorably than our sample perceived Carter and Ford. For example, the mean difference between Kennedy and Carter on comparable items was about .7 points. On the other hand, the 1960 candidates' images declined sharply between the first and last samplings (especially Nixon's), while the images of the 1976 candidates improved somewhat over time.

Candidate Images and Judgments of Who Won

Immediately following each debate, respondents were asked whom they thought did a better job of debating. At T_3 they were given an opportunity to reconsider their verdicts on the first debate. Then, at T_4 they were asked for retrospective judgments on debates 1 and 2. Favorable verdicts were considerably magnified over time. Ford initially "won" the first debate by a slight margin, but by T_4 a significantly greater proportion of the sample was willing to assign him the verdict. Differences between immediate versus delayed judgments of who won debate 2 were not significant, a slightly higher proportion of the sample casting their verdict with Carter at T_4. Of those who expressed a verdict a clear majority saw Carter as the better debater in the final debate.

A two-way analysis of variance, using shifts in image as the dependent variable and judgments of who won and party preference as the independent factors, indicated a significant relationship between these variables. There was a significant main effect for the debate verdict variable in the expected direction ($F = 8.63$; df $= 2,81$; $p < .001$) as well as a significant Party Preference X Debate Verdict interaction effect ($F = 6.47$; df $= 4,81$; $p < .001$).

Carter's favorable verdict on debate 2 matched Ford's significant image decline following that debate, but, surprisingly, our F-tests did not provide confirming evidence of a causal relationship between the two variables. In fact, no other F-tests proved significant between shifts in candidate images and either party preference or judgments of who won.

Candidate Images and Voting Intentions

We were unable in this study to establish clear links between shifts in composite images of the candidates and shifts in voting intentions. Certainly there were no dramatic shifts to Ford following his impressive image gains at T_2; nor were there demonstrable shifts away from Ford following the second debate. If anything, the shifts in voting intention toward Ford and Carter tended to counterbalance each other.

Voting Intentions and Judgments of Who Won the Debates

No clear pattern of relationships was found between judgments of who won a given debate and gross shifts (that is, to or from a candidate) in voting intention following that debate. For example, although our pro-Democratic, pro-Carter sample was willing to concede Ford the victory in the first debate, only two respondents, both of whom were initially undecided, placed themselves in the Ford camp at T_2. Perhaps others who had been impressed by Ford's performance waited longer before making so important a decision.

Summarizing the findings on relationships among judgments of who won, shifts in candidate images, and shifts in voting intentions, we can say that only limited support has been found for our hypothesis. Some evidence was found linking judgments of who won and shifts in candidate images. We are less confident that there was a consistent positive relationship between shifts in voting intentions and either of these variables.

Summary and Conclusions

The major findings from the study were as follows:

1. Although per-scale image shifts were generally not significant between adjoining time periods (given the stringent tests we applied), they added up to a picture of Ford as the more erratic campaigner, one who consistently lost after round 2 of the debates the more favorable impressions he had achieved after round 1, only to improve on almost all image dimensions, once again, after round 3. Overall, the composite images of both Carter and Ford improved slightly (nonsignificantly) over the course of the debates, in contrast to the steep declines which Tannenbaum et al. reported for Nixon and Kennedy in 1960.

2. Only limited support could be found for the hypothesis that shifts in candidate images, judgments of who won a given debate, and changes in voting intentions would parallel each other.

Notwithstanding Ford's clear defeat in round 2, his image improved somewhat more than Carter's did over the course of the debates. We are impressed, especially, with the fact that more persons in our heavily liberal, pro-Democratic, pro-Carter sample did not see the debates in a one-sided manner: that they did not award Carter all three verdicts; that their initially negative judgments of Ford were not intensified; that fewer initially undecided voters did not switch to Carter. If anything, the debates seemed to have had a moderating effect in this election, and that may be one good reason for holding presidential campaign debates again in 1980.

NOTE

1. The authors wish to thank statistical consultants Arthur Bochner, Richard Joslyn, and Thomas Steinfatt; student assistants Merri Berger, Susan Goldberg, George Gum; and the many persons in the senior author's classes who served as interviewers.

REFERENCES

Osgood, C., G. J. Suci, and P. H. Tannenbaum. *The Measurement of Meaning*. Urbana, Ill.: University of Illinois Press, 1967.

Tannenbaum, P. H., B. S. Greenberg, and F. R. Silverman. "Candidate Images" in S. Kraus (ed.), *The Great Debates: Background, Perspective and Effects*. Bloomington, Ind.: Indiana University Press, 1962, pp. 271–88.

23.

Media Influences and Their Anticipation

GARRETT J. O'KEEFE and HAROLD MENDELSOHN

The capacity of the mass media to "precondition" audiences has gone largely unexplored in the mass communications research literature. Too often attention has centered on reactions of audiences to an event as though the occurrences "just happened," without warning and time for preparation. While the press gave unprecedented coverage to post-debate public reaction, little concern was given to examining what citizens had been led to expect from the debates beforehand and what they wanted from them in terms of gratification. The research reported here[1] attempts to examine what audiences of the debates might have been anticipating in watching them on television and the extent to which the debates may or may have not met those anticipations.

As Americans moved into the era of the "new politics" over the past twenty years, their political behaviors have changed dramatically. Mendelsohn and Crespi (1970) have pointed out that the advent of television alone, accompanied by the displacement of "politicians" by the technocrats in political decision-making roles, greatly served to inhibit national parties as the exclusive political power brokers they previously had been.

Similarly, drastic shifts in the structure of American society that have occurred since the landmark sociopolitical studies Paul F. Lazarsfeld initiated at Columbia University in the 1940s have virtually obliterated the historical predictive power of demographic predispositions alone.

With several notable exceptions much of the contemporary efforts in this regard have sought to "explain" the political "effects" of the mass media as consequences either of demography or partisanship or both.

The cumulative results of these efforts have been considerably less than spectacular. At best, the research that has accumulated over the past three decades adds up to no more than an extension of a familiar aphorism—most mass-mediated political communications affect most types of voters very little or not at all most of the time. Here, rather than "explaining" voting behavior, the gross demographic, partisanship, and social-psychological variables merely describe who voted for whom under varying circumstances of media exposure. On the other hand several recent studies based on the "uses-gratifications" approach to examining audience behaviors imply that the needs, motives, and expectations individuals bring into their transactions with media are as important in determining media effects as are the actual structures and contents of messages and audiences' media attitude and exposure patterns. Blumler and

McQuail's (1969) analysis of British voting behavior in the mid-sixties suggested that the extent to which voters were influenced by television in their candidate evaluations was in part dependent on voters' reasons for watching political content on television. McLeod and Becker (1974) found that such motivations, or sought gratification, were often more direct and efficient predictors of political media effects than were the traditional factors related specifically to media exposure.

Such findings imply that the emphasis should be on examination of media use and exposure as behaviors functionally related to given antecedents, followed by study of the consequences of interactions of both the antecedents and media behaviors. Our own research (Mendelsohn and O'Keefe, 1976) on the 1972 presidential campaign led us to conclude that media influences on voter decision-making was explained by such factors as voters' difficulty of candidate choice, interest in the campaign, dependence on media for specific kinds of information, and anticipation of being influenced, as well as their degree of exposure and attention to campaign media content.

Examination of voters' anticipation of being influenced by media content presents a promising yet relatively unexplored line of inquiry derivable from the uses-gratification approach. Katz, Blumler, and Gurevitch (1974), in their seminal essay on uses-gratification, argue that consequences of media uses should in part depend on expectations that audience members have before such uses. This implies that individuals have certain expectations about the content of media they choose to attend, the kinds of gratifications they seek from such exposure, and presumably the probabilities they perceive of given exposures leading to given gratifications. In the 1972 Ohio study, we found not only that voters appeared aware of what to expect from media coverage of the campaign, but that they also anticipated the extent to which they would count on specific media as sources of influence. This finding may be explained in part by arguing that since voters do not enter a campaign tabula rasa in terms of political orientations, there is no reason to suspect they do so in terms of communications orientations. Individual media uses are apt to develop over years of communication experiences, with each experience serving at least in small part as a socializing agent for the next. Voter communication experiences over successive political campaigns should set the stage for anticipations of experiences in subsequent campaigns. And it seems reasonable to aver that such anticipations, coupled with individuals' needs for information, serve as contingent conditions under which given media use and exposure patterns may or may not have specific consequences.

Voters high in "anticipatory influence" in 1972 were found to differ from other voters in their media use patterns during the campaign, and they were as a group more likely to report having been influenced by media content during the campaign. In particular, those more expectant of influence who also decided for whom to vote later in the campaign were especially likely to report having been influenced by media content; indeed, anticipation of influence was the single best predictor of reported influence among late-deciding voters. In a related study Kraus, Davis, and Lee (1975) examined expectations in terms of credibility of media for audiences and found that greater "expectations" of media credibility led to greater media influence on a number of Watergate-related issues. Thus, there was considerable reason to believe that the anticipation of being influenced would most likely be followed by the experience of influence among viewers of the Carter–Ford encounters. The 1976 presidential debates provided an excellent basis for exploration of this issue in light of the possibility that great numbers of people had had their interest and presumably their expectations aroused by predebate media coverage.

The intent here is first to examine general orientations held by viewers before the debates, and then to attempt to relate certain of those orientations to viewers' reactions to the debates. We are especially concerned with the extent to which to which viewers anticipated having their choice of a presidential candidate influenced by what they saw in the debates, what other prior orientations such anticipation was related to, and the consequences of such anticipation.

We specifically sought to examine the relationship between anticipatory influence and informational, motivational, and decision-making predebate orientations of viewers. Information orientations measured before the debate included the extent to which viewers thought they had enough information about the candidates to decide between them as well as expressions of the kinds of added information they would most like to have.

Motivational orientations reflected general levels of interest in the campaign and specific gratifications sought by viewers in watching the debates, including issue and image surveillance, reinforcement, and decision-making assistance. Decision-making orientations turned on whether or not the viewer had decided on a candidate before the debate and, if so, how difficult the decision had been to make.

It was generally posited that greater anticipation of influence would yield greater post-debate "effects" on viewers along a number of dimensions. Informational effects included learning specific things about the candidates, including change in perception of candidates' issue positions. Motivational effects included increased desire to seek information and increased interest, campaign activity, and likelihood of voting. Effects pertaining to decision-making included reevaluation of choice of candidate and whether the decision was made easier or more difficult by exposure to the debate. Finally, affective reactions included change in attitudes toward the candidates, the debate situation itself, the government, and the nation.

Methodology and Results

The study examined anticipations of and reactions to the first Carter–Ford debate held Thursday night, September 23. Presumably, the first contest would be the one on which the most audience expectation would be brought to bear and, as it turned out, which also generated the largest audience and most extensive news coverage. Additionally, there was a methodological advantage in limiting the stimulus field to just one relatively easily defined event and eliminating concern with defining cumulative debate exposure over time. A two-wave panel design was used in which telephone interviews were conducted with the same respondents aged eighteen and over during the six days prior to the debate and again during the five days following it. The sample was selected randomly from the greater Akron, Ohio, telephone directory. Akron is the center of a medium-metropolitan industrial and commercial area reflecting diverse demographic and political characteristics not unlike those of the U.S. as a whole.[2] Four hundred interviews were completed before the debate (out of 583—a 69 percent response rate), and 312 interviews were completed with the same individuals afterward. Questionnaire items reflected the audience attributes and behaviors discussed above, and are listed in the tables that follow. Generally, the items ascertained respondent self-reports of their predebate orientations and post-debate reactions.

However, more objective change-score measures of specific criterion variables were also included. Specific items asked both before and after the first debate tapped respondents' perceptions of where the candidates stood on issues vis à vis respondents' own positions; respondents' perceptions of the "images" of the candidates; and respondents' likelihood of voting, their candidate preference, and the degree of difficulty they experienced in deciding on a candidate.

The Audience for the First Debate

Seventy-five percent of the Akron sample reported having watched fifteen minutes or more of the first Carter–Ford debate and were thus classified as "viewers." Overall, the audience cut across most demographic and political groups. As might be expected, minor variations occurred in that males, middle-aged persons, and the more affluent and the better educated were somewhat more likely to have tuned in the program. Exposure was evenly divided across political party lines, again raising questions about the power of party affiliation as controlling selective exposure. Overall, proportionately more Ford supporters watched than did Carter partisans or those who identified themselves as undecided, with Carter edging out Ford in overall popularity.

Viewers' Predebate Orientations

Before the event a surprising 65 percent of the viewers thought it likely that watching the debate would indeed influence their choice of a candidate in one way or another. A full one-fourth of them answered that it was "very likely" that they would be influenced. Moreover, 71 percent of the viewers had complained they had "too little" information on which to base a candidate choice, the majority of them having already decided to vote for either Carter or Ford. Three in ten of these said they had experienced difficulty reaching a decision.

For the most part viewers' predebate choices of candidates appeared not too well grounded in information, and it seems probable that many of the already-decided respondents were looking forward to the first debate as a vehicle for either rationalizing or justifying their early candidate commitments. Indeed, more detailed analyses show that 61 percent of Carter's supporters and 56 percent of Ford's had anticipated exposure-related influence to at least some degree. The relative uncertainty about Carter among the general electorate no doubt accounted in part for the proportionately greater anticipation among his early followers. Nonetheless, undecided viewers constituted the greatest proportion of individuals expecting influence—78 percent—at least suggesting the potential of the first debate for affecting the decision-making processes of this one crucial contingent of the electorate.

What kinds of information did viewers wish to get from the debate? Despite television's alleged power as an "image maker," the data reveal a preference among respondents for issue-oriented, as opposed to personality- or image-oriented, information. Nearly nine of every ten viewers in the panel said they wanted more information in general about the candidates' issue stances and plans and that an important reason for watching the debate was to find out more about the candidates' positions on issues.

It also appears that anticipatory influence is less a function of demographic attributes such as age and education and is more related to inadequate information, lack of interest in the campaign, and difficulty in deciding for whom to vote (Table 1).

Table 1: Post-Debate Reactions by Anticipatory Influence

	Anticipatory Influence		
	Low (n = 78)	High (n = 149)	Total (n = 234)
Learned about candidates or issues	8%**	29%**	21%
Learned about candidates as people	24	26	25
Increased information-seeking	37**	68**	59
Increased interest	32*	54*	47
Increased campaign activity	5	17	13
Increased likelihood of voting	28	34	32
Change in candidate preference	4	3	3
Increased satisfaction with preference	47	44	44
Decision became easier	37*	43*	41
Decision became more difficult	3*	18*	13
Thought debate was "good idea"	69	83	78
More optimistic about the nation	23*	37*	32
More optimistic about government	24	30	28

*$p < .05$ **$p < .01$, by chi-square test

Thus, it appears that on one level anticipatory influence is affected not only by previous experiences and personal attributes alone, but by feelings of specific information deprivation as well. If voters approach election campaigns with the notion that the events of the campaign will reflect themselves as usable (that is, persuasive) information, it is conceivable that debates can provide information which will not only contribute to their store of knowledge but will help voters make a decision one way or another. The more voters encounter difficulty in the decision-making process, the more likely are they to turn to a specific campaign event such as a debate in hopes of easing their travail through an encounter with persuasive rather than didactic information.

Viewers anticipating influence tended to be less interested in the campaign overall. Presumably, the more interested viewers were more firmly decided for one candidate or the other a priori. Consequently, they did not expect to be changing their minds simply as the result of any single encounter with any single campaign stimulus. Eighty-seven percent of the viewers who were "very interested" in the campaign already had a preferred candidate, versus 68 percent of those who expressed limited interest.

There was only a slight tendency for the more interested viewers to see themselves as being more informed. Even those who were more interested in the campaign seem to have believed they lacked enough prior information about the candidates; presumably these individuals turned to the debate as a possible source of additional material.

Particularly significant is the fact that viewers who anticipated influence, as compared to those who did not, attached greater importance to each of the specific gratifications that might have been sought from the debates. Here, the greatest disparity between the motivations of those anticipating influence versus those who did not lay in the desire to be provided with the kinds of information that would be of help in vote decision-making.

Post-Debate Reactions

Despite viewers' substantial desires to learn more about the candidates as people and their stands on issues and programs, roughly a fourth of all the viewers in the sample reported deriving such information from the first debate. Overall, then, in regard to these two factors, debate 1 seemed to generate more viewer disappointment than satisfaction (Table 1).

On the matter of learning about the candidates' stands on issues, however, viewers who were high in anticipatory influence were most likely to derive that particular gratification from the premier Carter–Ford confrontation. With regard to learning about the candidates as human beings, no differences between the low and high anticipatory subgroups could be noted. In brief, viewers who thought they would be influenced were least likely to be disappointed in learning about the candidates' positions on issues from the first debate.

If the acquisition of specific information from the first debate was relatively low among viewers, reactions in terms of increased motivations vis à vis the campaign were not. The majority of those watching the debate said they wanted to find out more about the candidates as a result of viewing, and nearly half said their interest in the campaign had been increased. Nearly twice as many of those who anticipated influence as those who didn't reported such increases. Anticipation of influence was also slightly and positively related to increases in likelihood of campaign activity and voting.

Altogether, only six respondents said they had changed their candidate preference as a result of viewing the initial debate, but almost half said they had become more satisfied with the candidate of their original choice, indicating a strong "reinforcement" effect deriving from the program.

The data in Table 1 show that although exposure to the debate was more likely than not to ease the burden of decision-making (for four of every ten viewers totally), the very same debate actually increased the difficulty of decision-making for 13 percent of the viewers. Moreover, viewers who scored high in anticipatory influence were more likely than the low scorers were to find themselves experiencing either greater ease or greater difficulty in making a vote decision as a consequence of viewing the first Carter–Ford encounter. This suggests that although some voters experiencing a particular campaign event such as a debate may approach it in the hope of easing their decision-making, the very opposite may and will often occur. That is to say, sheer information gain—

even for those who wish to be persuaded—often adds to discomfort rather than ameliorating it.

The possibility of boomerang effect notwithstanding, most viewers in the sample (78 percent) came away from the first debate endorsing the general idea of debates, and roughly three in ten reported the first debate left them feeling optimistic about both nation and government. In particular, viewers who anticipated being influenced by the debates were most likely to leave the first debate feeling optimistic about the future of the nation.

Change Scores as Indicators of Effect

Measures of actual change among viewers in their evaluations of where the candidates stood on issues and in their perceptions of candidates' "images" indicated a rather limited amount of net gain within the sample for either candidate (Table 2). Neither contender enjoyed a significant net advantage in convincing the viewers as a group that he was more in agreement with them on any of the issues, although Ford gained slightly on the inflation and Vietnam pardon issues, and Carter pulled a bit ahead on busing (a topic not directly addressed in the first debate) and improvement of government services. The change on the busing issue of course points to key methodological problems in the panel design utilized here: a lack of appropriate control over stimuli apart from the debate, which may have affected the sample, and potentially weak reliability of the

Table 2: Pre–Post Debate Net Change on Issues, Images, Vote Intention, and Candidates Choice among Viewers[1] (n = 234)

	Predebate	Post-Debate	Difference	t
Issues				
Inflation	1.88	1.93	.05	—
Employment	1.89	1.89	.00	—
Busing	2.07	2.02	−.05	—
Health insurance	2.03	2.03	.00	—
Pardon	2.06	2.10	.04	—
Service	1.87	1.82	−.05	—
Images				
Experience	2.49	2.49	.00	—
Appeal	1.75	1.70	−.05	—
Decisiveness	2.08	2.12	.04	—
Effective campaigner	1.39	1.54	.15*	2.08*
Confidence	1.73	1.97	.24**	3.06**
Credibility	2.01	2.01	.00	—
Empathy	1.65	1.54	−.11*	1.69*
Persuasiveness	1.62	1.83	.21**	2.91**
Voting intention	1.12	1.09	−.03	—
Candidate choice	1.93	1.89	−.04	—
Difficulty	2.36	2.32	−.04	—

[1]Positive change in direction of Carter.
*p < .05 by t-test.   **p < .01 by t-test.

measures. However, extended analyses not reported here indicated that the non-viewers shifted even less than the viewers on the above issues, including busing. These problems will be further addressed in the context of changes related to viewers' anticipation of influence.

Significant net shifts did occur on four of the eight candidate image attributes. Ford gained points in terms of being seen as a more effective campaigner than Carter and as exuding greater confidence and persuasiveness. This finding of course squares with press public opinion polls indicating that Ford gave the better "performance" in the first debate. On the other hand, it also points to some of the problems of "day-after" polls in oversimplifying the impact of such debates by focusing on "who won." While our own results likewise lead to a conclusion that Ford edged out Carter, the victory appears based on changes in but a few basic perceptions of Ford's personality, and not on any substantial shift in agreement with the former president's policy positions. Carter, on the other hand, was viewed as more emphatic after the debate than he had been before. No substantial net changes were found in viewers' voting intentions, their preferred candidate, or the difficulty they were having in choosing a candidate.

More meaningful for investigation of factors underlying audience predebate/post-debate change are analyses of individual changes, regardless of direction, exhibited by the viewers. Table 3 indicates that while viewers manifested higher change scores than nonviewers on most of the criterion attributes, in no case was the difference between the two groups statistically significant. This null result may in part be due to nonviewers' exposure to other political messages, particularly news reports concerning the debate itself.

Nonetheless, viewers high in anticipatory influence exhibited significantly greater change than the low-anticipation group on half of the issue and image attributes, as well as on candidate preference. Again, busing was one of the issues on which a significant shift occurred. Reliability of measures and extra-debate influences notwithstanding, the likelihood does exist that those anticipating influence who had some concern over the busing issue read into some of the candidates' general remarks about domestic issues information that they deduced was applicable to busing.

While the above data support the import of anticipatory influence, it is quite possible that viewers high in anticipatory influence also shared other characteristics that led them to exhibit greater change in the criterion variables. To explore this likelihood in at least a rudimentary way, six of the pre-campaign orientations, plus age and education level, were inserted along with anticipatory influence into multiple linear regression analyses of their relative impact on each of the criterion variables. Pre-campaign difficulty was excluded from this analysis because the attribute was ascertained only for already-decided voters.

Table 4 clearly suggests that anticipation of influence is the strongest of the factors examined in predicting overall variation in change scores. Anticipatory influence was positively and significantly correlated (Pearson r) with change in candidate choice, difficulty of decision, and summary additive indices of change scores derived from the issues items and the image items. More important, when the regression control procedure was inserted among all of the independent factors, anticipatory influence emerged with the highest standardized regression

412

Table 3: Pre–Post Debate Change Scores by Viewership,
Anticipatory Influence

	Viewers			Nonviewers
	Anticipatory Influence			
	Low (n = 85)	High (n = 149)	Total (n = 234)	Total (n = 78)
Issues				
Inflation	.35*	.49*	.44	.36
Employment	.44	.49	.47	.40
Busing	.34**	.52**	.46	.41
Health	.51	.46	.47	.44
Pardon	.56	.61	.59	.46
Service	.22**	.46**	.38	.31
Images				
Experience	.31	.35	.33	.47
Appeal	.28*	.44*	.39	.37
Decisiveness	.33**	.55**	.47	.44
Effectiveness	.38	.44	.42	.32
Confidence	.46*	.59*	.54	.59
Credibility	.25*	.38*	.33	.44
Empathy	.32	.41	.38	.32
Persuasiveness	.57	.55	.56	.50
Vote Intention	.07	.11	.09	.28
Candidate Choice	.20*	.32*	.28	.22
Difficulty	.06	.09	.08	.25

*p $<$ .05 by t-test.   **p $<$ .01 by t-test.

coefficients and proportions of variance explained vis à vis four of the criterion change variables. In contrast, anticipatory influence displayed a relatively weak relationship with change in vote intention.

While the overall variances explained (R^2) by the nine independent factors as a set were relatively low (all less than .10), these data build a strong case for anticipation of influence as a significant indicator of debate effect. It is particularly noteworthy that anticipatory influence predicted change to a greater degree than did interest in the campaign, information level, or gratifications sought from viewing the debates. Campaign interest and information level tended to be negatively associated with change.

More specifically, shift in candidate preference was most clearly explained by anticipatory influence alone, with that factor accounting for over two-thirds of the total variance explained. Viewers who changed the most in their issue perceptions appear to have been guided by more informationally based motivations than those who changed their perceptions of candidates' images. The former viewers tended to feel less informed about the candidates before the debate and also tended to indicate a desire to watch the debate to learn more about candidates' positions. On the other hand, those changing image perceptions

Table 4: Correlations (r) between Predebate Indicators and Regression Analyses on Criterion Change Variables (n = 234)

	Correlations									Pre–Post Debate Change in Regression Analyses[2]				
	Campaign Interest	Information Level	Issue Surveillance Gratification	Image Surveillance Gratification	Reinforcement Gratification	Vote Guidance Gratification	Anticipatory Influence	Difficulty	Age	Vote Intention	Candidate Choice	Issues Total	Images Total	Difficulty of Decision
Campaign interest	—									-.10	.02	-.03	.03	-.14
Information level	.04	—								-.10	-.02	-.08	.02	.02
Issue surveillance gratification	.15*	.04	—							-.10	.01	.06	-.02	-.01
Image surveillance gratification	.08	-.05	.15*	—						.02	-.04	-.03	.02	-.05
Reinforcement gratification	-.01	.01	.16*	.20*	—					-.07	.06	.08	.09	-.01
Vote guidance gratification	-.11	-.25**	.17*	.03	.14*	—								
Anticipatory influence	-.13*	-.23**	.27**	.10	.15*	.55*	—			.01	-.07	-.05	.03	.06
Difficulty[1]	.01	-.08	.00	-.03	.01	.13	.33**	—		.05	.19	.11	.16	.20
Age	.13*	.01	-.08	.07	.05	-.11	-.10	.07	—	-.12	.02	-.06	.08	.08
Education	.17*	.05	-.03	-.09	-.35**	-.09	-.05	.15*	.13*	-.09	-.01	.07	.03	.15
$R^2 =$										.066	.032	.040	.047	.094

[1]Includes only respondents with a preferred candidate (n = 179).
[2]Standardized regression coefficients are reported.
*p < .05. **p < .01.

were more likely to list that they sought general reinforcement or guidance in making a decision as their reasons for viewing. Change in perception of difficulty of decision among audience members who had already decided on a candidate was linked with lesser campaign interest and greater vote guidance seeking, as well as more anticipation of influence. Shifts in intention to vote appeared more a function of campaign interest and age, with the less-interested and younger respondents likelier to shift.

These results, combined with the finding that significant differences in change criteria were not found between viewers and nonviewers, imply that viewer anticipation played a critical role in determining how viewers were affected by the first debate. Of course, caution must be used in generalizing these data to other campaign situations. It has already been noted that media precoverage of the first debate had great potential for "setting up" viewers with great expectations that the presentation would in some way influence them in deciding for whom to vote. Most mass-mediated political communication situations do not have the advantage of such audience preconditioning. Moreover, little has been examined here regarding the assumed interaction between the pre-exposure attitudinal and motivational dispositions such as anticipatory influence and the actual strategies and tactics viewers use in attending to messages. A more comprehensive view of media effects will doubtless be found through the study of such interactions.

It is also important to delineate the conceptual and operational differences between need gratifications sought from the media, expectations that such gratifications will occur through specific media use patterns, and anticipation of influence, or "effect." While gratifications sought have emerged in recent years as major predictors of effect, the present work suggests that profitable results also develop from examining the degree of success expected or anticipated in being gratified by media messages.

Discussion

In his study of propaganda, Jacques Ellul (1965) asserts that the acceptance or rejection of mass-mediated messages of persuasion rests to a great extent on the degree to which audiences have been "preconditioned." In other words, mass-communications encounters never occur as unique and isolated instances in which prior expectations, themselves products of audience predispositions and preconditioning, play no part. To the contrary, it may be posited that in many mass-communications situations "effect" can be viewed as a function of the extent to which the prior expectations of audiences have been satisfied. This does not imply that effects cannot occur without prior expectations. The fact that the debates did appear to have observable effects on certain persons who did not anticipate influence is also important here.

In the political arena much research effort has been expended on election campaigns in an attempt solely to determine how the media may or may not contribute to the total store of "information" that citizens do or do not acquire in the course of such campaigns. Yet, for many voters, campaigns do not represent an opportunity for didactic experiences alone, wherein knowledge is acquired for its own sake. Instead, the events taking place during a given campaign are often perceived as either contributing or not contributing to the decision-making process into which every election forces citizens.

When citizens seek knowledge during an election campaign, they do so with many purposes in mind. Not all their objectives are purely cognitive, so that a debate for example can be perceived as potentially providing a basis for evaluating the personal attributes of candidates or for propelling some members of the audience into active campaign participation. Another way of viewing the functions of the media in political campaigns, then, is to consider them as providing their patrons with all three types of psychological nurturance—cognitive, affective, and conative.

Not only do voters learn to expect the media to furnish them with all three, but, as time goes by, many actually anticipate that their final choices of candidates will be influenced by what they encounter in the media. This is particularly true of voters who delay making up their minds for one or another candidate. The longer one puts off choosing a candidate, the more likely he or she is to look to the media for help: thus, the phenomenon of anticipatory influence. "Immunization" against campaign propaganda is not so much a function of how much "information" the voter accumulates, but rather of how early in a campaign the voter decides for a candidate, without the benefit of too much information.

The question regarding who the "winner" of a particular debate may be then becomes meaningless. Instead, we must gauge possible "effects" of debates in terms of whether and how they actually help those voters who anticipate help in order to arrive at a decision. It is important that in planning future debates attention is given not only to the debates themselves but to the predebate climate as well.

NOTES

1. The authors thank Columbia Broadcasting System, Inc., for the open and unrestrictive funding of the research reported here, and Donna Carlon for assistance in data analysis.
2. See Mendelsohn and O'Keefe (1976) for further description.

REFERENCES

Blumler, J. G., and D. McQuail. *Television in Politics: Its Uses and Influence.* Chicago: University of Chicago Press, 1969.
Ellul, J. *Propaganda.* New York: Knopf, 1965.
Katz, E., J. G. Blumler, and M. Gurevitch. "Utilization of Mass Communication by the Individual," in J. G. Blumler and E. Katz (eds.), *The Uses of Mass Communications.* Beverly Hills: Sage Publications, 1974.
Kraus, S., D. Davis, and J. Lee. "Public Opinion and the Resignation of Richard Nixon: A Study of Media Credibility and Political Cross Pressure." Paper presented to the American Association for Public Opinion Research. Itsaca, Illinois, 1975.

McLeod, J. M., and L. B. Becker. "Testing the Validity of Gratification Measures Through Political Effects Analysis," in J. G. Blumler and E. Katz (eds.), *The Uses of Mass Communications*. Beverly Hills: Sage Publications, 1974.

Mendelsohn, H., and I. Crespi. *Polls, Television and the New Politics*. Scranton: Chandler-Intext, 1970.

Mendelsohn, H., and G. J. O'Keefe. *The People Choose a President: Influences on Voter Decision Making*. New York: Praeger, 1976.

24.

Influence on Public Agendas

LEE B. BECKER, DAVID H. WEAVER,
DORIS A. GRABER, and MAXWELL E. McCOMBS

A variety of empirical evidence now in hand indicates that editors and news directors, in their day-by-day decisions about the coverage and play of the news, influence audience members' perceptions of what is important. Examining the normal, routine flow of the news during political campaigns, we found that over time what is important to the media—indexed by heavy play and coverage—also becomes salient and important to segments of the public. These studies detail the drop-by-drop, slow accretion of mass-communication effects (see Shaw and McCombs, 1977; Becker, McCombs, and McLeod, 1975).

The debates of 1976 provided an opportunity to examine the agenda-setting influence of the news media in a vastly grander setting than had been provided by recent political campaigns. The debates were among the most spectacular media events of this century. Certainly, they were the most concentrated instances of political communication in the 1976 presidential campaign. Representing the efforts of the League of Women Voters, the two major presidential candidates, and the TV networks, the debates received hours of valuable television time and publicity in all the news media.

The debates were designed to focus on issues. The issues placed before the voters by the debates should have been the ones voters subsequently thought were important. Issue saliences were given little attention in studies on the effects of the 1960 debates between John Kennedy and Richard Nixon. Katz and Feldman (1962), in their overview of research, did note two studies indicating foreign affairs—dealt with in detail in the 1960 encounters—was the most important issue during the entire campaign. There was some evidence as well that this issue increased in importance following the second, third, and fourth debates. While Katz and Feldman were ready to conclude that the debates made some issues more salient than others, the evidence was indirect and limited in scope. For the most part, researchers who examined the role of issues in the debates and the 1960 campaign were concerned with knowledge gain and change in candidate preference, not salience.

Research Design

In an effort to trace changes in issue saliences and other related political variables during the 1976 presidential campaign, a panel of approximately forty-five registered voters in each of three diverse communities was recruited in January of 1976. The panel members were interviewed in February, March, May, July, August, September, October, and November of that year and again in January of 1977, a total of nine interviews. Most of the interviews, which were designed to gather respondent-oriented reactions to the issues in the campaigns, were conducted by telephone. Interviewers attempted to gain unusual rapport with the panel members to facilitate acquisition of unanticipated reactions to the campaign.[1]

These interviews were conducted with voters in Evanston, Illinois, a suburban Chicago community; metropolitan Indianapolis, Indiana; and Lebanon, New Hampshire, a small New England town. The probability samples from which panel members were recruited were designed to overrepresent those persons in the communities who usually followed political campaigns either in their newspapers or on television. Those not using the media and those indicating no interest in politics were systematically eliminated from the sample pool.

The median age of the panel members was in the thirties. About 40 percent were college graduates. Approximately half of those working outside the home had jobs traditionally classified as white-collar. And 47 percent of the panel members were female.[2]

The September interviews were conducted before the first presidential debate between Jimmy Carter and Gerald Ford. The October wave was fielded after all four debates had been held. Inferences on debate effects come primarily from these two waves of the study.

To supplement data generated from panels in the three communities, a separate panel of twenty-one Evanston respondents was recruited for even more intensive interviewing during the campaign. The respondents in this panel were interviewed in person at approximately five-week intervals during the election year. The personal interviews generally began with very broad, open-ended questions and then switched to more structured questions. An unlimited number of probes was made to elicit as much information as possible. These probes routinely included questions calling for the reasons that caused the respondents to give specific answers.

In the course of the year, each respondent was interviewed for a total of twenty to thirty hours. All interviews were taped. In addition, members of the panel completed daily diaries listing news stories that had come to their attention.

The smaller Evanston panel provides qualitative data on reactions to the 1976 debates and to the campaign in general. No claims are being made here about the representativeness of the responses. Rather, the data are being used to provide insights into the effects of the political campaign which may be missed by standard survey practices.

The voter data gathered in both studies were supplemented by content analyses of the debates. Each question, answer, rebuttal comment, and closing statement was analyzed to determine which issues were covered in the debates. Coding allowed for up to three issue mentions in each of the questions, answers, rebuttal comments, and closing statements. If, for example, in answering a given question one of the candidates discussed both unemployment and inflation, that answer was coded into both categories.

Results: Three Communities

Three separate types of issue saliences were measured in the three-community study: intrapersonal salience—the extent to which an individual feels an issue is important to him or her; interpersonal salience—the amount of interpersonal discussion about an issue; and perceived community salience—the judgment of an individual about the salience rating of a given issue for others in the community.[3]

While most of the research on agenda-setting has examined the media's influence on intrapersonal saliences, there is no reason to believe the media's role is limited to that kind of an effect. The three types of measures have been included here to test for effects on various kinds of saliences and thereby expand the understanding of agenda-setting influences.[4]

Table 1 shows the percentages in the three-community panel listing each of eleven general issues as most important personally. Responses not fitting into the eleven categories were coded as "other." (Individuals unable to name a specific issue are eliminated from these analyses.)

The general dominance of economic issues is most obvious in Table 1. Indeed, by the final wave, almost 70 percent of the responses were for unemployment, inflation, taxes, or state of the economy. Almost 50 percent of the responses were economic at the outset of the study. By and large, however, the responses shown in Table 1 are relatively constant across time. There are no major shifts, for instance, during the spring primary period. And while there is a noticeable increase in the salience of inflation between the September and late October waves, which surround the debate period, a corresponding drop in the salience of the overall state of the economy partially erases this difference.

We found evidence that voters also talk about the things that are most important to them. Reports of *inter*personal salience were quite similar to the reports of *intra*personal salience shown in Table 1. The increase in the salience of economic matters was evidenced in these reports as well as in the intrapersonal reports.

Reports of community salience were very similar to reports of the other types of salience. Again, economic issues increase in salience over the campaign period. Overall, however, responses to this salience measure seem to be slightly more variable across time than was true for either the intrapersonal or the interpersonal measures. Inflation, for example, increases rather markedly from February to July, but drops off in August before increasing again in October. While there is a similar trend for the other measures, it isn't so marked.

There is little evidence in general, however, that the three measures vary independently. The October intrapersonal and interpersonal measures correlate .82 (Spearman's rho). The perceptual measure correlates .81 with the intrapersonal measure in October and .97 with the interpersonal.

When the three types of issue salience are viewed as a whole, they indicate the debates probably were not responsible for any massive shifts in saliences, as no such shifts appear during any of the campaign periods. Some fluctuation did seem to be taking place, however, and the debates may have contributed to that movement.

Table 2 shows the agendas presented to voters by the debates. The first

THE GREAT DEBATES

Table 1: Issues Considered Personally Important to Voters (Intrapersonal Measures)

	Feb.	March	May	July	Aug.	Sept.	Oct.	Nov.
Unemployment	9.9%	15.6%	10.4%	11.9%	10.7%	9.6%	11.9%	14.8%
Inflation	17.6	20.3	14.9	19.0	16.0	25.6	34.9	27.3
Taxes	2.3	3.9	1.5	0.8	4.6	5.6	5.6	7.0
State of the economy	15.3	20.3	20.1	19.8	25.2	27.2	18.3	19.5
Crime	7.6	0.8	5.2	7.9	9.2	4.8	1.6	3.9
Racial issues, busing	3.8	1.6	3.0	2.4	1.5	0.8	2.4	0.8
Health, welfare, education	14.5	5.5	5.2	6.3	6.9	2.4	7.1	3.1
Environment, energy	13.0	4.7	3.7	6.3	3.8	3.2	3.2	2.3
Credibility of government, leaders	4.6	3.9	5.2	7.1	5.3	3.2	4.0	6.3
Government spending, size	1.5	2.3	3.7	2.4	2.3	0.0	0.8	0.8
Foreign affairs, defense	3.8	15.6	20.1	8.7	8.4	8.8	4.0	5.5
Other	6.1	5.5	6.7	7.1	6.1	8.8	6.3	8.6
N	(131)	(128)	(134)	(126)	(131)	(125)	(126)	(128)

Table 2: Issues Covered in the Presidential Debates*

	Debate One	Debate Two	Debate Three	Total	Carter	Ford
Unemployment	8.9%	2.4%	12.3%	7.0%	8.6%	5.7%
Inflation	4.4	0.0	6.2	3.0	3.6	2.5
Taxes	22.2	0.0	2.5	7.4	6.5	8.2
State of the economy	6.7	0.8	7.4	4.4	5.0	3.8
Crime	2.2	0.0	1.2	1.0	.7	1.3
Racial issues, busing	0.0	0.0	3.7	1.0	.7	1.3
Health, welfare, education	8.9	0.8	7.4	5.0	6.5	3.8
Environment, energy	6.7	1.6	6.2	4.4	6.5	2.5
Credibility of government, leaders	8.9	9.5	18.5	11.8	13.7	10.1
Government spending, size	22.2	3.2	2.5	8.7	6.5	10.8
Foreign affairs, defense	0.0	77.0	12.3	36.0	30.2	41.1
Other	8.9	4.8	19.8	10.1	11.5	8.9
N	(90)	(126)	(81)	(297)	(139)	(158)

*Each question, answer, rebuttal comment, and closing statement was coded according to issues mentioned. Any given question, answer, rebuttal, or closing statement could be coded into up to three issue categories. Entries tabled here are the percentages of coded items for each of the issue categories.

debate, which was designed to focus on domestic issues, consisted of many references to economic matters, with taxes getting a large part of the mentions. Government size and spending also received a large percentage of the comments. The second debate was intended to focus on foreign affairs, and the content analysis indicates it did. While some of the comments strayed into matters of leadership, as the content analysis shows, the debate was clearly focused on foreign policy topics. The final presidential debate, which was open format, again turned heavily to economic matters. But even here foreign affairs was given some attention. The total presidential debate agenda is a summation across the three separate debates. As such, it presents a balance of domestic and foreign issues.[5]

The agendas also were divided into those associated with Carter and those associated with Ford to check for any strong imbalances. In general, there were none. More questions and answers on foreign affairs were associated with Ford, but even that difference is not overwhelming.

The match between these debate agendas and the agendas for the panel members in the waves surrounding the debates is shown in Table 3. The issue salience reports are correlated with the salience given these issues in the debates. All materials coded "other" were dropped from the analyses. Overall, there is little evidence of a strong relationship between the debate agendas and the panel agendas. Only the third debate agenda shows relatively consistent and positive relationships.

A closer examination of the issue reports provides a better understanding of the Table 3 correlations. While inflation was given relatively little play in the debates, it increased in salience in the issue reports from pre- to post-debate

THE GREAT DEBATES

waves. And while foreign affairs is dominant in the overall debate agenda, all issue reports show a slight decrease in the frequency of this response on the part of panel members.

The higher correlations of the panel agenda measures with the third debate agenda in Table 3 lend themselves to an interesting interpretation. The agendas of the first two presidential debates were constrained by the format adopted for them, domestic issues in the first, foreign affairs in the second. Only in the third presidential debate were journalists free to ask questions of concern to them. And the questions they asked show the best match with intrapersonal and interpersonal agendas even before the debates took place. Either the reporters were anticipating these saliences, or they were simply repeating past editorial behavior that had produced these saliences. Preliminary examination of the media content in the three communities studied suggests the second explanation is at least as plausible as the first. In other words, the third debate seems to have an agenda much like the media did during the extended campaign period.

The analyses in Table 3, of course, are aggregated analyses. As such, they do not test whether individual voters will reflect the agenda presented them by the debates. Rather, they present evidence that communities as a whole reflected agendas similar to those in the debates only in the case of the third debate.

In Table 4, data are presented that allow for a more direct test of the agenda-setting hypothesis. Here the intrapersonal salience of a specific issue, inflation, is examined. Inflation was paired with three other issues, unemployment, federal spending, and quality of national leadership, in a paired comparison measurement procedure.[6] Since these three issues were given prominent

Table 3: Correlations (Spearman's Rhos) between Presidential Debate Agendas and Respondent Agendas*

	Debate 1	Debate 2	Debate 3	Total
Intrapersonal Measures				
August	−.18	−.07	.34	−.12
September	−.20	−.10	.31	−.05
Debates held				
October	.07	−.14	.49	−.01
November	.05	−.12	.37	.05
Interpersonal Measures				
August	−.13	.12	.30	.03
September	−.18	−.10	.36	.00
Debates held				
October	.15	−.45	.12	−.33
November	.00	−.13	.40	.04
Perceptual Measures				
August	.21	−.56	.07	−.33
Debates held				
October	.12	−.53	.06	−.38

*The Ns for these correlations are all 11.

display in the debates and inflation was not, this comparison provides a rather straightforward test of the agenda-setting hypothesis in the context of the debates. If the debates influenced voters' agendas, the mean score for inflation should decrease from the predebate September wave to the post-debate October wave.

The data are not supportive of this expectation. In fact, for persons who viewed all of the debates, those who viewed some of them, and those who viewed none of them the change is in the reverse direction. The salience of inflation continued to increase during the debates. The upward change in Table 4 parallels the long-term upward trend in the salience of inflation previously seen in the issue salience reports. The debates simply did not offset or alter the trends already in motion. Analyses of individual data from the other two types of saliences reinforce this interpretation.

Table 4: Paired Comparison Analyses of Inflation Issue (Mean Scores)*

	September	October	Change	N
Viewed All Presidential Debates	1.39	1.76	+.37	(62)
Viewed Some of the Presidential Debates	1.36	1.56	+.20	(44)
Viewed None of the Presidential Debates	1.58	2.08	+.50	(12)

*A high score indicates inflation was considered important compared with unemployment, federal spending, and quality of national leadership. Range of scores was from 0 to 3.

Results: Evanston Intensive Panel

We had hoped to be able to turn to the Evanston panel to better understand the process by which voters acquired issue salience ratings from the debates. But the data from the three communities indicate little effect of the debates on the salience ratings assigned issues by the voters. As a consequence, the strength of the Evanston data would seem to lie in their ability to indicate why this effect, demonstrated in other campaign situations, had not surfaced here.

Because the acquisition of issue saliences from the media can be thought of as a type of learning, it is within the context of learning from the media that the Evanston intensive panel analyses are carried out. By understanding that general process, it is hoped, a better understanding of the process by which issue saliences are formed can be gained.

The Evanston intensive panel data are atypical of most data gathered to study the effects of the debates. The data are, in fact, much more like those from in-depth psychological interviews than those usually gained from survey instruments. They represent an attempt to be sensitive to the meaning of political campaigns for audience members. As such, the data are very respondent-oriented, rather than researcher-oriented, as is usually the case in much social research.

Most of the respondents in the Evanston panel expressed high interest in the prospective debates. Nevertheless, they failed to watch large portions of the broadcasts. Other demands on their time received priority, such as working late on their jobs even when it might have been avoided, attending dinner parties, going to church, having friends at their homes, babysitting, and, in a large number of instances, going to bed early. Attendance and attention declined with each successive debate.

Many respondents made absolute judgments about the quality of the debates. But others conditioned their answers, stating that the debates held more or less interest than expected or were more or less interesting, compared to other debates. Some pronounced certain aspects of a debate or certain portions of a discussion highly interesting while calling the rest dull. The predominant overall judgment was that the debates were boring, except for a few highlights.

The interviews suggest the debates came too late to fill major information needs of the voters. Panel members indicated they had already made a presidential choice and that nothing short of a spectacular disclosure was likely to change their views. A major reason for information acquisition—the need to make choices—had passed its peak in Evanston, at least among attentive voters.

Voters who had expressed a need for more information because they had learned little before the debates generally paid least attention to the debates and could not even mention the issues most prominently featured in them. The same factors which had made the information-poor what they were throughout the earlier stages of the 1976 campaign—lack of interest, lack of time, and lack of comprehension—also kept them from paying close attention to the debates and absorbing the available information.

Most respondents said they had not learned anything new about the issues during the debates. A variety of reasons were given for the lack of learning. The most prevalent one was that there was nothing new to be learned. The debates covered familiar ground and did not touch upon new facts or even deepen understandings. Another deterrent to learning seemed to be the manner of presentation. People were disappointed that these were lackluster, two-candidate news conferences which rehashed familiar facts and disclosed few real differences between the candidates. There were complaints that the presentations were unclear and overloaded with confusing statistics. Credibility was a factor as well. Some respondents questioned whether the facts presented to them were accurate or whether they were part of "campaign rhetoric." All these concerns diminished the impact of the debates.

The types of knowledge that the twenty-one respondents had about six key issues following the second debate were measured. In each case, varying degrees of knowledge were recorded, depending on whether the respondent was merely aware of the issue, could report facts about it, or was able to accurately state the position of one or both candidates on the issue.

The findings indicate that, even at the end of a presidential campaign, many panel members were barely aware of most widely reported issues. This finding did not seem to result from an inability of panel members to articulate political issues. Among those who claimed to be unfamiliar with the substance of a number of issues and who said that they could not state the issue positions of the candidates were experienced, articulate lawyers and business executives. On the other hand, the sample included people with partial grade-school educations and low-level occupations who found no difficulty in stating the issue positions of the candidates.

Neither the issue most frequently mentioned in the debates, foreign affairs, nor the ones with the highest impact on most respondents' lives, taxes and unemployment, were best understood among the issues. Rather, this distinction fell to the two issues which presented simple, dichotomous choices in the eyes of all respondents. The issues were national defense and amnesty, the least frequently mentioned of all issues examined here.[7] The national defense issue was perceived by all respondents as an either/or choice between spending more or less money for defense. Amnesty presented the poles of leniency and toughness. All of the other questions were perceived as involving a much wider, more confusing array of policy choices.

It should be kept in mind that the measures of knowledge used here are strict ones, requiring the ability to provide accurate factual information spontaneously. Other data, using less exacting standards, may well show gains in knowledge attributable to the debates. The Evanston panel data, however, suggest that such knowledge gains may be quite limited and superficial.

Interest in the debates, the fact of actual watching (as opposed to secondary information), and the degree of expressed need for additional information bore little relation to the level of learning attained. Initial level of political knowledge was a better predictor of high-level learning. This is consistent with the familiar finding that the knowledge-rich get richer and the knowledge-poor remain poor (Donohue, Tichenor, and Olien, 1975).

Conclusions

There is no evidence here that the debates had any significant impact on the public agenda. Despite an abundance of before–after measures on the salience of numerous issues, the agenda of public opinion did not show any marked shifts in priorities resulting from this colossal media event. Why did such a spectacular media effort fail to influence the public agenda? Our data here suggest three clusters of factors:

Timing,
Manner of presentation and content,
Orientations of audience members to the debates.

The debates came late in a political campaign that really began in New Hampshire during February 1976. The issues at the top of the agenda in October and November clearly were the culmination of trends running from the first of the year. Both the measures of the community agendas and the measures of individual agendas show identical trends. In the face of such long-running trends, perhaps it is unreasonable to expect significant impact from a short-term media effort.

The data suggest that the debates came too late to fill informational needs or seriously alter the perceived saliences of issues. A major motive for attending to information and reconsidering one's own agenda of issues—deciding on the presidential vote—was absent for many voters by the time of the debates. Most had already decided.

This lack of influence on the public agenda from debates so close to election day fits with the findings from a 1972 (Shaw and McCombs, 1977) election study where it was found that the major agenda-setting influence of mass communication appears gradually over a period of several months. From this perspective, the debates simply did not offer enough learning trials over a long enough period of time.

Voters also criticized the style and content of the debates. If voters are to learn from mass communication, the message should be interesting and useful. But many found the debates dull and boring. People also were disappointed that these media events were not exciting, point-counterpoint debates. Instead, the presentations were perceived as drawn-out news conferences. For many there was "nothing new." For others the new information was too fragmentary to be helpful.

The constraints of the format—debate 1 was limited to domestic issues and debate 2, foreign affairs—also appear in the agenda-setting measures of Table 3. There are substantial positive correlations only for the third debate, where the media were free to pursue the general array of issues that had been long on the media and public agendas.

Many of the criticisms of the message also index key aspects of the audience orientations to the debates. People found it hard to pay attention over long periods of time and difficult to sort out much of the information presented; often they very quickly forgot much of what they had attended to. Part of their difficulties may have stemmed from evaluations of the debates' credibility as a source of information. Some saw the debates as nothing beyond more campaign rhetoric, while others questioned the accuracy and utility of the facts tossed out by the candidates.

These data should not be interpreted as indicating the 1976 debates had no effect on voters. The analyses here have been narrowly focused—on issue saliences—and there is little evidence of effects here indeed. But other effects no doubt resulted, despite the limitations posed by timing, manner of presentation, and audience member orientations.

NOTES

1. Appreciation is expressed to Gary Kromer, Paula Poindexter, and Bob Burnham, Syracuse University graduate students; Roger Sanders, a graduate student at the University of Illinois Chicago Circle; and Douglas Dietsch, a graduate student at Indiana University.

2. Comparisons of the Lebanon panel with the cross-sectional sample of voters used to generate the panel indicate that there is little difference between panel and community members in terms of actual newspaper and television public affairs use. The panel members, however, were more interested in the campaign than the cross-sectional sample members were. Both groups were drawn from the voter registration lists, a process which tends to eliminate the very uninterested in any community. Panel members also tended to be younger and better educated than cross-section sample members.

3. The specific measures were the following: "Of the various problems and issues now facing the United States, which is most important to you personally?" (intrapersonal); "Which of these problems and issues have you talked about most often with others during the past month?" (interpersonal); "Now let's shift from the issues important to you to the issues most important to the entire community. They may or may not be concerned with the same issues as you are. Which issues do you think are most important to voters around here?" (perceived). Responses to these open-ended questions were content analyzed and coded as shown in Table 1.

4. See McLeod, Becker, and Byrnes (1974) for a conceptual discussion of these measures.

5. The vice-presidential debate agenda, though not included here, is relatively similar and would not have changed the picture appreciably. The vice-presidential debate, which was open-format, matches the second presidential debate agenda (rho = .65) better than either the first (rho = .42) or third debate (rho = .50). Fewer issue mentions (69) were coded here, however, than in the slightly longer presidential debates (297 overall). It also should be kept in mind that length of question or answer is not reflected in the coding here—only mention or nonmention of an issue.

6. The specific question was, "Now I would like to get your opinion on the relative importance of some of these issues. I will name two issues at a time. As I name each pair, please tell me which one you personally think is the most important issue in the presidential campaign." A high score in Table 4 indicates inflation "won" the pairing. Range of scores was from 0 to 3.

7. Amnesty was coded into the "other" category in Table 2. National defense was coded into the Foreign Affairs category. National defense independent of Foreign Affairs was not frequently mentioned in the debates.

REFERENCES

Becker, L. B., M. E. McCombs, and J. M. McLeod. "The Development of Political Cognitions," in S. H. Chaffee (ed.), *Political Communication.* Beverly Hills, Calif.: Sage Publications, 1975, pp. 21–63.

Donohue, G. A., P. J. Tichenor, and C. N. Olien. "Mass Media and the Knowledge Gap." *Communication Research* (January 1975), pp. 3–23.

Katz, E., and J. J. Feldman. "The Debates in the Light of Research: A Survey of Surveys," in S. Kraus (ed.), *The Great Debates.* Bloomington: Indiana University Press, 1962, pp. 173–223.

McLeod, J. M., L. B. Becker, and J. E. Byrnes. "Another Look at the Agenda-Setting Function of the Press." *Communication Research* (1974), pp. 131–66.

Shaw, D. L., and M. E. McCombs (eds.). *The Emergence of American Political Issues.* St. Paul, Minn.: West Publishing, 1977.

25.

Home State Voter Response and Secondary Media Coverage

CHARLES ATKIN, JOHN HOCKING,
and STEVEN McDERMOTT

A popular pursuit of mass-media researchers has been to analyze the influence of televised political events, such as the Carter–Ford debates. While most studies of campaign telecasts have focused on audience attitudinal yielding to the *initial broadcast* message, this survey investigation examines a variety of phenomena beyond direct persuasive impact.

The range of stimuli is broadened to include secondary mass-media reporting and analysis of the debate, such as radio news coverage, newspaper editorials, and opinion poll reports. The domain of response variables is widened to include interest and agenda salience, and absolute as well as positive attitude changes. A number of predebate predictor variables such as initial candidate preference, campaign interest, and demographic characteristics are related to exposure patterns and affective reactions. Among these attributes is the home state of the voter, which is expected to bias reactions toward the favorite son.

Theoretical expectations concerning differential response to Carter and Ford in Georgia and Michigan are based on the tendency for greater candidate familiarity and support to be exhibited in the home state. To the extent that the candidate is better known in his state than in the opponent's state, more stability of preference is anticipated due to well-established affect. To the extent that the home candidate is viewed more positively than the outsider, psychological defenses and sociological influences should contribute to reinforcement of predispositions: selective exposure and perception are expected to produce affective movement toward the home state contender and negative change toward the outside challenger; interpersonal messages more favorable to the insider should also lead to relatively positive change. Thus, it is predicted that Carter will be less successful in persuading Michigan viewers and Ford's impact on Georgians will be limited.

The debate selected for analysis in this study is the final encounter on October 22, 1976. Since this event came at the end of the debate series and late in a message-saturated campaign, it provides a tough test of the potency of the mass media. Compared to all of the prior persuasive communications, this broadcast constitutes a fairly weak stimulus that should have very limited effects.

429

Research Method

A panel survey was conducted with 466 voters, including 218 respondents in Michigan and 248 in Georgia. The first wave of telephone interviews took place the evening before the final debate (October 21), and the follow-up interviewing of the same sample occurred two nights after the debate (October 24). This design allowed measurement of change across a time period restricted enough to minimize nondebate campaign influences, yet long enough to provide opportunity for exposure to a wide range of relevant post-debate reports and interpretation in the broadcast and print media. In addition to seeing the Friday evening debate, voters could watch "instant analyses" later that night, attend radio and TV newscasts describing the debate late Friday night and Saturday, read newspaper accounts the following day, read Sunday morning newspaper analyses, and be exposed to reports of public opinion polls concerning the "winner" of the debate.

The limited research budget required use of the most convenient sample and interviewing staff: college-town voters and student interviewers. The sample was drawn randomly from telephone books in Lansing, Michigan, and Athens, Georgia. While the Lansing area is representative of the state of Michigan in many demographic characteristics, the smaller Athens population is somewhat younger and better educated than most other Georgians. Interviewers were 120 undergraduate students in communication courses who each completed approximately four pairs of interviews. Although these students were specially trained in interview techniques and the use of this survey instrument, many had no previous interviewing experience.

The basic design involved before and after measures on four sets of variables: (a) issue agenda, (b) campaign interest, (c) candidate attitudes, and (d) personality evaluations.

The second set of variables dealt with mass-media exposure, and interpersonal persuasion inputs were also measured.

Findings

The presentation of survey results is divided into five sections. The first set of findings describes the patterns to exposure to the debate and supplemental post-debate media content. Then the antecedent predictors of exposure are considered, including demographics, predispositions, and prior media exposure. Differences in reaction in the Michigan versus Georgia subsamples are covered next. The key data regarding the possible effects of debate and post-debate information are examined with correlational and mean change analyses. This is followed by an assessment of the role of persuasive influences, such as interpersonal interpretation and media analyses.

Exposure patterns

Viewership of the final debate was neither widespread nor attentive in Michigan and Georgia. Less than three-fifths of the sample watched the telecast, and only one voter in four reported seeing all of it. Those who did view were asked two follow-up questions about their degree of attention while watching. When asked how much attention they paid to "what the candidates said about the issues," just 11 percent of the viewers claimed to pay "close" attention, while

430   THE GREAT DEBATES

35 percent reported "some" attention, and 54 percent said "not much." The question probing attentiveness to "the way they looked and handled themselves on camera" yielded almost identical results: 12 percent "close," 36 percent "some," and 52 percent "not much" attention.

The network "instant analysis" programs that were broadcast a half-hour after the completion of the debate attracted one-sixth of all respondents. One-fifth to two-fifths were exposed to debate stories in each of the mass media in the days after the debate; the highest exposure was for radio news, followed by TV news and newspaper news and analysis. Across these different media, 70 percent were exposed to at least one post-debate story. On the average, the sample read, watched, or listened to 1.7 stories. Reports of the findings from voter opinion polls about the debate reached more than half of the sample.

The degree of exposure to the debate was positively but mildly related to post-debate exposure patterns. An index combining the six post-debate measures correlates +.27 with the debate exposure item. Nonviewers did not attempt to make up for the missed debate by seeking subsequent coverage; rather, those who had already seen it tended to seek secondary messages. There is a moderate interrelationship among these supplementary exposure measures.

Predictors of exposure

Viewership of the debate, ranging from nonexposure to full exposure, correlates moderately with campaign interest (+.27) and age level (+.25). Prior attitude toward each candidate is insignificantly correlated, indicating that supporters of either man were not much more likely to be in the audience. There is a modest tendency for voters with higher education (+.08) and occupational status (+.12) to view. Males watched slightly more (+.08) than females, and those from Michigan (+.08) saw more than Georgians.

Exposure to the six types of post-debate news coverage and analysis was weakly related to the predictor variables.

Differential response in Michigan and Georgia

Comparisons of voter reactions in the home states of each candidate are of interest primarily because of the assumption that favorite-son allegiances will be prevalent. This is not uniformly the case. We find that about twice as many home state voters strongly prefer the local candidate to the man from the other state. Nevertheless, approximately one-fifth of those from Athens rate Carter in the bottom half of the preference scale, and the same holds true for Lansing voter opinions about Ford. Thus, home state is only a rough locator variable representing candidate affect; theoretical predictions based on partisan predispositions and social influences cannot be fully examined with state analyses.

Given this qualification, the pattern of exposure to information and persuasion can be compared between the two states. Equivalent levels of exposure to the first debate are found in Michigan and Georgia, but voters from Michigan were more likely to remain attentive for the final debate.

There is a clear tendency for respondents to perceive that post-debate poll results showed the home state candidate as the "winner" of the debate. Athens voters were more likely to perceive newspaper commentary as mostly favorable to Carter, while Lansing voters reported reading pro-Ford analysis. Most respondents felt that the post-debate TV analyses were not biased toward either candidate. Interpersonal messages supporting the home state candidate were no more prevalent than communications favorable to the other candidate.

Change in attitude toward Carter after the debate was positive in the Michigan subsample (+.39 of a step on an eleven-step scale) and negative in the Georgia one (−.12). Ford attitude change was negative in Georgia (−.14) and near-zero in Michigan (+.01). Carter's personal image averaged across the four eleven-step evaluation scales improved in Michigan (+.37) and in Georgia (+.09). The evaluation of Ford also increased in Michigan (+.28) and in Georgia (+.12). The largest single change was in a jump of more than one point in Michigan voters' perception of Carter sincerity.

Examining these data by home state, we find a slight tendency for the outside candidate to gain relatively more support. On the average, the outsider increases +.13 of a step in attitude and +.25 in image, while the local candidate declines −.06 in attitude and rises +.18 in image. However, this pattern is mostly due to statistical regression fallacy: since the home state candidate is already high on the scale and the outside candidate is comparatively low, subsequent responses tend to regress toward the mean. This is not a complete explanation, since state of residence is less than perfectly related to prior attitude and evaluation scores. This issue will be examined more closely when changes among viewers and nonviewers are compared in the next section.

In terms of absolute amount of change, voters in Georgia showed more affective movement in either direction for Ford than for Carter; the shifting was greater for Carter than Ford among Michigan respondents.

Media Exposure and Change in Orientations

Between the first and second waves of the survey, there was a considerable amount of fluctuation in attitudes, evaluations, and interest and agenda ratings. On attitude toward Ford, 40 percent of the sample maintained the same position on the eleven-step scale over the three-day period. Favorable shifts of one or more steps occurred for 28 percent, and negative change was found for 32 percent. Carter attitude ratings were unchanged for 41 percent of the voters; 35 percent became more favorable, and 24 percent became less favorable. The Time 1–Time 2 correlation in attitude toward Ford was +.77, and a +.75 relationship was obtained for Carter across the three-day interval.

In the initial analysis the T_1–T_2 change scores are correlated with each of the exposure measures. In addition to examining directional change, the absolute amount of change regardless of direction is used as a correlate of exposure; a positive association means that exposure is related to general change, either favorable or unfavorable.

Debate effect: Our data show that viewing of the TV debate correlates +.03 with favorable attitude change toward Carter and +.10 with change on the summated Carter evaluative ratings. Debate viewing also correlates +.03 with positive change in Ford attitude, and +.11 with favorable evaluative change. Among the image measures, the strongest correlations are for ratings that the candidates are "concerned" (+.11 Carter, +.07 Ford) and "well-informed" (+.07 Carter, +.10 Ford). Change in perceived sincerity and confidence are very slightly related to exposure.

432

The *absolute* amount of change is slightly more correlated with exposure, on the average. Viewers are also more likely to become more interested in the campaign. These relational findings will be examined in more detail with mean change data below.

Debate effect by state: When correlations between viewing and change scores are examined, no significant differences are found. Affective change tends to be more positively correlated with debate exposure in the home state than in the outside state; the difference is +.06 versus .00 for attitude and +.16 versus +.06 for personality image. Relative to nonviewers, those who saw the debate became more favorable to the local candidate. Indeed, nonviewers moved .09 of a step negatively in attitude toward the home candidate and .13 of a step positively toward the outsider; this can be used as an indicator of magnitude of regression to the mean, so relative comparisons between viewers and nonviewers essentially account for regression fallacies.

Correlations of viewing with absolute change regardless of direction suggest that viewership is more positively related to changes on the outside candidate than on the home candidate. With respect to the out-of-state candidate, exposed respondents display more change than nonviewers, indicating that the debate serves to move attitudes and images favorably *or* unfavorably. On the other hand, absolute movement on the favorite son is only slightly greater for viewers, and this change is less sizable than the directional change; this indicates that the debate produces a small amount of predominantly positive change for the home man.

Post-debate effect: Exposure to post-debate coverage and analysis tends to be related positively with change in Carter attitude and negligibly with Ford attitude change and interest change. Changes in personality evaluation are not associated with post-debate exposure in most cases. Absolute change is not consistently related to exposure; there are about as many negative as positive associations. Among the various types of messages presented after the debate, only TV news and newspaper news have a consistently positive set of associations with changes on attitude, evaluation, and interest. The total variance in attitude change accounted for by debate and post-debate exposure is not impressive. The multiple correlation for all predictors used is .16 for Carter change and .07 for Ford.

Issue agenda changes: Among the five issues measured, inflation was most frequently discussed during the debate. The exposed group changed from 84 percent to 88 percent perceiving this issue to be important, while the nonexposed respondents changed from 87 percent to 85 percent; the net change of +6 percent between the two groups indicates that the debate emphasis did increase the salience of inflation as a campaign issue. Abortion, which was dealt with less prominently, had a net change of 0 percent.

Crime and Eastern Europe did not make the agenda, despite expectations that each topic would be debated; these unmentioned issues became relatively less important (net change of −10 percent and −9 percent, respectively).

Effects of Persuasive Interpretation

Four types of post-debate analysis appear to have the greatest potential for influencing how voters react to the event. Table 1 presents the mean changes in

Table 1: Mean Change in Affective Orientations, by Exposure to Partisan Analyses

Source and Valence of Persuasion

Affective Change	NP Analysis		Poll Analysis		TV Analysis		IP Analysis	
	Carter N = 24	Ford N = 19	Carter N = 86	Ford N = 36	Carter N = 16	Ford N = 10	Carter N = 58	Ford N = 51
Carter attitude	+ .16	+ .33	+ .16	+ .61	+ .06	+ .14	+ .48	− .18*
Carter evaluation	+ .33	− .19*	+ .21	+ .25	− .06	+ .18	+ .20	+ .12
Ford attitude	−1.05	+ .29*	− .41	+ .38*	− .01	+ .43	− .38	+ .57*
Ford evaluation	− .01	+ .21	− .02	+ .37*	+ .42	+1.39	+ .20	+ .42

*p < .05, by t-test between groups receiving pro-Carter vs. pro-Ford persuasion.
Table entries are mean change scores between Time 1 and Time 2 for those respondents exposed to persuasive messages primarily favorable to one of the debaters. Attitude was measured along 11-step scale; evaluation is averaged across the four 11-step scales. IP analysis refers to interpersonal communication from debate co-viewer(s).

attitude and image scores for groups of respondents who saw or heard interpretive commentary favoring either Ford or Carter.

There is evidence in Table 1 that interpersonal discussion significantly mediates the impact of the debate broadcast. Among debate viewers who heard predominantly favorable comments about one candidate from co-viewers, there is a half-step change in attitude toward that candidate and a quarter-step movement away from the opponent. Interpersonal discussion has less strong impact on personality evaluations. It should be noted that less than half of the viewers heard pro-Carter or pro-Ford interpretation.

Among the media inputs, most respondents perceived the polls as showing that Carter won the debate. Changes in Ford attitude and image are responsive to the direction of perceived poll results, but changes toward Carter are in the opposite direction (Table 1).

Small proportions of the sample felt that newspaper and television analysis favored one of the candidates. Those reading predominantly pro-Ford newspaper editorials and columns liked him better and viewed Carter less favorably. Carter's image increased or declined in direction consistent with the persuasive newspaper messages. The few who saw TV analyses favorable toward Ford changed favorably in response.

Reception of these valenced communications tends to be selective, as voters see and hear persuasive messages supportive of their favorite candidate. To describe the extent of partisan selectivity, the Time 1 attitude scales for each candidate were juxtaposed to produce a continuum of *relative* preference ranging from pro-Carter to equal liking to pro-Ford. This scale was derived by subtracting the Time 1 attitude toward Carter (ranging from 0 to 10) from the Time 1 attitude toward Ford. Each type of partisan message reception was likewise scaled from pro-Carter to equally valenced to pro-Ford. Prior preference correlates $+.45$ with receiving partisan interpersonal communication during the debate, $+.21$ with perception of supportive poll findings, and $+.20$ with perceived favorability of televised post-debate commentary. On the other hand, there is only a $+.05$ correlation with reading newspaper analysis favoring the preferred candidate.

Discussion

The final Carter–Ford debate did not attract an impressively large or attentive audience, even in the candidates' home states. However, more than two-thirds of the voters were exposed to secondary post-debate news and interpretation in the mass media. Since debate viewers were much more likely to attend these later messages than nonviewers, post-debate coverage seems primarily to serve a supplemental rather than a compensatory function for most voters.

The debate broadcast appears to have made a small but positive contribution to affect toward each candidate. Absolute amount of change is stimulated by the debate to a somewhat greater extent than positive directional change, as voters with differing predispositions react in contrasting fashion to the same ambiguous stimuli. The debate broadcast also makes a small contribution to a relatively heightened level of interest in the campaign.

Among the viewers of the debate, positive changes in affect occur regardless of initial predispositions. In addition, the debates actually seem to stimulate relatively more interest among those who are lower in initial interest. This pair of findings may reflect the unique power of a televised debate format to reach and influence many voters who would tune out or distort conventional campaign news and persuasion messages.

Issue agenda changes indicate that debaters can deemphasize issues by ignoring them as well as raising salience by dealing with a topic. Many voters originally thought that Ford's remark on Russian domination of Eastern Europe was an important campaign issue, but viewers accorded it less significance when it was not debated.

The post-debate coverage has limited effects on the variables considered in this study. A modest positive impact on attitude toward Carter and slight effects on Ford attitude can be detected, but personality image changes do not occur.

Some of the interpretive commentary is influential for certain voters. The combination of debate viewing with co-viewer conversations favorable to one of the candidates is moderately effective in producing positive attitude change.

Poll reports describing public reaction to the debate also seem to have an impact on affect toward Ford, as voters who perceived the polls showing a Carter victory became more negative and those sensing favorable public response to Ford's performance became more positive.

Finally, the differential responses of voters in Michigan and Georgia can be compared. There is evidence for selective exposure and perception in processing of partisan messages in the case of poll reports and newspaper analysis. Voters in Lansing exhibit more absolute affective change regarding Carter, while Athens voters change more on Ford; this may be due to the less strongly established predispositions toward the geographically distant candidate. In terms of directional change, attitude and image ratings of those who viewed the debate became somewhat more favorable toward the home state candidate than the outside candidate. Nevertheless, viewers do not become more negative toward the out-of-state candidate in attitude, and personality evaluations gain slightly. Thus, the favorite son appears to impress the home audience while the outsider makes minor progress in conveying good qualities to this potentially hostile audience. This indicates that the existence of debates may serve a positive function in generating support for the eventual winner of the presidential campaign.

26.

Impact of Ethnic Issues on Ethnic Voters

LEO W. JEFFRES and K. KYOON HUR

Ethnic voters received an unusual amount of attention during the 1976 presidential campaign, primarily because of two ethnic issues raised by the candidates. One was a comment by Carter endorsing the "ethnic purity" of neighborhoods, and the other was a statement by Ford during the second presidential debate that the Soviet Union does not dominate Eastern Europe. The Carter statement on ethnic purity stirred a heated debate and became an important campaign issue for Carter, who called on the Reverend Martin Luther King, Sr., for support among black voters. Some interpreted Carter's statement as anti-integrationist and consistent with his opposition to busing, an issue important to residents of primarily white ethnic neighborhoods. At the same time, the Ford statement "dumbfounded and dismayed" millions of voters of East European origin. Some observers considered the comment one of the most damaging statements of Ford's political career.

These two campaign issues were especially relevant to ethnic voters, and the present investigation attempts to examine the impact of the two issues by looking at the relationships between news media exposure, attention to the televised coverage of the 1976 presidential debates, awareness, evaluation and salience of the two ethnic issues, ethnicity, and subsequent voting behavior.

Ethnic voting may be with us for a long time. Wolfinger (1965) notes that the persistence of ethnic voting patterns may lie in the political system itself. Ethnic families pass along political party identification, ethnic candidates and issues may cause a realignment so that a particular party becomes the repository of ethnic loyalty even when the candidate or issue has passed, and ethnic identity remains despite the movement of many to the suburbs. Ethnic politics may survive both acculturation and assimilation. Dahl (1961) observes that in spite of growing assimilation of ethnics, ethnic factors continue to make themselves felt with astounding tenacity in local politics. Wolfinger (1965) similarly points out that ethnic voting patterns persist into the second and third generations and social changes have not reduced the political importance of national origins. Gordon (1970) found that ethnicity has been built into the political system in partisan cities; ethnic impact on voting turnout declined in partisan cities between 1934 and 1960 but not in nonpartisan cities.

Noting that ethnic politics have concentrated on local affairs, Busch (1976) points out that ethnics frequently broaden their perspective to include activities of the national government when the "mother country" is involved in American foreign policy. Thus, Ford's comment about Eastern Europe should have triggered political interests of ethnics from those countries.

The persistence of ethnic neighborhoods is supported by an analysis of census data for Cleveland, Boston, and Seattle for 1930, 1960, and 1970. Guest and Weed (1976) found few changes in patterns of ethnic segregation for the three cities. Though there were some sharp declines in residential segregation since 1930 for newer southern and East European ethnic groups, segregation of older ethnic groups actually increased. Though residential segregation was highly related to social status differences, ethnic segregation would continue to exist even if social status differences among ethnic groups disappeared.

Greeley (1974) argues that ethnicity is a predictor variable that can "no longer be ignored" by American social scientists. Looking at political participation among United States ethnic groups, he found the impact of ethnic background does not go away when social class is held constant. Greeley uses four political participation scales to examine thirteen ethnic groups that include Anglo-Saxons, Scandinavians, German and Irish Protestants, Irish Catholics, German Catholics, French, Italians, Slavs, Poles, blacks, Jews, and Spanish-speaking people. On the overall participation scale, the highest were Irish Catholics, followed by Scandinavians and Jews. Poles topped the voting scale, followed by Slavic Catholics and Anglo-Saxons. Irish were also highest on the political campaigning scale. Greeley also found positive correlations between ethnic identification and certain forms of political participation: Polish and Slavic voting, Jewish and Irish campaigning, and Italian political participation.

Our study tests whether the two ethnic issues were placed on the public "ethnic agenda" and whether they had any impact on ethnics' voting in the 1976 presidential election. A number of agenda-setting studies have demonstrated that (1) media exposure can increase the importance of issues like the two treated here, and (2) this increased relevance can, in turn, affect voters' candidate choice, turnout at the polls, or other relevant behaviors and attitudes (see McCombs and Shaw, 1972; McLeod, Becker, and Byrnes, 1974; McClure and Patterson, 1973; Kline, 1973; Gormley, 1975; Bowers, 1973; Shaw and Bowers, 1973; Shaw and McCombs, 1975; Tipton, Haney, and Basehart, 1973).

Although the present investigation has not included examination of media coverage of the two ethnic issues, we expect that ethnics' exposure to news media will increase their awareness of the two issues and the issues' salience. The increased issue salience is then expected to affect voting behavior. Our analysis takes several avenues.

Our framework includes a set of relationships between ethnicity, ethnic environment and origin, party affiliation, exposure to news media and the 1976 presidential debates, awareness of and reaction to the ethnic issues and their perceived importance in making the voting decision, and voting behavior. It was expected that East European background would have an impact on voter reaction to the Ford statement and subsequent voting behavior. We also expected that voters living in ethnic neighborhoods would find Carter's ethnic purity statement more important than those living in other situations. Thus, these two variables are included in the analysis. Debates exposure is an antecedent variable to the voters' reaction to Ford's comment on "Soviet domination" of Eastern Europe because the statement was made during the second presidential debate. However, debates exposure followed the appearance of Carter's ethnic purity statement.

Method

Using the 1974 Ethnic Directory of Greater Cleveland, we selected the most broadly based ethnic organizations representing thirteen of the largest ethnic groups in the metropolitan area. These ethnic organizations were contacted and asked to cooperate by providing their membership lists. Samples of 100 to 250 people were drawn from the lists. The ethnic groups included in the survey are Czech, Greek, Hungarian, Irish, Italian, Lebanese, Lithuanian, Polish, Puerto Rican, Romanian, Slovak, Slovenian, and Ukrainian. These people were sent a mail questionnaire and were later contacted by telephone to encourage cooperation and to answer questions. A total of 668 people returned the questionnaire, a response rate of 30 percent.

The questionnaire consisted of two parts. One contained items designed to measure ethnicity, ethnic activities, ethnic and general media use, and demographic factors. The other contained items designed to measure exposure to the 1976 presidential debates, awareness of and reaction to the two statements, party affiliation, and both 1972 and 1976 voting behaviors. The variables measured include party identification, ethnicity, ethnic neighborhood, news media exposure, debates exposure, ethnic issue awareness, reaction to ethnic issues, ethnic issue saliency, and voting behavior.

Results
Sample

The 768 respondents making up the sample consisted of 13 ethnic groups in the following proportions: Czech, 10.4 percent; Greek, 5.7 percent; Hungarian, 6.5 percent; Irish, 22.4 percent; Italian, 6.6 percent; Lebanese, 6.3 percent; Lithuanian, 8.2 percent; Polish, 6.5 percent; Puerto Rican, 7.8 percent; Romanian, 8 percent; Slovak, 4.8 percent; Slovenian, 9.1 percent; and Ukrainian, 3.3 percent. Some 57 percent are Eastern European, while 43 percent are non-East European ethnics. About 54 percent of the respondents are male and 46 percent, female. The average educational level achieved is high-school graduate, and the average income is between $10,000 and $15,000.

Though there is considerable variance and a wide range, respondents showed strong ethnicity. Most of the respondents reported that they belonged to at least one ethnic organization; the sample mean was a little over two ethnic organizations. Only 11 percent reported they did not belong to any ethnic organization. Respondents also showed strong ethnic attitudes: 46 percent recorded the highest score on the five-point Guttman scale that was indexed using five ethnic attitudes items.

About 55 percent of the respondents giving their partisan affiliation identified themselves as Democrats, while 22 percent said they were Republicans and 23 percent, independents. Aggregated voting behavior shows 36 percent voting for Ford, 47 percent Carter, 5 percent other, and 12 percent not voting. In the 1972 election the vote was 51 percent Nixon, 28 percent McGovern, 4 percent

other, and 18 percent not voting. Thus, there was a sizable shift in voting between the two elections in our samples.

Media and Debates Exposure

Respondents reported moderate to heavy media exposure, particularly newspaper reading and television news viewing. About 54 percent of the respondents
read a daily newspaper every day, and more than 40 percent said they read a
weekly newspaper regularly. About 56 percent reported watching national TV
news every day, and about 47 percent reported watching local TV news every
day.

Newspaper reading and general magazine reading were significantly related
to membership and activity in ethnic organizations but not to the ethnicity
attitudes measure. Also, total news media use was significantly related to the
former two ethnicity measures. Exposure to television and to television news
was not related to any ethnicity measures, however.

Our sample reported moderate exposure to the 1976 televised presidential
debates. Between 47 percent and 54 percent of the respondents said they
watched most of the three presidential debates, while 32 percent said they
watched most of the Mondale–Dole debate. Our data are, then, relatively similar to national data. There were strong relationships between the four debates
exposure, particularly between the first and the second debate ($r = .67$); it
seems that exposure to one debate led to another.

Debates exposure was significantly related to all of the media use measures
and news media measures in particular, suggesting that those who use media
heavily were more likely to watch debates. The relationship between debates
exposure and news media exposure held even after controlling for ethnicity
variables. Debates exposure was also related to two of the ethnicity measures—
membership and activity in ethnic organizations: those who are active in ethnic
organizations thus tend to watch more debates. However, debates exposure was
not related to the ethnic attitudes measure. Debates exposure was not related to
partisan affiliation: more Democrats than Republicans watched the first and the
second debates, while more Republicans watched the final debate. The difference
was not statistically significant in all debates, however. Finally, there was a weak
though significant relationship between debates exposure and education.

Ethnic Voting Results

People can register their feelings and act on campaign issues and personalities by failing to vote. Numerous observers have noted the importance of the
campaign in "getting out the vote." In our sample, voting (for any presidential
candidate) was related to viewing the debates ($r = .12*$) and attention to the
news media ($r = .20*$). Two of the ethnicity measures also are positively related to voting. Reactions to the two ethnic comments and the importance
attributed to them are all negatively related to voting, but only the relationship
between the importance of Ford's "Soviet domination" comment and voting is
statistically significant ($r = -.21*$). This is consistent with the absence of any
relationship with reaction, which was almost unanimous. Awareness was also
less important since almost 80 percent had heard Ford's comment before the

election. By contrast, awareness of Carter's "ethnic purity" statement predicts to voting; less than 70 percent had heard Carter's comment before the election, and a positive relationship is found between awareness and voting (partial $r = .13*$).

Did the ethnic comments affect the direction of people's voting? To determine this, we arrayed the variables in two path models designed to test the relationships between important factors for each of the two ethnic issues. The first model concerns Ford's East European statement (see Fig. 1). Traditional communication channels (news media exposure) and debate viewing are the most important factors leading to awareness of Ford's East Europe comment. Some selectivity is also noted in that Republicans are more likely than Democrats to have heard the comment before the election. Almost 80 percent of respondents had heard Ford's comment by election day. Reaction to the Ford statement followed our expectation that Eastern Europeans would respond negatively. Heavier news consumers also tended to disagree with Ford's comment more than did people who pay less attention to news. Less than 5 percent agreed with the statement. The response was more balanced, however, when people were asked how important the statement was in their voting decision. Greater importance is attributed to the comment by debate viewers, Democrats, Eastern European ethnics, and those with stronger ethnic identification.

With the exception of party affiliation, only two factors are significantly related to the direction of voting in the "Eastern European" model. Eastern European background is negatively related to voting for Carter; some of this is mediated by party affiliation. Ethnics from Eastern Europe tend to be Republicans more than do other ethnic groups in our sample, for example, Puerto Ricans and Irish.

The importance attributed to Ford's comment is also related to voting. Those who said the issue was important in their voting decision tended to vote for Carter. The model shows Ford's statement having little impact at the ballot box, but the skewed distribution on the voters' reaction to Ford's comment may obscure the situation somewhat. To examine such a possibility, we looked at how people learned of Ford's comment and we used a variety of measures to compare those who agreed and disagreed with Ford.

Only 4.5 percent of the 520 who had heard Ford's comment by election day agreed with the statement. However, the percentage is considerably higher among those who learned of the comment not from the debates but from other sources, for example, newspaper accounts, TV and radio news, and conversations with other people. Though 3.8 percent of debate viewers agreed with the comment, 7.2 percent of those learning about the statement from other sources agreed with Ford's assessment of the Soviet role in Eastern Europe. Direct exposure to the comment appears to have had more negative impact than mediated accounts, which would allow for others' interpretation. Debate viewers also attribute greater importance to the Ford statement than do those who learned of the comment from other channels. Only 27 percent of those learning of the statement from other channels said the comment was somewhat or very important in deciding which candidate to vote for; about 41 percent of those watching the second debate said the comment was somewhat or very important. Source of information about Ford's comment was compared with respondents' reaction

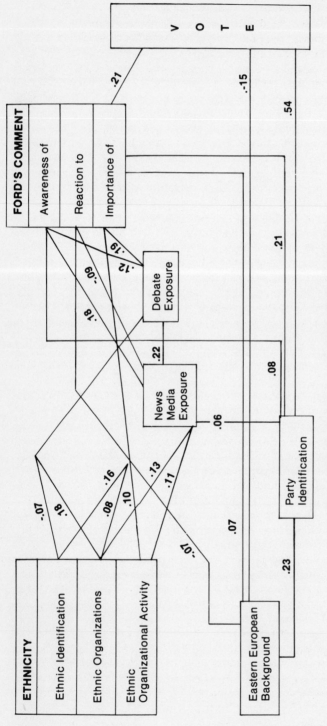

Fig. 1: Path Model for Ford's "Eastern Europe" Comment

Note: The figures in the model are partial correlation coefficients between the independent and dependent variables when all preceding variables in the model are held constant. Not all coefficients have been included to minimize complexity; those not included were not statistically significant. The correlations between ethnicity variables and Eastern European background are insignificant. Direct relations with the initial variables in the model are expressed in product–moment correlations. Ethnic identification is correlated at .23 with ethnic organizations, and at .16 with organizational activity; the latter variables are correlated at .77. Awareness is not related to reaction or salience, but the latter are correlated at −.11. For party affiliation, being Democrat = high; for vote, voting for Carter = high; for East European background, Eastern Europe ethics = high.

to Carter's statement to check for a response pattern effect. Those learning about Ford's comment from the debates are no more likely to approve or disapprove of Carter's comment than those who learned of Ford's statement from other sources. Furthermore, though more Democrats were unaware of Ford's comment, there is no relationship between party affiliation and how people learned of the statement—by viewing the debates or from other sources. There also is no relationship between how Eastern Europeans and other ethnics learned of the comment, though the former were more likely to be aware.

Those agreeing with Ford's comment include fewer Eastern European ethnics (40 percent) than those disagreeing with the comment about Soviet domination (54 percent). No significant differences are found between those who agreed and those who disagreed on radio listening, number of news magazines read, and national TV news viewing. Those who disagreed do tend to read more daily newspapers than do those who agreed and those who were unaware of the statement. Those agreeing with the Ford comment include more men (83 percent) than do those disagreeing (59 percent) or those unaware (50 percent). Differences are also noted on the amount of debate viewing: almost 60 percent of those disagreeing with Ford's comment were high debate viewers, in contrast to 46 percent of those agreeing and 41 percent of those unaware of the comment.

Carter's ethnic purity statement came at a time when the Cleveland school board was involved in a court battle over desegregation of the public schools; the NAACP suit generated much discussion of busing and concern for neighborhood schools. Some of the discussion included potential busing across city and suburb boundaries. Since many ethnic neighborhoods would be potential participants in any busing plan, Carter's comment struck a responsive note; almost two-thirds of the respondents aware of the comment before the election approved of the statement. News media exposure also led to awareness of Carter's "ethnic purity" statement, as illustrated in Figure 2. None of the other prior variables seem to be related to awareness. Reaction to the statement, however, is related to a number of factors, particularly ethnicity and living in an ethnic neighborhood. People who are heavier news consumers were more likely to disapprove of Carter's comment. Party affiliation is unrelated to issue reaction, though it does lead to increased salience; strong ethnic identification also appears to increase the importance of the issue among our respondents. People living in ethnic neighborhoods also considered the comment more important in making their voting decisions. The debates occurred after Carter made his comment about "ethnic purity." It was expected that the statement would stimulate some ethnics to watch the debates. The model shows this to be the case, with both awareness and salience of the "ethnic purity" issue leading to debate exposure. News media use and two ethnicity measures also are related to debate exposure.

A vote for Carter is predicted by three factors other than party affiliation, as the second path model illustrates. Living in an ethnic neighborhood is positively related to voting for Carter. Approving of Carter's comment and its perceived importance in the vote decision also are positive indicators of a Carter vote. Thus, it would seem that the "ethnic purity" issue helped Carter among ethnic voters.

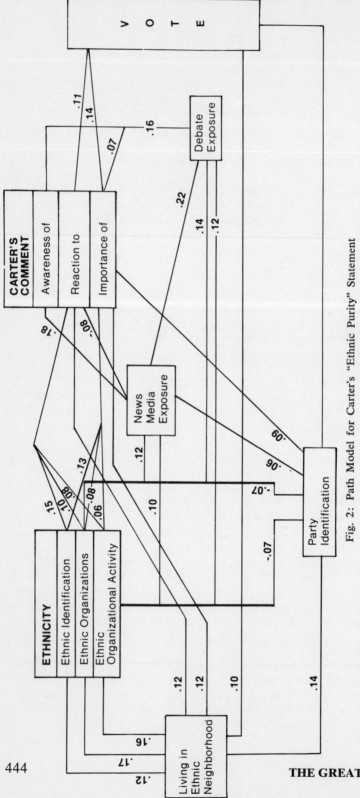

Fig. 2: Path Model for Carter's "Ethnic Purity" Statement

Note: The figures in the model are partial correlation coefficients between the independent and dependent variables when all preceding variables in the model are held constant. Not all coefficients have been included to minimize complexity; those not included were not statistically significant. The relationships between living in an ethnic neighborhood and ethnicity variables are expressed in product-moment correlations, as are other direct relations with the initial variable in the model. Reaction to Carter's statement and salience are correlated at .25 (p < .05). For party affiliation, being Democrat = high; for vote, voting for Carter = high.

THE GREAT DEBATES

REFERENCES

Bowers, T. A. "Newspaper Political Advertising and the Agenda Setting Function." *Journalism Quarterly*, 1973 (50), pp. 552–56.

Busch, R. J. "Ethnic Assimilation Versus Cultural Pluralism: Some Political Implications," in D. E. Weinberg (ed.), *Ethnicity: A Conceptual Approach.* Cleveland: Cleveland Ethnic Heritage Studies, Cleveland State University, 1976.

Gordon, M. *Assimilation in American Life.* New York: Oxford University Press, 1964.

Gormley, W. T. "Newspaper Agendas and Political Elites." *Journalism Quarterly*, 1975 (52), pp. 304–308.

Greeley, A. M. "Political Participation Among Ethnic Groups in the United States: A Preliminary Reconnaissance." *American Journal of Sociology*, 1974 (80), pp. 170–79.

Guest, A. M., and J. A. Weed. "Ethnic Residential Segregation: Patterns of Change." *American Journal of Sociology*, 1976 (81), pp. 1088–1111.

Kline, F. G. "Sources and Impact of Political Information in the 1972 Elections." Paper presented to the American Association for Public Opinion Research, Asheville, N.C., 1973.

McClure, R. D., and T. E. Patterson. "Television News and Political Advertising: The Impact of Exposure on Voter Belief." *Communication Research*, 1974 (1), pp. 3–31.

McCombs, M. E., and D. L. Shaw. "The Agenda-Setting Function of the Media." *Public Opinion Quarterly*, 1972 (36), pp. 176–87.

McLeod, J. M., L. B. Becker, and J. Byrnes. "Another Look at the Agenda-Setting Function of the Press." *Communication Research*, 1974 (1), pp. 131–66.

Shaw, D. L., and T. A. Bowers. "The Influence of TV Advertising on the Voter's Political Agenda." Paper presented to the Association for Education in Journalism, Fort Collins, Colorado, 1973.

Shaw, D. L., and M. E. McCombs. *The Emergence of Public Issues: Political News and Voter Learning.* University of North Carolina School of Journalism and Newhouse Communications Research Center, Syracuse University, 1975.

Tipton, L., R. D. Haney, and J. R. Basehart. "Media Agenda-Setting in City and State Election Campaigns." *Journalism Quarterly*, 1975 (52), pp. 15–22.

Wolfinger, R. "The Development and Persistence of Ethnic Voting." *American Political Science Review*, 1965 (59), 896–908.

Part III

Texts of the Debates

27.

The Significance of Written Texts

JESS YODER and HOWARD A. MIMS

The importance of written texts of speeches, debates, sermons, hearings, court proceedings, and other forms of oral discourse is evidenced by the numerous publications providing such documents. Lengthy sets of speeches have been published so that the spoken word can be communicated and studied long after messages are delivered. New editions of books comprising speeches by important national and world leaders are constantly coming on the market, and recently there has been a surge of publications containing speeches that serve as primary documents for historical studies. Special editions of speeches delivered by almost every American president since 1900 attest to the significance we give to the spoken word. Presidential candidates have often published volumes of their campaign speeches as a means of promoting their views. Other oral messages such as the selected verbatim transcripts of the Nixon White House tapes have received national attention. In addition to books, the texts of speeches, hearings, interviews, conference proceedings and the like can be found in newspapers, magazines, and special documents.

There are various reasons for publishing the spoken word rather than essays and position papers, which could state views more precisely. Psychologically, the reader of a speech becomes a "listener," particularly if he is familiar with the speaker's voice. The reader of the written word recreates the address and "witnesses" the speaker confronting a perceived audience in an imagined actual setting. Since speech acts are not impersonal presentations of concepts but speakers actively confronting listeners, it is commonly believed that more of the "real" person comes through in the oral presentation than in an essay.[1] The extensive publication of oral messages is in itself a tacit recognition of the power of the spoken word and its ability to reveal the speaker.

Clevenger, Parson, and Polisky, in their introduction to the Kennedy-Nixon debates, gave a detailed discussion of the problems of textual accuracy.[2] They outlined seven levels of textual accuracy. Patrick Henry's famous "Liberty or Death" speech, which was reconstructed by William Wirt fifty years after it was delivered, was given as an example of the lowest level of textual accuracy. Many available speech texts have been altered by the editor or speaker to make the material more readable or to make the views more palatable. We agree with their conclusion that the most accurate text is one based on audio-visual recordings.

While no written text can adequately recreate these presidential and vice-presidential debates, an accurate transcript of the debates that can be read and studied has value as a document. We believe it is important for the text to include excessively long pauses, stammering restarts, and mispronunciations. Our purpose has been to provide a transcription that reflects the verbal production of the speakers in these debates.

We started out by listening to tape recordings of the debates and comparing what we heard with the text provided by the *New York Times*. We soon discovered that although the *New York Times* text was highly reliable, it was not satisfactory for our purposes. Obviously, for the newspaper, an important priority was next-day publication. We have listed several illustrations taken from the first debate that show how our text differs from the text of the *New York Times*. The discrepancies between the texts are underlined.

The underlined portions in the selections above identify a number of words that are not easily discerned in rapid speech. We heard Mr. Carter saying "four"

The New York Times *Text*	*Our Text*
If you're going to increase domestic oil and gas production—and we have to—you have to give to those producers an opportunity to develop their land or their wealth.	If you're going to increase domestic oil and gas production—and we have to—you have to give to those producers an opportunity to uh develop their land or their wells.
There is an additional factor that needs to be done and cover it very succinctly, and that is to make sure that we have a good relationship between management business on the one hand and labor on the other.	There is uh—uh an additional factor that needs to be done . . . and covered very—very succinctly and that is, to make sure that we have a good relationship between management—business on the one hand, and labor, on the other.
We've got a short distinction between white collar crime. The big shots who are rich, or influential very seldom go to jail; those who are poor and who have no influence quite often are the ones who are punished.	We've got a short distinction between white collar crime—the—the—the big shots who are rich, who are influential uh very seldom go to jail; those who are poor and—and who have uh no influence —uh quite often are the ones who are punished.
But I believe by the end of the first full years of the next term, we could have the employment rate down to three percent adult unemployment which is about 4 to 4½ percent overall control inflation rates and have a balanced growth of about 46 percent around 5 percent which would give us a balanced budget.	But I believe that by the end of the first four years of uh—of the next term we could have the unemployment down to three percent adult unemployment, which is about four to four and a half percent overall, uh—controlled inflation rate and have a uh balance of growth of about —uh four to six percent, around five percent, which would give us a balanced budget.
(Entire sentence is omitted.)	We've got to have a firm way to handle the energy question.

not "full," "wells" not "wealth," and "four to six" not "46." When Mr. Carter said "the" three times in succession we wrote it down three times; the *New York Times* wrote it only once. We recorded interjections, long pauses, and sounds not intelligible as words; the *New York Times* did not. In cases where the speaker should have used a plural, the *New York Times* often corrected his grammar; we did not make such corrections. The illustrations above also show our disagreements on punctuation and grammatical constructions. In addition, the *New York Times* provided topical headings and paragraphing, which help the reader find materials discussed more readily. We did not edit the content in that manner.

The process used to produce our text went through several stages of production. We first made working copies of the debates by mounting a single column of the *New York Times* text in the center of 8½ x 11 paper. We then made photocopies of the mounted text.

Our next step was to formulate rules for recording fluency problems, interjections, mispronunciations, and punctuation. Initially we planned to work from video casettes, but we soon discovered that the replay system was not fast enough to obtain the quick repetitions that were needed to decipher utterances difficult to perceive. We found that working from audio tape recordings resulted in greater efficiency and accuracy.

In the next stage of production one person listened to the debates while following the working photocopy of the *New York Times* text. The wide margins provided space for corrections and comments. The next step was to type a rough draft from the corrected copy while listening to the debates a second time for making additional corrections.

The typed copy of the debates was then duplicated, and we both checked our texts while listening to the tapes the third time. During this stage we found it necessary to refine our guidelines and discuss problems that had arisen. A final copy was then made.

The following guidelines were used:

(1) *Contractions.* When the speakers used contractions, we recorded them as spoken. If the speaker said "gonna" for "going to" we recorded it as "gonna." However, if the speaker did not omit sounds but fused them so that "got to" sounded like "got'a" or "gotta" we recorded it as "got to."

(2) *Grammar.* If a speaker made a grammatical error such as using a singular verb with a plural subject, or if he used an incorrect pronoun or omitted an article, we did not correct the grammar. Often in rapid extemporaneous speaking such "errors" go unnoticed. As listeners we found ourselves "hearing" sounds that were not uttered.

(3) *Pauses.* Short pauses that came at the end of a phrase or clause are indicated by a comma. For this reason you may note commas that seem unnecessary for purposes of meaning but are helpful for knowing the manner of speaking. Long pauses are indicated by ellipses (. . .). Pauses that are associated with a break in thought or a restart are noted with the dash (—). The dash was also used to indicate a break in thought when there was no pause in speaking.

(4) *Interjections.* The most common interjection is the use of "uh" or "ah." If the speaker prolonged the sound we indicated that by "uhh." If the speaker

paused before the interjection we recorded it "—uh," if after the interjection, "uh—."

(5) *Unintelligible utterances.* Individual and combined speech sounds that we could not identify as recognizable words were transcribed phonetically using the International Phonetic Alphabet (IPA) enclosed in brackets. The brackets were used to indicate that the transcriptions are phonetic rather than phonemic, reflecting the absence of semantic content or our inability to discern the speakers' intended meaning, if indeed there was semantic intent. Some of the sounds were not clearly recognizable as standard English phonemes. Some utterances were clearly accidental "slips of the tongue," which resulted in unintelligible false starts. After listening carefully to each utterance of this type, phonetic transcriptions were used in an effort to reflect faithfully the acoustic nature of what was spoken.

We did not use the IPA in cases where the speaker apparently made a false start and then followed with the correct pronunciation, as in the case of Mr. Ford saying, "National Security coun—Council." There were cases such as Mr. Dole saying, "The difference between the Democratic congressional budget which I supported and the [rɪp]—and the President's budget . . . ," in which one could probably correctly infer that he started to say "Republican." However, in such cases, where the attempted word was not readily apparent, we did not try to guess what word the speaker had in mind; instead, we recorded the vocalization as illustrated above. We were less sure what Mr. Carter meant when he said, "I have also advocated that we stop the sale by Germany and France of [risa]—processing plants for Pakistan and Brazil."

(6) *Punctuation.* We have already commented on the uses of the comma, ellipses, and dash. We agree with Clevenger et al. that paragraphing represents judgments and implies interrelationships between a speaker's ideas; thus we have avoided this type of division.

Obviously each speaker has his own dialect and speech pattern that cannot be captured in print. For example, from these transcripts the reader cannot know that Mr. Carter spoke about 163 words per minute as compared to Mr. Ford's approximately 130 words per minute. But the transcripts as we have recorded them do show the speaker's nonfluencies, such as interjections, slips of the tongue, restarts, and the like. The reader may wish to correlate such behaviors with the questions being asked or topics discussed. From these transcripts one can readily observe that Mr. Carter used many more nonfluencies in the first debate than in the second. One can also note that the prepared statements in the introductory and summary comments are more fluent than the question-and-answer portions.

Certainly these transcripts can be used by those wishing to study the lines of argument, uses of evidence, audience appeals, self-concepts, language, and values reflected in what the speakers said. For many studies these transcripts will be of greatest value when used along with audio and video recordings. We believe that the texts that follow represent highly accurate accounts of what was said in these historic debates.

The First Ford-Carter Debate
Walnut Street Theater, Philadelphia
September 23, 1976, 9:30 p.m.

EDWIN NEWMAN, *Moderator*: Good evening. I'm Edwin Newman, moderator of this first debate of the 1976 campaign between Gerald R. Ford of Michigan, Republican candidate for president, and Jimmy Carter of Georgia, Democratic candidate for president. We thank you, President Ford and we thank you, Governor Carter, for being with us tonight. There are to be three debates between the presidential candidates and one between the vice-presidential candidates. All are being arranged by the League of Women Voters Education Fund. Tonight's debate, the first between presidential candidates in sixteen years and the first ever in which an incumbent president has participated, is taking place before an audience in the Walnut Street Theater in Philadelphia, just three blocks from Independence Hall. The television audience may reach a hundred million in the United States and many millions overseas. Tonight's debate focuses on domestic issues and economic policy. Questions will be put by Frank Reynolds of ABC News, James Gannon of the *Wall Street Journal*, and Elizabeth Drew of the *New Yorker* magazine. Under the agreed rules the first question will go to Governor Carter. That was decided by the toss of a coin. He will have up to three minutes to answer. One follow-up question will be permitted with up to two minutes to reply. President Ford will then have two minutes to respond. The next question will go to President Ford with the same time arrangements, and questions will continue to be alternated between the candidates. Each man will make a three-minute statement at the end, Governor Carter to go first. President Ford and Governor Carter do not have any notes or prepared remarks with them this evening. Mr. Reynolds, your question for Governor Carter.

MR. REYNOLDS: Mr. President, Governor Carter. Governor, in an interview with the Associated Press last week, you said you believed these debates would alleviate a lot of concern that some voters have about you. Well, one of those concerns, not an uncommon one about uh—candidates in any year, is that many voters say they don't really know where you stand. Now, you have made jobs your number one priority and you have said you are committed to a drastic reduction in unemployment. Can you say now, Governor, in specific terms, what your first step would be next January, if you are elected, to achieve that?

MR. CARTER: Yes. First of all is to recognize a tremendous economic strength in this country and to set the putting to—back to work of our people as a top priority. This is uh—an effort that ought to be done primarily by strong leadership in the White House, the inspiration of our people, the tapping of uh—business, agriculture, industry, labor and government at all levels to work on this uh project. We'll never have uh—an end to the inflationary spiral, and we'll never have a balanced budget until we get our people back to work. There are several things that can be done specifically that are not now being done. First of all, to channel research and development funds into areas that will provide uh large numbers of jobs. Secondly, we need to have a commitment in the uh private sector uh—to cooperate with government in matters like housing. Here a very small investment of taxpayer's money—in the housing field can bring large numbers of extra jobs, and the guarantee of mortgage loans, and the uh—putting forward of uh—two-O-two programs for housing for older people and so forth to cut down the roughly 20 percent unemployment that now exists in the—in the construction industry. Another thing is to deal with our—uh needs in the central cities, where the unemployment rate is extremely high: sometimes among minority groups, or those who don't speak English, or who're black, or young people, or—40 percent of the employment. Here a CCC type program would be appropriate . . . to channel money into the ah—cha—in—in into the sharing with the private sector and also local and state governments to employ young people who are now out of work. Another very important—uh aspect of our—uh economy would be to increase production in every way possible, uh to hold down—uh taxes on individuals, and to uh shift the tax burdens onto those who have avoided paying taxes in the past. These uh—kinds of specific things, uh none of which are being done now, would be a great help in—in reducing uh unemployment. There is uh—uh an additional factor that needs to be done . . . and covered very—very succinctly, and that is, to make sure that we have a good relationship between management—business on the one hand, and labor, on the other. In a lot of places where unemployment is very high, we might channel specific uh targeted job [im]—job—uh opportunities by paying part of the salary of unemployed people—uh and also sharing with uh—local governments the uh—payment of salaries which would uh—let us cut down the unemployment rate much lower, before we hit the inflationary level. But I believe that by the end of the first four years of uh—of the next term we could have the unemployment down to 3 percent adult unemployment, which is about uh—4 to 4 and a half percent overall uh controlled inflation rate and have a uh balance of growth of about—uh 4 to 6 percent, around 5 percent which would give us a balanced budget.

MR. REYNOLDS: Governor, uh—in the event you are successful and you do achieve a drastic drop (MR. CARTER: Yes) in unemployment that is likely to create additional pressure on prices, how willing are you to consider an incomes policy, in other words, wage and price controls?

MR. CARTER: Well—we now have such uh—a low utilization of uh—our productive capacity—uh about 73 percent; I think it's about the lowest since the Great Depression years—and such a high unemployment rate now—uh 7.9 percent—that—uh we have a long way to go in getting people to work before we have the inflationary pressures. And I think this would uh—this would be uh easy to accomplish, to get jobs down, without having strong in—inflationary pressures that—that would be necessary. I would not favor . . . the uh—payment of uh—of a given fixed income to people unless they are not able to work. But with tax incentives for the low-income groups we could build up their uh—income levels uh—above the poverty level and not uh make welfare more uh—profitable than—than work.

MR. NEWMAN: Mr. President, your response.

MR. FORD: I don't believe that uh that Mr. Carter's been any more specific in this case than he has been on many other instances. I notice particularly that he didn't endorse the Humphrey-Hawkins bill which he has on occasions and which is included as a part of the Democratic platform. That legislation uh allegedly would help our unemployment, but uh—we all know that it would've controlled our economy, it would've added uh—ten to thirty billion dollars each year in additional expenditures by the Federal Government. It would've called for export controls on agricultural products. . . . In my judgment the best way to get jobs is to uh—expand the private sector, where five out of six jobs today exist in our economy. We can do that by reducing Federal taxes as I proposed uh—about a year ago when I called for a tax reduction of $28 billion—three-quarters of it to go to private uh taxpayers and uh one-quarter to the business sector. We could add to jobs in the major metropolitan areas by a proposal that I recommended that would give tax incentives to business to move into the inner city and to expand or to build new plants so that they would take a plant, or expand a plant where people are, and people are currently unemployed. We could uh—also uh—help our youths with some of the proposals that uh—would give to young people an opportunity to work and learn at the same time just like we give money to young people who are going to college. Those are the kind of specifics that I think we have to discuss on these uh—debates, and these are the kind of programs that I'll talk about on my time.

MR. NEWMAN: Mr. Gannon, your question to President Ford.

MR. GANNON: Mr. President, I would like to continue for a moment on this uh question of taxes which you have just raised. You have said that you favor more tax cuts for middle-income Americans—even those earning up to $30 thousand a year. That presumably would cost the Treasury quite a bit of money in lost revenue. In view of the very large budget deficits that you have accumulated and that are still in prospect, how is it possible to promise further tax cuts and to reach your goal of balancing the budget?

MR. FORD: At the time, Mr. Gannon, that I made the recommendation for a $28 billion tax cut—three-quarters of it to go to individual taxpayers and 25 percent to American business. I said at the time that we had to hold the lid on federal spending, that for every dollar of a tax reduction we had to have an equal reduction in federal expenditures—a one-for-one proposition. And I recommended that to the Congress with a budget ceiling of three hundred and ninety-five billion dollars, and that would have permitted us to have a $25 billion tax reduction. In my tax reduction program for middle-income taxpayers, I recommended that the Congress increase personal exemptions . . . from seven hundred and fifty dollars per person to one thousand dollars per person. That would mean, of course, that for a family of four that that family would have a thousand dollars more personal exemption—money that they could spend for their own purposes, money that the government wouldn't have to spend. But if we keep the lid on federal spending, which I think we can—with the help of the Congress, we can justify fully a $28 billion tax reduction. In the budget that I submitted to the Congress in January this year, I re—recommended a 50 percent cutback in the rate of growth of federal spending. For the last ten years the budget of the United States has grown from uh—about 11 percent per year. We can't afford that kind of growth in federal spending. And in the budget that I recommended we cut it in half—a growth rate of 5 to 5 and one-half percent. With that kind of limitation, on federal spending, we can fully justify the tax reductions that I have proposed. And it seems to me with the stimulant of more money in the hands of the taxpayers, and with more money in the hands of business to expand, to modernize, to provide more jobs, our economy will be stimulated so that we'll get more revenue and we'll have a more prosperous economy.

MR. GANNON: Mr. President, to follow up a moment, uh—the Congress has passed a tax bill which is before you now, which did not meet exactly the uh—sort of outline that you requested. What is your intention on that bill, uh—since it doesn't meet your—your requirements? Do you plan to sign that bill?

MR. FORD: That tax bill does not entirely meet the criteria that I established. I think the Congress should have uh—added another $10 billion reduction in personal income taxes, including the increase of personal exemptions from seven hundred and fifty to a thousand dollars. And Congress could have done that if the budget committees of the Congress, and the Congress as a whole, had not increased the spending that I recommended in the budget. I'm sure that you know that in the resolutions passed by the Congress, that have added about $17 billion in more spending, by the Congress over the budget that I recommended. So I would prefer in that tax bill to have an additional tax cut and a further limitation on federal spending. Now this tax bill—that hasn't reached the White House yet, but is expected in a day or two—it's about fifteen hundred pages. It has some good provisions in it. It has—uh left out some that I have recommended, unfortunately. On the other hand, uh when you have a bill of that magnitude, with [ðə]—tho—those many provisions, a president has to sit and decide if there's more good than bad. And from the a—analysis that I've made so far, it seems to me that that tax bill does uh—justify my signature and my approval.

MR. NEWMAN: Governor Carter, your response.

MR. CARTER: Well, Mr. Ford is—is uh changing uh considerably his previous philosophy. The present tax structure is a disgrace to this country; it's just a welfare program for the rich. As a matter of fact, uh—25 percent of the total tax deductions, go for only 1 percent of the richest people in this country, and over 50 percent of the tax uh credits go for the 14 percent of the richest people in this country. When Mr. Ford first became president in [ɑkto]—in August of 1974, the first thing he did in—in October was to ask for a $4.7 billion increase in taxes on our people in the midst of the heaviest recession, since uh—since the great depression of nineteen uh—of the 1940s. In uh—January of 1975 he asked for a tax change: a $5.6 billion increase on low-and-middle-income private individuals, a six and a half billion dollar decrease on the corporations and the special interests. In uh—December of uh—1975 he vetoed the roughly 18 to 20 billion dollar uh tax-reduction bill that had been passed by the Congress, and then he came back later on in January of this year and he did advocate a $10 billion tax reduction, but it would be offset by a $6 billion increase this coming January in deductions for Social Security payments and for unemployment compensation. The whole philosophy of the Republican party, including uh—my opponent, has been to pile on taxes on low-income people to take 'em off on the corporations. As a matter fact, in—sin—since the late sixties when Mr. Nixon took office, we've had a reduction in uh—in the percentage of taxes paid by corporations from 30 percent down to about 20 percent. We've had an increase in taxes paid by individuals, payroll taxes, from

14 percent up to 20 percent. And this is what the Republicans have done to us. And this is why a tax reform is so important.

MR. NEWMAN: Mrs. Drew, your question to Governor Carter.

MS. DREW: uh Governor Carter, you proposed a number of new or enlarged programs, including jobs, health, welfare reform, child care, aid to education, aid to cities, changes in social security and housing subsidies. You've also said that you wanna balance the budget by the end of your first term. Now you haven't put a price tag on those programs, but even if we price them conservatively and we count for full employment by the end of your first term, and we count for the economic growth that would occur during that period, there still isn't enough money to pay for those programs and balance the budget by any [kŋ]—any estimates that I've been able to see. So, in that case what would give?

MR. CARTER: Well, as a matter of fact there is. If we assume the ah—uh— a rate of growth of our economy, equivalent to what it was during President Johnson, President Kennedy, even before the—the—the—uh wa uh—Vietnese —namese War, and if we assume that at the end of the four-year period we can cut our unemployment rate down to 4 to 4 and a half percent—under those circumstances, even assuming no elimination of unnecessary programs and assuming an increase in the ad—in the allotment of money to finance programs, increasing as the inflation rate does—my economic projections, I think confirmed by the House uh—and the Senate committees, have been with the $60 billion extra amount of money that can be spent in fiscal year '81 which will be the last year of this next term. Within that sixty-billion dollars increase there would be fit the programs that I promised the American people. I might say too, that—that if we see that these goals cannot be reached—and I believe they're reasonable goals—then I would cut back on the rate of implement— implementation of new programs in order to accommodate a balanced budget by fiscal year '81 which is the last year of the next term. I believe that we ought to have a balanced budget . . . during normal economic circumstances. And uh—these projections have been very carefully made. I stand behind them. And if they should be in error slightly on the down side, then I'll phase in the programs that we've uh—advocated, more slowly.

MS. DREW: Governor, uh—according to the budget committees of the Congress tha—tha—tha—that you referred to, if we get to full employment— what they project at a 4 percent unemployment—and, as you say, even allowing for the inflation in the programs, there would not be anything more than a surplus of $5 billion by the end of ninet—by 1981. And conservative estimates of your programs would be that they'd be about 85 to a hundred billion dollars. So how—how do you say that you're going to be able to do these things and balance the budget?

MR. CARTER: Well, the uh—the assumption that—that you uh—have described as different is in the rate of growth of our economy.

MS. DREW: No, they took that into account in those figures.

MR. CARTER: I believe that it's accurate to say that—that the—that the committees to whom you refer with the—the employment that you uh— state, and with the 5 to 5 and a half percent growth rate in our economy, that the uh—projections would be a uh—a $60 billion increase in the amount of money that we'd have to spend in 1981 compared to now. And uh—with that uh—in that framework would befit the—any improvements in the programs. Now this does not include uh—any uh—uh [dɛ] extra control over uh unnecessary spending, the weeding out of obsolete or obsolescent programs. Uh—we'll have uh—a safety version built in with complete reorganization of the executive branch of government which I am pledged to do. The present bureaucratic structure of the— of the Federal Government is a mess. And if I'm elected president that's gonna be a top priority of mine to completely revise the structure of the federal government, to make it economical, efficient, purposeful and manageable for a change. And also, I'm going to institute zero-based budgeting, which I used four years in Georgia, which uh—assesses every program every year, and eliminates those programs that are obsolete or obsolescent. But with these projections, we will have a balanced budget by fiscal year 1981, if I'm elected president. Keep my promises to the American people. And it's just predicated on very modest, but I think accurate, projections of employment increases and uh—a growth in our national economy equal to what was experienced under Kennedy, Johnson, before the Vietnam War.

Mr. Newman: President Ford.

Mr. Ford: If it is uh . . . true that there will be a $60 billion surplus by fiscal year 1981, rather than spend that money for all the new programs that Governor Carter recommends and endorses, and which are included in the Democratic platform, I think the American taxpayer ought to get an additional tax break—a tax reduction of that magnitude. I feel that the taxpayers are the ones that need the relief: I don't think we should add additional programs of the magnitude that Governor Carter talks about. It seems to me that our tax structure today . . . has rates that are too high. But I am uh—very glad to point out that since 1969, during a Republican administrations, we have had ten million people taken off of the tax rolls at the lower end of the taxpayer area. And at the same time, assuming that I sign the tax bill that was mentioned by Mr. Gannon, we will in the last two tax bills have increased the minimum tax on all wealthy taxpayers. And I believe that by eliminating ten million taxpayers in the last uh eight years, and by putting a heavier tax burden on those in the higher tax brackets, plus the other actions that've been taken, uh—we can give taxpayers adequate tax relief. Now it seems to me that uh— as we look at the recommendations of the budget committees and our own projections, there isn't going to be any $60 billion dividend. I've heard of those dividends in the past; it always happens. We expected one at the time of the Vietnam War, but it was used up before we ever ended the war and taxpayers never got the adequate relief they deserved.

Mr. Newman: Mr. Reynolds.

Mr. Reynolds: Mr. President, when you came into office you spoke very eloquently of the need for a time for healing, and very early in your administration you went out to Chicago and you announced, you proposed a program of uh case-by-case pardons for draft resisters to restore them to full citizenship. Some fourteen thousand young men took advantage of your offer, but another ninety thousand did not. In granting the pardon to former President Nixon, sir, part of your rationale was to put Watergate behind us to—if I may quote you again—truly end our long national nightmare. Why does not the same rationale apply now, today, in our Bicentennial year, to the young men who resisted in Vietnam, and many of them still in exile abroad?

MR. FORD: The amnesty program that I recommended in Chicago in September of 1974 would give to all draft evaders and—uh military deserters the opportunity to earn their uhh—good record back. About fourteen to fifteen thousand did take advantage of that program. We gave them ample time. I am against [ʌɛɪ]—an across-the-board pardon of draft evaders or military deserters. Now in the case of Mr. Nixon, the reason the—the pardon was given, was that, when I took office this country was in a very, very divided condition. There was hatred, there was divisiveness—uh people had lost faith in their government in many, many respects. Mr. Nixon resigned, and I became president. It seemed to me that if I was to uh adequately and effectively handle the problems of high inflation, a growing recession, the uh—involvement of the United States still in Vietnam that I had to give a hundred percent of my time to those two major problems. Mr. Nixon resigned. That is disgrace. The first President out of thirty-eight that ever resigned from public office under pressure. So when you look at the penalty that he paid, and when you analyze the requirements that I had—to spend all of my time working on the economy, which was in trouble, that I inherited; working on our problems in Southeast Asia—which were still plaguing us—it seemed to me that Mr. Nixon had been penalized enough by his resignation in disgrace and the need, and necessity for me to concentrate on the problems of the country fully justified the action that I took.

MR. REYNOLDS: I take it then, sir, that you do not believe that uh—it is— that you are going to reconsider and uh—think about those ninety thousand who are still abroad. Uh—have they not been penalized enough—many of 'em been there for years?

MR. FORD: Well, Mr. Carter has uh indicated that uh—he would give a blanket pardon to all uh—draft evaders. I do not agree with that point of view. I gave, in September of 1974, an opportunity for all draft evaders, all deserters, to come in voluntarily, clear their records by earning an opportunity to restore their good citizenship. I think we gave them a good opportunity—we're—I don't think we should go any further.

MR. NEWMAN: Governor Carter.

MR. CARTER: Well I think it's uh . . . very difficult for President Ford to uh—explain the difference between the pardon of President Nixon and—and uh—his attitude toward those who violated the draft laws. As a matter of fact— now [aʊ]—I don't advocate amnesty; I advocate pardon. There's a difference . . . in my opinion—uh and in accordance with the ruling of the Supreme Court and accordance with the definition in the dictionary. Amnesty means that—that you uh—that what you did was right. Pardon means that what you did, whether it's right or wrong, you're forgiven for it. And I do advocate a pardon for— for draft evaders. I think it's accurate to say that in uh—two years ago when Mr. Nixon—Mr. Ford put in this uh . . . amnesty that three times as many deserters were uh—excused as were—as were the uh—the ones who evaded the draft. But I think that now is the time to heal our country after the Vietnam War and I think that what the people are concerned about is not the—uh pardon or the amnesty of uh—those who evaded the draft, but—but whether or not our crime system is—is fair. We've got a—a sharp distinction drawn between white collar crime—the—the—the big shots who are rich, who are influential uh very seldom go to jail; those who are poor and—and who have uh no influence—uh quite often are the ones who are punished. And—and the whole uh subject of crime is one that concerns our people very much, and I believe that the fairness of it is—is what—uh—is a—is a major problem that addresses our—our leader and this is something that hasn't been addressed adequately by—by this administration. But I—I hope to have a complete uh—responsibility on my shoulders to help bring about a—a fair uh—criminal justice system and also to—to bring about uh—an end to the—to the divise— divisiveness that has occurred in our country uh as a result of the Vietnam War.

MR. NEWMAN: Mr. Gannon.

MR. GANNON: Governor Carter, you have promised a sweeping overhaul of the federal government, including a reduction in the number of government agencies—you say it would go down about two hundred from some nineteen hundred. That sounds, indeed, like a very deep cut in the federal government. But isn't it a fact that you're not really talking about fewer federal employees or less government spending, but rather that you are talking about reshaping the federal government, not making it smaller?

MR. CARTER: Well, I've been through this before, Mr. Gannon, as the governor of Georgia. When I took over we had uh a bureaucratic mess, like we have in Washington now, and we had three hundred agencies, departments, bureaus, commissions—uh some uh—fully budgeted, some not, but all having responsibility to carry out that was in conflict. And we cut those three hundred— uh agencies and so forth down substantially. We eliminated eliminated two hundred and seventy-eight of them. We set up a simple structure of government that could be administrated fairly and it was a—a tremendous success. It hasn't been undone since I was there. It resulted also in an ability to reshape our court system, our prison system, our education system, our mental health programs and—and a clear assignment of responsibility and—and authority and also to have uh our people once again understanding control our government.*
I intend to do the same thing if I'm elected president. When I get to Washington, coming in as an outsider, one of the major responsibilities that—that I will have on my shoulder is a complete reorganization of the [s]—of the executive branch of government. We now have uh—a greatly expanded White House staff. When Mr. Nixon went in office, for instance, we had three and a half million dollars spent on—on the White House and its staff. That has escalated now to sixteen and a half million dollars, in the last uh Republican administration. This needs to be changed. We need to put the responsibilities back on the cabinet members. We also need to have a great reduction in agencies and programs. For instance, we now have uh—in the health area three hundred and two different programs administered by eleven major departments and agencies, sixty other advisory commissions responsible for this. Medicaid's in one agency; Medicare is in a different one. The—the check on the quality of health care is in a different one. None of them uh are responsible for health care itself. This makes it almost impossible for us to have a good health program. We have

*Words were uttered rapidly and some final and weak sounds were omitted.

uh—just advocated uh—this past week . . . a consolidation of the responsibilities for energy. Our country now has no comprehensive energy program or policy. We have twenty different agencies in the federal government responsible for the production, the regulation, the uh—information about energy, the conservation of energy, spread all over government. This is a—a gross waste of money, so tough, competent management of government, giving us a simple . . . efficient . . . purposeful and manageable government would be a great step forward . . . and if I'm elected—and I intend to be—then it's gonna be done.

MR. GANNON: Well, I'd like to—to press my question on the number of federal employees—whether you would really plan to reduce the overall [s]—uh number, or—or merely put them in different departments and relabel them. Uh—in your energy plan, you consolidate a number of a—agencies into one, or you would, but uh does that really change the overall?

MR. CARTER: I can't say for sure that we would have fewer federal employees when I go out of office than when I come in. It took me about three years to completely reorganize the Georgia government. The last year I was in office uh—our budget was—was actually less than it was a year before, uh which showed a great uh improvement. Also, we had a—a 2 percent increase in the number of employees the last year. But it was a tremendous shift from administrative jobs into the delivery of services. For instance, we uh—completely revised our prison system. We established eighty-four new mental health treatment centers. And we shifted people out of administrative jobs into the field to deliver better services. The same thing will be done uh—at the federal government level. I—I accomplished this with s—substantial reductions in employees in some departments. For instance, in the Transportation Department uh we had uh—we cut back about 25 percent of the total number of employees. In giving our people better mental health care, we increased the number of employees. But the efficiency of it, the simplicity of it, the uh ability of people to understand their own government and control it was a—was a uh—substantial benefit derived from complete reorganization. We uh—have got to do that at the federal government level. If we don't, the bureaucratic mess is going to continue. There's no way for our people now to understand what their government is. There's no way to get the answer to a question. When you come to Washington to try to—as a governor—to try to begin a new program for your people, like uh the treatment of drug addicts, I found there were thirteen different federal agencies that I had to go to, to manage the uh drug treatment program. In the Georgia government we only had one agency responsible for drug treatment. This is the kind of change that would be made. And uh—it would be of—of tremendous benefit in long-range planning, in tight budgeting, uh saving the taxpayers's money, making the government more efficient, cutting down on bureaucratic waste, having a clear delineation of authority and responsibility of employees, and giving our people a better chance to understand and control their government.

MR. NEWMAN: President Ford.

MR. FORD: I think the record should show, Mr. Newman, that uh—the Bureau of Census—we checked it just yesterday—indicates that uh—in the four years that uh—Governor Carter was governor of the state of Georgia, uh—expenditures by the government went up over 50 percent. Uh—employees of the government in Georgia during his term of office went up over 25 percent; and the figures also show that the uh, uh—bonded indebtedness of the state of Georgia during his governorship went up over 20 percent. And there was some very interesting testimony given by uh—Governor Carter's successor, Governor Busby, before a Senate committee a few uh—months ago on how he found the Medicaid program when he came into office following Governor Carter. He testified, and these are his words—the present governor of Georgia—he says he found the Medicaid program in Georgia in shambles. Now let me talk about what we've done in the White House as far as federal employees are concerned. The first order that I issued after I became president was to cut or eliminate the prospective forty-thousand increase in federal employees that had been scheduled by my predecessor. And in the term that I've been president—some two years—we have reduced federal employment by eleven thousand. In the White House staff itself, when I became president, we had roughly five hundred and forty employees. We now have about four hundred and eighty-five employees, so we've made a rather significant reduction in the number of employees on the White House staff working for the president. So I think our record of cutting back employees, plus the . . . failure on the part of the Governor's programs to actually save employment in Georgia, shows which is the better plan.

MR. NEWMAN: Mrs. Drew.

MS. DREW: Mr. President, at Vail, after the Republican convention, you announced that you would now emphasize five new areas; among those were jobs and housing and health and improved recreational facilities for Americans. And you also added crime. You also mentioned [ps] education. For two years you've been telling us that we couldn't do very much in these areas because we couldn't afford it; and in fact we do have a $50 billion deficit now. In rebuttal to Governor Carter a little bit earlier, you said that if there were to be any surplus in the next few years you thought it should be turned back to the people in the form of tax relief. So how are you going to pay for any new initiatives in these areas you announced at Vail you were going to now stress?

MR. FORD: Well, in the uh—last two years, as I indicated before, we had a very tough time. We were faced with uh—heavy inflation, over 12 percent; we were faced with substantial unemployment. But in the last uh—twenty-four months we've turned the economy around and we've brought inflation down to under 6 percent, and we have reduced the uhh—well, we have added employment of about four million in the last seventeen months to the point where we have eighty-eight million people working in America today—the most in the history of the country. The net result is . . . we are going to have some improvement in our receipts. And I think we'll have some decrease in our disbursements. We expect to have a lower deficit in fiscal year 1978. We feel that with this improvement in the economy; we feel with more receipts and fewer disbursements we can in a moderate way increase, as I recommended, over the next ten years a new parks program that would cost a billion and a half dollars, doubling our national park system. We have recommended that in the h—housing program we can reduce down payments and moderate monthly payments. But that doesn't cost any more as far as the federal treasury is concerned. We believe that we can uh do a better job in the area of crime, but that requires a tougher sentencing, mandatory certain prison sentences for those who violate our criminal laws. We—uh believe that uh you can revise the federal criminal code, which has not been revised in a good many years. That doesn't cost any more money. We believe that you can uhh—do something more effectively with a moderate increase in money in the drug abuse program. We feel that uh—in education we can have a slight increase—not a major increase. It's my understanding that Governor Carter has indicated that uh—he approves of a $30 billion uh—expenditure by the federal government as far as education is concerned. At the present time we're spending roughly three billion five hundred million dollars. I don't know where that money would come from. But as we look at the quality-of-life programs—jobs, health, education, crime, recreation—we feel that as we move forward with a healthier economy, we can absorb the small necessary cost that will be required.

Ms. DREW: Sir, in the next few years would you try to reduce the deficit, would you spend more money for these programs that you have just outlined, or would you, as you said earlier, return whatever surplus you got to the people in the form of tax relief?

MR. FORD: We feel that uh—with the programs that I have recommended, the additional $10 billion tax cut, with the moderate increases in the quality-of-life area, we can still have a balanced budget which I will submit to the Congress in January of 1978. We won't wait one year or two years longer, as Governor Carter uh—indicates. As the economy improves, and it is improving, our gross national product this year will average about 6 percent increase over last year. We will have the lower rate of inflation for the uh—calendar year this year—something slightly under 6 percent. Employment will be up, revenues will be up. We'll keep the lid on some of these programs that we can hold down as we have a little extra money to spend for those quality-of-life programs which I think are needed and necessary. Now . . . I cannot, and would not, endorse the kind of program that uh—Governor Carter recommends. He endorses the Democratic uh—platform which, as I read it, calls for approximately sixty additional programs. We estimate that those programs would add a hundred billion dollars minimum and probably two hundred billion dollars—uhh maximum each year to the federal budget. Those programs you cannot afford and give tax relief. We feel that you can hold the line and restrain federal spending, give a tax reduction and still have a balanced budget by 1978.

MR. NEWMAN: Governor Carter.

MR. CARTER: Well, Mr. Ford takes the uh—same attitude that the Republicans always take. In the last three months before an election, they're always for the programs that they always fight the other three-and-one-half years. Uh—I remember when uh—Herbert Hoover was against uh—jobs for people. I remember when Alf Landon was against Social Security and uh—later President Nixon, sixteen years ago, was telling the public that John Kennedy's proposals would bankrupt the country and would double the cost. The best thing to do is to look at the record uh—of Mr. Ford's Administration and Mr. Nixon's before his. Uh—we had last year a $65 billion deficit—the largest deficit in the history of our country—more of a deficit spending than we had in the entire eight-year period under President Johnson and President Kennedy. We've got five hundred thousand more Americans out of jobs today than were out of work three months ago and since Mr. Ford's been in office two years, we've had a 50 percent increase in unemployment from five million people out of work to two and a half million more people out of work and a total of seven and a half million. We've also got uh—a comparison between himself and Mr. Nixon. He's got four times the size of the deficits that Mr. Nixon even had himself. This uh—talking about more people at work—uh is distorted because with a 14 percent increase in the cost of living . . . in the last uh—two years, it means that—that women and young people have had to go to work when they didn't want to because their fathers didn't make enough to pay the increased cost of uh—food and uh housing and clothing. We have uh—in this last uh two years alone a hundred and twenty billion dollars total deficits under President Ford and uh—at the same time we've had, in the last eight years, a doubling in the number of bankruptcies for small business: we've had a negative growth in our—in our national economy measured in real dollars. The take-home pay of a worker in this country is actually less now than it was in 1968—measured in real dollars. This is the kind of record that's there and talk about the future and a drastic change or conversion on the part of Mr. Ford as of last minute is one that just doesn't go.

MR. NEWMAN: Mr. Reynolds.

MR. REYNOLDS: Governor Carter, I'd like to turn uh—to what we used to call the energy crisis. Yesterday a British uh—government commission on air pollution, but one headed by a nuclear physicist, recommended that any further expansion of nuclear energy be delayed in Britain as long as possible. Now this is a subject that is quite controversial among our own people and there seems to be a clear difference between you and the President on the use of nuclear power plants, which you say you would use as a last priority. Why, sir, are they unsafe?

MR. CARTER: Well among my other experiences in the past, I've—I've been a nuclear engineer, and did graduate work in this field. I think I know the—the uh capabilities and limitations of atomic power. But the energy—uh policy of our nation is one that uh has not yet been established under this administration. I think almost every other developed nation in the world has an energy policy except us. We have seen uh—the Federal Energy Agency established, for instance. Uh—in the crisis of 1973 it was supposed to be a temporary agency, uh now it's permanent, it's enormous, it's growing every day. I think the *Wall Street Journal* uh reported not too long ago they have a hundred and twelve public relations experts working for the Federal Energy Agency to try to justify to the American people its own existence. We've got to have a—a firm way to handle the energy question. The reorganization proposal that I have put forward is one uh first step. In addition to that, we need to have—uh a realization that we've got uh about thirty-five years worth of oil left in the whole world. We're gonna run out of oil. When Mr. Nixon made his famous uh speech on Operation Independence we were importing about 35 percent of our oil. Now we've increased that amount 25 percent. We now import about 44 percent of our oil. We need to shift from oil to coal. We need to concentrate our research and development effort on uh coal burning and extraction, with safer mines, but also it's clean burning. We need to shift very strongly toward solar energy and have strict conservation measures. And then as a last resort only, continue to use atomic power. I would certainly uh—not cut out atomic power altogether.

We can't afford to give up that opportunity until later. But to the extent that we continue to use atomic power, I would be responsible as president to make sure that the safety precautions were initiated and maintained. For instance, some that have been forgotten: we need to have the reactor core—below ground level, the entire power plant that uses atomic uh—power tightly sealed and a heavy—heavy vacuum maintained. There ought to be a standardized design. There ought to be a full-time uh—atomic energy specialist, independent of the power company in the control room, full time, twenty-four hours a day, to shut down a plant if an abnormality develops. These kinds of uh—procedures, along with evacuation procedures, adequate insurance, ought to be initiated. So, shift from oil to coal, emphasize research and development on coal use and also on solar power, strict conservation measures, not yield every time that the special interest groups uh—put pressure on the president like uh this administration has done, and use atomic energy only as a last resort with the strictest possible safety precautions. That's the best overall energy policy in the brief time we have to discuss it.

MR. REYNOLDS: Well Governor, on that same subject, would you require mandatory conservation efforts to try to conserve fuel?

MR. CARTER: Yes, I would. Some of the things that can be done about this is a change in the rate structure . . . of electric power companies. We uh—now encourage people to waste electricity, and uh—by giving uh—the lowest rates to the biggest users. We don't do anything to cut down on peak load requirements. We don't have an adequate requirement for the insulation of homes, for the efficiency of automobiles. And whenever the uh—automobile manufacturers come forward and say they can't meet the uh—amendments that the Congress has put forward, this Republican administration has delayed the implementation dates. In addition to that, we ought to have a—a shift toward the use of coal, particularly in the Appalachian regions where the coal is located. A lot of uh— very high quality, low-carbon coal, uh—low-sulfur coal is there, it's where our employment is needed. Uh—this would—would help a great deal. So mandatory conservation measures—yes. Encouragement by the president for people to uh voluntarily conserve—yes. And also the private sector ought to be encouraged to—to bring forward to the public the benefits from efficiency. One bank in uh—Washington, fo—for instance, gives lower interest loans for people who adequately insulate their homes or who buy efficient automobiles. And some major uh—uh—manufacturing companies, like Dow Chemical, have through uh—very effective efficiency mechanism cut down the use of energy by uh—as much as 40 percent with the same out-product. These kinds of things uh—ought to be done, uh they ought to be encouraged and supported, and even required uh by the government, yes.

MR. NEWMAN: President Ford.

MR. FORD: Governor Carter skims over a very serious and a very broad subject. In January of uh—1975 I submitted to the Congress and to the American people the first comprehensive energy program recommended by any president. It called for an increase in the production of energy in the United States. It called for uh—conservation measures so that we would save the energy that we have. If you're going to increase domestic oil and gas production—and we have to—you have to give those producers an opportunity to uh—develop their land or their wells. I recommended to the Congress that we should increase coal production in this country from six hundred million tons a year to twel—a—a billion two hundred million tons by 1985. In order to do that we have to improve our extraction of coal from the ground; we have to improve our utilization of coal—make it more efficient, make it cleaner. In addition we uh—have to expand our research and development. In my program for energy independence we have increased, for example, solar energy research from about $84 million a year to about a hundred and twenty million dollars a year. We're going as fast as the experts say we should. In nuclear power we have increased the research and development, uh—under the Energy Research and Development Agency uh—very substantially, to insure that our ener—uh—nuclear power plants are safer, that they are more efficient, and that we have adequate safeguards. I think you have to have greater oil and gas production, more coal production, more nuclear production, and in addition you have to have energy conservation.

MR. NEWMAN: Mr. Gannon.

MR. GANNON: Mr. President, I'd like to return for a moment to this problem of unemployment. You have vetoed or threatened to veto number of job bills passed or uh—in development in the Democratic Congress—Democratic-controlled Congress. Yet at the same time the government is paying out, uh—I think it is $17 billion, perhaps $20 billion a year in unemployment compensation caused by the high unemployment. Why do you think it is better to pay out unemployment compensation to idle people than to put them to work in public service jobs?

MR. FORD: The bills that I vetoed, the one for an additional $6 billion, was not a bill that would have solved our unemployment problems. Even the proponents of it admitted that no more than four hundred thousand jobs would be uh—made available. Our analysis indicates that something in the magnitude of about one hundred fifty to two hundred thousand jobs would uh—be made available. Each one of those jobs would've cost the taxpayers $25 thousand. In addition, the jobs would not be available right now. They would not have materialized for about nine to eighteen months. The immediate problem we have is to stimulate our economy now so that we can get rid of unemployment. What we have done is to hold the lid on spending in an effort to reduce the rate of inflation. And we have proven, I think very conclusively, that you can reduce the rate of inflation and increase jobs. For example, as I have said, we have added some four million jobs in the last seventeen months. We have now employed eighty-eight million people in America, the largest number in the history of the United States. We've added five hundred thousand jobs in the last two months. Inflation is the quickest way to destroy jobs. And by holding the lid on federal spending we have been able to do an—a good job, an affirmative job in inflation and as a result have added to the jobs in this country. I think it's uh—also appropriate to point out that through our tax policies we have stimulated uhh—added employment throughout the country, the investment tax credit, the tax incentives for expansion and modernization of our industrial capacity. It's my—my opinion that the private sector, where five out of six jobs are, where you have permanent jobs, with the opportunity for advancement, is a better place than make-work jobs under the program recommended by the Congress.

MR. GANNON: Just to follow up, Mr. President: the—the Congress has just passed a three point seven billion dollar appropriation bill which would provide money for the public works jobs program that you earlier tried to kill by your veto of the authorization legislation. In light of the fact that uh—unemployment again is rising—or has in the past three months—I wonder if you have rethought that question at all; whether you would consider uh—allowing this program to be funded, or will you veto that money bill?

MR. FORD: Well, that bill has not yet come down to the Oval Office, so I am not in a position to make any judgment on it tonight. But that is an extra $4 billion that would uh—add to the deficit which would add to the inflationary pressures, which would help to destroy jobs in the private sector—not make jobs, where the jobs really are. These make-work, temporary jobs—dead end as they are—are not the kind of jobs that we want for our people. I think it's interesting to point out that uh—in the uh—two years that I've been president I've vetoed fifty-six bills. Congress has sustained forty-two vetoes. As a result, we have saved over $9 billion in federal expenditures. And the Congress by overriding the bills that I did veto, the Congress has added some $13 billion to the federal expenditures and to the federal deficit. Now Governor Carter complains about the deficits that uh—uh—this administration has had. And yet he condemns the vetoes that I have made that has—that have saved the taxpayer $9 billion and could have saved an additional $13 billion. Now he can't have it both ways. And therefore, it seems to me that we should hold the lid, as we have, to the best of our ability so we can stimulate the private economy and get the jobs where the jobs are—five out of six in this economy.

MR. NEWMAN: Governor Carter.

MR. CARTER: Well, Mr. Ford doesn't seem to put into perspective the fact that when—when uh five hundred thousand more people are out of work than there were three months ago, while we have two and a half million more people out of work than were when he took office, that this touches human beings. I was in uh—a city in uh—Pennsylvania not too long ago, near here, and uh—there were about four or five thousand people in the audience—it was on a—on a train trip. And I said, "How many uh—adults here are out of work?" About a thousand raised their hands. Mr. Ford uh—actually has fewer people now in the private sector in non-farm jobs than when he took office. And still he talks about—uh success. Seven point nine percent unemployment is a terrible tragedy in this country. He says he's learned how to match unemployment with inflation. That's right. We've got the highest inflation we've had in twenty-five years right now, except under this administration, and that was fifty years ago. And we've got uh—the highest unemployment we've had uh—under Mr. Ford's administration, since the Great Depression. This affects human beings, and—and his insensitivity in providing those people a chance to work has made this a welfare administration, and not a work administration. He hasn't saved $9 billion with his vetoes. There's only been uh—a net savings of $4 billion. And the cost in unemployment compensation, welfare compensation, and lost revenues has increased $23 billion in the last two years. This is a—a typical attitude that really causes havoc in people's lives, and then it's covered over by saying that our country has naturally got a 6 percent unemployment rate, or 7 percent unemployment rate and a 6 percent inflation. It's a travesty.

It shows a lack of leadership. And we've never had a president since the War between the States that vetoed more bills. Mr. Ford has vetoed four times as many bills as Mr. Nixon—per year. And eleven of 'em have been overriden. One of his bills that was overriden—he only got one vote in the Senate and seven votes in the House, from Republicans. (MR. NEWMAN: Governor Carter.) So this shows a breakdown in leadership.

MR. NEWMAN: Under the rules, I must stop you there. And Mrs. Drew.

Ms. DREW: Governor Carter, I'd like to come back to the subject of taxes. You have said that you want to cut taxes for the middle and lower income groups.

MR. CARTER: Right.

Ms. DREW: But unless you're willing to do such things as reduce the itemized deductions for charitable contributions or home mortgage payments, or interest, or taxes, or capital gains, you can't really raise sufficient revenue to provide an overall tax cut of any size. So how are you gonna provide that tax relief that you're talking about?

MR. CARTER: Now we have uh such a grossly unbalanced tax system—as I said earlier, that it is a disgrace—ah of all the tax—benefits now, 25 percent of 'em go to the 1 percent of the richest people in this country. Over 50 percent —53 to be exact—percent of the tax benefits go to the 14 percent richest people in this country, and we've had a 50 percent increase in payroll deductions since Mr. Nixon went in office eight years ago. Mr. Ford has—has advocated since he's been in office over $5 billion in reductions for corporations, special interest groups, and the very, very wealthy who derive their income—not from labor— but from investments. That's got to be changed. A few things that can be done: we have now a deferral system so that the multinational corporations who invest overseas—if they make a million dollars in profits overseas—they don't have to pay any of their taxes unless they bring their money back into this country. When they don't pay their taxes, the average American pays the taxes for them. Not only that, but it robs this country of jobs, because instead of coming back with that million dollars and creating a shoe factory, say in New Hampshire or Vermont, if the company takes the money down to Italy and— and builds a shoe factory, they don't have to pay any taxes on the money. Another thing is a system called DISC which was originally designed, proposed by Mr. Nixon, to encourage exports. This permits a company to create uh— a dummy corporation, to export their products, and then not to pay the full amount of taxes on them. This costs our uh—government about uh—$1.4 billion a year. And when those rich corporations don't pay that tax, the average American taxpayer pays it for 'em. Another one that's uh—that's very important is the uh—is the business deductions, uh—jet airplanes, uh—first class travel, the fifty-dollar martini lunch.[ɛ] The average working person can't—uh —can't take advantage of that, but the—the wealthier people—uh can. Uh— another system is where uhh—a dentist can invest money in say, raising cattle, and uh—can put in a hundred thousand dollars of his own money, borrow nine hundred thousand dollars—nine hundred mi—thousand dollars—that makes a million—and mark off a great amount of uh—of loss uh—through that procedure. Uh—there was one example, for instance, where uh—somebody uh—produced pornographic movies. They put in $30 thousand of their own money and got a hundred and twenty thousand dollars in tax savings. Well, these special kinds of programs have—have robbed the average taxpayer and have benefited those who are powerful, and who can employ lobbyists, and who can have their CPAs and their lawyers to help them benefit from the roughly uh—eight thousand pages of the tax code. The average uh American person can't do it. You can't hire a lobbyist uh out of unemployment compensation checks.

Ms. DREW: Ah—Governor, to follow up on your answer. Uh—in order for any kind of tax relief to really be felt by the middle and lower-income people (MR. CARTER: Yes) you need about, according to Congressional committees on this, you need about $10 billion. Now you listed some things—the uh—deferral on foreign income as estimated: that would save about $500 million. DISC, you said, was about 1.4 billion. uh—The estimate of the outside, if you eliminated all tax shelters, is 5 billion. So where else would you raise the revenue to provide this tax relief—would you, in fact, do away with all business deductions, and what other kinds of preferences would you do away with?

MR. CARTER: No, I wouldn't do away with all—uh business deductions. I think that would be a—a very serious mistake. But uh—if—if you could just do away with the ones that are unfair, you could lower taxes for everyone. I would never do anything that would increase the taxes for those who work for a living, or who are presently required to list all their income. What I wanna do is not to raise taxes, but to eliminate loopholes. And this is uh—the point of my first statistics that I gave you—that—that the present tax benefits that have been carved out over a long period of years—fifty years—by sharp tax lawyers and by lobbyists have benefited just the rich. These programs that I described to you earlier—the tax deferrals for overseas, the DISC, and the tax shelters, uh—they only apply to people in the $50 thousand-a-year bracket or up, and I think this is the very best way to approach it. It's to make sure that everybody pays taxes on the income that they earn and make sure that you take whatever savings there is from the higher income levels and give it to the lower- and middle-income families.

MR. NEWMAN: President Ford.

MR. FORD: Governor Carter's answer tonight does not coincide with the answer that he gave in an interview to the Associated Press a week or so ago. In that interview uh—Governor Carter indicated that uh—he would raise the taxes on those in the medium or middle-income brackets or higher. Now if you uh—take the medium or middle-income taxpayer—that's about $14 thousand per person—uh—Governor Carter has indicated, publicly, in an interview that he would increase the taxes on about 50 percent of the working people of this country. I think uh—the way to get tax equity in this country is to give tax relief to the middle-income people who have an income from roughly $8 thousand up to twenty-five or thirty thousand dollars. They have been short-changed as we have taken ten million taxpayers off the tax rolls in the last eight years, and as we have uh—added to the minimum tax uh—provision to make all people pay more taxes. I believe in tax equity for the middle-income taxpayer, increasing the personal exemption. Mr. Carter wants to increase taxes for roughly half of the taxpayers of this country. Now, the Governor has also played a little fast and loose with the facts about vetoes. The records show that President Roosevelt vetoed on an average of fifty-five bills a year. President Truman vetoed on the average, while he was president, about thirty-eight bills a year. I understand that Governor Carter, when he was Governor of Georgia, vetoed between thirty-five and forty bills a year. My average in two years is twenty-six. But in the process of that we have saved uhh—$9 billion. And one final comment, uh—Governor Carter talks about the tax bills and all of the inequities that exist in the present law. I must remind him the Democrats have controlled the Congress for the last twenty-two years and they wrote all the tax bills.

MR. NEWMAN: Mr. Reynolds.

MR. REYNOLDS: I suspect that uhh—we could continue on this tax argument for some time. But I'd like to move on to another area. Mr. President, uh—everybody seems to be running against Washington this year. And I'd like to raise two coincidental events and ask you whether you think perhaps this may have a bearing on the attitude throughout the country. The House Ethics Committee has just now ended its investigation of Daniel Schorr, after several months and many thousands of dollars, trying to find out how he obtained and caused to be published a report of the Congress that probably is the property of the American people. At the same time, the Senate Select Committee on Standards and Conduct has voted not really to begin an investigation of a United States senator because of allegations against him that he may have been receiving corporate funds illegally over a period of years. Do you suppose, sir, that events like this contribute to the feeling in the country that maybe there's something wrong in Washington, and I don't mean just in the executive branch but throughout the whole government?

MR. FORD: There is a considerable anti-Washington feeling throughout the country. But I think the feeling is misplaced. In the last two years, we have restored integrity in the White House, and we've set high standards in the executive branch of the government. The anti-Washington feeling, in my opinion, ought to be focused on the Congress of the United States. For example, this Congress, very shortly, will spend a billion dollars a year for its housekeeping, its salaries, its expenses and the like. It—the next Congress will probably be the first billion-dollar Congress in the history of the United States. I don't think the American people are getting their money's worth from the majority party that run this Congress. We, in addition, see that uh—in the last uh—four years the number of employees hired by the Congress has gone up substantial—uh much more than uh—the gross national product, much more than any other increase throughout our society. Congress is hiring people by the droves, and the cost as a result has gone up. And I don't see any improvement in the performance of the Congress under the present leadership. So it seems to me instead of the anti-Washington feeling being aimed at everybody in Washington, it seems to me that the focus should be where the problem is, which is the Congress of the United States, and particularly the majority in the Congress. They spend too much money on themselves. They have too many employees. There's some question about their morality. It seems to me that in this election, the focus should not be on the executive branch but the corrections should come as the voters vote for their members of the House of Representatives or for their United States senator. That's where the problem is and I hope there'll be some corrective action taken so we can get some new leadership in the Congress of the United States.

MR. REYNOLDS: Mr. President, if I may follow up. Uh—I think you've made it plain that you take a dim view of the uh—majority in the Congress. Isn't it quite likely, sir, that you will have a Democratic Congress in the next session, if you are elected president? And hasn't the country uh—a right to ask whether you can get along with that Congress, or whether we'll have continued confrontation?

MR. FORD: Well, It seems to me that uh—we have a chance—the Republicans—to get a majority in the House of Representatives. We will make some gains in the United States Senate. So there will be different ratios in the House, as well as in the Senate, and as president I will be able to uh—work with that Congress. But let me take the other side of the coin, if I might. Supposing we had—had a Democratic Congress for the last two years and we'd had uh—Governor Carter as President. He has, in effect, said that he would agree with all of—he would disapprove of the vetoes that I have made, and would have added significantly to expenditures and the deficit in the federal government. I think it would be contrary to one of the basic concepts in our system of government—a system of checks and balances. We have a Democratic Congress today, and fortunately we've had a Republican president to check their excesses with my vetoes. If we have a Democratic Congress next year, and a president who wants to spend an additional one hundred billion dollars a year, or maybe two hundred billion dollars a year, with more programs, we will have . . . . in my judgment, greater deficits with more spending, more dangers of inflation. I think the American people want a Republican president to check on any excesses that come out of the next Congress, if it is a Democratic Congress.

MR. NEWMAN: Governor Carter.

MR. CARTER: Well, it's not a matter of uh—Republican and Democrat. It's a matter of leadership or no leadership. President Eisenhower worked with a Democratic Congress very well. Even President Nixon, because he was a strong leader at least, worked with a Democratic Congress very well. Uh—Mr. Ford has vetoed, as I said earlier, four times as many bills per year as Mr. Nixon. Mr. Ford quite often puts forward a program just as a public relations stunt, and never tries to put it through the Congress by working with the Congress. I think under presidents For—uh—Nixon and Eisenhower they passed about 60 to 75 percent of their legislation. This year Mr. Ford will not pass more than 26 percent of all the legislative proposals he puts forward. This is government by stalemate, and we've seen almost a complete breakdown in the proper relationship between the president, who represents this country, and the Congress, who collectively also represent this country. We've had uh—Republican presidents before who've tried to run against a Democratic—uh Congress. And I don't think it's uh—the Congress is Mr. Ford's opponent; but if uh—if—if he insists that uh—that I be responsible for the Democratic Congress, of which I'm—have not been a part, then I think it's only fair that he be responsible for the Nixon administration in its [tʊ] entirety, of which he was a part. That, I think, is a good balance. But the point is, that—that a president ought to lead this country. Mr. Ford, so far as I know, except for avoiding another Watergate, has not accomplished one single major program for this country. And there's been a constant squabbling between the president and the Congress, and that's not the way this country ought to be run. I might go back to one other thing. Mr. Ford has uh—

misquoted an AP uh—news story that was in error to begin with. That uh—story reported several times that I would lower taxes for low and middle-income families and uh—that correction was delivered to the White House and I am sure that the president knows about this uh—correction, but he still insists uh—on repeating an erroneous statement.

MR. NEWMAN: President Ford, Governor Carter, we no longer have enough time for two complete sequences of questions. We have only about six minutes left for questions and answers. For that reason we will drop the follow-up questions at this point but each candidate will still be able to respond to the other's answers. Uh—to the extent that you can, gentlemen, please keep your remarks brief. Mr. Gannon.

MR. GANNON: Governor Carter, one uh—important uh—part of the Government's economic policy uh—apparatus we haven't talked about is the Federal Reserve Board. I'd like to ask you something about what you've said and that is that uh—you believe that a president ought to have a chairman of the Federal Reserve Board whose views are compatible with his own. Based on the record of the last few years, would you say that your views are compatible with those of Chairman Arthur Burns? And if not, would you seek his resignation if you are elected?

MR. CARTER: What I have said is that the president ought to have a chance to appoint a chairman of the Federal Reserve Board to have a coterminus uh—term; in other words, both of 'em serve the same four—four years. The Congress can modify the supply of money by modifying the income uh tax laws. The president can modify the uh—economic structure of a country by public statements and general attitudes in the budget that he proposes. The Federal Reserve has uh—an independent status that ought to be preserved. I think that Mr. uh—Burns did take a typical, erroneous Republican attitude in the 1973 year when inflation was so high. They assumed that the uh—inflation rate was because of excessive demand and uh—therefore put into effect tight constraint on the economy, very high interest rates, which is typical also of the Republican administration, uh—tried to increase the uh—the tax uh—payments by individuals, and cut the tax payments by corporations. I would have uh—done it opposite. I think the uh—problem should've been addressed by increasing productivity, by having uh—put—put people back to work so they could purchase more goods, lower income taxes on individuals, perhaps raise them, if necessary, on corporations in comparison. But uh—Mr. Burns uh—in that respect made a very serious mistake. I would not wanna destroy the—the independence of the uh Federal Reserve—uh Board. But I do think we ought to have a cohesive economic policy with at—at least the chairman of the Federal Reserve Board and the president's terms being uh—the same and letting the Congress, of course, be the third uh—entity with uh—with independence subject only to the president's veto.

MR. NEWMAN: President Ford, your response.

MR. FORD: The chairman of the Federal Reserve Board should be independent. Fortunately, he has been during Democratic as well as Republican administrations. As the result in the last uh—two years uh—we have had a responsible monetary policy. Uh the Federal Reserve Board indicated that the supply of money would be held between four to four and a half and seven and seven and a half. They have done a good job in integrating the money supply with the uh —fiscal policy of the uh—executive and legislative branches of the government. It would be catastrophic if the chairman of the Federal Reserve Board became the tool of the political uh—party that was in power. It's important for our future uhh—economic security that that job be nonpolitical and uh—separate from the executive and the legislative branches.

MR. NEWMAN: Mrs. Drew.

Ms. DREW: Uh Mr. President, the real problem with the FBI and, in fact, all of the intelligence agencies is there are no real laws governing them. Such laws as there are tend to be vague and open-ended. Now, you have issued some executive orders, but we've learned that leaving these agencies to executive discretion and direction can get them and, in fact, the country in a great deal of trouble. One president may be a decent man, the next one might not be. So, [wʊd] what do you think about trying to write in some more protection by getting some laws governing these agencies?

MR. FORD: You are familiar, of course, with the fact that I am the first president in thirty years who has reorganized the intelligence agencies in the federal government: the CIA, the Defense Intelligence Agency, the National Security Agency and the others. We've done that by executive order. Uhh—and I think uh—we've tightened it up; we've uh—straightened out their problems that developed over the last few years. It doesn't seem to me that it's needed or necessary to have legislation in this particular regard. Uhh—I have recommended to the Congress, however—I'm sure you're familiar with this—legislation that would uhh—make it uhh—very uhh—proper in—in the right way, that the attorney general could go in and get the right for wiretapping under security cases. This was an effort that was made by the attorney general and myself, working with the Congress. But even in this area, where I think new legislation would be justified, uh the Congress has not responded. So, I feel in that case, as well as in the reorganization of the intelligence agencies, as I've done, we have to do it by executive order. And I'm glad that we have a good director in George Bush. We have good executive orders, and the CIA and the DIA and NASA uh —uh—NSA are now doing a good job under proper supervision.

MR. NEWMAN: Governor Carter.

MR. CARTER: Well, one of the very serious things that's happened in our government in recent years, and has continued up until now, is a breakdown in the trust among our people in the [twenty-seven-minute delay]

MR. NEWMAN: . . . failure in the broadcasting of the debate, it occurred twenty-seven minutes ago. Uh the fault has been dealt with and uh—we want to thank President Ford and Governor Carter for being so patient and understanding while this uh delay went on. Uh we very much regret the technical failure that lost the sound as it—as it was leaving this theater. It occurred during uh Governor Carter's response to what would have been and what was the last question put to the candidates. That question went to President Ford. It dealt with the control of government intelligence agencies. Uh Governor Carter was making that response and had very nearly finished it. Uh—he will conclude his response now after which uh—President Ford and Governor Carter will make their closing statements. Governor.

MR. CARTER: There has been too much government secrecy and not uh—not enough respect for the personal privacy of American citizens.

MR. NEWMAN: It is now time for the closing statements, which are to be up to four minutes long. Governor Carter, by the same toss of the coin that directed the first question to you, you are to go first now.

MR. CARTER: Well, tonight we've had a chance to talk a lot about the past. But I think it's time to talk about the future. Our nation in the last eight years has been divided as never before. It's a time for unity. It's a time to draw ourselves together: to have a president and a Congress that can work together with mutual respect for a change, cooperating for a change, in the open for a change, so the people can understand their own government. It's time for government, industry, [æ] labor, manufacturing, agriculture, education, other entities in our society to cooperate. And it's a time for government to understand and to cooperate with our people. For a long time our American citizens have been excluded, sometimes misled, sometimes have been lied to. This is uh—not compatible with the purpose of our nation. I believe in our country. It needs to be competent. The government needs to be well-managed, efficient, economical. We need to have a government that's sensitive to our people's needs—to those who are poor, who don't have adequate health care, who have been cheated too long . . . with our tax programs, who've been out of jobs, whose families have been torn apart. We need to restore the faith and the trust of the American people in their own government. In addition to that, we've suffered because we haven't had leadership in this administration. We've got a government of stalemate. We've lost the vision of what our country can and ought to be. This is not the America that we've known in the past. It's not the America that we have to have in the future. I don't claim to know all the answers. But I've got confidence in my country. Our economic strength is still there. Our system of government—in spite of Vietnam, Cambodia, CIA, Watergate—is still the best system of government on earth. And the greatest resource of all are the two hundred and fifteen million Americans who have within us the strength, the character, the intelligence, the experience, the patriotism, the idealism, the compassion, the sense of brotherhood on which we can rely in the future to restore the greatness to our country. . . . We ought not to be excluded from our government anymore. We need a president who can go in—who derives his strength from the people. I owe the special interests nothing. I owe everything to you, the people of this country. And I believe that we can bind our wounds. I believe that we can work together. And I believe that [ʊɪ] if we can tap the tremendous untapped reservoir of innate strength in this country, that we can once again have a government as good as our people, and let the world know what we still know and hope for—that we still live in the greatest and the strongest and the best country on earth.

MR. NEWMAN: President Ford.

MR. FORD: On November second all of you will make a very, very important decision. One of the major issues in this campaign is trust. A president should never promise more than he can deliver and a president should always deliver everything that he's promised. A president can't be all things to all people. A president should be the same thing to all people. Another issue in this campaign, Governor Carter has endorsed the Democratic platform, which calls for more spending, bigger deficits, more inflation or more taxes. Governor Carter has embraced the record of the present Congress, dominated by his political party. It calls for more of the same. Governor Carter in his acceptance speech called for more and more programs, which means more and more government. I think the real issue in this campaign, and that which you must decide on November second, is whether you should vote for his promise or my performance in two years in the White House. On the fourth of July we had a wonderful two hundredth birthday—for our great country. It was [oʊ] a superb occasion. It was a glorious day. In the first century of our nation's history our forefathers gave us the finest form of government in the history of mankind. In the second century of our nation's history, our forefathers developed the most productive industrial nation in the history of the globe. Our third century should be the century of individual freedom for all our two hundred and fifteen million Americans today and all that join us. In the last few years government has gotten bigger and bigger; industry has gotten larger and larger; labor unions have gotten bigger and bigger; and our children have been the victims of mass education. We must make this next century the century of the individual. We should never forget that a government big enough to give us everything we want is a government big enough to take from us everything we have. The individual worker in the plants throughout the United States should not be a small cog in a big machine. The member of a labor union must have his rights strengthened and broadened and our children in their education should have an opportunity to improve themselves based on their talents and their abilities. My mother and father, during the Depression, worked very hard to give me an opportunity to do better in our great country. Your mothers and fathers did the same thing for you and others. Betty and I have worked very hard to give our children a brighter future in the United States, our beloved country. You and others in this great country have worked hard and done a great deal to give your children and your grandchildren the blessings of a better America. I believe we can all work together to make the individuals in the future have more and all of us working together can build a better America.

MR. NEWMAN: Thank you President Ford. Thank you Governor Carter. Our thanks also to the questioners and to the audience in this theater. Ahh— we much regret the technical failure that caused a twenty-eight-minute delay in the broadcast of the debate. We believe, however, that everyone will agree that it did not detract from the effectiveness of the debate or from its fairness. The next presidential debate is to take place on Wednesday, October sixth, in San Francisco at nine-thirty P.M., Eastern Daylight Time. The topics are to be foreign and defense issues. As with all three debates between the presidential candidates and the one between the vice-presidential candidates, it is being arranged by the League of Women Voters Education Fund in the hope of promoting a wider and better informed participation by the American people in the election in November. Now, from the Walnut Street Theater in Philadelphia, good night.

The Second Debate
Palace of Fine Arts Theater, San Francisco
October 6, 1976, 9:30 p.m.

Ms. FREDERICK: Good evening. I'm Pauline Frederick of NPR, moderator of this second of the historic debates of the 1976 campaign between Gerald R. Ford of Michigan, Republican candidate for president, and Jimmy Carter of Georgia, Democratic candidate for president. Thank you, President Ford and thank you, Governor Carter, for being with us tonight. This debate takes place before an audience in the Palace of Fine Arts Theater in San Francisco. An estimated one hundred million Americans are watching on television as well. San Francisco was the site of the signing of the United Nations Charter, thirty-one years ago. Thus, it is an appropriate place to hold this debate, the subject of which is foreign and defense issues. The questioners tonight are Max Frankel, associate editor of the *New York Times*, Henry L. Trewhitt, diplomatic correspondent of the *Baltimore Sun*, and Richard Valeriani, diplomatic correspondent of NBC News. The ground rules are basically the same as they were for the first debate two weeks ago. The questions will be alternated between candidates. By the toss of a coin, Governor Carter will take the first question. Each question sequence will be as follows: The question will be asked and the candidate will have up to three minutes to answer. His opponent will have up to two minutes to respond. And prior to the response, the questioner may ask a follow-up question to clarify the candidate's answer when necessary with up to two minutes to reply. Each candidate will have three minutes for a closing statement at the end. President Ford and Governor Carter do not have notes or prepared remarks with them this evening, but they may take notes during the debate and refer to them. Mr. Frankel, you have the first question for Governor Carter.

MR. FRANKEL: Governor, since the Democrats last ran our foreign policy, including many of the men who are advising you, country has been relieved of the Vietnam agony and the military draft, we've started arms control negotiations with the Russians, we've opened relations with China, we've arranged the disengagement in the Middle East, we've regained influence with the Arabs without deserting Israel, now, maybe we've even begun a process of peaceful change in Africa. Now you've objected in this campaign to the style with which much of this was done, and you've mentioned some other things that—that you think ought to have been done. But do you really have a quarrel with this Republican record? Would you not have done any of those things?

MR. CARTER: Well I think this Republican administration has been almost all style, and spectacular, and not substance. We've uh—got a chance tonight to talk about, first of all, leadership, the character of our country, and a vision of the future. In every one of these instances, the Ford administration has failed, and I hope tonight that I and Mr. Ford will have a chance to discuss the reasons for those failures. Our country is not strong anymore; we're not respected anymore. We can only be strong overseas if we're strong at home; and when I become president we'll not only be strong in those areas but also in defense—a defense capability second to none. We've lost in our foreign policy, the character of the American people. We've uh—ignored or excluded the American people and the Congress from participation in the shaping of our foreign policy. It's been one of secrecy and exclusion. In addition to that we've had a chance to become now, contrary to our longstanding beliefs and principles, the arms merchant of the whole world. We've tried to buy success from our enemies, and at the same time we've excluded from the process the normal friendship of our allies. In addition to that we've become fearful to compete with the Soviet Union on an equal basis. We talk about détente. The Soviet Union knows what they want in détente, and they've been getting it. We have not known what we've wanted and we've been out-traded in almost every instance. The other point I wanna make is about our defense. We've got to be a nation blessed with a defense capability that's efficient, tough, capable, well organized, narrowly focused —fighting capability. The ability to fight, if necessary, is the best way to avoid the chance for, or the requirement to fight. And the last point I wanna make is this: Mr. Ford, Mr. Kissinger have uh—continued on with the policies and failures of Richard Nixon. Even the Republican platform has criticized the lack of leadership in Mr. Ford and they've criticized the foreign policy of this administration. This is one instance where I agree with—with the Republican platform. I might say this in closing, and that is that as far as foreign policy goes, Mr. Kissinger has been the president of this country. Mr. Ford has shown an absence of leadership, and an absence of a grasp of what this country is and what it ought to be. That's got to be changed. And that's one of the major issues in this uh—campaign of 1976.

Ms. Frederick: President Ford, would you like to respond?

Mr. Ford: Governor Carter again is talking in broad generalities. Let me take just one question that he raises—the military strength and capability of the United States. Governor Carter in November of 1975 indicated that he wanted to cut the defense budget by $15 billion. A few months later, he said he wanted to cut the defense budget by eight or nine billion dollars. And more recently, he talks about cutting the defense budget by five to seven billion dollars. There is no way you can be strong militarily and have those kind of reductions in our military uh—appropriation. Now let me just tell you a little story. About uh— late October of 1975, I asked the then Secretary of Defense, Mr. Schlesinger, to tell me what had to be done if we were going to reduce the defense budget by uh—three to five billion dollars. A few days later, Mr. Schlesinger came back and said if we cut the defense budget by three to five billion dollars, we will have to cut military personnel by two hundred and fifty thousand, civilian personnel by a hundred thousand, jobs in America by a hundred thousand. We would have to stretch out our aircraft procurement, we would have to reduce our naval construction program, we would have to reduce the uh—research and development for the Army, the Navy, the Air Force and Marines by 8 percent. We would have to close twenty military bases in the United States immediately. That's the kind of defense program that uh—Mr. Carter wants. Let me tell you this straight from the shoulder. You don't negotiate with Mr. Brezhnev from weakness. And the kind of defense program that Mr. Carter wants will mean a weaker defense and a poor negotiating position.

Ms. Frederick: Mr. Trewhitt, a question for President Ford.

Mr. Trewhitt: Mr. President, my question really is the other side of the coin from Mr. Frankel's. For a generation the United States has had a foreign policy based on containment of Communism. Yet we have lost the first war in

Vietnam; we lost a shoving match in Angola. Uh—the Communists threatened to come to power by peaceful means in Italy and relations generally have cooled with the Soviet Union in the last few months. So le—let me ask you first, what do you do about such cases as Italy? And secondly, does this general drift mean that we're moving back toward something like an old cold—cold-war relationship with the Soviet Union?

MR. FORD: I don't believe we should move to a cold-war relationship. I think it's in the best interest of the United States, and the world as a whole, that the United States negotiate rather than go back to the cold-war relationship with the Soviet Union. I don't uh—look at the picture as bleakly as you have indicated in your question, Mr. Trewhitt. I believe that the United States ha—had many successes in recent years, in recent months, as far as the Communist movement is concerned. We have been successful in Portugal, where a year ago it looked like there was a very great possibility that the uh—Communists would take over in Portugal. It didn't happen. We have a democracy in Portugal today. A few uh—months ago, or I should say, maybe two years ago, the Soviet Union looked like they had continued strength in the Middle East. Today, according to Prime Minister Rabin, the Soviet Union is weaker in the Middle East than they have been in many, many years. The facts are, there —the Soviet Union relationship with Egypt is uh—at a low level. The Soviet Union relationship with Syria is at a very low point. The United States today, according to Prime Minister Rabin of Israel, is a—at a peak in its uh—influence and power in the Middle East. But let's turn for a minute to the uhh— southern African operations that are now going on. The United States of America took the initiative in southern Africa. We wanted to end the bloodshed in southern Africa. We wanted to have the right of self-determination in southern Africa. We wanted to have majority rule with the full protection of the rights of the minority. We wanted to preserve human dignity in southern Africa. We have taken the initiative, and in southern Africa today the United States is trusted by the black front-line nations and black Africa. The United States is trusted by other elements in southern Africa. The United States foreign policy under this administration has been one of progress and success. And I believe that instead of talking about Soviet progress, we can talk about American successes. And may I make an observation—part of the question you asked, Mr. Trewhitt? I don't believe that it's in the best interest of the United States and the NATO nations to have a Communist government in NATO. Mr. Carter has indicated he would look with sympathy to a Communist government in NATO. I think that would destroy the integrity and the strength of NATO, and I am totally opposed to it.

MR. CARTER: Well, Mr. Ford, unfortunately, has just made a statement that's not true. I have never advocated a Communist government for Italy. That would obviously be a ridiculous thing for anyone to do who wanted to be president of this country. I think that this is uh—an instance of uh—deliberate distortion, and this has occurred also in the question about defense. As a matter of fact, uh—I've never advocated any cut of $15 billion in our defense budget. As a matter of fact, Mr. Ford has made a political football out of the defense budget. About a year ago he cut the Pentagon budget six point eight billion dollars. After he fired James Schlesinger, the political heat got so great that he

478   **THE GREAT DEBATES**

added back about $3 billion. When Ronald Reagan won the Texas primary election, Mr. Ford added back another one and a half billion dollars. Immediately before the Kansas City convention, he added back another one point eight billion dollars in the defense budget. And his own uh—Office of Management and Budget testified that he had a $3 billion cut insurance added to the defense budget—defense budget under the pressure from the Pentagon. Obviously, this is another indication of trying to use the defense budget for political purposes, which he's trying to do tonight. Now, we went into south Africa late, after Great Britain, Rhodesia, the black nations had been trying to solve this problem for many, many years. We didn't go in until right before the election, similar to what was taking place in 1972, when Mr. Kissinger announced peace is at hand just before the election at that time. And we have weakened our position in NATO because the other countries in Europe supported the democ—democratic forces in Portugal long before we did; we stuck to the Portugal dictatorships much longer than other democracies did in this world.

Ms. FREDERICK: Mr. Valeriani, a question for Governor Carter.

MR. VALERIANI: Governor Carter, much of what the United States does abroad is done in the name of the national interest. What is your concept of the national interest? What should the role of the United States in the world be? And in that connection, considering your limited experience in foreign affairs, and the fact that you take some pride in being a Washington outsider, don't you think it would be appropriate for you to tell the American voters before the election the people that you would like to have in key positions, such as Secretary of State, Secretary of Defense, national security affairs advisor at the White House?

MR. CARTER: Well, I'm not gonna name my cabinet before I get elected. I've got a little ways to go before I start doing that. But I have uh—an adequate background, I believe. I am a graduate of the U.S. Naval Academy, the first military graduate since uh—Eisenhower. I've served as the Governor of Georgia and have traveled extensively in foreign countries and South America, Central America, Europe, the Middle East and in Japan. I've traveled the last twenty-one months among the people of this country. I've talked to them and I've listened. And I've seen at first hand, in a very vivid way, the deep hurt that's come to this country in the aftermath of Vietnam and Cambodia, Chile, and Pakistan, and Angola, and Watergate, CIA revelations. What we were formerly so proud of—the strength of our country, its uh—moral integrity, the representation in foreign affairs of what our people are, what our Constitution stands for, has been gone. And in the secrecy that has surrounded our foreign policy in the last few years, uh—the American people, the Congress have been excluded. I believe I know what this country ought to be. I've uh—been one who's loved my nation as many Americans do, and I believe that there's no limit placed on what we can be in the future, if we can harness the tremendous resources—militarily, economically, and the stature of our people, the meaning of the Constitution, in the future. Every time we've made a serious mistake in foreign affairs, it's been because the American people have been excluded from the process. If we can just tap the intelligence and ability, the sound common sense and the good judgment of the American people, we can once again have a foreign policy to make us proud instead of ashamed. And I'm not gonna exclude the American people from that process in the future, as Mr. Ford and Kissinger have done. This is what it takes to have a sound foreign policy strong at home, strong defense, permanent commitments, not betray the principles of our country, and involve the American people and the Congress in the shaping of our foreign policy. Every time Mr. Ford speaks . . . from a position of secrecy in negotiations, in secret [eɪgʰ]—in secret treaties that've been uh—pursued and achieved, in supporting dictatorships, in ignoring human rights, . . . we are weak and the rest of the world knows it. So these are the ways that we can restore the strength of our country, and they don't require long experience in foreign policy. Nobody has that except a president who has served a long time or a secretary of state. But my background, my experience, my knowledge of the people of this country, my commitment to our principles that don't change—those are the best bases to correct the horrible mistakes of this administration and restore our own country to a position of leadership in the world.

Mr. VALERIANI: How specifically, uh—Governor, are you going to bring the American people into the decision-making process in foreign policy? What does that mean?

Mr. CARTER: First of all, I would quit conducting the decision-making process in secret, as has been a characteristic of Mr. Kissinger and Mr. Ford. In many instances we've made agreements, like in Vietnam, uh—that have uh —been revealed later on to our uh—embarrassment. Recently Ian Smith, the uh—president of uh—Rhodesia, announced that he had unequivocal commitments from Mr. Kissinger that he could not reveal. The American people don't know what those commitments are. We've seen uh—in the past the destruction of elected governments, like in Chile, and the strong support of military dictatorship there. These kinds of things have hurt us very much. I would restore the concept of the fireside chat, which was an integral part of the administration of Franklin Roosevelt. And I would also restore the involvement of the Congress. When Harry Truman was president he was not afraid to have a strong secretary of defense. Dean Acheson, George Marshall were strong secretaries of uh—state—excuse me—state. But he also made sure that there was a bipartisan support. The members of Congress, Arthur Vandenberg, Walter George, were part of the process, and before our nation made a secret agreement, or before we made a bluffing statement, we were sure that we had the backing not only of the president and the secretary of state, but also of the Congress and the people. This is a responsibility of the president. And I think it's very damaging to our country for Mr. Ford to have turned over this responsibility to the secretary of state.

Ms. FREDERICK: President Ford, do you have a response?

Mr. FORD: Governor Carter again contradicts himself. He complains about secrecy and yet he is quoted as saying that in the attempt to find a solution in the Middle East that he would hold unpublicized meetings with the Soviet Union—I presume for the purpose of an—imposing a settlement on Israel and the Arab nations. But let me talk just a minute about what we've done to avoid secrecy in the Ford administration. After the United States took the initiative in working with Israel and with Egypt and achieving the Sinai II agreement— and I'm proud to say that not a single Egyptian or Israeli soldier has lost his life since the signing of the Sinai agreement. But at the time that uh—I submitted the Sinai agreement to the Congress of the United States, I submitted every single document that was applicable to the Sinai II agreement. It was the most complete documentation by any president of any agreement signed by a president on behalf of the United States. Now as far as meeting with the Congress is concerned, during the twenty-four months that I've been the president of the United States I have averaged better than one meeting a month with responsible groups or committees of the Congress—both House and Senate. The secretary of state has appeared in the several years that he's been the secretary before eighty different uh—committee hearings in the House and in the Senate. The secretary of state has made better than fifty speeches all over the United States explaining American foreign policy. I have made myself at least ten uh—speeches in various parts of the country where I have discussed with the American people defense and foreign policy.

Ms. FREDERICK: Mr. Frankel, a question for President Ford.

MR. FRANKEL: Mr. President, I'd like to explore a little more deeply our relationship with the Russians. They used to brag back in Khrushchev's day that because of their greater patience and because of our greed for—for business deals that they would sooner or later get the better of us. Is it possible that despite some setbacks in the Middle East, they've proved their point? Our allies in France and Italy are now flirting with Communism. We've recognized the permanent Communist regime in East Germany. We've virtually signed, in Helsinki, an agreement that the Russians have dominance in Eastern Europe. We've bailed out Soviet agriculture with our huge grain sales. We've given them large loans, access to our best technology and if the Senate hadn't interfered with the Jackson Amendment, maybe we—you would've given them even larger loans. Is that what you call a two-way street of traffic in Europe?

MR. FORD: I believe that we have uh—negotiated with the Soviet Union since I've been president from a position of strength. And let me cite several examples. Shortly after I became president in uh—December of 1974, I met with uh—General Secretary Brezhnev in Vladivostok and we agreed to a mutual cap on the ballistic missile launchers at a ceiling of twenty-four hundred—which means that the Soviet Union, if that becomes a permanent agreement, will have to make a reduction in their launchers that they now have or plan to have. I've negotiated at Vladivostok with uh—Mr. Brezhnev a limitation on the MIRVing of their ballistic missiles at a figure of thirteen-twenty, which is the first time that any president has achieved a cap either on launchers or on MIRVs. It seems to me that we can go from there to uh—the uh—grain sales. The grain sales have been a benefit to American agriculture. We have achieved a five and three quarter year uh—sale of a minimum six million metric tons, which means that they have already bought about four million metric tons this year and are bound to buy another two million metric tons to take the grain and corn and wheat that the American farmers have produced in order to uh—have full production. And these grain sales to the Soviet Union have helped us tremendously in meeting the costs of the additional oil and—the oil that we have bought from overseas. If we turn to Helsinki—I'm glad you raised it, Mr. uh—Frankel. In the case of Helsinki, thirty-five nations signed an agreement, including the secretary of state for the Vatican—I can't under any circumstances believe that the —His Holiness, the Pope would agree by signing that agreement that the thirty-five nations have turned over to the Warsaw Pact nations the domination of uh —Eastern Europe. It just isn't true. And if Mr. Carter alleges that His Holiness by signing that has done it, he is totally inaccurate. Now, what has been accomplished by the Helsinki agreement? Number one, we have an agreement where they notify us and we notify them of any uh—military maneuvers that are to be undertaken. They have done it. In both cases where they've done so, there is no Soviet domination of Eastern Europe and there never will be under a Ford administration. (MR. FRANKEL: Uh—uh—[ʊʊʊ]).

Ms. FREDERICK: Governor Carter?

MR. FRANKEL: I'm sorry, I [wɑ]—could I just follow—did I understand you to say, sir, that the Russians are not . . . using Eastern Europe as their own sphere of influence in occupying mo—most of the countries there and in [sʊ] and making sure with their troops that it's a—that it's a Communist zone, whereas on our side of the line the Italians and the French are still flirting with the possibility* of . . . Communism?

MR. FORD: I don't believe, uh—Mr. Frankel that uh—the Yugoslavians consider themselves dominated by the Soviet Union. I don't believe that the Rumanians consider themselves dominated by the Soviet Union. I don't believe that the Poles consider themselves dominated by the Soviet Union. Each of those countries is independent, autonomous: it has its own territorial integrity and the United States does not concede that those countries are under the domination of the Soviet Union. As a matter of fact, I visited Poland, uh—Yugoslavia and Rumania to make certain that the people of those countries understood that the president of the United States and the people of the United States are dedicated to their independence, their autonomy and their freedom.

Ms. FREDERICK: Governor Carter, may I have your response?

MR. CARTER: (chuckle) Well, in the first place, I'm not criticizing His Holiness the Pope. I was talking about Mr. Ford. The uh—fact is that secrecy has surrounded the decisions made by the Ford administration. In the case of uh—the Helsinki agreement—it may have been a good agreement at the beginning, but we have failed to enforce the so-called basket three part, which insures the right of people to migrate, to join their families, to be free, to speak out. The Soviet Union is still jamming Radio [fjʊr] Free Europe—Radio—uh—uh—Radio Free Europe is being jammed. We've also seen a very serious uh—problem with the so-called Sonnenfeldt document, which apparently Mr. Ford has just endorsed, which said that there's an organic linkage between the Eastern European countries and the Soviet Union. And I would like to see Mr. Ford convince the Polish-Americans and the Czech-Americans and the Hungarian-Americans in this country that those countries don't live under the domination and supervision of the Soviet Union behind the Iron [kʌnt]—uh—Curtain. We also have seen Mr. Ford exclude himself from access to the public. He hasn't had a tough cross-examination-type press conference in over thirty days. One press conference he had without sound. He's also shown a weakness in yielding to pressure. The Soviet Union, for instance, put pressure on Mr. Ford and he refused to see a symbol of human freedom recognized around the world, Aleksandr Solzhenitsyn. The Arabs have put pressure on Mr. Ford, and he's yielded,

*At this point Mr. Ford interrupted and partially masked Mr. Frankel's question.

and has permitted a boycott by the Arab countries of American businesses who trade with Israel, or who have American Jews owning or taking part in the management of American [kʌmp+kʌntrɪ]—companies. His own secretary of commerce had to be subpoenaed by the Congress to reveal the names of businesses who were subject to this boycott. They didn't volunteer the information. He had to be subpoenaed. And the last thing I'd like to say is this: This grain deal with the Soviet Union in '72 was terrible, and Mr. Ford made up for it with three embargoes, one against our own ally in Japan. That's not the way to run our foreign policy, including international trade.

Ms. FREDERICK: Mr. Trewhitt, a question for Governor Carter.

MR. TREWHITT: Governor, I'd like to pick up on that point, actually, and on your appeal for a greater measure of American idealism in foreign affairs. Foreign affairs come home to the American public pretty much in such issues as oil embargoes and grain sales, that sort of thing. Would you be willing to— to risk an oil embargo in order to promote human rights in Iran and Saudi Arabia, withhold arms from Saudi Arabia for the same purpose? Uh—or uh— I think you—matter of fact, you've perhaps answered this final part, but would you withhold grain from the Soviet Union in order to promote civil rights in the—in the Soviet Union?

MR. CARTER: I would never single out food . . . as a trade embargo item. If I ever decided to impose an embargo because of a crisis in international relationships, it would include all shipments of all equipment. For instance, if the Arab countries ever again declare an embargo against our nation on oil I would consider that not a military but an economic declaration of war, and I would respond instantly and in kind. I would not ship that Arab country anything— no weapons, no spare parts for weapons, no oil-drilling rigs, no oil pipe, no nothing. I wouldn't single out just food. Another thing that I'd like to say is this: In our international trade, as I said in my op—opening statement, we have become the arms merchant of the world. When this Republican administration came into office we were shipping about $1 billion worth of arms overseas, now ten to twelve billion dollars worth of arms overseas to countries that quite often use these weapons to fight each other. The shift in emphasis has been very disturbing to me, speaking about the Middle East. Under the last Democratic administration 60 percent of all weapons that went into the Middle East were for Israel. Nowadays—75 percent were for Israel before. Now 60 percent go to the Arab countries, and this does not include Iran. If you include Iran, our present shipment of weapons to the Middle East, only 20 percent goes to Israel. This is a deviation from idealism; it's a deviation from a commitment to our major ally in the Middle East, which is Israel; it's a yielding to economic pressure on the part of the Arabs on the oil issue; and it's also a tremendous indication that under the Ford administration we have not addressed the energy policy adequately. We still have no comprehensive energy policy in this country. And it's an overall sign of weakness. When we are weak at home [ɛə] economically—high unemployment, high inflation, a confused government, a wasteful defense establishment, this encourages the kind of pressure that's been put on us successfully. It would've been inconceivable ten—fifteen years ago, for us to be brought to our knees with an Arab oil embargo. But it was done three years ago and they're still putting pressure on us from the Arab countries to our discredit around the world. These are the weaknesses that I see, and I believe it's not just a matter of idealism. It's a matter of being tough. It's a matter of being strong. It's a matter of being consistent. Our priorities ought to be first of all to meet our own military needs, secondly to meet the needs of our allies and friends, and only then should we ship military equipment to foreign countries. As a matter of fact, Iran is gonna get eighty F-14s before we even meet our own Air Force orders for F-14s. And the shipment of Spruance-class destroyers to Iran are much more highly sophisticated than the Spruance-class destroyers that are present being delivered to our own Navy. This is ridiculous and it ought to be changed.

MR. TREWHITT: Governor, let me pursue that if I may. If I understand you correctly you would in fact to use my examples, withhold arms from Iran and Saudi Arabia even if the risk was an oil embargo and if they should be securing those arms from somewhere else, and then if the embargo came, then you'd respond in kind. Do I have it correctly?

MR. CARTER: If—Iran is not an Arab country, as you know, it is a Moslem country—but if Saudi Arabia should declare an oil embargo against us, then I would consider that an economic declaration of war. And I would make sure that the uh—Saudis understood this ahead of time so there would be no doubt in their mind. I think under those circumstances they would refrain from pushing us to our knees as they did in 1973 with their previous oil embargo.

MS. FREDERICK: President Ford?

MR. FORD: Governor Carter uh—apparently doesn't realize that since I've been president we have sold to the Israelis over $4 billion in military hardware. We have made available to the Israelis over 45 percent of the total economic and military aid since the establishment of Israel twenty-seven years ago. So the Ford administration has done a good job in helping our good ally, Israel, and we're dedicated to the survival and security of Israel. I believe that Governor Carter doesn't realize the need and necessity for arms sales to Iran. He indicates he would not make those. Iran is bordered very extensively by the Soviet Union. Iran has Iraq as one of its neighbors. The Soviet Union and the Communist-dominated government of Iraq are neighbors of Iran, and Iran is an ally of the United States. It's my strong feeling that we ought to sell arms to Iran for its own national security, and as an ally—a strong ally of the United States. The history of our relationship with Iran goes back to the days of President Truman when he decided that it was vitally necessary for our own security as well as that of Iran, that we should help that country, and Iran has been a good ally. In 1973 when there was an oil embargo, Iran did not participate. Iran continued to sell oil to the United States. I believe that it's in our interest and in the interest of Israel and Iran, and Saudi Arabia, for the United States to sell arms to those countries. It's for their security as well as ours.

MS. FREDERICK: Mr. Valeriani, a question for President Ford.

MR. VALERIANI: Mr. President, the policy of your administration is to normalize relations with mainland China. And that means establishing at some point full diplomatic relations and obviously doing something about the mutual defense treaty with Taiwan. If you are elected, will you move to establish full diplomatic relations with Peking, and will you abrogate the mutual defense treaty with Taiwan? And, as a corollary, would you provide mainland China with military equipment if the Chinese were to ask for it?

MR. FORD: Our relationship with the People's Republic of China is based upon the Shanghai Communique of 1972, and that communique calls for the normalization of relations between the United States and the People's Republic. It doesn't set a times schedule. It doesn't uh—make a determination as to how uh—that relationship should be achieved in relationship to our current uhh —diplomatic recognition and obligations to the Taiwanese Government. The Shanghai Communique does say that the differences between the People's Republic on the one hand and Taiwan on the other shall be settled by peaceful means. The net result is this administration, and during my time as the president for the next four years, we will continue to move for normalization of relations in the traditional sense, and we will insist that the disputes between Taiwan and the People's Republic be settled peacefully, as was agreed in the Shanghai Communique of 1972. The Ford administration will not let down, will not eliminate or forget our obligation to the people of Taiwan. We feel that there must be a continued obligation to the people, the some nineteen or twenty million people in Taiwan. And as we move during the next four years, those will be the policies of this administration.

MR. VALERIANI: And sir, the military equipment for the mainland Chinese?

MR. FORD: There is no policy of this government to give to the People's Republic, or to sell to the People's Republic of China, military equipment. I do not believe that we, the United States, should sell, give or otherwise transfer military hardware to the People's Republic of China, or any other Communist nation, such as the Soviet Union and the like.

MS. FREDERICK: Governor Carter.

MR. CARTER: Well, I'd like to go back just one moment to the previous question, where uh—Mr. Ford, I think, confused the issue by trying to say that we are shipping Israel 40 percent of our aid. As a matter of fact, during this current year uh we are shipping Iran, or have contracted to ship to Iran, about seven and a half billion dollars worth of arms and also to Saudi Arabia, about seven and a half billion dollars worth of arms. Also in 1975, we almost brought Israel to their knees after the uh—Yom Kippur War by the so-called reassessment of our relationship to Israel. We in effect tried to make Israel the scapegoat for the problems in the Middle East. And this weakened our relationships with Israel a great deal and put a cloud on the total commitment that our people feel toward the Israelis. There ought to be a clear, unequivocal commitment without change to Israel. In the Far East I think we need to continue to be uh —strong and uh—I would certainly uh—pursue the uh—normalization of uh —relationships with the People's Republic of China. We opened a great opportunity in 1972, which has pretty well been frittered [əreɪ]—frit—frittered away under Mr. Ford, that ought to be a constant uh—inclination toward—uh— toward friendship. But I would never let that friendship with the People's Republic of China stand in the way of the preservation of the independence and freedom of the people on Taiwan.

MS. FREDERICK: Mr. Frankel, a question for Governor Carter.

MR. FRANKEL: Governor, we always seem in our elections, and maybe in between too, to argue about uh—who can be tougher . . . in the world. Give or take a—a few billion dollars, give or take one weapons systems, our leading politicians, and I think you, too, gentlemen, seem to settle roughly on the same strategy in the world at roughly the same Pentagon budget cost. How bad do things have to get in our own economy, or how much backwardness and hunger would it take in the world to persuade you that our national security and our survival required very drastic cutbacks in arms spending and dramatic new efforts in other directions?

MR. CARTER: Well, always in the past we've had an ability . . . to have a strong defense and also have—to have a strong uh—domestic economy, and also to be strong in our reputation and influence within the community of nations. These . . . uh—characteristics of our country have been endangered under Mr. Ford. We're no longer respected . . . in a showdown vote in the United Nations or in—in any other international council we're lucky to get 20 percent of the other nations to vote with us. Our allies feel that we've neglected them. The so-called Nixon shock against Japan had weakened our relationships there. Under this administration we've also had an inclination to [s] keep separate the European countries, thinking that if they are separate, then we can dominate them and proceed with our secret, Lone Ranger-type diplomatic efforts. I would uh—also like to point out that we, in this country, have let our economy go down the drain. The worst inflation since the Great Depression. The highest unemployment of any developed nation of the world. We have a higher unemployment rate in this country than Great Britain, and West Germany. Our unemployment rate is twice as high as it is in Italy; it's three or four times as high as it is—as it is in Japan. And that . . . terrible circumstance in this country is exported overseas. We comprise about 30 percent of the world's economic trade power influence. And when we're weak at home—weaker than all our allies—that weakness weakens the whole free world. So strong economy is very important. Another thing that we need to do is to re-establish the good relationships that we ought to have between the United States and our natural allies and friends. They have felt neglected. And using that base of strength, and using the idealism, the honesty, the predictability, the commitment, the integrity of our own country, that's where our strength lies. And that would permit us to deal with the developing nations in a position of strength. Under this administration we've had a continuation of the so-called balance of power politics, where everything is looked on as a struggle between us on the one side, the Soviet Union on the other. Our allies—the smaller countries get trampled in the rush. What we need is to try to seek individualized bilateral relationships with countries, regardless of their size, and to establish world-order politics, which means that we want to preserve peace through strength. We also wanna revert back to the stature and the respect that our country had in previous administrations. Now, I can't say when this can come. But I can guarantee it will not come if Gerald Ford is reelected and this present policy is continued; it will come if I'm elected.

MR. FRANKEL: If I hear you right, sir, you're saying guns and butter both, but President Johnson also had trouble uh—keeping up both Vietnam and his domestic programs. I was really asking when do the—the needs of the cities and our own needs and those of other backward an—and—and even more needy countries and societies around the world take precedence over some of our military spending? Ever?

MR. CARTER: Well let me say very quickly that under President Johnson, in spite of the massive investment in the Vietnam War, he turned over a balanced budget to Mr. Nixon. The unemployment rate was less than 4 percent. The inflation rate under Kennedy and Johnson was about 2 percent—one-third what it is under this administration. So we did have at that time with good management, the ability to do both. I don't think that anybody can say that Johnson and Kennedy neglected the poor and the destitute people in this country or around the world. But I can say this: The number one responsibility of any president, above all else, is to guarantee the security of our nation—an ability to be free of the threat of attack, or blackmail and to carry out our obligations to our allies and friends, and to carry out a legitimate foreign policy. They must go hand in hand, but the security of this nation has got to come first.

MS. FREDERICK: President Ford.

MR. FORD: Let me say very categorically you cannot maintain the security and the strength of the United States with the kind of defense budget cuts that Governor Carter has indicated. In 1975 he wanted to cut the budget $15 billion. He's now down to a figure of five to seven billion dollars. Reductions of that kind will not permit the United States to be strong enough to deter aggression and maintain the peace. Governor Carter apparently doesn't know the facts. As soon as I became president, I initiated a meeting with the NATO heads of state and met with them in Brussels to discuss how we could improve the re— defense relationship in Western Europe. In uh—November of 1975 I met with the leaders of the five industrial nations in France for the purpose of seeing what we could do acting together to meet the problems of uh—the coming recession. In Puerto Rico this year, I met with six of the leading industrial nations' heads of state to meet the problem of inflation so we would be able to solve it before it got out of hand. I have met with the heads of government bilaterally as well as multilaterally. Our relations with Japan have never been better. I was the first United States president to visit Japan. And we uh—had the emperor of Japan here this uh—past year and the net result is Japan and the United States are working more closely together now than at any time in the history of our relationship. You can go around the world—and let me take Israel for example. Just recently, President Rabin said that our relations were never better.

MS. FREDERICK: Mr. Trewhitt, a question for President Ford.

MR. TREWHITT: Mr. President, uh—you referred earlier to your meeting with Mr. Brezhnev at Vladivostok in 1974. At—you agreed on that occasion to try to achieve another strategic arms limitation—SALT—agreement, ah—within the year. Ah—nothing happened in 1975, or not very much publicly at least. And those talks are still dragging and things got quieter as the current season approached. Is there—is there a bit of politics involved there, perhaps on both sides? Or perhaps more important . . . are interim weapons developments— and I'm thinking of such things as the cruise missile and the Soviet SS-20, an intermediate-range rocket—making SALT irrelevant, bypassing the SALT negotiations?

MR. FORD: First we have to understand that SALT I expires October third, 1977. Uh—Mr. Brezhnev and I met in Vladivostok in December of 1974 for the purpose of trying to take the initial step so we could have a SALT II agreement that would go to 1985. As I indicated earlier, we did agree on a twenty-four-hundred limitation on uh—uh—launchers of ballistic missiles. Uh—that would mean a cutback in the Soviet program; it would not interfere with our own program. At the same time, we put a limitation of thirteen hundred and twenty on MIRVs. Our technicians have been working since that time in Geneva, trying to put into technical language a—an agreement that can be verified by both parties. In the meantime, there has developed the problem of the Soviet Backfire—their high-performance aircraft which they say is not a long-range aircraft and which some of our people say is a intercontinental aircraft. In the interim, there has been the development on our part primarily, the cruise missiles; cruise missiles that could be launched from land-based mobile installations; cruise missiles that could be launched—launched from high-performance aircraft, like the B-52s or the B-1s, which I hope we proceed with; cruise missiles which could be launched from either surface or submarine uh—naval vessels. Those gray-area weapons systems are creating some problems in a—the agreement for a SALT II negotiation. But I can say that I am dedicated to proceeding, and I met just last week with the foreign minister of the Soviet Union, and he indicated to me that uh—the Soviet Union was interested in narrowing the differences and making a realistic and a sound compromise. I hope and trust, in the best interest of both countries, and in the best interests of all people throughout this globe, that the Soviet Union and the United States can make a mutually beneficial agreement. Because if we do not and SALT I expires on October three, 1977, you will unleash again an all-out nuclear arms race with the potential of a nuclear holocaust of unbelievable dimensions. So it's the obligation of the president to do just that, and I intend to do so.

MR. TREWHITT: Mr. President, let me follow that up by—I'll submit that the cruise missile adds a—a whole new dimension to the—to the arms competition—and then cite a statement by your office to the Arms Control Association a few days ago in which you said the cruise missile might eventually be included in a comprehensive arms limitation agreement but that in the meantime it was an essential of the American strategic arsenal. Now, uh—may I assume that from that you're tending to exclude the cruise missile from the next SALT agreement, or is it still negotiable in that context?

MR. FORD: I believe that the cruise missiles which we are now developing in research and development across the spectrum from air, from the sea, or from the land, uh—can be uh—included within a SALT II agreement. They are a new weapons system that has a great potential, both conventional and nuclear armed. At the same time, we have to make certain that the Soviet Union's Backfire, which they claim is not an intercontinental aircraft and which some of our people contend is, must also be included if we are to get the kind of agreement which is in the best interest of both countries. And I really believe that it—it's far better for us and for the Soviet Union, and more importantly for the people around the world, that these two superpowers find an answer for a SALT II agreement before October three, 1977. I think good will on both parts, hard bargaining by both parties and a reasonable compromise will be in the best interests of all parties.

Ms. FREDERICK: Governor Carter.

MR. CARTER: Well, Mr. Ford acts like he's uh—running for president for the first time. He's been in office two years, and there has been absolutely no progress made toward a new SALT agreement. He has learned the date of the expiration of SALT I, apparently. We've seen, in this world, a development of a tremendous threat to us. As a nuclear engineer myself, I know the limitations and capabilities of atomic power. I also [nʊni]—know that as far as the human beings on this earth are concerned that the nonproliferation of atomic weapons is number one. Only the last few days with the election approaching, has Mr. Ford taken any interest in a nonproliferation movement. I advocated last May in a speech at the United Nations that we move immediately as a nation to declare a complete moratorium on the testing of all nuclear devices, both weapons and peaceful devices; that we not ship . . . any more atomic fuel to a country that refuses to comply with strict [s] controls over the waste which can be reprocessed into explosives. I've also advocated that we stop the sale by Germany and France of [rɪsɑ]—processing plants for Pakistan and Brazil. Mr. Ford hasn't moved on this. We also need to provide an adequate supply of enriched uranium. Mr. Ford, again, under pressure from the atomic energy lobby, has insisted that this reprocessing or rather re-en—enrichment be done by private industry and not by the existing uh—government uh—plants. This kind of confusion and absence of leadership has let us drift now for two years with a constantly increasing threat of atomic weapons throughout the world. We now have five nations that have atomic bombs that we know about. If we continue under Mr. Ford's policy by 1985 or '90 we'll have twenty nations that have the capability of exploding atomic weapons. This has got to be stopped. That is one of the major challenges and major undertakings that I will assume as the next president.

Ms. FREDERICK: Mr. Valeriani, a question for Governor Carter.

MR. VALERIANI: Governor Carter, earlier tonight you said America is not strong any more; America is not respected any more. And I feel that I must ask you: Do you really believe that the United States is not the strongest country in the world, do you really believe that the United States is not the most respected country in the world? Or is that just campaign rhetoric?

MR. CARTER: No, it's not just campaign rhetoric. I think that militarily we are as strong as any nation on earth. I think we got to stay that way and continue to increase our capabilities to meet any potential threat. But as far as strength derived from commitment to principles, as far as strength derived from the unity within our country, as far as strength derived from the people, the Congress, the secretary of state, the president, sharing in the evolution and carrying-out of a foreign policy, as far as strength derived from the respect of our own allies and friends, their assurance that we will be staunch in our commitment, that we will not deviate and that we'll give them adequate attention, as far as—as strength derived from doing what's right—caring for the poor, providing food, becoming the breadbasket of the world instead of the arms merchant of the world—in those respects, we're not strong. Also, we'll never be strong again overseas, unless we're strong at home. And with our economy in such terrible disarray and getting worse by the month. We've got five-hundred thousand more Americans unemployed today than we had three months ago. We've got two and a half million more Americans out of work now than we had when Mr. Ford took office. This kind of deterioration in our economic strength is bound to weaken us around the world. And we not only have uh—problems at home but we export those problems overseas. So as far as the respect of our own people toward our own government, as far as participation in the shaping of uh—concepts and commitments, as far as the trust of our country among the nations of the world, as far as dependence of our country in meeting the needs and obligations that we've expressed to our allies, as far as the respect of our country—even among our potential adversaries—we are weak. Potentially we're strong. Under this administration that strength has not been realized.

Ms. FREDERICK: President Ford.

MR. FORD: Governor Carter uh—brags about the unemployment during Democratic administrations and condemns the unemployment at the present time. I must remind him that we're at peace and during the period that he brags about unemployment being low, the United States was at war. Now let me correct one other comment that uh—Governor Carter has made. I have recommended to the Congress that we develop the uranium enrichment plant at Portsmouth, Ohio, which is a publicly owned [gʌ]—U.S. government facility and have indicated that the private program which would follow on in Alabama is one that may or may not uhh—be constructed. But I am committed to the one at Portsmouth, Ohio. The governor also talks about morality in foreign policy. The foreign policy of the United States meets the highest standards of morality. What is more moral than peace, and the United States is at peace today? What is more moral in foreign policy than for the administration to take the lead in the World Food Conference in Rome in 1974 when the United States committed six million metric tons of food—over 60 percent of the food committed for the disadvantaged and underdeveloped nations of the world? The Ford administration wants to eradicate hunger and disease in our underdeveloped countries throughout the world. What is more moral than for the United States under the Ford administration to take the lead in southern Africa, in the Middle East? Those are initiatives in foreign policy which are of the highest moral standard and that is indicative of the foreign policy of this country.

Ms. FREDERICK: Mr. Frankel, a question for President Ford.

MR. FRANKEL: Mr. President, can we stick with morality? Uh—for a lot of people it seems to cover uh—a bunch of sins. Uh—Mr. Nixon and Mr. Kissinger used to tell us that instead of morality we had to worry in the—in the world about living and letting live all kinds of governments that we really don't like. North and South Korean dictators, Chilean fascists, uh—Chinese Communists, Iranian emperors and so on. They said the only way to get by in a wicked world was to treat others on the basis of how they treated us and not how they treated their own people. But more recently, uhh—we seemed to've taken a different tack. Uhh—we've seemed to have decided that it—that it is part of our business to tell the Rhodesians, for instance, that the way they're treating their own black people is wrong and they've got to change their government and we've put pressure on them. We were rather liberal in our advice to the Italians as to how to vote. Uhm—is this a new Ford foreign policy in the making? Can we expect that you are now going to turn to South Africa and force them to change their governments, to intervene in similar ways to end the bloodshed, as you called it, say, in Chile or Chilean prisons, and throw our weight around for the—for the values that [wʊ]—that we hold dear in the world?

MR. FORD: I believe that uh—our foreign policy must express the highest standards of morality. And the initiatives that we took in southern Africa are the best examples of what this administration is doing and will continue to do in the next four years. If the United States had not moved when we did in southern Africa, there's no doubt there would have been an acceleration of bloodshed in that tragic part of the world. If we had not taken our initiative, it's very, very possible that uh—the government of Rhodesia would have been overrun and that the Soviet Union and the Cubans would have dominated uh—southern Africa. So the United States, seeking to preserve the principle of self-determination, to eliminate the possibility of bloodshed, to protect the rights of the minority as we insisted upon the rights of the majority, uh—I believe followed the good conscience of the American people in foreign policy. And I believe that we used our skill. Secretary of State Kissinger has done a superb job in working with the black African nations, the so-called front-line nations. He has done a superb job in getting the prime minister of South Africa, Mr. Vorster, to agree that the time had come for a solution to the problem of Rhodesia. Secretary Kissinger, in his meeting with uh—Prime Minister Smith of Rhodesia, was able to convince him that it was in the best interests of whites as well as blacks in Rhodesia to find an answer for a transitional government and then a majority government. This is a perfect example of the kind of leadership that the United States, under this administration, has taken. And I can assure you that this administration will follow that high moral principle in our future efforts in foreign policy, including our efforts in the Middle East where it is vitally important because the Middle East is the crossroads of the world. There've been more disputes in its [ʌn] area where there's more volatility than any other place in the world. But because Arab nations and the Israelis trust the United States, we were able to take the lead in the Sinai II Agreement. And I can assure you that the United States will have the leadership role in moving toward a comprehensive settlement of the Middle Eastern problems, I hope and trust as soon as possible. And we will do it with the highest moral principles.

MR. FRANKEL: Mr. President, just clarify one point: There are lots of majorities in the world that feel they're being pushed around by minority governments. And are you saying they can now expect to look to us for not just good cheer but throwing our weight on their side—in South Africa, or on Taiwan, or in Chile, uh—to help change their governments, as in Rhodesia?

MR. FORD: I would hope that as we move to one area of the world from another—and the United States must not spread itself too thinly—that was one of the problems that helped to create the circumstances in Vietnam—but as we as a nation find that we are asked by the various parties, either one nation against another or individuals within a nation, that the United States will take the leadership and try to resolve the differences. Let me take uh—uh—South

Korea as an example. I have personally told President Pack* that the United States does not condone the kind of repressive measures that he has taken in that country. But I think in all fairness and equity we have to recognize the problem that South Korea has. On the north they have North Korea with five-hundred thousand well-trained, well-equipped troops—they are supported by the People's Republic of China; they are supported by the Soviet Union. South Korea faces a very delicate situation. Now the United States, in this case, this administration, has recommended a year ago and we have reiterated it again this year, that the United States, South Korea, North Korea and the uh—People's Republic of China sit down at a conference table to resolve the problems of the Korean peninsula. This is a leadership role that the United States under this administration is carrying out, and if we do it, and I think the opportunities and the possibilities are getting better, we will have solved many of the internal domestic problems that exist in South Korea at the present time.

Ms. FREDERICK: Governor Carter.

Mr. CARTER: I notice that Mr. Ford didn't comment on the uh—prisons in Chile. This is an—a typical example, maybe of many others, where this administration overthrew an elected government and helped to establish a military dictatorship. This has not been . . . an ancient history story. Last year under Mr. Ford, of all the Food for Peace that went to South America, 85 percent went to the military dictatorship in Chile. Another point I wanna make is this. He says we have to move from one area of the world to another. That's one of the problems with this administration's so-called shuttle diplomacy. While the secretary of state's in one country, there are almost a hundred and fifty others that are wondering what we're gonna do next, what will be the next secret agreement. We don't have a comprehensive understandable foreign policy that deals with world problems or even regional problems. Another thing that concerned me was what Mr. Ford said about unemployment, that—insinuating that under Johnson and Kennedy that unemployment could only be held down when this country is at war. Karl Marx said that the free enterprise system in a democracy can only continue to exist when they are at war or preparing for war. Karl Marx was the grandfather of Communism. I don't agree with that statement. I hope Mr. Ford doesn't either. He has put pressure on the Congress—and I don't believe Mr. Ford would even deny this—to hold up on nonproliferation legislation until the Congress agreed for an $8 billion program for private industry to start producing enriched uranium. And the last thing I wanna make is this. He talks about peace and I'm thankful for peace. We were peaceful when Mr. Ford went into office. But he and Mr. Kissinger and others tried to start a new Vietnam in Angola, and it was only the outcry of the American people and the Congress when their secret deal was discovered that prevented our involvement in that conflagration which was taking place there.

Ms. FREDERICK: Gentlemen, I'm sorry we do not have time enough for two complete sequences of questions. We now have only twelve minutes left. Therefore, I would like to ask for shorter questions and shorter answers. And we also will drop the follow-up question. Each candidate may still respond, of course, to the other's answer. Mr. Trewhitt, a question for Governor Carter.

*He obviously meant President Park.

THE GREAT DEBATES

MR. TREWHITT: Governor Carter, before this event the most communications I received concerned Panama. Is—would you as president be prepared to sign a treaty which at a fixed date yielded administrative and economic control of the Canal Zone and shared defense, which, as I understand it, is the position the United States took in 1974?

MR. CARTER: Well, here again, uh—the Panamanian question is one that's been confused by Mr. Ford. Uh—he had directed his uh—diplomatic relation —uh—[rɛl]—uh—representative to yield to the Panamanians full sovereignty over the Panama Canal Zone at the end of a certain period of time. When Mr. Reagan raised this uh—question in Florida uh—Mr. Ford not only disavowed his instructions, but he also even dropped, parenthetically, the use of the word "détente." I would never give up complete control or practical control of the Panama Canal Zone, but I would continue to negotiate with the Panamanians. When the original treaty was signed back in the early 1900s, when Theodore Roosevelt was president, Panama retained sovereignty over the Panama Canal Zone. We retained control as though we had sovereignty. Now I would be willing to go ahead with negotiations. I believe that we could share more fully responsibilities for the Panama Canal Zone with Panama. I would be willing to continue to raise the payment for shipment of goods through the Panama Canal Zone. I might even be willing to reduce to some degree our military emplacements in the Panama Canal Zone, but I would not relinquish practical control of the Panama Canal Zone any time in the foreseeable future.

MS. FREDERICK: President Ford.

MR. FORD: The United States must and will maintain complete access to the Panama Canal. The United States must maintain a defense capability of the Panama Canal. And the United States will maintain our national security interest in the Panama Canal. The negotiations for the Panama Canal started under President Johnson and have continued up to the present time. I believe those negotiations should continue. But there are certain guidelines that must be followed, and I've just defined them. Let me take just a minute to comment on something that Governor Carter said. On non—nu—oh—uh—nonproliferation, in May of 1975, I called for a conference of uh—nuclear suppliers. That conference has met six times. In May of this year, Governor Carter took the first initiative, approximately twelve months after I had taken my initiative a year ago.

MS. FREDERICK: Mr. Valeriani, a question for President Ford.

MR. VALERIANI: Mr. President, the Government Accounting Office has just put out a report suggesting that you shot from the hip in the Mayaguez rescue mission and that you ignored diplomatic messages saying that a peaceful solution was in prospect. Uh—why didn't you do more diplomatically at the time; and a related question: Did the White House try to prevent the release of that report?

MR. FORD: The White House did not uh—prevent the release of that report. On July twelfth of this year, we gave full permission for the release of that report. I was very disappointed in the fact that the uh—GAO released that report because I think it interjected political partisan politics at the present time. But let me comment on the report. Somebody who sits in Washington, D.C., eighteen months after the Mayaguez incident, can be a very good grandstand quarterback. And let me make another observation. This morning, I got a call from the skipper of the Mayaguez. He was furious because he told me that it was the action of me, President Ford, that saved the lives of the crew of the Mayaguez. And I can assure you that if we had not taken the strong and forceful action that we did, we would have been uh—criticized very, very uh—severely for sitting back and not moving. Captain Miller is thankful. The crew is thankful. We did the right thing. It seems to me that those who sit in Washington eighteen months after the incident are not the best judges of the decision-making process that had to be made by the National Security Council and by myself at the time the incident was developing in the Pacific. Let me assure you that we made every possible overture to the People's Republic of China and through them to the Cambodian Government. We made uh—diplomatic uh—protests to the Cambodian government through the United Nations. Every possible diplomatic means was utilized. But at the same time, I had a responsibility, and so did the National Security Coun—Council, to meet the problem at hand. And we handled it responsibly and I think Captain Miller's testimony to that effect is the best evidence.

Ms. FREDERICK: Governor Carter.

MR. CARTER: Well, I'm reluctant to uh comment on the recent report—I haven't read it. I think the American people have only one—uh requirement—that the facts about Mayaguez be given to them accurately and completely. Mr. Ford has been there for eighteen months. He had the facts that were released today immediately after the Mayaguez incident. I understand that the report today is accurate. Mr. Ford has said, I believe, that it was accurate, and that the White House made no attempt to block the issuing of that report. I don't know if that's exactly accurate or not. I understand that both the [sɛk]—the uh—Department of State and the Defense Department have approved the accuracy of today's report, or yesterday's report, and also the National Security Agency. I don't know what was right, or what was wrong, or what was done. The only thing I believe is that whatever the—the knowledge was that Mr. Ford had should have been given to the American people eighteen months ago, immediately after the Mayaguez uh—incident occurred. This is uh—what the American people want. When something happens that endangers our security, or when something happens that threatens our stature in the world, or when American people are endangered by the actions of a foreign country, uh—just forty uh sailors on the Mayaguez, we obviously have to move aggressively and quickly to rescue them. But then after the immediate action is taken, I believe the president has an obligation to tell the American people the truth and not wait eighteen months later for the report to be issued.

Ms. FREDERICK: Gentlemen, at this time we have time for only two very short questions. Mr. Frankel, a question for Governor Carter.

MR. FRANKEL: Governor Carter, if the price of uh—gaining influence among the Arabs is closing our eyes a little bit to their boycott against Israel, how would you handle that?

MR. CARTER: I believe that the boycott of American businesses by the Arab countries because those businesses trade with Israel or because they have American Jews who are owners or directors in the company is an absolute disgrace. This is the first time that I've—[ɛ] remember in the history of our country when we've let a foreign country circumvent or change our Bill of Rights. I'll do everything I can as president to stop the boycott of American businesses by the Arab countries. It's not a matter of diplomacy or trade with me. It's a matter of morality. And I don't believe that Arab countries will pursue it when we have a strong president who will protect the integrity of our country, the commitment of our Constitution and Bill of Rights and protect people in this country who happen to be Jews. It may later be Catholics; it may be—later be Baptists who are threatened by some foreign country. But we ought to stand staunch. And I think it's a disgrace that so far Mr. Ford's administration has blocked the passage of legislation that would've revealed by law every instance of the boycott and it would've prevented the boycott from continuing.

Ms. FREDERICK: President Ford.

MR. FORD: Again Governor Carter is inaccurate. The Arab boycott action was first taken in 1952. And in November of 1975 I was the first president to order the executive branch to take action, affirmative action, through the Department of Commerce and other cabinet departments, to make certain that no American businessman or business organization should discriminate against Jews because of an Arab boycott. And I might add that uh—my administration —and I'm very proud of it—is the first administration that has taken an antitrust action against companies in this country that have allegedly cooperated with the Arab boycott. Just on Monday of this week I signed a tax bill that included an amendment that would prevent companies in the United States from taking a tax deduction if they have in any way whatsoever cooperated with the Arab boycott. And last week when we were trying to get the Export Administration Act through the Congress—necessary legislation—my administration went to Capitol Hill and tried to convince the House and the Senate that we should have an amendment on that legislation which would take strong and effective action against those who uh—participate or cooperate with the Arab uh boycott. One other point. Because the Congress failed to act, I am going to announce tomorrow that the Department of Commerce will disclose those companies that have uh—participated in the Arab boycott. This is something that we can do; the Congress failed to do it, and we intend to do it.

Ms. FREDERICK: Mr. Trewhitt, a very brief question for President Ford.

MR. TREWHITT: Mr. President, if you get the accounting of missing in action you want from North Vietnam—or from Vietnam, I'm sorry, now . . . would you then be prepared to reopen negotiations for restoration of relations with that country?

MR. FORD: Let me restate uh—our policy. As long as Vietnam, North Vietnam, does not give us a full and complete accounting of our missing in action, I will never uh—go along with the admission of Vietnam to the United Nations. If they do give us a bona fide, complete uh—accounting of the eight hundred MIAs, then I believe that the United States should begin negotiations for the uh—admission of Vietnam to the United Nations. But not until they have given us the full accounting of our MIAs.

Ms. FREDERICK: Governor Carter.

MR. CARTER: One of the uh—most embarrassing uh—failures of the Ford administration, and one that touches specifically on human rights, is his refusal to appoint a presidential commission . . . to go to Vietnam, to go to Laos, to go to Cambodia and try to trade for the release of information about those who are missing in action in those wars. This is what the families of MIAs want. So far, Mr. Ford has not done it. We've had several fragmentary efforts by members of the Congress and by—by private citizens. Several months ago the Vietnam government said, "We are ready to sit down and negotiate for release of information on MIAs. So far, Mr. Ford has not responded. I would never normalize relationships with Vietnam, nor permit them to join the United Nations until they've taken this action. But that's not enough. We need to have an active and aggressive action on the part of the president, the leader of his country, to seek out every possible way to get that information which has kept the MIA families in despair and doubt, and Mr. Ford has just not done it.

Ms. FREDERICK: Thank you Governor Carter. That completes the questioning for this evening. Each candidate now has up to three minutes for a closing statement. It was determined by the toss of a coin that Governor Carter would take the first question, and he now goes first with his closing remarks. Governor Carter.

Mr. CARTER: The purpose of this debate and the outcome of the election will determine three basic things: Leadership, upholding the principles of our country, and proper priorities and commitments for the future. This election will also determine what kind of world we leave our children. Will it be a nightmare world threatened with the proliferation of atomic bombs, not just in five major countries but dozens of smaller countries that have been permitted to develop atomic weapons because of a failure of our top leadership to stop proliferation? Will we have a world of hunger and—and hatred, and will we be living in an armed camp stripped of our friendship and allies . . . hiding behind a tight defense that's been drawn in around us because we are fearful of the outside world? Will we have a government of secrecy that excludes the American people from participation in making basic decisions and therefore covers up mistakes and makes it possible for our government—our government —to depart from the principles of our Constitution and Bill of Rights? Or will we have a world of peace with the threat of atomic weapons eliminated, with full trade, with our people at work, inflation controlled, openness in government, our people proud once again, Congress, citizens, president, secretary of state working in harmony and unity toward a common future? Or world where people have enough to eat and a world where we care about those who don't? Can we become a breadbasket of the world instead of the arms merchant of the world? I believe we can and we ought to. Now we've been hurt in recent years in this country. In the aftermath of Vietnam, Cambodia, Chile, Pakistan, Angola, Watergate, CIA, we've been hurt. Our people feel that we've lost something precious. That's not necessary. I wanna see our nation [rɛs]—return to a posture and an image and a standard to make us proud once again. I remember the world with NATO, and the world of Point Four, and the world of the Marshall Plan, and the world of the Peace Corps. Why can't we have that once again? We ought to be a beacon for nations who search for peace and who search for freedom, who search for individual liberty, who search for basic human rights. We haven't been lately. We can be once again. We'll never have that world leadership until we are strong at home, and we can have that strength if we return to the basic principles. It ought not to be a strength of bombast and threats. It ought to be a quiet strength based on the integrity of our people, the vision of the Constitution, an in—innate strong will and purpose that God's given us in the greatest nation on earth—the United States.

Ms. FREDERICK: President Ford.

MR. FORD: As we have seen tonight, foreign policy and defense policy are difficult and complex issues. We can debate methods, we can debate one decision or another, but there are two uh things which cannot be debated—experience and results. In the last two years, I have made policy decisions involving long-range difficulties and policies and made day-to-day judgments . . . not only as president of the United States but as the leader of the free world. . . . What is the result of that leadership? America is strong. America is free. America is respected. Not a single young American today is fighting or dying on any foreign battlefield. America is at peace and with freedom. Thank you, and good night.

Ms. FREDERICK: Thank you, President Ford. Thank you, Governor Carter. I also want to thank our questioners and the audience here this evening. The third and final debate between President Ford and Governor Carter will take place on October the twenty-second at nine-thirty P.M. Eastern daylight time on the campus of the College of William and Mary in Williamsburg, Virginia. The subject matter will cover all issues. These debates are sponsored by the League of Women Voters Education Fund to help voters become better informed on the issues and to generate greater voter turnout in the November election. Now, from the Palace of Fine Arts Theater in San Francisco, good night.

The Vice-Presidential Debate
Alley Theater, Houston
October 15, 1976, 9:00 p.m.

MR. HOGE: Good evening, I'm James Hoge, editor of the *Chicago Sun Times*, and moderator of this third of the historic debates of the 1976 campaign. Tonight we have the vice-presidential candidates: for the Democrats, Senator Walter Mondale of Minnesota; for the Republicans, Senator Robert Dole of Kansas. Thank you, Senator Mondale, and thank you, Senator Dole, for being with us this evening. This debate is taking place before an audience in the Alley Theater in Houston, Texas. It is also being broadcast by radio and television to an audience estimated at some eighty-five million persons in this nation and overseas. As far as we can tell this is the first formal debate ever held between vice-presidential candidates. Their views are important not only because they seek the second highest office in the land, but because as potential vice presidents, they must be judged on their capacities to serve as president of the United States. For example, of the last five presidents, three have become president due to death, or resignation, by a chief executive. We will begin this debate tonight with opening statements of up to two minutes by each candidate. By the toss of a coin it was determined that Senator Dole would go first. Senator Dole, your opening statement.

MR. DOLE: Thank you very much. First, I wish to thank the League of Women Voters, and this is a great privilege and honor for me. I also wanna thank my many friends in Russell, Kansas, for that big long telegram I received today. I think tonight may be sort of a fun evening. It's a very important evening; it's a very historic evening. But I've known ah my counterpart for some time, and we've been friends and we're—we'll be friends when this debate is over and we'll be friends when the election is over and he'll still be in the Senate. (laughter) And . . . I think first of all I should make it very clear that I'm . . . most proud to be on the ticket with President Ford. I've known President Ford for sixteen years—sixteen years. It's a long time. He's known me for that long. I know him to be a man of compassion and competence. He has that confidence . . . and he projects that leadership that America needs and that you need right now. Now, I don't know much about uh—Governor Carter. I've tried to find out. I know he's very ambitious. I know he wants to be president. He's been running for three years. But I know he said uh—at least one thing—that he does agree with my opponent, my friend, uh—Walter Mondale, probably the most liberal senator in the United States Senate. And that's really what this debate's all about. If by some uh—tragic circumstance one of us should become president of the United States, where do we stand on the issues? I would just say in a very uh—summary way that I have a great deal of faith in you, the American people. I'm concerned about farmers and housewives and young people and professional people, working men and women. I think we can find our solutions working together. My opponent has a record of voting for ever—every inflationary spending program except in defense, where he votes for every cut. And we'll explore that as this debate goes on.

MR. HOGE: Thank you, Senator Dole. Senator Mondale, your opening statement.

MR. MONDALE: I believe that most Americans would agree on the problems that this country faces and that the next—and which the next administration must solve. They include the need once again for an economy that works. The economy today is in very, very bad shape—the highest unemployment since the Great Depression, 50 percent higher than when Mr. Ford took office; raging inflation, with the latest uh—wholesale price indexes once again su—raising the specter of double-digit inflation. The purchasing power of the average American has slipped so much that it is now the equivalent of the purchasing power in 1965. It is not getting better. It is getting worse. All the leading indicators now point downward, and stock investors are now losing confidence and over $50 billion of value has disappeared from the stock market in less than a month. We need a government that works, and we need a government that cares, and once again we have to get back to work on education, on health, on housing, on the environment, on energy; and we need a foreign policy that once again reflects the values and the beliefs of the American people. This will take leadership, and we need leadership, too. The Republican administration, the Republican party has had eight years to solve these problems. All of them have gotten worse. The Republican ticket does not offer new plans for their solution but is engaged in a frantic effort to defend the past. This nation desperately needs new leadership. The Carter-Mondale ticket would offer a new generation of leadership dedicated to solu—to solving the problems which I have listed, and that is the basis of our appeal.

MR. HOGE: Thank you gentlemen. The subject matter of tonight's debate, like that of the first two presidential debates, covers domestic and economic policies, and foreign and defense issues. The questioners tonight are Hal Bruno, chief political correspondent of *Newsweek* magazine; Marilyn Berger, White House correspondent of NBC News; and Walter Mears, special correspondent for the Associated Press. Questions will be alternated between the two candidates. After a question is asked, the candidate will have up to two and a half minutes to respond. His opponent will then have two and a half minutes to reply to that. The first candidate then may reply to those remarks for up to one minute. I should mention at this point that I will intervene if a candidate is not addressing the question which has been posed to him. At the conclusion of the questioning, each candidate will be allowed up to three minutes for a closing remark. Senator Mondale and Senator Dole do not have prepared notes or comments with them this evening. However, they may make notes and refer to them during the debate. We now begin with questions on domestic and economic policies. The first question goes to Senator Dole, as was determined by the coin toss. Mr. Bruno, you have the first question.

MR. BRUNO: Uh—Senator Dole, presidential candidates uh—always promise that their vice president will play an important role. But it seldom turns out that way and they usually wind up uh—as standby equipment, which is the way Vice President Rockefeller once described the job. What's your view of this office that you're seeking? Has President Ford told you what your role might be, and what would you like it to be?

MR. DOLE: Well, I've said, as I've traveled around the country, in—mostly in jest, that [ɛsɛ]*—why you are running for vice president, I said, well, it's

*Probably "they say."

indoor work and no heavy lifting. (laughter) But . . . I've also thought very seriously about it. President Ford has discussed it with me. It's a great opportunity. It's a great responsibility. I can't stand here tonight uh—in Houston, Texas, and say that come uh—January when I'll be sworn in as vice president that I'm gonna do anything in the first hundred days, or even the second hundred days. But I have discussed it with President Ford. He's indicated two uh—responsibilities that he's going to designate. One will be having some role in increasing our agricultural exports, because we believe—we believe together—that the future of American agriculture lies in its exports. Also, because of my long association with families who had uh—their sons or husbands as missing in action and prisoners of war—he indicated to me last week that I would have a role as his representative—try to get some accounting for the missing in action in Southeast Asia. But beyond that, of course, our constitutional duty is to preside over the Senate, and vote in case of a tie. We also serve on the National Security Council, Domestic Council, and whatever other assignments we may have from time to time. I think probably one important aspect that we ought to talk about—and that's our vision of America. I believe the people viewing tonight—people who watching us tonight—may well determine the role I play as vice president. I believe that we're going forward in America under the leadership of President Ford, and I believe there'll be more and more challenges, positive challenges, to those of us who hold high office, to serve the American people. And that's really what it's all about: whether we're vice president, on the city council, member of the legislature, or whatever. Our obligation is to the people. We must have faith in the American people—and I have that faith. But I think the opponents have more faith in bigger government, more controls and more interference with their everyday lives.

Mr. Hoge: Senator Mondale, your response.

Mr. Mondale: The problems that our country faces are so great that a very strong role is required of the vice president and of all federal officials. I've discussed this matter—uh extensively with Governor Carter and as vice president I would have such a substantial role in both domestic and foreign policy. I would work with the president, for example, in this long overdue effort to basically restructure and reorganize the federal government. Today it's a mess. There's no one in charge. There's great waste, great duplication, and the time has come for a long overdue reorganization. That would be one of the first tasks that I would have working with the new president. There would be a whole range of duties that I would have working with the president and uh—on problems of economic growth, we got to get people back to work, attacking inflation and finally getting a policy to—to keep the dollar worth a dollar, and the other problems that we face here at home. One of the specific suggestions that uh—we are considering now is that I would head up the task force to deal with the federal aspects of crime in America. Today, the federal function in law enforcement is in disarray. The Drug Enforcement Ad—Administration is totally demoralized. The FBI is also under great difficulty. We need to have a coordinated, effective, and national attack on organized and hard crime, those crimes prohibited by federal law. We need to finally get a national effort that really makes sense, that stops the importation of those death-dealing imported illegal drugs. We need to have a new look at official lawlessness at the federal level, because we've seen too many instances where people in high public office —uh violate the law themselves. And one of the things that we're considering is establishing an interdepartmental agency under the chairmanship of the vice president to finally, at long last, put some strength behind a national effort to deal with these uh—terrible problems in American life. And may I close by saying that uh—one of the reasons that I believe I am gonna be the vice president, is one of the reasons that uh—my opponent mentioned, and that is the present president imposed an embargo on farm exports four times in three years, and they want a change.

MR. HOGE: Senator Dole, do you have a further comment?

MR. DOLE: Well, I would just say to my good friend, uh—I'm happy that you're going to be responsible uh—for reorganization. I hope you don't pattern it after Governor Carter's efforts in Georgia. They added more bureaucrats to the government in Georgia, the cost of government went up, his Human Resources uh—Committee or whatever it's called was called an organizational nightmare by Governor Buzzy—Busbee, his successor. I understand from Bobby Smith, who's supposed to be the ag expert in the Carter campaign, that you're gon' do 'way* with the Department of Agriculture. That's in essence what he said. You're gonna put it together with a lot of other things. And I know the farmers who may be viewing will be pleased to know that. They should also be pleased to know that uh—Senator Mondale—uh sponsors export licensing proposals in the Congress, which would make it necessary for farmers to get an export license before they could ship their goods overseas. And under his proposal—which is still pending, thank goodness it hasn't passed, we'd all be in difficulty—we wouldn't be able to ship anything out.

MR. HOGE: Miss Berger, your question to Senator Mondale.

MS. BERGER: Senator Mondale, the polls indicate that less than half of those eligible will vote in this coming election. And although you and Senator Dole have both touched on the very important issues that are before the country, many Americans feel that they're being shortchanged by a campaign that has descended into a name-calling contest. For example, Governor Carter has said that President Ford has been brainwashed; President Ford says that Carter is slandering America. If the tone of the campaign worries the electorate, does it worry you, Senator Mondale?

MR. MONDALE: There are many things that I think have contributed to this phenomenon that I find very, very discouraging. And that is, the great numbers of Americans do not plan to participate in the electoral process which is so crucial to uh—a sound and effective nation. We can't solve our problems unless everyone helps. There've been so many things that have dispirited the American people, that have fed frustration and despair. We've gone through the worst war in American history, that divided this country perhaps just as much it's ever been divided. [u] We then went through the worst political scandal in American history, with the highest officers in government being found guilty or at least charged with guilt in very serious crimes. We then saw evidence that even our own intelligence agencies and law enforcement agencies, charged to enforce the law, had themselves violated the law. And then we've seen a government that

*He actually said [ju ɡʌn du weɪ wɪə] for "you are going to do away with."

is unable to deal with the real problems that the American people face. People need jobs. It's a tragedy every time an able-bodied American is denied the opportunity to make—to work. There are now eight million Americans who can't find work. It's a tragedy when Americans work and find the value of their dollar disappearing. It's a tragedy when children can't get educated, when health care wipes them out, when senior citizens find that the attention and the credit they're entitled to—through Social Security and Medicaid—is being taken from them. These things have all contributed to a growing feeling in America that government does not respond to solve people's problems, that government lives by one standard and expects Americans to live by another, and because of that we have this large feeling in America, reflected in those surveys that were suggested in your question, that has contributed to this feeling that involvement in politics does not count. And if there's one hope that Governor Carter and I have, if there's one objective that's central above all, is that we can restore the faith in the American people by simply telling the truth, obeying the law, seeing problems as they really are, attacking the real questions, the real problems that fect—affect Americans, and then I think we will see the restoration of public trust.

MR. HOGE: Senator Dole, your response.

MR. DOLE: Well I think it's a very good question. It goes back to the party institutions. Uh—maybe it's uh—an indictment uh—in that sense of uh—those of us who seek office. It goes back to my basic premise—and that's faith in the people. It just seems to me that some of those who lust for power are not really concerned about the people. They say they're concerned, and they talk about the people. They never give us [u] their positions. And so I think many Americans are sort of turned off, and they were turned off by the war in Southeast Asia. They were turned off by Watergate—I'll say that word first—they were turned off by Watergate. But we're looking ahead. They were probably turned off by what they saw in U.S. House of Representatives. They've been turned off by a lot of things they've seen in politics. But I think they've been turned off too by promises and promises, and bigger and bigger spending programs, and more and more inflation. They're looking for leadership. They yearn for leadership and they found that leadership in President Ford. And Governor Carter talks about tax reform, talks about taxing the rich. He talks about nearly everyone. He said former president Johnson lied and cheated and distorted the facts. I think that turns a lot of people off. He was quick to apologize to Mrs. Johnson. He insulted Governor Wallace, but he was quick to apologize to Governor Wallace. Someone in the family insulted Billy Graham but they were quick to apologize to Billy Graham. I think it's time we stopped uh—apologizing and talked—it's time we started talking to you, the American people. We need your help. We wanna restore faith in this system and I think we can. Let's not promise what we can't deliver. Let's uh—be honest with you, the voter, with you the taxpayer. It's fine to talk about education, more this, more that, and more that. But there're eighty-eight million people working in America . . . that are gonna pay the taxes—the highest number every* working in America—some 40 percent of the population, the highest in history, working now in America. And

*Probably meant to say "ever."

THE GREAT DEBATES

we're concerned about the 7.8 percent unemployed. We'll be concerned until that's reduced to 4 percent or 3 percent or wherever. But we can't lose sight of the number one enemy, and that number one en—enemy is inflation. And I think the American people are coming around—they're beginning to understand that President Ford says what he means and does what he says.

MR. HOGE: Senator Mondale.

MR. MONDALE: Well, who really has faith in the people? A candidate like Governor Carter, who campaigns for the people, is out every day meeting and talking with the people, holds news conferences and answers questions of the —of the news media as he has every day for twenty-four months, or a president who's in the White House, not through election but through appointment, who has held only two preannounced news conferences since February? Who trusts the people more—Governor Carter and Senator Mondale, who have disclosed our income-tax returns so the American people can look at our private financial affairs and determine [hɔɑ] how we conducted our affairs, or President Ford and Senator Dole, who refuse to let the American people see their tax returns? Who trusts the people? A candidate like Governor Carter, who tells the truth, or a president like Mr. Ford, who last week told the American people that he had fought the Arab boycott and sought legislation and sanctions against it when the whole record shows he's proc—proceeded in just the opposite direction?

MR. HOGE: Thank you. Mr. Mears, your question for Senator Dole.

MR. MEARS: Senator Dole, prior to your current campaign you sometimes expressed concern about a negative image of the Republican party. You're quoted as having said last spring that, "We're in the unfortunate position of having a president vetoing bills and getting on the wrong side of people issues. He's vetoed the education bill, the jobs bill, you name it." Are you still concerned about the risk that Republicans will be perceived as opposed to what you call vet—uh—"people issues" and do you think that President Ford has exercised the veto too frequently?

MR. DOLE: Well, I might say at the outset I haven't always agreed with President Ford and I've voted to override on occasion—but not every time, as my counterpart has. I think President Ford uh—and hindsight's very good, particularly when you're on the ticket. And my hindsight is, the president's been very courageous. And there is a difference. You know, we look at our states and we look at the bills and we decide to sustain or override. The president—and particularly this president, who has courage—President Ford looks at the nation; he looks at all the American people, and he makes that judgment: Should I sign, can I sign, or must I veto this bill? And so he's vetoed sixty-two bills—I think the sixty-second happened today. And I say that's uh—a courageous act repeated sixty-two times, because much of that legislation sounded good, some of it was good [ʌ] some of it we just couldn't have unless we're gonna fuel the fires of inflation. I don't suggest that every veto uh—I must agree with. But I also suggest that I'm a Republican. I'm proud to be a Republican. We're sometimes perceived, as I've said before, as the antipeople party because we're not for more spending. We're not for more government; we're for a strong defense. We're for peace in the world. Those aren't very attractive to some people. They wanna know how much we're gonna spend for this, and how much we're gonna spend for that. Well Senator Mondale could tell 'em that because he votes for every piece of spending legislation that comes down the pike . . . unless it's in the area of defense, and then he votes for every budget cut. I think he's voted to cut the budget—in addition to what had already been cut in the Congress—some $16 billion: against the B-1 bomber, which means a lot of jobs, against the C5-A, against the Trident submarine. And the list goes on and on and on and on. I believe the American people want us to be responsible. We've got to make the tough decisions. It's one thing to be in the office of the president or a senator of the United States and vote for every spending program, never concern ourselves with inflation or the total cost. But I would only close by saying that I hope the viewers remember . . . we had a Democratic Congress, we've had one for twenty-two straight years. And so if anyone stands up to debate this Republican senator and tries to dump all the responsibility on a Republican president by the name of Gerald Ford, I'd just ask that question: Where have you been for twenty-two years?

MR. HOGE: Senator Mondale, your response.

MR. MONDALE: Perhaps the most pronounced difference that ref—separates the Democratic and the Republican candidates is reflected in the question that was just asked. There is practically no difference between the two parties in terms of how much they would spend. The Senate Budget Committee estimated that the Republican platform cost $50 billion, the Democratic platform cost $40 billion. The difference between the Democratic Congressional budget which I supported and the [rıp]—and the president's budget was only $3 billion in deficit, and if you removed the gimmickry in the president's budget it was exactly the same. The difference is in how we spend those resources. And I am unashamed of my support for programs to put people back to work. I am unashamed of my support for programs to build housing so the families of this country can live in decent housing. I'm unashamed of supporting education programs that give our kids a decent education. I'm unashamed of supporting health programs that give people who get ill a chance to have decent health without being totally wiped out. And I'm unashamed of supporting programs such as Medicare. My opponent voted against Medicare. Can you imagine voting against program, as did the president, that would provide help for senior citizens after they're past their earning years so that they could have decent health care without being wiped out? Now, where do the Republicans want to spend their money? Well, I'll tell you. First of all, this year they're spending $55 billion in the cost of the recession that they created. We didn't give 'em this recession. We had full employment when they took over. Mr. Ford, in just two years, has increased unemployment by two and a half million Americans. They haven't solved inflation and they—and instead of trying to deal with the problem of unemployment, instead of that they proposed a $20 billion tax cut for wealthy corporations, despite the fact that just yesterday a newspaper carried a story that ten major corporations made massive amounts of money and didn't owe a dime in federal taxes. Ford Motor Corporation earned $800 million and didn't owe a dime to the federal government; in fact, got a hundred and eighty million dollars back. So between those tax cuts and between the massive costs of unemployment, they spend much more than we would. But what do they get for it? We wanna see money spent to help problems that people really face in their lives.

MR. HOGE: Senator Dole.

MR. DOLE: Well, we're all for those programs. Uh—but it's uh—we just don't believe in excesses. I think in retrospect uh—the elder-care program that I voted for instead of Medicare is probably a better program because Medicare, everybody gets the benefits, whether you're in need or not, once you reach the age of sixty-five. Now they're having a lot of problems in Medicare. I'm glad you mentioned Ford Motor Company not paying taxes. Again the Democrats control the committee. I'm on the committee. Senator Mondale's on the Finance Committee. Henry Ford happens to be supporting Governor Carter, maybe that's why. Governor Carter did have a little meeting with him at the Twenty-One Club, had some small businessmen there, said don't worry about taxes, I won't be doing anything for at least a year. That's after he said the tax system was a disgrace. We have peace in this country today. That's important to me—important to mothers who may be listening. They talk about their full employment when we took over—that's because they had a full-grown war in Southeast Asia. That's not the way we try to end unemployment in the Republican party.

MR. HOGE: Mr. Bruno, your question to Senator Mondale.

MR. BRUNO: Uh—Senator Mondale, uh—everyone seems to agree that solving the economic problems of inflation and unemployment has to be given top priority. Uh—you and Governor Carter have a whole shopping list of things that you wanna do. After [ʌnǝ] after the ec—economic problem, what do you see as the next most urgent and crucial domestic problems? In what order of importance would you go to work on such problems as the decay and bankruptcy of the cities, uh—tax reform, health insurance, uh—help for the poor and the elderly—in short, after the economy, what would be the very specific priorities of a Carter administration?

MR. MONDALE: You have to work on several problems at once, because they all demand the attention of the American people. One of the key problems would be to try to finally get a health insurance program to deal with the health crisis in America. In just the past two years, health costs in America have risen in the cities by over 25 percent. We have to do something about that. There's no hope under the ad—Republican administration. Mr. Ford said he vet—he would veto any legislation if we sent it. We have to do something about housing. We're in a housing depression. Today, nearly 20 percent of the building tradesmen in America are unemployed. We need to put them back to work—to build housing that Americans need. We need to continue to—to build support, as the budget permits, for education. We need to—to get back to work on the problems of senior citizens. Now, all of this has to be done prudently, within a budget, and within the constraints that our resources permit; but once we put people back to work, once we end this recession—which we will do—even the president's own estimates indicates that we will have somewhere between sixty and seventy billion dollars of increased revenues on existing tax rates just from economic growth which we can use to work on these programs. Then we'll have tax reform, and I wanna deal with this problem just a moment. Mr. Dole has probably the worst record in favor of loopholes of any senator in the United States Senate. Mr. Ford has one of the worst records in favor of tax loopholes in the history of the House of Representatives. I have one of the best records of tax reform in the United States Senate, and it—I find it very peculiar to find two people who spent their congressional careers trying to block tax reform that permits very wealthy Americans to avoid most of their taxes to suddenly complain when the Congress hadn't passed the kind of legislation that we're talking about. What we're basically talking about is presidential leadership. We need leadership in the presidency to help support those of us in the Congress that have been pushing for tax reform and then we will have it. It is now possible for people of great wealth, by using complete tax fictions, to avoid all or most their taxes. But most Americans listening to me tonight could hire the best tax lawyer in America and you couldn't save a dime. There are no loopholes for you.

MR. HOGE: Senator Dole, your response.

MR. DOLE: W'I* think Senator Mondale is a little nervous, but uh—time I think of loophole, I think of Governor Carter. I don't know why it comes to me, but uh—uh—I remember his '75 tax return—you've probably seen it, since it's public. His tax liability was $58 thousand. Not many Americans—I don't imagine many of you in the viewing audience—uh had to worry about a $58 thousand tax bill. I didn't. But Governor Carter did . . . until he took off $41 thousand. That's called the investment tax credit—he bought some peanut machinery—gonna use it next year. So he took $41 thousand off his tax and sent the government a check for $17 thousand. So how much did he pay on his income? Well, he paid about twelve point eight percent. This that same man, that same Governor Carter who runs around the country talking about tax reform, loopholes, and the rich. I don't know who uh—rates uh—Senator Mondale on the Finance Committee. I don't know how they rated him on the Honeywell amendment he offered and the IDS amendment he offered. They never passed, they never got out of the Senate. They're both special interest amendments. That's all right, because those were his amendments. I don't know where Governor Carter's corporate returns are and partnership returns—I haven't seen those published anywhere. But I know about his tax reform. I wanna get back to the question, if that's all right. We're talking about the economy. What are we go'n† do after the economy's taken care of? Well, I don't know, it's occurred to me, and I'm certain it hasn't occurred to my counterpart—we might—it's not illegal, to take some of that surplus and apply it to the national debt. We've never done it, but we wouldn't be put in jail if Congress voted to try to retire some of that debt, to take some of the pressure off the American working man, and the American working woman. And I get a little tired of Governor Carter's antibusiness attitude. I know they get great support, monetary support, from George Meany. In fact I've been suggesting that George Meany was probably Senator Mondale's makeup man—he may or may not have been, they did a good job. (laughter from audience) But I think it's time the American people understand that this [n] a very serious election; and we got a tough choice to

*[wəaɪ]
†"going" was pronounced as [gʌn].

make. Governor Carter talks about raising everyone's taxes above the median income. He didn't know what the median income was, of course. It's $14 thousand per American family, that's what it is. So I say, take a look and you'll vote for Ford.

Mr. Hoge: Senator Mondale.

Mr. Mondale: The question was, what would we do to deal with the human problems in America? The first thing we would do is to put people back to work. The most atrocious result of the Republican policy is massive unemployment. It costs us $50 billion this year. Secondly, we will fight inflation. Today, inflation is three times worse than it was under the Democrats. And the latest indexes indicate that it's back on its way up. No effort to fight this at all. We will have tax reform. There's no question about our commitment to tax reform. My record proves it. Governor Carter's uh—positions prove that. We are fully committed to tax reform, and when the Republicans are raising money around the country, they say give us some money to defeat Governor Carter because if he gets elected there'll be a tax reform. And they are right when they say that, because we'll have tax reform and bring relief to the average income earner in this country. They know what Governor Carter is talking about. He's talking about the loopholes that favor Americans, usually earning above $50 thousand a year.

Mr. Hoge: Thank you, Senator Mondale. We now turn to questions on foreign and defense issues. Miss Berger, you have the first question in this subject area and it is for Senator Dole.

Miss Berger: Senator Dole, President Ford said in an interview this week that if he's elected he would like to see Henry Kissinger stay on as secretary of state. This hardly seems to square with the Republican platform which appears to repudiate much of Kissinger's foreign policy. Which way do you go, Senator Dole, with President Ford or with the Republican platform?

Mr. Dole: I go with both and stay with Henry. Uhh—you know if you look back over history, uh—President Washington had Thomas Jefferson for his secretary of state, uh—Harry Truman had Dean Acheson for his secretary of state, both very strong men, both very active men, both very powerful men. Henry Kissinger is a powerful man. And I haven't always agreed with Heny— Henry Kissinger but I—when I start disagreeing with Henry I start looking at what he's done for America—uh what he's done for the free world. I think about the breakthrough in China. I think about our increased responsive relations with—with the Soviet Union. I think about winding down the war that we inherited from another Democrat administration in Southeast Asia. I think most recently about his efforts in South Africa, where he's trying to protect the rights of the majority and the rights of the minority. [ju nə]* we sort of thought that Henry might'a had a role to play in grain embargoes, so we weren't totally happy at that time. We're not happy with embargoes; there'll not be any more embargoes except in extreme circumstances under a Ford-Dole Administration. So I agree with the president. Uh Secretary Kissinger's performed yeoman service. Anywhere you look you find Henry's tracks and they're tracks that are right for America. They're tracks that are right for the free world. And I

*Probably "you know."

wonder how many mothers and how many fathers and how many young men
. . . and young women who may be viewing tonight . . . have really stopped to
think about what this Republican administration has done. No one's being
drafted; no one's going off to war; no one's being shot at; no one's being hos-
pitalized; no one's being buried in America; not a single shot being fired in
anger. And this is a Republican administration, this is a Republican policy.
And this policy by and large has been spearheaded by one Henry Kissinger.
And we have our differences. And I looked at the platform—I was on the Platform Committee. I don't see any contradiction on that platform. I've read the
morality section. I think it sustains President Ford, and sucksta—sustains Henry
Kissinger.

MR. HOGE: Senator Mondale, your response.

MR. MONDALE: The real question of the foreign policy of the next administration is the responsibility of the president of the United States. He is the
person elected to discharge the responsibility of foreign policy. He is the person
that must conduct it and lead this nation's efforts. And that's where I think the
key difference between the two parties lie. We want a change. We want new
leadership. And above all we want a change of philosophy and direction.
America's greatest strength is to be found in its values and its beliefs. And
every time in our pursuit of foreign policy that we disregard those basic values,
of freedom, of democracy, of national independence, we pursue a policy that
is not credible, is not sustainable, either overseas or at home. Now let me say
what I mean. For example, in Africa, for seven and a half years it was the
policy of this administration to support the colonial control of black Africa and
support white minority rule in majority black states. That was our explicit
policy. And after that failed, and on the eve of this election, suddenly we've
turned around and wanted to be believed as we pursued the policy that we
should'a pursued in the first place. Failure to follow our beliefs in the first instance is causing us great trouble in Africa. Look at Greece. During the
whole period that the military junta controlled Greek government, this administration cozied up to that military dictatorship, befriended them, did everything they could to support them, but once Greek restored their own democracy,
we've turned our back on them and have not assisted them in seeking a just and
final settlement on the island of Cyprus. Take the issue of the Middle East. This
government of ours is pursuing a policy of permitting the vicious Arab boycott
to continue in this country. They have not sought any reform. They are pursuing an arms-peddling policy in this world which—in which we s—sell more
arms by double of all the rest of the world put together. And last year alone,
or this year, we're selling and contracting for seven and a half billion dollars
of arms for Saudi Arabia and only a billion four for Israel. We've lost our way.
We need a new sense of values, and we intend to restore them.

MR. HOGE: Senator Dole.

MR. DOLE: Well, I noticed in all that discussion he never once [ɛ] criticized
Secretary Kissinger; I don't recall Senator Mondale ever criticizing Secretary
Kissinger. As I think back uh—the Democrat policies that—and their secret
agreements at Yalta and Potsdam and how this had the effect of enslaving
Eastern Europe, and as I think of uh—the leadership of President Roosevelt—

THE GREAT DEBATES

and I think about that every day because of a personal experience in World War II—I'm kind of thankful we have somebody who's concerned about peace. And whether Senator Mondale likes it or not, or whether Governor Carter likes it or not—and Governor Carter won't tell us who he's gonna to put in the cabinet. He probably doesn't know—I think it's kinna nice to be at peace in the world, to be respected in the world. We've had more respect than we've ever had. Prime Minister Rabin said our relations to [1:]—Israel are at a peak, the highest they've been. The same is true of France and West Germany. We have a balanced peace in the Mideast because of our leadership.

MR. HOGE: Mr. Mears, your question to Senator Mondale.

MR. MEARS: Senator Mondale, you and Governor Carter have made an issue of President Ford's statement that there is no Soviet domination of Eastern Europe—a statement the president now says was in error. I'd like to know whether there's any real difference between the two tickets on Eastern Europe or whether this is simply an effort by the Democrats to attract voters of Eastern European backgrounds. What would a Democratic administration do that the Republicans are not doing to foster freedom in Eastern Europe? And what would a new administration do on the question that the president declined to answer yesterday? If an Eastern European nation attempted to overthrow Soviet domination, should the United States help?

MR. MONDALE: Well, there're several things we would do. The first thing we would do was—is to make clear consistently what the facts are in Eastern Europe. The comment that the president made that Eastern Europe was independent and aut—autonomous from Soviet control is probably one of the most outrageous statements made by a president in recent political history. It's caused great confusion in Europe. Communist newspapers in Poland are praising the president because the statement helped give credibility to Soviet control. I'm glad the president finally apologized for that remark, but it's surprising that it took six days and several attempts before we finally received that apology. What we think is needed in our policies with Eastern Europe is not to deal with Eastern Europe as a bloc as does this administration, but to deal with each country individually on its own status directly and not through the Soviet Union; to continue to identify with their aspirations for national independence, not because we are any—under any illusions about how easy it would be for them to become independent, but because it's important for us to identify as the nation which above all stands for freedom and independence with the aspirations of all people around the world for those same objectives. Secondly, we would push the—that part of the Helsinki accords known as Basket Three, which requires . . . much opening up—much more opening up in people-to-people contacts and informational contacts. This administration signed the Helsinki accords but don—has done practically nothing to push those agreements which would open up communications between our nation and our peoples and the peoples of Eastern Europe and the Soviet Union. As a matter of fact it was just the other day, after several weeks delay, before they even finally appointed ahh—representatives of the administration to the commission looking into the enforcement of that provision. And finally, I think it's important that we honor people from Eastern Europe who stand as symbols of the human spirit's ability to stand up to police oppression. And I will never understand why this president of the United States refused to even receive and honor Mr. Solzhenitsyn,* who perhaps above all people in the human race stands as a symbol for the ability and the strength of spirit against police oppression.

MR. HOGE: Senator Dole, your response.

MR. DOLE: Well, I'm glad you mentioned Solzhenitsyn. I checked today with his interpreter and I understand you've never met Mr. Solzhenitsyn, and neither has Mr. Carter. Now I've had the privilege of meeting uh—uh—Mr. Solzhenitsyn—maybe you've shook his hand somewhere—but uh—I want to move into the Eastern Europe sector. I'm reminded of how the Berlin Wall went up and who was in power when it went up. I think if we take a hard look at President Ford's record . . . rather than all the rhetoric that followed uh—a mistake in the last debate about uh Poland, uh we'd know very clearly where President Ford not only stands but has stood for twenty some years. . . . I think one way to let the people in Eastern Europe know of our concern is by trade. As President Ford said, they've never really given up hope. Their government may be dominated, their leaders of that government may be dominated by Soviet Russia, but the hearts and the minds of the Polish people, or the Yugoslavs or Rumanians, or the Czechs, or whoever, have never been dominated. And they're good customers. You know we have a favorable balance of trade with Eastern Europe. I think last year they exported almost a half-billion dollars' worth of goods and material and we sent in about a billion dollars' worth. I just wish Governor Carter had a foreign policy. He doesn't have any—doesn't have any experience. He made some statement about Italy that bothers me because I was in World War II in Italy. My whole life changed because of my experience in Italy. I know the Italian people. I know they're God-fearing, freedom-loving people. I couldn't quite understand what Governor Carter meant in *Playboy* magazine. I couldn't understand frankly why he was in *Playboy* magazine. But he was, and we'll give him the bunny vote. But I couldn't understand what he meant when he said that we ought to extend the hand of friendship to Communists in Portugal and governments of France and Italy, because by doing that he simply invites . . . difficulty from Communist leaders in those countries. So I say, oh we're strong, we're firm, President Ford understands, we're still at peace, we still have those same hopes and aspirations of the Eastern Europeans. And that's what it's all about: freedom, peace, no bloodshed.

MR. HOGE: Senator Mondale.

MR. MONDALE: Well, I regret that uh—Mr. Dole made that statement about Mr. Solzhenitsyn, because it's false. I've repeatedly spoken out in admiration of him. I served on the host committee receiving Mr. Solzhenitsyn in the United States Senate. He's a man that deserved to be honored and it was a shame to me that the president of the United States, because we were fearful of offending the Soviet Union, failed to accord that high honor to Mr. Solzhenitsyn. I'm also sorry that he's tried to misrepresent Governor Carter's position on the government that should control Portugal and Italy. The governor made

*Was pronounced as: [zoʊlsʊnitzn̩].

it very clear that he hoped the noncommunists would continue to control*
those countries. The biggest thing that we're doing today that is undermining
those forces of democracy is the disarray of our economy here at home. With
our tremendous unemployment, with our tremendous inflation, and the dominance of our economy on the economies of Western Europe, of Japan and
Canada, we have contri—contributed to such conditions that it has strengthened
the radical forces in those countries. And that's what we need to do to best help
the democratic forces of those nations.

MR. HOGE: Thank you, Senators. We have reserved time this evening for
questions on general subjects. The first question in this area is from Mr. Bruno,
and it is for Senator Dole.

MR. BRUNO: Senator Dole, out there in the campaign trail uh—you been
saying that a Carter-Mondale Administration would take its orders from George
Meany and the AFL-CIO. Yet Mr. Meany was among those who influenced
President Ford on the grain embargo, which you personally opposed. Now how
do you know that Mr. Meany will influence Governor Carter any more than he
already has influenced President Ford? And what, if anything, is wrong with
labor or business or farmers making their views known in the White House as
long as it's done openly and honestly?

MR. DOLE: [ɔ], I don't have any quarrel, uh—say, first of all, with anybody making their views known. I wish more businessmen would participate
in active politics. In fact, I've held up labor as an example . . . for others to
follow because they are very active. I just don't believe that uh—labor leaders,
whether it's Leonard Woodcock or George Meany or Jerry Wurf†, whoever,
ought to make a decision for thousands and millions of working men and
women who are concerned about spending; they're concerned about taxes;
they're concerned about the gun control that Mondale and Carter favor. They're
concerned about abortion. They're concerned about a lot of things, . . . and
their labor leader makes the decision, "We're gonna support the Carter-Mondale
ticket." Now, George Meany did exercise some influence on the first embargo.
I don't know how much because I wasn't privy to those meetings. He said he
did it in the name of the consumer, when he really did it in the name of
organized labor to increase the shipping subsidy at the taxpayers' expense.
Working with Mr. Gleason and the Longshoremen's Union they refused to load
the ships, and it really put the president in a very difficult spot. As I think back
of all the Democrat senators who now talking about embargoes, uh I can only
recall one who spoke out at the time, that was Senator George McGovern. He
had no allegiance and owed nothing to Mr. Meany because, as you know,
Meany didn't support him in 1972. But, all of a sudden embargoes've cropped
up as a great big issue. I know how much strength uh—labor leaders have. I
know how much they're out pushing voter registration. I know how much
they—control they have in the Democratic party. And that's their right, to
have influence, but not to take over the party. They have great influence on
Senator Mondale, always have had. He's got a 95 percent labor rating or

*"to control" spoken as: [ku kətroʊl].
†Was pronounced as: [wɜˑk].

higher, the most liberal senor—senator in the United States Senate, and that's his right. He wants to be liberal and spend your money and tax and tax and spend and spend. That's his right. He gets—when he first—he was appointed as attorney general, then appointed to the Senate. Some of us had to run for what we have. When you have had things given to you, you like to give something else to someone else. You give away your tax money back to the taxpayers. And I just think that George Meany has every right to have influence, but not domination of a great party like the Democratic party.

MR. HOGE: Senator Mondale.

MR. MONDALE: Well, there are many things that could be said about that. I might begin first with voting records. Uh—there are many organizations that uh—prepare voting records. I'm pleased to have a very high rating in small business groups, among farmer groups, a much higher rating than my opponent from—the senator from Kansas; good ratings, high ratings in housing, in health and education; good ratings from organizations dealing with economic management—and I'm pleased by that. But perhaps one that's most appropriate tonight is an independent dispassionate organization that represents the views of all Americans: conservative, liberal, moderate, and so on—called the League of Women Voters. For five years the League has prepared the list of the most crucial issues that they believe affects governmental effectiveness, that affects governmental honesty, that affects dealing with America's real problems. And I'm proud of the fact that in each of those five years the League of Women Voters has rated me one hundred percent in favor of every one of those issues that they, on an independent and a bipartisan basis, have believed to be the most important to this country. And I note in that same record that my opponent was wrong half the time. He only was there 50 percent of the time. And I noted that the president of the United States, Mr. Ford, when he was in the Congress was right only 35 percent of the time. And I think that says something about balance. We are in the mainstream of public life. We want to get along with business, we want to get along with farmers, we want to get along with labor. We think the president has to lead everyone. And that's the only way that a president can lead. This president and his running mate think they can get elected by whipping labor on the back. Well labor's got a right to participate in the public life of this country as well as anyone else. Just take the embargo, for example. I was opposed, and said so at the time, of all the embargoes: the four imposed by the Republicans and the short one imposed by members of the labor movement. I thought it was wrong in both instances. This—this particular ticket here uh—is—selects out Mr. Meany as the scapegoat. Well, you can't run this country trying to scapegoat Americans. You have to bring everybody together and have a united country working together to solve our real problems. And that's another reason why we need Governor Carter.

MR. HOGE: Senator Dole, any further response?

MR. DOLE: Well, I'd say as far as the League of Women Voters—uh concerned, you can look at that two ways—either I was wrong half the time or they were wrong half of the time. (laughter) And I think, knowing the League of Women Voters, I think I'll take my interpretation. But with reference to uh—and they—cause they—very fine, but they tend to be a little bit liberal.

Now, George Meany, he wants the right-to-work law repealed in Texas, in my state. Senator Mondale's for the repeal of right-to-work laws. He wants to force you to join a labor union. Seventy-five percent of America's working men and women don't belong to labor unions, but they will if George Meany and Governor Carter and Senator Mondale have their way. They've also got some big Proposition Fourteen out in California where organizers come on your property three hours a day and organize farmers, unionize farmers. Governor Carter's for that. I assume Senator Mondale's for that. Certainly Cesar Chavez is, and other labor leaders. I just say they ought to have influence; they shouldn't have domination. What about your national security voting record where you get a zero every year—to talk about our defense?

Mr. Hoge: Thank you. Miss Berger, your question to Senator Mondale.

Ms. Berger: Senator Mondale, you've criticized Mr. Ford for having defended Richard Nixon—that is, while Mr. Ford was vice president—and you did see in your own political career that Hubert Humphrey suffered a great deal politically by standing with Lyndon Johnson almost to the end on Vietnam. And now you've acknowledged that you have differences with Governor Carter. You've said that an important mark of national leadership is the ability to put loyalty to principle above loyalty to party, or even to the president of the United States. If push came to shove, would you put principle above loyalty to your running mate, and possibly to the president of the United States? And what issues are important enough to do that?

Mr. Mondale: The answer is, yes I would. But I would not have accepted a place as the running mate of Governor Carter if I thought that was a real possibility. We had a long talk about the problem of independence between the two—the president and the vice president. And I made it clear to him that I was not interested in serving in a role that was ceremonial, or serving in a role where if I really felt deeply about something I was prevented from saying so. I did not wanna go through that; I did not wanna give up my position in the Senate where I have that right. We agreed that that would be the relationship. And during this campaign on three separate occasions where I've agreed with Mis—disagreed with Mr. Carter, I've said so in the course of this campaign. And I think the whole issue of public trust and public faith is bound up very closely with that question. We have had so much politics-as-usual, so much political trimming, that Americans have lost faith in public leadership. For example, in Watergate, when this nation's whole system of liberty was at stake, and the Ervin Committee was established to investigate wrongdoing by the president of the United States, my opponent introduced a resolution to slam the door shut on the Ervin Committee so the people could not see and hear what was going on. In the [sɛ?]*—night of the Saturday Night Massacre, perhaps the most treacherous moment in the history of American liberty, when the high officers—Richardson and Ruckelshaus—were fired for enforcing the law, . . . fired by the president of the United States, both Mr. Ford and Mr. Dole stood up and defended Mr. Nixon. And if Mr. Nixon had gotten away with that massacre that night he would [strɑ?]—probably still be president of the United States and we would not have taught that crucial lesson that not

*Probably meant to say, "And the Saturday . . . "

even the highest officials in government can violate the law. Never again can we permit that kind of politics-above-all to dominate this country. Even today this administration is fighting all the Watergate reforms, opposed the appointment of a special prosecutor, opposed the reforms that [kʰǫ] were cried out for adoption following the revelations of the abuse of the CIA and the FBI. And with a record like that, and with all of the abuse of public faith and trust that we've been through, surely that, too, is another reason for a new generation of leadership.

MR. HOGE: Senator Dole.

MR. DOLE: Well, Watergate is a Republican problem, and I voted for the Watergate investigation. My opponent was absent—which is—we're all absent sometimes, but he's absent more than others. I think also it's well to point up that uh—I did introduce a resolution to shut off the public hearings and to get down to business and get Watergate behind us. Democrats didn't wanna do that. They were having great fun on TV every day . . . it looked for a while they didn't want to find a solution. I remember Senator Ervin's report, the chairman of the Watergate committee, and he said in that report—and I was chairman of the Republican party during the Watergate years, and I'm very proud to have been chairman. I've always said that the night Watergate happened was my night off, so can't hook me for that. But Senator Ervin said . . . had Senator Dole been in charge, there wouldn't have been a Watergate, so I don't want any rub-off from Senator Mondale's statements to want any of you people to believe that he might be suggesting that somehow President Ford or Senator Dole was in any way involved in Watergate; we were not. He brings it up all the time, he brings up the pardon all the time. He didn't bring up the fact that we tried to extend the investigation of Watergate back into other areas that were voted down along straight party lines. That's their right. They control the Senate. He didn't bring up the fact that uh—on the problems in the House uh—Democrats this year, the speaker appointed three Democrats to investigate the Democrats. Can you imagine the hue and cry in America had the Republicans done that? Why Mondale would've dropped dead. And that's the way it's been—that's the way it's been. But Watergate's our burden. We're going forward. It's behind us, and Governor Carter can talk about it, and Senator Mondale can talk about it, but beyond that I think we must say as Senator Mondale has—and I don't quarrel with him—that if there comes a time when I'm the vice president I can't agree with the president, then I must say so. I think that's fundamental. I think we're both honorable men, I think we both make that judgment. The only mystery to me is how do you know what Governor [kə]—Carter stands for? I've been trying to find out for six weeks. He has three positions on everything—that's why they're having three TV debates. (laughter) So I just suggest that uh—maybe in the time remaining Senator Mondale can tell us what his running mate stands for. The American people would like to know.

MR. HOGE: Senator Mondale.

MR. MONDALE: My candidate stands for jobs for all Americans. He stands for a government that fights inflation. He stands for tax reform and to take those revenues and reduce taxes for the average American. He stands for a program at long last to solve the high—[hɑl]—health crisis in America. He stands for—at long last, to get the housing industry back on its feet. He will

THE GREAT DEBATES

support programs to give senior citizens a decent break. He will not try, as Mr. Ford did, to put a cap on Social Security so senior citizens were robbed of their inflationary adjustments. He will not destroy the housing programs for senior citizens as this Republican administration has done. Governor Carter stands for leadership. He's gonna take charge. We need someone to lead this country. We haven't had it. Governor Carter will provide that leadership. And Governor Carter will restore to this nation a foreign policy that operates in the public and on the basis of the beliefs of the American people.

MR. HOGE: Gentlemen, we have about five minutes left for short questions and short answers. Each sequence from now on will consist only of the question, the answer and the other candidate's response. We'll drop the further response. The first question is from Mr. Mears to Senator Dole.

MR. MEARS: Senator Dole, ten days ago when Senator Mondale raised the issues of Watergate and the Nixon pardon, you called it the start of a campaign mud-slinging. Two years ago when you were running for the Senate you said that the pardon was prematurely granted and that it was a—and that it was a mistake. You were quoted by the *Kansas City Times* as saying, "You can't ignore our tradition of equal application of the law." Did you approve of the Nixon pardon when President Ford granted it? Do you approve of it now, and if the issue was fair game in your 1974 campaign in Kansas, why is it not an appropriate topic now?

MR. DOLE: Well it—(cough) [ɪ:] it is an appropriate topic, I guess, but it's not a very good issue any more than the war in Vietnam would be or World War II, or World War I, or the war in Korea, all Democrat wars, all in this century. I figured up the other day, if we added up the killed and wounded in Democrat wars in this century, it'd be about one point six million Americans —enough to fill the city of Detroit. Now if we wanna go back and rake that over and over and over, we can do that. I assume Senator Mondale doesn't want to do that. But it seems to me that the pardon of Richard Nixon is behind us, Watergate's behind us. If we have this vision for American, if we're really concerned about those people out there and their problems, yes, and their education and their jobs, we ought to be talking about that. I know it strikes a responsive chord in some to kick Richard Nixon around. I don't know how long you can keep that up. How much mileage is there in someone who's been kicked, whose wife suffered a serious stroke, who's been disgraced in office and stepped down from that office, and I think after two years and some months that it's probably a dead issue. But let 'em play that game. That's the only game they know.

MR. HOGE: Senator Mondale.

MR. MONDALE: I think uh—Senator Dole has richly earned his reputation as a hatchet man tonight, by implying, and stating, that World War II and the Korean War were Democratic wars. Does he really mean to suggest to the American people that there was a partisan difference over our involvement in the war to fight Nazi Germany? I don't think any reasonable American would accept that. Does he really mean to suggest that it was only partisanship that got us into the war in Korea? Does he really mean to forget that part of the record where Mr. Nixon and the Republican party wanted us to get involved earlier in the war in Vietnam, and long after Mr. Nixon and the Republican party promised to finish the war in Vietnam, they kept urging us forward, and that in fact it was the Democratic Congress that passed the law ending the war in Vietnam and preventing a new war in Angola? Now, on Watergate, we're not charging, and he knows it, his involvement in Watergate. What we're saying is that they defended Mr. Nixon up to the last.

MR. HOGE: Mr. Bruno, your question to Senator Mondale.

MR. BRUNO: Senator Mondale, uh—you cited the priorities of a Carter administration. At the same time Governor Carter has promised to balance the federal budget within four years. Now can we take just one of those items that you gave very high priority to that would be very costly, uh—national health insurance? Now, realistically, what are the chances of getting this program in a Carter-Mondale administration, or would it have to be postponed until the budget is balanced? Which comes first?

MR. MONDALE: Well, I think both the presidential budget and our estimates agree that if we move back to full employment, as we intend to do, and achieve a five and a half percent real growth rate, as we did under Truman, and as we did under Kennedy and Johnson, that within four years the revenues generated by that growth, without increasing taxes, will pay for the costs of the programs now in place, such as Social Security, pensions and the rest, the ongoing programs that are essential in America—the defense program and the rest—and that we will have a full employment yield of somewhere between seventy and eighty billions of dollars. Some of that could be used for tax relief and it should be. Some of it should be, however, used for programs that at long last start dealing with the real problems that America faces, such as health care. Now, there are many different versions of health care; but we would work closely with Senator Kennedy, with Paul Rogers and ev—others to develop a health program. Now there's no question about the difference in spending. The Republicans would spend more than we do during that same period, but they would spend it first by $20 billion in tax relief for wealthy businessmen or wealthy corporations, and secondly by the continuation of these economic policies that are costing us over $50 billion a year. So the question is not spending, the question is the priorities.

MR. HOGE: Senator Dole.

MR. DOLE: Well, I would remind uh—those who may be still tuned in that the Democrats still control the Congress. They did when we started this debate an hour and twenty minutes ago; they still do . . . by two-to-one margins almost, and they're responsible for legislation. I know Senator Long, who's the chairman of our finance committee, be very pleased to learn what Senator Mondale is gonna do now with Governor Carter. Now if they're talking about full employment they're talking about the Humphrey-Hawkins bill, which they support. We don't know what it costs—twenty billion dollars? forty billion dollars? or more? Another government employment program. I'd like to add up the number of jobs Senator Mondale has cost this country in defense plants, defense jobs, in all his anti-defense votes. They'd be hundreds and hundreds of thousands, . . . and he knows it. He wants bigger welfare programs, bigger giveaway programs. We wanna take care of those out of work; we wanna take care of those in need. Let's not wreck our business system, let's not wreck our free enterprise system . . . just to prove a point.

MR. HOGE: Thank you, Senators. That concludes the questioning for this evening. Each candidate now has up to three minutes for a closing statement. By the coin toss, it was determined that Senator Dole would make the first opening statement and take the first question. He now also goes first with his closing statement. Senator Dole.

MR. DOLE: Well, first I wish to thank the panel for their indulgence and of course all those in the viewing audience who may still be with us. I really hope—and I haven't prepared any final statement in advance—I really hope you were listening and we were able to tell you who's concerned about the American people, which party has faith in the American people, which party and which candidates want bigger and bigger and bigger government, which candidates want more and more spending, more and more interference. And we added up five of the programs that Governor Carter and Mondale talk about—only five, they really want sixty some new programs in their platform or expanded programs—they wanna create twenty-two new agencies, or expand that many existing agencies. We only added up five programs and the cost is a hundred and three billion dollars, a hundred and three billion! That would cost every taxpayer in America several hundred dollars. They don't care about inflation—the cruelest tax of all. And if you're in your living room watching tonight and you're making six thousand dollars a year on a fixed income and there's a six percent inflation, that's three hundred and sixty dollars a year, that's thirty dollars a month. That affects everybody in America. And add up your inflation if you let Carter and Mondale have their way—one spending program after another. We're concerned about the poor. We're concerned about the sick. We're concerned about the disabled. We're concerned about those on Social Security. And we have programs for that. We're concerned about housing—Carla Hills announced one today to reduce the interest payments from eight and a half percent to eight percent for FHA and VA homes. Governor Carter wants to preclude you from taking off your interest, your mortgage interest as a tax reduction. He says nobody wants their taxes lowered. Well, maybe not if they're getting a forty-one thousand dollar tax credit as he is. I just say in my final minute, it's a great honor and privilege to even be standing here—whatever happens on November second—it's an honor and a privilege. It's an honor and a privilege to have known President Ford for sixteen years, sixteen years, as I said at the outset. He's a man of unparalleled decency and honesty and courage; he's a man we can be proud of; he's gonna give us that leadership that America needs—all Americans—white, blacks, Spanish-speaking, rich, poor. Don't be fooled by the words, don't be fooled by the rhetoric, don't be fooled by the promises because somebody has to pay for those promises. Just take a look at the leadership. Take a look at President Ford. And thank President Ford for the fact that we live in peace and freedom and your sons and your husbands and your relatives are home and they're safe. It could only happen in America. Thank you.

MR. HOGE: Senator Mondale.

MR. MONDALE: Americans are not interested in partisan debating points. They're not interested in how many uh—debate points are scored. That means little to the lives of Americans. What really counts is whether this country can begin to solve those problems that are overwhelming so many Americans:

record unemployment—the highest since the Great Depression, and getting worse; runaway inflation—three times worse than that under the Democratic party; deficits that're unbelievable. Just last year, under this administration, we had a deficit larger than all of the deficits created in the eight years of the Democratic administration, and under this Republican party higher deficits than in the previous one hundred and ninety two years of this government's history. Now we recognize that you have to be prudent, that you have to live within a budget, that you have to deal with the resources that are at hand. There's no dispute on that. The question is how will those resources be used? And we believe that we need a government that works, that's efficient, but we also think that we need a government that cares. We've cared too little for people in this country that have gotten sick and can't afford decent health care. We've cared too little for the thousands and thousands of American families that cannot get or afford decent housing. This administration has fought time and time again to cut back support for our senior citizens. They have no energy policy. They have no environmental policy. Those things must change. We believe in a strong defense. We're not going to let this nation's defenses drop. But there's a big difference between waste and strength, and what we've been attacking is waste because waste does not contribute to strength—it contributes to weakness. There are many problems in the Defense Department that require better management in order to get that increased strength. We need leadership in this country to do all of those things. For eight years now the Republicans have controlled government. For eight years they've controlled the White House, and every one of those problems has gotten worse. They are not now proposing new policies and new directions. Tonight you heard what they are doing. They are defending the past. Everything is all right. The problems are not as bad as the statistics or the people believe, and therefore they might go away. That is not enough. This country cries out for new leadership. We need a fresh start. And the Carter-Mondale ticket promises that start. Not because we know all the answers—we know better. Not because we can do everything at once—because we know better than that. But because a good nation requires that we begin the effort.

MR. HOGE: Thank you, Senator Mondale and thank you, Senator Dole. I want to thank as well the audience here tonight and my colleagues who were our questioners. The final debate in this series will be between the presidential candidates, Gerald Ford and his challenger, Jimmy Carter. It will be held on October twenty-second at nine-thirty P.M. Eastern Daylight Time on the campus of William and Mary College in Williamsburg, Virginia. The subject matter will cover all issues. The sponsors of these debates is the League of Women Voters Education Fund, whose purpose is to promote greater participation by a better informed electorate in the election on November second. Now, from the Alley Theater, Houston, Texas, goodnight.

The Third Presidential Debate
College of William and Mary, Williamsburg, Va.
October 22, 1976, 9:30 p.m.

Ms. WALTERS: Good evening, I'm Barbara Walters, moderator of the last of the debates of 1976 between Gerald R. Ford, Republican candidate for president, and Jimmy Carter, Democratic candidate for president. Welcome, President Ford. Welcome, Governor Carter. And thank you for joining us this evening. This debate takes place before an audience in Phi Beta Kappa Memorial Hall on the campus of the College of William and Mary in historic Williamsburg, Virginia. It is particularly appropriate that in this Bicentennial year we meet on these grounds to hear this debate. Two hundred years ago, five William and Mary students met at nearby Raleigh Tavern to form Phi Beta Kappa, a fraternity designed, they wrote, to search out and dispel the clouds of falsehood by debating without reserve the issues of the day. In that spirit of debate, without reserve, to dispel the clouds of falsehood, gentlemen, let us proceed. The subject matter of this debate is open, covering all issues and topics. Our questioners tonight are Joseph Kraft, syndicated columnist; Robert Maynard, editorial writer for the *Washington Post*; and Jack Nelson, Washington bureau chief of the *Los Angeles Times*. The ground rules tonight are as follows: Questioners will alternate questions between the candidates. The candidate has up to two and one-half minutes to answer the question. The other candidate has up to two minutes to respond. If necessary, a questioner may ask a follow-up question for further clarification, and in that case the candidate has up to two minutes to respond. As was initially agreed to by both candidates, the answers should be responsive to the particular questions. Finally, each candidate has up to three minutes for a closing statement. President Ford and Governor Carter do not have prepared notes or comments with them this evening, but they may make notes and refer to them during the debate. It has been determined that President Ford would take the first question in this last debate, and Mr. Kraft, you have that first question for President Ford.

MR. KRAFT: Mr. President, uh—I assume that the Americans all know that these are difficult times and that there's no "pie in the sky" and that they don't expect something for nothing. Uh—so, I'd like to ask you as a first question as you look ahead in the next four years, [el] what sacrifices are you going to call on the American people to make, what price are you going to ask them to pay uh—to realize your objectives? Uh—let me add, uh—Governor Carter, that if—if you felt uh—that it was appropriate to answer that question in—in your comments uh—as to what price it would be appropriate for the American pay—people to pay uh—for a Carter administration, I think that would be proper too. Mr. President?

MR. FORD: Mr. Kraft, I believe that the American people, in the next four years under a Ford administration, will be called upon to make those necessary sacrifices to preserve the peace which we have. Which means, of course, that uh—we will have to maintain an adequate military capability—which means, of course, that we will have to add a uh—I think uh—a few billion dollars to our defense appropriations to make certain that we have adequate uh—strategic forces—adequate conventional forces. I think the American people will be called upon to uh—uh—be in the forefront in giving leadership to the solution of those problems that must be solved in the Middle East, in southern Africa, and any problems that might arise in the Pacific. The American people will be called upon to tighten their belts a bit in meeting some of the problems that we face domestically. I don't think that uh—America can go on a big spending spree with a whole lot of new programs uh—that would add significantly to the federal budget. I believe that the American people, if given the leadership that I would expect to give, would be willing to give this thrust to preserve the peace and the necessary restraint at home to hold the lid on spending so that we could, I think, have a long overdue and totally justified tax decrease for the middle-income people. And then, with the economy that would be generated from a restraint on spending, and a tax uh reduction primarily for the middle-income people, then I think the American people would be willing to make those sacrifices for peace and prosperity in the next uh—four years.

MR. KRAFT: Could I be a little bit more specific, Mr. President? (MR. FORD: Surely, surely. *overlapping*) Doesn't your policy really imply that we're going to have a fairly high rate of unemployment over a fairly long time, that growth is gonna be fairly slow, and that we're not gonna be able to do much—very much in the next four or five years to meet the basic agenda of our national needs in the cities, in health, uh in transit and a whole lot of things like that (MR. FORD: Not at all. *overlapping*), aren't those the real costs?

MR. FORD: No, Mr. Kraft, we're spending very significant amounts of money now, some $200 billion a year, almost 50 percent of our total federal expenditure uh—by the federal government at the present time for human needs. Now we will probably need to increase that to some extent. But we don't have to have [ɛʌ]—growth in spending that will blow the lid off and add to the problems of inflation. I believe we can meet the problems within the cities of this country and still uh—give a tax reduction. I proposed, as you know, a reduction to increase the personal exemption from seven hundred and fifty to a thousand dollars. With the fiscal program that I have, and if you look at the projections, it shows that we will reduce unemployment, that we will continue to win the battle against inflation, and at the same time give the kind of quality of life that I believe is possible in America. Uh—a job, a home for all those that'll work and save for it, uh—safety in the streets, uh—health that is a—health care that is affordable. These things can be done if we have the right vision and the right restraint and the right leadership.

MS. WALTERS: Thank you. Governor Carter, your response please.

MR. CARTER: Well I might say first of all that I think in . . . case of the Carter administration the sacrifices would be much less. Mr. Ford's own uh—environmental agency has projected a 10 percent unemployment rate by 1978 if he's uh—president. The American people are ready to make sacrifices if they are part of the process. If they know that they will be helping to make decisions and won't be excluded from being an involved party to the national purpose. The major effort we must put forward is to put our people back to work. And I think that this uh—is one example where uh—a lot of people have selfish, grasping ideas now. I remember 1973 in the depth of the uh—energy crisis when President Nixon called on the American people to make a sacrifice, to cut down on the waste of uh—gasoline, to cut down on the uh—speed

THE GREAT DEBATES

of automobiles. It was a—a tremendous surge of patriotism, that "I want to make a sacrifice for my country." I think we uh—could call together, with strong leadership in the White House, business, industry and labor, and say let's have voluntary price restraints. Let's lay down some guidelines so we don't have continuing inflation. We can also have a—an end to the extremes. We now have one extreme for instance, of some welfare recipients, who by taking advantage of the welfare laws, the housing laws, the uh—Medicaid uh—laws, and the uh—food stamp laws, make over $10 thousand a year and uh—they don't have to pay any taxes on it. At the other extreme, uh—just 1 percent of the richest people in our country derive 25 percent of all the tax benefits. So both those extremes grasp for advantage and the person who has to pay that expense is the middle-income family who's still working for a living and they have to pay for the rich who have privilege, and for the poor who are not working. But I think uh—uh—a balanced approach, with every-body being part of it and a striving for unselfishness, could help as it did in 1973 to let people sacrifice for their own country. I know I'm ready for it. I think the American people are too.

Ms. WALTERS: Thank you. Mr. Maynard, your question for Governor Carter.

MR. MAYNARD: Governor, by all indications, the voters are so turned off by this election campaign so far that only half intend to vote. One major reason for this apathetic electorate appears to be the low level at which this campaign has been conducted. It has digressed frequently from important issues into allegations of blunder and brainwashing and fixations on lust and *Playboy*. What responsibility do you accept for the low level of this campaign for the nation's highest office?

MR. CARTER: I think the major reason for a decrease in participation that we have experienced ever since 1960 has been the deep discouragement of the American people about the performance of public officials. When you've got seven and a half, eight million people out of work, and you've got three times as much inflation as you had during the last eight-year Democratic administration, when you have the highest deficits in history; when you have it uh—becoming increasingly difficult for a family to put a child through college or to own a home, there's a natural inclination to be turned off. Also, in the aftermath of Vietnam and Cambodia and uh—Watergate and uh—the CIA revelations, people have feel—have felt that they've uh been betrayed by public officials. I have to admit that in the uh—heat of the campaign—I've been in thirty primaries during the springtime, I've been campaigning for twenty-two months—I've made some mistakes. And I think this is uh—uh—part of uh—of just being a human being. I—I have to say that my campaign has been an open one. And uh—the *Playboy* thing has been of great—very great concern to me. I don't know how to deal with it exactly. Uh—I uh—agreed to give the interview uh—to *Playboy*. . . . Other people have done it who are notable—uh—Governor Jerry Brown, uh—Walter Cronkite, uh—Albert Schweitzer, Mr. Ford's own secretary of the treasury, Mr. Simon, uh—William Buckley—many other people. But they weren't running for president, and in retrospect, from hindsight, I would not have given that uh—interview had I do it—had it—I to do it over again. If I should ever decide in the future to discuss my—my deep Christian beliefs and uh—condemnation and sinfulness, I'll use another forum besides *Playboy*. But I can say this, uh—I'm doing the best I can to get away from that, and during the next ten days, the American people will not see the Carter campaign running uh—television advertisements and newspaper advertisements based on a personal attack on President Ford's character. I believe that the opposite is true with President Ford's campaign, and uh—I hope that we can leave those issues in this next ten days about personalities and mistakes of the past—we've both made some mistakes—and talk about unemployment, inflation, housing, education, taxation, government organization, stripping away of secrecy, and the things that are crucial to the American people. I regret the things in my own long campaign that have been mistaken, but I'm trying to do away with those the last ten days.

Ms. WALTERS: Thank you, Governor Carter. President Ford, your response.

MR. FORD: I believe that the uh—American people have been turned off in this election, uh—Mr. Maynard, for a variety of reasons. We have seen on Capitol Hill, in the Congress, uh—a great many uh—allegations of wrongdoing, of uh—alleged immorality, uh—those are very disturbing to the American people. They wonder how an elected representative uh—can serve them and participate in such activities uh—serving in the Congress of the United States. Yes, and I'm certain many, many Americans were turned off by the revelations of Watergate, a very, very uh—bad period of time in American political history. Yes, and thousands, maybe millions of Americans were turned off because of the uh—problems that came out of our involvement in Vietnam. But on the other hand, I found on July fourth of this year, a new spirit born in America. We were celebrating our Bicentennial; and I find that uh—there is a—a movement as I travel around the country of greater interest in this campaign. Now, like uh—any hardworking uh—person seeking public office uh—in the campaign, inevitably sometimes you will use uh—rather graphic language and I'm guilty of that just like I think most others in the political arena. But I do make a pledge that in the next ten days when we're asking the American people to make one of the most important decisions in their lifetime, because I think this election is one of the most vital in the history of America, that uh—we do together what we can to stimulate voter participation.

Ms. WALTERS: Thank you, President Ford. Mr. Nelson, your question to President Ford.

MR. NELSON: Uh—Mr. President, you mentioned Watergate, and you became president because of Watergate, so don't you owe the American people a special obligation to explain in detail your role of limiting one of the original investigations of Watergate, that was the one by the House Banking Committee? And, I know you've answered questions on this before, but there are questions that still remain and I think people want to know what your role was. Will you name the persons you talked to in connection with that investigation, and since you say you have no recollection of talking to anyone from the White House, would you be willing to open for examination the White House tapes of conversations uh—during that period?

MR. FORD: Well, Mr. uh—Nelson, uh—I testified before two committees, House and Senate, on precisely the questions that you have asked. And the testimony under oath was to the effect that I did not talk to Mr. Nixon, to Mr. Haldeman, to Mr. Ehrlichman, or to any of the people at the White House. I said I had no recollection whatsoever of talking with any of the White House legislative liaison people. I indicated under oath that the initiative that I took was at the request of the ranking members of the House Banking and Currency Committee on the Republican side, which was a legitimate request and a proper response by me. Now that was gone into by two congressional committees, and following that investigation, both committees overwhelmingly approved me, and both the House and the Senate did likewise. Now, in the meantime, the special prosecutor, within the last few days, after an investigation himself, said there was no reason for him to get involved because he found nothing that would justify it. And then just a day or two ago, the attorney general of the United States made a further investigation and came to precisely the same conclusion. Now, after all of those investigations by objective, responsible people, I think the matter is closed once and for all. But to add one other feature, I don't control any of the tapes. Those tapes are in the jurisdiction of the courts and I have no right to say "yes" or "no." But all the committees, the attorney general, the special prosecutor, all of them have given me a clean bill of health. I think the matter is settled once and for all.

MR. NELSON: Well, Mr. President, if I do say so though, the question is that I think that you still have not gone into details about what your role in it was. And [nætðe] I don't think there is any question about whether or not uh—there was criminal prosecution, but whether—whether you have told the American people your entire involvement in it. And whether you would be willing, even if you don't control the tapes, whether you would be willing to ask that the tapes be released for examination.

MR. FORD: That's for the uh—proper authorities who have control over those tapes to make that decision. I have given every bit of evidence, answered every question that's as—been asked me by any senator or any member of the House. Plus the fact, that the special prosecutor, on his own initiation, and the attorney general on his initiation, the highest law enforcement official in this country, all of them have given me a clean bill of health. And I've told everything I know about it. I think the matter is settled once and for all.

MS. WALTERS: Governor Carter, your response.

MR. CARTER: I don't have a response.

MS. WALTERS: Thank you. Then we'll have the next question from Mr. Kraft to Governor Carter.

MR. KRAFT: Uh—Governor Carter, the next big crisis spot in the world may be Yugoslavia. Uh—President Tito is old and sick and there are divisions in his country. Uh—it's pretty certain that the Russians are gonna do everything they possibly can after Tito dies to force Yugoslavia back into the Soviet camp. But last Saturday you said, and this is a quote, "I would not go to war in Yugoslavia, even if the Soviet Union sent in troops." Doesn't that statement practically invite the Russians to intervene in Yugoslavia? Ah—doesn't it discourage Yugoslavs who might be tempted to resist? And wouldn't it have been wiser on your part uh—to say nothing and to keep the Russians in the dark as President Ford did, and as I think every president has done since—since President Truman?

MR. CARTER: In the last uh—two weeks, I've had a chance to talk to uh—two men who have visited uh—the Soviet Union, Yugoslavia and China. One is Governor Avell—Averell Harriman, who visited the Soviet Union and Yugoslavia, and the other is James Schlesinger, whom I think you accompanied to uh—China. I got a—a complete report back from those countries from these two distinguished—uh—gentlemen. Mr. Harriman talked to the leaders in Yugoslavia, and I think it's accurate to say that there is no uh—prospect in their opinion, of the Soviet Union invading uh—Yugoslavia should uh—Mr. Tito pass away. The present leadership uh—there is uh—is fairly uniform in—in their purpose, and I think it's a close-knit group, uh—and uh— I think it would be unwise for us to say that we will go to war uh—in Yugoslavia uh—if the Soviets should invade, which I think would be an extremely unlikely thing. I have maintained from the very beginning of my campaign, and this was a standard answer that I made in response to the Yugoslavian question, that I would never uh—go to war or become militarily involved, in the internal affairs of another country unless our own security was direc—rectly threatened. And uh—I don't believe that our security would be directly threatened if the Soviet Union went uh—into Yugoslavia. I don't believe it will happen. I certainly hope it won't. I would take eh—the strongest possible measures short of uh—actual military uh—action there by our own troops, but I doubt that that would be an eventuality.

MR. KRAFT: One quick follow-up question. (GOVERNOR CARTER: Yes.) Did you clear the response you made with Secretary Schlesinger and Governor Harriman?

MR. CARTER: No, I did not.

Ms. WALTERS: President Ford, your response.

MR. FORD: W'I firmly believe, uh—Mr. Kraft, that it's unwise for a president to signal in advance what uh—options he might exercise if any uhh—international problem arose. I think we all recall with some sadness that at uh—the period of the nin—late nineteen forties, early nineteen fifties, there were some indications that the United States would not include uh—South Korea in an area of defense. There are some who allege, I can't prove it true or untrue, that uh—such a statement uh—in effect invited the North Koreans to invade South Korea. It's a fact they did. But no president of the United States, in my opinion, should signal in advance to a prospective enemy, what his uhh—decision might be or what option he might exercise. It's far better for a person sitting in the White House uh—who has a number of options to make certain that the uh—other side, so to speak, doesn't know precisely what you're going to do. And therefore, that was the reason that I would not uh—identify any particular course of action uh—when I responded to a question a week or so ago.

Ms. WALTERS: Thank you, Mr. Maynard, your question to President Ford, please.

MR. MAYNARD: Sir, this question concerns your administrative performance as president. The other day, General George Brown, the chairman of the Joint

Chiefs of Staff, delivered his views on several sensitive subjects, among them Great Britain, one of this country's oldest allies. He said, and I quote him now, "Great Britain, it's a pathetic thing. It just makes you cry. They're no longer a world power. All they have are generals, admirals, and bands," end quote. Since General Brown's comments have caused this country embarrassment in the past, why is he still this nation's leading military officer?

MR. FORD: I have indicated to General Brown that uh—the words that he used in that interview, in that particular case and in several others, were very ill advised. And General Brown has indicated uh—his apology, his regrets, and I think that will, uh—in this situation, settle the matter. It is tragic that uh—the full transcript of that interview was not released and that there were excerpts, some of the excerpts, taken out of context. Not this one, however, that you bring up. General Brown has an exemply [sic] record of military performance. He served this nation with great, great skill and courage and bravery for thirty-five years. And I think it's the consensus of the people who are knowledgeable in the military field, that he is probably the outstanding military leader and strategist that we have in America today. Now he did use uh—ill-advised words, but I think in the fact that he apologized, that he was reprimanded, uh—does permit him to stay on and continue that kind of leadership that's we so badly need as we enter into uh—negotiations uh—under the SALT II agreement, or if we have operations that might be developing uh in the Middle East or southern Africa, in the Pacific, uh—we need a man with that experience, that knowledge, that know-how, and I think, in light of the fact that he has uh—apologized, uh—would not have justified my asking for his resignation.

MS. WALTERS: Thank you. Governor Carter, your response.

MR. CARTER: Well, just briefly, I—I think this is uh—the second time that General Brown has made a statement that—for which he did have to apologize. And I know that everybody uh—makes mistakes. I think the first one was related to uh—the unwarranted influence of American Jews on the media and uh—in the Congress. This one concerned uh—Great Britain. I think he said that Israel was a—a military burden on us and that Iran hoped to reestablish the Persian Empire. Ah—I'm not uh—sure that I remembered earlier that President Ford had—had expressed uh—his concern about the statement or apologized for it. This is uh—something, though, that I think uh—is indicative of the need among the American people to know how its commander-in-chief, the president, feels and—and—and I think the only criticism that I would have uh—on—of Mr. Ford is that uh—immediately when the statement was re—re—revealed, uh—perhaps a—a statement from the president would have been a clarifying and a very beneficial thing.

MS. WALTERS: Mr. Nelson, your question now to Governor Carter.

MR. NELSON: Governor, despite the fact that uh—you've been running for president a long time now, uh—many Americans uh—still seem to be uneasy about you. Uh—they don't feel that uh—they know you or the people around you. And one problem seems to be that you haven't reached out to bring people of broad background or national experience into your campaign or your presidential plans. Most of the people around you on a day-to-day basis are the people you've kno—known in Georgia. Many of them are young and relatively inexperienced in national affairs. And uh—doesn't this raise a serious question as to uh—whether you would bring into a Carter administration uh people with the necessary background to run the federal government?

MR. CARTER: I don't believe it does. Uh—I began campaigning uh—twenty-two months ago. At that time, nobody thought I had a chance to win. Uh—very few people knew who I was. I came from a tiny town, as you know, Plains, and didn't hold public office, didn't have very much money. And my first organization was just four or five people plus my wife and my children, my three sons and their wives. And we won . . . the nomination by going out into the streets—barbershops, beauty parlors, restaurants, stores, in factory shift lines . . . also in farmers' markets and livestock sale barns—and we talked a lot and we listened a lot and we learned from the American people. And we built up uh—an awareness among the uh—voters of this country, particularly those in whose primaries I entered—thirty of them, nobody's ever done that before—about who I was and what I stood for. Now we have a very, very wide-ranging group of advisers who help me prepare for these debates and who teach me about international economics, and foreign affairs, defense matters, health, education, welfare, government reorganization. I'd say, several hundred of them. And they're very fine and very highly qualified. The one major decision that I have made . . . since acquiring the nomination, and I share this with President Ford, is the choice of a vice president. I think this should be indicative of the kind of leaders I would choose to help me if I am elected. I chose Senator Walter Mondale. And the only criterion I ever put forward in my own mind was who among the several million people in this country would be the best person qualified to be president, if something should happen to me and to join me in being vice president if I should serve out my term. And I'm convinced now, more than I was when I got the nomination, that Walter Mondale was the right choice. And I believe this is a good indication of the kind of people I would choose in the future. Mr. Ford has had that same choice to make. I don't want to say anything critical of Senator Dole, but I've never heard Mr. Ford say that that was his prim—primary consideration—Who is the best person I could choose in this country . . . to be president of the United States? I feel completely at ease knowing that someday Senator Mondale might very well be president. In the last five pres—vice presidential uh—nominees, uh—incumbents, three of them have become president. But I think this is indicative of what I would do.

MS. WALTERS: President Ford, your response, please.

MR. FORD: The Governor may not have heard my uh—established criteria for the selection of a vice president, but uh—it was a well-established criteria that the person I selected would be fully qualified to be president of the United States. And Senator Bob Dole is so qualified: sixteen years in the House of Representatives and in the Senate, uhh—very high responsibilities on important committees. I don't mean to be critical of uh—Senator Mondale, but uh—I was uh—very, very surprised when I read that uh—Senator Mondale made a very derogatory, very personal comment about General Brown uh—after the news story that uh—broke about General Brown. If my recollection is correct he indicated that uh—General Brown was not qualified to be a sewer commissioner. I don't think that's a proper way to describe aayuh—chairman of the

Joint Chiefs of Staff who has fought for his country for thirty-five years, and I'm sure the governor would agree with me on that. Uh—I think Senator Dole would show more good judgment and discretion than to so describe uh—a heroic and brave and very outstanding leader of the military. So I think our selection uh—of Bob Dole as vice president uh—is based on merit. And if he should ever become uh—the president of the United States, with his vast experience as member the House and a member of the Senate, as well as a vice president, I think he would do an outstanding job as president of the United States.

Ms. WALTERS: Mr. Kraft, your question to President Ford.

MR. KRAFT: Uh—Mr. President, uh—uh—let me assure you then maybe some of the uh viewing audience that being on this panel hasn't been as it may seem, all torture and agony. Uh—one of the heartening things is that uh—I and my colleagues have received uh—literally hundreds and maybe even thousands of suggested questions from ordinary citizens all across the country . . . who want answers.

MR. FORD: That's a tribute to their interest in this election.

MR. KRAFT: I'll give you that. Ahh—but, uh—let me go on, because one main subject on the minds of all of them has been the environment. Uh—they're particularly curious about your record. People—people really wanna know why you vetoed the strip-mining bill. They wanna know why you worked against strong controls on auto emissions. They wanna know why you aren't doing anything about pollution uh—of the Atlantic Ocean. Uh—they wanna know why a—a bipartisan organization such as the National League of Conservation Voters says that when it comes to environmental issues, you are—and I'm quoting—"hopeless."

MR. FORD: Well, first, uh—let me set the record straight. I vetoed the strip-mining bill, Mr. Kraft, because it was the overwhelming consensus of knowledgeable people that that strip-mining bill would have meant the loss of literally uh—thousands of jobs, something around a hundred and forty thousand jobs. Number two, that strip-mining bill would've severely set back our need for more coal, and Governor Carter has said repeatedly that coal is the resource that we need to use more in the effort to become independent of the uh—Arab oil supply. So, I vetoed it because of a loss of jobs and because it would've interfered with our energy independence program. The auto emissions—uh—it was agreed by Leonard Woodcock, the head of the UAW, and by the uh—heads of all of the automobile industry, we had labor and management together saying that those auto emission standards had to be modified. But let's talk about what the Ford administration has done in the field of environment. I have increased, as president, by over 60 percent the funding for water treatment plants in the United States, the federal contribution. I have fully funded the land and water conservation program; in fact, have recommended and the Congress approved a substantially increased land and water conservation program. Uh—I have uh—added in the current year budget the funds for the National Park Service. For example, we uh—proposed about $12 million to add between four and five hundred more employees for the National Park Service. And a month or so ago I did uh—likewise say over the next ten years we should expand—double—this national parks, the wild wilderness areas, the scenic river areas. And then, of course, the—the final thing . . . is that I have signed and approved of more scenic rivers, more wilderness areas, since I've been president than any other president in the history of the United States.

Ms. WALTERS: Governor Carter.

MR. CARTER: Well, I might say that I think the League of Conservation Voters is absolutely right. This uh—administration's record on environment is very bad. Uh—I think it's accurate to say that the uh—strip-mining law which was passed twice by the Congress—uh—and was only like two votes I believe of being overriden—would have* been good for the country. The claim that it would have* put hundred and forty thousand miners out of work is uh—hard to believe, when at the time Mr. Ford vetoed it, the United Mine Workers was uh—supporting the bill. And I don't think they would have supported the uh—bill had they known that they would lose a hundred and forty thousand jobs. There's been a consistent policy on the part of this administration to lower or delay enforcement of air pollution standards and water pollution standards. And under both President Nixon and Ford, monies have been impounded that would've gone to uh—cities and others to control uh—water pollution. We have no energy policy. We, I think, are the only developed nation in the world that has no comprehensive energy policy, to permit us to plan in an orderly way how to shift from increasing the scarce uh—energy uh—forms: oil, and have research and development concentrated on the increased use of coal, which I strongly favor. The research and development to be used primary to make the coal burning uh—be clean. We need a heritage trust program, similar to the one we had in Georgia, to set aside additional lands that have uh—geological and archeological importance, uh natural areas for enjoyment. Uh—the lands that Mr. Ford uh—brags about having approved are in Alaska and they are enormous in uh—in size. But as far as the accessibility of them by the American people, it's very uh—far in the future. We've taken no strong position in the uh—control of pollution of our oceans, and I would say the worst uh—threat to the environment of all is nuclear proliferation. And this administration, having been in office now for two years or more, has still not taken strong and bold action to stop the proliferation of nuclear waste around the world, particularly plutonium. Those are some brief remarks about the failures of this administration. I would do the opposite in every respect.

Ms. WALTERS: Mr. Maynard, to Governor Carter.

MR. MAYNARD: Governor, federal policy in this country since World War II has tended to favor the development of suburbs at the great expense of central cities. Does not the federal government now have an affirmative obligation to revitalize the American city? We have heard little in this campaign suggesting that you have an urban reconstruction program. Could you please outline your urban intentions for us tonight?

MR. CARTER: Yes, I'd be glad to. In the first place, uh—as is the case with the environmental policy and the energy policy that I just described, and the policy for nonproliferation of uh—of nuclear waste, this administration has no urban policy. It's impossible for mayors or governors to cooperate with the president, because they can't anticipate what's gonna happen next. A mayor of

*"would have" was spoken as [wʊdə].

a city like New York, for instance, needs to know uh—eighteen months or two years ahead of time what responsibility the city will have in administration and in financing—in things like housing, uh—pollution control, uh—crime control, education, welfare and health. This has not been done, unfortunately. I remember the headline in the *Daily News* that said, "Ford to New York: Drop Dead." I think it's very important that our cities know that they have a partner in the federal government. Quite often Congress has passed laws in the past designed to help people with uh—the ownership of homes and with the control of crime and with adequate health care and education programs and so forth. Uh—those uh programs were designed to help those who need it most. And quite often this has been in the very poor people and neighborhoods in the downtown urban centers. Because of the uh—great—ly—greatly uh—advantaged uh—tho—per—persons who live in the suburbs, better education, better organization, more articulate, more aware of what the laws are, quite often this money has been channeled out of the downtown centers where it's needed. Also I favor all revenue sharing money being used for local governments, and also to remove prohibitions in the use of revenue sharing money so that it can be used to improve education, and health care. We have now uh—for instance only 7 percent of the total education cost being financed by the federal government. When uh—the Nixon-Ford Administration started, this was 10 percent. That's a 30 percent reduction in the portion that the federal government contributes to education in just eight years. And as you know, the education cost has gone up uh—tremendously. The last point is that the major—uh thrust has gotta be to put people back to work. We've got an extraordinarily high unemployment rate among downtown urban ghetto areas, uh—particularly among the very poor and particularly among minority groups, sometimes 50 or 60 percent. And the concentration of employment opportunities in those areas would help greatly not only to reestablish the tax base, but also to help reduce the extraordinary welfare cost. One of the major responsibilities on the shoulders of uh—New York City is to—is to finance welfare. And I favor a shifting of the welfare cost away from the local governments altogether. And over a longer period of time, let the federal government begin to absorb part of it that's now paid by the state governments. Those things would help a great deal with the cities, but we still have a—a very serious problem there.

Ms. WALTERS: President Ford.

MR. FORD: Let me uh—speak out very strongly. The Ford administration does have a very comprehensive program to help uh—our major metropolitan areas. I fought for, and the Congress finally went along with a general revenue sharing program, whereby cities and uh—states, uh—the cities two-thirds and the states one-third, get over six billion dollars a year in cash through which they can uh—provide many, many services, whatever they really want. In addition we uh—in the federal government make available to uh—cities about uh—three billion three hundred million dollars in what we call community development. In adesh—in addition, uh—uh—as a result of my pressure on the Congress, we got a major mass transit program uh—over a four-year period, eleven billion eight-hundred million dollars. We have a good housing program, uh—that uh—will result in cutting uh—the down payments by 50 percent and uh—having mortgage payments uh lower at the beginning of any mortgage period. We're expanding our homestead uh—housing program. The net result is, uh—we think under Carla Hills, who's the chairman of my uh—urban development and uh—neighborhood revitalization program, we will really do a first-class job in helping uh—the communities throughout the country. As a matter of fact, that committee under Secretary Hills released about a seventy-five-page report with specific recommendations so we can do a better job uh—the weeks ahead. And in addition, the tax program of the Ford administration, which provides an incentive for industry to move into our major uh—metropolitan areas, into the inner cities, will bring jobs where people are, and help to revitalize those cities as they can be.

MS. WALTERS: Mr. Nelson, your question next to President Ford.

MR. NELSON: Uh—Mr. President, your campaign has uh—run ads in black newspapers saying that quote, "for black Americans, President Ford is quietly getting the job done." Yet, study after study has shown little progress in desegregation and in fact actual increases in segregated schools and housing in the Northeast. Now, civil rights groups have complained repeatedly that there's been lack of progress and commitment to an integrated society uh—during your —your administration. So how are you getting the job done for blacks and other minorities and what programs do you have in mind for the next four years?

MR. FORD: Let me say at the outset, uh—I'm very proud of the record of this administration. In the cabinet I have one of the outstanding, I think, administrators as the secretary of transportation, Bill Coleman. You're familiar, I'm sure, with the recognition given in the Air Force to uh—General James, and there was just uh—approved a three-star admiral, the first in the history of the United States Navy, so uh—we are giving full recognition to individuals of quality in the Ford administration in positions of great responsibility. In addition, uh—the Department of Justice is fully enforcing, and enforcing effectively, the Voting Rights Act, the legislation that involves jobs, housing for minorities, not only blacks but all others. Uh—the Department of uh—uh—HUD is enforcing the new legislation that uhh—outlaws, that takes care of redlining. Uh—what we're doing is saying that there are opportunities, business opportunities, educational opportunities, responsibilities uh—where people with talent, black . . . or any other minority, can fully qualify. The Office of Minority Business in the Department of Commerce has made available more money in trying to help uh—black businessmen or other minority businessmen than any other administration since the office was established. The Office of Small Business, under Mr. Kobelinski, has a very massive program trying to help the black community. The individual who wants to start a business or expand his business as a black businessman is able to borrow, either directly or with guaranteed loans. I believe on the record that this administration has been more responsive and we have carried out the law to the letter, and I'm proud of the record.

MS. WALTERS: Governor Carter, your response, please.

MR. CARTER: The uh—description just made of this administration's record is hard to uh—recognize. I think it's accurate to say that Mr. Ford voted against the uh—Voting Rights Acts and the uh—Civil Rights Acts in their uh—debative stage. I think once it was assured they were going to pass he finally voted for it. This country uh—changed drastically in 1969 when the uh—terms of John

Kennedy and Lyndon Johnson were over and Richard Nixon and—and Gerald Ford became the presidents. There was a time when there was hope for those who uh—were poor and downtrodden and who were—uh elderly or who were —uh ill or who were in minority groups, but that time has been gone. I think the greatest thing that ever happened to the South was the passage of the Civil Rights Act and the opening up of opportunities—uh to black people—the chance to vote, to hold a job, to buy a house, to go to school, and to participate in public affairs. It not only liberated—uh black people but it also liberated the whites. We've seen uh—in many instances in recent years a minority affairs uh—section of uh Small Loan Administration, uh—Small Business Administration lend uh—a black entrepreneur just enough money to get started, and then to go bankrupt. The bankruptcies have gone up—uh in an extraordinary degree. Uh—[fɪʔ] FHA, which used to be a very responsible agency, uh—that everyone looked to to help own a home, lost six million dollars last year. There've been over thirteen hundred indictments . . . in HUD, over eight hundred convictions . . . relating just to home loans. And now the federal government has become the world's greatest slum landlord. We've got a 30 percent or 40 percent unemployment rate among minority uh—young people. And there's been no concerted effort given to the needs of those who are both poor and black, or poor and who speak a foreign language. [æ] And that's where there's been a great uh generation . . . of despair, and ill health, and the lack of education, lack of purposefulness, and the lack of hope for the future. But it doesn't take just a quiet uh—dormant* uh minimum enforcement of the law. It requires an aggressive searching out and reaching out to help people who especially need it. And that's been lacking in the last eight years.

Ms. WALTERS: Mr. Kraft, to Governor Carter.

MR. KRAFT: Ah—Governor Carter, ah—in the nearly two-hundred-year history of the Constitution, there've been only uh—I think it's twenty-five amendments, most of them on issues of the very broadest principle. Uh—now we have proposed amendments in many highly specialized causes, like gun control, school busing, balanced budgets, school prayer, abortion, things like that. Do you think it's appropriate to the dignity of the Constitution to tack on amendments in wholesale fashion? And which of the ones that I listed—that is, uh—balanced budgets, school busing, school prayer, abortion, gun con—control—which of those would you really work hard to support if you were president?

MR. CARTER: I would not work hard to support any of those. Uh—we've always had, I think, a lot of constitutional amendments proposed, but the passage of them has been uh—fairly slow, and uh—few and far between. In the two-hundred-year history there's been a very uh—cautious approach to this. We—quite often we have a transient problem. I—I'm strongly against a—abortion. I think abortion's wrong. I don't think the government oughta do anything to encourage abortion. But I don't favor a constitutional amendment on the subject. But short of the constitutional amendment, and within the confines of the Supreme Court rulings, I'll do everything I can to minimize the need for abortions with better sex education, family planning, with better adoptive pro-

*Phonetically spoken as [doʊlmənt].

cedures. I personally don't believe that the federal government oughta finance abortions, but I—I draw the line and don't support a constitutional amendment. However, I honor the right of people who seek the constitutional amendments on school busing, on uh—prayer in the schools and on abortion. But among those you named, I won't actively work for the passage of any of them.

Ms. WALTERS: President Ford, your response, please.

MR. FORD: I support the uh—Republican uh—platform, which calls for the constitutional amendment that would uh—outlaw abortions. I favor the particular constitutional amendment that would turn over to the states the uh—individual right to the voters in those states uh—the chance to make a decision by public referendum. Uh I call that the people amendment. I think if you really believe that the people of a state ought to make a decision on a matter of this kind that uh—we ought to have a federal constitutional amendment that would permit each one of the fifty states to make the choice. Uh—I think this is a responsible and a proper way to proceed. Uhh—I . . . believe also that uh— there is some merit to a—an amendment that uh—uh—Senator Everett Dirksen uh—proposed very frequently, an amendment that would uh—change the court decision as far as voluntary prayer in public schools. Uh—it seems to me that there should have—be an opportunity, uh—as long as it's voluntary, as long as there is no uh—compulsion whatsoever, that uh—an individual ought to have that right. So in those two cases I think uh—such uh—a constitutional amendment would be proper, and I really don't think in either case they're trivial matters. I think they're matters of very deep conviction, as far as many, many people in this country believe. And therefore, they shouldn't be treated lightly. But they're matters that are ah—important. And in those two cases, I would favor them.

Ms. WALTERS: Mr. Maynard to President Ford.

MR. MAYNARD: Mr. President, twice you have been the intended victim of would-be assassins using handguns. Yet, you remain a steadfast opponent of substantive handgun control. There are now some forty million handguns in this country, going up at the rate of two point five million a year. And tragically, those handguns are frequently purchased for self-protection and wind up being used against a relative or a friend. In light of that, why do you remain so adamant in your opposition to substantive gun control in this country?

MR. FORD: Uh—Mr. Maynard, uh—the record of gun control, whether it's one city or another or in some states, does not show that the registration of a gun, handgun, or the registration of the gun owner, has in any way whatsoever decreased the crime rate or the use of that gun in the committing of a crime. The record just doesn't prove that such legislation or action by a local city council is effective. What we have to do, and this is the crux of the matter, is to make it very, very uh—difficult for a person who uses a gun in the commission of a crime to stay out of jail. If we make the use of a gun in the commission of a crime a serious criminal offense, and that person is prosecuted, then, in my opinion, we are going after the person who uses the gun for the wrong reason. I don't believe in the registration of handguns or the registration of the handgun owner. That has not proven to be effective, and therefore, I think the better way is to go after the criminal, the individual who commits a crime in the possession of a gun and uses that gun for a part of his criminal activity.

Those are the people who ought to be in jail. And the only way to do it is to pass strong legislation so that once apprehended, indicted, convicted, they'll be in jail and off the streets and not using guns in the commission of a crime.

MR. MAYNARD: But Mr. President, don't you think that the proliferation of the availability of handguns contributes to the possibility of those crimes being committed. And, there's a second part to my follow-up, very quickly. There are, as you know and as you've said, jurisdictions around the country with strong gun-control laws. The police officials in those cities contend that if there were a national law, to prevent other jurisdictions from providing the weapons that then come into places like New York, that they might have a better handle on the problem. Have you considered that in your analysis of the gu—the hand-gun proliferation problem?

MR. FORD: Yes, I have. And uh—the individuals that uh—with whom I've consulted have not uh—convinced me that uh—a national registration of hand-guns or handgun owners will solve the problem you're talking about. The person who wants to use a gun for an illegal purpose can get it whether it's registered or outlawed. They will be obtained. And they are the people who ought to go behind bars. You should not in the process penalize the legitimate handgun owner. And when you go through the process of registration, you in effect, are penalizing that individual who uses his gun for a very legitimate purpose.

MS. WALTERS: Governor Carter.

MR. CARTER: I—I think it's accurate to say that Mr. Ford's position on gun control has changed. Uh—earlier, uh—Mr. Levi, his uh—attorney general, put forward a gun control proposal, which Mr. Ford later, I believe, espoused, that called for the prohibition against the uh sale aw—of the uh—so-called Saturday Night Specials. And it would've put uh—very strict uh—uh—control over who owned a handgun. I have been a hunter all my life and happen to own both shotguns, rifles, and a handgun. And uh—the only purpose that I would see in registering uh—handguns and not long guns of any kind would be to prohibit the uh—ownership of those guns by those who've used them in the commission of a crime, or who uh—have been proven to be mentally incompetent to own a gun. I believe that limited approach to the—to the question would be uh—advisable, and—and I think, adequate. But that's as far as I would go with it.

MS. WALTERS: Mr. Nelson to Governor Carter.

MR. NELSON: Uh Governor, you've said the uh—Supreme Court of today is, uh—as you put it, moving back in a proper direction uh—in rulings that have limited the rights of criminal defendants. And you've compared the present Supreme Court under Chief Justice Burger very favorably with the more liberal court that we had under Chief Justice Warren. So exactly what are you getting at, and can you elaborate on the kind of court you think this country should have? And can you tell us the kind of qualifications and philosophy you would look for as president in making Supreme Court appointments?

MR. CARTER: While I was governor of Georgia, although I'm not a lawyer, we had complete reform of the Georgia court system. We uh—streamlined the structure of the court, put in administrative officers, put a unified court system in, required that all uh—severe sentences be reviewed for uniformity. And, in addition to that put forward a proposal that was adopted and used throughout my own term of office of selection of—for all judges and district attorneys or prosecuting attorneys, on the basis of merit. Every time I had a vacancy on the Georgia Supreme Court—and I filled five of those vacancies out of seven total and about half the court of appeals judges, about 35 percent of the trial judges—I was given from an objective panel the five most highly qualified persons in Georgia. And from those five, I always chose the first one or second one. So merit selection of judges is the most important single criterion. And I would institute the same kind of procedure as president, not only in judicial appointments, but also in diplomatic appointments. Secondly, I think that the Burger Court . . . has fairly well confirmed the major and—and most far-reaching and most controversial decisions of the Warren Court. Civil rights—uh has been confirmed by the Burger Court, hasn't been uh—reversed, and I don't think there's any inclination to reverse those basic decisions. The one-man, one-vote rule, which is a very important one that uh—s—struck down the unwarranted influence in the legislature of parsley [spoʊʔ]—uh populated areas of—of the states. The uh—right of indigent or very poor accused persons to uh—legal counsel. Uh—I think the Burger Court has confirmed that basic and very controversial decision of the Warren Court. Also the—the protection of an arrested person against unwarranted persecution in trying to get a false uh—confession. But now I think there have been a couple of instances where the Burger Court has made technical rulings where an obviously guilty person was later found to be guilty. And I think that in that case uh—some of the more liberal uh—members of the uh—so-called Warren Court agreed with those decisions. But the only uh—thing I uh—have pointed out was, what I've just said, and that there was a need to clarify the technicalities so that you couldn't be forced to release a person who was obviously guilty just because of a—of a small technicality in the law. And—and that's a reversal of position uh by the Burger Court with which I do agree.

MR. NELSON: [wə] Governor, I don't believe you ans—you answered my question though about the kinds of uh people you would be looking for the court, the type of philosophy uh—you would be looking for if you were making (MR. CARTER: [əɑː]) appointments to the Supreme Court as president.

MR. CARTER: Okay, I thought I answered it by saying that it would be on the basis of merit. Once the uh—search and analysis procedure had been completed, and once I'm given a list of the five or seven or ten uh—best qualified persons in the country, I would make a selection from among those uh—persons. If the uh—list was, uh—in my opinion, fairly uniform, if there was no outstanding person, then I would undoubtedly choose someone who would most accurately reflect my own basic polisi—political philosophy as best I could determine it. Which would be uh—to continue the progress that has been made under the last two uh—courts—the Warren Court and the Burger Court. I would also like to uh—completely revise our criminal justice system—to do some of the things at the federal level in court reform that I've just described, as has been done in Georgia and other states. And then I would like to appoint people who would be interested in helping with that. I know that uh Chief Justice Burger is. He hasn't had help from the administration, from the Congress, to carry this out. The uh—emphasis, I think, of the—of the court system uh—should be to interpret the uh—the Constitution and the laws uh—

equally between property protection and personal protection. But when there's uh—a very narrow decision—which quite often there's one that reaches the Supreme Court—I think the choice should be with human rights. And uh—that would be another factor that I would follow.

Ms. WALTERS: President Ford.

MR. FORD: Well, I think the answer uh—as to the kind of person that I would select uh—is obvious. I had one opportunity to nominate uh—an individual to the Supreme Court and I selected the Circuit Court of Appeals judge from Illinois, uh—John Paul Stevens. I selected him because of his outstanding record as a Circuit Court of Appeals judge, and I was very pleased that uh—an overwhelming Democratic United States Senate, after going into his background, came to the conclusion that he was uh—fit and should serve, and the vote in his behalf was overwhelming. So, I would say somebody in the format of uh—Justice Stevens would be the kind of an individual that I would uh—select in the future, as I did him in the past. I uh—believe, however, a comment ought to be made about the direction of the uh—Burger Court, vis-à-vis the uh—court uh— that preceded it. It seems to me that . . . the *Miranda* case . . . was a case that really made it very, very difficult for the—uh police, the law enforcement people in this country to uh—do what they could to make certain that the victim of a crime was protected and that those that commit crimes uh—were properly handled and uh—sent to jail. The *Miranda* case, uh—the Burger Court uh—is gradually changing, and I'm pleased to see that there are some steps being made by the uh—Burger Court to modify the so-called *Miranda* decision. Uh—I might make a correction uh—of what uh—Governor Carter said, uh speaking of uh— uh—gun control, uh—yes, it is true, I believe that the sale of uh—Saturday Night S—Specials should be cut out, but he wants the registration of handguns.

Ms. WALTERS: Mr. Kraft.

MR. KRAFT: Uh—Mr. President, uh—the country is now uh—in uh—in something that your uh—advisors call an economic pause. I think to most Americans that sounds like a—a antiseptic term for uh—low growth, uh—unemployment standstill at a high, high level, uhh—decline in take-home pay, uh—lower factory earnings, more layoffs. Uh, isn't that a really rotten record and doesn't your administration bear most of the blame for it?

MR. FORD: Well, Mr. Kraft, uh—I violently disagree with your assessment. And I don't think the record justifies the conclusion that you come to. Uh—let me uh—talk about uh—the economic announcements that were made just this past week. Yes, it was announced that the uh—GNP real growth in the third quarter was at 4 percent. But do you realize that over the last ten years that's a higher figure than the average growth during that ten-year period? Now it's lower than the nine-point-point-two percent growth in the first quarter, and it's lower than the ehuh 5 percent growth in the second quarter. But every economist—liberal, conservative that I'm familiar with—recognizes that in the fourth quarter of this year and in the fifth quar—uh—the first quarter of next year that we'll have an increase in real GNP. But now let's talk about the pluses that came out this week. We had an 18 percent increase in housing starts. We had a substantial increase in new permits for housing. As a matter of fact, based on the announcement this week, there will be at an annual rate of a million, eight hundred and some thousand new houses built, which is a tremendous increase over last year and a substantial increase over the earlier part of this year. Now in addition, we had . . . a very—some very good news in the reduction in the rate of inflation. And inflation hits everybody: those who are working and those who are on welfare. The rate of inflation, as announced just the other day, is under 5 percent; and the uh—4.4 percent that was indicated at the time of the 4 percent GNP was less than the 5.4 percent. It means that the American buyer is getting a better bargain today because inflation is less.

MR. KRAFT: Mr. President, let me ask you this. Uh—there has been an increase in layoffs and that's something that bothers everybody because even people that have a job are afraid that they're going to be fired. Did you predict that layoff, uh—that increase in layoffs? Didn't that take you by surprise? Hasn't the gov—hasn't your administration been surprised by this pause? Uh— in fact, haven't you not—haven't you been so obsessed with saving money uh— that you didn't even push the government to spend funds that were allocated?

MR. FORD: Uh Mr. Kraft, uh—I think the record can be put in this uh—in this way, which uh—is the way that I think satisfies most Americans. Since the depths of the recession, we have added four million jobs. Im—most importantly, consumer confidence as surveyed by the reputable organization at the University of Michigan is at the highest since 1972. In other words, there is a growing public confidence in the strength of this economy. And that means that there will be more industrial activity. It means that there will be a reduction in the uhh—unemployment. It means that there will be increased hires. It means that there will be increased employment. Now we've had this pause, but most economists, regardless of their political philosophy, uh—indicate that this pause for a month or two was healthy, because we could not have honestly sustained a 9.2 percent rate of growth which we had in the first quarter of this year. Now, uh—I'd like to point out as well that the United States' economic recovery from the recession of a year ago is well ahead of the economic recovery of any major free industrial nation in the world today. We're ahead of all of the Western European country. We're ahead of Japan. The United States is leading the free world out of the recession that was serious a year, year and a half ago. We're going to see unemployment going down, more jobs available, and the rate of inflation going down. And I think this is a record that uh—the American people understand and will appreciate.

MS. WALTERS: Governor Carter.

MR. CARTER: With all due respect to President Ford, I think he ought to be ashamed of mentioning that statement, because we have the highest unemployment rate now than we had at any time between the Great Depression caused by Herbert Hoover and the time President Ford took office. We've got seven and a half million people out of jobs. Since he's been in office, two and a half million more American people have lost their jobs. In the last four months alone, five hundred thousand Americans have gone on the unemployment roll. In the last month, we've had a net loss of one hundred and sixty-three thousand jobs. Anybody who says that the inflation rate is in good shape now ought to talk to the housewives. One of the overwhelming results that I've seen in the polls is that people feel that you can't plan anymore. There's no way to make a prediction that my family might be able to own a home or to put my kid through college. Savings accounts are losing money instead of gaining money. Inflation is robbing us. Under the present administration—Nixon's and Ford's—we've had three times the inflation rate that we experienced under President Johnson and President Kennedy. The economic growth is less than half today what it was at the beginning of this year. And housing starts—he compares the housing starts with last year. I don't blame him, because in 1975 we had fewer housing starts in this country, fewer homes built, than any year since 1940. That's thirty-five years. And we've got a 35 percent unemployment rate in many areas of this country among construction workers. And Mr. Ford hasn't done anything about it. And I think this shows a callous indifference to the families that have suffered so much. He has vetoed bills passed by Congress within the congressional budget guidelines . . . job opportunities for two million Americans. We'll never have a balanced budget, we'll never meet the needs of our people, we'll never control the inflationary spiral, as long as we have seven and a half or eight million people out of work, who are looking for jobs. And we've probably got two and a half more million people who are not looking for jobs any more, because they've given up hope. That is a very serious indictment of this administration. It's probably the worst one of all.

Ms. WALTERS: Mr. Maynard.

MR. MAYNARD: Governor Carter, you entered this race against President Ford with a twenty-point lead or better in the polls. And now it appears that this campaign is headed for a photo finish. You've said how difficult it is to run against a sitting president. But Mr. Ford was just as much an incumbent in July when you were twenty points ahead as he is now. Can you tell us what caused the evaporation of that lead in your opinion?

MR. CARTER: Well, that's not exactly an accurate description of what happened. When I was that far ahead, it was immediately following the Democratic Convention, and before the Republican Convention. At that time, uh—25 or 30 percent of the Reagan supporters said that they would not support President Ford. But as occurred at the end of the con—Democratic Convention, the Republican Party unified itself. And I think immediately following the Republican Convention, there was about a ten-point spread. I believe that to be accurate, I had 49 percent; President Ford, 39 percent. Uh—the polls uh—are good indications of fluctuations, but they vary widely one from another. And the only poll I've ever followed is the one that uh—you know, is taken on election day. I was in uh—thirty primaries in the spring, and uh—at first it was obvious that I didn't have any standing in the poll. As a matter of fact, I think when Gallup ran their first poll in December of 1975 they didn't put my name on the list. They had thirty-five people on the list. My name wasn't even there. And at the beginning of the year I had about 2 percent. So the polls to me are interesting, but they don't determine, you know, my hopes or—or my despair. I campaign among people. I've never depended on powerful political figures to put me in office. I have a direct relationship with hundreds of people around— hundreds of thousands around the country who actively campaign for me. In Georgia alone, for instance, I got 84 percent of the vote, and I think there were fourteen people uh—in addition to myself on the ballot, and Governor Wallace had been very strong in Georgia. That's an overwhelming support from my own people who know me best. And today, we have about five hundred Georgians at their own expense—just working people who believe in me—spread around the country uh—involved in the political campaign. So, the polls are interesting, but uh—I don't know how to explain the fluctuation. I think a lot of it uh—depends on current events—uh—sometimes foreign affairs, sometimes domestic affairs. But I think our hold uh—of support among those who uh—are crucial to the election has been fairly steady. And my success in the primary season was, I think, notable for a newcomer, from someone who's from outside Washington, who—who never has been a part of the Washington establishment. And I think that we'll have good results uh—on November the second for myself and I hope for the country.

MS. WALTERS: President Ford, your response.

MR. FORD: I think uh—the uh—increase and the uh—prospects as far as I'm concerned and the l—less favorable prospects for Governor Carter, reflect that Governor Carter uh—is inconsistent in many of the positions that he takes. He tends to distort on a number of occasions. Uh—just a moment ago, for example, uh—he uh—was indicating that uh—uh—in the 1950s, for example, uh—unemployment was very low. He fails to point out that uh—in the 1950s we were engaged in the war in Vietnam. We—I mean in Korea—we had uh—three million five hundred thousand young men uh—in the Army, Navy, Air Force and Marines. That's not the way to end unemployment or to reduce unemployment. At the present time we're at peace. We have reduced the number of people in the Army, Navy, Air Force and Marines from three million, one hundred [uu]—three million, five hundred thousand to two million one hundred thousand. We are not at war. We have reduced the military manpower by a million four hundred thousand. If we had that many more people in the Army, the Navy, the Air Force, and Marines, our unemployment figure would be considerably less. But this administration doesn't believe the way to reduce unemployment is to go to war, or to increase the number of people in the military. So you cannot compare unemployment, as you sought to, uh—with the present time with the 1950s, because the then administration had people in the military—they were at war, they were fighting overseas, and this administration . . . has reduced the size of the military by a million four hundred thousand. They're in the civilian labor market and they're not fighting anywhere around the world today.

MS. WALTERS: Thank you, gentlemen. This will complete our questioning for this debate. We don't have uh—time for more questions and uh—full answers. So now each candidate will be allowed up to four minutes for a closing statement. And at the original coin toss in Philadelphia a month ago it was determined that President Ford would make the first closing statement tonight. President Ford.

MR. FORD: For twenty-five years I served in the Congress under five presidents. I saw them work, I saw them make very hard decisions. I didn't always agree with their decisions, whether they were Democratic or Republican presidents. For the last two years, I've been the president, and I have found from experience that it's much more difficult to make those decisions than it is to second-guess them. I became president at the time that the United States was in a very troubled time. We had inflation of over 12 percent, we were on the brink of the worst recession in the last forty years, we were still deeply involved in the problems of Vietnam. The American people had lost faith and trust and confidence in the presidency itself. That uh—situation called for me to first put the United States on a steady course and to keep our keel well balanced, because we had to face the difficult problems that had all of a sudden hit America. I think most people know that I did not seek the presidency. But I am asking for your help and assistance to be president for the next four years. During this campaign we've seen a lot of television shows, a lot of bumper stickers, and a great many uh—slogans of one kind or another. But those are not the things that count. What counts is, that the United States celebrated its 200th birthday on July fourth. As a result of that wonderful experience all over the United States, there is a new spirit in America. The American people are healed, are working together. The American people are moving again, and moving in the right direction. We have cut inflation by better than half. We have come out of the recession and we're well on the road to real prosperity in this country again. There has been a restoration of faith and confidence and trust in the presidency because I've been open, candid and forthright. I have never promised more than I could produce and I have produced everything that I promised. We are at peace. Not a single young American is fighting or dying on any foreign soil tonight. We have peace with freedom. I've been proud to be president of the United States during these very troubled times. I love America just as all of you love America. It would be the highest honor . . . for me to have your support on November second and for you to say, "Jerry Ford, you've done a good job, keep on doing it." Thank you, and good night.

Ms. WALTERS: Thank you President Ford, Governor Carter.

MR. CARTER: Thank you Barbara (barely audible). The major purpose of an election for president is to choose a leader. Someone who can analyze the depths of feeling in our country to set a standard for our people to follow, to inspire our people to reach for greatness, to correct our defects, to answer difficult questions, to bind ourselves together in a spirit of unity. I don't believe the present administration has done that. We have been discouraged and we've been alienated. Sometimes we've been embarrassed and sometimes we've been ashamed. Our people are out of work, and there's a sense of withdrawal. But our country is innately very strong. Mr. Ford is a good and decent man, but he's in—been in office now more than eight hundred days, . . . approaching almost as long as John Kennedy was in office. I'd like to ask the American people what, what's been accomplished. A lot remains to be done. My own background is different from his. I was a school board member, and a library board member. I served on a hospital authority. And I was in the state senate and I was governor and I'm an engineer, a Naval officer, a farmer, a businessman. And I believe we require someone who can work harmoniously with the Congress, who can work closely with the people of this country, and who can bring a new image and a new spirit to Washington. Our tax structure is a disgrace, it needs to be reformed. I was Governor of Georgia for four years. We never increased sales taxes or income tax or property tax. As a matter of fact, the year before I went out of office we gave a $50 million refund to the property taxpayers of Georgia. We spend six hundred dollars per person in this country— every man, woman and child—for health care. We still rank fifteenth among all the nations of the world in infant mortality. And our cancer rate . . . is uh—

higher than any country in the world. We don't have good health care. We could have it. Employment ought to be restored to our people. We've become almost a welfare state. We spend now 700 percent more on unemployment compensation than we did eight years ago when the Republicans took over the White House. Our people wanna go back to work. Our education system can be improved. Secrecy ought to be stripped away from government and a maximum of personal privacy ought to be maintained. Our housing programs have uh—gone bad. It used to be that the average—uh family could own a house. But now less than a third of our people can afford to buy their own homes. The budget was more grossly out of balance last year than ever before in the history of our country—$65 billion—primarily because our people are not at work. Inflation is robbing us, as we've already discussed, and the government bureaucracy is uh—just a horrible mess. This doesn't have to be. Now I don't know all the answers. Nobody could. But I do know that if the president of the United States and the Congress of the United States and the people of the United States said, "I believe our nation is greater than what we are now." I believe that if we are inspired, if we can achieve a degree of unity, if we can set our goals high enough and work toward recognized goals with industry and labor and agriculture along with government at all levels, then we can achieve great things. We might have to do it slowly. There are no magic answers to do it. But I believe together we can make great progress. We can correct our difficult mistakes and answer those very tough questions. I believe in the greatness of our country, and I believe the American people are ready for a change in Washington. We've been drifting too long. We've been dormant too long. We've been discouraged too long. And we have not set an example for our own people. But I believe that we can now establish in the White House a good relationship with Congress, a good relationship with our people, set very high goals for our country. And with inspiration and hard work we can achieve great things. And let the world know—that's very important. But more importantly, let the people in our own country realize . . . that we still live in the greatest nation on earth. Thank you very much.

Ms. WALTERS: Thank you, Governor Carter, and thank you, President Ford. I also would like to thank the audience and my three colleagues—Mr. Kraft, Mr. Maynard and Mr. Nelson—who have been our questioners. This debate has, of course, been seen by millions of Americans and, in addition, tonight is being broadcast to one hundred and thirteen nations throughout the world. This concludes the 1976 presidential debates, a truly remarkable exercise in democracy, for this is the first time in sixteen years that the presidential candidates have debated. It is the first time ever that an incumbent president has debated his challenger. And the debate included the first between the two vice presidential candidates. President Ford and Governor Carter, we not only want to thank you, but we commend you for agreeing to come together to discuss the issues before the American people. And our special thanks to the League of Women Voters for making these events possible. In sponsoring these events, the League of Women Voters Education Fund has tried to provide you with the information that you will need to choose wisely. The election is now only eleven days off. The candidates have participated in presenting their views in three ninety-minute debates, and now it's up to the voters, now it is up to you, to participate. The League urges all registered voters to vote on November second for the candidate of your choice. And now, from Phi Beta Kappa Memorial Hall on the campus of the College of William and Mary, this is Barbara Walters wishing you all a good evening.

NOTES

1. Carrol C. Arnold, "Oral Rhetoric, Rhetoric, and Literature," *Philosophy and Rhetoric* I (January 1968), pp. 191–210.

2. Theodore Clevenger, Jr., Donald W. Parson, and Jerome B. Polisky, "The Problem of Textual Accuracy," in *The Great Debates*, ed. Sidney Kraus (Bloomington: Indiana University Press, 1962), pp. 341–47.

CONTRIBUTORS

CHARLES ATKIN, Professor, Department of Communication, Michigan State University

WARREN E. BECHTOLT, JR., Mass Communication Research Center, University of Wisconsin-Madison

LEE B. BECKER, Associate Professor, School of Journalism, Ohio State University

SAMUEL L. BECKER, Professor and Chairman, Department of Speech and Dramatic Art, University of Iowa

CHARLES BENTON, President, Benton Foundation

CARL R. BYBEE, Assistant Professor, Department of Communication, Purdue University

STEVEN H. CHAFFEE, Vilas Research Professor of Journalism and Mass Communication, University of Wisconsin-Madison

SUN YUEL CHOE, doctoral candidate, Mass Communication Research Center, University of Wisconsin-Madison

RICHARD L. COHEN, Former Staff Director, Public Agenda Foundation; Executive Assistant to the Director, International Communications Agency

DENNIS K. DAVIS, Associate Professor, Department of Communication, Cleveland State University

JACK DENNIS, Professor and Chairperson, Department of Political Science, University of Wisconsin-Madison

JEAN A. DURALL, Assistant Professor, Department of Communication Studies, Northwestern University

STUART EIZENSTAT, Special Assistant to the President for Domestic Affairs

DORIS A. GRABER, Professor, Department of Political Science, University of Illinois-Chicago Circle

ROBERT P. HAWKINS, Assistant Professor, School of Journalism and Mass Communication, University of Wisconsin-Madison

JOHN HOCKING, Assistant Professor, Department of Speech Communication, University of Georgia

K. KYOON HUR, Assistant Professor, Department of Radio and Television, University of Texas

LEO W. JEFFRES, Assistant Professor, Department of Communication, Cleveland State University

542

JIM KARAYN, Former Executive Director, 1976 Presidential Debates, League of Women Voters; President, WHYY, Inc., Philadelphia-Wilmington

JIN KEON KIM, Assistant Professor, Department of Communication and Theatre, University of Illinois-Chicago Circle

SIDNEY KRAUS, Professor and Chairman, Department of Communication, Cleveland State University

PEGGY LAMPL, Former Executive Director, League of Women Voters; Deputy Assistant Director for Congressional Relations, U.S. Department of State

GLADYS ENGEL LANG, Professor, Departments of Sociology and Communication, State University of New York at Stony Brook

KURT LANG, Professor, Department of Sociology, State University of New York at Stony Brook

KENNETH LEIBOWITZ, Instructor in Communications, Philadelphia College of Pharmacy

ELMER W. LOWER, Former President, ABC News; Professor, School of Journalism, University of Missouri

MICHAEL MacKUEN, Assistant Professor, Department of Political Science, University of Michigan

MAXWELL E. McCOMBS, John Ben Snow Professor, S. I. Newhouse School of Public Communications, Syracuse University

STEVEN McDERMOTT, Assistant Professor, Department of Speech Communication, San Jose State University

JACK M. McLEOD, Professor, School of Journalism and Mass Communication, and Chairman, Mass Communications Research Center, University of Wisconsin-Madison

HAROLD MENDELSOHN, Professor, Department of Mass Communications, University of Denver

LOUIS T. MILIC, Professor, Department of English, Cleveland State University

ARTHUR H. MILLER, Study Director, Center for Political Studies, Institute for Social Research, and Associate Professor, Department of Political Science, University of Michigan

HOWARD A. MIMS, Associate Professor, Department of Speech and Hearing, Cleveland State University

GARRETT J. O'KEEFE, Associate Professor, Department of Mass Communications, University of Denver

ROBERT PEPPER, Associate Professor and Co-Director of Broadcasting and Film Division, Department of Speech and Dramatic Art, University of Iowa

SUZANNE PINGREE, Mass Communication Research Center, University of Wisconsin-Madison

GENE POKORNY, Executive Vice-President, Cambridge Reports, Inc.

MICHAEL RAOUL-DUVAL, Former Special Counsel to President Ford; President, Industrial Products Group, Mead Corporation

JOHN P. ROBINSON, Professor, Department of Communication, and Director, Communication Research Center, Cleveland State University

RICHARD S. SALANT, Former President, CBS News; Vice-Chairman of the Board, NBC

DAVID O. SEARS, Professor, Departments of Psychology and Political Science, University of California, Los Angeles

HERBERT A. SELTZ, Professor, Department of Telecommunications, Indiana University

HERBERT W. SIMONS, Professor, Department of Speech, Temple University

KIM A. SMITH, University College, University of Louisville

JOHN STENSRUD, Teaching Assistant, Department of Sociology, State University of New York at Stony Brook

HERBERT A. TERRY, Assistant Professor, Department of Telecommunications, Indiana University

DAVID H. WEAVER, Associate Professor, School of Journalism, Indiana University

LAWRENCE A. WENNER, Assistant Professor, Department of Human Communication, University of Kentucky

RICHARD D. YOAKAM, Professor, School of Journalism and Department of Telecommunications, Indiana University

JESS YODER, Professor, Department of Communication, Cleveland State University

DEAN A. ZIEMKE, graduate student in Mass Communication and Project Assistant, Mass Communications Research Center, University of Wisconsin-Madison

CONTRIBUTORS

INDEX

Hovland, Carl, 298
Hruska, Roman, 32
Huddleston, Walter D., 32
Hughes, Charles Evans, 14
Hughes, Harold, 30
Humphrey, Hubert, 22, 23, 25, 26, 27, 28, 42, 43, 92
Huntley, Chet, 24
"Huntley-Brinkley Report," 144

images: of candidates, 4, 5, 7, 11, 34, 97, 106, 107, 109, 122, 131, 185, 229, 236, 237, 240, 258, 265, 270, 274, 278, 279, 280, 282, 291, 304, 306, 307, 310, 315, 317, 321, 322, 327, 331–347, 358, 359, 382, 390, 393, 396, 398–404, 411, 412, 433; of ideal president, 34, 399. *See also* issues
Internal Revenue Service (IRS), 70, 72
Interpublic Group of New York, 20
Interstate and Foreign Commerce Subcommittee on Communication and Power, 16, 43
issues: 7, 8, 54–65, 108, 109, 111, 114, 143, 187, 208, 210, 212, 216, 233–261, 269–297, 306–308, 314–330, 332, 336, 348–367, 374–377, 418–428; abortion, 235, 307, 308, 321, 323, 336, 366, 374, 376, 377, 433; amnesty, 203, 216, 235, 306, 426; Arab oil embargo, 206; B-1 bomber, 235, 236, 358; bureaucracy in government, 355; busing, 235, 336, 412; cities, 11, 21, 78, 193, 195; constitutional amendment, 190; crime, 433; defense, 213, 244, 308, 318, 323, 376, 377, 426; domestic affairs, 88, 93, 94, 99, 108, 137, 145, 216, 234, 237; the economy, 55, 56, 63, 74, 75, 93, 99, 108, 137, 192, 193, 206, 217, 225, 228, 229, 230, 321; energy, 203, 204; environment, 216, 217, 235, 308; "ethnic purity," 440, 441, 443; farm subsidies, 308; Ford's Eastern Europe remark, 187, 194–195, 216, 233, 234, 235, 247, 252, 255, 279–281, 283, 433, 436–441; foreign affairs, 56, 57, 63, 64, 79, 88, 93, 94, 101, 106, 108, 141, 145, 147, 187, 191, 192, 195, 216, 217, 229, 234, 280, 418, 438, 439, 440, 441; government reorganization, 235, 236, 358, 374, 376; government responsiveness, 56; government spending, 195, 235, 306; grain embargo, 206; gun control, 235, 236; home mortgage interest deduction, 75, 77; human rights, 206; inflation, 57, 58, 60, 244, 306, 424; intelligence agencies, 165; invasion of privacy, 307; minorities, 190, 192, 437, 443; national security, 93, 141; moral

leadership in government, 57, 61, 63, 64; national health care program, 216, 336; national responsibility, 76, 77; Nixon's pardon, 203, 255; priorities, 58; racial protest, social upheaval, 21, 55; role of the presidency, 88; role of the vice-presidency, 88; tax reform, 56, 235, 306, 318, 321, 323, 354, 374, 376, 377, 426; unemployment, 57, 58, 60, 234, 235, 306, 321, 323, 336, 354, 374, 376, 426; Vietnam, 11, 21, 30, 55, 56, 203, 224, 225, 348; Watergate, 11, 55, 56, 203, 224, 225, 245, 256
"Issues and Answers," 117

Jackson, Henry, 32, 74, 76, 77, 78, 84
Jackson, Read, 96, 118
Jagoda, Barry, 90, 94, 95, 97, 98, 113, 115, 116, 117, 121, 122, 126, 130, 131, 135, 140, 147
Jasinowski, Jerry, 105
Javits, Jacob, 17, 23, 143
Jeffersonian exposition, 328
Jeffres, Leo W., 437
John Hancock Hall (Boston), 76
Johnson Advertising Agency, 19
Johnson, Claudia, 164–165
Johnson, Lyndon Baines, 4, 15, 18, 19, 20, 21, 22, 23, 29, 30, 42, 92
Jordan, Hamilton, 105, 106
Jordan, Vernon, Jr., 56

Karayn, Jim, 7, 61, 69, 70, 71, 78, 83, 84, 85, 86, 87, 89, 90, 91, 92, 94, 96, 98, 99, 101, 102, 103, 110, 111, 112, 113, 114, 115, 116, 117, 118, 119, 120, 121, 122, 123, 124, 125, 131, 134, 136, 137, 142, 143, 148, 150, 153, 169, 170, 172
Katz, Elihu, 224, 225, 226, 249, 351, 406, 418
KCET (Los Angeles), 70
Kelley, Clarence, M., 165
Kelly, Jack, 137, 138, 139, 140, 141
Kennedy, Edward M., 11, 15, 28. *See also* debate
Kennedy, John F., 3, 4, 6, 13, 14, 15, 16, 18, 21, 22, 29, 30, 41, 42, 48, 85, 92, 96, 105, 111, 122, 148, 152, 162, 175, 176, 204, 209, 213, 256, 318, 369, 398, 401, 402, 418. *See also* debate
Kennedy, Robert F., 16, 21, 22. *See also* debate
Kent, Frank H., 205
Kerlinger, F. N., 350, 385
Kerr, Clark, 8, 56
Kessel, J. H., 314
Key, V. O., Jr., 4, 327
KGW-TV (Portland), 35
Kiker, Douglas, 160, 163, 164, 165, 166

Murphy, George, 16
Murray, George, 133
Muskie, Edmund, 24, 27, 28, 29, 256

NAACP, 178
National Association of Broadcasters (NAB), 16, 19
National Broadcasting Company (NBC), 14, 16, 20, 24, 25, 62, 65, 84, 90, 91, 98, 110, 115, 119, 120, 121, 125, 126, 127, 136, 141, 144, 145, 146, 147, 148, 158–174
National Council of Churches, 76
national debate commission, 218–219
National Educational Television (NET), 110
National Organization for Women (NOW), 46
National Public Affairs Center for Television (NPACT), 69, 83, 110
National Public Radio Network (NPR), 75, 84
Nelson, Jack, 149
Nessen, Ron, 147, 162, 163, 164, 166
New Orleans *Times-Picayune*, 64
Newman, Edwin, 132, 134, 137, 170, 171, 300, 303
Newsday, 299
News Election Service (NES), 13, 20
news panel. *See* press panel
Newsweek, 62, 145, 229
Newton, Carroll, 13
New Yorker, 137
New York Times, 5, 62, 64, 141, 177, 184, 262–268, 298, 450, 451
Nie, Norman H., 314, 315, 332
Nielsen, A. C., 75, 262–268
Nielsen, Waldemar, 56
Nielsen ratings, 78, 230–231
Nimmo, Dan, 13, 270
Nixon, Richard, 3, 4, 6, 13, 14, 15, 16, 18, 22, 25, 26, 27, 28, 29, 30, 31, 41, 42, 43, 44, 48, 85, 96, 105, 111, 115, 122, 123, 125, 148, 152, 162, 175, 176, 188, 203, 204, 213, 291, 298, 318, 332, 398, 401, 402, 418, 439, 449. *See also* debate; issues; Watergate

O'Connor, E. F., Jr., 227
Office of Minority Business, 190
O'Keefe, Garrett J., 269
Olien, C. N., 426
Ordeshook, P. C., 327
Osgood, Charles, 400

Page, Benjamin I., 314
Palace of Fine Arts Theater (San Francisco), 101, 102, 106, 137–142
Palmgreen, P., 269
panelists. *See* debate

panel surveys, 59, 60, 63
Parson, Donald W., 449, 452
Pastore, John, 17, 22, 32, 43, 44, 45, 86, 90, 91
Patterson, T. E., 278, 354, 438
Paulsen, Pat, 27
Pearson, Carl, 412
Pearson, Drew, 24
Pearson, James, 22
Peckman, Joseph, 105
Pedhazur, E. J., 350, 385
Pengra, Mike, 96, 101, 138, 139, 140, 141
persuasion, 223, 224, 227. *See also* images; issues
Petrocik, J. R., 314, 315, 332
Pfister, Walter, 118, 120, 125, 126, 136
Phi Beta Kappa Memorial Hall (Williamsburg), 101, 132, 143, 146–149, 184
Pike, Donald, 149
Playboy, 164, 255
Pokorny, Gene, 7, 68, 72
Polisky, Jerome B., 449, 452
polls, 262–268. *See also* Associated Press; CBS; Gallup; Harris; NBC; *New York Times*; Nielsen; public opinion; ratings; Roper; Yankelovich
Pomper, Gerald M., 314
Pool, I., 325
Powell, Jody, 90, 91, 94, 95, 105, 106, 113, 115, 116, 163, 164, 165, 166, 209
Presidential Forums, 7, 8, 9, 68–82, 83, 84, 85, 86, 103, 110, 116, 121, 212; audience reaction, 112, 113; evaluation of, 80, 81, 82; financial support, 69, 70, 71, 83, 85; Los Angeles, 79–80; Miami or Southern, 75–77; Midwest, 78–79; Northeast, 74–75; steering committee, 72, 73, 86, 87, 88
Presidential primaries, 7, 27, 28, 33, 55, 61, 74, 77, 79, 80, 209, 211; Florida, 34, 75, 77; Maryland, 79; Massachusetts, 74, 76, 84; New Hampshire, 34, 74, 75, 77, 84; North Carolina, 34, 78; Oregon, 80; Pennsylvania, 78; Texas, 34
press conference, 15, 18, 34, 87, 89, 180, 185, 197, 210
press coverage, 15, 35, 158–186, 187
press panel (news panel). *See* debate: panelists
production, 8, 110–157. *See also* audio failure; lighting; set; sound system
Progressive Party, 181
Proxmire, William, 32
Public Agenda Foundation, 8, 54–67
Public Broadcasting Service (PBS), 62, 65, 69, 70, 71, 73, 75, 76, 91, 98, 110, 119, 123, 130, 132, 143, 144, 145; stations: KCET (Los Angeles), 70; WGBH (Boston), 70; WNET (New

DATE DUE

NO 30 '83			
NOV 8 84			
DEC 1 84			
FEB 2 0 '89			
MAR 1 6 '89			
MAR 3 0 '89			
GAYLORD			PRINTED IN U.S.A.